# Borland® C++ 4

## By EXAMPLE

que

**Stephen Potts**
**Timothy S. Monk**

## Borland® C++4 By Example

Library of Congress Catalog No.: 94-65887

ISBN: 1-56529-756-3

97  96  95  94      4  3  2  1

Interpretation of the printing code: the rightmost double-digit number is the year of the book's printing; the rightmost single-digit number, the number of the book's printing. For example, a printing code of 94-1 shows that the first printing of the book occurred in 1994.

**Publisher:** *David P. Ewing*

**Associate Publisher:** *Michael Miller*

**Publishing Director:** *Joseph B. Wikert*

**Managing Editor:** *Michael Cunningham*

**Product Marketing Director:** *Greg Wiegand*

# Credits

**Publishing Manager**
*Brad Koch*

**Acquisitions Editor**
*Angela J. Lee*

**Product Director**
*C. Kazim Haidri*

**Production Editor**
*Mike La Bonne*

**Technical Editor**
*Russell Jacobs*

**Acquisitions Coordinator**
*Patricia Brooks*

**Book Designer**
*Jean Bisesi*

**Graphic Image Specialists**
*Teresa Forrester*
*Tim Montgomery*
*Dennis Sheehan*
*Sue VandeWalle*

**Production Team**
*Stephen Adams*
*Nick Anderson*
*Claudia Bell*
*Cameron Booker*
*Paula Carroll*
*Scott Cook*
*Karen Dodson*
*Rich Evers*
*Brook Farling*
*Bob LaRoche*
*Joy Dean Lee*
*G. Alan Palmore*
*Linda Quigley*
*Kris Simmons*
*Michael Thomas*
*Tina Trettin*
*Lillian Yates*

**Indexer**
*Jeanne Clark*

# Dedications

*To my wife, Suzanne, and to my six children, James, Jessica, Jeremy, Julie, Jenny, and Jake for understanding why I had to do this.*
*S.P.*
*To my mother, Claudia, and my grandmother, Claudia, thank you for everything.*
*T.M.*

# About the Authors

Stephen Potts has been designing and writing software systems for 12 years. He received a degree in computer Science from Georgia Tech. He is currently a consultant in Windows-based technologies, and owns NoBoredom Classes, a computer education company in Atlanta, Ga.

Timothy S. Monk is a senior software engineer for the Follett Software Company, a leader in school library automation software. He also is the author of the book *Windows Programmer's Guide to Serial Communications*, published by Sams Publishing in 1992. He has been involved in all areas of microcomputer development since 1979.

# Acknowledgments

Thanks to Mike Schinkel for talking me into becoming an author, and to Angela Lee of Que for taking a chance on me.

  S.P.

My thanks to Angela Lee and Joe Wikert of Que for the opportunity to be a part of this project. Also, many thanks to my wife, Patricia, for her love and support.

  T.M.

## Trademark Acknowledgments

Que Corporation has made every attempt to supply trademark information about company names, products, and services mentioned in this book. Trademarks indicated below were derived from various sources. Que Corporation cannot attest to the accuracy of this information.

  ANSI is a registered trademark of American National Standards Institute.

  Borland is a registered trademark of Borland International, Inc.

  DEC is a registered trademark of Digital Equipment Corporation.

  DR DOS is a registered trademark of Digital Research, Inc.

  IBM and OS/2 are registered trademarks of International Business Machines Corporation.

  Microsoft and MS-DOS are registered trademarks of Microsoft Corporation. Windows is a trademark of Microsoft Corporation.

  Visual C and Turbo C++ are registered trademarks of Microsoft, Inc.

  UNIX is a trademark of AT&T.

  X Window System is a trademark of the Massachusetts Institute of Technology.

### We'd Like To Hear from You!

As part of our continuing effort to produce books of the highest possible quality, Que would like to hear your comments. To stay competitive, we *really* want you, as a computer book reader and user, to let us know what you like or dislike most about this book or other Que products.

You can mail comments, ideas, or suggestions for improving future editions to the address below, or send us a fax at (317) 581-4663. For the on-line inclined, Prentice Hall Computer Publishing now has a forum on CompuServe (type **GO QUEBOOKS** at any prompt) through which our staff and authors are available for questions and comments. In addition to exploring our forum, please feel free to contact me personally on CompuServe at 74143,1574 to discuss your opinions of this book.

Thanks in advance—your comments will help us to continue publishing the best books available on computer topics in today's market.

  Christopher Haidri
  Product Development Specialist
  Que Corporation
  201 W. 103rd Street
  Indianapolis, Indiana 46290
  USA

# Overview

# Contents

# Contents

Contents

Contents

Contents

Contents

# Introduction

*Borland C++ 4 By Example* is one of several books in Que's line of *By Example* titles. The philosophy of these books is a simple one: computer programming concepts are best taught with multiple examples. Command descriptions, format syntax, and language references are not enough for a newcomer to learn a programming language. Only by looking at many examples, where new commands are used immediately, and by running sample programs can programming students get more than just a "feel" for the language.

## Who Should Use This Book?

This book teaches on three levels of examples: beginning, intermediate, and advanced. Text accompanies the many examples at each level. If you are new to C++, and even if you are new to computers, this book attempts to put you at ease and gradually builds your C++ programming skills. If you are an expert at C++, this book tries to provide a few extras for you along the way.

## The Book's Philosophy

This book focuses on programming *well* in C++ by teaching programming techniques and proper program design. Emphasis is always placed on a program's readability instead of "tricks of the trade" code examples. In this changing world, programs should be clear, properly organized, and well-documented, and this book does not waver from the importance of this philosophy.

The book teaches you C++ by using a holistic approach; you learn the mechanics of the language, tips and warnings, and how to use C++ for different types of applications, as well as a little history and interesting "sidebars" on the computing industry.

Although many other books build single applications, adding to them a little at a time with each chapter, the chapters of this book are stand-alone chapters showing you complete programs that fully illustrate the commands discussed. There is a program for every level of reader, from beginning to advanced.

More than 200 sample program listings are provided. These programs show ways that C++ can be used for personal finance, school and business record keeping, math and science, and general-purpose applications that almost everybody with a computer can use. This wide variety of programs shows you that C++ is a very powerful language that is easy to learn and use.

# Overview of This Book

*Borland C++ 4 By Example* is divided into nine parts and six appendixes. Part I introduces you to the C++ environment and introductory programming concepts. Starting with Part II, the book presents the C++ programming language commands and library functions. After mastering the language, you can then use the book as a handy reference. When you need help with a specific C++ programming problem, turn to the appropriate area that describes that part of the language to see various examples of code. The following sections describe the parts of this book:

## Part I: Introduction to C++

Part I explains what C++ is by describing a brief history of the C++ programming language and then presenting an overview of C++'s advantages over other languages. This part of the book describes your computer's hardware, how you develop C++ programs, and the steps you follow to enter and run programs. You will write your first C++ program in the fourth chapter.

## Part II: C++ Operators

Part II covers the entire set of C++ operators. The rich assortment of operators (more than in any other programming language except APL) makes up for the fact that the C++ programming language is very small. The operators and their order of precedence are more important to C++ than to most programming languages.

## Part III: C++ Constructs

C++ data processing is most powerful because of the looping, comparison, and selection constructs that C++ offers. This part of the book shows you how to write programs that correctly flow with control computations to produce accurate and readable code.

## Part IV: Functions

To support true structured programming techniques, C++ must allow for local and global variables, as well as offer several ways to pass and return variables between functions. These subjects are the focus of Part IV. C++ is a very strong structured language that attempts, if the programmer is willing to "listen to the language," to protect local variables by making them visible only to the parts of the program that need those variables.

## Part V: Input/Output

C++ contains no commands that perform input or output. To make up for this apparent oversight, C++ compiler writers supply several useful input and output functions, described in this part of the book. By separating input and output functions from the language, C++ achieves better portability between computers; if your program runs on one computer, it should work on any other.

In addition, Part V describes several of the math, character, and string library functions available with C++. These functions keep you from having to write your own routines to perform common tasks.

## Part VI: Arrays and Pointers

C++ offers single-dimensional arrays and multidimensional arrays—the subjects of Part VI. A multidimensional array holds multiple occurrences of repeating data but does not require lots of effort on your part to process.

Unlike many other programming languages, C++ uses pointer variables a great deal. Pointer variables and arrays work together to give you flexible data storage, allowing for easy sorting and searching of data.

## Part VII: Data Structures

Variables, arrays, and pointers are not enough to hold the types of data your programs will require. Structures and classes, discussed in Part VII, allow for more powerful grouping of many different kinds of data into manageable units.

Your computer would be too limiting if you could not store data to disk and retrieve that data back into your programs. Disk files are required by most "real world" applications. This part of the book describes how C++ processes sequential and random access files, as well as teaches the fundamental principles needed to save data to the disk effectively.

## Part VIII: Object-Oriented Programming

This section looks at using the object-oriented programming features of Borland C++. You'll learn about objects and classes. You'll see how to implement data hiding and to define an object's public interface. Finally, you'll learn about the advanced topics of class inheritance and object polymorphism.

## Part IX: Borland's ObjectWindows Library

This section introduces you to Borland's ObjectWindows Library. You'll see how to use OWL to write programs for Microsoft Windows. You'll learn about OWL's application and window classes. You'll learn about event-driven programming, and how OWL implements this concept. You'll also learn about adding functionality to your programs by using menus, controls, toolbars, status bars, and dialog boxes.

## Appendixes

The appendixes provide support information for the nine main parts of the book. You will find among the appendixes a review of binary and hexadecimal numbers, answers to the review questions for each chapter, a comprehensive ASCII table, a C++ precedence table, a keyword and function reference, and a complete mailing list application.

# Conventions Used in This Book

The following typographic conventions are used in this book:

- Code lines, variable names, and any text that you see on-screen are in monospace.

- Placeholders on format lines are in *italic monospace*.

- User input following a prompt is in **bold monospace**.

- File names are in regular text.

- Optional parameters on format lines are enclosed in flat brackets ([ ]). You do not type the brackets when you include these parameters.

- New terms, which can be found in the Glossary, are in *italic*.

## Index to the Icons

The following icons appear throughout this book:

Level 1

Level 2

Level 3

Tip

Caution

Note

Pseudocode

This icon appears beside pseudocode, which is typeset in *italic* just after the program. The pseudocode consists of one or more sentences indicating what the program instructions would say if their functions could be stated aloud, in English. Pseudocode appears for selected programs.

The pseudocode, program listings, and detailed program descriptions presented in this book should give you many vehicles for learning the C++ programming language.

# Part I

*Introduction to C++ 4*

# CHAPTER 1

# Welcome to Borland C++

## Introduction

This book teaches you how to use Borland C++ to write programs. In this chapter, you learn about the history of C and C++, and review the PC system. You also learn how Borland C++ supports programming for IBM PCs and compatible systems.

Borland C++ is Borland's compiler for the C and C++ computer languages. It is designed to run under Windows 3.X. It can create programs that execute under MS-DOS, Windows, or Windows NT systems.

## Defining a Computer Language

A *compiler* is a computer program that translates another program written in a computer language (such as C, or COBOL) into a form that the computer can understand. The output from a compiler is a file with a suffix *obj*. This stands for *object*.

Remember that a computer, for all its speed and power, is merely a device that manipulates binary numbers. Some of the binary numbers are interpreted by the computer as instructions; others are translated as data.

A *program* is a set of instructions that causes the computer to manipulate data. A *programming language* is a means for you to generate those instructions. Originally, programming was done using instructions that the computer recognized directly. This proved to be so tedious and slow that programmers began to write "higher level" programming languages that were easier to use. These languages could not be understood by the computer directly, so special programs called *compilers* had to be written to translate this new language into the machine's instruction set. *Borland C++* is a software development environment that includes a *compiler* as well as a number of other tools.

An *executable file* is one that contains a program that has been compiled and is ready to run. It is nearly impossible for humans to read. However, it is exactly what the computer needs to operate. Sometimes people call an executable file by other names, such as an *image*, or simply a *program*.

In the computing field there are dozens of programming languages. For each language, there are many different compilers, sold by a variety of vendors. The choice between competing compilers is a matter of taste and opinion. In recent years, the competition among compiler vendors has become so intense that product quality is generally very high.

## Low-Level Languages

*Low-level language* statements resemble the computer's native set of instructions. Such languages are very close to the computer. Therefore, the program can achieve a high degree of efficiency. The problem is that a program written in a low-level language is difficult to read and write; the program might use several lines of code to do something as simple as print a character. Low-level languages are specific to a computer's CPU chip. A program written in a low-level language for a Motorola 68000 would have to be completely rewritten on an Intel 80486.

Low-level languages offer little or no portability because of the bond between the language and the computer. Another consequence of this tight coupling between the hardware and software is the absence of standards for languages at this level. Most experts feel that if chip technology is to advance, the chip designers must have complete control over the instruction set. Low-level language is often referred to as *assembly language*.

## High-Level Languages

*High-level languages* are designed with the human programmer in mind. Programs written in high-level languages are generally not as efficient as those written in low-level languages. However, programs written in high-level languages are easier to write. High-level languages are usually more hardware-independent; a program written in a high-level language on one hardware platform can generally be made to run on another hardware platform, though usually not without some modification.

Many high-level languages have been standardized by organizations, such as the American National Standards Institute (ANSI). This standardization generally makes the language more portable. Examples of high-level languages include FORTRAN, COBOL, and Pascal.

## What Is C?

C is a programming language that falls somewhere between a low-level and a high-level language. C is similar to a high-level language in that it is block-structured and procedural. A well-written C program can be very readable. It resembles a low-level language in that it contains operators that manipulate individual bits. The authors of the first C implementation, Brian W. Kernighan and Dennis M. Ritchie, wrote C to exploit the native capabilities of the computer on which they were working. Thus, you can use C to write very efficient programs, though not as proficient as those written in a purely low-level language. C programs are usually more efficient than programs written in other high-level languages. An ANSI standard for the C language now exists, and writing portable programs in C is very common. The existence of this standard makes C popular with software vendors who must port their applications to a number of operating systems and hardware platforms.

## What Is C++?

C++ is an object-oriented programming language. As software systems develop into more powerful instruments, they also become more complex. Every new release of a word processor, database, or spreadsheet program is larger than the previous one, and contains more features. This increasing size and complexity makes it difficult to manage the software development process. As programmers struggle to deal with this complexity, new ideas emerge. One collection of these ideas is based on a philosophy called *object-oriented programming*.

While object-oriented programs can be written in languages such as C or BASIC, these languages lack certain features. For example, C provides no mechanism to hide variables from unauthorized access. C also does not enable one class to be declared as a subclass of another. These and other features were added to the C language by Dr. Bjarne Stroustrup at AT&T's Bell Labs in the early 1980s. He called this new language C++.

Borland C++ can be used as a development platform for both procedural and object-oriented programs. Both approaches are referred to in this book. Object-oriented design is a field of its own; therefore, it is recommended that interested readers obtain a book on that specific area of computer science.

## The History of Borland C++

Turbo C was the first C offering from Borland. Patterned after Borland's very successful Turbo Pascal compiler, Turbo C offered PC-based programmers a C programming environment. Turbo C not only provided the traditional command-line interface, but also exploited the PC's unique capabilities, offering an environment with a built-in text editor from which you could compile your program. If an error occurred during the compilation, the programmer was returned to the file. The offending line of code was identified, and a description of the error given.

Turbo C++ followed Turbo C as Borland's C++ offering. Although many competing C++ vendors were offering C++ as a preprocessor that would translate C++ additions into equivalent C code, Turbo C++ was a true C++ compiler.

# C++ and the PC System

C++ has become the language of choice for developers on many sizes and types of computers. Nowhere is it more popular than on the PC.

## Operating Systems

Several operating systems are supported on PCs, such as DOS, Windows, OS/2, and UNIX. These operating systems provide a means of controlling the computer's hardware. Programming the PC through the operating system's Application Programming Interface (API) is the only portable way to control the PC hardware.

An *operating system* is a collection of programs that provides an environment in which to operate the computer. The Operating System gives the user a set of commands, such as **DIR** in DOS, or File | **O**pen in Windows. The operating system also provides a set of functions referred to as an Applications Programming Interface (API). The programmer puts API function calls in his programs to perform work, such as reading data from a disk drive, or reading the computer's clock. Thus, he doesn't need to write the code to do these tasks. This architecture also enables the operating system to prevent one application from damaging another.

## BIOS

In the early days of DOS programming, it was common for programmers to make calls directly to the Basic Input/Output Subsystem (BIOS). These calls enabled more direct control of the computer than the operating system's service calls provided. Windows and Windows NT forbid this approach.

## Borland C++ and the PC System

In addition to offering compliance with the ANSI C standard, Borland C++ gives the programmer the ability to create programs that run under MS-DOS, Windows 3.1, Win32s, and Windows NT.

If you want to create a program that is intended exclusively for MS-DOS computers, a number of built-in functions can help you. These functions include graphics and BIOS calls. All six traditional memory models (tiny, small, medium, compact, large, and huge) are supported.

Borland C++ supports the programming of Windows 3.1 applications in two ways. First, you can write C++ code and include calls to the Windows API. Alternatively, you can call the ObjectWindows Class Library (OWL) member functions. Making calls to the OWL member functions requires an understanding of object-oriented programming principles.

You can write code for more advanced operating systems, such as the upcoming 32-bit version of Windows and WindowsNT, using the same Integrated Development Environment (IDE) as you currently do for Windows and DOS development. In fact, you can build an executable program for each of these environments using a single project file.

## Summary

In this chapter, you learned the history of C and C++. Also, you saw how Borland C++ supports programming for IBM PC systems.

## Review Questions

The answers to the Review Questions are in Appendix B.

1. Describe the differences between low-level and high-level languages.

2. Is C a low-level or high-level language?

3. How is C++ different from C?

4. How did Turbo C stand apart from the other C compilers in its day?

5. What operating systems does Borland C++ support?

# CHAPTER 2

# The Borland C++ Environment

Among the innovations found in Borland C++ 4.0 are a Windows-based debugger, enhanced project management, support for Windows NT, and a Windows version of the Borland C++ Integrated Development Environment (IDE). The IDE offers an array of helpful tools, such as a full-screen editor, pull-down menus, interactive help, and a debugger.

This chapter introduces the following topics:

♦ Starting Borland C++

♦ Understanding Borland C++'s screen

♦ Understanding projects

♦ Getting help in Borland C++

♦ Exiting Borland C++

The chapter provides the tools necessary for you to begin entering your Borland C++ programs.

## Starting Borland C++

To begin using Borland C++, install it according to the directions in the box. This creates a program group named *Borland C++ 4.0* (see figure 2.1). Within that group you will see 15-20 icons, depending on the options that you selected during installation. The most important icon is named *Borland C++*; this icon starts the Integrated Development Environment (IDE). The other icons represent some very useful facilities that are beyond the scope of this book. You should become familiar with them after you master the IDE.

**Figure 2.1.**

The Borland C++
opening screen.

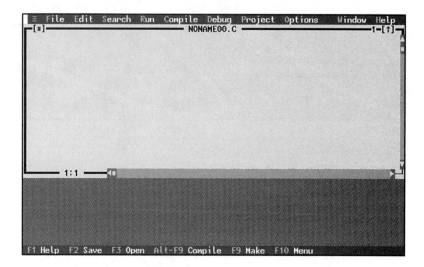

When you double-click on the Borland C++ icon, the main IDE screen appears.

**Power Up Properly**

There is a proper sequence to follow when turning on your computer. The sequence is easy to remember with the following rule: *The boss always comes to work last and is the first to go home.*

Have you had bosses like that? Your computer's power-up sequence should follow a similar rule: *The system unit (the "boss" that holds the CPU) should come to work last.*

In other words, turn on everything else first, including the printer, monitor, and modem. Only then should you turn on the system unit. This keeps system-unit power surges to a minimum and protects the circuits inside the unit.

When you are ready to turn off the computer, turn off the system unit first (the boss goes home first). Then turn off the rest of the equipment in whatever order is most convenient.

**Tip:** If your computer equipment is plugged into a switched surge protector, it is fine to use the single switch for all your equipment, including the system unit. The surge protector ensures that power gets to the system unit as evenly as possible.

# The Borland C++ Screen

Figure 2.2 shows the parts of the Borland C++ screen. From this screen, you create, modify, and execute Borland C++ programs.

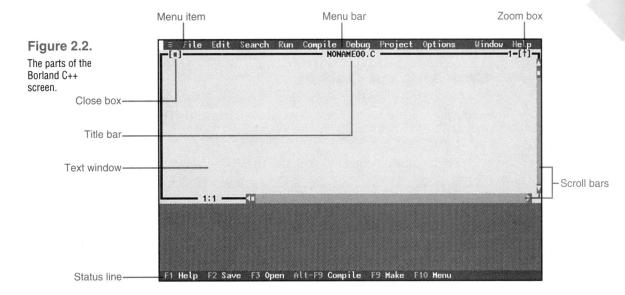

**Figure 2.2.**

The parts of the Borland C++ screen.

---

### Using the Mouse

You use the mouse to move the cursor around on the screen quickly. Before mouse devices became common, users had to press the arrow keys continually to move the cursor from one location to another. Now you can move the cursor by moving the mouse across the desk and clicking the mouse when the cursor is at the desired position.

To *click* the mouse, you press and immediately release the left mouse button. Clicking the mouse might select an item from a menu or move the text cursor on the screen. Sometimes you click the mouse after moving the mouse cursor over a **Y**es or **N**o answer in response to a question.

To *double-click* the mouse, you press the left mouse button twice in rapid succession. You might need to double-click the mouse to execute a menu command.

To *drag* the mouse, you press and hold down the left mouse button while moving the mouse cursor across the screen. Usually, the area you drag the mouse across is highlighted on-screen so that you can see the path the mouse leaves. When you are finished marking the path, release the mouse button. This is one way to select several lines from a Borland C++ program so that you can move or erase them.

At first glance, the IDE looks like a normal, if rather empty, Windows 3.X application. You will see a familiar menu bar across the top and a row of tiny icons just below it. These icons represent the most common menu selections. At the bottom of the screen is a window named Message. It is within this window that the IDE communicates warnings, error messages, and status to the programmer. At the very bottom of the screen is a one-line rectangle called the *status line*. This line contains useful communications from time to time.

## Choosing an Option

When you display a pull-down menu, you must tell Borland C++ which command on the menu to perform. You can request a command in one of three ways:

- ◆ Click on the command with the mouse.
- ◆ Highlight the command with the arrow keys and then press Enter.
- ◆ Press the command's underlined letter.

For example, to request the New project command, move the mouse cursor until it rests anywhere on the word New. One click of the mouse chooses the New command. Keyboard users can press the down-arrow key until the New command is highlighted; pressing the Enter key carries out the command. Keyboard users also have a shortcut: simply typing the highlighted letter of the command. By typing N or n, the keyboard user can execute the New command. Note that you can use an uppercase letter or a lowercase letter to select any command or option.

If you begin to select from a menu but then change your mind, press Esc to close the menu and return to the program-editing window; alternatively, click the mouse outside the pull-down menu area to close the menu.

> **Tip:** The best way to learn how to choose from Borland C++'s pull-down menus is to experiment. As long as you don't save anything to disk, you won't harm existing Borland C++ program files or data.

Sometimes commands appear in gray and are not as readable as others. For example, most of the options on the Project pull-down menu are in gray. You cannot choose any of these commands. Borland C++ displays the unavailable commands so that you will remember where they are when you need them. These commands return to their normal colors whenever they are available in the current context of your Borland C++ session.

## The Menu Shortcut Keys

After using Borland C++ for a while, you will become familiar with the commands on the pull-down menus. Despite the ease of using Borland C++ menus, there is a faster way to select some of these commands. Borland C++'s *shortcut keys* are faster to use than the menus, whether you use a mouse or the keyboard.

Many of the function keys execute menu commands when you press them. For instance, to choose Help | Keyword search, you could display the **Help** pull-down menu and then select Keyword search (or type Alt-H | s). Rather than go through these menu steps, however, you can press **F1** to immediately run the Keyword search command. The key or key combination listed beside a given menu option is the shortcut key for that option. Notice that the Help | Keyword search menu option has **F1** listed to the right of it. You will understand the function of each of these shortcut keys as you learn more about Borland C++.

## The Project

In the old days, when programmers had hair on the top of their heads as well as on the sides, programming on personal computers was simple. All of the PC world ran MS-DOS, and complete C programs were contained in source files. You invoked the compiler, which transformed those files into an executable program file. You then ran it and amazed everyone with your great talent.

Now, all of that has changed. Modern programs can be designed for DOS, Windows 16 bit, Windows 32 bit, or Windows NT. Many of them must run on all four operating systems. In the Windows programs, you not only have source files (with CPP file extensions), you also have resource files (RC), module-definition files (DEF), project files (PRJ), header files (H), and four different types of executable files (EXE), one for each "target" operating system. In short, the programmer's life is becoming increasingly complex.

In response, Borland has beefed up its project management in this release. In C++ 4.0, a *project* is the set of all files and option settings needed to build executable files for all of that application's target operating systems. The target is the operating system(s) where the completed program will run. This information is kept in a file called XXX.PRJ, where XXX represents a project name chosen by the programmer.

All of the examples in this book should be built by using a project. These projects can all be built to an EasyWin target, except for a few that should be built to a DOS target (the latter are clearly indicated). An EasyWin target is one that is mainly text in a window. All the examples should be run in this configuration unless otherwise noted. In Chapter 3, you will create a program in an EasyWin target. The following example illustrates the use of a DOS target.

## Example

In order to understand how to use the IDE, you will proceed to create a project that builds to a DOS target:

1. In Windows, open the Borland C++ 4.0 program group.

2. Double-click on the Borland C++ icon. This brings you to the IDE.

   On the menu bar across the top of the window you will see a selection labeled Project.

3. Choose **Project** | **New project**.

4. Select Application [.exe] from the Target Type list and DOS Standard from the Platform list.

5. Click on the Advanced button (the one marked by the propeller-head symbol).

6. Select .cpp as the Initial Node; then choose OK.

7. Accept the defaults for the rest of the settings by choosing OK in the New Project window.

   At this point a Project window appears with an outline of the project components. The [.exe] represents the target, and the [.cpp] represents the one and only component. Normally, you will have many components, and possibly many targets, in the same project.

8. Double-click on the [.cpp] entry in the Project window.

9. At this point, an editing window appears. Type the program that follows. Be as accurate as possible, because a single typing error can cause the C++ compiler to generate a series of errors. This program's purpose is simply to give you practice using the Borland C++ editor and compiler.

*Comment your program with the program name.*
*Include the header file iostream.h.*
 *Start the main() function.*
  *Print "Hello, World!" to the screen*
   *Exit the main() function.*

> **Note:** The preceding description is the design of the C2SAMPLE.CPP program. This mixture of plain English and commands from a programming language is called *pseudocode*. Pseudocode is used by some programmers to put their ideas on paper quickly. Throughout this book, pseudocode descriptions are presented immediately before sections of actual code.

```
// Filename: C2SAMPLE.CPP
// Prints "Hello, World!"

#include <iostream.h>

main()
    {
    int i;
    cout << "Hello, World! Press 1 to return.";
    cin >> i;
    return 0;                        // Return status
    }
```

**10.** Choose **D**ebug | **R**un from the menu bar. After a few dialog boxes appear and disappear, the screen goes black and Hello, World! appears. Press 1 and then press Enter to return to the IDE.

## Getting Help

When using Borland C++, you can get help at any time by using the on-line help feature. The help system provides several kinds of help that explain virtually every aspect of Borland C++. Depending on your request, the Help system may even offer sample programs that you can merge into your own programs.

Selecting **H**elp | **C**ontents gives the Borland C++ programmer a "road map" to the various categories of help available. When you double-click on a topic shown, you get a help screen specific to that topic. The **H**elp | **C**ontents screen is shown in figure 2.3.

**Figure 2.3.**

The **H**elp|**C**ontents screen.

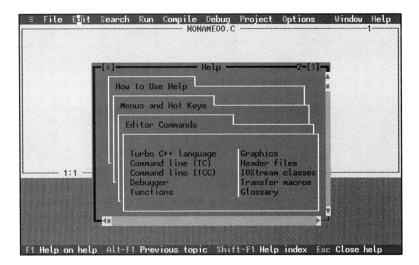

Choosing **Search** from the button bar displays a dialog box with a list of more than 1,000 functions, constants, variables, and topics used in Borland C++. At this point, most of the entries probably make little sense to you. As you learn more about Borland C++, you will understand these topics better.

### Example

The Borland C++ on-line help system is so complete that it even offers help about using the help system. Select the **Help** menu, then choose Using **help**. A window appears that walks you through all aspects of using the help system (see figure 2.4). You can click on any of the words highlighted in green to get additional details on that topic.

After you become familiar with Borland C++, the *context-sensitive help* feature relieves some of your programming frustration. Whenever you request context-sensitive help by pressing Ctrl+F1, Borland C++ "looks" at what you are doing and gives you help with your current problem. For example, if you are working on the Borland C++ `iostream.h` header and the cursor is on the word `iostream.h`, when you press Ctrl+F1 Borland C++ displays help on the *iostream class*.

Choosing **Help** | **About** displays a dialog box in the center of the screen that shows which version of Borland C++ you are using. This is helpful when you call Borland for support and need to supply the version number. Pressing Esc or choosing OK removes this dialog box from the screen and returns you to the program-editing window.

**Figure 2.4.**

Getting help from the help system.

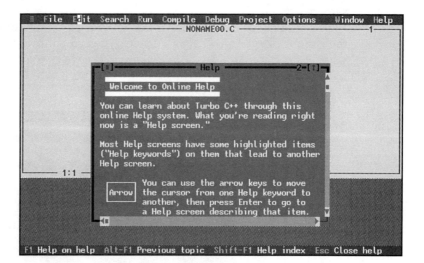

## Quitting Borland C++

When you finish your session, you can exit Borland C++ and return to the program manager by choosing **File** | **Exit**. If you made changes to a project and you try to exit without saving the changes to disk, Borland C++ displays a warning message in a dialog box. It asks if you want to save your changes. You may answer Yes to save them, No to discard them, or Cancel to remain in the IDE.

## Summary

This chapter introduced you to the Borland C++ environment. The major advantages of Borland C++ over its predecessors. In this chapter, you learned how to start Borland C++, create a project, request on-line help, and exit Borland C++.

## Review Questions

Answers to Review Questions are in Appendix B.

1. What is a project?
2. What is a target?
3. How do you display the **Help** | **Contents** screen?

4. What does *context-sensitive help* mean?
5. What are keyboard shortcut keys used for?

6. What is an integrated development environment?
7. How does an EasyWin target differ from a DOS target?
8. How do you build a C++ executable program file? a C executable program file?

## Review Exercises

1. Find out the version of Borland C++ that you are running.

2. Use the Help menu to find instruction on how to use the project management features of Borland C++?

3. Create a new project. Make its target type an application for a Win32 platform. Be sure that it is a C++ program (rather than a C program).

# CHAPTER 3

# C++ Programs

This chapter introduces you to fundamental programming concepts. The task of programming computers has been described as rewarding, challenging, easy, difficult, fast, and slow. It is all of these, and more. Programming your computer takes some time to do well, but you will have fun along the way, especially with the rich assortment of features offered by C++. Writing complex programs to solve advanced problems takes time and can be frustrating, but once you get a complex program working, the feeling is gratifying.

In this chapter, you will learn about the concept of programming from a program's design to its execution on your computer. Before you finish the chapter, you will have typed and executed a simple C++ program.

This chapter covers the following topics:

+ The concept of programming

+ Running C++ programs

+ The program's output

+ Program design

+ Using the Borland C++ editor

+ Using the Borland C++ compiler

## Computer Programs

As you learned in Chapter 1, a program is a set of instructions that causes the computer to manipulate data.

Keep in mind that computers are just machines. They will not do anything until they are given very detailed instructions. If you use your computer for word processing, the word processor is actually a program that someone wrote (in a language such as C++) that tells the computer exactly how to behave when you type words into it.

You are familiar with the concept of programming if you have ever followed a recipe. A recipe is just a program (a set of instructions) that tells the cook how to make a certain dish. A good recipe gives the instructions in the proper order and provides a complete description so that the cook can make everything successfully and with no assumptions.

If you want your computer to help with your budget, keep track of names and addresses, or compute gas mileage for your car travel, the computer needs a program that tells it how to do those things. There are two ways to supply that program for your computer:

◆ Buy a program written by somebody else that does the job you want done.

◆ Write the program yourself.

Writing the program yourself has an advantage for some applications: the program will do exactly what you want it to do. If you buy one that is already written, you will have to adapt your needs to those of the designers of the program. That is where C++ comes into the picture. With the C++ programming language (and enough study), you can make your computer perform almost any reasonable task.

To create a C++ program for your computer, you must have an *editor* and a C++ *compiler*. Similar to a word processor, an editor is a program that lets you type a C++ program into memory, make changes to it (such as move, copy, insert, and delete text), and save that program more permanently in a disk file.

After you type the program by using the editor, you must compile the program before you run it. C++ is implemented as a *compiled* language. You run a program on your computer until you have compiled it. A C++ compiler translates the instructions into a form executable by your computer.

If you know the BASIC programming language, you may not have heard of a compiler or understand the need for one. That is because BASIC (as well as APL and some versions of other computer languages) is not a compiled language but an *interpreted* language. Rather than translate the entire program into machine-executable form (as a compiler does), an interpreter translates each program instruction and then executes it before translating the next one. The difference between a compiler and an interpreter is subtle, but the bottom line is not: compilers produce *much* more efficient and faster-running programs than interpreters do. In addition, the program you've written does not require its user to have a copy of the interpreter in order to run the program; the compiler will produce an independently executable program. The seemingly extra step of compiling is thus worth the effort (and with today's compilers, there is not much extra effort needed).

Because computers are machines, the instructions you write in C++ must be very detailed. You cannot assume that the computer understands what to do if an instruction is missing from your program, or if you include an instruction that does not conform to C++ language requirements.

---

**The Program and Its Output**

While programming, remember the difference between the program and its output. Your program contains the instructions you write by using C++. Only after you run the program does the computer actually follow your instructions.

Throughout this book, you often will see a program listing (the C++ instructions in the program) followed by the program's results (whatever occurs when you run it). The results, which are the output of the program, go to an output device, such as the screen, the printer, or a disk file.

---

## Program Design

Design your programs before typing them into the computer.

The most important part of programming is designing. Learning the C++ language is a requirement, but that is not the only thing to consider. There are two basic approaches to program design that you should learn. The first is called *structured programming*. To write a program using the structured programming methodology, you should follow these steps:

1. Define the problem to solve with the computer.

2. Design the output of the program (what the user sees).

3. Break down the program into logical steps to achieve the program's output.

4. Write the program (this is where the editor is useful).

5. Compile the program.

6. Test the program to make sure that it performs as expected.

As you can see, the actual typing of the program occurs toward the end of programming. The order of these steps is important, as you must plan how to tell a computer the way to perform a certain task.

The second approach is called *object-oriented programming*. To write a program using the object-oriented methodology, you should follow these steps:

1. Define the problem to solve with the computer.

2. Identify the unique objects in the problem domain.

3. Identify the interactions among objects.

4. Create classes of objects by defining variables that represent the possible states that the object may be in during the life of the program.

5. Identify the messages that each object should accept, and code the routines to cause the objects to react properly to these messages. Attach these message-handling routines to the object classes as member functions. Test each class as you complete it.

6. Declare objects of these classes.

7. Decide what the state of the system should be at startup.

8. Compile, link, and execute the system.

For many of you, the structured approach will be more familiar. Good systems can be written using either approach, but the object-oriented way is gaining converts at a rapid pace. It would be a wise investment of your time to study object-oriented programming carefully in Chapters 33 through 36.

Your computer can only perform instructions step by step. You must assume that the computer has no previous knowledge of the problem, and it is up to you to supply it with that knowledge. That is what good recipes do. It would be foolish if a recipe for baking a cake simply said, "Bake the cake." Why? Because it assumes far too much on the part of the cook. Even if the recipe is written out step by step, care must be taken (through advance planning) to be sure that the steps are in the proper sequence. Putting the ingredients in the oven *before* stirring them would not be prudent!

In programs presented throughout this book, this programming process is adhered to. Before seeing a program, you will read about its design. The goals of the program will be presented, those goals will be broken down into logical steps, and then the program will be written.

Designing the program in advance makes the entire program structure more accurate and keeps you from having to make many changes. A builder knows that a room is much harder to add after the house is built. If you do not plan properly and think out every aspect of your program's steps, it will take you longer to create the final, working program. Making major changes to programs is more difficult after they are written.

Using a formal approach to developing programs will become more important to you as you write longer and more complicated programs. Throughout this book, you will see tips for program design. Now is the time to launch C++, so that you can see what it's like to create your own program and watch it run.

# Using the Borland C++ Editor

The instructions in your C++ program are called *source code*. You type source code into your computer's memory with your editor. Once you type the C++ source code (your program), you should save it to a disk file before compiling and running it. Most C++ compilers expect C++ source programs to be stored in files with names ending in CPP. For example, all of the following are valid file names for most C++ compilers:

MYPROG.CPP     SALESACT.CPP          EMPLYEE.CPP ACCREC.CPP

Figure 3.1 shows a Borland C++ screen. Across the top of the screen is a menu bar that offers pull-down menus for editing, compiling, and running options. Without Borland C++'s integrated environment, you would have to start an editor, type your program, save the program to disk, exit the editor, run the compiler, and only then run the compiled program from the operating system. With this integrated environment, you just type the program into the editor and then select the proper menu option that compiles and runs the program in one step.

**Figure 3.1.**

Borland C++'s integrated environment.

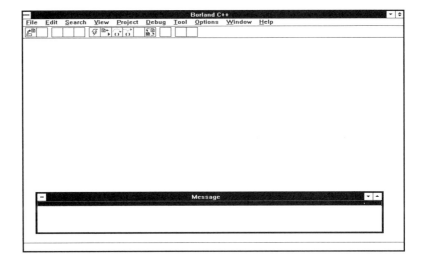

# Using the C++ Compiler

Once you type and edit your C++ program's source code, you must compile the program. When you compile the program on your PC, the compiler will eventually produce an executable file whose name begins with the same name as the source code but ends in an EXE file extension. For example, if your source program is named GRADEAVG.CPP, you will wind up with a compiled file called GRADEAVG.EXE, which you could execute from the DOS prompt by typing the name GRADEAVG.

> **Note:** Each program in this book contains a comment that specifies a recommended file name for the source program. You do not have to follow the file-naming conventions used in this book. The file names in the program listings are only suggestions. If, however, you decide to obtain the sample diskette that contains a listing of each program in this book, the file names of the program listings will match those on the diskette you receive.

Unlike many other programming languages, C++ normally routes programs through a *preprocessor* before they are compiled. C++ source code can contain *preprocessor directives* that control the way your programs compile. The preprocessor step is performed automatically by Borland C++, so it requires no additional effort or commands to learn on your part.

There is one additional step your program must go through after compiling and before running. This step is called the *linking* stage. When your program is linked, needed runtime information (which is not always available to the compiler) is supplied to your program. You can also take several compiled programs and combine them into one executable program by linking them together. Borland C++ initiates the linking stage automatically, so you do not have to worry about the process.

Figure 3.2 shows the steps that Borland C++ performs to produce an executable program.

**Figure 3.2.**

Compiling C++ source code into an executable program.

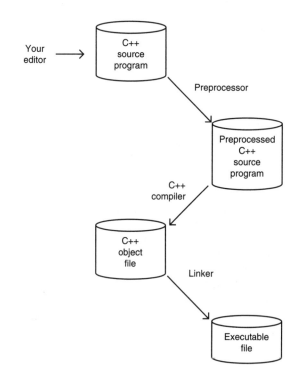

# Running a Sample Program

Before delving into the specifics of the C++ language, you should take a few moments to get familiar with the Borland C++ Integrated Development Environment (IDE). You start the IDE by performing the following steps:

1. Install Borland C++ 4.0 according to the installation instructions in the box.

2. Start Microsoft Windows.

3. Open the Borland C++ 4.0 program group.

4. Double-click the mouse (press the left button twice rapidly) on the icon named Borland C++.

   Your screen should resemble figure 3.1 at this point. On the menu bar across the top of the window you will see a selection labeled Project. The *project* is the main working unit in Borland C++ 4.0. The reason for this is simple. Most of the program development now taking place is for the Windows family of operating systems. Windows programs require multiple files. Managing these separate files is difficult if the tools don't support it. Borland's way of supporting multifile programming is the project. As long as the programs you write are simple ones, the *project* feature will seem like overkill. As your programs increase in complexity, however, you will begin to appreciate it more and more.

5. Choose **P**roject | **N**ew Project.

   Your screen should look like figure 3.3.

**Figure 3.3.**

Creating a new project.

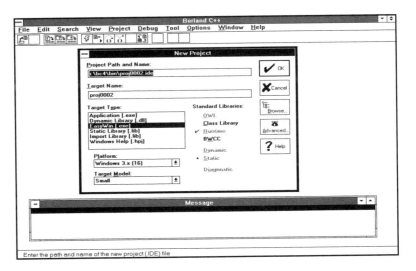

6. Choose EasyWin as your Target Type. This is a simple window that displays text.

7. Click on the Advanced button (marked by the clever propeller-head symbol).

8. Select the .cpp option as the Initial Node, then click on OK.

9. Click on OK in the New Project window.

At this point, a new window appears with an outline of the project components (see figure 3.4) The [.exe] represents the target, and the [.cpp] represents the one and only component. Normally you will have many components and possibly many targets in the same project.

**Figure 3.4.**
The Project Outline.

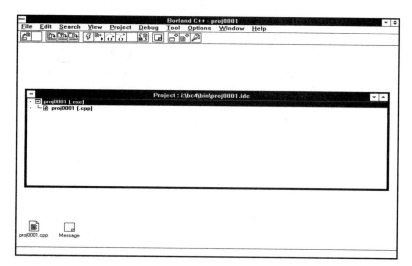

10. Double-click on the [.cpp] entry in the Project Window.

11. At this point, a window will appear. Type in the following program. Be as accurate as possible, because a single typing error can cause the C++ compiler to generate a series of errors. You do not have to understand the program's content; its purpose is simply to give you practice in using the Borland C++ editor and compiler. (Do not type in the Pseudocode. It is a design aid, not part of the actual program.)

*Comment your program with the program name.*
*Include the header file iostream.h.*
*Define the variable BELL as the character code \a, which is a beep.*
*Start of the main() function.*
    *Initialize the integer variable ctr to a zero.*
    *Define the character array fname to hold 20 elements.*

*Print to the screen What is your first name?*
*Accept a string from the keyboard.*
*Process a loop while the variable ctr is less than 5.*
    *Print the string accepted from the keyboard.*
    *Increment the variable ctr by one.*
*Print to the screen the character code that will make the beep.*
*Return out of the main() function.*

**Note:** The preceding description is the design of the C3SAMPLE.CPP program. This is called *pseudocode*. Pseudocode is simply an informal narrative, in English, that help a programmer organize his/her thoughts before beginning to code. Pseudocode is one of several design methods you might use; it is particularly good for writing code in C++.

```cpp
// Filename: C3SAMPLE.CPP
// Requests a name, rings a bell, and prints the name
// 5 times

#include  <iostream.h>

#define   BELL '\a'

main()
    {
    int  ctr = 0;          // Integer variable to count
                           // through loop
    char fname[ 20 ];      // Define character array to hold
                           // name

    cout << "What is your first name? "; // Prompt the user
    cin >> fname;                        // Get the name from
                                         // the keyboard
    while (ctr < 5)                      // Loop to print the
        {                                // name exactly 5
times
        cout << fname << "\n";
        ctr++;
        }
    cout << BELL;                        // Ring the bell
    return 0;                            // Return status
}
```

Again, be as accurate as possible. In most programming languages, and especially in C++, the characters you type in a program must be accurate. In this sample C++ program, there are parentheses ( ( ) ), brackets ( [ ] ), and braces ( { } ); none can be used interchangeably.

Although the comments to the right of some of the lines (the words after the / / ) do not have to end in the same columns as shown in this listing, if you enter the program exactly as shown, you will familiarize yourself with the editor while learning to be accurate with the characters you type.

**12.** Choose **Debug** | **Run** from the menu bar. After a few dialog boxes appear and disappear, you will see another window pop up. This is the EasyWin target that you specified. The program that you entered will appear in this window. Answer the questions and observe the behavior of the program.

## If Errors Are Reported

You are typing instructions for a machine, so you must be very accurate. If you misspell a word, leave out a quotation mark, or make another mistake, your C++ compiler will inform you with an error message. The error will appear in a separate message window, as shown in figure 3.5. The most common error is a *syntax error*, which usually means that a statement is not in the correct form.

**Figure 3.5.**

The compiler reporting program errors.

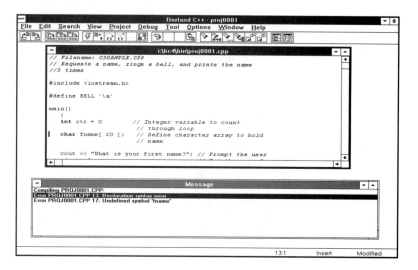

When you get an error message (or more than one), you should return to the editor window and fix the problem. The error message will usually tell you which line contains the error, and double-clicking on the error message will put the cursor on the offending line in the editor window. If you don't understand the error, you may have to check your reference manual or simply scour your program's source code until you find the problem.

---

**Getting the Bugs Out**

One of the first computers, owned by the military, refused to print some important data one day. After programmers tried for many hours to find the solution within the program, a lady named *Grace Hopper* decided to check out the printer.

She found a small moth lodged between two important wires. When she removed the moth, the printer started working perfectly (although the moth did not have as much luck).

Grace Hopper is now a retired admiral, and although she is responsible for developing many important computer concepts (she was the author of the original COBOL language), she may be best known for discovering the first computer *bug*.

Since Admiral Hopper discovered that moth, errors in computer programs have been known as *computer bugs*. When you test your programs, you may have to *debug* them; that is, get the bugs out by fixing your typing errors and by changing the logic so that the program does exactly what you want it to do.

---

Once you have typed in your program correctly and you get no compile errors, the program will run properly by asking for your first name and then by printing it five times on the screen. After the fifth time, your computer's bell will ring.

## Summary

This chapter helped you understand the steps required to write a program using Borland C++. You know now that advanced planning makes program writing much easier and that the program's instructions produce output only after you run the program.

You also saw how to use Borland C++'s editor and compiler. Now that you know how to run a C++ program, it is time to start learning the actual C++ programming language.

## Review Questions

Answers to Review Questions are in Appendix B.

1. What is a program?

2. What do you use to type C++ programs into the computer?

3. What file name extension do C++ programs typically have?

4. What does the term *debug* mean?

5. True or false: You must link a program before compiling it.

CHAPTER 4

# Running a Program

Before looking at the specifics of the C++ language, many people like to walk through a few simple programs to get a feel for what a C++ program is like. This chapter introduces a few C++ language commands and elements.

The following topics are covered:

♦ An overview of C++ programs and their structure

♦ Including comments in C++ programs

♦ Variables and constants—what they are and their types

♦ Simple math operators

♦ Screen output

Some of the commands mentioned in this chapter are covered more formally in later chapters.

## Looking at a C++ Program

Figure 4.1 shows the outline of a typical small C++ program. No C++ commands are shown in the figure. Although there is much more to a program than the outline suggests, this is the general format of the early programs in this book.

To get acquainted with C++ programs as quickly as possible, you should begin by looking at a C++ program in its entirety. Following is a listing of a very simple C++ program. It does not do much, but it lets you get familiar with the general format of the C++ language. The next few sections discuss elements in this program. You may not understand everything in the program (even after finishing this chapter), but it is a good place to start. If there is something specific that you do not understand, that is okay for now.

```
// Filename: C4FIRST.CPP
// Initial C++ program that demonstrates the C++ comments
// and shows a few variables and their declarations

#include     <iostream.h>

main()
    {
    int      i;   // These 4 lines declare 4 variables
    int      j;
    char     c;
    float    x;

    i = 4;        // i and j are assigned integer constants

    j = i + 7;

    c = 'A';      // All character constants are enclosed in
                  // single quotes

    x = 9.087;    // x requires a floating-point value
                  // since it was declared as a
                  // floating-point variable

    x = x * 4.5;  // Change what was in x with a formula
    // Send the values of the variables to the screen
```

**Fig. 4.1.**

A skeleton outline for a simple C++ program.

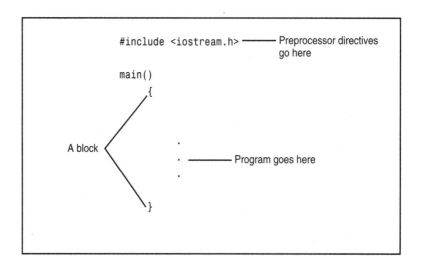

```
    cout << i << j << c << x;

        return 0;       // ALWAYS end programs and functions with
                        // return

    }
```

For now, just familiarize yourself with the overall program. Look through it to see whether you can understand parts or all of it. If you are new to programming, you should know that the computer will look at each line of the program, starting with the first line and working its way down, until all the instructions given in the program have been performed. (Of course, the program first has to be compiled, as described in the last chapter.)

The output of this program is minimal; it simply displays four values on the screen after performing some assignments and calculations of arbitrary values. Just concentrate on the general format at this point.

## The Format of C++ Programs

C++ is a free-form language.

Unlike some other programming languages, such as COBOL, C++ is a *free-form* programming language. This means that programming statements can start in any column of any line. You can insert blank lines in a program if you want. This chapter's sample program, called C4FIRST.CPP, contains several blank lines. (You can find the name of each program in this book in the first line of each listing.) These blank lines help separate parts of the program. In a simple program like this, the separation is not as critical as it might be in a longer, more complex program.

Generally, spaces within C++ programs are free-form as well. Your goal should not be to make your programs as compact as possible but to make them as readable as possible. For example, the C4FIRST.CPP program *could* be rewritten as follows:

```
// Filename: C4FIRST.CPP Initial C++ program that
// demonstrates the C++ comments and shows a few variables
// and their declarations
#include <iostream.h>
main() {int i;
// These 4 lines declare 4 variables
int j;char c;float x;i=4;//i and j are assigned integer
// constants
j=i+7;c='A';// All character constants are enclosed in single
// quotes
x=9.087;// x requires a floating-point value since
// it was declared as a floating-point variable
x=x*4.5;// Change what was in x with a formula
```

```
cout<<i<<j<<c<<x; // Send the values of the variables
// to the screen
return 0;}// ALWAYS end programs and functions with return
```

To your C++ compiler, these two programs are exactly the same and will produce the same results. However, to people who must read the program, the first style is *much* more readable. Granted, this is an extreme example, but programmers have been known to write code without any blank lines.

## Readability Is the Key

As long as programs do their job and produce correct output, who cares how well they are written? Well, in today's world of fast computers and abundant memory and disk space, *you* should care. Even if no one else ever looks at your C++ program, you might need to make a change to it at a later date. The more readable you make it, the faster you will be able to find what needs to be changed and to make those changes.

If you work as a programmer for a company, you will almost certainly be expected to modify someone else's source code, and others will modify your programs. In programming departments, it is said that long-term employees write readable programs. Given the new global economy and all of the changes facing businesses in the years ahead, companies are seeking programmers who write for the future; that is, their programs are straightforward, readable, and don't include hard-to-read programming tricks.

Put some *white space* into your programs. White space consists of the blank lines and spaces placed throughout a program. Notice that the first few lines in C4FIRST.CPP start in the first column, but the body of the program is indented a few spaces. This helps programmers "zero in" on the important code. When you write programs that contain several sections (called *blocks*), white space helps the programmer's eye drop down more easily to the next indented block.

## Using Uppercase and Lowercase Letters

Uppercase and lowercase letters are much more significant in C++ than in most other programming languages. You will find that most of C4FIRST.CPP is typed in lowercase letters. The C++ keywords are all in lowercase letters. For example, you must type the keywords int, char, and return in lowercase characters in your programs. If you used uppercase letters, your C++ compiler would think that they were variable names. Appendix E shows a list of every command in the C++ programming language. You will find that none of the commands are in uppercase letters.

Most C++ programmers reserve uppercase characters for specific instances. Constants are generally defined in all capitals. The first letter of a class name is generally capitalized, which means that its constructor and destructor functions will be also. (See Chapter 33.)

## Braces and *main()*

All C++ programs require the following lines:

```
main()
    {
```

A C++ block is enclosed between a pair of braces.

The statements following `main()` will be the first statements executed. The section of a C++ program that begins with `main()`, followed by an opening brace (`{`), is called the *main function*. A C++ program is actually a group of functions (small sections of code), and the function called `main()` is required and is always the first function executed.

In the sample program shown here, almost the entire program is `main()` because the closing brace (`}`) that follows `main()`'s opening brace is at the end of the program. Everything between the two braces is called a *block*. You will read more about blocks later. For now, you should realize that this sample program contains only a single function, `main()`, and that the entire function is a single block because there is only one pair of braces.

All executable C++ statements must end with a semicolon (`;`).

In addition, you should realize that many statements have a semicolon (`;`) after them. Every executable C++ statement must be followed by a semicolon so that C++ will know where the statements end. The computer ignores all comments, so you don't need to put semicolons after comments. The lines with `main()` and braces do not end with semicolons either; these lines simply define the beginning and the end of the function and do not actually execute.

Figure 4.2 repeats the sample program and contains additional markings to help acquaint you with these new terms. Also included are a few other items that are described later in the chapter.

**Figure 4.2.**

The parts of the sample program.

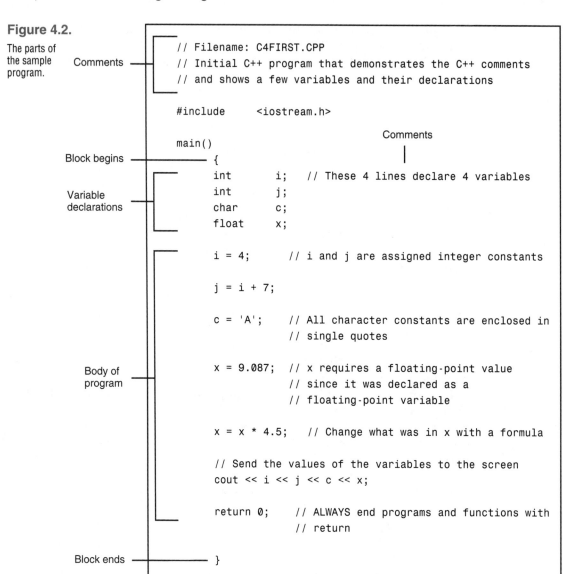

## Comments in C++

In Chapter 3, you learned the difference between a program and its output. Most users of a program do not see the program itself; they see the output from the execution of the program's instructions. Programmers, however, look at the program listings, add new routines, change old ones, and add new features.

As explained earlier, the readability of a program is important. Nevertheless, no matter how clearly you write C++ programs, you can always improve readability by putting *comments* throughout the program listings.

A comment is a message that explains what is going on at a given point in the program. For example, if you wrote a payroll program, you might put a comment before the check-printing routine to describe what was about to happen. You do not put C++ language statements inside a comment—a comment is a message to people looking at your programs, not a message to the computer. Your C++ compiler ignores all comments in a program.

Comments can span more than one line. Notice in the sample program, C4FIRST.CPP (figure 4.2), that the first three lines are actually a single comment. This comment explains the file name and a little about the program.

Comments can also share lines with C++ commands. There are several comments off to the right of much of the C4FIRST.CPP program. These comments explain what the individual lines do. Use abundant comments, but remember who they are for: *people, not computers.* Use comments if they help explain the code, but do not *over*comment. For example, even though you may not be familiar with C++ yet, the following statement is easy to understand; it prints the words Borland C++ By Example on the screen:

> Comments describe to people what the program is doing.

```
cout << "Borland C++ By Example"; // Print Turbo C++ By
                                  // Example on the screen
```

This comment is redundant and adds nothing to the understanding of the line of code. It would be much better in this case to leave the comment out completely. Comment only when necessary.

If a comment does not span more than one line in your program file, you can start the comment with //. The comment is read from the // to the end of the line. If the comment does span more than one line, you can either start each subsequent line with a //, or you can wrap the comment by starting it with /* and ending it with */.

The following example shows the use of /* and */ on a two-line comment:

```
/* Print Borland C++ By Example
   on the screen */
cout << "Borland C++ By Example";
```

> **Note:** C++ comments usually begin with the // symbol.

Of course, it does not matter whether you use uppercase letters, lowercase letters, or both in comments because C++ ignores comments. Most C++ programmers capitalize the first letter of sentences in comments, just as they would in everyday writing. Since people, not computers, read your comments, use whatever case seems most appropriate for the message in the comment.

### Comment as You Go

Put comments in your programs *as you write them.* You are most familiar with your program logic at the time you are typing the program in the editor. Some people put off including comments until after the program is written. More often than not, the comments never get put in, or only a half-hearted attempt is made to do so.

If you comment as you write your code, you can glance up at the comments while working on later sections of the program, instead of having to decipher the previous code. This helps greatly when you want to look at something you wrote earlier in the program.

## Examples

1. Suppose that you wanted to write a C++ program to produce a fancy boxed title with your name in it and flashing dots around it (like a marquee). The C++ code required to do this may be difficult to understand and may not, by itself, be understandable to others who look at the program. Before such code, then, you might want to insert the following comment:

```
// The following lines draw a box around
// a name and then display flashing dots around it
// to look like a movie marquee.
```

This would not tell C++ to do anything, because a comment is not a C++ command. The comment would, however, make the next few lines of code more understandable to you and to others. The comment explains in English, for the people reading the program, exactly what the program will be doing next.

**2.** You should put the disk file name of the program in an early comment. For example, in the C4FIRST.CPP program shown earlier, the first line is the beginning of a comment:

```
// Filename: C4FIRST.CPP
```

The comment continues on the next two lines, but this part of it explains to anyone who might look at the program listing exactly which disk file it is in. Throughout this book, each program has a comment that includes a suggested file name under which the program can be stored. Each file name begins with C*x*, where *x* represents the chapter number in which the program appears. For example, C6INIT.CPP is in Chapter 6 and C10PAY1.CPP is in Chapter 10. This will help you find the programs in case another section of the book refers to them later.

**Tip:** It also may be a good idea to put your name in a comment at the top of every program. If someone has to modify your program at a later date, that person may want to (or need to) speak with you before changing it.

## The Sample Program Summarized

Now that you have an overview of a C++ program, its structure, and its comments, the rest of this chapter walks you through the entire sample program. Do not attempt to become a C++ expert after you complete this section—that is what the rest of the book is for! Just sit back and follow the discussion of the code.

As described earlier, the C4FIRST.CPP program contains several comments. The first three lines of the program are:

```
// Filename: C4FIRST.CPP
// Initial CPP program that demonstrates the C++ comments
// and shows a few variables and their declarations
```

This comment gives the file name and explains the purpose of the program. This comment is not the only one in the program; others appear throughout the rest of the code.

The next two lines (following the blank separating line) are:

```
main()
    {
```

This begins the `main()` function. Basically, the `main()` function's opening and closing braces enclose the body of this program and the instructions that actually execute. Many times, C++ programs contain more than one function, but they always contain one called `main()`. The `main()` function does not have to be the first one, but it usually is. The opening brace begins the first (and only) block of this program.

When this program is compiled and run, the computer looks for `main()` and starts executing whatever instruction follows `main()`'s opening brace. Here are the next four lines:

```
int        i;      // These 4 lines declare 4 variables
int        j;
char       c;
float      x;
```

These four lines declare variables. A *variable declaration* describes all variables used in that block of code. A C++ program takes data and processes it into meaningful results. All C++ programs include the following:

◆ Commands

◆ Data

The data is made up of *variables* and *constants*. As the name implies, a *variable* is data that can change as the program runs. A *constant* is data that remains the same. In real life, a variable might be your age or salary. Both increase over time (if you are lucky!). Your first name and social security number are constants because they remain unchanged throughout your life.

Chapter 5, "Variables and Constants," fully explains these concepts. However, for an overview of the sample program's elements, the following discussion explains the variables and constants in this program.

C++ allows several kinds of constants. For now, you simply need to understand that a C++ constant is any number, character, word, or phrase. All of the following are valid C++ constants:

```
5.6          -45     'Q'     "Mary"     18.67643     0.0
```

As you can see, some constants are numeric and some are character-based. The single and double quotation marks around two of the constants are not part of the constants themselves. A single-character constant requires single quotes around it, whereas a string of characters, such as `Mary`, requires double quotation marks.

If you look for the constants in the sample program, you will find the following:

```
4          7     'A'     9.087     4.5
```

A variable is like a box inside your computer that holds something. That something might be a number or a character. You can have as many variables as your program needs in order to hold data that changes in the program. Once you put a value into a variable, it stays in that variable until you do one of the following: change it, end the block of code in which it is defined, or turn off your computer.

Variables have names so you can tell them apart. You use the *assignment operator*, the equal sign (=), to assign values to variables. The statement

```
sales = 25000;
```

puts the constant value 25000 into the variable named sales. In the sample program, you will find the following variables:

```
i    j    c    x
```

The four lines of code that follow the opening brace of the sample program declare these variables. This variable declaration lets the rest of the program know that two integer variables named i and j, as well as a character variable called c and a floating-point variable called x, will appear throughout the program. If the terms *integer* and *floating point* are new to you, these refer to two different types of numbers: integers are whole numbers, and floating-point numbers contain decimal points.

You can see the variables being assigned values in the next few statements in the sample program:

```
i = 4;        // i and j are assigned integer constants

j = i + 7;

c = 'A';      // All character constants are enclosed in
              // single quotes

x = 9.087;    // x requires a floating-point value
              // since it was declared as a
              // floating-point variable

x = x * 4.5;  // Change what was in x with a formula
```

The first line puts a 4 in the integer variable i. The second line adds a 7 to variable i's value to get an 11, which then gets assigned to (put into) the variable called j. The plus sign (+) in C++ works the same way it does on calculators. The other primary math operators are shown in table 4.1.

**Table 4.1. The primary math operators.**

| Operator | Meaning | Example |
|---|---|---|
| + | Addition | 4 + 5 |
| - | Subtraction | 7 - 2 |
| * | Multiplication | 12 * 6 |
| / | Division | 48 / 12 |

The character constant A is assigned to the c variable. The number 9.087 is assigned to the variable called x, and then x is immediately overwritten with a new value: itself (9.087) times 4.5. This helps illustrate why computer designers use an asterisk (*) for multiplication and not a small x as people do when multiplying on paper. If both were allowed, the computer would confuse the variable x with the multiplication symbol $x$.

> **Tip:** If there are mathematical operators on the right side of the equal sign, the math is done completely before the assignment is performed.

The next line (after the comment) includes the following special (and at first confusing) statement:

```
cout << i << j << c << x;
```

When the program runs and gets to this line, it prints the contents of the four variables on the screen.

The actual output from this line is

```
4 11 A 40.891499
```

The cout is not a C++ command but is actually the name of an object that controls your monitor's screen; the << is an operator defined by the person who implemented the stream classes. You'll learn about classes in Chapter 33.

```
return 0;      // ALWAYS end programs and functions with
               // return

}
```

*Put a return state-
ment at the end
of each function.*

The return statement simply tells C++ that this function is finished and to return a value of zero to DOS.

The return statement is optional. C++ would know when it reached the end of the program without a return. It is a good programming practice, however, to put a return statement at the end of every function, including main().

The closing brace after the return does three things in this program: it signals the end of a block (which was begun earlier with the opening brace), the end of the main() function, and the end of the program.

## Summary

This chapter focused on commenting your programs well. You also learned a little about variables and constants, which hold the program's data.

Now you can begin to write your own programs. Chapter 5 takes a detailed look at constants and variables, describes their uses, and explains how you choose names for them.

## Review Questions

Answers to Review Questions are in Appendix B.

1. What must go before and after each multiline comment in a C++ program?

2. What is a variable?

3. What is a constant?

4. True or false: Semicolons are optional in C++.

5. What are four C++ math operators?

6. What operator puts a value into a variable? (*Hint*: It is called the *assignment operator*.)

7. True or false: A variable can consist of only two types: integer and character.

8. Is the following a variable name or a string constant?

    ```
    city
    ```

9. What, if anything, is wrong with the following C++ statement?

    ```
    RETURN;
    ```

# Variables and Constants

To understand programming with C++, you must comprehend how C++ creates, stores, and manipulates data. This chapter introduces the following topics:

- Defining variables and constants
- Naming and using C++ variables
- The types of C++ variables
- Declaring variables
- Assigning values to variables
- The types of C++ constants
- Special constants

Now that you have an overview of C++, you can begin to write your own programs. Before you are done with this chapter, you will be writing your own simple C++ programs from scratch.

You learned in the last chapter that C++ programs consist of commands and data. Data is the heart of all C++ programs; if you do not correctly declare or use variables and constants, your data will be inaccurate. Your results will be incorrect, as well. An old computer adage says that if you put "Garbage in, you will get garbage out!" Most of the time, people blame computers for mistakes that are made. The computers themselves are probably not to blame; the data was most likely entered into the programs incorrectly.

This chapter focuses on both numeric variables and constants. If you are not a "numbers" person, don't be alarmed. Working with numbers is the computer's job. You just have to understand how to let the computer know what you want it to do.

> **Note:** A computer's memory is divided into small blocks of space. Each of these blocks is large enough to hold one instance of a certain type of data. Each block of space is called a *memory location*. If the program specifies that a location should be reserved to hold changing values, it is called a variable. A *variable* has the following characteristics:
>
> ◆ An address in memory that the computer uses to locate the variable
>
> ◆ A name, so that the programmer doesn't have to remember an address
>
> ◆ A type which tells the compiler what kind of operations can legally be performed on the variable
>
> ◆ A value

# Variables

Variables have characteristics. When you decide that your program needs another variable, you simply declare a new one. C++ makes sure that you get it. You declare all C++ variables within whatever block of code needs them. To declare a variable, you must give it the following:

◆ A name

◆ A type

◆ A value

The computer assigns the address. You usually don't need to know the address. If you do, however, you can get the address by using the **&** in front of the name. The following sections explain these characteristics.

## Naming Variables

You can have many variables in a single program. Therefore, you must assign names to each so that you can keep track of them. Variable names are unique, as are house addresses. If two variables had the same name, C would not know which variable you wanted when you requested one of them.

Variable names can be as short as a single letter. Their names must begin with a letter of the alphabet or an underscore (_). After the first letter or underscore, they can contain letters, numbers, and additional underscores.

> **Tip:** The underscore (_) helps separate parts of the variable name. The reason the underscore is used is that the name cannot contain spaces.

The following variable names are valid:

```
salary      aug91_sales    _i      index_age      amount
```

It is customary to use lowercase letters for C++ variable names, and to capitalize the first letter of a class name. You do not have to follow this convention. However, you should know that the compiler interprets uppercase and lowercase letters in variable names differently. Therefore, each of the following four variables appears completely different to your C++ compiler:

```
sales   Sales   SALES   sALES
```

Do not give a variable the name of a command or library function.

Be very careful with the Shift key when you type a variable name. Do not inadvertently change the case of a variable name throughout a program; if you do, C++ thinks that they are distinct and separate variables, and does not operate on them properly.

Variables cannot have the same name as a C++ command or a library function. Appendix E contains a list of all C++ command and library function names. Avoid these when naming variables.

Some *invalid* variable names are as follows:

```
81_sales    Aug91+Sales    MY AGE    cout
```

---

**Use Meaningful Variable Names**

Although you can call a variable any name that fits the naming rules (as long as the name is not being used by another variable in the program), you should always use meaningful variable names. Use names that help describe the values held by the variables.

For example, keeping track of total payroll in a variable referred to as `total_payroll` is more descriptive than using the variable name `XYZ34`. Even though both names are valid, `total_payroll` is easier to remember. You also have a good idea of what the variable holds by looking at its name.

---

## Variable Types

Variables can hold different *types* of data. Table 5.1 lists the different types of C++ variables. For instance, if a variable holds an integer, C++ assumes that no decimal point or fractional part (the number(s) to the right of the decimal point) exists for the variable's value. Many types are possible in C++. For now, the most important types on which you should concentrate are `char`, `int`, and `float`. Using the `unsigned` prefix lets them hold positive numbers only.

**Table 5.1. Possible C++ variable types that can hold data.**

| Declaration Name | Type |
| --- | --- |
| char | Character |
| unsigned char | Unsigned character |
| signed char | Signed character (same as char) |
| int | Integer |
| unsigned int | Unsigned integer |
| signed int | Signed integer (same as int) |
| short int | Short integer |
| unsigned short int | Unsigned short integer |
| signed short int | Signed short integer (same as short int) |
| long | Long integer |
| long int | Long integer (same as long) |
| signed long int | Signed long integer (same as long int) |
| unsigned long int | Unsigned long integer |
| float | Floating-point |
| double | Double floating-point |
| long double | Long double floating-point |

The next section describes each of these types in more detail. For now, you need to concentrate on the importance of declaring these variable types before using them. You can declare a variable in two places:

◆ Inside a block of code

◆ Preceding a function name, such as before main()

The first of these locations is the most common, and is used throughout much of this book. (If preceding a function name you declare a variable, it is referred to as a *global* variable. Later chapters address the pros and cons of global variables.) To declare a variable, you must state its type followed by its name. In the last chapter, you saw a program that declared four variables in the following way:

*Start of the main() function.*
   *Declare the variables i and j as integers.*
   *Declare the variable c as a character.*
   *Declare the variable x as a floating-point variable.*

```
main()

    {
    int      i;   // These four lines declare four
    int      j;   // variables
    char     c;
    float    x;
    // Rest of program follows
```

This declares two integer variables named i and j. You have no idea, however, what is inside those variables. You generally cannot assume that a variable holds zero, or any other number, until you assign a value to it. The first two lines basically tell C++ the following:

"This program is going to use two integer variables. Expect them. They are to be named i and j. Please ensure that the value put into i or j is an integer and not a floating-point number or anything else."

The second line in this example declares a character variable referred to as c. Only single characters should be placed there. A floating-point variable referred to as x is declared next.

You must declare all variables in a C++ program before you use them.

## Examples

**1.** Suppose that you have to keep track of a person's first, middle, and last initials. An initial is obviously a character. Therefore, it would be prudent to declare three character variables to hold the three initials. In C++, you can do that with the following statement:

```
main()
    {
    char     first, middle, last;
    // Rest of program follows
```

This statement can go after the opening brace of main(), and lets the rest of the program know that you require these three character variables.

**2.** You also can declare these three variables on three separate lines, improving readability and maintainability:

```
main()
    {
    char     first;
    char     middle;
    char     last;
    // Rest of program follows
```

**3.** Suppose that you want to keep track of a person's age and weight. If you want to store these values as whole numbers, they can probably go into integer variables. The following statement declares these variables:

```
main()
    {
    int      age, weight;
    // Rest of program follows
```

4. The next section explores each of the variable types in detail. Many types exist for you to use. However, you typically employ character, integer, and floating-point variables more than any other. In short, a character variable holds a single character, and an integer variable—a single whole number. A float variable holds a number that contains a decimal point.

Suppose that a teacher wants to keep track of the average of each of these: a class score and the letter grade. The teacher also wants to keep a log of the number of students in the class. Notice that the following program fragment uses all three common types of variables:

```
main()
    {
    char          letter_grade;
    float     class_avg;
    int           class_size;
    // Rest of program follows
```

## Looking at Data Types

You might be wondering why it's important to have so many variable types. After all, a number is just a number. C++ has more data types than just about any other programming language. The type of a variable is very important. It is used by the the compiler to tell when we try to do something obviously wrong, such as add two characters together. For the programmer, knowing the correct type to use is not as difficult as it might seem at first.

The character variable is very easy to understand. This variable can hold only a single character. You cannot put more than a single character into a character variable.

> **Note:** C++ does not have a string variable, as do many other programming languages. You cannot hold more than a single character in a C++ character variable. To store a string of characters, you must use an *aggregate* variable type, which combines other fundamental types from table 5.1 to create an array. Chapter 6, "Character Strings and Character Arrays," explains this in more detail.

Integer variables hold whole numbers. Although mathematicians might cringe at this definition, an *integer* is really just any number that does not contain a decimal point. All the following are integers:

```
45     -932     0     12     5421
```

Floating-point numbers contain decimal points. They are known as *real* numbers to mathematicians. Whenever you need to store salaries, temperatures, or any other numbers that might have a fractional part (a decimal portion), you must store them in a floating-point variable. All the following are floating-point numbers, and any of the floating-point variables can hold them:

```
45.12    -2344.5432    0.00    .04594
```

Sometimes you have to keep track of very large numbers or very small ones. Table 5.2 shows a list of ranges that each C++ variable type might hold. *Use this table only as a guide*; varying types of compilers and computers might enable different ranges.

**Table 5.2. These are typical ranges of numbers that C++ variables can hold.**

| Type | Range |
| --- | --- |
| char | −128 to 127 |
| unsigned char | 0 to 255 |
| signed char | −128 to 127 |
| int | −32768 to 32767 |
| unsigned int | 0 to 65535 |
| signed int | −32768 to 32767 |
| short int | −32768 to 32767 |
| unsigned short int | 0 to 65535 |
| signed short int | −32768 to 32767 |
| long int | −2147483648 to 2147483647 |
| signed long int | −2147483648 to 2147483647 |
| unsigned long int | 0 to 4294967295 |
| float | −3.4E+38 to 3.4E+38 |
| double | −1.7E+308 to 1.7E+308 |
| long double | −1.7E+308 to 1.7E+308 |

**Note:** The table shows floating-point ranges in scientific notation. To determine the actual range, multiply the number before the E (meaning exponent) by 10 raised to the power after the plus sign. For instance, a floating-point number (a type float) can contain a number as small as −3.4 * $10^{38}$.

> **Caution:** All true C++ programmers know that they cannot count on employing this exact table on every computer that uses C++. These ranges might be much different on another computer. Remember to use this table only as a guide.

Notice that both integers and doubles that are long tend to hold larger numbers (and, therefore, higher precision) than both integers and double floating-point variables that are regular. The reason is that a larger number of memory locations are used by many of the C++ compilers for these data types. Again, you cannot count on this always being the case. However, generally it is.

---

**Accommodating the Size of Your Data**

If the long variable types hold larger numbers than the regular ones, you might initially want to use long variables for all your data. This is not required in most cases and will slow down your program's execution.

As Appendix A explains, the more memory locations used by data, the larger that data can be. However, every time your computer has to access more storage for a single variable (which is usually the case for long variables), the CPU takes much longer to access it, calculate with it, and store it. As designed by Kernighan and Ritchie, the basic data types (`char`, `int`, and `float`) should be optimized for the computer. In Borland C++, they are.

Use long variables only if you fear that your data might overflow the normal data type ranges. Although the ranges vary on other computers, you should have an idea of whether your numbers might exceed the computer's storage ranges. If you are working with extremely large numbers (or extremely small fractional numbers), use long variables so they hold the extra data width.

---

Generally, all numeric variables should be signed (the default) unless you know for certain that your data is to contain only positive numbers. Some values, such as age and distance, are always positive. Other data can be negative. By making a variable unsigned, you gain a little extra storage range (as explained in Appendix A). However, that extra range of values must always be positive.

Obviously, you must be very aware of what kinds of data your variables are to hold. You certainly do not always know exactly what all of them are to hold, but you have a general idea. For example, if you want to store a person's age, you know that a long integer variable would probably be a waste of space. The reason is that nobody would live longer than a regular integer could hold.

At first, it might seem strange that table 5.2 states that character variables can hold numeric values. In C++, integers and character variables can be used interchangeably in many cases. As explained in Appendix A, each of the ASCII table characters has a unique number that corresponds to the character's location in the table. If you store a number in a character variable, C++ actually treats the data as if it were the ASCII character which matched that number in the table. Conversely, you can store character data in an integer variable. C++ finds that character's ASCII number, and stores it instead of the character. Examples that help illustrate this appear later in this chapter.

## Assigning Values to Variables

Now that you are familiar with the C++ variable types, you are ready to learn how to put values into those variables. You do this with the *assignment* statement. The equal sign (=) is used for assigning values to variables. The format of the assignment statement is

```
variable = expression;
```

The Variable is any variable you declared earlier. The expression is any variable, constant, expression, or combination that produces a resulting data type that is the same as the variable's data type.

Think of the equal sign (=) as a left-pointing arrow. Interpreted loosely, the equal sign means that you put the number, variable, or expression that is on the right side of the equal sign into the variable on the left side of it.

---

### Designating Long, Unsigned, and Floating-Point Values

When you type a number, C++ interprets its type as the smallest type that can hold the number. For example, if you type **63**, C++ knows that this number fits into a signed integer memory location. C++ does not treat the number as a long integer. The reason is that **63** is not large enough to warrant a long integer constant size.

You can, however, append a suffix character to numeric constants to override the default type. If you put an **L** at the end of an integer, C++ interprets that integer as a long one. The number **63** is an integer constant, whereas the number **63L** is a long integer constant.

Assign the **U** suffix to designate an unsigned integer constant. The number **63** is, by default, a signed integer constant. If, however, you type **63U**, C++ treats it as an unsigned integer. The suffix **UL** indicates an unsigned long constant.

C++ interprets all floating-point constants (numbers that contain decimal points) as double floating-point constants. This assures the maximum accuracy in such numbers. If you used the constant **6.82**, C++ treats it as a double floating-point data type, even though it would fit in a regular float. You can append the floating-point suffix, **F**, or the long double floating-point suffix, **L**, to constants that contain decimal points in order to represent either a floating-point constant or a long double floating-point constant instead of the default double constant value.

You might rarely use these suffixes. However, if you have to assign a constant value to an extended or unsigned variable, appending the **U**, **L**, **UL**, or **F** (their lowercase equivalents work, too) at the end of the constant might assure more accuracy.

---

## Examples

1. If you want to keep track of your current age, salary, and dependents, you can store these values in three C++ variables. You first declare the variables by choosing correct types and good names for them. Then, you assign values to them. Later in the program, these values might change—for example, if the program calculates a new pay increase for you.

   Good variable names are age, salary, and dependents. To declare these three variables, the first part of the main() function might resemble this:

   ```
   // Declare and store three values
   main()
       {
           int         age;
           float     salary;
           int         dependents;
   ```

   Notice that you do not have to declare all integer variables together. However, you can if you want to. Once these variables are declared, the next three statements can assign them values:

   ```
   age = 39;
   salary = 25000.00;
   dependents = 2;
   ```

   Notice that this program is not complete. After these assignment statements come other statements, then a closing brace.

2. The preceding example is not very long, and it does not do much. It does, however, illustrate using values, and assigning them to variables. Do not put commas in values you assign to variables. Numeric constants should *never* contain commas. The following statement is invalid:

   ```
   salary = 25,000.00;
   ```

3. You can assign variables to other variables. Alternatively, you can assign mathematical expressions to other variables. Suppose that you stored your tax rate in a variable referred to as tax_rate earlier in a program. Then, you decide to use your tax rate for your spouse's rate, as well. At the proper point in the program, you can code the following:

   ```
   spouse_tax_rate = tax_rate;
   ```

   Putting the spaces around the equal sign is acceptable to the C++ compiler. However, you do not have to include them. Use whatever method with which you are most comfortable.
   The value in tax_rate is, at this line's point in the program, copied to a new variable named spouse_tax_rate. The value in tax_rate is still there after this line finishes. The variables have been declared earlier in the program.

If your spouse's tax rate is going to be 40 percent of yours, you can assign an expression to the spouse's variables, as follows:

```
spouse_tax_rate = tax_rate * .40;
```

Any of the four mathematical symbols you learned in the last chapter, as well as those you encounter later in this book, can be part of the expression you assign to a variable.

4. If you want to assign character data to a character variable, you must enclose the character in single quote marks. All C++ character constants must be enclosed in single quote marks.

The following section of a program declares three initial variables, then assigns three initials to them. The initials are character constants. The reason is that they are enclosed in single quotes.

```
main()
    {
    char    first, middle, last;
    first = 'G';
    middle = 'M';
    last = 'P';
    // Rest of program follows
```

mu can put other values into these variables later, if the program warrants it.

---

**Caution:** Do not mix types. In most cases, C++ lets you. However, the results are unpredictable. For instance, you could have stored a floating-point constant in `middle`, as shown in the following:

```
middle = 345.43244;    // Do not do this!
```

If you did so, `middle` would hold a strange value that seems to be meaningless garbage. Make sure that values you assign to variables match the variable's type. The only major exception to this occurs when you assign an integer to a character variable, or a character to an integer variable, as you will see shortly.

---

5. C++ gives you the ability to declare *and* initialize variables with values at the same time. For example, the following section of code declares an integer `age`, a floating-point `salary`, and three character variables. This code also initializes all of these at the time of declaration:

```
main()
    {
    int       age = 30;
    float     salary = 25000.00;
    char      first = 'G', middle = 'M', last = 'P';
    // Rest of program follows
```

This is a little easier than first declaring them, then initializing them with values. As the preceding chapter discussed, cout is used to print the values of variables and constants. Chapter 8, "Simple Input and Output," explains cout in more detail. In a short preview, the following cout statements will print the variables declared in the preceding section of code:

```
cout << age << ' ' << salary << ' ';
cout << first << ' ' << middle << ' ' << last;
```

Putting all of these together into one commented (short) program produces the following code:

```
// Filename: C5VAR.CPP
// Program that initializes and prints five variables

#include  <iostream.h>

main()
    {
    int     age = 30;
    float    salary = 25000.00;
    char     first = 'G', middle = 'M', last = 'P';

    cout << age << ' ' << salary << ' ';
    cout << first << ' ' << middle << ' ' << last;
    return 0;
    }
```

If you were to compile and run this program, you would see the following output:

```
30 25000 G M P
```

The numbers are not formatted very well (especially salary). However, you soon will learn how to produce the desired output.

# Constants

As with variables, C++ has several types of *constants*. Remember that a constant does not change. Integer constants are whole numbers that do not contain decimal points. Floating-point constants are numbers that contain a fractional portion (an optional value to the right of the decimal point).

## Special Integer Constants

You already know that an integer is any whole number without a decimal point. C++ lets you assign integer constants to variables. You also can use integer constants for calculations and print them with cout.

A regular integer constant cannot begin with a leading 0. To C++, the number 012 is *not* the number twelve. If you precede an integer constant with a leading 0, C++ thinks that it is an octal constant. An *octal constant* is a base-8 number. The octal numbering system is not used much in today's computer systems. The newer versions of C++ retain octal capabilities for compatibility with previous versions when octal played a more important role in computers.

An octal integer constant contains a leading 0. A hexadecimal constant contains a leading 0x.

Another special integer that is still used today in C++ is a base-16 or *hexadecimal* constant. Appendix A describes the hexadecimal numbering system. If you want to represent a hexadecimal integer constant, append the 0x prefix to it. All of the following are hexadecimal numbers:

```
0x10     0x2C4     0xFFFF     0X9
```

Notice that it does not matter whether you use a lowercase or an uppercase X after the leading zero, or a lowercase or an uppercase hexadecimal digit (for hex numbers A through F). If you write business application programs in C++, you might think that you'll never need to use hexadecimal numbers. You might be correct. However, for a complete understanding of C++, and your computer in general, you should be familiar with the fundamentals of hexadecimal numbers.

Table 5.3 shows a few integer constants represented in their regular decimal, hexadecimal, and octal notations. Each row contains the same number in all three bases.

**Table 5.3. Integer constants are represented in three different bases.**

| Base-10 Decimal | Base-16 Hexadecimal | Base-8 Octal |
|---|---|---|
| 8 | 0x08 | 010 |
| 10 | 0x0A | 012 |
| 16 | 0x10 | 020 |
| 65536 | 0x10000 | 0200000 |
| 25 | 0x19 | 031 |

**Note:** Floating-point constants might begin with a leading zero. They will be properly interpreted by C++. The reason is that only integers are possible hexadecimal and octal constants.

> **Your Computer's Word Size Is Important**
>
> If you write many system programs that use hexadecimal numbers, you probably want to store those numbers in unsigned variables. This keeps C++ from improperly interpreting positive numbers as negative ones.
>
> For example, your computer stores integers in two-byte words. The hexadecimal constant 0xFFFF represents either -1 or 65535, depending on how the sign bit is interpreted. If you declare an unsigned integer, such as
>
> ```
> unsigned int i_num = 0xFFFF;
> ```
>
> C++ knows that you want it to use the sign bit as data and not as the sign. If, however, you declare the same value as a signed integer, as in
>
> ```
> int i_num = 0xFFFF;   // The word "signed" is optional
> ```
>
> C++ thinks that this is a negative number (-1) because the sign bit is turned on (if you were to convert 0xFFFF to binary, you would get 16 ones). Appendix A describes these concepts in more detail.

## String Constants

*A string constant is always enclosed in double quotes.*

One type of C++ constant, referred to as the *string constant*, does not have a matching variable. A string constant is *always* enclosed within double quote marks. The following are examples of string constants:

```
"C++ Programming"    "123"   " "   "4323 E. Oak Road"    "x"
```

Any string of characters, or single ones, enclosed in double quotes, is considered a string constant. A single space, word, or group of words between double quotes is a C++ string constant. If the string constant contains only numeric digits, it is *not* a number, but a string of numeric digits with which you cannot perform mathematical calculations. You can perform mathematical calculations with numbers only—not with string constants that contain numbers, or even a character constant that might contain a number (enclosed in a single quote).

> **Note:** A string constant is *any* character, digit, or group of characters enclosed in double quotes. A character constant is any character enclosed in single quotes.

The double quotes are never considered part of the string constant. The double quotes surround the string and simply inform your C++ compiler that the constant is a string constant, not some other type of constant.

You can easily print string constants. Simply put the string constants in a cout call, as the following line shows:

*Print Turbo C++ By Example to the screen.*

```
cout << "Turbo C++ By Example";
```

## Examples

**1.** The following program displays a simple message to the screen. No variables are needed because no data is stored or calculated.

```cpp
// Filename: C5ST1.CPP
// Displays a string on the screen

#include  <iostream.h>

main()
    {
    cout << "C++ programming is fun!";
    return 0;
    }
```

Remember to make the last line in your C++ programs (before the closing brace) a `return` statement.

**2.** You want to label the output from your programs. Do not print the value of a variable unless you also print a string constant that describes the variable. The following program computes sales tax for a sale, then prints the tax. Notice that a message is printed first, which tells the user of the program what the next number means.

```cpp
// Filename: C5ST2.CPP
// Computes sales tax with an appropriate message

#include     <iostream.h>

main()
    {
    float    sale, tax;
    float    tax_rate = .08;      // Sales tax percentage

    // Determine the amount of the sale
    sale = 22.54;

    // Compute the sales tax
    tax = sale * tax_rate;

    // Print the results
    cout << "The sales tax is: " << tax;

    return 0;
    }
```

## The Tail of String Constants

An additional aspect of string constants sometimes confuses C++ programmers who are beginners. All string constants end with a zero. You do not see the zero. However, C++ makes sure that the zero is stored at the end of the string in memory. Figure 5.1 shows how the string "Turbo C++ Program" appears in memory.

**Figure 5.1.**

A string constant always ends with a zero in memory.

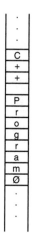

You do not have to worry about putting the zero at the end of a string constant; C++ does this for you whenever it stores a string. If your program were to contain the string "Borland C++ Program", the compiler would recognize it as a string constant (from the double quotes), and store the zero at the end.

The zero, referred to as the *string delimiter*, is important to C++. Without this delimiter, C++ would not know in which place the string constant ended in memory. (Remember that the double quotes are not stored as part of the string. Therefore, C++ cannot use them to determine in which place the string ends.)

The string-delimiting zero is *not* the same as a character zero. If you look at the ASCII table in Appendix C, you see that the first entry, ASCII number 0, is the *null* character. This null character, ASCII zero, is what actually delimits strings in C++. (If you are unfamiliar with the ASCII table, read Appendix A for a review.) Sometimes you hear that C++ string constants end in *ASCII 0*, or the *null zero*. This differentiates the string-delimiting zero from the character '0', whose ASCII value is 48.

*All string constants end in a null zero, sometimes called the binary zero or ASCII zero.*

As explained in Appendix A, all memory locations in your computer hold bit patterns for characters. If the letter A is stored in memory, an A is not really there. The binary bit pattern for the ASCII A (01000001) is stored there. The binary bit pattern for the null zero is 00000000. Therefore, the string-delimiting zero is also referred to as a *binary zero*.

To illustrate this concept further, figure 5.2 shows the bit patterns for the following string constant when stored in memory:

```
"I am 30."
```

**Figure 5.2.**

The bit pattern shows the difference between the null zero and the character zero.

|   |          |
|---|----------|
| I | 01001001 |
|   | 00100000 |
| a | 01100001 |
| m | 01101101 |
|   | 00100000 |
| 3 | 00110011 |
| Ø | 00110000 |
|   | 00000000 |

This concept is fairly advanced. However, you need to understand it before you continue. If computers are new to you, read Appendix A. Figure 5.2 shows how a string is stored in your computer's memory at the binary level. It is important for you to recognize that the character 0 inside the number 30 is not the same zero (at the bit level) as the string-terminating null zero. If it were, C++ would think that this string ended early (after the 3), which is incorrect.

## The Length of Strings

Many times, your program needs to know the length of a string. This becomes critical when you learn how to accept string input from the keyboard.

> **Note:** The length of a string is the number of characters up to, but not including, the delimiting null zero.

The length of a string constant does not include the null binary zero.

In other words, when you need to know how long a string constant is, or when you must tell C++ how long it is (as you will see later), you need to count the number of characters in the string. Do not include the null character in that count, even though you know that C++ will add it to the end of the string.

### Examples

1. The following includes some string constants:

```
"0"      "C++"       "A much longer string constant"
```

**2.** Note these string constants and their corresponding string lengths:

| String | Length |
|---|---|
| `"C++"` | 3 |
| `"0"` | 1 |
| `"Hello"` | 5 |
| `" "` | 0 |
| `"30 oranges"` | 10 |

## Special Character Constants

All C++ character constants should be enclosed in single quotes. The single quotes are not part of the character. However, they serve to delimit it. All the following are valid C++ character constants:

```
'w'      'W'      'C'      '7'      '*'      '='      '.'      'K'
```

C++ does not append a null zero to the end of character constants. Be aware that the following constants are very different to C++:

```
'R'      "R"
```

The first `'R'` is a single character constant. It is one character long, as *all* character constants (and variables) are one character long. The second `"R"` is a string constant because it is delimited by double quotes. Its length also is one. However, it includes an extra null zero in memory so that C++ knows in which place the string ends. This difference prevents you from mixing character constants and character strings. Figure 5.3 shows how these two constants are stored in memory.

**Figure 5.3.**

The character constant `'R'` and the string constant `"R"` are stored in memory.

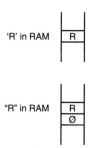

'R' in RAM

"R" in RAM

All the alphabetic, numeric, and special characters on your keyboard can be character constants. There are some characters, however, that cannot be represented with your keyboard. These include some of the higher ASCII characters, such as the Spanish Ñ. You do not have keys for every character in the ASCII table. Therefore, C++ provides a way for you to represent these characters by typing the character's ASCII hex number inside the single quotes.

For example, to store the Spanish Ñ in a variable, look up its hexadecimal ASCII number in Appendix C. You find that it is A5. Append the prefix \x to it, and enclose it in single quotes. Now, C++ knows to use the special character. You can do this with the following code:

```
char sn='\xA5';      // Puts the Spanish N into the variable
                     // called sn
```

This is the way to store (or print) any character from the ASCII table, even if the character does not have a key on your keyboard.

The single quote marks still tell C++ that a *single* character is inside the quotes. Even though '\xA5' contains four characters inside the quotes, those four characters represent a single character, not a character string. If you were to include these four characters inside a string constant, C++ would treat them as a single character within the string. The string constant

```
"An accented a is \xA0"
```

is a C++ string that is 18 characters long. C++ interprets the \xA0 character as the á, just as it should.

> **Caution:** If you are familiar with entering ASCII characters by typing their ASCII numbers with the Alt-*number* key (from the keypad), do not use this method in your C++ programs. Although the Borland C++ compiler supports the method, your program might not be portable to another C++ compiler.

Any characters interpreted with a backslash (\), such as those in this discussion, are called *escape sequences* or *escape characters*. Table 5.4 shows some additional escape sequences that come in handy when you want to print special characters.

**Table 5.4. These special C++ escape sequences can help in printing certain characters.**

| Escape Sequence | Meaning |
| --- | --- |
| \a | Alarm (the terminal's bell) |
| \b | Backspace |
| \f | Formfeed (for the printer) |
| \n | Newline (carriage return and linefeed) |
| \r | Carriage return |
| \t | Tab |
| \v | Vertical tab |

*continues*

**Table 5.4. Continued**

| Escape Sequence | Meaning |
|---|---|
| \\ | Backslash (\) |
| \? | Question mark |
| \' | Single quote |
| \" | Double quote |
| \ooo | Octal number |
| \xhh | Hexadecimal number |
| \0 | The null zero (or binary zero) |

**Tip:** Include \n in a cout if you want it to skip to the next line.

**Math with C++ Characters**

C++ links characters very closely with their ASCII numbers. For this reason, you can actually perform arithmetic on character data. Note the following section of code:

```
char  c;
c = 'T' + 5;      // Add 5 to the ASCII character
```

This actually stores a Y in c. The ASCII value of the letter T is 84. Adding 5 to 84 produces 89. The variable c is not an integer variable, but a character variable. For this reason, C++ knows to put the ASCII character for 89 (rather than the number itself) in **c**

Conversely, you can store character constants in integer variables. If you do, C++ actually stores the matching ASCII number for that character. Note this section of code:

```
int i = 'P';
```

This does *not* put a letter P in i, because i is not a character variable. C++ assigns the number 80 to the variable, as 80 is the ASCII number for the letter P.

## Examples

**1.** To print two names on two different lines, you include \n between them.

*Print* Harry *to the screen. Then, drop the cursor down to a
new line. Next, print Jerry.*

```
cout << "Harry" << '\n' << "Jerry";
```

*When the program gets to this line, it prints*

```
Harry

Jerry
```

**2.** The following short program rings the bell on your computer. The reason is that the program assigns the \a escape sequence to a variable, then prints it:

```
// Filename: C5BELL.CPP
// Rings the bell

#include  <iostream.h>

main()
    {
    char    bell='\a';

    cout << bell;
    return 0;
    }
```

**3.** Without these escape sequences, you would have no way to print double quote marks. Double quote marks delimit strings. Therefore, C++ would think that the string you were printing ended too early. The backslash and single quote cannot print regularly either; C++ interprets the backslash as an escape sequence prefix and the single quote as a character constant delimiter. Therefore, the three escape sequences \", \\, and \' let you print these characters, as the following program shows:

```
// Filename: C5SPEC2.CPP
// Prints quotes and a backslash

#include  <iostream.h>

main()
    {
    cout << "Albert said, \"I will be going now.\" \n";
    cout << "The backslash character looks like this: \\ \n";
    cout << "I\'m learning C++ \n";
    return 0;
    }
```

The \n is included to send the cursor to the next line after each cout. The output from this program resembles this:

```
Albert said, "I will be going now."
The backslash character looks like this: \
I'm learning C++
```

# Summary

A firm grasp of C++'s foundation is critical. In this chapter, you learned about variable types and constant types, how to name variables, and how to assign values to them. These issues are important to your understanding of the rest of C++.

This chapter showed you how to store in variables almost every type of value. There is no string variable, so you cannot store string constants in string variables as you can in other programming languages. However, you can "fool" C++ into thinking that it has a string variable by using a character array to hold strings. The next chapter teaches this important concept.

# Review Questions

The answers to Review Questions are in Appendix B.

1. Which of the following variable names are valid?

```
my_name     89_sales     sales_89     a-salary
```

2. Which of the following constants are characters, strings, integers, and floating-point constants?

```
0     -12.0     "2.0"     "X"     'X'     65.4     -708     '0'
```

3. How many variables do the following statements declare, and what are their types?

```
int       i, j, k;
char      c, d, e;
float     x = 65.43;
```

4. With what do all string constants end?

5. True or false: An unsigned variable can hold a larger value than a signed variable.

6. How many characters of storage does the following constant take?

```
'\x41'
```

7. How is the following string stored at the bit level?

```
"Order 10 of them."
```

8. How is the following string (referred to as a *null string*) stored at the bit level? (*Hint*: The length is zero, but there is still a terminating character.)

```
""
```

# Review Exercises

1. Write a C++ program to store your initials in three variables.

2. Write the C++ code to store in three variables: your weight, height in feet, and shoe size. Declare the variables, and assign them values in the body of the program.

3. Rewrite the program in the preceding exercise, adding proper cout statements to print the values to the screen. Use appropriate messages (by printing string constants) to describe the numbers that are printed.

4. Write a program that declares an integer value and then adds 10000 to it several times until it stops working. Observe the reaction of the computer.

5. Write a program that stores a value in every type of variable that C++ allows. You must first declare each variable at the top of the program. Put numbers in the variables, and print them to see how C++ stores and prints them.

6. Test the effect of the unsigned keyword by declaring an unsigned integer and then adding 10000 to it repeatedly until it stops working. Compare the result to exercise 4. Compare it to table 5.2.

# CHAPTER 6

# Character Strings and Character Arrays

Even though C++ has no string variables, you can make C++ think that it has them by using character arrays. The concept of arrays may be new to you, but this chapter shows how easily you can declare and use them. Once you declare an array, it can hold character strings as though they were actual string variables.

This chapter introduces the following topics:

- ◆ Character arrays
- ◆ Assigning string values to character arrays
- ◆ Printing character arrays
- ◆ How character arrays differ from strings

After you finish this chapter, you'll be on your way to manipulating almost every type of variable C++ offers. Being able to manipulate characters and words is one thing that separates your computer from powerful calculators, giving the computer true data processing capabilities.

## Character Arrays

*A string constant can be stored in an array of characters.*

There's a variable for almost every type of data in C++, but no variable exists that will hold character strings. The authors of C++ realized that users needed some way to store strings in variables. Instead of storing strings in string variables (some languages, such as BASIC and Pascal, have string variables), you must store them in an array of characters.

An *array* is a set of objects of the same type that can be operated on at least some of the time in the same manner as the other objects. Most programming languages allow the use of arrays. An array is a list (sometimes called a *table*) of variables. Suppose you have to keep track of the sales of 100 salespersons. You could make up 100 variable names and assign each one a different salesperson's sales. All those variable names, however, would be difficult to track. If you were to put them into an array of floating-point variables, you would only have to keep track of a single name (the array name) and then reference each of the 100 values with a numeric subscript.

Chapter 28, "Pointers and Arrays," covers the processing of arrays in more detail. However, to work with character string data in your early programs, you need to become familiar with the concept of an array of characters, or *character array*.

Because a string is simply a list of one or more characters, a character array is a perfect place to hold strings of information. Suppose you want to keep track of a person's full name, age, and salary by placing these items in variables. The age and salary are easy; there are variable types to hold them. You can code the following to declare those variables:

```
int     age;
float   salary;
```

There is no string variable that can hold the name, but you can create an array of characters (one or more character variables stored next to each other in memory) with the following declaration:

```
char name[ 15 ];
```

This reserves space in memory for an array of characters. An array declaration always includes brackets ([ ]), which declare the storage that C++ needs to reserve for the array. This array will be 15 characters long, and the array name is name. You also can assign a value to the character array at the time you declare it. The following declaration statement not only declares the character array, but also puts the name "Michael Jones" into it.

*Declare the character array name as 15 characters long and assign Michael Jones to that array.*

```
char name[ 15 ] = "Michael Jones";
```

Figure 6.1 shows what this array looks like in memory. Each of the 15 boxes of the array is called an *element*. Notice that there is a null zero (the string-terminating character) at the end of the string. Notice also that the last character of the array, the 15th element, has no data in it. There is a value there, even though the program didn't place any data there. It is not necessary to be concerned with what follows the string's null zero.

**Figure 6.1.**

A character array after being declared and assigned a string value.

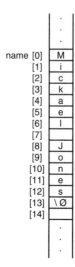

```
name [0]   M
     [1]   i
     [2]   c
     [3]   h
     [4]   a
     [5]   e
     [6]   l
     [7]
     [8]   J
     [9]   o
    [10]   n
    [11]   e
    [12]   s
    [13]  \Ø
    [14]
```

You can access individual elements in an array or the array as a whole. This is the primary advantage of an array over a number of variables with different names. You can assign values to individual array elements by putting each element's location, called a *subscript*, in brackets. Note an example:

```
name[ 3 ] = 'k';
```

All array subscripts begin with 0.

This overwrites the h in the name with a k. The string now looks like the one shown in figure 6.2.

**Figure 6.2.**

The array contents after changing one of the elements.

```
name [0]   M
     [1]   i
     [2]   c
     [3]   k
     [4]   a
     [5]   e
     [6]   l
     [7]
     [8]   J
     [9]   o
    [10]   n
    [11]   e
    [12]   s
    [13]  \Ø
    [14]
```

All array subscripts start at zero. Therefore, to overwrite the first element, you have to use a 0 as the subscript. Assigning name[ 3 ], as just shown, changes the fourth value in the array.

You can print the entire string, or more accurately the entire array, with a single cout:

```
cout << name;
```

Notice that when you print an array, you don't put the brackets after the array name.

You must be sure that you reserve enough characters in the array to hold the entire string, including the terminating null zero. For example, the following won't work:

```
char name[ 5 ] = "Michael Jones";
```

This reserves only 5 characters for the array, but the name and its null zero takes 14 characters. C++ will not give you an error if you try to do this; instead, C++ overwrites whatever follows the array name in memory. This will cause unpredictable results and is certainly not correct.

Always reserve enough array elements to hold the string, plus its terminating null character. It's easy to forget the null zero at the end, but don't. If your string contains 13 characters, it must have a 14th (the null zero), or the string will never be treated as a string. To help eliminate this error, C++ provides a shortcut. The following character array statements do exactly the same thing:

```
char horse[ 9 ] = "Stallion";
char horse[ ] = "Stallion";
```

If you assign a value to a character array at the same time that you declare the character array, C++ counts the string's length, adds one for the null zero, and reserves that much array space for you.

Never declare a character array (or any other type of array) with empty brackets if you don't also assign values to the array at the same time. The statement

```
char people[ ];
```

does *not* reserve any space for the array called people. Because you did not assign the array a value when you declared it, C++ assumes that this array contains 0 elements. Therefore, there isn't enough room to put values into the array later.

## Character Arrays versus Strings

In the preceding section, you saw how to put a string in a character array. Strings can exist in C++ only as string constants or as values stored in character arrays. As you read through this book and familiarize yourself with the use of arrays and strings, you will become more comfortable with them. At this point, you should understand the following fundamental rule about C++ character arrays and character strings:

Strings must be stored in character arrays, but not all character arrays contain strings.

To understand this point, look at the two arrays illustrated in figure 6.3. The first one, called cara1, does *not* contain a string. It is, however, a character array, containing a list of several characters. The second array, called cara2, does contain a string because there is a null zero at the end.

**Figure 6.3.**

Two character arrays, one containing characters and the other containing a character string.

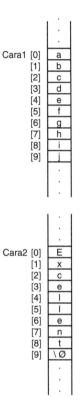

These arrays could be initialized with the following declaration statements.

*Declare the array cara1 with 10 individual characters.*
*Declare the array cara2 with the character string Excellent.*

```
char cara1[ 10 ] = { 'a', 'b', 'c', 'd', 'e', 'f', 'g',
                     'h', 'i', 'j' };
char cara2[ 10 ] = "Excellent";
```

If you want to put individual characters into an array, you must enclose the list of characters in braces, as shown in the preceding statements. You also could initialize cara1 later in the program, using assignment statements, such as the following statement:

```
char cara1[ 10 ];
cara1[ 0 ] = 'a';
cara1[ 1 ] = 'b';
cara1[ 2 ] = 'c';
cara1[ 3 ] = 'd';
cara1[ 4 ] = 'e';
cara1[ 5 ] = 'f';
cara1[ 6 ] = 'g';
cara1[ 7 ] = 'h';
cara1[ 8 ] = 'i';
cara1[ 9 ] = 'j';    // Last element possible, since started
                     // with 0 subscript
```

This character array doesn't contain a null zero, so it does not contain a string of characters. It contains characters that can be stored there and used individually, but in a program, they cannot be treated as if they were a string.

**Caution:** You cannot assign string values to character arrays in a regular assignment statement, except when you declare them. A character array is not a string variable (the array is used only to hold a string), so the array cannot go on the left side of an equal sign.

The following program is *invalid*:

```
main()
    {
    char    petname[ 20 ];     // Reserve space for
                               // the pet's name
    petname = "Alfalfa";       // INVALID!
    cout << petname;
    return 0;
    }
```

Because the pet's name was not assigned *at the time the character array was declared*, petname cannot be assigned a value later. The following is allowed, however, because you can assign values individually to a character array:

```
main()
    {
    char    petname[ 20 ];     // Reserve space for
                               // the pet's name
    petname[ 0 ] = 'A';        // Assign values one
                               // element at a time
    petname[ 1 ] = 'l';
    petname[ 2 ] = 'f';
    petname[ 3 ] = 'a';
    petname[ 4 ] = 'l';
    petname[ 5 ] = 'f';
    petname[ 6 ] = 'a';
```

```
petname[ 7 ] = '\0';        // Needed to ensure that
                            // this is a string!
  cout << petname;          // Now the pet's name
                            // prints properly
  return 0;
  }
```

The petname character array now holds a string since the last character is a null zero. How long is the string in petname? It is seven characters long—the length of a string never includes the null zero.

You cannot assign more than 20 characters, which is this array's reserved space. However, you can store any string of 19 or fewer characters (leaving one for the null zero) in the array. If you put the "Alfalfa" string into the array and then assign a null zero to petname[ 3 ], as in

```
petname[ 3 ] = '\0';
```

the string in petname is now just three characters long. You have, in effect, shortened the string. There are still 20 characters reserved for petname, but the data inside it is the string "Alf" that ends with a null zero.

The strcpy() function puts string constants in string arrays.

There are many other ways to assign a string a value, such as using a strcpy() (for "string copy") function. This is a library function that lets you copy a string constant into a string. To copy the "Alfalfa" pet name into the petname array, you could type

```
strcpy(petname, "Alfalfa"); // Copy Alfalfa into the array
```

The strcpy() function assumes that the first value within its parentheses is a character array name and that the second value is either a valid string constant or another character array that holds a string. You must be sure that the first character array within the parentheses is long enough (has enough elements reserved) to hold whatever string you copy into it.

Other methods of initializing arrays are explored throughout this book.

### Examples

1

**1.** Suppose you want to keep track of your aunt's name in a program so that you can print the name. If your aunt's name is Ruth Ann Cooper, you would have to reserve at least 16 elements—15 to hold the name and another to hold the null character. The following statement properly reserves a character array to hold the name:

```
char aunt_name[ 16 ];
```

**2.** If you want to put your aunt's name in the array while you reserve the array storage, you can do so as follows:

```
char aunt_name[ 16 ] = "Ruth Ann Cooper";
```

You also can leave out the array size and let C++ count the number of elements needed:

```
char aunt_name[ ] = "Ruth Ann Cooper";
```

3. Suppose you want to keep track of three friends' names. The longest name is 20 characters (including the null zero). You just have to reserve enough character array space to hold each friend's name:

```
char friend1[ 20 ];
char friend2[ 20 ];
char friend3[ 20 ];
```

These declarations can go toward the top of the block, along with any integer, floating-point, or character variables you need to declare.

4. The following program asks the user for his or her first and last name. It then prints the user's initials to the screen by printing the first character in each name array. To do so, the program must print each array's 0 subscript because the first subscript of any array begins at 0, not 1.

```
// Filename: C6INIT.CPP
// Prints the user's initials

#include <iostream.h>

main()
    {
    char    first[ 20 ];    // Holds the first name
    char    last[ 20 ];     // Holds the last name

    cout << "What is your first name? ";
    cin >> first;
    cout << "What is your last name? ";
    cin >> last;

    // Print the initials
    cout << "Your initials are " << first[0] << '.'
        << last[0] << '.';
    return 0;
    }
```

5. The following program takes those three friends' character arrays and assigns them string values in the three ways shown in this chapter:

```
// Filename: C6STR.CPP
// Stores and initializes 3 character arrays for 3 friends

#include     <iostream.h>
#include     <string.h>

main()
    {
```

```
// Declare all arrays and initialize the first one
   char      friend1[ 20 ] = "Johann Paul Johnson";
   char      friend2[ 20 ];
   char      friend3[ 20 ];

// Use a function to initialize the second array
   strcpy(friend2, "Julie L. Roberts");

   friend3[ 0 ] = 'A';        // Initialize the last string
                              // an element at a time
   friend3[ 1 ] = 'd';
   friend3[ 2 ] = 'a';
   friend3[ 3 ] = 'm';
   friend3[ 4 ] = ' ';
   friend3[ 5 ] = 'G';
   friend3[ 6 ] = '.';
   friend3[ 7 ] = ' ';
   friend3[ 8 ] = 'S';
   friend3[ 9 ] = 'm';
   friend3[ 10 ] = 'i';
   friend3[ 11 ] = 't';
   friend3[ 12 ] = 'h';
   friend3[ 13 ] = '\0';

   // Print all three names out
   cout << friend1 << '\n';
   cout << friend2 << '\n';
   cout << friend3 << '\n';
   return 0;
   }
```

Obviously, the last method of initializing a character array with a string—one element at a time—is not used as often as the other two ways.

## Summary

In this chapter, you learned about character arrays that hold strings. Even though C++ has no string variables, character arrays can hold string constants. Once you put a string into a character array, you can print it or manipulate it as if it were a string.

Starting with the next chapter, you will begin to hone the C++ skills you are building. Chapter 7 introduces preprocessor directives, which are not really part of the C++ language itself, but which help you work with your source code as a whole before your program is compiled.

## Review Questions

Answers to Review Questions are in Appendix B.

1. How would you declare a character array, called `my_name`, that will hold the following string constant?

   ```
   "This is C++"
   ```

2. How long is the string shown in Review Question 1?

3. How many bytes of storage does the string shown in Review Question 1 take?

4. What do all string constants end with?

5. How many variables do the following statements declare, and what are their types?

   ```
   char name[ 25 ];
   char address[ 25 ];
   ```

6. True or false: The following statement assigns a string constant to a character array.

   ```
   myname[]="Kim Langston";
   ```

7. True or false: The following declaration puts a string into the character array named `city`.

   ```
   char city[ ] = { 'M', 'i', 'a', 'm', 'i', '\0' };
   ```

8. True or false: The following declaration puts a string into the character array named `city`.

   ```
   char city[ ] = { 'M', 'i', 'a', 'm', 'i' };
   ```

## Review Exercises

1. Write the C++ code to store your weight (you can fib), height in feet, shoe size, and name in four separate variables. Declare the variables, then assign them appropriate values in the body of the program.

2. Rewrite the program in Exercise 1 by adding proper `cout` statements to print the values to the screen. Use appropriate messages (by printing string constants) to describe the values that are printed.

3. Write a program to store and print the names of your two favorite television programs. Store these programs in two character arrays. Initialize one of the strings (assign it the first program's name) at the time you declare the array. Initialize the second value in the body of the program with the `strcpy()` function.

4. Write a program that puts 10 different initials into 10 elements of a single character array. Do not store a string-terminating null zero. Print the list backward, one initial on each line.

# CHAPTER 7

# Preprocessor Directives

As you might recall from Chapter 3, the C++ compiler routes your programs through a *preprocessor* before compiling your programs. The preprocessor could be called a "precompiler" because it changes your source code before the compiler ever sees it.

The preprocessor is so important to the C++ programming language that you should familiarize yourself with it before learning more regular commands within the language. A preprocessor is a program that translates code. Regular C++ commands do not affect the preprocessor. You must supply special non-C++ commands, called *preprocessor directives*, that the preprocessor looks at. These directives make changes to your source code before the C++ compiler looks at it. It is sometimes useful to give instructions to the compiler to tell it how to treat a certain situation. In C++, the preprocessor passes through your code, looking to see if you have started any statement with a pound character (#). If you have, it reads the line, reacts to it properly, and then removes it from the executable code.

This chapter introduces the following topics:

- ♦ What preprocessor directives are
- ♦ The #include preprocessor directive
- ♦ The #define preprocessor directive

Almost every proper C++ program contains preprocessor directives. In this chapter, you learn about the two most common directives: #include and #define.

# What Are Preprocessor Directives?

*Some preprocessor directives temporarily change your source code.*

As indicated, preprocessor directives are commands you supply to the preprocessor. All preprocessor directives begin with a pound sign (#). Because they are not C++ commands but are C++ preprocessor commands, never put a semicolon at the end of a preprocessor directive. These directives typically begin in column 1 of your source program. They can begin in any column, but in the interest of code portability, stay with tradition and start each one in the first column on the line where the directive appears. Figure 7.1 shows a program that contains three preprocessor directives.

**Figure 7.1.**

A program that contains three preprocessor directives.

Preprosessor directives ⎯⎯

```
// Filename: C7PRE.CPP
// C++ program that demonstrates preprocessor directives

#include <iostream.h>
#define AGE 28
#define MESSAGE "Hello, world."

main()
{
   int i = 10, age;  // i is assigned a value at declaration
                     // age is still UNDEFINED

   age = 5;          // Put 5 in the variable age

   i = i * AGE;   // AGE is not the same as the variable age

   cout << i << age << AGE;   // Print 280 5 28
   cout << MESSAGE;   // Hello, world gets printed on screen

   return 0;
}
```

Some preprocessor directives are commands that tell the C++ preprocessor to change your source code temporarily. These changes last only as long as the compile process does. When you look at your source code again, the preprocessor will be through with your file, and its changes will no longer be in the file. Your preprocessor does not in any way compile your program or look at your actual C++ commands. Some beginning C++ students tend to get confused by this, but you won't be confused if you understand that your program has yet to be compiled when your preprocessor directives execute.

A preprocessor is similar to a word processor or an editor and does similar things with your program. This analogy applies throughout this chapter.

# The *#include* Preprocessor Directive

The `#include` preprocessor directive merges a disk file into your source program. Remember that a preprocessor directive is like a word processor command. Word processors are capable of file merging, which is what the `#include` directive does. The `#include` preprocessor directive takes one of the following formats:

```
#include <filename>
#include "filename"
```

In the `#include` directive, the file name must be an ASCII text file (as your source file is) that resides on your disk. Take a look at figure 7.2, which shows the contents of two files on disk. One file is called OUTSIDE, and the other file is called INSIDE. Notice that OUTSIDE includes the following preprocessor directive:

*Include the file INSIDE in your source file.*

```
#include <INSIDE>
```

**Figure 7.2.**

Two files that illustrate the `#include` directive.

> The file called OUTSIDE contains the following text:
> ```
> Now is the time for all good men
>
> #include INSIDE
>
> to come to the aid of their country.
> ```
> The file called INSIDE contains the following text:
> ```
> A quick brown fox jumped
> over the lazy dog.
> ```

Assume that you are able to run the OUTSIDE file through the C++ preprocessor. The preprocessor finds the `#include` directive and replaces it with the entire file called INSIDE. In other words, the C++ preprocessor directive merges the INSIDE file into the OUTSIDE file, at the place of the `#include` statement. OUTSIDE is expanded to include its original text *plus* the merged text. Figure 7.3 shows what OUTSIDE looks like after the preprocessor gets through with it.

**Figure 7.3.**

The OUTSIDE file after the preprocessor finishes with the `#include` statement.

> OUTSIDE now includes the INSIDE file:
> ```
> Now is the time for all good men
>
> A quick brown fox jumped
> over the lazy dog.
>
> to come to the aid of their country.
> ```

The INSIDE file remains in its original form on the disk. Only the file that contains the #include directive is changed. Note that this change is *temporary*; that is, OUTSIDE is expanded by the included file only as long as it takes to compile the program.

Because the OUTSIDE and INSIDE files are not C++ programs, consider a few examples that are more usable to the C++ programming language. You might want to #include a file that contains common code you use often. Suppose that you print your name and address many times in your C++ programs. You *could* type the following few lines of code, which print your name and address, into each of your programs:

```
cout << "Kelly Jane Peterson\n";
cout << "Apartment #217\n";
cout << "4323 East Skelly Drive\n";
cout << "New York, New York\n";
cout << "            10012\n";
```

Instead of typing the same five lines everywhere you want your name and address printed, you could type them *once* and then save them in a file called MYADD.CPP. Later, you just type the following line when you want your name and address to be printed:

```
#include <myadd.cpp>
```

This method not only saves keystrokes but also maintains consistency and accuracy. (Sometimes this kind of repeated text is known as *boilerplate* text.)

You usually can use either angle brackets (<>) or double quotes ("") around the included file's name and get the same results. The angle brackets tell the preprocessor to look for the included file in a default include directory set up by your compiler. The double quotes inform the preprocessor to look for the included file first in the directory where the source code is stored and then, if not found there, in the system include directory.

The #include directive is most often used for system header files.

Most of the time, you will see angle brackets around the included file name. If you want to include sections of code in other programs, be sure to store that code in the system include directory if you use angle brackets. Even though #include works well for inserted source code, there are more efficient ways to include common source code. You will learn about these methods, called *external functions*, in Part IV of this book.

The preceding #include example for source code has served well in explaining what the #include preprocessor directive does. However, #include is not often used to include source code text, but to include special system files called *header* files.

*Header files* inform C++ how to interpret the many library functions you use. Your C++ compiler comes with its own header files. When you installed your compiler, these header files were automatically stored on your disk in the system include directory. Their file names always end in .h to distinguish them from regular C++ source code.

The most common header file is named `iostream.h`. This gives your C++ compiler information it needs about the library `cout` and `cin` functions, as well as other common library routines that perform input and output.

At this point, you do not have to fully understand the `iostream.h` file. You should, however, place this file before `main()` in every program you write. It is rare when a C++ program does *not* need `iostream.h` included, and it doesn't harm anything if you include `iostream.h` when it isn't needed.

Throughout this book, whenever a new library function is described, the matching header file for that function is also given. Because almost every C++ program that you write includes a `cout` to print to the screen, almost every program contains the following line:

```
#include <iostream.h>
```

In the last chapter, you saw the `strcpy()` function. Its header file is called `string.h`. Therefore, if you write a program that contains `strcpy()`, you should also include its matching header file at the time you include `<iostream.h>`. These items should go on separate lines:

```
#include <iostream.h>
#include <string.h>
```

The order of your `include` files does not matter as long as you place them before the functions that need them. Most C++ programmers place all their needed header files before the first function in the file.

These header files are nothing more than text files. You may want to search your disk with the editor and find one of them, such as `iostream.h`, so that you can open it and look at it. It may seem very complex at this point, but there is nothing unusual about these files. If you do look at some of these files, do *not* change them in any way. If you make any changes, you may have to reload them from scratch to get the original versions back.

## Examples

1

1. The following program is very short. It includes the printing routine for name and address, which was described in this section. After printing the name and address, the program ends.

```
// Filename: C7INC1.CPP
// Illustrates the #include preprocessor directive

#include  <iostream.h>

main()
    {
#include "myadd.cpp"
    return 0;
    }
```

The double quotes are used because the file named MYADD.CPP is stored in the same directory as the source file. You should realize that if you type this program into your computer (after typing and saving the MYADD.CPP file) and then compile the program, the MYADD.CPP file is included only as long as it takes to compile the program. Your compiler will not see the file as shown here. The compiler will see (and think you typed) the following:

```
// Filename: C7INCL1.CPP
// Illustrates the #include preprocessor directive

#include  <iostream.h>

main()
    {
    cout << "Kelly Jane Peterson\n";
    cout << "Apartment #217\n";
    cout << "4323 East Skelly Drive\n";
    cout << "New York, New York\n";
    cout << "             10012\n";
    return 0;
    }
```

This explains what is meant by the term *preprocessor*: the changes are made to your source code *before* it is compiled. Your original source code is restored as soon as the compile is finished. When you look at your program again, it is back in its original form, as originally typed, with the #include statement.

2. The following program copies a message into a character array and prints it to the screen. Because both cout and strcpy() library functions are used, both of their header files should be included as well.

```
// Filename: C7INCL3.CPP
// Uses two header files

#include <iostream.h>
#include <string.h>

main()
    {
    char message[ 20 ];

    strcpy(message, "This is fun!");
    cout << message;
    return 0;
    }
```

# The *#define* Preprocessor Directive

#define replaces every occurrence of the first argument with the second argument.

The #define preprocessor directive is also commonly used in many C++ programs. The #define directive may seem strange at first, but it really does nothing more than a word processor's find-and-replace command. The format of #define is

```
#define ARGUMENT1 argument2
```

where ARGUMENT1 is a single word containing no spaces. Use the same naming rules for the #define statement's first argument that you follow for variables (refer to Chapter 4). It is traditional to use uppercase characters for ARGUMENT1; this is one of the few uses of uppercase letters in the C++ language. At least one space separates ARGUMENT1 from argument2, which can be any character, word, or phrase. argument2 can contain spaces or anything else you can type at the keyboard. Because #define is a preprocessor directive and not a C++ executable statement, do not put a semicolon at the end of #define.

The #define preprocessor directive replaces every occurrence of ARGUMENT1 in your program with the contents of argument2. In most cases, the #define directive should go before main(), along with the #include directive. Look at the following #define directive:

*Define the constant AGELIMIT to 21.*

```
#define AGELIMIT 21
```

If your program includes one or more occurrence of the word AGELIMIT, the preprocessor replaces each instance with the number 21. Your compiler will think that you actually typed 21 instead of AGELIMIT, because the preprocessor finishes its work before your compiler sees the source code. Again, though, the changes are temporary. After your program is compiled, you will see it as you originally typed it, with the #define statement and AGELIMIT occurrences still intact.

AGELIMIT is *not* a variable. Variables get declared and assigned values only when your program is compiled and run. The preprocessor changes your source file *before* it gets compiled.

#define creates defined constants.

You might wonder why you should go to this much trouble. If you wanted 21 everywhere that AGELIMIT occurs, you could have typed 21 to begin with! The advantage to using #define instead of constants is that if the age limit ever changes (is reduced, for example, to 18), you have to change only one line in the program; you do not have to look for every occurrence of 21 and change each one—and maybe miss one in the process.

Because the `#define` preprocessor directive lets you easily define and change constants, the replaced arguments of the `#define` directive are sometimes called *defined constants*. You can define any type of constant, including string constants. The following program contains a defined string constant that replaces a string in two places:

```
// Filename: C7DEF1.CPP
// Defines a string constant and uses it twice

#include <iostream.h>
#define MYNAME "Phil Ward"

main()
    {
    char name[ ] = MYNAME;
    cout << "My name is " << name << '\n';        // Print the
                                                  // array
    cout << "My name is " <<   MYNAME << '\n';    // Print the
                                                  // defined constant

    return 0;
    }
```

The first argument of the `#define` directive is in uppercase letters to distinguish it from variable names in the program. Variables are usually entered in lowercase. Although your preprocessor and compiler would not get confused, people who look at your program can quickly scan it and tell which items are defined constants and which items are not. When they see an uppercase word (if you follow the recommended standard for the first `#define` argument), they will know to look at the top of the program for its actual defined value.

The fact that defined constants are not variables is made even clearer in the following program, which prints five values. Try to guess what those five values are before looking at the answer following the program.

```
// Filename: C7DEF2.CPP
// Illustrates that #define constants are not variables

#include <iostream.h>

#define X1 (b +c)
#define X2 (X1 + X1)
#define X3 (X2 * c + X1 - d)
#define X4 (2 * X1 + 3 * X2 + 4 * X3)

main()
    {
    int  b = 2;     // Declare and initialize 4 variables
    int  c = 3;
    int  d = 4;
    int  e = X4;

    cout << e << "   " << X1 << "   " << X2 << "   " << X3
         << "   " << X4;
    return 0;
    }
```

Here is the output from this program:

```
164   5   10   31   164
```

If you treated X1, X2, X3, and X4 as variables, you would not get the correct answers. X1 through X4 are not variables, but are defined constants. Before your program is compiled, the preprocessor looks at the first line and knows to change every occurrence of X1 to (b + c). This happens before the next #define is processed. Therefore, after the first #define, the source code looks like this:

```
// Filename: C7DEF2.CPP
// Illustrates that #define constants are not variables

#include <iostream.h>

#define X2 ((b + c) + (b + c))
#define X3 (X2 * c + (b + c) - d)
#define X4 (2 * (b + c) + 3 * X2 + 4 * X3)

main()
    {
    int  b = 2;      // Declare and initialize 4 variables
    int  c = 3;
    int  d = 4;
    int  e = X4;

    cout << e << "   " << (b + c) << "   " << X2 << "   "
        << X3 << "   " << X4;
    return 0;
    }
```

After the first #define directive finishes, the second one takes over and changes every occurrence of X2 to ((b + c) + (b + c)). At that point, your source code looks like this:

```
// Filename: C7DEF2.CPP
// Illustrates that #define constants are not variables

include <iostream.h>

#define X3 (((b + c) + (b + c)) * c + (b + c) - d)
#define X4 (2 * (b + c) + 3 * ((b + c) + (b + c)) + 4 * X3)

main()
    {
    int  b = 2;      // Declare and initialize 4 variables
    int  c = 3;
    int  d = 4;
    int  e = X4;

    cout << e << "   " << (b + c) << "   " << ((b + c) +
            (b + c)) << "   " << X3 << "   " << X4);
    return 0;
    }
```

After the second #define directive finishes, the third one takes over and changes every occurrence of X3 to ((b + c) + (b + c) * c + (b + c) - d). Your source code then looks like this:

```
// Filename: C7DEF2.CPP
// Illustrates that #define constants are not variables

#include <iostream.h>

#define X4 (2 * (b + c) + 3 * ((b + c) + (b + c)) + 4 *
        (((b +c) + (b + c)) * c + (b + c) - d))


main()
    {
    int  b = 2;      // Declare and initialize 4 variables
    int  c = 3;
    int  d = 4;
    int  e = X4;

    cout << e << "   " << (b + c) << "   " << ((b + c) +
            (b + c) << "   " << (((b + c) + (b + c)) * c +
            (b + c) - d) << "   " << X4;
    return 0;
    }
```

The source code is growing rapidly! After the third #define directive finishes, the fourth and last one takes over and changes every occurrence of X4 to (2 * (b + c) + 3 * ((b + c) + (b + c)) + 4 * (((b + c) + (b + c)) * c + (b + c) - d)). Your source code looks like this at this point:

```
// Filename: C7DEF2.CPP
// Illustrates that #define constants are not variables

#include <iostream.h>

main()
    {
    int  b = 2; // Declare and initialize 4 variables
    int  c = 3;
    int  d = 4;
    int  e = (2 * (b + c) + 3 * ((b + c) + (b + c)) + 4 *
            (((b + c) + (b + c)) * c + (b + c) - d))

    cout << e << "   " << (b + c) << "   " << ((b + c) +
            (b + c) << "   " << (((b + c) + (b + c)) * c +
            (b + c) - d) << "   " << (2 * (b + c) + 3 *
            ((b + c) + (b + c)) + 4 * (((b + c) +
            (b + c)) * c + (b + c) - d));
    return 0;
    }
```

This is what your compiler actually sees. You did not type this complete listing; you typed only the original listing that was first shown. The preprocessor expanded the source into this longer form, as though you *had* typed it this way.

Borland C++ has an alternative to #define for defining constants. The keyword const placed before a variable accomplishes the same thing. Note the following lines:

```
const int      i = 12;
const char     c = 'A';
const float    f = 3.1415926;
```

i, c, and f are now constants and cannot be changed.

What are the advantages of using #define instead of const? They have to do with several points that haven't been made yet.

First, a #define directive allocates no storage, but a const variable does. This is important if you're trying to keep your executable program size to a minimum.

Second, a #define directive is visible from where it is located in the source file all the way to the end of the file. That is, when the compiler does its search and replace, it will replace every instance from the point of definition on. A const variable has visibility only within the program block in which it is defined. In other words, if a const is defined inside a block bounded by braces ({ }), the const has no visibility outside its block. The search and replace is restricted.

The third point has to do with arrays. You can create an array, which is a list of values, by using a #define directive or a const variable. With arrays, the first point in favor of #define over const is reversed. Every time you use an array created by the #define directive, that array is duplicated. Every time you use an array created as a const variable, a reference to the variable is created; this takes less room in memory than making another copy of the array.

This example may be extreme, yet it illustrates how #define works on your source code and does not define any variables at all. The #define directive does nothing more than a word processor's find-and-replace command does. Because of this, you can even rewrite the C++ language. If you are used to BASIC, you might be more comfortable typing PRINT instead of C ++'s cout when printing to the screen. The #define statement

```
#define PRINT cout
```

allows you to print in C++ with the following statements:

```
PRINT << "This is a new printing technique\n";
PRINT << "I could have used cout instead.\n";
```

This works because your compiler, by the time it sees the program, will see the following:

```
cout << "This is a new printing technique\n";
cout << "I could have used printf() instead.\n";
```

You cannot replace a defined constant if it resides in another string constant. For example, you cannot use the #define statement

```
#define AGE
```

to replace information in the following cout:

```
cout << "AGE";
```

AGE is a string constant and will print literally as it appears inside the double quotes. As long as the defined constant does not reside between double quotes, the processor will make the replacement.

---

**Do Not Overuse #define**

Many early C++ programmers enjoy redefining parts of the language to suit what they are used to in another language. The cout-to-PRINT example is just one illustration. You can redefine virtually any C++ statement or function so that it "looks" the way you prefer.

There is a danger here, and you should be wary of using #define for this purpose. Redefining the language becomes very confusing to others who may need to modify your programs later. In addition, as you become familiar with C++, you will start to use the true C++ language more and more. Any older programs that you redefined will be confusing to you.

If you are going to program in C++, use the language elements supplied by C++. Shy away from redefining commands in the language. The #define directive is a great way to define numeric and string constants. If those constants change, you only have to change one line in your program. Resist the temptation to define commands and built-in functions.

---

## Examples

1
1. Suppose you want to keep track of your company's target sales amount of $55,000.00. That target amount has not changed for the last two years. Since it probably will not change in the near future (sales are flat), you decide to start using a defined constant to represent the target sales amount. Then if the target amount does change, you only have to change it on the #define line. The #define statement would look like this:

```
#define TARGETSALES 55000.00
```

This line defines a floating-point constant. You then can assign TARGETSALES to floating-point variables and print it, just as if you had typed 55000.00 throughout your program.

2. If you find yourself defining the same constants in many programs, you might consider putting them in their own file on disk and then include them. This saves typing the defined constants at the top of every program. If you stored that file in a file called MYDEFS.h in your program's directory, you could include it with the following #include statement:

```
#include "mydefs.h"
```

(To use angle brackets, you would have to store the file in your system's include directory.)

3. Defined constants are good for array sizes. Suppose, for example, that you declare an array for a customer's name. When you write the program, you know that none of your customers' names is longer than 22 characters (including the null zero). Therefore, you can use the following:

```
#define CNMLENGTH 22
```

When you define the array, you could use this:

```
char cust_name[ CNMLENGTH ]
```

Other statements that need to know the array size also can use CNMLENGTH.

4. Many C++ programmers define a list of error messages. Once the messages are defined with easy-to-remember names, you can print those constants if an error occurs while maintaining consistency throughout your programs. You might see something like the following toward the top of C++ programs:

```
#define DISKERR "Your disk drive seems not to be working"
#define PRNTERR "Your printer is not responding"
#define AGEERR  "You cannot enter an age that small"
#define NAMEERR "You must enter a full name"
```

## Summary

This chapter covered the #include and #define preprocessor directives. Although these are the only two preprocessor directives you know so far, they are the two most often used in C++ programs. Although these directives are not executed, they change your source file by merging and defining constants in your programs.

The next chapter explains cout in more detail. There are many cout options that you will want to use as you write programs. You also will see a way to allow keyboard input in your C++ programs.

# Review Questions

Answers to Review Questions are in Appendix B.

1. True or false: You can define variables with the preprocessor directives.

2. Which preprocessor directive will merge another file into your program?

3. Which preprocessor directive will define constants throughout your program?

4. True or false: You can define character, string, integer, and floating-point constants with the #define directive.

5. Which happens first: compile or preprocess?

6. When would you use the angle brackets in an #include statement, and when would you use double quotes?

7. Which are easier to change: defined constants or constants you type throughout a program? Why?

8. Which header file should be included in almost every C++ program you write?

9. True or false: The line

```
#define MESSAGE "Please press Enter to continue..."
```

would change the statement

```
cout << "MESSAGE";
```

10. What is the output from the following program?

```
// Filename: C7EXER.CPP

#include <iostream.h>
#define AMT1 a+a+a
#define AMT2 AMT1 - AMT1

main()
    {
    int  a = 1;

    cout << "Amount is " << AMT2;
    return 0;
    }
```

# Review Exercises

1. Write a program that prints your name to the screen. Use a defined constant for the name. Do not use a character array and do not type your actual name inside the `cout`.

2. Suppose your boss wants you to write a program that produces an exception report. If the company's sales are lower than $100,000.00 or more than $750,000.00, your boss wants the program to print a message accordingly. You will learn how to produce this type of report later in this book, but for now, write the `#define` statements that define these two floating-point constants.

3. Write the `cout` statements that print your name and birth date to the screen. Store these statements in a separate file. Write a second program that includes the first file to print your name and birth date. Be sure to include `<iostream.h>`, because the included file contains `cout` statements.

4. Write a nonsense program that defines 10 digits—0 through 9—as constants `ZERO` through `NINE`. Add these 10 defined digits together and print the results.

# CHAPTER 8

# Simple Input and Output

You have already seen the word cout appear in your code next to a "<<" operator. cout is an *object* that is the software representative of your monitor's screen. Don't worry about objects too much for now; we'll learn more about them in later chapters. For now, just think of cout as your screen and cin as your keyboard. Because the screen is such a common output device, you need to understand how to take advantage of cout to print data the way you want to see it. In addition, your programs will become more powerful if you learn to get input from the keyboard. cin is an object that mirrors cout; instead of sending output values to the screen, cin accepts values that the user types at the keyboard.

The cout and cin objects offer the beginning C++ programmer simple input and output. Both objects allow you to send output from and receive input to your programs.

This chapter covers the following topics:

♦ Using the cout object

♦ Using manipulators

♦ Using the cin object

You will be surprised at how much more advanced your programs can be after you learn these input and output objects.

## The *cout* Object

cout sends
output to the
screen.

The cout object sends data to the standard output device. This is the screen, unless you have redirected the standard output to another device. At this point, if you do nothing special, cout sends all output to the screen.

The format of cout is a little different than that of regular C++ commands:

```
cout << data [ << data ];
```

The data can be variables, constants, expressions, or a combination of all three.

Note that in this book it is sometimes necessary to define C++ constructs that have an indefinite number of parameters or arguments, or that have optional parameters that may or may not be present. In such cases, the optional parameter appears in square brackets ([ ]). The text enclosed in square brackets may be present one or more times, or not at all.

## Printing Strings

The easiest data to print to cout is a string. To print a string constant, you simply put the string constant after the cout operator. For example, to print the string "The rain in Spain," type the following cout:

*Print the phrase "The rain in Spain" to the screen.*

```
cout << "The rain in Spain";
```

You must remember, however, that cout does *not* perform an automatic carriage return. This means that the screen's cursor will remain after the last character that is printed. Subsequent couts begin right after the last character that was printed. To understand this better, try to predict the output from the following three cout operators:

```
cout << "Line 1";
cout << "Line 2";
cout << "Line 3";
```

These couts produce the output

```
Line 1Line 2Line 3
```

which is probably not what was intended. You must include the "newline" character, \n, whenever you want to move the cursor to the next line. The following three cout operators produce a three-line output:

```
cout << "Line 1\n";
cout << "Line 2\n";
cout << "Line 3\n";
```

Here is the output from these couts:

```
Line 1
Line 2
Line 3
```

The \n character sends the cursor to the next line no matter where you insert the character. The following three cout operators also produce the correct three-line output:

```
cout << "Line 1";
cout << "\nLine 2\n";
cout "Line 3";
```

The second cout prints a newline before it prints anything else. It then prints its string, followed by another newline. The third string prints on that new line.

You also can print strings stored in character arrays by putting the array name inside the cout. If you were to store your name in an array defined as

```
char my_name[ ] = "Lyndon Harris";
```

you could print the name with the following cout:

```
cout << my_name;
```

## Examples

1. The following section of code prints three string constants on three different lines:

```
cout << "Nancy Carson\n";
cout << "1213 Oak Street\n";
cout << "Fairbanks, Alaska\n";
```

2. The following program stores a few values in three variables and prints the result:

```
// Filename: C8PRNT1.CPP
// Prints values in variables

#include <iostream.h>

main()
    {
    char        first = 'E';        // Store some character,
    char        middle = 'W';       // integer, and
    char        last = 'C';         // floating-point
                                    // variables

    int         age = 32;
    int         dependents = 2;
    float       salary = 25000.00;
    float       bonus = 575.25;
```

```
// Print the results
cout << first << middle << last;
cout << age << dependents;
cout << salary << bonus;
return 0;
}
```

**3.** The program in Example 2 does not help the user at all. The output is not labeled, and all of it prints on a single line. Here is the same program with a few messages printed before the numbers and some newline characters placed where they are needed.

```
// Filename: C8PRNT2.CPP
// Prints values in variables with appropriate labels

#include <iostream.h>

main()
    {
    char        first = 'E';     // Store some character,
    char        middle = 'W';    // integer, and
    char        last = 'C';      // floating-point
                                 // variables
    int         age = 32;
    int         dependents = 2;
    float       salary = 25000.00;
    float       bonus = 575.25;

    // Print the results
    cout << "Here are the initials:\n";
    cout << first << middle << last << \n\n;
    cout << "The age and number of dependents are:\n";
    cout << age << "   " << dependents << "\n\n";
    cout << "The salary and bonus are:\n";
    cout << salary << ' ' << bonus;
    return 0;
    }
```

Note the output from this program:

```
Here are the initials:
EWC

The age and number of dependents are:
32   2

The salary and bonus are:
25000 575.25
```

**4.** The cout is often used to label output. Before printing an age, an amount, a salary, or any other numeric data, you should print a string constant that tells the user what the number means. The following cout lets the user know that the next number printed will be an age. Without this cout, the user may not know that the number represents an age.

```
cout << "Here is the age that was found in our files:";
```

5. All four of the following couts produce different output because all four string constants are different:

```
cout << "Come back tomorrow\n";
cout << "Come  back  tomorrow\n";
cout << "cOME BACK TOMORROW\n";
cout << "C o m e  b a c k  t o m o r r o w\n";
```

6. You can print a blank line by printing two newline characters next to each other (\n\n) after your string:

```
cout << "Prepare the invoices...\n\n";
```

7. If you need to print a table of numbers, you can use the \t tab character. Place the tab character between the numbers that print. The following program prints a list of team names and number of hits for the first three weeks of the season:

```
// Filename: C8TEAM.CPP

// Prints a table of team names and hits for three weeks

#include <iostream.h>

main()
    {
    cout << "Parrots\tRams\tKings\tTitans\tChargers\n";
    cout << "3\t5\t3\t1\t0\n";
    cout << "2\t5\t1\t0\t1\n";
    cout << "2\t6\t4\t3\t0\n";
    return 0;
    }
```

This program produces the following table. You can see that even though the names have different widths, the numbers print correctly beneath them. The \t character forces the next name or value into the next tab position (every eight characters).

| Parrots | Rams | Kings | Titans | Chargers |
|---------|------|-------|--------|----------|
| 3 | 5 | 3 | 1 | 0 |
| 2 | 5 | 1 | 0 | 1 |
| 2 | 6 | 4 | 3 | 0 |

## The *hex* and *oct* Manipulators

The hex and oct manipulators are used to print hexadecimal and octal numbers. Even if you store a hexadecimal number in an integer variable (with the leading 0x characters, such as 0x3C1), that variable will print as a decimal value. To print the value in hex, you must use the hex manipulator.

> **Tip:** You can print any integer value as a hexadecimal number if you use the hex conversion character. You do not have to store the integer as a hex number first.

### Examples

1. Suppose you are working on a systems program and need to add five hexadecimal values together to test the results. You can write a short C++ program that does just that. You can then print the answer as a hexadecimal number by using the hex manipulator. Note the following program:

```
// Filename: C8HEX.CPP
// Adds five hexadecimal numbers and prints the answer

#include <iostream.h>

main()
    {
    // Store the five numbers to add together
    int     num1 = 0x4c, num2 = 0x52, num3 = 0xd1,
            num4 = 0xdc, num5 = 0x1f;
    int     hex_ans;      // This will hold the result

    hex_ans = num1 + num2 + num3 + num4 + num5;

    // Print the answer
    cout << "The hexadecimal numbers add up to:"
        << hex << hex_ans << " \n";
    return 0;
    }
```

This program produces a single line of output:

```
The hexadecimal numbers add up to: 26a
```

The syntax "cout << hex " can be thought of as a message that you are sending to your screen that says, "Please display the numbers that you are sent as hexadecimal numbers."

2. If you use octal, you might need this type of routine to add octal (base 8) numbers. The preceding program can be rewritten with octal numbers and printed with the oct manipulator as follows:

```
// Filename: C8OCT.CPP
// Adds five octal numbers and prints the answer

#include <iostream.h>

main()
    {
    // Store the five numbers to add together
    int     num1 = 054, num2 = 067, num3 = 011, num4 = 031,
            num5 = 056;
    int     oct_ans;    // This will hold the result

    oct_ans = num1 + num2 + num3 + num4 + num5;

    // Print the answer
    cout << "The octal numbers add up to:"
         << oct << oct_ans << " \n";
    return 0;
    }
```

This program produces the following output:

```
The octal numbers add up to: 263
```

The answer, 263, is an octal number (not a decimal) because you printed it with the oct manipulator.

3. Use of the hex or oct manipulator sets integer output to octal or hexadecimal until another oct, hex, or dec manipulator is encountered. The dec manipulator returns output to decimal.

## Other Manipulators

You have already seen the need for additional program output control. Some floating-point numbers print with too many decimal places for most applications. What if you want to print only dollars and cents (two decimal places) or print an average with a single decimal place? If you want to change the way these conversion characters produce output, you need to use a *manipulator*. A manipulator changes the value of a variable in the cout object. These variables are called state flags because they flag your request. When the cout object sends the data to the screen, it checks these flags to see how to perform the task.

*You can modify the way numbers print.*

You can specify how many print positions to use in printing a number. For example, the following cout prints the number 456, using three positions (the length of the data):

```
cout << 456;
```

If 456 were stored in an integer variable, it would still use three positions to print, because the number of digits printed is three. However, you can specify how many positions will print. The following cout prints the number 456 in five positions (with two leading spaces):

```
cout << setw(5) << setfill(' ') << 456;
```

The syntax of setw() and setfill() indicates they are functions. They are, in reality, *member functions* that can change the state variables of the object cout. A member function is one that works only with a specific group of objects of the same class. See Chapter 33 for a detailed description of classes and member functions.

You typically use the setw manipulator when you want to print data in uniform columns. The following program shows you the importance of the width number. Each cout output is shown in the comment to its left.

```
// Filename: C8MOD1.CPP
// Illustrates various integer width cout modifiers

#include <iostream.h>
#include <iomanip.h>

main()
    {                              // The output appears below
    cout << 456 << 456 << 456;  // 456456456
    cout << setw(5) << 456 << setw(5) << 456 << setw(5)
         << 456;                   // 456  456  456
    cout << setw(7) << 456 << setw(7) << 456 << setw(7)
         << 456 << " \n";          // 456    456    456
    return 0;
    }
```

In this example, we see a new header file. This file, iomanip.h, gives us access to a manipulator function like setw. When you use a setw manipulator inside a conversion character, C++ right-justifies the number within the width you specify. When you specify an eight-digit width, C++ prints a value inside the eight digits, padding the number with leading blanks if it does not fill the whole width.

**Note:** If you do not specify a width large enough to hold the number, C++ ignores your width request and prints the number in its entirety.

You can control the width of strings in the same manner, again using the setw manipulator. If you don't specify enough width to print the full string, C++ ignores the width. The mailing list application in the back of this book uses this technique to print names on mailing labels.

**Note:** setw() becomes more important when you want to print floating-point numbers.

setprecision(2) tells C++ to print a floating-point number with two decimal places. If C++ has to round off the fractional part, it will do so. The line

```
cout << setw(6) << setprecision(2) << 134.568767;
```

produces the following output:

```
134.57
```

Without the setw or setprecision manipulator, C++ would print this:

```
134.568767
```

> **Tip:** When printing floating-point numbers, C++ always prints the entire portion to the left of the decimal (to maintain as much accuracy as possible), no matter how many positions you specify for width. Therefore, many C++ programmers ignore the setw manipulator for floating-point numbers and specify only the precision, as in setprecision(2).

## Examples

1. You saw earlier how the \t tab character can be used to print columns of data. The tab character is limited to eight columns. If you want more control of the width of your data, use a setw manipulator. The following program is a modified version of C8TEAM.CPP, using the width specifier instead of the tab character. This specifier ensures that each column is 10 characters wide.

```cpp
// Filename: C8TEAMMD.CPP
// Prints a table of team names and wins for three weeks,
// using width-modifying conversion characters

#include <iostream.h>
#include <iomanip.h>

main()
    {
    cout << setw(10) << "Parrots" << setw(10) << "Rams"
         << setw(10) << "Kings" << setw(10) << "Titans"
         << setw(10) << "Chargers" << "\n";
    cout << setw(10) << 3 << setw(10) << 5 << setw(10) << 3
         << setw(10) << 1 << setw(10) << 0 << "\n";
cout << setw(10) << 2 << setw(10) << 5 << setw(10) << 1
         << setw(10) << 0 << setw(10) << 1 << "\n";
cout << setw(10) << 2 << setw(10) << 6 << setw(10) << 4
         << setw(10) << 3 << setw(10) << 0 << "\n";
    return 0;
    }
```

**2.** The following program revises the payroll program shown earlier (C8PAY1.CPP). The output is "cleaned up" because the dollar amounts now print properly to two decimal places.

```cpp
// Filename: C8PAY1.CPP
// Computes and prints payroll data properly
// in dollars and cents

#include <iostream.h>
#include <iomanip.h>

main()
    {
    char        emp_name[ ] = "Larry Payton";
    char        pay_date[ ] = "03/09/94";
    int         hours_worked = 40;
    float    rate = 7.50;        // Pay per hour
    float    tax_rate = .40;       // Tax percentage rate
    float    gross_pay, taxes, net_pay;

    // Compute the pay amount
    gross_pay = hours_worked * rate;
    taxes = tax_rate * gross_pay;
    net_pay = gross_pay - taxes;

    // Print the results
    cout << "As of: " << pay_date << "\n";
    cout << emp_name << " worked " << hours_worked
         << " hours\n";
    cout << "and got paid " << setw(2) << setprecision(2)
         << setiosflags(ios::fixed) << gross_pay << "\n";
    cout << "After taxes of: " << setw(5) << setprecision(2)
         << taxes << "\n";
    cout << "his take-home pay was: " << setw(6)
         << setprecision(2) << net_pay << "\n";
    return 0;
    }
```

The following is the output from this program. You should remember that the floating-point variables still hold the full precision (to six decimal places), as they did in the last program. The modifying setw manipulators affect only how the variables are printed, not what is stored in them.

```
As of: 03/09/92
Larry Payton worked 40 hours
and got paid 300.00
After taxes of: 120.00
his take-home pay was: 180.00
```

**3.** Most C++ programmers do not use the setw manipulator to the left of the decimal point when printing dollars and cents. Here is the payroll program again, using the shortcut floating-point width method. Notice that the last three cout statements include no setw manipulator. C++ knows to print the full number to the left of the decimal, but only two places to the right.

```
// Filename: C8PAY2.CPP
// Computes and prints payroll data properly, using the
// shortcut modifier

#include <iostream.h>
#include <iomanip.h>

main()
    {
    char         emp_name[ ] = "Larry Payton";
    char         pay_date[ ] = "03/09/92";
    int          hours_worked = 40;
    float    rate = 7.50;        // Pay per hour
    float    tax_rate = .40;     // Tax percentage rate
    float    gross_pay, taxes, net_pay;

    // Compute the pay amount
    gross_pay = hours_worked * rate;
    taxes = tax_rate * gross_pay;
    net_pay = gross_pay - taxes;

    // Print the results
    cout << "As of: " << pay_date << "\n";
    cout << emp_name << " worked " << hours_worked
         << " hours\n";
    cout << "and got paid " << setiosflags(ios::fixed)
         << setprecision(2) << gross_pay << "\n";
    cout << "After taxes of: " << setprecision(2) << taxes
         << "\n";
    cout << "his take-home pay was: " << setprecision(2)
         << net_pay << "\n";
    return 0;
    }
```

This program's output is the same as that of the last program.

The setiosflags and resetiosflags manipulators are used to set certain global flags that the C++ iostream class uses in establishing the default behavior of its input and output. These flags are referred to as *state variables*. The function setiosflags() sets the flags indicated; resetiosflags() clears (or resets) them. These manipulators take as arguments any of the values shown in table 8.1. These manipulators may be used in combination.

For example, the `setiosflags( ios::left)` function instructs the `cout` object to left-justify its output:

```
cout << setw(20) << "Hello\n";
cout << setw(20) << setiosflags(ios::left) << "Hello\n" ;
```

produces the following output:

```
                Hello
Hello
```

## Table 8.1. Arguments for *setiosflags* and *resetiosflags*.

| Value | Meaning If Set |
|---|---|
| ios::skipws | Skip white space on input |
| ios::left | Left-adjust output |
| ios::right | Right-adjust output |
| ios::internal | Pad after the sign or base indicator |
| ios::dec | Decimal conversion |
| ios::oct | Octal conversion |
| ios::hex | Hexadecimal conversion |
| ios::showbase | Show base indicator on output |
| ios::showpoint | Show decimal point |
| ios::uppercase | Uppercase hexadecimal output |
| ios::showpos | Show '+' with positive integers |
| ios::scientific | Use scientific notation |
| ios::fixed | Use fixed notation |
| ios::unitbuf | Flush all streams after insertion |
| ios::stdio | Flush stdout, stderr after insertion |

# The *cin* Operator

You now understand how C++ represents data and variables, and you know how to print that data. There is one additional part of programming that you have not seen: inputting data into your programs.

Until this point, every program has had no input of data. All data you worked with was assigned to variables within the program. However, this is not always the best way to get the data into your programs; you rarely know what your data is going to be when you write your programs. The data is known only when you run the programs (or another user runs them).

The cin operator stores keyboard input in variables.

You can use the cin operator to get input from the keyboard. When your programs reach the line with a cin, the user at the keyboard can enter values directly into variables. Your program can then process those variables and produce output. Figure 8.1 illustrates the difference between cout and cin.

**Figure 8.1.**

The actions of cout and cin.

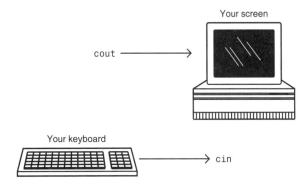

**The *cin* Operator Fills Variables with Values**

There is a major difference between cin and the assignment statements (such as i = 17;) you have seen. Both fill variables with values. However, an assignment statement is assigned specific values to variables *at programming time*. When you run a program with assignment statements, you know from the program's listing exactly what values will go into the variables, because you wrote the program to store those values there. Every time you run the program, the results are exactly the same since the same values go into (are *assigned* to) the same variables.

When you write programs that use cin, you have no idea what values will go into the cin's variables because the values are not known *until the program is run and the user enters those values*. This means more flexible programs that can be used by a variety of people. Whenever the program is run, different results are printed, depending on what is typed at each cin in the program.

The cin operator has its drawbacks. However, if you understand the cout operator, cin should not pose much of a problem. Therefore, the next few chapters make use of cin, until you learn the more powerful (and flexible) input methods.

The cin operator looks very much like cout, containing one or more variables to the right of the operator name. The format of cin is

```
cin [>> values];
```

The iostream.h header file contains the information C++ needs for cin, so include that file when using cin. The cin operator uses the same manipulators as the cout operator. The values are the variables into which the data will be placed.

The cin operator requires that the user type correct input. This is not always possible to guarantee!

As mentioned, cin poses a few problems. The cin operator requires that your user type the input *exactly* as cin expects it. Because you cannot control the user's typing, its accuracy cannot be ensured. You might want the user to enter an integer value followed by a floating-point value, which your cin operator might expect, yet your user decides to enter something else! If that happens, there is not much you can do; the resulting input will be incorrect, and your C++ program has no reliable method for testing user accuracy.

For the next few chapters, you can assume that the user knows to enter the proper values. But for your own programs used by others, you will want to be on the lookout for other methods that get better input, starting in Part V of this book.

## Examples

1. If you want a program that computes a seven percent sales tax, you can use the cin statement to get the sales figure, compute the tax, and print the result. The following program shows you how to do this:

```cpp
// Filename: C8SLTX1.CPP
// Gets a sales amount and prints the sales tax

#include <iostream.h>
#include <iomanip.h>

main()
    {
    float     total_sale;   // User's sales amount
                            // will go here
    float     stax;

    // Get the sales amount from user
    cin >> total_sale;

    // Calculate sales tax
    stax = total_sale * .07;

    cout << "The sales tax for " << setprecision(2)
         << total_sale << " is " << setprecision (2)
         << stax;
    return 0;
    }
```

If you run this program, it will wait for you to enter a value for the total sale. After you press the Enter key, the program calculates the sales tax and prints the result.

If you entered 10.00 as the sales amount, you would see the following output:

```
The sales tax for 10.00 is 0.70
```

2. The preceding program is fine for introducing cin but contains a serious problem. The problem is not in the code itself, but in the assumption made about the user. The program does not indicate what it expects the user to enter. The cin assumes too much already, so your programs that use cin should inform the user exactly what they should type. The following revision of this program prompts the user with an appropriate message before getting the sales amount:

```
// Filename: C8SLTX2.CPP
// Prompts for a sales amount and prints the sales tax

#include <iostream.h>
#include <iomanip.h>

main()
    {
    float      total_sale;    // User's sales amount
                              // will go here
    float      stax;

    // Display a message for the user
    cout << "What is the total amount of the sale? ";

    // Get the sales amount from user
    cin >> total_sale;

    // Calculate sales tax
    stax = total_sale * .07;

    cout << "The sales tax for " << setprecision(2)
        << total_sale << " is " << setprecision (2)
        << stax;
    return 0;
    }
```

Because the first cout does not contain a newline character, \n, the user's response to the prompt will appear directly to the right of the question mark.

3. In inputting keyboard strings into character arrays with cin, you are limited to getting one word at a time. The cin will not let you type more

than one word at a time into a single character array. The following program asks for the user's first and last names. It has to store those two names in two different character arrays because cin cannot get both names at once. The program then prints the names in reverse order.

```cpp
// Filename: C8PHON1.CPP
// Program that gets the user's name and prints it
// to the screen as it would appear in a phone book

#include <iostream.h>
#include <iomanip.h>

main()
    {
    char    first[ 20 ], last[ 20 ];

    cout << "What is your first name? ";
    cin >> first;
    cout << "What is your last name? ";
    cin >> last;
    cout << "\n\n";        // Print 2 blank lines
    cout << "In a phone book, your name would look like this:\n";
    cout << last << ", " << first;
    return 0;
    }
```

Figure 8.2 shows a sample run from this program.

**Figure 8.2.**

Getting strings
from the keyboard.

```
What is your first name? Martha
What is your last name? Roberts


In a phone book, your name would look like this:
Roberts, Martha
```

4. Suppose you want to write a program that does simple addition for your seven-year-old daughter. The following program prompts her for two numbers and then waits for her to type an answer. When she gives her answer, the program displays the correct result, so that she can see how well she did. (Later, you will learn how you can let her know immediately whether her answer is correct.)

```cpp
// Filename: C8MATH.CPP
// Program to help children with simple addition
// Prompts child for two values, after printing a title message
#include <iostream.h>
#include <iomanip.h>
```

```
main()
   {
   int     num1, num2, ans;
   int     her_ans;

   cout << "*** Math Practice ***\n\n\n";
   cout << " What is the first number? ";
   cin >> num1;
   cout << "What is the second number? ";
   cin >> num2;

   // Compute answer and give her a chance to wait for it
   ans = num1 + num2;

   cout << "\nWhat do you think is the answer? ";
   cin >> her_ans;      // Nothing is done with this

   // Print answer after a blank line
   cout << "\n" << num1 << " plus " << num2 << " is: "
        << ans << "\n\nHope you got it right!";
   return 0;
   }
```

## Summary

You now can print almost anything to the screen. By studying the manipulators and how they behave, you can control your output more thoroughly than ever before. Furthermore, because you can receive keyboard values, your programs are much more powerful. No longer do you have to know your data values when you write the program. With cin you can ask the user to enter values into variables for you.

You have the tools to begin writing programs that fit the data processing model of *input -> process -> output*. This chapter concludes the preliminary discussion of the C++ language. Part I provided an overview of the language and showed you enough of its elements so that you can begin writing useful programs as soon as possible.

The next chapter begins a new kind of discussion. You will learn how C++'s math and relational operators work on data, and you will learn the importance of the precedence table of operators.

## Review Questions

Answers to Review Questions are in Appendix B.

1. What is the difference between cout and cin?

2. Why is displaying a prompt message important before using cin for input?

3. How many values are entered with the following cin?

   ```
   cin >> i >> j >> k >> l;
   ```

4. Because both methods put values into variables, is there any difference between assigning values to variables and using cin to give them values?

5. What is the output produced by the following cout?

   ```
   cout << "The backslash, \"\\\" character is special";
   ```

6. What is the result of the following cout?

   ```
   cout << setw(8) << setprecision(3) << 123.456789;
   ```

## Review Exercises

1. Write a program that prompts for the user's name and weight. Store these values in separate variables and print them to the screen.

2. Assume that you are a college professor who needs to average the grades of 10 students. Write a program that prompts for 10 different grades and displays an average of them.

3. Modify the program in Exercise 2 to ask for each student's name as well as grade. Print the grade list to the screen, with each student's name and grade in two columns. Make sure that the columns align by using a setw manipulator on the grade. At the bottom, print the average of the grades. (*Hint:* Store the 10 names and 10 grades in different variables with different names.) This program is easy but takes about 30 lines, plus lines for appropriate comments and prompts. Later, you will learn ways to streamline this program.

4. Write a program that prompts for the user's full name, hours worked, hourly rate, and tax rate, and then displays the taxes and net pay in the appropriate dollars and cents. Store the first, middle, and last names in three separate character arrays.

5. Modify the child's math program (C8MATH.CPP), shown earlier in this chapter, so that it practices subtraction, multiplication, and division after it finishes the addition.

6. This exercise tests your understanding of the backslash conversion character. Write a program that uses cout operators to produce figure 8.3 on-screen:

**Fig. 8.3.**

Writing a program that uses cout operators produces this kind of results.

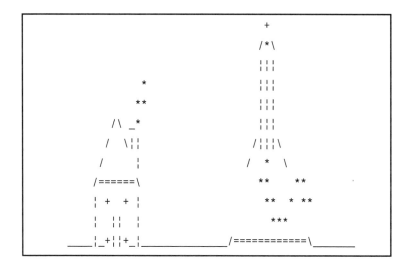

# Part II

*C++ Operators*

# CHAPTER 9

# Using C++ Math Operators and Their Order of Precedence

You might be dreading this chapter if you don't like math. Relax! C++ does all your math for you. It's a misconception that you have to be good at math to understand how to program computers. The opposite is true. The computer is there to be your slave, follow your instructions, and do all the calculations.

This chapter shows how C++ computes by introducing these topics:

- ♦ C++'s primary math operators
- ♦ The operator precedence table
- ♦ Multiple assignments
- ♦ Compound operators
- ♦ Mixed data type conversions
- ♦ Type casting

Many people who dislike math actually enjoy learning how the computer does calculations. After seeing the operators and a few simple ways in which C++ uses them, you will feel comfortable putting calculations in your programs. Computers are very fast, and they are capable of performing math operations many times faster than people can.

## The Primary Math Operators

C++ *math operators* are symbols used for addition, subtraction, multiplication, and division, as well as other similar operations. C++ operators are not always mathematical in nature, but many are. Table 9.1 lists the primary C++ operators and their meanings.

**Table 9.1. Many of the symbols for the C++ primary operators have a mathematical function.**

| Symbol | Meaning |
| --- | --- |
| * | Multiplication |
| / | Division and integer division |
| % | Modulus or remainder |
| + | Addition |
| - | Subtraction |

Most of these operators work in ways familiar to you. Multiplication, addition, and subtraction produce the same results (and the division operator usually does) that you get when you do these math functions with a calculator. Table 9.2 shows examples that illustrate four of these simple operators.

**Table 9.2. When you use these four C++ operators, you can get these typical results.**

| Formula | Result |
| --- | --- |
| 4 * 2 | 8 |
| 64 / 4 | 16 |
| 80 - 15 | 65 |
| 12 + 9 | 21 |

Table 9.2 contains examples of *binary operations* performed with four different operators.

When you use these operators (with respect to assigning their results to variables), C++ does not care whether you put spaces around the operators.

> **Note:** Use the asterisk (*) for multiplication, and not an *x*, which you normally use when you multiply by hand. An *x* cannot be used because C++ would confuse it with a variable referred to as x. C++ would not know whether you wanted to multiply, or use the value of that variable.

## The Unary Operators

You can use the addition and subtraction operators by themselves. When you do, they are called *unary operators*. A unary operator operates on, or affects, a single value. For instance, you can assign a variable a positive or negative number by using a unary + or -. In addition, you can assign a variable the negative of the value of another variable by using a unary -.

### Examples

**1.** The following section of code assigns four variables a positive or negative number. All the plus signs (+) and minus signs (-) are unary because they are not used between two values.

*The variable a becomes equal to negative 25.*
*The variable b becomes equal to positive 25.*
*The variable c becomes equal to negative a.*
*The variable d becomes equal to positive b.*

```
a = -25;   // Assign 'a' a negative 25
b = +25;   // Assign 'b' a positive 25 (The plus sign is
           // not needed)
c = -a;    // Assign 'c' the negative of 'a' (25)
d = +b;    // Assign 'd' the positive of 'b' (The plus sign
           // is not needed)
```

**2.** You generally don't have to use the unary plus sign. C++ assumes that a number or variable is positive even if you don't put a + in front of it. The following four statements are equivalent to the last ones, except that these don't contain plus signs:

```
a = -25;   // Assign 'a' a negative 25
b =  25;   // Assign 'b' a positive 25
c = -a;    // Assign 'c' the negative of 'a' (-25)
d =  b;    // Assign 'd' the positive of 'b'
```

**3.** The unary negative comes in handy when you want to negate a single number or variable. The negative of a negative is positive. Therefore, the following short program assigns a negative number (using the unary -) to a variable. Then, the program prints the negative of that variable. Because it had a negative number to begin with, the cout produces a positive result.

```
// Filename: C9NEG.CPP
// The negative of a variable that contains a negative value

#include <iostream.h>

main()
    {
    signed int      temp = -12;     // 'signed' is not
                                    //   needed
                                    //   because that is
                                    //   default

    cout << -temp;      // Produce a 12 on the screen
    return 0;
    }
```

The variable declaration did not need the `signed` prefix because all integer variables are `signed` by default.

4. If you want to subtract the negative of a variable, make sure that you put a space before the unary minus sign. For example, the line

```
new_temp = old_temp - -inversion_factor;
```

temporarily negates the `inversion_factor`, then subtracts that negated value from `new_temp`.

## Division and Modulus

The modulus operator (%) computes the remainder of division.

The division operator (/) and the modulus operator (%) might operate in ways unfamiliar to you. They are usually as easy to use, though, as the other operators previously discussed.

The forward slash (/) always divides. However, it produces an integer division if integer values (constants, variables, or a combination of both) appear on both sides of the /. If there is a remainder, C++ discards it.

The percent sign (%) produces a modulus, or a remainder, of an integer division. This operator requires integers on both sides. Otherwise, it does not work.

### Examples

1. Suppose that you want to compute your weekly pay. The following program asks for your yearly pay, divides it by 52, and prints the results to two decimal places:

```
// Filename: C9DIV.CPP
// Displays user's weekly pay
```

```
#include <iostream.h>
#include <iomanip.h>

main()
    {
    float    weekly, yearly;

    cout << "What is your annual pay? ";  // Prompt user
    cin >> yearly;

    weekly = yearly / 52;  // Compute the weekly
    cout << "\n\nYour weekly pay is "
        << setprecision(2) << setiosflags(ios::fixed) << weekly;
    return 0;
    }
```

A floating-point number is used in the division; therefore, C++ produces a floating-point result. The following is a sample run from this program:

```
What is your annual pay? 38000.00
Your weekly pay is $730.77
```

2. Integer division does not round its results. If you divide two integers, and the answer is not a whole number, C++ ignores the fractional part. The following couts help show this. The output that would result from each cout appears in the comment to the right of each line.

```
cout << 10 / 2 << " \n";     // 5  (no remainder)
cout << 300 / 100 << " \n";  // 3  (no remainder)
cout << 10 / 3 << " \n";     // 3  (discarded remainder)
cout << 300 / 165 << " \n";  // 1  (discarded remainder)
```

3. The modulus operator produces an integer remainder. If the preceding four couts used the modulus operator, the output would show only the remainder of each division, as in the following:

```
cout << 10 % 2 << " \n";     // 0  (no remainder)
cout << 300 % 100 << " \n";  // 0  (no remainder)
cout << 10 % 3 << " \n";     // 1 (Answer: 3 with 1 remaining)
cout << 300 % 165 << " \n";  // 135 (Answer: 1 with 135
                             // remaining)
```

Once you learn a few more commands, the modulus operator comes in handy for several types of applications. You can use the modulus to make sure that the user has entered an odd or even number, and to check whether a year is a leap year. You can employ the modulus to test for several other helpful values, as well.

# The Order of Precedence

Knowing the meaning of the math operators is the first of two steps toward understanding C++ calculations. You also must understand the *order of precedence*. This order (sometimes referred to as the *math hierarchy* or *order of operators*) determines exactly how C++ computes formulas.

Perform multiplication, division, and modulus before addition and subtraction.

The precedence of operators is the same as that used in high school algebra courses. To see how the order of precedence works, try to determine the result of the following simple calculation:

    2 + 3 * 2

If you said 10, you would not be alone; many people would respond with 10. However, 10 is correct only if you interpret the formula from left to right. What if you calculated the multiplication first? If you computed the value of 3 * 2 and got an answer of 6, then added it to 2, the result would be 8. This is exactly the answer—8—that C++ computes!

C++ always performs multiplication, division, and modulus first, then computes addition and subtraction. Table 9.3 shows the order of the operators you have seen so far. There are many more levels to C++'s precedence table of operators than those that table 9.3 shows. Appendix D contains the complete table of precedence. Notice in Appendix D's precedence table that multiplication, division, and modulus reside on level 3, one level higher than level 4's addition and subtraction. In the next few chapters, you learn how to use the rest of the precedence table in your C++ programs.

**Table 9.3. The order of precedence for the primary operators begins with multiplication.**

| Order | Operators |
|-------|-----------|
| First | Multiplication, division, modulus remainder (*, /, %) |
| Second | Addition, subtraction (+, -) |

## Examples

1. Following C++'s order of operators is easy if you look at the intermediate results one at a time. The three calculations in figure 9.1 show you how to do this.

**Figure 9.1.**

These sample
calculations show
C++'s order of
operators.

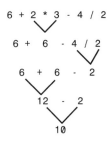

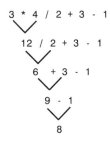

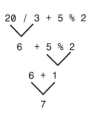

**2.** Referring back at the order of the precedence table again, you notice that multiplication, division, and modulus are on the same level. This implies that there is no hierarchy on that level. If more than one of these operators appear in a calculation, C++ performs the math from left to right. The same is true of addition and subtraction; the calculation to the far left is performed first. Figure 9.2 shows an example.

**Figure 9.2.**

This sample
calculation shows
C++'s order of
operators from
left to right.

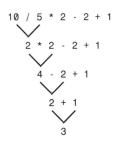

In figure 9.2, the division appears to the left of the multiplication. Therefore, the division is computed first because both are on the same level in the precedence table (Appendix D).

Now, you should be able to follow the order of these C++ operators. You really do not need to worry about the math because C++ does all the work. However, you should understand the order of operators, so that you know how to structure your calculations. You are now ready to see how you can override the order of precedence with parentheses.

# Using Parentheses

Parentheses override the normal precedence of math operators.

If you want to override the order of precedence, put parentheses in your calculations. The parentheses actually reside on a level above the multiplication, division, and modulus in the precedence table. In other words, any calculation in parentheses—whether it is addition, subtraction, division, or something else—is always performed before the rest of the line. The other calculations are performed in their normal operator order.

The first formula in this chapter, 2 + 3 * 2, produced an 8 because the multiplication was performed before addition. However, by adding parentheses around the addition, as in (2 + 3) * 2, the answer becomes 10.

In the precedence table that Appendix D shows, the parentheses reside on level 1, the highest level in the table. Being higher than the other levels means that the parentheses take precedence over multiplication, division, and all the other operators you have seen.

## Examples

1. The calculations in figure 9.3 illustrate how parentheses override the regular order of operators. These are the same three formulas that the last section showed, except that their results are calculated differently due to the use of parentheses.

**Figure 9.3.**

The use of parentheses is at the highest level of precedence.

```
6 + 2 * (3 - 4) / 2
         \   /
6 + 2 *  -1  / 2
       \   /
6  +  -2   / 2
    \    /
6 +    - 1
  \    /
     5
```

*continues*

**Figure 9.3.**

continued

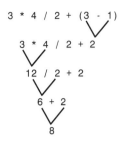

$$3 * 4 / 2 + (3 - 1)$$
$$3 * 4 / 2 + 2$$
$$12 / 2 + 2$$
$$6 + 2$$
$$8$$

$$20 / (3 + 5) \% 2$$
$$20 / 8 \% 2$$
$$2 \% 2$$
$$0$$

**2.** If an expression contains parentheses within parentheses, C++ evaluates the contents of the innermost parentheses first. The expression in figure 9.4 illustrates this concept.

**Figure 9.4.**

C++ performs the calculations of the innermost parentheses first.

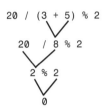

$$5 * (5 + (6 - 2) + 1)$$
$$5 * (5 + 4 + 1)$$
$$5 * (9 + 1)$$
$$5 * 10$$
$$50$$

**3.** The following program produces an incorrect result, even though it appears as if it should work. Try to spot the error.

*Comments to identify your program.*
*Include the header file* iostream.h.
*Include the header file* iomanip.h.
*Start of the* main() *function.*
    *Declare the variables* avg, grade1, grade2, *and* grade3
    *as floating-point integers.*
    *Set the variable* grade1 *to* 85.0.
    *Set the variable* grade2 *to* 80.0.
    *Set the variable* grade3 *to* 75.0.
    *The variable* avg *becomes equal to* grade1 *plus* grade2

*plus* grade3 *divided by 3.0.*
*Print to the screen* The average is *and the average of*
*the 3 grade variables.*
*Return from the* main() *function.*

```
// Filename: C9AVG1.CPP
// Computes the average of three grades

#include <iostream.h>
#include <iomanip.h>

main()
    {
    float     avg, grade1, grade2, grade3;

    grade1 = 85.0;
    grade2 = 80.0;
    grade3 = 75.0;
    avg = grade1 + grade2 + grade3 / 3.0;
    cout << "The average is "
        << setprecision(1) << setiosflags(ios::fixed) << avg;
    return 0;
    }
```

The problem is that division is performed first. Therefore, the third grade is divided by three. Then, the other two grades are added to that result. To fix the problem, you just need to add one set of parentheses, as the following shows:

```
// Filename: C9AVG2.CPP
// Computes the average of three grades

#include <iostream.h>
#include <iomanip.h>

main()
{
float     avg, grade1, grade2, grade3;

grade1 = 85.0;
grade2 = 80.0;
grade3 = 75.0;
avg = (grade1 + grade2 + grade3) / 3.0;
cout << "The average is "
    << setprecision(1) << setiosflags(ios::fixed) << avg;
return 0;
}
```

**Tip:** Use plenty of parentheses in your C++ programs to make the order of operators clearer, even when you don't have to override their default order. This makes the calculations easier to understand when you later modify the program.

**Shorter Is Not Always Better**

When you program computers for a living, it is much more important to create programs that are easy to understand than to write ones that are short, or include tricky calculations.

*Maintainability* is a measure of the ease with which a program can be updated or changed. Avoiding tricky code enhances the maintainability of a program. The business world is changing rapidly, and the programs that companies used for years must be updated to reflect the changing environment. Businesses do not always have the resources to write programs from scratch. Therefore, they have to make do by modifying the ones they have.

Years ago, when computer hardware was much more expensive (and computer memories were much smaller), it was important that you write more compact programs, despite the problems they caused when they needed to be changed. This was aggravating when the original programmers left and someone else (you!) had to step in and modify another person's code. One of the principal reasons for the growing popularity of object-oriented programming with C++ is its positive effect on maintainability. If the vast majority of a program is written as member functions of classes, the people maintaining the system are able to locate and change the source code quickly. They also must  be sure that they have isolated 100 percent of the side effects of this change. Side effects are the curse of maintenance programming. Just when you think that you have made a successful change, some seemingly unrelated part of the system stops functioning. C++, when used in a strictly object-oriented system, can eliminate this problem.

Companies are realizing the importance of spending time to write programs that are easy to modify, and that do not rely on tricks or quick routines that are hard to follow. You will be a more valuable programmer if you write clean programs, with lots of white space, many remarks, and straightforward code. Put parentheses around formulas to make them clearer, and use variables for storing results in case you need the same answer later in the program. Break long calculations into several smaller ones. Later in the book, when we study the object-oriented constructs of C++, you learn to view maintainability as a primary goal.

Throughout this book, you learn tips on writing maintainable programs. You and your colleagues will appreciate these tips when you incorporate them into your own C++ programs.

# The Assignment Statement

In C++, the assignment operator, =, is used more extensively than in other languages such as Basic or Fortran. So far, you have seen this operator used for the simple assignment of values to variables. This is consistent with its use in most programming languages.

If more than one equal sign appears in an expression, each = performs an assignment. This multiple use introduces a new aspect of the precedence order. Consider the following expression:

```
a = b = c = d = e = 100;
```

This might seem confusing at first, especially if you know other computer languages. To C++, the equal sign always means to "assign the value on the right to the variable on the left." This right-to-left order is described in Appendix D's precedence table. The forth column in the table is labeled *Associativity*. The *Associativity column* describes the direction of the operation. The assignment operator associates from right to left, whereas some of the other operators associate from left to right.

The assignment associates from right to left. Therefore, the preceding expression first assigns the 100 to the variable named e. This produces a value, 100, of the expression. In C++, all expressions produce values, typically the result of assignments. Therefore, this value (100) is then assigned to the variable d. The value of that, 100, is assigned to c, then to b, and finally to a. Whatever values were in the five variables previous to this statement are replaced, after it finishes, by 100.

C++ does not automatically set variables to zero before you use them. Therefore, you might want to zero them out with a single assignment statement. The following section of variable declarations and initialization is performed with multiple assignment statements:

```
#include <iostream.h>
main()
{
int        ctr, num_emp, num_dep;
float     sales, salary, amount;

ctr = num_emp = num_dep = 0;
sales = salary = amount = 0;
// Rest of program follows
```

In C++, you can include the assignment statement almost anywhere in a program, even within another calculation. For example, note this statement:

```
value = 5 + (r = 9 - c);
```

This is a perfectly legal C++ statement. The assignment operator resides on the first level of the precedence table and always produces a value. Its associativity is from right to left; therefore, the r is first assigned 9 - c. The reason is that the equal sign on the right is evaluated first. The subexpression (r = 9 - c) produces a value— whatever is placed into r—which is added to 5 before that result is stored in value.

## Examples

**1.** C++ does not initialize variables to zero before you use them. Therefore, you might want to include a multiple assignment operator to zero them out before using them. The following section of code ensures that all variables are initialized before the rest of the program uses them:

```
#include <iostream.h>
main()
    (
    int        num_emp, dependents, age;
    float      salary, hr_rate, taxrate;

    // Initialize all variables to zero
    num_emp = dependents = age = hours = 0;
    salary = hr_rate = taxrate = 0.0;

    // Rest of program follows
```

**2.** The two statements

```
gross = hr_rate * hours;
```

```
salary = taxrate * gross;
```

can be combined into one with the multiple assignment operator, as the following line shows:

```
salary = taxrate * (gross = hr_rate * hours);
```

Use these types of statements judiciously. Even though employing combined statements can be more efficient than using two statements, the former are harder to read.

## Compound Assignment

Many times in programming, you will want to update the value of a variable. That is, you will need to take a variable's current value, add or multiply that value by an expression, and then assign it back to the original variable. The following assignment statement demonstrates this:

```
salary = salary * 1.2;
```

This expression multiplies the old value of salary by 1.2 (in effect, raising the value in salary by 20 percent), then reassigns it to salary. C++ provides several operators, referred to as *compound operators*, that you can use whenever the same variable appears on both sides of the equal sign. Table 9.4 shows the compound operators.

### Table 9.4. C++ provides these compound operators.

| Operator | Example | Equivalent |
|---|---|---|
| += | bonus += 500; | bonus = bonus + 500; |
| -= | budget -= 50; | budget = budget - 50; |
| *= | salary *= 1.2; | salary = salary * 1.2; |
| /= | factor /= .50; | factor = factor / .50; |
| %= | daynum %= 7; | daynum = daynum % 7; |

The compound operators are low in the precedence table. They are typically evaluated very late in equations that use them.

### Examples

1. Suppose that you have been storing your factory's production amount in a variable referred to as prod_amt, and your supervisor has just informed you of a new addition that needs to be applied to that production value. You can code this update in a statement that resembles the following:

```
prod_amt = prod_amt + 2.6;   // Add 2.6 to current production
```

Instead of this formula, you should use C++'s compound addition operator by coding the update in this way:

```
prod_amt += 2.6;   // Add 2.6 to current production
```

2. Suppose that you are a high school teacher who wants to adjust your students' grades upward. You gave a test that seemed too difficult, and the grades were not up to your expectations. If you had stored each student's grade in variables named grade1, grade2, grade3, and so on, you could update the grades from within a program with the following section of compound assignments:

```
grade1 *= 1.1;      // Increase each student's grade by 10%
grade2 *= 1.1;
grade3 *= 1.1;
// Rest of grade changes follow
```

3. The precedence of the compound operators requires important consideration when you decide how to code compound assignments. Notice in Appendix D that the compound operators are on level 14, much lower than the regular math operators. This means you must be careful how you interpret them.

Suppose, for example, that you want to update the value of a sales variable with the following formula:

```
4 - factor + bonus
```

You can update the sales variable with the statement

```
sales += 4 - factor + bonus;
```

This applies the new formula, 4 - factor + bonus, to sales. This is *not* the same as

```
sales = sales + 4 - factor + bonus;
```

The += operator is much lower in the precedence table than + or -. Therefore, += is performed last and with right-to-left associativity. Consequently, the following two statements *are* equivalent:

```
sales += 4 - factor + bonus;
sales = sales + (4 - factor + bonus);
```

**4.** To give you a better idea of the compound operators and their precedence level, the following program uses each compound operator, and prints a result based on the operators. The program and its output will help you understand how to use the compound operators and their levels in the precedence table.

```cpp
// Filename: C9CMP.CPP
// Illustrates each compound operator

#include <iostream.h>

main()
    {
    int     i = 4;
    int     j = 8;
    int     k = 12;
    int     ans;                // Will hold various results

    ans = i + j;
    cout << ans << " \n";       // Print a 12
    ans += k;
    cout << ans << " \n";       // Print a 24
    ans /= 3;
    cout << ans << " \n";       // Print an 8
    ans -= 5;
    cout << ans << " \n";       // Print a 3
    ans *= 2;
    cout << ans << " \n";       // Print a 6
    ans %= 4;
    cout << ans << " \n";       // Print a 2
```

```
// Order of precedence affects the following
    ans *= 5 + 3;
    cout << ans << " \n";        // Print a 16
    ans += 4 - 2;
    cout << ans << " \n";        // Print an 18

    return 0;
    }
```

## Mixing Data Types in Calculations

C++ attempts to convert the smaller data type to the larger one in a mixed data type expression.

You can mix data types in C++, such as adding together an integer and a floating-point value. C++ generally converts the smaller type to the larger type. For instance, if you add a double to an integer, C++ first converts the integer to a double value, then performs the calculation. This produces the most accurate result possible. The automatic conversion of data types is only temporary; the converted value is back in its original data type as soon as the expression is finished.

If C++ converted two different data types to the smaller value's type, the higher-precision value would be truncated (shortened) too much and accuracy would be lost. For example, in the following short program the floating-point value of `sales` is added to an integer referred to as `bonus`. Before computing the answer, C++ converts `bonus` to a floating-point value, which results in a floating-point answer.

```
// Filename: C9DATA.CPP
// Demonstrates mixed data type in an expression

#include <iostream.h>
#include <iomanip.h>

main()
{
int        bonus = 50;
float    salary = 1400.50;
float    total;

total = salary + bonus;    // bonus becomes
                           // floating-point temporarily
cout << "The total is "
     << setprecision(2) << setiosflags(ios::fixed) << total;
return 0;
}
```

## Type Casting

Most of the time, you do not have to worry about C++'s automatic conversion of data types. However, problems can occur if you mix unsigned variables with variables of other data types. Unsigned variables do not always convert to the larger data type due to differences in computer architecture. Therefore, the result might be loss of accuracy. Even incorrect results are possible.

You can override C++'s default conversions by specifying your own temporary type change. This is referred to as *type casting*. When you type cast, you temporarily change a variable's data type from its declared data type to a new one. The format of a type cast is

```
(data type) expression
```

in which data type can be any valid C++ data type, and the expression can be a variable, a constant, or an expression. The following line of code type casts the integer variable age into a double floating-point variable temporarily, so that it can be multiplied by the double floating-point factor.

*Assign the variable* age_factor *the value of the variable* age
*(now a double floating-point variable). Then, multiply by
the variable* factor.

```
age_factor = (double)age * factor;   // Temporarily change
                                     // age to double
```

## Examples

1. Suppose that you want to verify the interest calculation used by your bank on a loan. The interest rate is 15.5 percent, stored as 0.155 in a floating-point variable. The amount of interest you owe is computed by multiplying the interest rate by the amount of the loan balance, then multiplying that by the number of days in the year since the loan was originated. The following program finds the daily interest rate by dividing the annual interest rate by 365, the number of days in a year. C++ must convert the integer 365 to a floating-point constant automatically because it is used in combination with a floating-point variable.

```
// C9INT1.CPP
// Calculates interest on a loan

#include <iostream.h>
#include <iomanip.h>

main()
    {
    int        days = 45;  // Days since loan origination
    float      principal = 3500.00;   // Original loan amount
    float      interest_rate = 0.155; // Annual interest rate
    float      daily_interest;        // Daily interest rate

    daily_interest = interest_rate / 365;   // Compute
                                            // floating-point value
```

```
// Days is an integer. It too will be converted
// to float next
daily_interest = principal * daily_interest * days;
principal += daily_interest;    // Update the principal
                                // with interest
cout << "The balance you owe is "
     << setiosflags(ios::fixed) << setprecision(2)
     << principal;
return 0;
}
```

The following is the output of this program:

```
The balance you owe is 3566.88
```

2. Instead of letting C++ perform the conversion, you might want to type cast all mixed expressions to ensure that they convert to your liking. The following is the same program that appears in Example 1, except that type casts are used to convert the integer constants to floating-point values before they are used:

```
// C9INT2.CPP
// Calculates interest on a loan using type casting

#include <iostream.h>
#include <iomanip.h>

main()
    {
    int         days = 45;   // Days since loan origination
    float       principal = 3500.00;   // Original loan amount
    float       interest_rate = 0.155; // Annual interest rate
    float       daily_interest;        // Daily interest rate

    // Type cast days to float
    daily_interest = interest_rate / (float)365;

    // Days is an integer. Convert it to float
    daily_interest = principal * daily_interest * (float)days;
    principal += daily_interest;    // Update the principal
                                    // with interest
    cout << "The balance you owe is "
         << setiosflags(ios::fixed) << setprecision(2)
         << principal;
    return 0;
    }
```

The output from this program and the first one is exactly the same.

## Summary

You now understand C++'s primary math operators and the important precedence table. Parentheses group operations together so that they override the default precedence levels. Unlike some operators in other programming languages, every operator in C++ has a meaning, no matter in which place the operator appears in an expression. You can, therefore, use the assignment operator (=) in the middle of other expressions.

When performing math with C++, you must be aware of how C++ interprets data types, especially when you mix them within the same expression. You can temporarily type cast a variable or constant in order to override its default data type.

This chapter introduced you to C++ operators. The next two chapters extend this discussion to include relational and logical operators, which enable you to compare data, and compute accordingly.

## Review Questions

The answers to Review Questions are in Appendix B.

**1.** What is the result of each of the following expressions?

    A. `1 + 2 * 4 / 2`

    B. `(1 + 2) * 4 / 2`

    C. `1 + 2 * (4 / 2)`

**2.** What is the result of each of these expressions?

    A. `9 % 2 + 1`

    B. `(1 + (10 - (2 + 2)))`

**3.** Convert each of the following formulas into its C++ assignment equivalents:

    A. $a = \dfrac{3+3}{4+4}$

    B. $x = (a - b) * (a - c)2$

    C. $f = \dfrac{a1/2}{b1/3}$

    D. $d = \dfrac{(8 - x2)}{(x - 9)} - \dfrac{(4 * 2 - 1)}{x3}$

4. Write a short program that prints the area of a circle with a radius of 4 and pi = 3.14159. (The area of a circle is computed using the equation `pi * radius2`.)

5. Write the assignment and `cout` statement that prints the remainder of 100 / 4.

## Review Exercises

1. Write a program that prints each of the first 8 powers of 2—that is, $2^1, 2^2, 2^3,$ ..., $2^8$. Please include a comment to indicate your name at the top of the program. Print string constants that describe each answer printed. The first two lines of your output should resemble this:

```
2 raised to the first power is: 2

2 raised to the second power is: 4
```

2. Change C9PAY.CPP, shown earlier in the chapter, so that it computes and prints a bonus of 15 percent of the gross pay. Taxes are not to be taken out of the bonus. After printing the four variables `gross_pay`, `tax_rate`, `bonus`, and `gross_pay`, print a check on the screen that resembles a printed check. Add string constants so that it prints the name of the payee, and puts your name as the payer at the bottom of the check.

3. Store in variables the weights and ages of three people. Print a table, with titles, of the weights and ages. At the bottom of the table, print the average of the weights and heights, as well as their totals.

4. Assume that a video store employee worked 50 hours. The worker gets paid $4.50 for the first 40 hours, gets time and a half (1.5 times the regular pay rate) for the first 5 hours over 40. The employee also gets double time for all hours over 45. Assuming a 28 percent tax rate, write a program that prints the gross pay, taxes, and net pay to the screen. Label each amount with appropriate titles (using string constants), and add appropriate comments in the program.

# CHAPTER 10

# Relational Operators

At times, you don't want every statement in your C++ program to execute whenever the program runs. So far, each program you have seen began executing at the top and continued, line by line, until the last statement was executed. Depending on your application, you might not always want this to happen.

Most programs are *data-driven*. That is, the data should dictate what the program does. You would not want the computer to print paychecks for all employees every pay period; some employees might have taken a leave of absence. Alternatively, they could have been on a sales commission and not made a sale during a particular pay period. Printing paychecks with zero dollars would be ridiculous. You want the computer to print checks to employees who have pay coming to them, but not to others.

In this chapter, you learn how to create data-driven programs. Such programs do not execute the same way every time they are run. The use of *relational operators* makes this possible. These operators conditionally control other statements. The relational operators examine the constants and variables in the program, and operate based on what they find.

This chapter introduces the following topics:

♦ Relational operators

♦ The `if` statement

♦ The `else` statement

Besides introducing these comparison commands, this chapter also prepares you for much more powerful programs. You can work with powerful programs once you learn the comparison commands.

# Making Data Comparisons by Using Relational Operators

Relational operators compare data.

In addition to using the math operators discussed in the last chapter, you can use other operators to make data comparisons. These operators are called *relational operators*. They compare data, letting you know whether two variables are equal or not equal, or which one is less or more than the other. Table 10.1 lists the relational operators and their meanings.

**Table 10.1. You use relational operators to compare data.**

| Operator | Description |
|---|---|
| == | Equal to |
| > | Greater than |
| < | Less than |
| >= | Greater than or equal to |
| <= | Less than or equal to |
| != | Not equal to |

The six operators in table 10.1 provide the foundation for comparing data in C++. Each operator always appears with two constants, variables, expressions, or a mix of these—one on each side of the operator. Many of the relational operators are probably familiar to you. You should learn them as well as you know the +, -, *, /, and % mathematical operators.

> **Note:** Unlike many programming languages, C++ tests for equality with a double equal sign (==). The single equal sign (=) is reserved for assignment of values only.

## Examples

1. Assume that a program initializes four variables in this way:

        int  a = 5;

        int  b = 10;

        int  c = 15;

        int  d = 5;

The following statements are then true:

> a is equal to d so a == d.
>
> b is less than c so b < c.
>
> c is greater than a so c > a.
>
> b is greater than or equal to a so b >= a.
>
> d is less than or equal to b so d <= b.
>
> d is not equal to c so d != c.

These are not C++ statements. However, they are statements of relational fact about the values in the variables. Relational logic is easy.

Relational logic always produces a *True* or *False* result. In some programming languages, you cannot directly use the True or False result of relational operators inside other expressions. However, in C++ you can. You will soon see how to do this, but for now, the following True and False evaluations are correct:

> A True relational result evaluates to 1.
>
> A False relational result evaluates to 0.
>
> Each of the examples presented earlier in this example evaluate to a 1, or True, result.

**2.** Assuming the values in the last example's four variables, each of the following statements about those values is False (0):

> a == b
>
> b > c
>
> d < a
>
> d > a
>
> a != d
>
> b >= c
>
> c <= b

You should study these statements to see why each one is False and evaluates to 0. The variables a and d are equal to the same value (5). Therefore, neither is greater or less than the other.

You deal with relational logic in everyday life. Think of the following statements you might make:

"The generic butter costs less than the name brand."

"My child is younger than Johnny."

"Our salaries are equal."

"The dogs are not the same age."

Each of these statements is either True or False. There is no other possible outcome.

---

**Watch the Signs!**

Many people say that they are "not inclined toward math" or "not very logical." You might be one of them. As mentioned earlier, you do not have to be good in math to be an excellent computer programmer. Also, you should not be frightened by the term "relational logic," because, as you just learned, you use it all the time. Nevertheless, some people get confused about its meaning.

The two primary relational operators, less than (<) and greater than (>), are easy to remember. You might have been taught to distinguish between the two in school, but you could have forgotten them. Actually, their symbols tell you what they mean.

The "arrow points" of the < and > indicate the smaller of the two values. Notice in the True statements in Example 1 that the point of each < and > always goes toward the smaller number. The large, open part of the operators points to the larger values.

The relation is False if the point goes in the wrong direction. In other words, 4 > 9 is False because the point of the operator is pointing to the 9. Alternatively, in English, "4 is greater than 9 is a False statement because 4 is really less than 9.

---

# The *if* Statement

You incorporate relational operators in C++ programs with the if statement. This statement is called a *decision statement* because it tests a relationship, using the relational operators. Then it makes a decision about which statement to execute next, based on the result of that decision. The if statement has the following format:

if (*condition*)

{ *A block of 1 or more C++ statements* }

The condition includes any relational comparison, and must be enclosed within parentheses. You saw several relational comparisons earlier, such as a == d and c < d. The block of one or more C++ statements can be any legal C++ statement, such as an assignment or the cout operator, enclosed within braces. The block of the if, sometimes called the body of the if statement, is usually indented a few spaces for readability. This lets you see at a glance exactly what executes if the condition is True.

> **Caution:** Do not put a semicolon after the parentheses of the relational test. Semicolons go after each statement inside the block.

If only one statement follows the if, the braces are not required, but they are helpful to include. The block executes *only if the condition is True.* If the condition is False, C++ ignores the block, and simply executes the next statement in the program following the if.

The if statement makes a decision.

Basically, you can read an if statement in the following way: "If the condition is True, perform the block of statements inside the braces. Otherwise, the condition must be False. Therefore, do *not* execute the block, but continue execution as though the if did not exist."

The if statement is employed to make a decision. The block of statements following the if executes if the decision (the result of the relation) is True. Otherwise, the block does not execute. As with relational logic, you use "if" logic every day. Consider the following:

"If the day is warm, I will go swimming."

"If I make enough money, we will build a new house."

"If the light is green, go."

"If the light is red, stop."

Each of these statements is *conditional.* That is, you will perform the action if and only *if* the condition is True.

## Expressions as Conditions

C++ always interprets any nonzero value as True, and any zero value as False. This lets you insert regular nonconditional expressions within the if logic. To see this, consider the following section of code:

```
main()
   {
   int     age = 21;      // Declare and assign age a
                          // value of 21
```

```
if (age = 85)
    {
    cout << "You have lived through a lot!";
    // Rest of program goes here
```

At first, it might seem as though the `cout` does not execute, *but it does*. A regular assignment operator, =, is used and not a relational operator, ==. Therefore, C++ performs the assignment of 85 to `age`. As in all the assignments you saw in the last chapter, this produces a value for the expression of 85. Because 85 is nonzero, C++ interprets the `if` condition as True, and performs the body of the `if` statement.

> **Note:** Confusing the relational equality test (==) and the regular assignment operator (=) is a common error made in C++ programs. The nonzero True test makes this bug even more difficult to find.
>
> The designers of C++ did not intend for this to confuse you. They want you to take advantage of this feature when you can. Instead of putting an assignment before an `if`, then testing the result of that assignment, you can combine the assignment and the `if` into a single statement.
>
> To test your understanding, would C++ interpret the following condition as True or False?
>
> ```
> if (10 == 10 == 10) ...
> ```
>
> Be careful. At first glance, it seems True. However, C++ thinks that the expression is False! The == operator associates from left to right, so the first `10` is compared to the second `10`. They are equal; therefore, the result is 1 (for True). Then, the 1 is compared to the third `10`, which results in a `0` (False) result!

## Examples

1. All the statements in this example are valid C++ `if` statements.

> *If (the variable `sales` is greater than `5000`),*
> *the variable bonus becomes equal to `500`.*

```
if (sales > 5000)
    {
    bonus = 500; }
```

If this were part of a C++ program, the value inside the variable `sales` would determine what happens next. If `sales` contains more than `5000`, the next statement that executes is the one inside the block that initializes `bonus`. If, however, `sales` contains `5000` or less, the block does not execute, and the line following the `if`'s block executes.

*If (the variable age is less than or equal to 21),*
> *print* You are a minor. *to the screen and go to a*
> *new line,*
> *print* What is your grade? *to the screen,*
> *and accept an integer from the keyboard.*

```
if (age <= 21)
    {
    cout << "You are a minor.\n";
    cout << "What is your grade?";
    cin >> grade;
    }
```

If the value in age is less than or equal to 21, the lines of code in the block executes next. Otherwise, C++ skips the entire block, and continues with the program.

*If (the variable balance is greater than the variable*
low_balance)*,*
> *print* Past due! *to the screen. Then, move the cursor to*
> *a newline.*

```
if (balance > low_balance)
    {
    cout << "Past due!\n";
    }
```

If balance is more than low_balance, execution of the program continues at the block, and the message Past due! prints to the screen. You can compare two variables (as in the preceding code fragment ), a variable to a constant (as in the previous fragment), one constant with another (although that is rarely done), or an expression in place of any variable or constant. The following if statement shows an expression included in the if.

*If (the variable pay multiplied by the variable* tax_rate
*equals the variable* minimum)*,*
> *the variable* low_salary *becomes equal to* 1400.60*.*

```
if (pay * tax_rate == minimum)
    {
    low_salary = 1400.60;
    }
```

The precedence table of operators in Appendix D includes the relational operators. They are on levels 6 and 7, lower than the other primary math operators. When using expressions such as this one, you can make them much more readable if you use parentheses (even though they are not required) around the expressions. The following is a rewrite of this if statement with additional parentheses.

*If ((the variable pay multiplied by the variable tax_rate)
equals the variable minimum),
        the variable low_salary becomes equal to 1400.60.*

```
if ((pay * tax_rate) == minimum)
    {
    low_salary = 1400.60;
    }
```

**2.** The following is a simple program that computes the pay of a salesperson. The salesperson gets a flat pay rate of $4.10 per hour. In addition, if the sales total more than $8,500, the salesperson gets an additional $500. This is a good introductory example of conditional logic that depends on a relation of two values: sales and $8,500.

```
// Filename: C10PAY1.CPP
// Calculates a salesperson's pay based on that person's
// sales

#include <iostream.h>
#include <iomanip.h>

main()
    {
    char        sal_name[ 20 ];
    int         hours;
    float       total_sales, bonus, pay;

    cout << "\n\n";      // Print 2 blank lines
    cout << "Payroll Calculation\n";
    cout << "-------------------\n";

    // Ask the user for needed values
    cout << "What is salesperson's last name? ";
    cin >> sal_name;
    cout << "How many hours did the salesperson work? ";
    cin >> hours;
    cout << "What were the total sales? ";
    cin >> total_sales;

    bonus = 0;      // Initially, there is no bonus

    // Compute the base pay
    pay = 4.10 * (float)hours;      // Type cast the hours

    // Add bonus only if sales were high
    if (total_sales > 8500.00)
        {
        bonus = 500.00;
        }
```

```
        cout << sal_name << " made " << setiosflags(ios::fixed)
            << setprecision(2) << pay << " \n";
        cout << "and got a bonus of " << setprecision(2)
            << bonus << "\n";

        return 0;
}
```

Now, note the results of running this program twice, each time with different input values. Notice what the program does: it computes a bonus for one employee, but not for the other. The $500 bonus is a direct result of the if statement. The assignment of $500 to bonus is executed only if the total_sales is more then $8,500.

```
Payroll Calculation
------------------
What is salesperson's last name? Harrison
How many hours did the salesperson work? 40
What were the total sales? 6050.64
Harrison made 164.00
and got a bonus of 0.00
Payroll Calculation
------------------
What is salesperson's last name? Robertson
How many hours did the salesperson work? 40
What were the total sales? 9800
Robertson made 164.00
and got a bonus of 500.00
```

**3.** When getting input from users, it is often wise to perform *data validation* on the values they type. If a user enters a bad value—for instance, a negative number when you know the input cannot be negative—you can inform the user of the problem, and ask that the input be reentered.

Not all data can be validated. However, most of it can be checked to be certain that it's reasonable. For example, if you were writing a student record-keeping program to track each student's name, address, age, and other pertinent data, you could check to see whether the age falls within a reasonable range. If the user enters 213 for the age, you know that the value is incorrect. If the user enters -4 for the age, you know that the input value is incorrect, also. Not all incorrect input can be checked. If the student is 21 and the user types 22, your program would have no way of knowing whether the age is correct. The reason is that 22 falls within a reasonable range.

The following program is a routine that requests an age, then checks to make sure that it is more than 10. This is certainly not a foolproof test, as the user can still enter incorrect ages. However, it does take care of extremely low values. If the user enters a bad age, the user is requested for it again, inside the if statement.

```
// Filename: C10AGE.CPP
// Program to help ensure that age values are reasonable

#include <iostream.h>

main()
    {
    int     age;

    cout << "\nWhat is the student's age? ";
    cin >> age;

    if (age < 10)
        {
            cout << "*** The age cannot be less than 10 ***\n";

        }
    return 0;
    }
```

This routine can be a section of a longer program. Later, you will learn how to prompt repeatedly for a value until a valid input is given.

If the entered age is less than 10, the user gets an error message.

Observe the output of this program. The program knows, because of the if statement, whether age is more than 10.

```
What is the student's age? 3
*** The age cannot be less than 10 ***
```

4. Unlike many languages, C++ does not include a square operator. You can take the square of a number by multiplying it by itself. Many computers don't let integers hold more than the square of 180; therefore, this program uses if statements to make sure that the number fits into an integer answer when it is computed.

The following program takes a value from the user and prints the square of it, unless it is more than 180. The message I cannot square numbers that large appears if the user types too large a number.

```
// Filename: C10SQRT1.CPP
// Prints the square of the input value
// if the input value is less than 180

#include <iostream.h>

main()
    {
    int     num, square;
```

```
    cout << "\n\n";       // Print 2 blank lines
    cout << "What number do you want to see the square of? ";
    cin >> num;

    if (num < 180)
        {
        square = num * num;
        cout << "The square of " << num << " is " << square;
        }

    if (num >= 180)
        {
        cout << "\n*** Square is not allowed for ";
        cout << "numbers over 180 ***";
        cout << "\nRun this program again and try ";
        cout << "a smaller value.";
        }

    cout << "\nThank you for requesting squares.";
    return 0;
    }
```

The following includes the results of a couple of sample runs from this program. Notice that both conditions work: if the user enters a number below 180, the user sees the square. If the user enters a larger number, an error message appears.

```
What number do you want to see the square of? 45
The square of 45 is 2025
Thank you for requesting squares.

What number do you want to see the square of? 212

*** Square is not allowed for numbers over 180 ***
Run this program again and try a smaller value.
Thank you for requesting squares.
```

You will be able to improve on this program when you learn to use else later in this chapter. The program's problem is its redundant check of the user's input. The variable num has to be checked once to print the square if it is below 180. Then, it must be checked again for the error message if it is above 180.

5. The value of 1 for True or 0 for False can help save you an extra programming step that other languages do not necessarily allow you. To see how, study the following section of code:

```
commission = 0;                    // Initialize commission

if (sales > 10000)
    {
```

```
commission = 500.00;
    }

pay = net_pay + commission;    // commission is 0
                               // unless high sales
```

This program can be made more efficient by combining the if's relational test with the assignments to commission and pay, knowing that it will return 1 or 0:

```
pay = net_pay + (commission = (sales > 10000) * 500.00);
```

This single line does what the previous four lines did. The assignment to the far right has precedence; therefore, it gets computed first. The variable sales is compared to 10000. If it is more than 10000, a True result of 1 is returned. That 1 is multiplied by 500.00, and stored in commission. If, however, sales is not more than 10000, 0 is the result. And 0 multiplied by 500.00 still leaves 0.

The value (500.00 or 0) that is assigned to commission becomes the value of that expression. That value is then added to net_pay, and stored in pay.

# The *else* Statement

The else statement never appears in a program without an if- statement. This section introduces the else statement by showing you the popular if-else combination statement. The following illustrates its format:

```
if (condition)
    {
    A block of 1 or more C++ statements
    }
else
    {
    A block of 1 or more C++ statements
    }
```

The first part of the if-else is identical to the if-statement. If the condition is True, the block of C++ statements following the if executes. However, if the condition is False, the block of C++ statements following the else executes. Although the simple if-statement determines only what happens when the condition is True, the if-else determines what happens if the condition is False. No matter what the outcome, the statement following the if-else executes next.

**Note:** The following describes the nature of `if-else`:

If the condition is True, the entire block of statements following the `if` is performed. If the condition is False, the entire block of statements following the `else` is performed.

**Tip:** You can compare characters, not just numbers. When you compare characters, C++ uses the ASCII table to determine which character is "less than" (lower in the ASCII table) the other. You cannot compare character strings or arrays of character strings directly with the relational operators.

## Examples

1. The following program asks the user for a number. The program then prints a line indicating that the number is greater than zero or that it is not, using the `if-else` statement.

```cpp
// Filename: C10IFEL1.CPP
// Demonstrates if-else by printing whether an input value
// is greater than zero or not

#include <iostream.h>

main()
    {
    int     num;

    cout << "What is your number? ";
    cin >> num;     // Get the user's number

    if (num > 0)
        {
        cout << "More than 0\n";
        }
    else
        {
        cout << "Less or equal to 0\n";
        }

    // No matter what the number was, the following executes
    cout << "\n\nThanks for your time!\n";
    return 0;
    }
```

You do not need to test for *both* possibilities when you use an `else`. The `if` tests to see whether the number is greater than zero. The `else` takes care of all other possibilities automatically.

**2.** The following program asks for the user's first name, and stores it in a character array. The first character of the array is then checked to see whether it falls in the upper half of the alphabet. If it does, an appropriate message displays.

```cpp
// Filename: C10IFEL2.CPP
// Tests the user's first initial, and prints a message

#include <iostream.h>

main()
    {
    char    last[ 20 ];     // Holds the last name

    cout << "What is your last name? ";
    cin >> last;

    // Test the initial - must be uppercase
    if (last[ 0 ] <= 'P')
        {
        cout << "Your name is early in the alphabet.\n";
        }
    else
        {
        cout << "You have to wait awhile ";
        cout << "for YOUR name to be called!";
        }
    return 0;
    }
```

Notice that because a character array element is being compared to a character constant, you must enclose the latter in single quotes. The data types on both sides of each relational operator must match.

**3.** The following program is a more complete payroll routine than you have seen. It uses the `if` statement to illustrate how to compute overtime pay. Note the logic of this program as outlined in the following explanation:

If an employee works 40 hours or fewer, this worker gets paid regular pay (the hourly rate times the number of hours worked). If the employee works between 40 and 50 hours, this worker gets one and a half times the hourly rate for the hours over 40. The employee still gets regular pay for the first 40 hours. All hours over 50 earn double time.

```cpp
// Filename: C10PAY2.CPP
// Computes the full overtime pay possibilities

#include <iostream.h>
#include <iomanip.h>
```

```
main()
    {
    int         hours;
    float       dt, ht, rp, rate, pay;

    cout << "\n\nHow many hours were worked? ";
    cin >> hours;
    cout << "\nWhat is the regular hourly pay?";
    cin >> rate;

    // Compute pay here
    // Double-time possibility
    if (hours > 50)
        {
        dt = 2.0 * rate * (float)(hours - 50);
        ht = 1.5 * rate * 10.0; // Time + 1/2 for 10 hours
        }
    else
        {
        dt = 0.0;
        } // Either none or double for those hours over 50

    // Time and a half
    if (hours > 40)
        {
        ht = 1.5 * rate * (float)(hours - 40);
        }

    // Regular pay
    if (hours >= 40)

        {
        rp = 40 * rate;
        }
    else
        {
        rp = (float)hours * rate;
        }

    pay = dt + ht + rp;    // Add up three components of payroll

    cout << "\nThe pay is "
        << setprecision(2) << setiosflags(ios::fixed) <<  pay
        << '\n';
    return 0;
    }
```

4. The block of statements following the if can contain any valid C++ statement, even another if statement. This sometimes comes in handy.

The following program could be run to give an award to employees based
on their years of service to your company. You are giving a gold watch to
those with more than 20 years, a paperweight to those with more than 10
years, and a pat on the back to everyone else.

```
// Filename: C10SERV.CPP
// Prints a message depending on years of service

#include <iostream.h>

main()
    {
    int     yrs;

    cout << "How many years of service? ";
    cin >> yrs;      // Get the years employee has worked

    if (yrs > 20)
        {
        cout << "Give a gold watch\n";
        }
    else
        {
        if (yrs > 10)
            {
            cout << "Give a paper weight\n";
            }
        else
            {
            cout << "Give a pat on the back\n";
            }
        }
    return 0;
    }
```

You should probably not rely on if-else-if to take care of too many conditions. The reason is that more than three or four conditions add confusion. You get into messy logic, such as: "If this is True, then if this is True, then do something else if this is True, and so on…" The switch statement, covered in a later chapter, handles these types of multiple if selections better than a long if-else.

## Summary

You now have the tools to write powerful data-driven programs. This chapter showed you how to compare constants, variables, and combinations of both by using the relational operators. The if and if-else statements rely on these comparisons of data to determine which code to execute next. You can now *conditionally execute* statements within your programs.

The next chapter goes one step further by combining relational operators to create *compound relational conditions*. These logical operators improve your program's capability to make selections based on data comparisons.

# Review Questions

Answers to Review Questions are in Appendix B.

**1.** What operator tests for equality?

**2.** Please state whether the following relational tests are True or False:

A. `4 >= 5`

B. `4 == 4`

C. `165 >= 165`

D. `0 != 25`

**3.** True or false: `C++ is fun` prints on-screen when the following statement is executed.

```
if (54 <= 54)
   {

   cout << "C++ is fun";

   }
```

**4.** What is the difference between an `if` statement and an `if-else` statement?

**5.** Will the following `cout` execute?

```
if (3 != 4 != 1)
   {

   cout << "This will print";

   }
```

**6.** Using the ASCII table in Appendix C, please state whether these character relational tests are True or False:

A. `'C' < 'c'`

B. `'0' > '0'`

C. `'?' > ')'`

## Review Exercises

1. Write a weather-calculator program than asks for a temperature, and prints Brrrr! whenever a temperature falls below freezing.

2. Write a program that asks for a number and prints its square and cube. If that number is less than 2, then print nothing.

3. Ask the user for two numbers. Print a message explaining how the first one relates to the second. In other words, if the user entered 5 and 7, you would print 5 is less than 7.

4. Prompt the user for an employee's pretax salary. Print the employee's salary taxes. The taxes are 10 percent if the employee made less than $10,000, and 15 percent if the worker earned between $10,000 and $20,000. The taxes are 20 percent if the employee earned more than $20,000.

# CHAPTER 11

# Logical Operators

By combining *logical operators* with relational operators, you can create more powerful data-testing statements. The logical operators are sometimes referred to as *compound relational operators*. As C++'s precedence table shows, the relational operators take precedence over the logical operators when you combine them. The precedence table plays an important role in these types of operators.

In this chapter, you learn about the following topics:

♦ The && AND operator

♦ The ¦¦ OR operator

♦ The ! NOT operator

This chapter concludes your learning of the conditional testing that C++ enables. Presented here are many examples of if statements in programs that work on compound conditional tests.

## Logical Operators

At times, you might need to test more than one set of variables. You can combine more than one relational test into a *compound relational test* by using the logical operators in table 11.1.

**Table 11.1. You can create compound relational tests by using logical operators.**

| Operator | Meaning |
|----------|---------|
| && | AND |
| ¦¦ | OR |
| ! | NOT |

You use logical operators for compound relational tests.

The first two logical operators, && and ¦¦, never appear by themselves. They typically are placed between two or more relational tests.

Tables 11.2, 11.3, and 11.4 illustrate how the logical operators work. These tables are referred to as *truth tables* because they show how to achieve True results from an if statement that uses them. Study the tables so that they become familiar to you.

**Table 11.2. When using the && (AND) operator, both sides of the operator must be True.**

| True | AND | True | = True |
|------|-----|------|--------|
| True | AND | False | = False |
| False | AND | True | = False |
| False | AND | False | = False |

**Table 11.3. When using the ¦¦ (OR) operator, one or the other side of the operator must be True.**

| True | OR | True | = True |
|------|----|------|--------|
| True | OR | False | = True |
| False | OR | True | = True |
| False | OR | False | = False |

**Table 11.4. When you use the ! (NOT) operator, an opposite relation is the result.**

| NOT | True | = False |
|-----|------|---------|
| NOT | False | = True |

# The Use of Logical Operators

The True and False on each side of the operators represent a relational if test. For instance, the following tests are valid if tests that use logical operators (sometimes referred to as *compound relational operators*).

*If ((the variable a is less than the variable b) AND (the variable c is greater than the variable d)),*
   *print* Results are invalid. *to the screen.*

```
if ((a < b) && (c > d))
    {

    cout << "Results are invalid.";

    }
```

For the cout to execute, the variable a must be less than b and, at the same time, c must be greater than d. The if statement still requires parentheses around its complete conditional test.

```
if ((sales > 5000) || (hrs_worked > 81))
    {

    bonus = 500;

    }
```

The || is
sometimes
referred to as the
"inclusive or."

Here, the sales must be greater than 5000, or the hrs_worked must be more than 81 before the assignment executes.

```
if (!(sales < 2500))
    {

    bonus = 500;

    }
```

In this example, if sales is greater than or equal to 2500, bonus is 500. This illustrates an important programming tip: "Use ! sparingly." (Alternatively, as some so wisely state, "Do not use ! or your programs will not be !(unclear).") It would be much clearer to rewrite the preceding example by turning it into a positive relational test:

```
if (sales >= 2500)
    {

    bonus = 500;

    }
```

The ! operator is sometimes helpful, especially when testing for end-of-file conditions later. Most of the time, you can avoid ! by using reverse logic:

!(var1 == var2) is exactly the same as (var1 != var2)

!(var1 <= var2) is exactly the same as (var1 > var2)

!(var1 >= var2) is exactly the same as (var1 < var2)

!(var1 != var2) is exactly the same as (var1 == var2)

!(var1 > var2) is exactly the same as (var1 <= var2)

!(var1 < var2) is exactly the same as (var1 >= var2)

Notice that the overall format of the if statement is retained when you use logical operators. However, the relational test has been expanded to include more than one relation. You can even have three or more tests:

```
if ((a == B) && (d == f) || (1 = m) || !(k != 2)) ...
```

However, this is a little too much. Good programming practice dictates using, at most, two relational tests inside a single if statement. If you need to combine more than two tests, use more than one if statement.

As with other relational operators, you use these logical operators in everyday conversation. Note some examples:

"If my pay is high *and* my vacation time is long, we can go to Italy this summer."

"If you take the trash out *or* clean your room, you can watch TV tonight."

"If you are *not* good, you will be punished."

---

**Internal Truths**

The True or False results of relational tests occur internally at the bit level. For example, consider the following if test:

```
if (a == 6) ...
```

To determine the truth of the relation, (a == 6), the computer takes a binary 6, or 00000110, and compares it, bit by bit, to the variable a. If a contains 7, a binary 00000111, the result of the equal test is False because the right bit (referred to as the least significant bit) is different.

# C++'s Logical Efficiency

C++ attempts to be more efficient than other languages. If you combine multiple relational tests with one of the logical operators, C++ does not always interpret the full expression. This ultimately makes your programs run faster. However, you should be aware of some dangers. Given the conditional test

```
if ((5 > 4) || (sales < 15) && (15 != 15)) ...
```

C++ "looks at" only the first condition, (5 > 4), and realizes that it doesn't have to look further. Because (5 > 4) is True, and because True || (or) anything that follows is still True, C++ does not bother with the rest of the expression. The same holds for the following:

```
if ((7 < 3) && (age > 15) && (initial == 'D')) ...
```

C++ looks only at the first condition, which is False. Because False && (and) anything else that follows is also False, C++ does not interpret the expression to the right of (7 < 3). Most of the time, this does not pose a problem. However, you should be aware that the following expression might not fulfill your expectations:

```
if ((5 > 4) || (num = 0)) ...
```

The (num = 0) assignment never executes because C++ has to interpret only the (5 > 4) to see whether the entire expression is True or False. Due to this danger, do not include assignment expressions in the same condition as a logical test. The single `if` condition

```
if ((sales > old_sales) || (inventory_flag = 'Y')) ...
```

should be broken into two statements, such as

```
inventory_flag = 'Y';
if ((sales > old_sales) || (inventory_flag)) ...
```

so that `inventory_flag` is always assigned the 'Y' value, no matter how (sales > old_sales) tests.

## Examples

1. The Summer Olympics are held every four years. Each year during which the Olympics take place is divisible evenly by 4. The U.S. Census is taken every 10 years, at the start of each decade. Each year during which the Census is conducted is evenly divisible by 10. The following short program asks for a year. Then, it tells the user whether it is a year of the Summer Olympics, or of the census, or both. The program uses both relational and logical operators, and the modulus operator to determine the output.

```
// Filename: C11YEAR.CPP
// Determines if it is Summer Olympics year, US Census year,
// or both

#include <iostream.h>

main()
    {
    int     year;

    // Ask for a year
    cout << "What is a year for the test? ";
    cin >> year;

    // Test the year
    if ((year % 4) == 0 && (year % 10) == 0)
        {
        cout << "\nBoth Olympics and US Census!\n";
        }
    else
        {
        if ((year % 4) == 0)
            {
            cout << "\nSummer Olympics only\n";
            }
        else
            {
            if ((year % 10) == 0)
                {
                cout << "\nUS Census only\n";
                }
            else
                {
                cout << "\nNeither\n";
                }
            }
        }
    return 0;
    }
```

2. Now that you know about compound relations, you can write an age-checking program.

```
// Filename: C11AGE.CPP
// Program to help ensure that age values are reasonable

#include <iostream.h>

main()
    {
    int     age;

    cout << "What is your age? ";
```

```
    cin >> age;
    if ((age > 10) && (age < 100))
        {
        cout << "\nYou entered a valid age.\n";
        }
    else
        {
        cout << "\n*** The age must be ";
        cout << "between 10 and 100 ***\n";
        }
    return 0;
    }
```

3. The following program might be used by a video store to calculate a discount based on the number of rentals a customer makes, and the customer's status. Customers are classified as R for Regular, or S for Special Status. Special Status customers have been members of the rental club for more than one year. They automatically receive a 50-cent discount on all rentals. The store also holds value days several times a year. On value days, all customers get the 50-cent discount. Special Status customers do not get an additional 50 cents off during value days because every day is a discount for them.

The program asks for the customer status and whether it is a value day. The program then uses the | | operator to test for the discount. Even before you started learning C++, you might have studied this problem with the following idea:

If a customer has Special Status, or if it is a value day, deduct 50 cents from the rental.

This is basically the idea of the if decision in the program. Even though Special Status customers do not get an additional discount on value days, there is one final if test for them that prints an extra message at the bottom of the screen's bill.

```
// Filename: C11VIDEO.CPP
// Program to compute video rental amounts and give
// appropriate discounts based on the day or customer status

#include <iostream.h>
#include <iomanip.h>

main()
    {
    float       tape_charge, discount, rental_amt;
    char        first_name[ 15 ];
    char        last_name[ 15 ];
    int         num_tapes;
    char        val_day, sp_stat;
```

```
cout << "\n\n *** Video Rental Computation ***\n";
cout << "         -----------------------\n";
// Underline title

tape_charge = 2.00;     // The before-discount tape fee
                        // per tape

// Get input data
cout << "\nWhat is customer's first name? ";
cin >> first_name;
cout << "What is customer's last name? ";
cin >> last_name;

cout << "\nHow many tapes are being rented? ";
cin >> num_tapes;

cout << "Is this a Value day (Y/N)? ";
cin >> val_day;

cout << "Is this a Special Status customer (Y/N)? ";
cin >> sp_stat;

// Calculate rental amount
discount = 0.0;     // Increase the discount IF they
                    // are eligible
if ((val_day == 'Y') || (val_day == 'y')
    || (sp_stat == 'Y') || (sp_stat == 'y'))
    {
    discount = 0.5;
    rental_amt = (num_tapes * tape_charge)
    - (discount * num_tapes);
    }
else
    {
    rental_amt = num_tapes * tape_charge;
    }

// Print the bill
cout << "\n\n** Rental Club **\n\n";
cout << first_name << ' ' << last_name
    << " rented " << num_tapes << " tapes\n";
cout << "The total was "
    << setiosflags(ios::fixed) << setprecision(2)
    << rental_amt << "\n";
cout << "The discount was " << setprecision(2)
    << discount << " per tape\n";

// Print extra message for Special Status customers
if ((sp_stat == 'Y') || (sp_stat == 'y'))
```

```
        {
        cout << "\nThank them for being ";
        cout << "a Special Status customer";
        }
    return 0;
    }
```

Figure 11.1 shows the output from a sample run of this program. Notice that Special Status customers get the extra message at the bottom of the screen. This program, because of its `if` statements, performs differently depending on the data entered. No discount is applied for Regular customers on nonvalue days.

**Figure 11.1.**

The logical `if` helps give special discounts to certain customers.

```
*** Video Rental Computation ***
------------------------
What is the customer's first name? Diane
What is the customer's last name? Moore

How many tapes are being rented? 3
Is this a Value day (Y/N)? N
Is this a Special Status customer (Y/N)? Y

** Rental Club **

Diane Moore rented 3 tapes
The total was 4.50
The discount was 0.50 per tape

Thank them for being a Special Status customer
```

# The Precedence of Logical Operators

The math precedence order you read about in Chapter 9, "Using C++ Math Operators and Precedence," did not include the logical operators. To be thorough, you should be familiar with the entire order presented in Appendix D. As you can see, the math operators take precedence over the relational operators. And the relational operators take precedence over the logical operators.

You might wonder why the relational and logical operators are included in a precedence table. The following statement helps illustrate the reason:

```
if ((sales < min_sal * 2 && yrs_emp > 10 * sub) ...
```

Without the complete order of operators, it would be impossible to determine how such a statement would execute. According to the precedence order, the `if` statement executes in this way:

```
if ((sales < (min_sal * 2)) && (yrs_emp > (10 * sub))) ...
```

This might still be confusing, but less so. The two multiplications are performed first, followed by the operators < and >. The && is performed last because it is lowest in the order of operators.

To avoid ambiguity, use plenty of parentheses, even if the default precedence order is intended. It is also wise to resist combining too many expressions inside a single if relational test.

Notice that ¦¦ (OR) has lower precedence than && (AND). Therefore, the following if tests are equivalent:

```
if ((first_initial == 'A') && (last_initial == 'G')
    ¦¦ (id == 321)) ...
if (((first_initial == 'A') && (last_initial == 'G'))
    ¦¦ (id == 321)) ...
```

The second test is clearer because of the extra parentheses. However, the precedence table makes the tests identical.

## Summary

This chapter extended the if statement to include the &&, ¦¦, and ! logical operators. These operators enable you to combine more than one relational test into a single test. C++ does not always have to look at every relational operator when you combine several in an expression. This chapter concludes this book's explanation of the if statement.

The next chapter explains the rest of the regular C++ operators. As you learned in this chapter, the precedence table is very important to the C++ language. When evaluating expressions, keep the precedence table in mind (or at your fingertips) at all times.

## Review Questions

The answers to Review Questions are in Appendix B.

1. What are the three logical operators?

2. The following compound relational tests produce True or False comparisons. Determine which are True and which are False.

    A. ! (true ¦¦ false)

    B. (true && false) && (false ¦¦ true)

    C. ! (true && false)

    D. true ¦¦ (false && false) ¦¦ false

**3.** Consider the following statement:

```
int i = 12, j = 10, k = 5;
```

What are the results (True or False) of the following statements? (*Hint:* Remember that C++ interprets *any* nonzero statement as True.)

  A. i && j

  B. 12 - i ¦¦ k

  C. j != k && i != k

**4.** What is the value printed in the following program? (HINT: Do not be confused by the assignment operators on each side of the ¦¦.)

```
// Filename: C11LOGO.CPP
// Logical operator test

#include <iostream.h>

main()
    {
    int     f, g;

    g = 5;
    f = 8;
    if ((g = 25) ¦¦ (f = 35))
        {
        cout << "g is " << g << " and f got changed to: "
            << f << '\n';
        }
    return 0;
    }
```

# Review Exercises

**1.** Write a program to determine whether the user entered an odd, positive number. Use a single compound if statement.

**2.** Write a program that asks the user for two initials. Print a message letting the user know whether the first initial falls alphabetically before the second.

**3.** Write a number-guessing game. Assign a variable referred to as number a value at the top of the program. Give a prompt that asks for five guesses. Get the user's five guesses with a single cin. See whether any guess matches the number, and print an appropriate message if one does.

**4.** Write a tax-calculation routine. A family pays no tax if its members' combined salaries are less than $5,000. The family pays a 10 percent tax if the combined salaries are between $5,000 and $9,999, and a 20 percent tax if the combined salaries are between $10,000 and $19,999. Otherwise, the family pays a 30 percent tax.

# CHAPTER 12

# Additional C++ Operators

Several other C++ operators exist that you haven't learned about yet. C++ has more operators than most programming languages. At first glance, you might think that these operators make C++ programs cryptic and difficult to follow. After you learn them, however, you realize that C++'s operators simplify your coding tasks, and make your programs run smoother and faster.

This chapter introduces the following topics:

- The ?: conditional operator
- The ++ increment operator
- The -- decrement operator
- Postfix and prefix operation
- The sizeof operator
- The , sequence point operator

Most of the operators described in this chapter are unlike those found in any other programming language. Even if you have programmed in other languages for many years, you might be surprised at the power of some of these operators.

## The *?:* Conditional Operator

The conditional operator is a ternary operator.

The conditional operator, ?:, is C++'s only ternary operator. A *ternary* operator requires three operands (instead of the single and double operands of unary and binary operators). The conditional operator is used to replace `if-else` logic in some situations. The format of the conditional operator is

```
conditional_expression ? expression1 : expression2;
```

in which `conditional_expression` is any expression in C++ that results in a True (nonzero) or False (zero) answer. If the result of the `conditional_expression` is True, `expression1` executes. If the result of the `conditional_expression` is False, `expression2` executes. Only one of the expressions following the question mark ever executes. You should put a single semicolon at the end of `expression2`. The internal expressions, such as `expression1`, should not have a semicolon.

Figure 12.1 shows the conditional operator a little more clearly.

**Figure 12.1.**

At times, you can use the conditional operator to replace `if-else` logic.

```
                      If conditional       If conditional
                      expression is        expression is
                           True                False
                         execute             execute
                           this                this
                            ↓                   ↓
    conditional_expression ? expression1 : expression2 ;


                       If sales > 8000    If sales is not
          Example:        execute          > 8000 only
                            only             execute
                            this              this
                             ↓                 ↓
       (sales > 8000) ?   bonus = 500  :   bonus = 0 ;
```

If you require simple `if-else` logic, the conditional operator usually provides a more direct and succinct method. However, you should always prefer readability over compact code.

To get a glimpse of how useful the conditional operator is, consider the following section of code.

*If (the variable a is greater than the variable b), the variable ans becomes equal to 10.*
*Otherwise, the variable ans becomes equal to 25.*

```
if (a > b)
    {
    ans = 10;
    }
else
    {

    ans = 25;
    }
```

You can easily rewrite this kind of `if-else` code with a single conditional operator, as in the following example:

*If the variable `a` is greater than the variable `b`, the variable `ans` becomes equal to `10`; otherwise, `ans` becomes equal to `25`.*

```
a > b ? (ans = 10) : (ans = 25);
```

The conditional operator has very low precedence; therefore, parentheses are not required around the `conditional_expression` to make this work. However, they usually improve readability. This statement could be rewritten, using parentheses, as

```
(a > b) ? (ans = 10) : (ans = 25);
```

Each C++ expression has a value—in this case, the value that is assigned. Therefore, this statement can be made even more succinct, without loss of readability, by assigning `ans` the answer to the left of the conditional:

```
ans = (a > b) ? (10) : (25);
```

This expression now says the following: If `a` is more than `b`, assign `ans` a `10`; otherwise, assign `ans` a `25`. Almost any `if-else` statement can be rewritten as a conditional, and a conditional can be rewritten as an `if-else`. You should practice converting one to the other to acquaint yourself with the conditional operator's purpose.

---

**Tip:** Any valid C++ statement can be the `conditional_expression`, including all relational and logical operators, as well as any combination of them.

---

## Examples

**1.** Suppose that you are looking over your early C++ programs, and you notice the following section of code:

```
if (production > target)
    {
    target *= 1.10;
    }
else
    {
    target *= .90;
    }
```

You realize that such a simple `if-else` statement can be rewritten with a conditional operator and that more efficient code will result. You can change the code to this single statement:

```
(production > target) ? (target *= 1.10) : (target *= .90);
```

**2.** Using a conditional operator, you can write a routine to find the lowest value between two variables. This is sometimes called a *minimum routine*. The statement to do this is

```
minimum = (var1 < var2) ? var1 : var2;
```

If var1 is less than var2, the value of var1 is assigned to minimum. If var2 is less, it is assigned to minimum. If the variables are equal, var2 is assigned to minimum (because it doesn't matter which one is assigned).

**3.** A maximum routine can be written just as easily:

```
maximum = (var1 > var2) ? var1 : var2;
```

**4.** Taking the preceding examples a step farther, you can test for the sign of a variable. The following conditional expression assigns -1 to the variable referred to as sign if testvar is less than 0, 0 to sign if testvar is 0, and +1 to sign if testvar is more than 1:

```
sign = (testvar < 0) ? -1 : (testvar > 0);
```

It might be easy to spot why the less-than test results in -1. However, the second part can be confusing. This technique works well because of C++'s 1 (True) and 0 (False) return values from a relational test. If testvar is 0 or greater, sign is assigned the answer to (testvar > 0). The value of (testvar > 0) is 1 if True (therefore, testvar is more than 0), or 0 if testvar is equal to 0.

This technique takes advantage of C++'s efficiency and conditional operator very well. It might be helpful to rewrite this statement with a typical if-else. The following is the same problem written with a typical if-else statement:

```
if (testvar < 0)
    {
    sign = -1;
    }
else
    {

    sign = (testvar > 0);

    }      // testvar can be only 0 or more here
```

# The Increment *(++)* and Decrement *(--)* Operators

C++ offers two unique operators that add 1 to or subtract 1 from variables. These are the increment (++) and decrement (--) operators. Table 12.1 shows how these operators relate to other types of expressions you have seen. Notice that the ++ or

- - can go on either side of the variable it modifies. If the ++ or - - appears on the left, it is known as a *prefix* operator. If the operator appears on the right, it is a *postfix* operator.

**Table 12.1. The ++ and -- operators can go on either side of the variable that is modified.**

| Operator | Example | Description | Equivalent Statements |
|---|---|---|---|
| ++ | i++; | Postfix | i = i + 1;  i += 1; |
| ++ | ++i; | Prefix | i = i + 1;  i += 1; |
| — | i—; | Postfix | i = i - 1;  i -= 1; |
| — | —i; | Prefix | i = i - 1;  i -= 1; |

Whenever you need to either add 1 to or subtract 1 from a variable, use one of these operators. As table 12.1 shows, if you need to increment or decrement just a single variable, these operators provide the means to do so.

**Increment and Decrement Efficiencies**

The increment (++) and decrement (- -) operators are straightforward, efficient methods to either add 1 to or subtract 1 from a variable. Often you need to do this when counting or processing loops, which are covered in Part III of this book.

These two operators compile directly into their assembly language equivalents. Almost all computers include, at their lowest binary machine-language commands, increment and decrement instructions. If you use C++'s increment and decrement operators, you ensure that they will compile into these low-level equivalents.

If, however, you code expressions to add or subtract 1, such as i = i - 1, as you would in other programming languages, you do not ensure that the C++ compiler will compile this instruction into its machine-language efficient equivalent.

++ adds 1 to a variable, and -- subtracts 1 from a variable.

The choice you use, prefix or postfix, does not matter if you are incrementing or decrementing single variables on lines by themselves. However, when you combine these two operators with other ones in a single expression, you must be aware of their differences. Consider the following section of a program. (All variables in the next few examples are integers because the increment and decrement work only on integer variables.)

*The variable a becomes equal to 6.*
*The variable b becomes equal to the variable a incremented once, minus 1.*

```
a = 6;
b = ++a - 1;
```

What are the values of a and b after these two statements finish? The value of a is easy to determine; it gets incremented in the second statement, so the value is 7. However, b is either 5 or 6, depending on *when* the variable a increments. To determine when a increments, consider the following rules:

♦ If a variable is incremented or decremented with a prefix operator, the increment and decrement occur *before* the variable's value is used in the rest of the expression.

♦ If a variable is incremented or decremented with a postfix operator, the increment and decrement occur *after* the variable's value is used in the rest of the expression.

In the preceding code, a contains a prefix increment. Therefore, its value is first incremented to 7. Then, the 1 is subtracted from 7. The result, 6, is assigned to b. If a postfix increment had occurred, as in

```
a = 6;
b = a++ - 1;
```

the a would still be 7. However, a 5 would be assigned to b because a did not increment until after its value was used in the expression. The precedence table in Appendix D shows that prefix operators contain higher precedence than almost every other operator, especially postfix increments and decrements that occur last.

> **Tip:** If the order of prefix and postfix confuses you, break your expressions into two lines of code. Then, put the increment or decrement before or after the expression that uses it. The preceding example could be rewritten as
>
> ```
> a = 6;
> b = a - 1;
> a++;
> ```
>
> Now, there is no doubt as to when a gets incremented. Despite this tip, you should learn how these operators work because they are efficient and easy to use.

Even parentheses cannot override the postfix rule. Consider the following statement:

```
x = p + (((amt++)));
```

There are too many unnecessary parentheses here. However, even the redundant parentheses are not enough to increment amt before adding its value to p. Postfix increment and decrement *always* occur after their variables are used in the surrounding expression.

**Caution:** Do not attempt to increment or decrement an expression. You can apply these operators only to variables. The following expression is *invalid*:

```
sales = ++(rate * hours);   // NOT ALLOWED!
```

### Examples

**1.** As with all other C++ operators, keep the precedence table in mind when evaluating expressions that use increment and decrement. Figure 12.2 shows some examples that illustrate these operators.

**Figure 12.2.**

The precedence table helps you understand how these operators are used to increment and decrement within expressions.

```
int i = 1;
int j = 2;
int k = 3;
ans = i++ + j - --k;

        i++ + j - 2

          2 - 2

            0
```

Then, i increments by 1 to its final value of 2.

```
int i = 1;
int j = 2;
int k = 3;
ans = ++i * j - k--

        2 * j - k--

          4 - k--

            1
```

Then, k decrements by 1 to its final value of 2.

**2.** The precedence table takes on even more meaning when you see a section of code such as the one figure 12.3 shows.

**3.** Considering the precedence table, and more important, what you know about C++'s relational efficiencies, what is the value of ans in the following section of code?

```
int    i=1, j=20, k=-1, l=0, m=1, n=0, o=2, p=1;
ans = i || j-- && k++ || ++l && ++m || n-- & !o || p--;
```

**Figure 12.3.**

This section of code further illustrates the C operators and the precedence table.

```
int i = 0;
int j = -1;
int k = 0;
int l = 1;

ans = i++ && ++j || k || l++

        i++ && 0 || k || l++

            0  || k || l++

                0  ||  l++

                    1
```

Then, i and l increment by 1 to their final values of 1 and 2.

At first, this seems to be extremely complicated. Nevertheless, you can simply glance at it and determine the value of ans, as well as the ending value of the rest of the variables.

Recall that when C++ performs a relation || (OR), it ignores the right side of the || if the value on the left is True (any nonzero value is True). Because True or any other value is still True, C++ does not think that it has to look at the values on the right. Therefore, C++ performed this expression in the following way:

```
ans = i || j-- && k++ || ++l && ++m || n-- & !o || p--;
      |
      1 (true)
```

i is true; therefore, C++ knows that the entire expression is True, and ignores the rest of it after the first ||. Therefore, *every other increment and decrement expression is ignored.* The result is that only ans is changed by this expression. Also, the rest of the variables, j through p, are never incremented or decremented, even though several of them contain increment and decrement operators. If you use relational operators, be aware of this problem, and place all increment and decrement operators into statements by themselves before relational statements.

## The *sizeof* Operator

Another operator in C++ does not resemble an operator at all, but looks like a library function. It is the sizeof operator. If you think of sizeof as a function call, you won't get too confused. The reason is that sizeof works in a similar way. The sizeof operator has one of the following formats:

```
sizeof data
sizeof(data type)
```

The `sizeof` operator is a unary operator. The reason is that it operates on a single value. This operator produces a result that is the size, in bytes, of the data or data type specified. Most data types and variables require different amounts of internal storage on different computers. Therefore, the `sizeof` operator was provided to enable the same programs to be run on different kinds of computers.

> **Tip:** Most C++ programmers use parentheses around the `sizeof` argument, whether that argument is *data* or *data type*. Parentheses are required around data type arguments, and are optional around data arguments. Therefore, you might want to get in the habit of using them all the time.

The `sizeof` operator returns the size, in bytes, of its argument.

The `sizeof` operator is sometimes referred to as a *compile-time operator*. At compile time, not runtime, the compiler replaces each occurrence of `sizeof` in your program with an `unsigned` integer value. The `sizeof` operator is used in advanced C++ programming.

If you use an array as the `sizeof` argument, C++ returns the size, in bytes, of the number of bytes you originally reserved for the array. The data in the array, even if it is a short string inside a character array, has nothing to do with the array's size.

### Example

Suppose that you want to know the size, in bytes, of floating-point variables for your computer. You can determine this by putting the word `float` in parentheses, as the following program shows:

```
// Filename: C12SIZE1.CPP
// Prints the size of floating-point values

#include <iostream.h>

main()
    {
    cout << "The size of floating-point variables ";
    cout << "on this computer is: " << sizeof(float) << '\n';
    return 0;
    }
```

This program produces different results on various kinds of computers. You can use any valid data type as the `sizeof` argument. Compiled under Borland C++, this program produces the following output:

```
The size of floating-point variables on this computer is: 4
```

# The Comma Operator

An additional operator (,), sometimes referred to as a *sequence point,* is used a little differently from most C++ operators. The comma operator does not directly operate on data, but produces a left-to-right evaluation of expressions. The comma enables you to put more than one expression, separated by commas, on a single line.

You have already seen one use of the sequence point comma when you learned how to declare and initialize variables. In the following section of code, the comma separates statements. The comma associates from left to right; therefore, the first variable, i, is declared and initialized before the second variable, j.

```
main()
    {
    int     i = 10, j = 25;



    // Rest of program follows
```

The comma is not a sequence point when used inside function parentheses; instead, it is *separating arguments.*

## Examples

**1.** You can put more than one expression on a line, using the comma as a sequence point. Note the following program:

```
// Filename: C12COM1.CPP
// Illustrates the sequence point

#include <iostream.h>

main()
    {
    int     num, sq, cube;

    num = 5;

    // Calculate the square and cube of the number
    sq = (num * num), cube = (num * num * num);

    cout << "The square of " << num << " is " << sq
         << " and the cube is " << cube << "\n";
    return 0;
    }
```

This technique is not necessarily recommended, as it does not add anything to the program, and even decreases readability. The square and cube are probably better computed on two separate lines.

**2.** The comma enables some interesting statements. Consider the following section of code:

```
i = 10;
j = (i = 12, i + 8);
```

When this section of code finishes, the value of j is 20, even though this is not necessarily clear. In the first statement, i is assigned 10. In the second statement, the comma causes the i to be assigned a value of 12. Then, i + 8, or 20, is assigned to j.

**3.** In the following section of code, ans is assigned the value of 12, because the assignment before the comma is performed first. Despite the right-to-left associativity of the assignment operator, the comma's sequence point, in the last step, forces the assignment of 12 into x before x is assigned to ans.

```
ans = (y = 8, x = 12);
```

When this completes, y contains an 8 and x contains a 12. ans contains a 12, also.

## Summary

You are now familiar with the majority of the C++ operators. The conditional, increment, and decrement operators make C++ stand apart from many other programming languages. As with all operators, you must be aware of the precedence table at all times when using these operators.

The sizeof and sequence point operators are unlike most other operators. sizeof is a compile-time operator that works in a manner similar to the #define preprocessor directive; sizeof is replaced by its value at compile time. The sequence point operator (,) lets you put multiple statements on a line or within a single expression. However, you should reserve this operator for initializing variables because it might be unclear if combined with other expressions.

The next chapter discusses the *bitwise* operators. They operate on a very low binary level on your computer's variables. There are programmers who have used C++ for years, but have yet to learn the bitwise operators. If you are just learning C++, and are not interested in doing bit-level operations, you might want to skim the next chapter. You can return to it later when you need those operators.

## Review Questions

The answers to Review Questions are in Appendix B.

**1.** Which set of statements does the conditional operator replace?

**2.** Why is the conditional operator referred to as a ternary operator?

3. Rewrite the following conditional operator as an `if-else`:

```
ans = (a == b) ? c + 2 : c + 3;
```

4. True or false: The following statements produce the same result.

```
var++;
var = var + 1;
```

5. Why is using the increment and decrement operators more efficient than employing the addition and subtraction operators?

6. What is a sequence point?

7. Can the output of the following section of code be determined?

```
age = 20;
cout << "You are now " << age << ", and will be "
     << age++ << " in one year";
```

8. What is the output of the following section of a program?

```
char    name[ 20 ] = "Mike";
cout << "The size of name is: " << sizeof(name);
```

# Review Exercises

1. Write a program that prints the numbers 1 to 10. Use 10 different `cout`s and only one variable named `result` to hold the value before each `cout`. Use the increment operator to add 1 to `result` before each `cout`.

2. Write a program that asks for the user's age. Using a single `cout` that includes a conditional operator, print the following if the age is over 21:

```
You are not a minor.
```

Otherwise, print the following:

```
You are still a minor.
```

This `cout` might be long. However, it helps illustrate how the conditional operator can be used within other statements when the `if-else` cannot.

3. Use the conditional operator (not `if-else` statements) to write a tax-calculation routine. A family pays no tax if the members' combined salaries are less than $5,000. The family pays a 10 percent tax if the combined salaries are between $5,000 and $9,999, and a 20 percent tax if the combined salaries are between $10,000 and $19,999. Otherwise, the family pays a 30 percent tax. This is similar to an exercise in the preceding chapter, except for the conditional operator.

# CHAPTER 13

# Bitwise Operators

This chapter introduces the *bitwise operators*. The existence of these operators is one reason for the popularity of C++ among programmers who write both device drivers and operating system internal code. These features enable C++ to behave similarly to an assembly language, if needed. They operate on internal representations of data, not just "values in variables," as the other operators do. Bitwise operators require an understanding of both Appendix A's binary numbering system and your PC's memory. If you don't think that you are ready to tackle the bitwise operators, you can skim this chapter and return to it later.

Some people program in C++ for years and don't know how to work with the bitwise operators. Nevertheless, understanding them can help improve the efficiency of your programs, and let you operate at a level deeper than you could using many other programming languages.

In this chapter, you learn about the following topics:

♦ The bitwise logical operators

♦ Performing bitwise operations internally

♦ The bitwise shift operators

This chapter concludes the discussion of C++ operators for now. After you master this chapter, you will be able to perform almost any operation on your C++ variables and constants.

## Bitwise Logical Operators

Table 13.1 shows four bitwise logical operators. These operators work on the binary representation of integer data; therefore, systems programmers can manipulate internal bits in memory and variables. The bitwise logical operators are not just for systems programmers, however. Application programmers can also improve portions of their programs by learning how to use these operators.

**Table 13.1. You can use bitwise logical operators to manipulate data bits.**

| Operator | Meaning |
|----------|---------|
| & | Bitwise AND |
| \| | Bitwise inclusive OR |
| ^ | Bitwise exclusive OR |
| ~ | Bitwise 1's complement |

Bitwise logical operators perform bit-by-bit operations on internal data.

Each bitwise logical operator performs a bit-by-bit operation on internal data. Bitwise operators apply only to char, int, and long variables and constants, not to floating-point data. Binary numbers consist of 1s and 0s; therefore, these 1s and 0s (referred to as *bits*) are manipulated to produce the desired result of each bitwise operator.

Before looking at examples, you should understand tables 13.2 through 13.5. They contain truth tables that describe the actions of the bitwise operators on the internal bit patterns of an int (or char or long) variable.

**Table 13.2. The bitwise & (AND) truth table shows the actions of this operator on certain internal bits.**

| First Bit | AND | Second Bit | Result |
|-----------|-----|------------|--------|
| 1 | & | 1 | 1 |
| 1 | & | 0 | 0 |
| 0 | & | 1 | 0 |
| 0 | & | 0 | 0 |

In bitwise truth tables, you can replace the 1 and 0 with TRUE and FALSE, respectively, to understand the result better. For the & (AND) bitwise truth table, both bits that are operated on with & must be TRUE for the result to be TRUE. In other words, "TRUE AND TRUE is equal to TRUE."

**Tip:** By replacing the 1s and 0s with TRUE and FALSE, you might be able to relate the bitwise operators to the regular logical operators && and ¦¦, which you used with if comparisons.

**Table 13.3. The bitwise ¦ (*OR*) truth table illustrates how this operator performs on certain bits.**

| First Bit | OR | Second Bit | Result |
|---|---|---|---|
| 1 | ¦ | 1 | 1 |
| 1 | ¦ | 0 | 1 |
| 0 | ¦ | 1 | 1 |
| 0 | ¦ | 0 | 0 |

The ¦ bitwise operator is sometimes referred to as the *inclusive bitwise OR operator*. Either side of the ¦ operator, or both sides, must be 1 (TRUE) for the result to be 1 (TRUE).

**Table 13.4. The bitwise ^ (exclusive *OR*) operator acts a certain way on internal data.**

| First Bit | XOR | Second Bit | Result |
|---|---|---|---|
| 1 | ^ | 1 | 0 |
| 1 | ^ | 0 | 1 |
| 0 | ^ | 1 | 1 |
| 0 | ^ | 0 | 0 |

For the bitwise ^ operator, one side or the other must be 1, but not both sides.

The ^ bitwise operator is referred to as the *exclusive bitwise OR* operator. Either side of the ^ operator must be 1 (TRUE) for the result to be 1 (TRUE). However, both sides cannot be 1 (TRUE) at the same time.

**Table 13.5. The bitwise ~ (1's complement) operator reverses the bit pattern of numbers.**

| 1's Complement | Bit | Result |
|---|---|---|
| ~ | 1 | 0 |
| ~ | 0 | 1 |

The ~ bitwise operator, referred to as the *bitwise 1's complement* operator, reverses each bit to its opposite value.

> **Note:** The bitwise 1's complement does *not* negate a number. As Appendix A shows, the PC uses a 2's complement to negate numbers. The bitwise 1's complement reverses the bit pattern of numbers, but does not add the additional 1, as the 2's complement requires.

You can test and change individual bits inside variables to check for patterns of data. The examples in the next section help illustrate the bitwise logical operators.

## Examples

1. If you apply the bitwise & operator to the numbers 9 and 14, you get a result of 8. Figure 13.1 shows the reason this is so. When the binary values of 9 (1001) and 14 (1110) are operated on with a bitwise &, the resulting bit pattern is 8 (1000).

**Figure 13.1.**

The bitwise & is performed on two numbers.

```
    1  0  0  1  (9)
    ↓  ↓  ↓  ↓
    &  &  &  &
    1  1  1  0  (14)
=   1  0  0  0  (8)
```

In a C++ program, you could code this bitwise operation in the following way:

*result becomes equal to the binary value of 9, which is 1001, AND the binary value of 14, which is 1110.*

```
result = 9 & 14;
```

The result variable will hold 8 (1000), which is the result of the bitwise &. The 9 or 14 (or both) could also be stored in variables, with the same result.

2. When applying the bitwise ¦ operator to the numbers 9 and 14, the result is 15. When the binary values of 9 (1001) and 14 (1110) are operated on with a bitwise ¦, the resulting bit pattern is 15 (1111). The reason is that the result's bits are 1 (True) in every position in which a bit is 1 in either of the two numbers.

In a C++ program, you could code this bitwise operation in this way:

```
result = 9 ¦ 14;
```

The `result` variable will hold 15, which is the result of the bitwise ¦. The 9 or 14, or both, could also be stored in variables, with the same result.

3. The bitwise ^, when applied to 9 and 14, produces a 7 (0111). The bitwise ^ sets the resulting bit to 1 if one number's bit or the other's bit is on, but not both.

In a C++ program, you could code this bitwise operation in this way:

```
result = 9 ^ 14;
```

The `result` variable holds 7, which is the result of the bitwise ^. The 9 or 14, or both, could also be stored in variables, with the same result.

4. The bitwise ~ simply negates each bit. ~ is a unary bitwise operator because you can apply it to only a single value at one time. The bitwise ~ applied to 9 results in several values, depending on the size of the 9 and whether it is a `signed` value or not, as figure 13.2 shows.

**Figure 13.2.**

The bitwise ~ is applied to the number 9.

```
~ 1  0  0  1   (9)
= 0  1  1  0   (6)
```

In a C++ program, you could code this bitwise operation in this way:

```
unsigned char  uc_result = ~9;

signed char    sc_result = ~9;

unsigned int   ui_result = ~9;

signed int     si_result = ~9;

unsigned long  ul_result = ~9;

signed long    sl_result = ~9;
```

The `uc_result` variable will hold 246, the result of the bitwise ~ on the `unsigned char` 9. The `sc_result` variable will hold-10, the result of the bitwise ~ on the `signed char` 9. The `ui_result` variable will hold 65526, the result of the bitwise ~ on the `unsigned int` 9. The `si_result` variable will hold -10, the result of the bitwise ~ on the `signed int` 9.

The `ul_result` variable will hold 4294967286, the result of the bitwise ~ on the `unsigned long` 9.

The `sl_result` variable will hold -10, the result of the bitwise ~ on the `signed long` 9.

In any case, the 9 could have been stored in a variable, with the same result.

**5.** You can take advantage of the bitwise operators to perform tests on data that you couldn't execute as efficiently in other ways.

Suppose, for example, that you want to know whether the user typed an odd or even number (assuming that the input is integers). You could use the modulus operator (`%`) to see whether the remainder, after dividing the input value by 2, is 0 or 1. If the remainder is 0, the number is even. If the remainder is 1, the number is odd.

The bitwise operators are more efficient than other operators. The reason is that bitwise operators directly compare bit patterns without using any mathematical operations. Because a number is even if its bit pattern ends in 0, and odd if its bit pattern ends in 1, you can also test for odd or even numbers by applying the bitwise `&` to the data and to a binary 1. This technique is more efficient than using the modulus operator. The following program tells the user whether the input value is even or odd.

> *Comments to identify the file.*
> *Include the header file `iostream.h`.*
> *Start of the `main()` loop.*
> > *Declare the variable input as an integer.*
> > *Print the statement* `What number do you want me to test?` *on-screen.*
> > *Obtain a value for input from the user.*
> > *If the least-significant bit of input is 1, print the statement* `The number <the actual number that the user entered> is odd.`
> > *If the least significant bit of input is 0, print the statement* `The number <the actual number that the user entered> is even.`

```
// Filename: C13ODEV.CPP
// Uses a bitwise & to see if a number is odd or even

#include <iostream.h>

main()
    {
    int  input;      // Will hold user's number

    cout << "What number do you want me to test? ";
    cin >> input;

    if (input & 1) // True if result is 1; otherwise, it is
                   // False (0)
        {
        cout << "The number " << input << " is odd\n";
        }
    else
        {
        cout << "The number " << input << " is even\n";
        }
    return 0;
    }
```

6. The only difference between the bit patterns for uppercase and lowercase characters is bit number 5 (the third bit from the left, as Appendix A shows). For lowercase letters, bit 5 is a 1. For uppercase letters, bit 5 is a 0. Figure 13.3 shows how A and B differ from a and b by a single bit.

**Figure 13.3.**

The only difference between uppercase and lowercase ASCII letters is bit number 5.

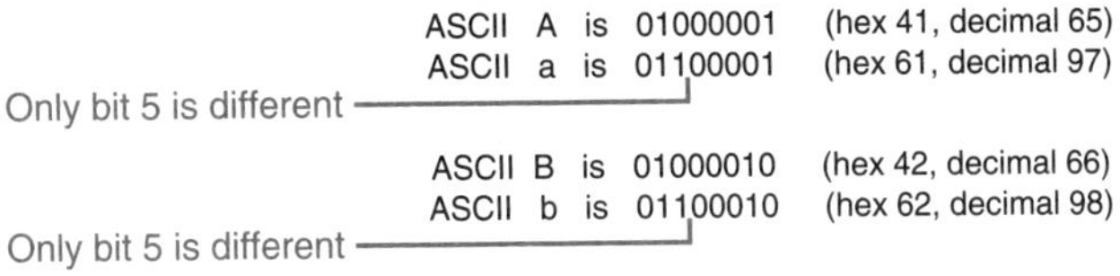

```
                         ASCII  A  is  01000001    (hex 41, decimal 65)
                         ASCII  a  is  01100001    (hex 61, decimal 97)
Only bit 5 is different ─────────────────────┘

                         ASCII  B  is  01000010    (hex 42, decimal 66)
                         ASCII  b  is  01100010    (hex 62, decimal 98)
Only bit 5 is different ─────────────────────┘
```

To convert a character to uppercase, you have to turn off (change to a 0) bit number 5. You can apply a bitwise & to the input character and 223 (which is 11011111 in binary) to turn off bit 5 and convert any input character to its uppercase equivalent. If the character is already in uppercase, this bitwise & does not change it.

The 223 (binary 11011111) is referred to as a *bit mask* because it "masks off" (just as masking tape masks off areas to be painted) bit 5 so that it becomes 0 (if it isn't already). The following program does this to ensure that the user typed uppercase characters when asked for initials:

```
// Filename: C13UPCS1.CPP
// Converts the input characters to uppercase if they aren't
// already

#include <iostream.h>
```

```
#define   BITMASK   (0xDF)       // 11011111 in binary

main()
    {
    char    first, middle, last;  // Will hold user's initials

    cout << "What is your first initial? ";
    cin >> first;
    cout << "What is your middle initial? ";
    cin >> middle;
    cout << "What is your last initial? ";
    cin >> last;

    // Ensure that initials are in uppercase
    first = first & BITMASK;      // Turn off bit 5 if
    middle = middle & BITMASK;    // it isn't already
    last = last & BITMASK;        // turned off

    cout << "Your initials are: " << first << ' '
        << middle << ' ' << last << '\n';
    return 0;
    }
```

The following output shows what happens when two of the initials are typed with lowercase letters. The program converts them to uppercase before printing them again. Although there are other ways to convert letters to lowercase, none are as efficient as using the & bitwise operator.

What is your first initial? g

What is your middle initial? M

What is your last initial? p

Your initials are: G M P

## Compound Bitwise Operators

As with most of the mathematical operators, you can combine the bitwise operators with the equal sign (=) to form *compound bitwise operators*. When you want to update the value of a variable, using a bitwise operator, you can shorten the expression. You do this by using the compound bitwise operators, as table 13.6 shows.

**Table 13.6. You can use the compound bitwise operators to shorten expressions.**

| Operator | Description |
|----------|-------------|
| &= | Compound bitwise AND assignment |
| ¦= | Compound bitwise inclusive OR assignment |
| ^= | Compound bitwise exclusive OR assignment |

The preceding example for converting lowercase initials to their uppercase equivalents can be rewritten with compound bitwise & operations:

```cpp
// Filename: C13UPCS2.CPP
// Converts the input characters to uppercase if they aren't
// already

#include <iostream.h>

#define   BITMASK   (0xDF)      // 11011111 in binary

main()
    {
    char    first, middle, last;  // Will hold user's initials

    cout << "What is your first initial? ";
    cin >> first;
    cout << "What is your middle initial? ";
    cin >> middle;
    cout << "What is your last initial? ";
    cin >> last;

    // Ensure that initials are in uppercase
    first &= BITMASK;      // Turn off bit 6 if it isn't
    middle &= BITMASK;     // already turned off
    last &= BITMASK;

    cout << "Your initials are: " << first << ' '
        << middle << ' ' << last << '\n';
    return 0;
    }
```

**Mathematics of the Binary Bitwise Operators**

There are three important mathematical properties of the binary bitwise operators. The first property is associativity: the action of any of the binary bitwise operators on any three objects does not depend on how these objects are grouped. Note the following examples:

(A ¦ B) ¦ C = A ¦ (B ¦ C)

(A & B) & C = A & (B & C)

(A ^ B) ^ C = A ^ (B ^ C)

The second property is commutativity: the action of any of the binary bitwise operators on any two objects does not depend on the order in which the objects are given. Note these examples:

A ¦ B = B ¦ A

A & B = B & A

A ^ B = B ^ A

The third property is that of having an identity value: each of the binary bitwise operators has an identity, which is a value e for which A ∘ e = e ∘ A = A, in which ∘ represents the operator. Study these examples:

A ¦ 0 = 0 ¦ A = A

A & 1 = 1 & A = A

A ^ 0 = 0 ^ A = A

The important feature to remember about this last property is that it applies, as the binary bitwise operators do, bit by bit. Although this isn't a problem for the inclusive and exclusive OR operators, it can pose a dilemma for the AND operator. When applying the AND operator, don't forget to include enough 1 bits for the bits you don't want to touch.

# Bitwise Shift Operators

Table 13.7 shows the bitwise shift operators. They shift bits inside a number to the left or right. The number of bits shifted depends on the value to the right of the bitwise shift operator. The formats of the bitwise shift operators are

```
value << number_of_bits
value >> number_of_bits
```

The value can be an integer or character variable, or a constant. The `number_of_bits` determines how many bits are to be shifted. Figure 13.4 shows what happens when the number 29 (binary 00011101) is shifted to the left three bits with a bitwise left shift (<<). Notice that each bit "shifts over" to the left three times, and 0s fill in from the right. If this were a bitwise right shift (>>), the 0s would fill in from the left as the rest of the bits are shifted to the right three times.

**Figure 13.4.**

The bits in binary 29 are shifted to the left.

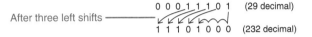

After three left shifts ———  0 0 0 1 1 1 0 1  (29 decimal)
1 1 1 0 1 0 0 0  (232 decimal)

**Table 13.7. The bitwise shift operators shift bits inside a number to the left or right.**

| Operator | Description |
| --- | --- |
| << | Bitwise left shift |
| >> | Bitwise right shift |

**Caution:** The results of bitwise shift operators are not consistent when applied to `signed` values. On the PC, the sign bit *propagates* with each shift. That is, for every shift position, the sign bit shifts. However, the original sign is retained, as well. The end result is that negative numbers fill in from the left with 1s, and not with 0s, when a bitwise right shift is applied to them.

You've probably noticed that the bitwise shift operators are the same operators used in `cout` and `cin`. This advanced feature of C++ is referred to as *operator overloading*. Although the concept of operator overloading is beyond the scope of this book, the Turbo C++ compiler can understand from context which meaning you intend.

## Examples

1. The following program shifts two values—first, three bits to the left, then to the right. This program illustrates how to code the bitwise left- and right-shift operators.

```
// Filename: C13SHFT1.CPP
// Demonstrates bitwise left- and right-shift operators

#include <iostream.h>

main()
```

```
{
int     num1 = 25;          // 00011001 binary
int     num2 = 102;         // 01100110 binary
int     shift1, shift2;     // Will hold shifted numbers

shift1 = num1 << 3;      // Bitwise left shift
cout << "25 shifted left 3 times is " << shift1
     << " \n";
shift2 = num2 << 3;      // Bitwise left shift
cout << "102 shifted left 3 times is " << shift2
     << " \n";

shift1 = num1 >> 3;      // Bitwise right shift
cout << "25 shifted right 3 times is " << shift1
     << " \n";
shift2 = num2 >> 3;      // Bitwise right shift
cout << "102 shifted right 3 times is " << shift2
     << " \n";

return 0;
}
```

The following is the output for this program:

25 shifted left three times is 200

102 shifted left three times is 816

25 shifted right three times is 3

102 shifted right three times is 12

**2.** You should learn another useful feature of bitwise shifting: If you bitwise left-shift a variable by a certain number of bit positions, the result will be the same as multiplying that same number by a power of 2. In other words, 15 left-shifted four times results in the same value as 15 times $2^4$, or 15 times 16, which equals 240.

If you bitwise right-shift a number by a certain amount of bit positions, the result will be the same as dividing that number by a power of 2. In other words, 64 right-shifted by 2 results in the same value as 64 divided by $2^2$, or 64 divided by 4, which equals 16. This property is retained in signed arithmetic by the sign propagation feature mentioned earlier. For this reason, a shift right on an unsigned value is often referred to as a logical shift right. And a shift right on a signed value is often referred to as an arithmetic shift right.

If you have to multiply or divide a variable by a power of 2, you can do it much faster by simply shifting the number. In fact, this is an optimization frequently used internally by the Turbo C++ compiler. The following program illustrates this:

```
// Filename: C13SHFT2.CPP
// Demonstrates multiplication and division by
// bitwise shifting

#include <iostream.h>

main()
    {
    signed int      num1 = 15;        // Numbers to be shifted
    signed int      num2 = -15;
    unsigned int    num3 = 15;
    unsigned int    num4 = 0x8000;

    num1 = num1 << 4;       // Multiply num1 by 16
    num2 = num2 >> 3;       // Divide num2 by 8
    num3 = num3 << 2;       // Multiple num3 by 4
    num4 = num4 >> 1;       // divide num4 by 2

    cout << "15 multiplied by 16 is " << num1 << " \n";
    cout << "-15 divided by 8 is " << num2 << " \n";
    cout << "15 multiplied by 4 is " << num3 << " \n";
    cout << "0x8000 divided by 2 is 0x" << hex << num4
         << " \n";

    return 0;
    }
```

## Compound Bitwise Shift Operators

As with most of the mathematical operators, you can combine the bitwise operators with the equal sign (=) to form *compound bitwise shift operators*. When you want to update the value of a variable by using a bitwise shift operator, you can shorten the expression by using the compound bitwise operators, shown in table 13.8.

**Table 13.8. You can combine the bitwise operators with the = sign to form compound bitwise shift operators.**

| *Operator* | *Description* |
|---|---|
| <<= | Compound bitwise left shift |
| >>= | Compound bitwise right shift |

The preceding example demonstrates math using shift operators, which can be rewritten with compound bitwise & operations:

```
// Filename: C13SHFT3.CPP
// Demonstrates multiplication and division by
// bitwise shifting

#include <iostream.h>

main()
    {
    signed int      num1 = 15;        // Numbers to be shifted
    signed int      num2 = -15;
    unsigned int    num3 = 15;
    unsigned int    num4 = 0x8000;

    num1 <<= 4;      // Multiply num1 by 16
    num2 >>= 3;      // Divide num2 by 8
    num3 <<= 2;      // Multiple num3 by 4
    num4 >>= 1;      // divide num4 by 2

    cout << "15 multiplied by 16 is " << num1 << " \n";
    cout << "-15 divided by 8 is " << num2 << " \n";
    cout << "15 multiplied by 4 is " << num3 << " \n";
    cout << "0x8000 divided by 2 is 0x" << hex << num4
        << " \n";

    return 0;
    }
```

## Summary

The bitwise operators work at the bit level; therefore, they are not often used in application programs. You must be comfortable with the binary numbering system before you can fully understand their operations. However, the bitwise operators offer a very efficient method of changing individual bits or groups of bits in variables. With these operators, you can test for odd and even numbers, and multiply and divide by powers of two. You can also perform other tasks for which you would normally use less efficient operators and commands.

The bitwise operators, despite their efficiency, do not always lend themselves to code that is readable. Generally, most people reserve them for systems-level programming, and use the easier-to-read, higher-level operators for most data processing.

# Review Questions

The answers to Review Questions are in Appendix B.

1. What are the four bitwise logical operators, the three compound bitwise logical operators, and the two bitwise shift operators?

2. What is the result of each of the following bitwise true-false expressions?

    A. 1 ^ 0 & 1 & 1 ¦ 0

    B. 1 & 1 & 1 & 1

    C. 1 ^ 1 ^ 1 ^ 1

    D. ~(1 ^ 0)

3. True or false: 7 (binary 111) can be used as a bit mask to test whether the three bits to the far right in a variable are 1s.

4. What is the difference between the bitwise ~ (1's complement) and 2's complement?

# Review Exercises

1. Write a program that converts an entered uppercase letter to a lowercase letter by applying a bit mask and one of the bitwise logical operators. If the character is already in lowercase, do not change it.

2. Write a program that asks the user for a number. Multiply that number by each power of 2, from $2^1$ to $2^7$. Then, divide that number by each power of 2, from $2^1$ to $2^7$. Use shift operators, not math operators.

3. Write a program that swaps the contents of two variables without using any other variable. Use one of the bitwise variables.

# Part III

*C++ Constructs*

# *while* Loops

The capabilities to repeat tasks make computers good tools for processing large amounts of information. This chapter and the next few present C++ constructs. *Constructs* are the control and looping commands in programming languages. C++ constructs include powerful as well as succinct and efficient looping commands similar to those of other programming languages with which you might already be familiar.

The while loops let your programs repeat a series of statements, over and over, as long as a certain condition is met. Computers don't get bored when performing the same tasks repeatedly. That's one reason they are so important in business data processing.

This chapter introduces the following topics:

- ◆ The while loop

- ◆ The do-while loop

- ◆ The exit() function

- ◆ The break statement

- ◆ Counters and totals

After completing this chapter, you will know the first of several methods available in C++ for repeating sections of a program. This chapter's discussion of loops includes one of the most important uses for looping: creating counter and total variables.

## The *while* Statement

The while statement is one of several C++ construct statements. A construct (from *construc*tion) is a programming language statement or a series of statements that controls looping. The while is a looping statement. Looping statements control execution of a series of other statements, causing parts of a program to execute repeatedly, as long as a certain condition is met.

The format of the while statement is

```
while (test expression)
    {
    block of one or more C++ statements;
    }
```

The parentheses around the test expression are required. As long as the test expression is True (nonzero), the block of one or more C++ statements executes repeatedly until the test expression becomes False (evaluates to zero). If you want to execute just one statement in the body of the while loop, you do not have to enclose the statement in braces. Each statement within the body of the while loop requires semicolons at the end.

The body of the while loop executes repeatedly as long as the test expression is True.

The test expression usually contains relational and possibly logical operators. These operators provide the True-False condition checked for in the test expression. If the test expression is False when the program reaches the while loop for the first time, the entire body of the while loop does not execute at all. Whether the body of the while loop executes zero times, one time, or many times, the statements following the while loop's closing brace execute when the test expression becomes False.

The test expression determines when the loop finishes; therefore, the body of the while loop *should* change variables used in the test expression. Otherwise, the test expression will never change, and the while loop will repeat forever. This is known as an *infinite loop*, and constitutes a serious programming error.

> **Tip:** The braces surrounding the body of the while loop are not required if it contains only one statement. It is a good habit, however, to enclose all while loop statements with braces. If you have to add more statements to the body of the while loop later, the braces will already be there.

## The Concept of Loops

You use the loop concept on a daily basis. Whenever you have to repeat a certain procedure several times, you are performing a loop, just as your computer does with the while construct. Suppose that you are wrapping holiday gifts. The following include the looping steps, in a while-like format, that you go through to wrap them:

```
while (There are still unwrapped gifts)
    {
    Get the next gift;
    Cut the wrapping paper;
    Wrap the gift;
    Put a bow on the gift;
    Fill out a name card for the gift;
    Put the wrapped gift with the others;
    }
```

Whether you had 3, 15, or 100 gifts to do, you would go through this procedure (loop) repeatedly until every gift was wrapped. To use an example that might be more easily computerized, suppose that you want to add up all the checks you wrote last month. You perform the following step:

*You have a total for all check amounts written last month. To this total add all of last month's checks that remain.*

The body of the pseudocode while loop has only one statement. However, that statement must be performed until you have totaled all the checks from last month. When this loop ends (when there are no more checks from last month), you have the total.

The body of the while loop can contain one or more C++ statements, even additional while loops. Your program will be more readable if you indent the body of a while loop a few spaces to the right. The following examples illustrate this.

## Examples

1. Some of the programs you saw in earlier chapters required user input with cin. If the user did not enter the appropriate values, the programs displayed an error message. Then, the user was asked again to enter the values. This was fine. However, now that you understand the while loop construct, you should put the error message inside a loop. In this way, the user sees it not once but continually, until the proper input values are typed.

   The following program is short. However, it demonstrates a while loop used to ensure valid user input. The program asks the user whether to continue with the program. You might want to incorporate this program into a larger one that needs the user's permission to continue. Put a prompt, such as the one shown here, at the bottom of a screenful of text. The text remains on the screen until the user tells the program to continue with the rest of the execution.

*Comments to identify the program.*
*Include the header file `iostream.h`.*
*Start of the `main()` function.*
  *Declare the variable `ans` as a character.*
  *Print to the screen `Do you want to continue (Y/N)?`*
  *Obtain a character from the keyboard.*
  *While the character typed is not a Y or an N (or a y or an n), go through the loop.*
      *Print to the screen `You must type a Y or an N.`*
      *Print to the screen `Do you want to continue (Y/N)?`*
      *Obtain another character from the keyboard.*
*Return.*

```cpp
// Filename: C14WHIL1.CPP
// Input routine to ensure that user types a correct response
// This routine might be part of a larger program.

#include <iostream.h>

main()
    {
    char    ans;

    cout << "Do you want to continue (Y/N)? ";
    cin >> ans;      // Get user's answer

    while ((ans != 'Y') && (ans != 'y') && (ans != 'N')
         && (ans != 'n'))
        {
        cout << "\nYou must type a Y or an N\n";
            // Warn and ask again
        cout << "Do you want to continue (Y/N) ?";
        cin >> ans;
        }    // Body of while loop ends here

    return 0;
    }
```

Notice that there are two `cin` functions which do the very same thing. An initial `cin`, outside the `while` loop, must be used to get an answer for which the `while` loop can check. If the user types something other than Y or N (or y or n), the program prints an error message. Then, the program asks for another answer, and loops back to check it again. This method of data-entry validation is preferred to giving the user only one additional chance to get it right.

The `while` loop tests the expression at the top of the loop. This is the reason the loop might never execute; if the test is initially False, the loop does not execute even once. Notice the following output from this program. The program repeats indefinitely, until the relational test is True (until the user types Y, y, N, or n).

```
Do you want to continue (Y/N)? k

You must type a Y or an N
Do you want to continue (Y/N)? c

You must type a Y or an N
Do you want to continue (Y/N)? s

You must type a Y or an N
Do you want to continue (Y/N)? 5

You must type a Y or an N
Do you want to continue (Y/N)? Y
```

**2.** The following program is an example of an *invalid* while loop. See if you can find the problem.

```cpp
// Filename: C14WHBAD.CPP
// Bad use of a while loop

#include <iostream.h>

main()
    {
    int    a = 10, b = 20;

    while (a > 5)
        {
        cout << "a is " << a << ", and b is " << b
            << " \n";
        b = 20 + a;
        }
    return 0;
    }
```

This while loop is an example of an infinite loop. It is vital that at least one of the statements inside the while changes a variable in the test expression (in this example, the variable a); otherwise, the condition will always be True. Because a does not change inside the while loop, the program never ends without the user's intervention.

---
**Tip:** If you inadvertently write an infinite loop, you must stop the program yourself. This typically means pressing Ctrl+Break, if not Ctrl+Alt+Del.

---

**3.** The following program asks for the user's first name, then uses a `while`
loop to count the characters in the name. This is a string-length program.
That is, it counts the number of characters in the name until it reaches the
null zero. The length of a string is the number of characters it contains up
to, but not including, the null zero.

```cpp
// Filename: C14WHIL2.CPP
// Counts the number of letters in the user's first name

#include <iostream.h>

main()
    {
    char    name[ 15 ];    // Will hold user's first name
    int     count = 0;     // Will hold total characters in
                           // name

    // Get the user's first name
    cout << "What is your first name? ";
    cin >> name;

    while (name[ count ] != 0)      // Loop until the null
                                    // zero is reached
        {
        count++;                    // Add 1 to the count
        }

    cout << "Your name has " << count << " characters\n";
    return 0;
    }
```

The loop continues as long as the value of the next character in the `name`
array is more than zero. The last character in the array is a null zero;
therefore, the test fails on the name's last character, and the statement
following the body of the loop continues.

> **Note:** A library function referred to as `strlen()` determines the length of
> strings. You learn about this function in Chapter 23, "Character, String, and
> Numeric Functions."

**4.** The string-length program's `while` loop is not as efficient as it should be.
A `while` loop fails when its test expression is zero. Therefore, there is no
need for the inequality-to-zero test. By changing the test expression, as
the following program shows, you can improve the efficiency of the
string-length count.

```
// Filename: C14WHIL3.CPP
// Counts the number of letters in the user's first name

#include <iostream.h>

main()
    {
    char      name[ 15 ];    // Will hold user's first name
    int       count = 0;     // Will hold total characters in
                             // name

    // Get the user's first name
    cout << "What is your first name? ";
    cin >> name;

    while (name[ count ])    // Loop until the null zero
                             // is reached
        {
        count++;             // Add 1 to the count
        }

    cout << "Your name has " << count << " characters\n";
    return 0;
    }
```

## The *do-while* Loop

The do-while statement controls the do-while loop. This loop is similar to the while loop, except that with do-while, the relational test occurs at the *bottom* of the loop. This ensures that the body of the loop executes at least once. The do-while loop tests for a positive relational test; as long as the test is True, the body of the loop continues to execute.

The format of the do-while loop is

```
do
    {
    block of one or more C++ statements;
    }
while (test expression)
```

The body of the do-while loop executes at least once.

As with the while statement, the test expression must have parentheses around it.

### Examples

1. The following program is very similar to the earlier one with the while loop (C14WHIL1.CPP), except that a do-while loop is used instead. Notice the placement of the test expression. It is at the end of the loop; therefore, the user input does not have to appear before the loop, then again in its body.

```
// Filename: C14WHIL4.CPP
// Input routine to ensure that user types a correct response
// This routine might be part of a larger program.

#include <iostream.h>

main()
    {
    char    ans;

    do
        {
        cout << "\nYou must type a Y or an N\n";
                // Warn and ask again
        cout << "Do you want to continue (Y/N) ?";
        cin >> ans;
        }       // Body of while loop ends here
    while ((ans != 'Y') && (ans != 'N'));
    return 0;
    }
```

2. Suppose that you are entering sales amounts into the computer to calculate extended cost. You need the computer to print the quantity sold, part number, and extended cost (quantity times the price per unit). The following program accomplishes this:

```
// Filename: C14INV1.CPP
// Gets inventory information from user, and prints
// an inventory detail listing with extended cost

#include <iostream.h>
#include <iomanip.h>

main()
    {
    int         part_no, quantity;
    float       cost, ext_cost;

    cout << "*** Inventory Computation ***\n\n";    // Title
    // Get inventory information
    do
        {
        cout << "What is the next part number ";
        cout << "(-999 to end)? ";
        cin >> part_no;
        if (part_no != -999)
            {
            cout << "How many were bought? ";
            cin >> quantity;
            cout << "What is the unit price ";
            cout << "of this item? ";
            cin >> cost;
```

```
        ext_cost = cost * quantity;
        cout << "\n" << quantity << " of # "
             << part_no << " will cost "
             << setiosflags(ios::fixed) << setprecision(2)
           ➡<< ext_cost;
        cout << "\n\n\n";     // Print two blank lines
        }
  }
while (part_no != -999);      // Loop only if part
                              // number is not -999

cout << "End of inventory computation\n";
return 0;
}
```

Figure 14.1 shows the output from this program.

```
*** Inventory Computation ***

What is the next part number (-999 to end)? 123
How many were bought? 4
What is the unit price of this item? 5.43

4 of # 123 will cost 21.72


What is the next part number (-999 to end)? 523
How many were bought? 26
What is the unit price of this item? 1.25

26 of # 523 will cost 32.50


What is the next part number (-999 to end)? -999
End of inventory computation
```

The do-while loop controls the entering of the customer sales information. Notice the trigger that ends the loop. If the user enters -999 for the part number, the do-while loop quits. The reason is that no part number -999 exists in the inventory.

This program can be improved in several ways. The invoice should be printed to the printer, not to the screen. You learn how to direct your output to a printer in Part V, "Input, Output." The inventory total (the whole amount of the entire order) should also be computed. You learn how to total such data in the section "Counters and Totals," later in this chapter.

## The *if* Loop versus the *while* Loop

Some beginning programmers confuse the `if` statement with the loop constructs. The `while` and `do-while` loops repeat a section of code a number of times, depending on the condition being tested. The `if` statement may or may not execute a section of code. However, if the section does execute, it does so only once.

Use an `if` statement when you want to conditionally execute a section of code once. Use a `while` or `do-while` loop if you want to execute the section of code more than once. Figure 14.2 shows the differences between the `if` statement and the two `while` loops.

**Figure 14.2.**

There are differences between the `if` statement and the two `while` loops.

```
    if (conditional test)

        {

            // Body of if statements

        }                                 ──── Test at top of loop

    while (conditional test)

        {

            // Body of while statements

        }
                                          ── Body loops continuously
    do                                       as long as test is true

        {

            // Body of do statements

    while (conditional test)───── Test at bottom of loop
```

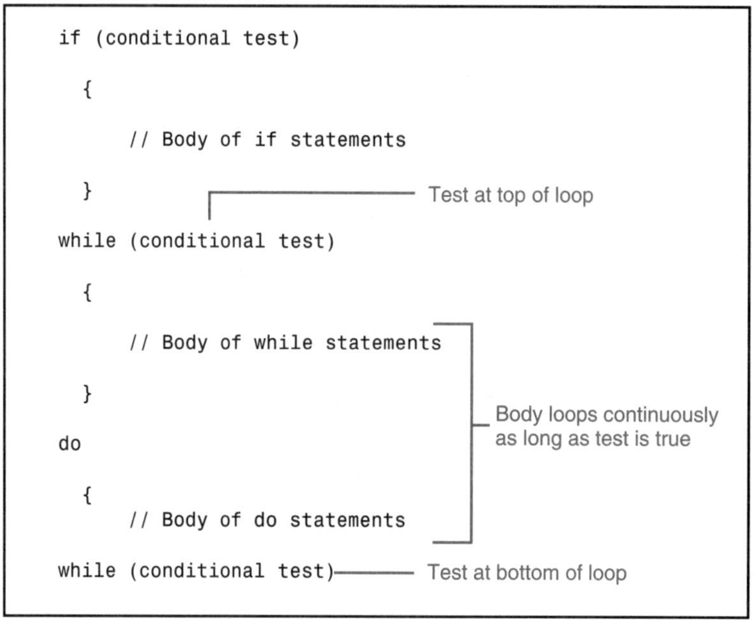

## *exit()* and *break*

C++ provides a way to leave a program early (before its natural finish) with the `exit()` function. The format of `exit()` is

```
exit(status);
```

in which status is an `int` variable or constant. The status is sent to the operating system's *error-level* environment variable. Here, the status can be tested by batch files.

The `exit()` function provides an early exit from your programs.

Often something happens in a program that requires its termination. What occurs can be a major problem such as a disk drive error. Alternatively, the user might simply indicate a desire to quit the program. (You can tell this by giving the user a special value to type in `cin` functions that triggers the user's intent.) You can put the `exit()` function on a line by itself, or anywhere a C++ statement or function can appear. Typically, `exit()` is placed in the body of an `if` statement to end the program early, depending on the result of a relational test.

You must include the `stdlib.h` header file when using `exit()`. This file defines the operation of `exit()` to your program. Whenever you use a function in a program, you must include its corresponding `#include` header file, which is listed in the library reference manual.

Instead of exiting an entire program, you can use the `break` statement to exit the current loop. The format of `break` is

```
break;
```

*The break statement ends the current loop.*

The `break` statement goes any place in a C++ program that another statement can go. However, `break` typically appears in the body of a `while` or `do-while` loop so that you can leave the loop early. The following examples illustrate the `exit()` function and the `break` statement. The `break` statement is covered more extensively in Chapter 16.

> **Note:** The `break` statement exits only the most current loop. If you have a program with a `while` loop that is within another `while` loop, `break` exits only the internal loop.

## Examples

**1.** The following is a simple program that shows how the `exit()` function works. This program seems to print several messages on-screen, but that is misleading. The `exit()` that appears early in the program causes it to quit immediately after `main()`'s opening brace.

```cpp
// C14EXIT1.CPP
// Quits very early because of exit() function

#include <iostream.h>
#include <stdlib.h>    // Required for exit()

main()
    {
    exit(0);            // Force program to end here

    cout << "C++ programming is fun.\n";
    cout << "I like learning Borland C++ by example!\n";
    cout << "C++ is a powerful language ";
    cout << "that is not difficult to learn.";

    return 0;
    }
```

**2.** The `break` statement is not intended to be as strong a program exit as the `exit()` function. Whereas `exit()` ends the entire program, `break` quits only the loop that is active at the time. In other words, `break` is usually placed inside a `while` or `do-while` loop to make the program think that the loop is finished. The statement following the loop executes after a `break` occurs. However, the program does not quit, as it does with `exit()`.

The following program appears to print `C++ is fun!` until the user types `N` or `n` to stop it. The program prints the message only once, however, because the `break` statement forces an early exit from the loop.

```cpp
// Filename: C14BRK.CPP
// Demonstrates the break statement

#include <iostream.h>

main()
    {
    char     user_ans;

    do
        {
        cout << "C++ is fun! \n";
        break;      // Cause early exit
        cout << "Do you want to see ";
        cout << "the message again (N/Y)? ";
        cin >> user_ans;
        }
    while (user_ans == 'N' && user_ans == 'n');

    cout << "That's all for now\n";
    return 0;
    }
```

This program always produces the following output:

```
C++ is fun!
That's all for now
```

You can tell from this program's output that the `break` statement does not enable the `do-while` loop to reach its natural conclusion, but causes the loop to finish early. The final `cout` prints because the entire program does not exit with the `break` statement; only the current loop exits.

**3.** Unlike the `break` in the last program, `break` is usually placed after an `if` statement. This makes it a *conditional break*. The break occurs only if the relational test of the `if` statement is True.

A good illustration of this is the inventory program you saw earlier (C14INV1.CPP). Even though the user enters `-999` to quit the program, an additional `if` test is needed inside the `do-while`. The `-999` ends the `do-while` loop. However, the body of the `do-while` still needs an `if` test so that the remaining quantity and cost prompts are not given.

If you insert a `break` after the test for the end of the user's input, as the next program shows, the `do-while` does not need the `if` test. The `break` quits the `do-while` as soon as the user signals the end of the inventory by entering `-999` as the part number.

```
// Filename: C14INV2.CPP
// Gets inventory information from user and prints
// an inventory detail listing with extended cost

#include <iostream.h>
#include <iomanip.h>

main()

    {
    int        part_no, quantity;
    float      cost, ext_cost;

    cout << "*** Inventory Computation ***\n\n";   // Title

    // Get inventory information
    do
        {
        cout << "What is the next part number ";
        cout << "(-999 to end)? ";
        cin >> part_no;
        if (part_no == -999)
            {
            break;
            }    // Exit the loop if no more part numbers
        cout << "How many were bought? ";
        cin >> quantity;
        cout << "What is the unit price of this item? ";
        cin >> cost;
        cout << "\n" << quantity << " of # "
             << part_no << " will cost " << setprecision(2)
             << ext_cost;
        cout << "\n\n\n";    // Print two blank lines
        }
    while (part_no != -999);   // Loop only if part number
                               // is not -999

    cout << "End of inventory computation\n";
    return 0;
    }
```

**4.** The following program might be used to control two other programs. It illustrates how C++ can pass information to the operating system with exit(). This is your first example of a *menu* program. Similar to a menu in a restaurant, a menu program lists possible choices. The user decides which choice from the menu's options the computer is to perform. The mailing list application in Appendix F employs a menu for its user options.

This program returns a 1 or 2 to its operating system, depending on the user's selection. Then, the operating system tests the exit value, and handles the running of the appropriate program.

```
// Filename: C14EXIT2.CPP
// Asks user for selection, and returns it
// to the operating system with exit()

#include <iostream.h>
#include <stdlib.h>

main()
    {
    int    ans;

    do
        {
        cout << "Do you want to:\n\n";
        cout << "\t1.  Run the word processor \n\n";
        cout << "\t2.  Run the database program \n\n";
        cout << "What is your selection? ";
        cin >> ans;
        }
    while ((ans != 1) && (ans != 2));        // Ensure that
                                             // user enters 1 or 2

    exit(ans);      // Return value to operating system
    return 0;
    }
```

# Counters and Totals

Counting is important for many applications. For example, you might need to know how many customers you have, or how many people scored above an average in a class. Alternatively, you might want to count how many checks you wrote last month with your computerized checkbook system.

Before developing C++ routines to count occurrences, think of how you count in an abstract way. If you were adding up a total number of items, such as the stamps in your stamp collection or the number of wedding invitations you sent out, you would do the following:

Start at 0, and add 1 to it for each item you are counting. When you finish, you have the total number (the total count) of items.

This is all you do when counting with C++. Assign 0 to a variable and add 1 to it every time you process another data value. The increment operator (++) is especially useful when counting.

### Examples

1. To illustrate the use of a counter, the following program prints Computers are fun! exactly 10 times on-screen. You could write a program that actually had 10 cout operators, but that would not be very elegant. It would also be too cumbersome to have 5,000 cout operators if you wanted to print that same message 5,000 times.

   By adding a while loop and a counter that stops after a certain total is reached, you can control the printing, as the following program shows:

```
// Filename: C14CNT1.CPP
// Program to print a message 10 times

#include <iostream.h>

main()
    {
    int     ctr = 0;    // Holds the number of times printed

    do
        {
        cout << "Computers are fun!\n";
        ctr++;    // Add one to the count, after each cout
        }
    while (ctr < 10); // Print again if fewer than 10 times
    return 0;
    }
```

   The following is the output from this program. Notice that the message prints exactly 10 times.

```
Computers are fun!
Computers are fun!
Computers are fun!
Computers are fun!
Computers are fun!
Computers are fun!
Computers are fun!
Computers are fun!
Computers are fun!
Computers are fun!
```

The heart of the counting process in this program is the following statement.

*Increment the variable* ctr *by 1.*

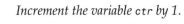

```
ctr++;
```

You learned earlier that the increment operator adds 1 to a variable. In this program, the counter variable is incremented each time the do-while loops. The only operation performed on this line is the increment of ctr; therefore, the prefix increment (++ctr) would produce the same result.

2. Notice that the last program not only added to the counter variable, but also performed a loop a specific number of times. This is a common method of conditionally executing parts of a program a fixed number of times.

The following program is a password program. A password is stored in an integer variable. The user must correctly enter the matching password in three attempts. If the user does not type the correct password in three tries, the program ends. This is a common method that dial-up computers use. They let the caller try the password a fixed number of times; then, they hang up the phone if that limit is exceeded. This helps deter people from trying hundreds of different passwords at one sitting.

If the user guesses the correct password within three tries, a secret message displays.

```
// Filename: C14PASS1.CPP
// Program to prompt for a password, and check it against an
// internal one

#include <iostream.h>
#include <stdlib.h>

main()
    {
    int     stored_pass = 11862;
    int     num_tries = 0;              // The counter for
                                        // password attempts
    int     user_pass;

    while (num_tries < 3)               // Loop only 3 times
        {
        cout << "\nWhat is the password ";
        cout << "(You get 3 tries...)? ";
        cin >> user_pass;
        num_tries++;                    // Add 1 to counter
        if (user_pass == stored_pass)
            {
```

```
                    cout << "You entered the correct password.\n";
                    cout << "The cash safe is behind ";
                    cout << "the picture of the ship.\n";
                    exit(0);
                    }
            else
                {
                cout << "You entered the wrong password.\n";
                if (num_tries == 3)
                    {
                    cout << "Sorry, you get no more chances";
                    }
                else
                    {
                    cout << "You get " << 3 - num_tries
                         << " more tries...\n";
                    }
                }
            }     // End of while loop
    exit(1);
    }
```

This program gives the user three chances in case one or two typing errors occur. Following three attempts, however, the program quits after refusing to let the user see the secret message.

**3.** The following program is a letter-guessing game. It includes a message that tells the user how many tries were made before guessing the letter. A counter keeps track of the number of tries.

```
// Filename: C14GUES.CPP
// Letter-guessing game

#include <iostream.h>

main()
    {
    int     tries = 0;
    char    comp_ans, user_guess;

    // Save the computer's letter
    comp_ans = 'T';      // Change to a different letter
                         // if desired

    cout << "I am thinking of a letter...";
    do
        {
        cout << "What is your guess? ";
        cin >> user_guess;
        tries++;             // Add 1 to the guess-counting
                             // variable
```

```
        if (user_guess > comp_ans)
            {
            cout << "Your guess was too high\n";
            cout << "\nTry again...\n";
            }
        if (user_guess < comp_ans)
            {
            cout << "Your guess was too low\n";
            cout << "\nTry again...\n";
            }
        }
    while (user_guess != comp_ans);        // Quit when match
                                           // found

    // User got it rcorrect; let the user know
    cout << "*** Congratulations!  You got it right! \n";
    cout << "It took you only " << tries
         << " tries to guess.";
    return 0;
    }
```

Figure 14.3 shows the output from this program.

**Figure 14.3.**

Counting the number of guesses.

```
I am thinking of a letter...What is your guess? A
Your guess was too low

Try again...What is your guess? Z
Your guess was too high

Try again...What is your guess? N
Your guess was too low

Try again...What is your guess? W
Your guess was too high

Try again...What is your guess? S
Your guess was too low

Try again...What is your guess? T
*** Congratulations!  You got it right!
It took you only 6 tries to guess.
```

# Producing Totals

Writing a routine that adds up values is as easy as counting. Instead of adding 1 to the counter variable, you add a value to the total variable. For instance, if you want to find the total dollar amount of checks you wrote in December, you would do the following: Begin at 0 (nothing). Then, add to that each check written in December. Instead of building a count, you are building a total.

When you want C++ to add up values, initialize a total variable to zero. Then, add each value to the total until you have gone through all the values. The following examples show you how to produce totals.

## Examples

1. Suppose that you want to write a program to add your grades for a class you are taking. The teacher has informed you that if you get over 450 points, you will receive an A.

   The following program keeps asking you for values until you type -1. The -1 is a signal that you are finished entering grades, and you want to see the total. The program also prints a congratulatory message if you earn an A.

```
// Filename: C14GRAD1.CPP
// Adds up grades and determines if an A was made

#include <iostream.h>
#include <iomanip.h>

main()
    {
    float    total_grade=0.0;
    float    grade;   // Holds individual grades

    do
        {
        cout << "What is your grade? (-1 to end) ";
        cin >> grade;
        if (grade >= 0.0)
            {
            total_grade += grade;
            }     // Add to total
        }
    while (grade >= 0.0);    // Quit when -1 entered

    // Control begins here if no more grades
    cout << "\n\nYou made a total of "
        << setiosflags(ios::fixed) << setprecision(1)
        << total_grade << " points\n";
    if (total_grade >= 450.00)
        {
        cout << "** You made an A!!";
        }

    return 0;
    }
```

   Notice that the -1 response does *not* get added into the total grade. The program checks for -1 before adding to total_grade. Figure 14.4 shows the output from this program.

**Figure 14.4.**

This shows the
output from the
program that
computes the
total grade.

```
What is your grade? (-1 to end) 87
What is your grade? (-1 to end) 89
What is your grade? (-1 to end) 96
What is your grade? (-1 to end) 78
What is your grade? (-1 to end) 99
What is your grade? (-1 to end) 87
What is your grade? (-1 to end) 89
What is your grade? (-1 to end) -1


You made a total of 625.0 points
** You made an A!!
```

**2.** The following program is an extension of the grade-calcuation program. This program not only totals the grades, but also computes an average.

The program must know how many grades were entered before the average calculation can work. This is a subtle problem; the number of grades entered is unknown in advance. Therefore, every time the user enters a valid grade (not -1), the program must add 1 to a counter as well as add that grade to the total variable. This kind of routine, which combines a counter with totaling, is common in many programs.

```cpp
// Filename: C14GRAD2.CPP
// Adds up grades, computes average, and determines if an
// A was made

#include <iostream.h>
#include <iomanip.h>

main()
    {
    float       total_grade = 0.0;
    float       grade_avg = 0.0;
    float       grade;
    int         grade_ctr = 0;

    do
        {
        cout << "What is your grade? (-1 to end) ";
        cin >> grade;
        if (grade >= 0.0)
            {
            total_grade += grade;       // Add to total
```

```
            grade_ctr ++;                    // Add to count
            }
        }
    while (grade >= 0.0);        // Quit when -1 entered

    // Control begins here if no more grades
    if (grade_ctr != 0)
        {
        grade_avg = (total_grade / grade_ctr);   // Compute
                                                  // average
        cout << "\nYou made a total of "
             << setiosflags(ios::fixed) << setprecision(1)
             << total_grade << " points.\n";
        cout << "Your average was " << setprecision(1)
             << grade_avg << " \n";
        if (total_grade >= 450.0)
            {
            cout << "** You made an A!!";
            }
        }
    return 0;
    }
```

Figure 14.5 shows the result of running this program.

**Figure 14.5.**

This output from the program computes the total grade and the average.

```
What is your grade? (-1 to end) 88
What is your grade? (-1 to end) 98
What is your grade? (-1 to end) 97
What is your grade? (-1 to end) 87
What is your grade? (-1 to end) 94
What is your grade? (-1 to end) 96
What is your grade? (-1 to end) -1

You made a total of 560.0 points.
Your average was 93.3
** You made an A!!
```

## Summary

This chapter showed you two ways to produce a C++ loop: the while loop and the do-while loop. The two variations of the while loop differ in how they test for ending the loop. The while loop tests at the top, while the do-while loop tests at the bottom.

The end result is that the body of the do-while always executes at least once. To add to the while loop's flexibility, you learned the exit() function, which terminates a program. You were also introduced to the break statement, which terminates the current loop.

You learned about counters and totals, which are two of the most important applications of loops. Your computer is a wonderful tool for adding and counting due to the repetitive capability of the while loop.

The next chapter extends your knowledge of loops by showing you how to create a *determinate* loop called the for loop. The for loop is useful when you want a section of code to loop a specific number of times.

## Review Questions

The answers to Review Questions are in Appendix B.

1. What is the difference between the while loop and the do-while loop?

2. What is the difference between a counter variable and a total variable?

3. Which C++ operator is most useful for counting?

4. True or false: The braces are not required around the body of while and do-while loops.

5. What is wrong with the following code?

```
while (sales > 50)
    cout << "Your sales are very good this month.\n";
    cout << "You will get a bonus for your high sales\n";
```

6. What file must you include as a header file if you use exit()?

7. How many times will this cout print?

```
int     a = 0;
do
    {
    cout << "Careful \n";
    a++;
    }
while (a > 5);
```

8. How can you inform the operating system of the program exit status?

9. What is printed in the following section of code?

```
a = 1;
while (a < 4)
    {
    cout << "This is the outer loop\n";
```

```
        a++;
        while (a <= 25)
            {
            break;
            cout << "This prints 25 times\n";
            }
        }
```

10. In program C14GRAD2.CPP, what could have happened if you hadn't checked for a grade counter of zero?

## Review Exercises

1. Write a program with a while loop that prints the numbers from 10 to 20, adding a blank line between the numbers. Make sure you write the program so that it adds a blank line between the numbers.

2. Write a weather-calculator program that asks for a list of the last 10 day's temperatures, computes the average, and prints the results. You will have to compute the total as the input occurs, then divide that total by 10 to find the average. Use a while loop for the 10 repetitions.

3. Rewrite the program in exercise 1, using a do-while loop.

4. Write a program similar to the weather-calculator program in Exercise 2. However, make it a general-purpose program that computes the average of any number of days. You will have to count the number of temperatures entered so that you'll have that total when you compute the final average.

5. Write a program to produce your own ASCII table on-screen. Do not print the first 31 characters, because they are nonprintable.

# *for* Loops

The for loop offers a way to repeat sections of your program a specific number of times. Unlike the while and do-while loops, the for loop is referred to as a *determinate loop*. This means that at programming time, you usually determine exactly how many times the loop takes place. You saw that the while and do-while loops continue to operate until a certain condition is met. The for loop does that and more; it continues looping until a specific count (up or down) is reached. Once the final for loop count is reached, execution continues at the next statement in the sequence.

This chapter introduces the following topics:

♦ The for loop

♦ Nested for loops

The for loop is a helpful way of looping through a section of code when you want to count or total amounts. Although the for loop does not replace the while and do-while loops, there are instances in which the for loop is more readable than a corresponding while loop.

## The *for* Statement

The for statement encloses one or more C++ statements that form the body of the loop; the statements in the loop repeat continuously a certain number of times. You, as programmer, control the number of times the loop repeats.

The format of the for loop is

```
for (start expression; test expression; count expression)
    {
    Block of one or more C++ statements;
    }
```

The for loop
continues to
operate for a
specific number
of times.

C++ evaluates the start expression before the loop begins. This expression is typically an assignment statement (such as `ctr = 1;`). However, it can be any legal expression you specify. C++ looks at and evaluates the start expression only once, at the top of the loop. Then, C++ never evaluates the start expression again.

> **Caution:** Do not put a semicolon after the right parenthesis. If you do, the for loop will think that there are no statements to execute. It will continue looping, doing nothing each time, until the test expression becomes False.

Every time the body of the loop repeats, the count expression executes, typically incrementing or decrementing a variable. The test expression evaluates to True (nonzero) or False (zero,) and determines whether the body of the loop will repeat again.

> **Tip:** If only one C++ statement resides in the for loop's body, the braces are not required. However, they are recommended. If you add more statements later, the braces will already be there. Then, you will not inadvertently leave them out.

## The Concept of *for* Loops

You use the concept of for loops in your daily life. Whenever you have to repeat a certain procedure a specified number of times, it is a good candidate for a computerized for loop.

To illustrate further the concept of a for loop, suppose that you need to put up 10 new shutters on your house. You must do the following steps for each shutter:

```
Move the ladder to the location of the next shutter.
Take a shutter, hammer, and nails up the ladder.
Hammer the shutter to the side of the house.
Climb down the ladder.
```

You have 10 shutters; therefore, you must perform each of these steps exactly 10 times. After 10 times, the job is finished. You loop through a procedure that has several steps. These steps are the body of the loop. It is certainly not an endless loop because there is a fixed number of shutters; you run out of shutters after 10 of them.

To use another example that might be more easily computerized, suppose that you have to fill out three tax returns for each of your teenage children. For each child, you must perform the following steps:

```
Add up the total income.
Add up the total deductions.
Fill out a tax return.
Put it in an envelope.
Mail it.
```

Then, you must repeat this procedure twice.

Notice how the sentence before these five steps begins: "For each child...." This signals a `for` loop construct.

> **Note:** The `for` loop tests at the top of the loop. If the test expression is False when the `for` loop begins, the body of the loop never executes.

### The Choice of Loops

You can write any loop construct with a `for` loop, `while` loop, or `do-while` loop. All these loop constructs are candidates for virtually any loop you need C++ to perform. The `for` loop is a good choice when you want to count or loop a specific number of times.

Although the `while` and `do-while` loops continue looping until a certain condition is met, the `for` loop continues until a specific value is reached. Because of the close connection of C++'s True-False test to an expression's result (an expression is True if it is nonzero), any loop construct can be used for any loop your programs require.

Generally, you use `for` loops when you want to perform a procedure a specific number of times. You reserve `while` loops for looping until a condition is met.

## Examples

**1.** To give you a glimpse of the `for` loop's capabilities, the first program in this example contains a `for` loop. The second program does not. The first program is a counting program. Study the program and its output. The results basically speak for themselves, and illustrate the `for` loop very well.

The following is a program with a `for` loop:

*Comments to identify the program.*
*Include the header file `iostream.h`.*
*Start of the `main()` function.*
    *Declare the variable `ctr` as an integer.*
    *Start at the variable `ctr` equal to 1 and go through*
    *the loop, incrementing `ctr` by 1, while the variable*
    *`ctr` is less than or equal to 10.*
        *Print to the screen the value of `ctr`.*
    *Return from the `main()` function.*

```
// Filename: C15FOR1.CPP
// Introduces the for loop

#include <iostream.h>

main()
    {
    int     ctr;

    for (ctr = 1; ctr <= 10; ctr++)        // Start ctr at 1,
                                           // increment through loop
        {
        cout << ctr << "\n";      // Body of for loop
        }
    return 0;
    }
        Here is this program's output:
1
2
3
4
5
6
7
8
9
10
```

Now, consider the same program with a `while` loop.

*Comments to identify the program.*
*Include the header file* stdio.h.
*Begin the program by calling the* main() *function.*
  *Initialize* ctr *to 1.*
  *If* ctr <= 10 *is True, perform body of loop (do the* cout
  *operator, and increment* ctr *by 1).*
  *If it is False (evaluates to 0), skip the loop, and*
  *continue with the rest of the program.*
  *Return from the* main() *function.*

```
// Filename: C15WHI1.CPP
// Simulating a for loop with a while loop

#include <iostream.h>

main()
    {
    int     ctr = 1;

    while (ctr <= 10)
        {
```

```
        cout << ctr << "\n";      // Body of while loop
        ctr++;
        }

    return 0;
    }
```

Notice that the `for` loop is a cleaner way of controlling the looping process. The `for` loop does several things that a `while` loop will not do, unless you write extra statements.

With `for` loops, you do not have to write extra code to initialize variables and increment or decrement them. You can see at a glance (in the expressions within the `for` statement) exactly how the loop will execute. This is not the case with the `while` loop, which forces you to look inside the loop to see how it is controlled.

2. Both of the following programs add the numbers from 100 to 200. The first program uses a `for` loop. The second program does not. The first example shows how using a start expression other than 1 begins the loop with a bigger count expression.

The following is a program with a `for` loop:

```
// Filename: C15FOR2.CPP
// Demonstrates totaling by using a for loop

#include <iostream.h>

main()
    {
    int     total, ctr;

    total = 0;      // Will hold total of 100 to 200

    for (ctr = 100; ctr <= 200; ctr++)  // ctr is 100, 101,
                                         // 102, ..., 200

        {
        total += ctr;
        }          // Add value of ctr each iteration

    cout << "The total is " << total << "\n";
    return 0;
    }
```

The following is the same program without a `for` loop, but it does use a `do-while` loop instead:

```
// Filename: C15WHI2.CPP
// A totaling program that uses a do while loop
#include <iostream.h>
```

```
main()
    {
    int    total = 0;      // Initialize total
    int    num = 100;      // Starting value

    do
        {
        total += num;      // Add to total
        num++;             // Increment counter
        }
    while (num <= 200);
    cout << "The total is " << total << "\n";
    return 0;
    }
```

Both programs produce the following output:

```
The total is 15150
```

The body of the loop in both programs executes only 100 times. The starting value is 100, not 1 (as in the C15WHI1.CPP example). Note that the for loop is less complex than the do-while loop. The reason is that the initialization, testing, and incrementing are performed in the single for statement.

> **Tip:** Notice how the body of the for loop is indented. This is a good habit to develop; it makes the beginning and end of the loop's body easier to locate.

3. The body of the for loop can have more than one statement. The following program requests five pairs of data values: children's first names and their ages. Then, it prints the name of the child's teacher, based on the youngster's age. This program illustrates a for loop with couts, a cin, and an if statement in its body. There are exactly five children to check; therefore, the for loop ensures that the program ends after the fifth child is checked.

```
// Filename: C15FOR3.CPP
// Program that receives input on five children, and prints
// the names of their teachers inside a loop

#include <iostream.h>

main()
    {
    char    child[ 25 ];   // Holds child's first name
    int     age;           // Holds child's age
    int     ctr;           // The for loop counter variable
```

```
for (ctr = 1; ctr <= 5; ctr++)
    {
    cout << "What is the next child's name? ";
    cin >> child;
    cout << "What is the child's age? ";
    cin >> age;
    if (age <= 5)
        {
        cout << "\n" << child
            << " has Mrs. Jones for a teacher\n";
        }
    if (age == 6)
        {
        cout << "\n" << child
            << " has Miss Smith for a teacher\n";
        }
    if (age >= 7)
        {
        cout << "\n" << child
            << " has Mrs. Anderson for a teacher\n";
        }
    }     // Quits after 5 times

return 0;
}
```

Figure 15.1 shows the output from this program. You will be able to improve the program after you learn to use the switch statement discussed in Chapter 17, "The switch and goto Statements."

**Figure 15.1.**

The result of the program shows input values inside a for loop.

```
What is the next child's name? Jim
What is the child's age? 5

Jim has Mrs. Jones for a teacher
What is the next child's name? Kerry
What is the child's age? 8

Kerry has Mrs. Anderson for a teacher
What is the next child's name? Julie
What is the child's age? 6

Julie has Miss Smith for a teacher
What is the next child's name? Ed
What is the child's age? 10

Ed has Mrs. Anderson for a teacher
What is the next child's name? Cherie
What is the child's age? 7

Cherie has Mrs. Anderson for a teacher
```

**4.** The preceding examples use an increment as the count expression. You can make the for loop increment the loop variable by any value. It does not have to be a 1.

The following program prints the even numbers from 1 to 20, followed by the odd ones from 1 to 20. To do this, 2 (instead of 1) is added to the counter variable each time the loop executes.

```
// Filename: C15EVOD.CPP
// Prints the first few odd and even numbers

#include <iostream.h>

main()
    {
    int     num;      // The for loop variable

    cout << "Even numbers below 21\n";    // Title
    for (num = 2; num <= 20; num += 2)
        {
        cout << num << " ";
        }               // Print every other number
    cout << "\nOdd numbers below 20\n";   // A second title
    for (num = 1; num <= 20; num += 2)
        {
        cout << num << " ";
        }       // Print every other number
    cout << "\n";
    return 0;
    }
```

The first `for` loop variable, `num`, is 2 and not 1. If it were 1, the number 1 would print first, as it does in the odd-number section. There are two loops in this program. The body of each one consists of the single `cout` function.

Two of the `cout`s, the titles, are not part of either loop. If they were, the titles would print before each number prints. When the program is run, the following is the result:

```
Even numbers below 21
2 4 6 8 10 12 14 16 18 20
Odd numbers below 20
1 3 5 7 9 11 13 15 17 19
```

5. You can decrement the loop variable, as well. If you do, the value is subtracted from the loop variable each time through the loop. The following example is a rewrite of the counting program, producing the reverse effect by showing a countdown:

```
// Filename: C15CNTD1.CPP
// Countdown to the lift-off

#include <iostream.h>
```

```
main()
    {
    int     ctr;

    for (ctr = 10; ctr != 0; ctr--)
        {
        cout << ctr << "\n";
        }        // Print ctr as it counts down
    cout << "*** Blast off! ***";
    return 0;
    }
```

When decrementing a loop variable, the initial value should be larger than the end value *for* which the program is testing. In this case, 10 is counted down to 1. The loop variable, ctr, decrements each time. By studying this program's output, you can see how easy it is to control a loop:

```
10
 9
 8
 7
 6
 5
 4
 3
 2
 1
*** Blast off! ***
```

**Tip:** This countdown program's for loop illustrates a redundancy you can eliminate in code, thanks to C++. The test expression, ctr != 0;, tells the for loop to continue looping until ctr equals zero. However, if ctr becomes zero, that is a False value in itself; there is no reason to add the additional != 0, except for clarity. The for loop can be rewritten as

```
for (ctr = 10; ctr; ctr—)
```

without loss of meaning, and with more efficiency. This technique is such an integral part of C++ that you should become comfortable with it. You will experience very little loss of clarity once you get used to writing your code this way.

6. You can make a for loop test for something other than a constant value. The following program combines much of what you have learned so far. It asks for student grades, and computes an average. There might be a different number of students each semester; therefore, the program first

asks the user for the number of students whose grades are about to be entered. Then, the program loops until the user enters that many scores, and computes the average based on the total scores and the number of grades entered.

```cpp
// Filename: C15FOR4.CPP
// Computes a grade average with a for loop

#include <iostream.h>
#include <iomanip.h>
#include <stdlib.h>              // Why?...

main()
    {
    float       grade, avg;
    float       total = 0.0;
    int         num;            // Total number of grades
    int         loopvar;        // Used to control for loop

    cout << "\n*** Grade Calculation ***\n\n";      // Title
    cout << "How many students are there? ";
    cin >> num;        // Get total number to enter
    if (num < 1)
        {
        exit(0);
        }

    for (loopvar = 1; loopvar <= num; loopvar++)
        {
        cout << "\nWhat is the next student's grade? ";
        cin >> grade;
        total += grade;
        }       // Keep a running total

    avg = total / num;
    cout << "\n\nThe average of this class is: "
         << setiosflags(ios::fixed) << setprecision(1) << avg <<
"\n";
    return 0;

    }
```

Neither the total nor the average calculations have to be altered if the number of students changes because of the way the `for` loop is set up.

**7.** Characters and integers are so closely associated in C++ that you can actually increment character variables in a `for` loop. The following program prints the letters A through Z with a simple `for` loop:

```cpp
// Filename: C15FOR5.CPP
// Prints the alphabet with a simple for loop

#include <iostream.h>
```

```
main()
    {
    char    letter;

    cout << "Here is the alphabet\n";
    for (letter = 'A'; letter <= 'Z'; letter++)  // Loops
                                                 // 'A' through 'Z'

        {
        cout << letter << " ";
        }
    cout << "\n";
    return 0;
    }
```

The program produces the following output:

```
Here is the alphabet
A B C D E F G H I J K L M N O P Q R S T U V W X Y Z
```

**8.** You can leave any of the for loop's expressions blank. The following for loop leaves all the expressions blank (they are called *null expressions*):

```
for ( ; ; )
    {

    cout << "Over and over...";

    }
```

This executes forever in an infinite loop. Although you should avoid infinite loops, your program might dictate that you leave one expression or another in a for loop blank. If you already initialized the start expression earlier in the program, you would be wasting computer time to repeat that expression in the for loop, and C++ does not require it. The following program leaves the start expression and the count expression blank, leaving only the for loop's test expression.

```
// Filename: C15FOR6.CPP
// Uses only the test expression in the for loop to count
// by 5's

#include <iostream.h>

main()
    {
    int    num = 5;                     // Starting value

    cout << "\nCounting by 5's: \n";    // Title
    for ( ; num <= 100; )  // Only contains test expression
        {
        cout << num << "\n";
```

```
            num += 5;   // Increment expression outside of loop
            }           // End of the loop's body
    return 0;
    }
```

Note the following output from this program which illustrates the optional `for` loop expressions. Most of the time, you need to leave out just one of them. If you find yourself using a `for` loop without two of its expressions, you might want to consider replacing it with a `while` or `do-while` loop.

```
Counting by 5s:
5
10
15
20
25
30
35
40
45
50
55
60
65
70
75
80
85
90
95
100
```

# Nested *for* Loops

Use nested loops when you want to repeat a loop more than once.

Any C++ statement can go inside the body of a `for` loop—even another `for` loop! When you put one loop within another, you are creating *nested loops*. The clock in a sporting event works similar to a nested loop. You might think that this is stretching an analogy a little far. However, it truly works. A football game counts down from 15 minutes to 0. It does this four times. The first countdown is a loop going from 15 to 0 (for each minute), and that loop is nested within another counting from 1 to 4 (for each of the four quarters).

Whenever your program needs to repeat a loop more than once, it is a good candidate for a nested loop. Figure 15.2 shows two outlines of nested loops. You can think of the inside loop as looping "faster" than the outside loop. In the first outline, the `for` loop, counting from 1 to 10, is the inside loop. It loops faster. The reason is that the variable `in` goes from 1 to 10 before the outside loop, the variable `out`, finishes its first iteration. Because the outside loop does not repeat until the body of the loop ends, the inside `for` loop has a chance to finish in its entirety. When the outside loop finally does iterate a second time, the inside one starts all over again.

**Figure 15.2.**

This drawing includes outlines of two nested loops.

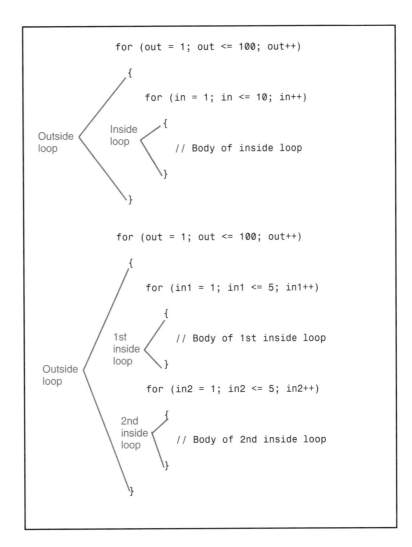

The second outline shows two loops within an outside loop. Both inside loops execute in their entirety before the outside loop finishes its first iteration. When the outside loop starts its second iteration, the two inside loops repeat all over again.

Notice the order of the braces in each of the outlines. The inside loop *always* finishes; therefore, its ending brace must come before the outside loop's ending brace. Indentation makes this much clearer. The reason is that you can "line up" the braces of each loop.

To sum up nested loops, follow this rule of thumb: In nested loops, the inside loop or loops execute completely before the outside loop's next iteration. Nested loops become important later when you use them for array and table processing.

## Examples

1. The following program contains a nested loop (one loop within another). The inside loop counts and prints from 1 to 5. The outside loop counts from 1 to 3. Therefore, the inside loop repeats, in its entirety, three times. In other words, this program prints the values 1 to 5. It prints them three times.

```cpp
// Filename: C15NEST1.CPP
// Prints the numbers from 1 to 5 three times, using a
// nested loop

#include <iostream.h>

main()
    {
    int     times, num;     // Outer and inner for
                            // loop variables

    for (times = 1; times <= 3; times++)
        {
        for (num = 1; num <= 5; num++)
            {
            cout << num << "\n";
            }        // Inner loop body
        }            // End of outer loop

    return 0;
    }
```

Notice that the inside loop, which prints from 1 to 5, repeats three times.

The indentation maintains the standard of `for` loops; every statement in each loop is indented a few spaces. The inside loop is already indented; therefore, its body is indented another few spaces.

The following is the result of running this program:

```
1
2
3
4
5
```

```
1
2
3
4
5
1
2
3
4
5
```

**2.** The outside loop's counter variable changes each time through the loop. If one of the inside loop's control variables is the outside loop's counter variable, you see effects similar to those that the following program shows:

```cpp
// Filename: C15NEST2.CPP
// An inside loop controlled by the outer loop's counter
// variable

#include <iostream.h>

main()
    {
    int     outer, inner;

    for (outer = 5; outer >= 1; outer—)
        {
        for (inner = 1; inner != outer; inner++)
            {
            cout << inner << "\n";
            }       // End of inner loop
        }
    return 0;
    }
```

Note the following output from this program. The inside loop repeats five times (as outer counts down from 5 to 1), and prints from 4 numbers down to 1 number.

```
1
2
3
4
1
2
3
1
2
1
```

Table 15.1 shows the two variables that are traced through this program. Sometimes you have to "play computer" when learning a new concept such as nested loops. By executing a line at a time, and writing down each variable's contents, you can produce this table.

**Table 15.1. Two variables are traced through this program.**

| Variable<br>outer | Value<br>inner |
|---|---|
| 5 | 1 |
| 5 | 2 |
| 5 | 3 |
| 5 | 4 |
| 4 | 1 |
| 4 | 2 |
| 4 | 3 |
| 3 | 1 |
| 3 | 2 |
| 2 | 1 |

**Tip (for mathematicians):** The for statement is identical to the mathematical summation symbol. When you write programs to simulate the summation symbol, the for statement is an excellent candidate. Also, a nested for statement is good for double summations.

For example, the summation

$$\sum_{i = 1}^{i = 30} (i / 3 * 2)$$

can be rewritten as

```
total = 0;
for (i = 1; i <= 30; i++)
    {
    total += (i / 3 * 2);
    }
```

**3.** A factorial is a mathematical number used in probability theory and statistics. A *factorial* of any number is the multiplied product of every number from that number down to 1. For instance, the factorial of 4 is 24 because

4 * 3 * 2 * 1 = 24

The factorial of 6 is 720 because

6 * 5 * 4 * 3 * 2 * 1 = 720

The factorial of 1 is 1 by definition.

Nested loops are good candidates for writing a factorial number-generating program. The following program asks the user for a number. Then, the program prints every factorial up to, and including, that number:

```
// Filename: C15FACT.CPP
// Computes the factorial of numbers through the
// user's number

#include <iostream.h>

main()
    {
    int     outer, num, fact, total;

    cout << "What factorial do you want to see? ";
    cin >> num;

    for (outer = 1; outer <= num; outer++)
        {
        total = 1;   // Initialize total for each factorial
        for (fact = 1; fact <= outer; fact++)
            {
            total *= fact;
            }      // Compute each factorial
        }

    cout << "The factorial for " << num << " is " << total
        << "\n";
    return 0;
    }
```

The following is the output:

```
What factorial do you want to see? 7
The factorial for 7 is 5040
```

You can run this program, entering different values when asked, and see various factorials. Be careful, however, because factorials multiply quickly; a factorial of 8 or so no longer fits in an `int` variable.

## Summary

This chapter showed you how to control loops. Instead of writing extra code around a `while` loop, you can use the `for` loop to control the number of iterations at the time you define the loop. All `for` loops contain three parts: a start expression, a test expression, and a count expression.

You have now seen C++'s three loop constructs: the `while` loop, the `do-while` loop, and the `for` loop. These are similar. However, they behave differently in the testing or initialization of loops. All three loops are equally useful; there is no specific advantage to employing one over the other. Your programming problem should dictate which loop is appropriate. The next chapter shows you additional ways to control the loops you write.

## Review Questions

The answers to Review Questions are in Appendix B.

1. What is a loop?

2. True or false: The body of a `for` loop contains, at most, one statement.

3. What is a nested loop?

4. Why would you want to leave one or more expressions out of the `for` statement's parentheses?

5. Which loop "moves faster"—the inside loop or the outside one?

6. What is the output from the following program?

```
for (ctr = 10; ctr >= 1; ctr -= 3)
   {

   cout << "ctr \n";

   }
```

7. True or false: A `for` loop is better to use than a `while` loop when you know in advance exactly how many iterations a loop requires.

8. What happens when the test expression becomes False in a `for` statement?

9. True or false: The following program contains a valid nested loop.

```
for (i = 1; i <= 10; i++);
   {
   for (j = 1; j <= 5; j++)
      {
      cout << i << " " << j << "\n";
      }
   }
```

**10.** What is the output of the following section of code?

```
start = 1;
end = 5;
step = 1;

for ( ; start >= end; )
        {
.       cout << i << "\n";
        start += step;
        end—;
        }
```

# Review Exercises

**1.** Write a program that prints the numbers from 1 to 15 on-screen. Use a for loop to control the printing.

**2.** Write a program that prints the values from 15 to 1 on-screen. Use a for loop to control the printing.

**3.** Write a program that uses a for loop to print every odd number from 1 to 100.

**4.** Write a program that asks for the user's age. Use a for loop to print Happy Birthday! once for every year of the age.

**5.** Write a program that uses a for loop to print the ASCII characters from 32 to 255 on-screen.

**6.** Using the ASCII table numbers, write a program that prints the following output, employing a nested for loop:

```
A
AB
ABC
ABCD
ABCDE
```

**Tip:** The outside loop should loop from 1 to 5;  the inside loop's start variable should be 65 (the value of ASCII "A").

# CHAPTER 16

# Advanced Control of *for* Loops: *break* and *continue*

This chapter focuses on two techniques for refining control of a for loop: the break statement, and the continue statement. These statements give you the power (depending on the data being processed) to break out of a for loop early, or skip processing the rest of the loop body.

This chapter covers the following topics:

♦ Using break inside a for loop

♦ Using the continue statement

## The *break* and *for* Statements

The for loop was designed to execute a loop a specified number of times. However, there can be rare instances when the for loop should quit before the for's counting variable has reached its final value. As with while loops, you can use the break statement to quit a for loop early.

The break statement goes in the body of the for loop. Programmers rarely put break on a line by itself; it almost always appears after an if test. If the break were on a line by itself, the loop would always quit early, defeating the purpose of the body of the for loop.

## Examples

1. The following program shows what can happen when C++ encounters an unconditional `break` statement—that is, one *not* preceded by an `if` statement.

*Comments to identify the program*
*Include the header file* `iostream.h`.
*Start of the* `main()` *function.*
> *Declare the variable* `num` *as an integer.*
> *Print* `Here are the numbers from 1 to 20` *on-screen and return to the next line.*
> *The variable* `num` *starts at 1 and is incremented by 1 while* `num` *is less than or equal to 20.*
> > *Print the value of* `num` *and return to the next line.*
> > *Break immediately out of the* `for` *loop.*
> *Print* `That's all, folks!` *on-screen.*
> *Exit the* `main()` *function.*

```
// Filename: C16BRAK1.CPP
// A for loop defeated by the break statement

#include <iostream.h>

main()
    {
    int     num;

    cout << "Here are the numbers from 1 to 20\n";
    for (num = 1; num <= 20; num++)
        {
        cout << num << "\n";
        break;     // This exits the for loop immediately
        }

    cout << "That's all, folks!";
    return 0;
    }
```

The following is this program's output:

```
Here are the numbers from 1 to 20
1
That's all, folks!
```

Notice that the `break` immediately terminates the `for` loop before it has completed one cycle. The `for` loop might as well not be in this program.

**2.** The following program is an improved version of the program in Example 1. This program asks whether the user wants to see another number. If the user does, the `for` loop continues its next iteration. If the user does not, the `break` statement terminates the `for` loop.

```
// Filename: C16BRAK2.CPP
// A for loop running at the user's request

#include <iostream.h>

main()
    {
    int     num;          // Loop counter variable
    char    ans;

    cout << "Here are the numbers from 1 to 20\n";

    for (num = 1; num <= 20; num++)
        {
        cout << num << "\n";
        cout << "Do you want to see another (Y/N)? ";
        cin >> ans;
        if ((ans == 'N') || (ans == 'n'))
            {
            break;       // Will exit the for loop if
                         // user wants
            }
        }

    cout << "\nThat's all, folks!";
    return 0;
    }
```

Note the following sample run of this program. The `for` loop prints 20 numbers, as long as the user does not answer N or n to the prompt. Otherwise, the `break` takes over and terminates the `for` loop early. The statement after the body of the loop always executes next if the `break` occurs.

```
Here are the numbers from 1 to 20
1
Do you want to see another (Y/N)? Y
2
Do you want to see another (Y/N)? Y
3
Do you want to see another (Y/N)? Y
4
Do you want to see another (Y/N)? Y
5
Do you want to see another (Y/N)? Y
6
```

```
Do you want to see another (Y/N)? Y
7
Do you want to see another (Y/N)? Y
8
Do you want to see another (Y/N)? Y
9
Do you want to see another (Y/N)? Y
10
Do you want to see another (Y/N)? N
That's all, folks!
```

If you nest one loop inside another, the break terminates the "most active" loop—that is, the innermost loop in which the break statement resides.

**3.** Use the *conditional* break (an if statement followed by a break) when you are missing data. When you process data files or large amounts of user data entry, you might expect 100 input numbers, and get only 95; you can use a break to terminate the for loop before it cycles through its 96th iteration.

Suppose that the teacher using C15FOR4.CPP, the grade-averaging program presented in the last chapter, entered an incorrect number of total students. Maybe she typed 16 when there were only 14 students. The preceding for loop would loop 16 times, no matter how many students there really were. The reason is that this loop relies on the teacher's count.

The following grade-averaging program is more sophisticated. It asks the teacher for the total number of students. However, if the teacher wants to, she can enter -99 as a student's score. The –99 is not actually averaged in, but is used as a trigger value to break out of the for loop before its normal conclusion. A counter has to be placed in the loop as well. The reason is that the total number of grades entered might not match the number the teacher originally entered.

```cpp
// Filename: C16BRAK3.CPP
// Computes a grade average with a for loop,
// allowing for an early exit with a break statement

#include <iostream.h>
#include <iomanip.h>

main()
    {
    float       grade, avg;
    float       total = 0.0;
    int         num, count = 0;   // Total number of grades
                                  // and counter
    int         loopvar;          // Used to control for loop

    cout << "\n*** Grade Calculation ***\n\n";      // Title
    cout << "How many students are there? ";
    cin >> num;     // Get total number to enter
```

```
        for (loopvar = 1; loopvar <= num; loopvar++)
            {
            cout << "\nWhat is the next student's grade? ";
            cout << "(-99 to quit) ";
            cin >> grade;
            if (grade < 0.0)    // A negative number triggers
                                // break
                {
                break;          // Leave the loop early
                }
            count++;
            total += grade;     // Keep a running total
            }

    if (count != 0)
            {
            avg = total / count;
            cout << "\n\nThe average of this class is: "
                << setiosflags(ios::fixed)  << setprecision(1) << avg <<
"\n";
            }
    return 0;
    }
```

Notice that the grade is tested for less than zero, not –99.0. Floating-point values do not compare well for equality (because of their bit-level representations). No grade will be negative. Therefore, any negative number will trigger the break statement. This program works as follows:

```
*** Grade Calculation ***

How many students are there? 10

What is the next student's grade? (-99 to quit) 87

What is the next student's grade? (-99 to quit) 97

What is the next student's grade? (-99 to quit) 67

What is the next student's grade? (-99 to quit) 89

What is the next student's grade? (-99 to quit) 94

What is the next student's grade? (-99 to quit) -99

The average of this class is: 86.8
```

# The *continue* Statement

The continue
statement causes
C++ to skip the
remaining
statements and
return to the top
of the loop.

The continue statement does the opposite of the break statement; instead of exiting a loop early, continue forces the computer to perform *another* iteration of the loop. If you put a continue statement in the body of a for or while loop, the computer ignores any statement in the loop that follows continue.

The format of continue is

```
continue;
```

You use the continue statement when data in the body of the loop is bad, out of bounds, or unexpected. Instead of acting on the bad data, you might want to return to the top of the loop to get another data value. The following examples help illustrate the use of continue.

> **Tip:** The continue statement forces a new iteration of any of the three loop constructs: for, while, and do-while.

Figure 16.1 shows the difference between the break and continue statements.

**Figure 16.1.**

The break and
continue
statements
operate differently.

```
for (i = 0; i <= 10; i++)

    {

        break; ─────────────────┐
                                │
        cout << "loop it\n";   // Never prints     break terminates
                                                    loop immediately
    }
                                │
// Rest of program  ◄───────────┘


for (i = 0; i <= 10; i++) ◄─────┐
                                │   continue causes loop to
    {                           │   perform another iteration
                                │
        continue; ──────────────┘

        cout << "loop it\n";   // Never prints

    }

// Rest of program
```

## Examples

**1.** The following program appears to print the numbers 1 through 10, each
followed by C++ Programming. It doesn't. The continue in the body of the
for loop causes an early finish to the loop. The first cout in the for loop
executes. However, the second cout does not execute because of the
continue.

```
// Filename: C16CON1.CPP
// Demonstrates use of continue statement

#include <iostream.h>

main()
    {
    int     ctr;

    for (ctr = 1; ctr <= 10; ctr++)      // Loop 10 times
        {
        cout << ctr << " ";
        continue;             // Cause body to end early
        cout << "C++ Programming\n";
        }
    cout << "\n";
    return 0;
    }
```

Note this program's output:

```
1 2 3 4 5 6 7 8 9 10
```

If you have such warnings enabled, Borland C++ gives you a warning
message when you compile this type of program. The compiler recognizes
that the second cout is unreachable code. The reason is that it will never
execute because of the continue. Therefore, most programs do not use a
continue, except after an if statement. This makes it a conditional continue
statement, which is much more useful. The next two examples demonstrate the conditional use of continue.

**2.** The following program asks the user for five lowercase letters, one at a
time, then prints their uppercase equivalents. The program uses the ASCII
table to ensure that the user entered lowercase letters. (These are the letters
whose ASCII numbers range from 97 to 122.) If the user does not type a
lowercase letter, the program ignores it with the continue statement.

```
// Filename: C16CON2.CPP

// Prints uppercase equivalents of five lowercase letters

#include <iostream.h>
```

```
main()
    {
    char    letter;
    int     ctr;

    for (ctr = 1; ctr <= 5; ctr++)
        {
        cout << "Please enter a lowercase letter ";
        cin >> letter;
        if ((letter < 'a') || (letter > 'z')) // See if
                                               // out of range
            {
            continue;    // Go get another
            }
        letter -= 32;    // Subtract 32 from ASCII value
                         // to get uppercase
        cout << "The uppercase equivalent is: "
             << letter << "\n";
        }
    return 0;
    }
```

Only lowercase letters get converted to uppercase because of the `continue` statement.

**3.** Suppose that you want to average the salaries of employees who made over $10,000 a year in your company. However, you only have their monthly gross pay figures. The following program prompts for each employee's monthly salary, and annualizes it (by multiplying it by 12). Then, the program computes an average. It does not average in any salary that is less than $10,000 a year. The `continue` ensures that those salaries are ignored in the average calculation, letting the other salaries fall through.

If you enter –1 as the monthly salary, the program prints the result of the average and terminates.

```
// Filename: C16CON3.CPP
// Average salaries over $10,000 annually

#include <iostream.h>
#include <iomanip.h>

main()
    {
    float   month, year;    // Monthly and yearly salaries
    float   avg = 0.0, total = 0.0;
    int     count = 0;

    do
        {
        cout << "What is the next monthly salary ";
        cout << "(-1 to quit)? ";
```

```
cin >> month;
        if ((year = month * 12.00) < 10000.00)  // Do not
                                                 // add low salaries

            {
            continue;
            }
        if (month < 0.0)
            {
            break;          // Quit if user entered -1
            }
        count++;            // Add 1 to valid counter
        total += year;      // Add yearly salary to total
        }
    while (month > 0.0);

    if (count)
        {
        avg = total / (float)count;     // Compute average
        cout << "\n\nThe average of high salaries is $"
             << setiosflags(ios::fixed) << setprecision(2)
             << avg << "\n";
        }
    return 0;
    }
```

Notice that this program uses both a continue statement and a break statement. The program does one of three set things, depending on the user's input: adds to the total, continues another iteration if the salary is too low, or completely exits the while loop (and average calculation) if the user types a -1.

The following is the output from a sample run of this program:

```
What is the next monthly salary (-1 to quit)? 500.00
What is the next monthly salary (-1 to quit)? 2000.00
What is the next monthly salary (-1 to quit)? 750.00
What is the next monthly salary (-1 to quit)? 4000.00
What is the next monthly salary (-1 to quit)? 5000.00
What is the next monthly salary (-1 to quit)? 1200.00
What is the next monthly salary (-1 to quit)? -1


The average of high salaries is $36600.00
```

## Summary

In this chapter, you learned several more ways to use and modify your program's loops. By adding continue and break statements, you can better control how the loop behaves. Being able to exit early (with the break statement) or begin the next loop iteration in a timely fashion (with the continue statement) enables more freedom in processing different types of data.

The next chapter shows you a construct of C++ that does not loop but relies on the break statement to work properly. This construct is the switch statement, which makes creating your program's choices much easier.

## Review Questions

The answers to Review Questions are in Appendix B.

1. What is the purpose of a loop?

2. What is the difference between a break statement and a continue statement?

3. Why do continue and break statements rarely appear without an if statement controlling them?

4. What is the output from this section of code?

```
for (i = 1; i <= 10; i++)
    {
    continue;
    cout << "***** \n";
    }
```

5. What is the output from this section of code?

```
for (i = 1; i <= 10; i++)
    {
    cout << "***** \n";
    break;
    }
```

6. What is a the purpose of a nested loop?

7. Can a nested loop be used to measure elapsed time?

## Review Exercises

1. Write a program that prints c++ is fun on-screen for 10 seconds. (*Hint:* Use a loop and vary the number of iterations to consume the desired amount of time. This kind of loop is called a timing loop.)

2. Make the program in Exercise 1 flash the message c++ is fun on and off for 10 seconds. (*Hint:* You might have to use several timing loops.)

3. Write a grade-averaging program for a class of 20 students. Ignore any grade less than 0. Continue until all 20 student grades are entered. You can stop if the user types -99 to end early.

4. Write a program that prints the numbers from 1 to 15 in one column. To the right of each *even* number, print its square. To the right of each *odd* number, print its cube (the number raised to the 3rd power).

# CHAPTER 17

# The *switch* and *goto* Statements

The switch statement improves on the if and else-if constructs by streamlining the multiple-choice decisions your programs make. The switch statement does not replace the if statement. However, the switch construct is better to use when your programs have to perform one of *many* different actions.

The switch and break statements work together. Almost every switch statement you use will include at least one break statement in its body. As a conclusion to Part III on C++ constructs, this chapter presents the goto statement for completeness, although you rarely use it.

The following topics are introduced in this chapter:

♦ The switch statement

♦ The goto statement

If you have mastered the if statement presented in Chapter 10, you should have little trouble with the concepts presented here. After learning about the switch statement, you will be able to write menus and multiple-choice, data-entry programs with ease.

## The *switch* Statement

The switch statement, sometimes referred to as the *multiple-choice statement*, lets your program choose from several alternatives. The format of the switch statement is a little longer than that of other statements you have seen. The following presents its format:

```
switch (expression)
{
case (expression1):
    C++ statements;
case (expression2):
    C++ statements;
case (expression3):
    C++ statements;
  :
  :
default:
    C++ statements;
}
```

Use the `switch` statement when your program makes a multiple-choice selection.

The expression can be any `int` or `char` expression, constant, or variable. The subexpressions—`expression1`, `expression2`, and so on—can be any other `int` or `char` constant. The number of `case` expressions following the `switch` line is determined by your application. The C++ statements can be any block of C++ code.

The `default` line is optional; not all `switch` statements include this line, although most do. It does not have to be the last line of the body of the switch statement.

If the expression matches the first `case`, `expression1`, the statements that are usually under `expression1` execute. If the expression matches the second `case`, `expression2`, the statements that are usually under `expression2` execute. If none of the `case` expressions matches that of the `switch` expression, the `default` case block executes.

The `case` expression value does not have to have parentheses around it. However, using them makes the value easier to find.

**Tip:** Use a `break` statement after each `case` block to keep execution from "falling through" to the rest of the `case` statements.

Using the `switch` statement is easier than its format might lead you to believe. You can usually use a `switch` statement that is more easily understood in the place in which you would otherwise put an `if-else-if` combination of statements. The `switch` statement also is much easier to follow than an `if` within an `if` within an `if`, which you have had to write until now.

The `if` and `else-if` combinations of statements are neither poor choices to use nor difficult to follow. When the relational test that determines the choice is complex, and contains many `&&` and `||` operators, `if` might be a better candidate. The `switch` statement is preferable when multiple-choice possibilities are based on a single constant, a variable, or an expression.

**Tip:** To improve your program's speed, arrange the cases so that the ones that are executed most frequently appear at the top of the list.

The following examples clarify the `switch` statement. They compare `switch` and `if` statements to help you see the difference.

## Examples

1. Suppose that you want to write a program to teach your child how to count. The program should ask the child for a number, then beep (ring the computer's alarm bell) that many times.

The program assumes that the child enters a number from 1 to 5. The following program uses the `if-else-if` combination to accomplish the beeping-counting program.

*Comments to identify the program.*
*Include the header file `iostream.h`.*
*Comment to identify what is about to happen in the program.*
*Globally define BEEP to print to the screen a control character that will make a beep sound, then move the cursor to a newline.*
*Start of the `main()` function.*
  *Declare the variable `num` as an integer.*
  *Comment to identify what is about to happen in the program.*
  *Print to the screen `Please enter a number`.*
  *Obtain an integer from the keyboard.*
  *Comment to identify what is about to happen in the program.*
  *If the variable obtained is equal to a 1, cause the computer to make a beep sound, and return to a newline.*
    *Otherwise, if the variable obtained is equal to a 2, cause the computer to make two beep sounds, and return to a newline.*
      *Otherwise, if the variable obtained is equal to a 3, cause the computer to make three beep sounds, and return to a newline.*
        *Otherwise, if the variable obtained is equal to a 4, cause the computer to make four beep sounds, and return to a newline.*
          *Otherwise, if the variable obtained is equal to a 5, cause the computer to make five beep sounds, and return to a new line.*
  *Return from the `main()` function.*

```cpp
// Filename: C17BEEP1.CPP
// Beeps a certain number of times

#include <iostream.h>

// Define a beep cout to save repetitiveness of the program
#define BEEP cout << "\a\n"

main()
    {
    int    num;

    // Get a number from the child (you might have to help
    // the child)
    cout << "Please enter a number ";
    cin >> num;

    // Use multiple if statements to beep
    if (num == 1)
        {
        BEEP;
        }
    else
        {
        if (num == 2)
            {
            BEEP;
            BEEP;
            }
        else
            {
            if (num == 3)
                {
                BEEP;
                BEEP;
                BEEP;
                }
            else
                {
                if (num == 4)
                    {
                    BEEP;
                    BEEP;
                    BEEP;
                    BEEP;
                    }
                else
                    {
                    if (num == 5)
                        {
                        BEEP;
                        BEEP;
                        BEEP;
```

```
                                    BEEP;
                                    BEEP;
                                    }
                              }
                        }
                  }
            }
      return 0;
      }
```

This program assumes that if the child enters something other than 1 through 5, no beeps are sounded. The program takes advantage of the #define preprocessor directive to define a shortcut to an alarm cout function. In this case, the BEEP is a little clearer to read, as long as you remember that BEEP is not a command; instead, everywhere it appears, it is replaced with the cout.

One drawback to this type of "if within an if" program is reduced readability. By the time you indent the body of each if and else, the program is shoved too far to the right. There is room for no more than five or six possibilities. Also, this type of logic is difficult to follow. A switch statement is much better to use because it involves a multiple-choice selection, as the following, improved version of the preceding program illustrates:

```
// Filename: C17BEEP2.CPP
// Beeps a certain number of times, using a switch

#include <iostream.h>

// Define a beep cout to save repetitiveness of the program
#define BEEP cout << "\a\n"

main()
    {
    int     num;

    // Get a number from the child (you might have to help
    // the child)
    cout << "Please enter a number ";
    cin >> num;

    switch (num)
        {
        case 1:
              BEEP;
              break;
        case 2:
              BEEP;
              BEEP;
              break;
        case 3:
```

```
                BEEP;
                BEEP;
                BEEP;
                break;
        case 4:
                BEEP;
                BEEP;
                BEEP;
                BEEP;
                break;
        case 5:
                BEEP;
                BEEP;
                BEEP;
                BEEP;
                BEEP;
                break;
        }
    return 0;
    }
```

This version is much clearer than the previous one. It is obvious that the value of num controls the execution. Only the case that matches num executes. The indentation helps separate the cases from each other.

If the child types a number other than 1 through 5, no beeps are sounded. The reason is that there is not a case expression to match any other value, nor is there a default case.

If two or more of the case expressions are the same, an error results, and the program does not compile.

2. If the child did not type a 1, 2, 3, 4, or 5, nothing happened in the preceding program. The following program is the same one modified to take advantage of the default option. The default block of statements executes if none of the previous cases matched.

```
// Filename: C17BEEP3.CPP
// Beeps a certain number of times, using a switch

#include <iostream.h>

// Define a beep cout to save repetitiveness of the program
#define BEEP cout << "\a\n"

main()
    {
    int     num;

        // Get a number from the child (you might have to help
        // the child)
        cout << "Please enter a number ";
        cin >> num;
```

```
switch (num)
    {
    case 1:
        BEEP;
        break;
    case 2:
        BEEP;
        BEEP;
        break;
    case 3:
        BEEP;
        BEEP;
        BEEP;
        break;
    case 4:
        BEEP;
        BEEP;
        BEEP;
        BEEP;
        break;
    case 5:
        BEEP;
        BEEP;
        BEEP;
        BEEP;
        BEEP;
        break;
    default:
        cout << "You must enter a number ";
        cout << "from 1 to 5\n";
        cout << "Please run this program again\n";
        break;
    }
return 0;
}
```

The break at the end of the default case might seem redundant. After all, there are no other case statements that execute by "falling through" from the default case. It is a good habit to put a break after the default case anyway.

3. To illustrate the importance of using break statements in each case expression, here is the same beeping-counting program without any break statements:

```
// Filename: C17BEEP4.CPP
// A program that incorrectly beeps, using a switch

#include <iostream.h>

// Define a beep cout to save repetitiveness of the program
#define BEEP cout << "\a\n"
```

```
main()
    {
    int     num;

    // Get a number from the child (you might have to help
    // the child)
    cout << "Please enter a number ";
    cin >> num;

    switch (num)
        {
        case 1:
            BEEP;
        case 2:
            BEEP;
            BEEP;
        case 3:
            BEEP;
            BEEP;
            BEEP;
        case 4:
            BEEP;
            BEEP;
            BEEP;
            BEEP;
        case 5:
            BEEP;
            BEEP;
            BEEP;
            BEEP;
            BEEP;
        default:
            cout << "You must enter a number ";
            cout << "from 1 to 5\n";
            cout << "Please run this program again\n";
            break;
        }
    return 0;
    }
```

If the child types a 1, the program beeps 15 times! The break is not there to stop the execution from falling through to the other cases. Unlike other programming languages, such as Pascal, C++'s switch statement requires that you handle the case code in this way.

This is not necessarily a drawback. Having to specify breaks gives more control in how you handle the specific cases, as the next example shows.

4. The following program controls the printing of end-of-day sales totals. The program first asks for the day of the week. If the day is Monday through Thursday, a daily total prints. If the day is a Friday, a weekly as well as a daily total prints. If the day happens to be the end of the month, a monthly sales total prints.

In reality, these totals would come from the disk drive instead of being assigned at the top of the program. Furthermore, instead of individual sales figures being printed, a full daily, weekly, and monthly report of many sales totals would probably be printed. You are on your way to learning more about expanding the power of your C++ programs in the upcoming chapters. For now, concentrate on the switch statement and its possibilities.

The sales figures are handled through a hierarchy of cases. Because the daily amount is the last case, it is the only report printed if the day of the week is Monday through Thursday. If the day of the week is Friday, the second case executes, printing the weekly sales total and then falling through to the daily total (as Friday's total has to be printed, as well). If it is the end of the month, the first case executes, falling through to the weekly total, then to the daily sales total. In this example, the use of a break statement would be harmful. Other languages that do not offer this "fall through" flexibility are more limiting.

```cpp
// Filename: C17SALE.CPP
// Prints daily, weekly, and monthly sales totals

#include <iostream.h>
#include <iomanip.h>

main()
    {
    float    daily = 2343.34;      // Later, these figures
// will come from a disk file instead of being so obviously
// assigned as they are here.
    float    weekly = 13432.65;
    float    monthly = 43468.97;
    char     ans;
    int      day;                  // Day value to trigger
                                   // correct case

// Month will be assigned 1 through 5 (for Mon - Fri)
// or 6 if it is the end of the month. Assume weekly AND
// daily prints if it is the end of month no matter what the
// day is.
    cout << "Is this the end of the month? (Y/N) ";
    cin >> ans;
    if ((ans=='Y') || (ans=='y'))
        {
        day = 6;      // Month value
        }
    else
        {
        cout << "What day number, 1 through 5 ";
        cout << "(for Mon-Fri) is it? ";
        cin >> day;
        }
```

```
        switch (day)
          {
          case 6:
              cout << "The monthly total is: $"
              << setiosflags(ios::fixed) << setprecision(2)
              << monthly << "\n";
          case 5:
              cout << "The weekly total is: $"
                << setiosflags(ios::fixed) << setprecision(2)
                << weekly << "\n";
          default:
              cout << "The daily total is: $"
                << setiosflags(ios::fixed) << setprecision(2)
                << daily << "\n";
          }
        return 0;
        }
```

**5.** The order of the case statements is not fixed. You can rearrange them so that they are more efficient. If you know that most of the time only one or two cases will be selected, put them toward the top of the switch statement.

For example, suppose that most of the company's employees in the next program are engineers. Their option is third in the case statements. By rearranging the case statements so that Engineering is at the top, you could speed up this program. C++ does not have to scan two case expressions that it rarely executes.

```
// Filename: C17DEPT2.CPP
// Prints message, depending on the department entered

#include <iostream.h>

main()
    {
    char    choice;

    do    // Display menu and check that the user enters
          // a correct option
        {
        cout << "\nChoose your department:\n";
        cout << "S - Sales\n";
        cout << "A - Accounting\n";
        cout << "E - Engineering\n";
        cout << "P - Payroll\n";
        cout << "What is your choice? ";
        cin >> choice;
        // Convert choice to uppercase (if the user
        // entered lowercase) with the ASCII table
        if ((choice >= 'a') && (choice <= 'z'))
            {
            choice -= 32;       // Subtract enough to make
                                // uppercase
```

```
            }
        }
    while ((choice != 'S') && (choice != 'A')
        && (choice != 'E') && (choice != 'P'));

        // Put the Engineering first as it occurs most
        // often

    switch (choice)
        {
        case 'E':
            cout << "\n Your meeting is at 2:30\n";
            break;
        case 'S':
            cout << "\n Your meeting is at 8:30\n";
            break;
        case 'A':
            cout << "\n Your meeting is at 10:00\n";
            break;
        case 'P':
            cout << "\n Your meeting has been canceled\n";
            break;
        }
    return 0;
    }
```

**6.** When you use menus, it is best to give the user a chance to choose no
option. Perhaps the user started the program, then decided against continuing. If so, the user might not want to choose *any* option on the menu.
Most programmers give the user a chance to exit earlier than the normal
conclusion of the program, as the following example shows. The menu
now has a fifth option. If the user types **Q**, the program exits to the operating system early.

```
// Filename: C17DEPT3.CPP
// Prints message, depending on the department entered,
// giving the user a chance to stop the program early

#include <iostream.h>
#include <stdlib.h>

main()
    {
    char      choice;

    do      // Display menu and check that the user enters
            // a correct option
        {
        cout << "\nChoose your department:\n";
        cout << "S - Sales\n";
        cout << "A - Accounting\n";
        cout << "E - Engineering\n";
        cout << "P - Payroll\n";
```

```
            cout << "Q - Quit the program\n";
            cout << "What is your choice? ";
            cin >> choice;
            // Convert choice to uppercase (if the user
            // entered lowercase) with the ASCII table
            if ((choice >= 'a') && (choice <= 'z'))
                {
                choice -= 32;      // Subtract enough
                                   // to make uppercase
                }
        }
    while ((choice != 'S') && (choice != 'A')
        && (choice != 'E') && (choice != 'P')
        && (choice != 'Q'));

        // Put the Engineering first as it occurs most
        // often

    switch (choice)
        {
        case 'E':
            cout << "\n Your meeting is at 2:30\n";
            break;
        case 'S':
            cout << "\n Your meeting is at 8:30\n";
            break;
        case 'A':
            cout << "\n Your meeting is at 10:00\n";
            break;
        case 'P':
            cout << "\n Your meeting has been canceled\n";
            break;
        case 'Q':
            exit(0);       // Give the user a chance
                           // to change mind
            break;
        }
    return 0;
}
```

# The *goto* Statement

Early programming languages did not offer the flexible constructs that C++ gives you, such as for and while loops, and switch statements. The only means of looping and comparing was with the goto statement. C++ still includes a goto. However, the other constructs are more powerful and flexible and easier to follow in a program.

The goto statement causes your program to jump to a different location, instead of executing the next statement in the sequence. The format of the goto statement is

```
goto statement label
```

goto causes execution to jump to a statement other than the next one in order.

A statement label is named, as are variables (refer to Chapter 5, "Variables and Constants"). A statement label also cannot have the same name as a C++ command or function. If you use a goto statement, there must be a statement label elsewhere in the program to which the goto can branch. Execution then continues at the statement with the statement label.

The statement label precedes a line of code. Follow all such labels with a colon (:). C++ then knows that they are labels, and does not confuse them with variables. You haven't seen such labels in the C++ programs thus far in this book. The reason is that none of the programs needed them. These labels are optional, unless you have a goto that branches to one.

Each of the following four lines of code has a different statement label. These lines are not a program; they are individual lines that might be included in a program. Notice that each statement label appears to the left of its line:

```
pay:        cout << "Place checks in the printer \n;

Again:      cin >> name;

EndIt:      cout << "That is all the processing.\n";

CALC:       amount = (total / .5) * 1.15;
```

Such labels give goto statements a tag to which to go. When your program encounters a goto statement, it branches to the line beginning with the statement label indicated in the goto statement. The program then continues to execute sequentially until another goto changes the order again (or until the program ends).

**Tip:** These labels are not intended to replace comments. However, label names should reflect something of the code that follows. A repetitive calculation deserves a label such as CalcIt and not x15z. Even though the system enables you to use both, the first one is a better indication of the code's purpose.

### Use *goto* Judiciously

Overusing the goto statement is not considered good practice in programming. Some programmers, especially those who are beginners, tend to include too many gotos in a program. When a program branches all over the place, following its execution becomes as difficult as trying to trace a single strand of spaghetti through a plate of noodles. This is referred to as *spaghetti code*.

Using a few gotos here and there is not necessarily a bad practice. Usually, however, you can substitute better code. To eliminate gotos, and write more structured programs, you should use the other looping and switch constructs that the last few chapters discussed. They are better alternatives to the goto.

*continues*

> *continued*
>
> The goto should be used judiciously. Starting with the next chapter, you begin to break your programs into smaller modules referred to as functions. And the goto becomes less important as you write more functions.
>
> For now, become familiar with goto so that you can understand programs that use it. Someday, you might be asked to fix someone else's code that contains a goto. The first step you probably take will be to substitute something else for the goto!

## Examples

1. The following program has a problem that is directly the result of the goto, but is one of the best illustrations of this statement. The program consists of an *endless loop* (sometimes referred to as an *infinite loop*). The first three lines (after the opening brace) execute, and then the fourth line, the goto, causes execution to loop back to the beginning and repeat the first three lines. The goto continues to do this until you press Ctrl+Break.

*Comments to identify the program.*
*Include the header file iostream.h.*
*Start of the main() function.*
*Label the line as Again:*
    *and print This message to the screen and return to the next line.*
    *Tab over and print keeps repeating and return to the next line.*
    *Tab over twice, and print over and over and return to the next line.*
    *Go to the line labeled as Again:.*
    *Return out of the main() function.*

```cpp
// Filename: C17GOTO1.CPP
// Program to show use of goto
// (This program ends only when user presses Ctrl+Break.)

#include <iostream.h>

main()
    {
Again:
    cout << "This message\n";
    cout << "\t keeps repeating\n";
    cout << "\t\t over and over\n";

    goto Again;     // Repeat continuously

    return 0;
    }
```

Figure 17.1 shows the result of running this program.

**Figure 17.1.**

In this program, the goto statement causes repeat printing.

```
             keeps repeating
                      over and over
This message
             keeps repeating
                      over and over
This message
             keeps repeating
                      over and over
This message
             keeps repeating
                      over and over
This message
             keeps repeating
                      over and over
This message
             keeps repeating
                      over and over
This message
             keeps repeating
                      over and over
This message
             keeps repeating
                      over and over
This message
```

Of course, you do not want to write programs with infinite loops. The goto is a statement best preceded with an if; therefore, eventually the goto stops branching without the user having to intervene.

2. The following program is one of the worst written ones ever! It is the epitome of spaghetti code! However, do your best to follow it and understand its output. Familiarizing yourself with the program's flow helps you better understand the goto. You also will appreciate the fact that the rest of this book uses goto only when needed to make the program clearer.

```cpp
// Filename: C17GOTO2.CPP
// Program that demonstrates overuse of goto

#include <iostream.h>

main()
    {
    goto Here;
First:    cout << "A\n"; goto Final;
There:    cout << "B\n"; goto First;
Here:     cout << "C\n"; goto There;
Final:    return 0;
    }
```

At first glance, this program appears to print the first three letters of the alphabet. However, the gotos make them print in reverse order: C, B, A. Although the program is not well designed, some indentation of the lines without statement labels makes the program a little more readable. Indenting lets you quickly separate the statement labels from the rest of the code, as you can see in the following program:

```
// Filename: C17GOTO3.CPP
// Program that demonstrates overuse of goto

#include <iostream.h>
main()
    {
    goto Here;

First:
    cout << "A\n";
    goto Final;

There:
    cout << "B\n";
    goto First;

Here:
    cout << "C\n";
    goto There;

Final:
    return 0;
    }
```

This program's listing is slightly easier to follow than the last one, even though each does the same thing. In this book, the rest of the programs that use statement labels also use indentation.

Note that the following three lines would better produce this output:

```
cout << "C\n";
cout << "B\n";
cout << "A\n";
```

The goto warning is worth repeating: Employ goto sparingly, and only when its use makes the program more readable and maintainable. Usually, there are better commands to use.

## Summary

In this chapter, you examined the switch statement and its related options. It can help improve the readability of a complicated if-else-if selection. The switch statement is especially good when several outcomes are possible based on a certain choice. You also can use the exit() function (first mentioned in Chapter 13) to end a program earlier than its normal conclusion.

The goto statement causes an unconditional branch, and can be difficult to follow at times. However, you should be acquainted with as much C++ as possible to prepare yourself to work on programs that others have written. Remember that goto is not employed often these days; you almost always can find a better construct to use.

# Review Questions

The answers to Review Questions are in Appendix B.

1. How does goto change the order in which parts of a program would normally execute?

2. What statement can substitute for an if-else-if construct?

3. What statement almost always ends each case statement in a switch?

4. True or false: The order of your case statements has no bearing on the efficiency of your program.

5. Rewrite the following section of code by using a switch statement:

```
if (num == 1)
    {
    cout << "Alpha";
    }
else if (num == 2)
    {
    cout << "Beta";
    }
else if (num == 3)
    {
    cout << "Gamma";
    }
else
    {

    cout << "Other";

    }
```

6. Rewrite the following program by using a do-while loop to eliminate the goto:

```
Ask:
    cout << "What is your first name? ";
    cin >> name;
    if ((name[0] < 'A') || (name[0] > 'Z'))
        {
        goto Ask;      // Keep asking until the user
                       // types a valid letter

        }
```

## Review Exercises

**1.** Write a program that uses a `switch` statement. The program should ask for the user's age. It should use the `switch` statement to print a message based on the age entered. Print You can vote! if the user is 18 or older, You can adopt! if the user is 21 or older, and Are you REALLY that young? for any other age.

**2.** Write a program, driven by a menu, for your local TV cable company. It charges the customers in the following way:

If you live within 20 miles outside the city limits, you pay $12.00 a month. If you live within 20 to 30 miles outside the city limits, you pay $23.00 a month. If you live within 30 to 50 miles outside the city limits, you pay $34.00 a month. No one living outside 50 miles can connect into the service. Use a menu to prompt for the number of miles the user lives from the city limits.

**3.** Write a program that calculates parking fees for a multilevel parking garage. Ask whether the driver is in a car or truck. Charge the driver $2.00 for parking the first hour, $3.00 for the second hour, and $5.00 for more than two hours. For a truck, add an extra $1.00 to the total fee. (*Hint:* Use one `switch` statement and one `if` statement.)

**4.** Modify the preceding program to charge depending on the time of day the car or truck is parked. If it is parked before 8 a.m., charge the fees given in Exercise 3. If the car or truck is parked after 8 a.m. and before 5 p.m., charge an extra usage fee of 50 cents. If the car or truck is parked after 5 p.m., deduct 50 cents from the computed price. You must prompt the user for the starting time in a menu that includes the following:

    A. Before 8 a.m.

    B. Before 5 p.m.

    C. After 5 p.m.

# Part IV

*Functions*

# CHAPTER 18

# Writing C++ Functions

A computer doesn't get bored. It performs the same input, output, and computations your programs require, as long as you want it to. You can take advantage of the computer's repetitive nature by looking at your programs in a new way: as a series of small routines that execute whenever you need them, as many times as necessary.

This chapter approaches its subject a little differently from the preceding chapters. It concentrates on teaching the need for writing your own *functions*, which are modules or sections of code that you execute and control from the main() function. So far, all programs in this book have consisted of one single, long function referred to as main(). As you learn here, main()'s primary purpose is to control the execution of other functions that follow it.

This chapter covers the following topics:

- The need for functions

- Tracing functions

- Writing functions

- Calling functions

This chapter plays a key role in helping you understand object-oriented programming. Later, when *classes* are discussed, you learn how functions and variables are combined into classes. You then declare *objects* of these classes to do the work inside your programs. All of the functions that you see in this chapter are independent of a *class* or *structure*. This is done to keep matters simple. Much of the power of C++, however, comes from *encapsulating* variables and functions into *objects*.

# An Overview of Functions

When you approach an application problem that needs to be programmed, it's best not to sit down at the keyboard and start typing. Instead, you should think about the program and its purpose. One of the best ways to attack a program is to start with the overall goal; then, break it into several smaller tasks. You should never lose sight of the overall goal of the program. However, you should try to ascertain how the individual objects fit together to accomplish this goal.

When you finally do sit down to start coding the program, continue to think in terms of the objects that fit together. Do not approach it as one giant program; it is to your advantage to continue to develop the individual objects.

main() doesn't have to be the first function in a program. However, it usually is.

# Programming with Functions

Each function should perform one task. For instance, if you were writing a C++ program to obtain a list of characters from the keyboard, alphabetize them, then print them to the screen, you *could* write all of this in one large main() function. Listing 18.1 shows how this was done in the C++ skeleton (program outline) as follows:

**Listing 18.1. A *main()* Function Skeleton Outlines an Entire C++ Program**

```
main()
    {
    // :
    // C++ code to get a list of characters
    // :
    // C++ code to alphabetize the characters
    // :
    // C++ code to print the alphabetized list on-screen
    // :

    return 0;
    }
```

The skeleton in Listing 18.1 is *not* a good way to write the program. Even though you could type this program in just a few lines of code, it would be much better to get in the habit of breaking up every program into distinct tasks. You should not use main() to do everything. In fact, you should use main() to do very little except call each of the other functions that actually do the work.

A better way to organize this program is to write separate functions for each task. This does not mean that each function should be only one line long; simply make sure that each function acts as a building block, and performs one distinct task in the program.

The skeleton in listing 18.2 shows a much better way to write the program just described.

**Listing 18.2. This Skeleton of the Same Program Uses Separate Functions for Each Task**

```
main()
    {
    getletters();       // Call a function that gets the
                        // numbers
    alphabetize();      // Call a function that alphabetizes
                        // the letters
    printletters();     // Call a function that prints
                        // letters on the screen
    return 0;           // Return to DOS
    }

getletters()
    {
    // :
    // C++ code to get a list of characters
    // :

    return;     // Return to main()
    }

alphabetize()
    {
    // :
    // C++ code to alphabetize the characters
    // :
    //
    return;     // Return to main()
    }

printletters()
    {
    // :
    // C++ code to print the alphabetized list on screen
    // :

    return;     // Return to main()
    }
```

The program outlined in listing 18.2 takes longer to type; however, the program is much better organized. The only thing that main() does is to control the other functions by showing, in one place, the order in which they are called. Each separate function does its thing, then returns to main(). The main() function then calls the next function until there are no more. The main() function then returns control to DOS.

> **Tip:** A good rule of thumb is that a function should not perform more than one task. If it does, you are probably doing too much in the function. You should break it into two or more functions.

The main() function is usually a calling function that controls the rest of the program.

Until now, you have typed the full program in the first function, main(). From this point on, in all but the smallest of programs, main() is simply a control of other functions that do the work.

These listings are not intended to be examples of real C++ programs; they are simply skeletons, or outlines, of programs. From these types of outlines, it is easier to write the actual full program. Before you write such a program, you know that it will have four distinct sections: a primary function-calling main() function, a keyboard data-entry function, an alphabetizing function, and a printing function.

You should never lose sight of your original programming problem. With the approach just described, you never do! Once again, study the main() calling routine in listing 18.2. Notice that you can glance at main() and get a feel for the overall program. And the rest of the program's statements won't get in the way. A large programming problem has been broken into distinct, separate tasks called functions; each function performs one primary job.

## More on Function Mechanics

Up to this point, very little has been said about naming and writing functions. However, you probably understand many of the goals of listing 18.2. A C++ function generally has the following properties:

♦ Each function must have a name.

♦ A function name is created and assigned by you, the programmer, and follows the naming rules for variables. A function name must begin with a letter or underscore (_). The name can contain letters, numbers, and the underscore.

♦ Each function name has one set of parentheses immediately following it. This helps you (and C++) distinguish functions from variables. The parentheses do not necessarily have to contain something. So far, all such parentheses in this book have been empty.

♦ The body of each function, starting immediately after the closing parenthesis of its name, must be enclosed by braces. This means that a block of one or more statements makes up the body of each function.

Use meaningful
function names;
for instance,
calc_balance()
is more descriptive
than xy3().

Although the outline that listing 18.2 shows is a good example of readable code, it can be improved (besides putting the actual C++ statements inside it to make it work). It might be better to use the underscore character (_) in the function names. The functions get_letters() and print_letters() are much easier to read than getletters() and printletters().

> **Caution:** Be sure to use the underscore character (_), and not a hyphen (-), when naming functions and variables. If you use a hyphen, C++ gets very confused, and produces misleading error messages.

All programs must
have a main()
function.

Listing 18.3 shows an example of a C++ function. You can already tell a lot about this function. You know that it isn't a complete program because it does not contain a main() function. All programs must have a main() function. The function name is calc_it. You know this because parentheses follow the name. These parentheses happen to have something in them. The body of the function is enclosed within a block of braces. Inside that block is a smaller block—the body of the while loop. A return statement is the last line of the function.

> **Tip:** Not every function requires a return statement as its last line. However, including a return is recommended: The compiler issues a warning if you don't. The return statement helps show your intent to return to the calling function at that point. Later, you learn when return is required. For now, however, get in the habit of including it anyway.

**Listing 18.3. This Function, Named *calc_it()*, Is an Example of a C++ Function**

```
calc_it(int     n)
    {
    // Function to print the square of a number
    int     square = 0;

    while (square <= 250)
        {
        square = n * n;
        cout << "The square of " << n << " is "
            << square << "\n";
        n++;
        }     // A block within the function
    return;
    }
```

## Calling and Returning Functions

A function call is similar to a temporary program detour.

You have been reading a lot about *function calling* and *returning control*. Although you might already understand these phrases from the description of functions so far, an illustration of a function call can be helpful.

A function call in C++ is similar to a detour on a highway. You are traveling along in the primary function referred to as main(), then run into a function-calling statement. You must temporarily leave the main() function and go execute the function's code. Once that function finishes (its return statement is reached), program control reverts back to main(). When you finish the detour, you end up back in your main routine to continue the trip. Control continues as main() proceeds to call other functions.

**Note:** Generally, the *calling function* controls function calls and their order. The *called functions* are controlled by the calling function.

A complete C++ program, with functions, will make all of this very clear. The following program, named C18FUN1.CPP, prints several messages to the screen. Each message printed is determined by the order of the functions.

Before worrying too much about what this program does, take a little time to study its structure. You ought to be able to see that three functions are defined in the program: main(), next_fun(), and third_fun(). The three functions appear sequentially. The body of each is enclosed within braces. At the end of each function is a return statement.

```
// C18FUN1.CPP
// This program illustrates function calls

#include <iostream.h>

void    next_fun(void)    // Second function - parentheses
                          // always required
    {
    cout << "Inside next_fun()\n";  // No variables defined
                                    // in function
    return;                         // Control is now returned
                                    // to main()
    }

void    third_fun(void)   // Last function called in program
    {
    cout << "Inside third_fun()\n";
    return;                   // Always return from
                              // all functions
    }
```

```
main()     // main() is ALWAYS the first C function executed
    {
    cout << "First function called main()\n";
    next_fun();      // Second function is called here
    third_fun();     // This function is called here
    cout << "main() is completed\n";   // All control
                                       // returns here
    return 0;                // Control is returned to DOS
    }                        // This brace concludes main()
```

The following is the output of this program:

```
First function called main()
Inside next_fun()
Inside third_fun()
main() is completed
```

Figure 18.1 shows a trace of this program's execution. Notice that main() controls which of the other functions are called, as well as the order in which they are called. Control *always* returns to the calling function once the called function finishes.

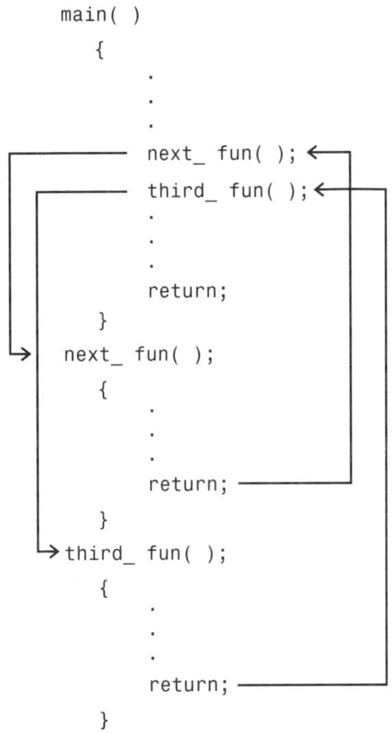

**Figure 18.1.**

The function calls involved in this program's execution are traced.

Notice in the listing that the user functions are preceded by void, and include void inside the parentheses. C++ requires this because it is a strongly typed language. Chapter 21, "Function Return Values and Prototypes", discusses the meaning of void.

To call a function, you just type its name, including the parentheses. Then, you type a semicolon. Remember that semicolons follow all executable statements in C++. And a function call (sometimes referred to as a *function invocation*) is an executable statement. The execution is the function's code that is called. Any function can call any other function. It just happens that main() is the only function that calls other user-written functions in this program.

You can tell that the following statement is a function call:

```
print_total();
```

print_total is not a C++ command or library function name; therefore, it must be the name of a variable or user-written function. Only function names end with the parentheses. Therefore, print_total(); must be a function call or the start of a function's code. Of these two possibilities, it must be a call to a function. The reason is that it ends with a semicolon. Without the semicolon, it would have to be the start of a function definition.

When you define a function—that is, when you type the function name and its subsequent code inside braces—you *never* follow the name with a semicolon. Notice in the previous program that main(), next_fun(), and third_fun() have no semicolons in the place in which these functions appear in the body of the program. Only in main(), where these two functions are called, does a semicolon follow the function names.

> **Caution:** You cannot define a function within another one. All function code must be listed sequentially, one after the other, throughout the program. One function's closing brace must appear before another's code can be listed.

## Examples

**1.** Suppose that you are writing a program to do the following:

Ask for the user's department. If it is Accounting, the user should receive the Accounting Department's report; if it is Engineering, the user should get this department's report. If the user's department is Marketing, this report should be given.

The following is a skeleton of such a program. It shows the code for main() in its entirety. The switch statement is a perfect function-calling statement for such a multiple-choice selection. The following shows only a skeleton of the other functions:

```
// Skeleton of a departmental report program

#include <iostream.h>

void    acct_report(void)
    {
    // :
    // Accounting report code goes here
    // :

    return;
    }

void    eng_report(void)
    {
    // :
    // Engineering report code goes here
    // :

    return;
    }

void    mtg_report()
    {
    // :
    // Marketing report code goes here
    // :

    return;
    }

main()
    {
    int    choice;

    do
        {
        cout << "Choose your department from ";
        cout << "the following list\n";
        cout << "\t1.   Accounting\n";
        cout << "\t2.   Engineering\n";
        cout << "\t3.   Marketing\n";
        cout << "What is your choice? ";
        cin >> choice;
        }
    while ((choice < 1) || (choice > 3)); // Ensure 1, 2,
                                          //   or 3

    switch (choice)
        {
        case    1:
            acct_report(); // Call accounting function
            break;         // Don't fall through
```

```
            case     2:
                eng_report();     // Call engineering function
                break;
            case     3:
                mtg_report();     // Call marketing function
                break;
        }
    return 0;        // Program returns to DOS when done
    }
```

The body of switch statements usually contains function calls. You can tell that these case statements execute functions. For instance, acct_report();, which is the first line of the first case, is not a variable name or C++ command. Instead, it is the name of a function defined in the program. If the user enters a 1 at the menu, the function named acct_report() executes. Once it finishes, control returns to the first case body, whose break; statement causes the switch to end. The main() function returns to DOS (or to your integrated C++ environment, if you are using it) when the return statement executes.

2. In the preceding example, the main() routine itself is not very well designed. The displaying of the menu should be done in a separate function.

The following is a rewrite of this sample program, with a fourth function added that prints the menu to the screen. This is a good example in which each function performs a single task. Again, the first three functions show only skeleton code. The reason is that the goal of these examples is to illustrate function calling and returning.

```
// 2nd skeleton of a departmental report program

#include <iostream.h>

void     menu_print(void)
    {
    cout << "Choose your department from ";
    cout << "the following list\n";
    cout << "\t1.   Accounting\n";
    cout << "\t2.   Engineering\n";
    cout << "\t3.   Marketing\n";
    cout << "What is your choice? ";
    return;       // Return to main()
    }

void     acct_report(void)
    {
    // :
    // Accounting report code goes here
    // :
```

```
    return;
    }

void    eng_report(void)
    {
    // :
    // Engineering report code goes here
    // :

    return;
    }

void    mtg_report(void)
    {
    // :
    // Marketing report code goes here
    // :

    return;
    }

main()
    {
    int     choice;

    do
        {
        menu_print();      // Call a function to do printing
                           // of menu
        cin >> choice;
        }
    while ((choice < 1) || (choice > 3)); // Ensure 1, 2,
                                          // or 3

    switch (choice)
        {
        case    1:
            acct_report();  // Call accounting function
            break;          // Don't fall through
        case    2:
            eng_report();   // Call engineering function
            break;
        case    3:
            mtg_report();   // Call marketing function
            break;
        }
    return 0;     // Program returns to DOS when done
    }
```

The menu-printing function does not have to follow main(); however, as it is the first function called, it seems best to define it there.

**3.** Readability is the key; therefore, programs broken into separate functions result in better code that is easier to read. You can write and test each function, one at a time. Once you write a general outline of the program, you can list a number of function calls in `main()`, and define their skeletons after `main()`.

The body of each function initially consists of `return` statements; therefore, the program compiles in its skeleton format. As you complete each function, you can compile and test the program *as you write it*. This approach results in more accurate programs. The separate functions let others who might later modify the program "zero in" on the code they need to change, without affecting the rest of the program.

Another useful habit, popular with many C++ programmers, is to separate functions from each other with a comment consisting of a line of asterisks (`*`) or hyphens (`·`). This makes it easy, especially in longer programs, to see in which place a function begins and ends. The following is another listing of the preceding program; however, it includes comments that help break up the program listing, making it even easier to see the four distinct functions:

```cpp
// 3nd skeleton of a departmental report program

#include <iostream.h>

void     menu_print(void)
    {
    cout << "Choose your department from ";
    cout << "the following list\n";
    cout << "\t1.   Accounting\n";
    cout << "\t2.   Engineering\n";
    cout << "\t3.   Marketing\n";
    cout << "What is your choice? ";
    return;      // Return to main()
    }

//***********************************************************

void     acct_report(void)
    {
    // :
    // Accounting report code goes here
    // :

    return;
    }
```

```
//***********************************************************

void    eng_report(void)
    {
    // :
    // Engineering report code goes here
    // :

    return;
    }

//***********************************************************

void    mtg_report(void)
    {
    // :
    // Marketing report code goes here
    // :

    return;
    }

//***********************************************************

main()
    {
    int    choice;

    do
        {
        menu_print();    // Call a function to do printing
                         // of menu
        cin >> choice;
        }
    while ((choice < 1) || (choice > 3)); // Ensure 1, 2,
                                          // or 3

    switch (choice)
        {
        case    1:
            acct_report();  // Call accounting function
            break;          // Don't fall through
        case    2:
            eng_report();   // Call engineering function
            break;
        case    3:
            mtg_report();   // Call marketing function
            break;
        }
    return 0;    // Program returns to DOS when done
    }
```

Because of space limitations, not all program listings in this book show functions separated in this manner. You might find, however, that your listings are easier to follow if you put the separating comments between your functions. The mailing list application in Appendix F uses these types of comments to separate its functions visually.

4. You can execute a function more than once simply by calling it from more than one place in a program. Alternatively, if you put a function call in the body of a loop, the function executes repeatedly until the loop finishes.

The following program uses functions to print the message C++ is Fun! both forward and backward several times on-screen. Notice that main() does not make every function call. The second function, name_print(), calls the function named reverse_print(). Trace the execution of the program's couts. Figure 18.2 shows the output from the program to help you trace its execution.

```cpp
// Filename: C18FUN2.CPP
// Prints C++ is Fun! several times on-screen

#include <iostream.h>

//*************************************************************

void      reverse_print(void)
    {
    // Print several C++ is Fun! messages, in reverse,
    // separated by tabs
    cout << "!nuF si ++C\t!nuF si ++C\t!nuF si ++C\t\n";
    return;     // Return to name_print()
    }

//*************************************************************

void      name_print(void)
    {
    // Print C++ is Fun! across a line, separated by tabs
    cout << "C++ is Fun!\tC++ is Fun!\t";
    cout << "C++ is Fun!\tC++ is Fun!\n";
    cout << "C + +  i s  F u n !\tC + +  i s  F u n !\t";
    cout << "C + +  i s  F u n !\n";

    reverse_print();     // Call next function from here
    return;              // Return to main()
    }

//*************************************************************

void      one_per_line(void)
    {
    // Print C++ is Fun! down the screen
    cout << "C\n+\n+\n \ni\ns\n \nF\nu\nn\n!\n";
    return;              // Return to main()
    }
```

```
main()
    {
    int     ctr;          // To control loops

    for (ctr = 1; ctr <= 5; ctr++)
        {
        name_print();  // Call function 5 times
        }

    one_per_line();     // Call last function once
    return 0;
    }
```

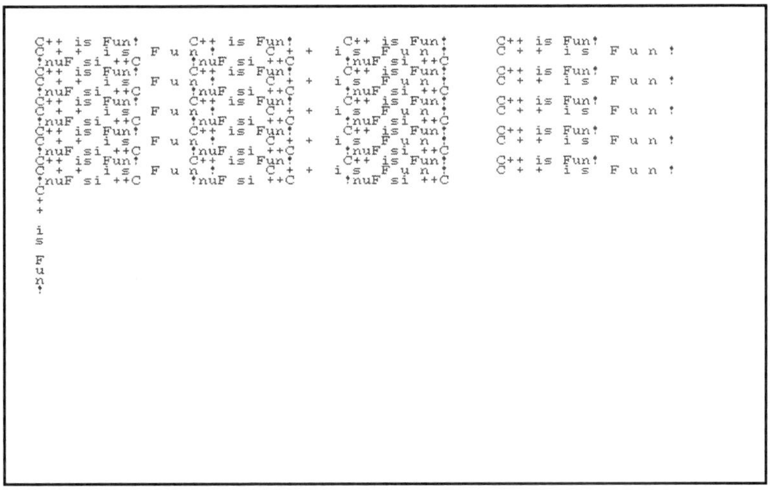

**Figure 18.2.**

A message is
printed several
times on-screen.

## Summary

Instead of typing long programs, you can break them up into separate functions.
That way, you can isolate your routines so that surrounding code doesn't get in the
way when you are concentrating on a section of your program.

There are other aspects of functions that add to their complexity, especially in the
way that variable values are recognized by all the program's functions. The next
chapter shows you how variables are handled between functions, and helps
strengthen your programming skills.

# Review Questions

The answers to Review Questions are in Appendix B.

**1.** True or false: A function should always include a `return` statement as its last command.

**2.** What is the name of the first function executed in a C++ program?

**3.** Which is better—one long function, or several smaller functions? Why?

**4.** How do function names differ from variable names?

**5.** How can you use comments to help visually separate functions from each other?

**6.** What is wrong with the following section of a program?

```
void     calc_it(void)
    {
    cout << "Getting ready to calculate the square of 25\n";

    sq_25()
        {
        cout << "The square of 25 is: "
            << (25 * 25) << "\n";
        return;
        }

    cout << "That is a big number!\n";
    return;
    }
```

**7.** Is the following a variable name, a function call, a function definition, or an expression?

```
scan_names();
```

# Review Exercises

**1.** Complete the program skeleton in the section of this chapter called "Calling and Returning Functions." Code the bodies of the functions and run it.

**2.** Write a program that prints the phrase It was the night before Christmas. Implement it as a group of functions. Have each one of the functions print one word to the screen, call the function that prints the next word. The output should be the phrase It was the night before Christmas.

**3.** Write a program that declares a global variable called ival and initializes it to 0. Write a function inc_ival() that print the value of ival to the screen, increments ival by 1, then calls itself if ival is less than 10. A function calling itself is called *recursion*, and is perfectly legal in C++. Write a main() function to call inc_ival().

# CHAPTER 19

# Variable Scope

The concept of *variable scope* is most important when you write functions. Variable scope determines which functions recognize certain variables. If a function recognizes a variable, the variable is visible to that function. Variable scope protects variables from inadvertant change by another function. A function should not be able to see or change a variable to which it does not need access.

This chapter introduces the following topics:

♦ Local variables

♦ Global variables

♦ Passing arguments

♦ Receiving parameters

♦ Automatic and static variables

The concept introduced in the last chapter, multiple functions, is much more useful when you learn about local and global variable scope.

## Global versus Local Variables

If you have programmed in BASIC only, the concept of local and global variables might be new to you. In many interpreted versions of BASIC, all variables are global. That is, the entire program knows what every variable is, and has the capability to change any variable. If you use a variable named SALES at the top of the program, even the last line in the program can use SALES.

Global variables can be dangerous. Parts of a program can inadvertently change a variable that shouldn't be altered. Suppose, for instance, that you need to write a program to keep track of grocery store inventory. You might keep track of sales percentages, discounts, retail and wholesale prices, and costs of produce and dairy products. Other areas over which you might want control include delivered prices, price changes, sales tax percentages, holiday markups, post-holiday markdowns, and so on.

The huge number of prices in such a system would be confusing. You would have to write a program to keep track of each kind of price. It would be easy to call the dairy prices d_prices, but also label the delivered prices d_prices. Either C++ will not enable you to do this (it will not let you define the same variable twice), or you will overwrite a value used for something else. Whatever happens, keeping track of all the different, but similarly named, prices would make the program confusing to write.

Global variables are visible across many program functions. Such variables can be dangerous because code can inadvertently overwrite a variable that has been initialized elsewhere in the program. It is better to have every variable local in your program; that way, only the functions that should be able to change the variables can do so.

A local variable can be seen (and changed) only from within the function in which it is defined. The variable cannot be used, changed, or erased from any other function without special programming that you learn about in Chapter 20, "Passing Values."

If you use only one function, main(), the question of global versus local variables is moot. You know, however, from reading the last chapter, that single-function programs are not recommended. When you type functions into your program, you must understand how to define variables to be local to the functions that need them. Later, when you learn about classes you learn how to protect variables even better.

## Defining Variable Scope

In Chapter 5, "Variables and Constants," you learned about two methods of defining variables:

- ◆ You can define a variable within the braces of a block of code (usually at the top of a function).

- ◆ You can define a variable before a function name, such as main().

Until now, all the program examples in this book have contained variables defined with the first method. You have yet to see the second way employed.

Because most of these programs consisted entirely of a single function referred to as main(), there was no reason to distinguish between the two methods. It is only when you use multiple functions in programs that these two variable definitions become critical.

Local variables are visible only in the block in which they are defined. These two methods of variable definitions describe the way local and global variables are defined. The following rules, specific to local and global variables, are very important:

- A variable is local *only if* you define it within the braces of a block.

- A variable is global *only if* you define it outside a function.

All variables you have seen so far have been local. They were all defined immediately after the opening braces of main(). Therefore, they were local to main(): only main() could use them. Other functions would have no idea that these variables existed, as they belonged to main() only. Once the function (or block) ends, all its local variables are destroyed.

> **Tip:** All local variables disappear when their block ends. A global variable is visible from its point of definition down into the source file.

A global variable is visible ("known") from its point of definition down into the source file. That is, if you define a global variable, any line in the rest of the program (no matter how many functions and lines of code follow) is capable of using that variable.

### Examples

**1.** The following section of code defines two local variables, i and j:

```
main()
    {
    int  i, j;      // Local since defined after brace

    // Rest of main() goes here
    }
```

These variables are visible to main() and not to any other function that might follow or be called by main().

**2.** The following section of code defines two global variables, g and h:

```
int  g, h;              // Global since defined before a function

main()
    {
    // main()'s code goes here
    }
```

It really doesn't matter if your #include lines go before or after global variable declarations.

**3.** Global variables can appear before any function. In the following program, main() uses no variables at all. However, both functions before main() can use sales and profit because these variables are global.

```
// Filename: C19GLO.CPP
// Program that contains 2 global variables

#include <iostream.h>
#include <iomanip.h>

float     sales, profit; // 2 global variables

void third_fun(void)
    {
    cout << "In the third function: \n";
    cout << "The sales in 3rd function is: "
        << setiosflags(ios::fixed) << setprecision(2) << sales <<
        ➥"\n";
    cout << "The profit in 3rd function is: "
        << setiosflags(ios::fixed) << setprecision(2) << profit
        ➥<< "\n";
    // If sales and profit were local, they would not be
    // visible by more than one function
    return;
    }

void do_fun(void)
    {
    sales = 20000.00;   // This variable is visible from
                        // this point down.
    profit = 5000.00;   // So is this one. They are both
                        // global.
    cout << "The sales in the 2nd function is: "
        << setiosflags(ios::fixed) << setprecision(2)
        << sales << "\n";
    cout << "The profit in the 2nd function is: "
        << setiosflags(ios::fixed) << setprecision(2) << profit
        ➥<< "\n\n";
    third_fun();        // Call 3rd function to show that
                        // globals are visible
    return;
    }

main()
    {
    cout << "No variables defined in main()\n\n";
    do_fun();            // Call the first function
    return 0;
    }
```

A global variable is visible from its point of definition down into the program. Statements appearing before global variable definitions cannot use those variables. Figure 19.1 shows the result of running the preceding program.

**Figure 19.1.**

Any line in a
program can use
global variables
once they are
defined.

```
No variables defined in main()

The sales in the 2nd function is: 20000.00
The profit in the 2nd function is: 5000.00

In the third function:
The sales in 3rd function is: 20000.00
The profit in 3rd function is: 5000.00
```

**Tip:** Declare all global variables at the top of your programs. Even though you can
define such variables later, you will be able to spot the variables faster if they are
at the top.

4. The following program uses both local and global variables. It should now
be obvious to you that j and p are local, and that i and z are global.

```cpp
// Filename: C19GLLO.CPP
// Program with both local and global variables
// Global Variables      Local Variables
//     i, z                   j, p

#include <iostream.h>
#include <iomanip.h>

float     z = 9.0;  // Global variable since defined before
                    // a function

void pr_again(void)
    {
    int  j = 5;    // Local to pr_again() only

    cout << j << " " << z << "\n";
        // This couldn't print p or i!
    return;   // Return to main()
    }

int  i = 0;          // Global variable since defined outside
                     // main()
```

```
main()
   {
   float    p;    // Local to main() only

   p = 9.0;       // Put value in global variable
   cout << i << "   " << p << " " << z << "\n";
   // Print global i and local p
   pr_again();    // Call next function
   return 0;      // Return to DOS
   }
```

j is defined in a function that main() calls. However, main() cannot use j because this variable is local to pr_again(). When pr_again() finishes, j completely disappears. The variable z is global from its point of definition on. That is the reason pr_again() cannot print i. The function pr_again() cannot print p because this variable is a local one to main() only.

Make sure that you can recognize local and global variables before continuing. If you are able to do this, the rest of the chapter will seem very easy.

**5.** Two variables, local to two different functions, can have the same name. They are distinct variables, stored in two different places in memory even though their names are identical.

The following short program uses two variables, both named age. They have two different values, and they are considered two very distinct variables. The first age is local to main(); the second age is local to get_age().

```
// Filename: C19LOC2.CPP
// Two different local variables with the same name

#include <iostream.h>

void get_age(void)
   {
   int  age;      // A different age - this one is local
                  // to get+age()

   cout << "What is your age again? ";
   cin >> age;
   return;
   }

main()
   {
   int  age;

   cout << "What is your age? ";
   cin >> age;
```

```
      get_age();      // Call the second function
      cout << "main()'s age is still: " << age << "\n";
      return 0;
      }
```

The output of this program is shown next. Study it carefully. Notice that main()'s last cout << does not print the newly changed age. Instead, cout << prints the only age known to main()—the age that is local to main(). Even though these variables have the same name, main()'s age has nothing to do with get_age()'s age. They might as well have different variable names.

```
What is your age? 28
What is your age again? 56
main()'s age is still 28
```

You should be careful when naming variables. Having two variables with the same name is misleading. It would be easy to become confused when changing this program later. If these variables truly need to be separate, name them differently, such as old_age and new_age, or ag1 and ag2. That convention helps you notice immediately that they are quite different.

6. There are a few times when overlapping the names of local variables does not add to confusion. However, you should be careful about overdoing it. Sometimes programmers use the same variable name as the name of the counter variable in a for loop. The following program illustrates an acceptable use of two local variables with the same name:

```
// Filename: C19LOC3.CPP
// Using two local variables with the same name as counting
// variables

#include <iostream.h>

void do_fun(void)
    {
    int  ctr;

    for (ctr = 10; ctr >= 0; ctr−)
        {
        cout << "do_fun()'s ctr is: " << ctr << "\n";
        }
    return;         // Return to main()
    }

main()
    {
    int  ctr;       // Loop counter

    for (ctr = 0; ctr <= 10; ctr++)
        {
```

```
        cout << "main()'s ctr is: " << ctr << "\n";
        }
    do_fun();      // Call second function
    return 0;
    }
```

Although this program simply prints 0 through 10, then 10 through 0, the use of ctr in both functions is not a problem. These variables do not hold important data that is to be processed; instead, they serve as for loop counting variables. Naming them both ctr causes little confusion, as their use is limited to control for loops only. Because a for loop initializes and increments variables, neither function relies on the other's ctr to do anything.

**7.** Be very careful about creating local variables with identical names in the same function. If a local variable is defined early in a function, and another local variable with the same name is defined again inside a new block, C++ uses only the innermost variable, until its block ends.

The following example helps clarify this confusing problem. The program contains one function with three local variables. See if you can find the three variables.

```
// Filename: C19MULI.CPP
// Program with multiple local variables called i

#include <iostream.h>

main()
    {
    int  i;        // Outer i

    i = 10;
        {
        int  i;    // New block's i

        i = 20;    // Outer i STILL holds a 10
        cout << i << " " << i << "\n";      // Print 20 20
            {
            int  i;    // Another new block and local
                       // variable

            i = 30;    // Innermost i only
            cout << i << " " << i << " " << i << "\n";
                // Print 30 30 30
            }    // Innermost i is now gone forever
        }        // Second i is gone forever (its block ended)
    cout << i << " " << i << " " << i << "\n";
        // Print 10 10 10
    return 0;
    }    // main() ends, and so does its variables
```

All local variables are local to the block in which they are defined. This program has three blocks, each one nested within another. You can define local variables immediately after an opening brace of a block; therefore, there are three distinct i variables in this program.

The local i disappears completely when its block ends (that is, when the closing brace is reached). C++ always prints the variable it sees as the "most local."

---

**Use Global Variables Rarely**

You might be asking yourself, "Why do I need to know about global and local variables?" At this point, that's an understandable question, especially if you've programmed only in BASIC until now. The bottom line is this: global variables can be dangerous. Code can inadvertently overwrite a variable that was initialized in another place in the program. It is better to have every variable in your program local to the function that needs to access it.

Please read that last sentence once more. Even though you now know how to make variables global, you should not do so without a compelling reason. Try to stay away from using global variables. It might seem easier to use global variables when writing programs with more than one function; if you make every variable that is used by each function global, you never have to worry whether or not one is visible to a certain function. However, a function can accidentally change a global variable. If you keep variables local to functions that need them, you protect their values.

---

# The Need for Passing Variables

You just learned the difference between local and global variables. You saw that by making your variables local, you protect their values. The reason is that the function which sees a variable is the only one that can modify the variable.

What do you do, though, if you have a local variable that you want to use in two or more functions? In other words, you might need a variable to be typed from the keyboard in one function. However, that same variable needs to be printed in another function. If the variable is local to the first function, how can the second one access it?

If two functions need to share a variable, you have two alternatives. One way is to declare the variable globally. This alternative is not preferred because you want only those two functions to "see" the variable. However, all functions could "see" it if it were global. The better way is to pass the local variable from one function to another. This alternative has a large advantage—the variable is known only to the two functions, and the rest of the program will not be able to access the variable.

> **Caution:** Never pass a global variable. C++ will get confused. There is no reason to pass global variables, as they are already visible to all functions.

You pass an argument when you pass one local variable to another function.

When you pass a local variable from one function to another, you are passing an argument from the first function to the next. You can pass more than one argument (variable) at a time if you want several local variables sent from one function to another. The receiving function gets parameters (variables) from the function that sent them. You should not worry too much about what you call these variables—either arguments or parameters. What is important to remember is that you are simply sending local variables from one function to another.

You need to know some additional terminology before you study some examples. When a function passes parameters, it is referred to as the *calling function*. The function that receives those arguments (which are named parameters when they are received) is referred to as the *receiving function*. Figure 19.2 shows a diagram that explains these new terms.

**Figure 19.2.**

You use the calling and receiving functions to pass a local variable from one function to another.

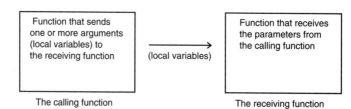

You must place the local variable in parentheses in both the calling and receiving functions to pass it from one function to another. For example, the local and global examples presented earlier did not pass local variables from main() to do_fun(). If a function name has empty parentheses, nothing is being passed to it. Given this, the following line passes two variables, total and discount, to a function named do_fun():

```
do_fun(total, discount);
```

It is sometimes said that a variable or function is defined. This has absolutely nothing to do with the #define preprocessor directive that defines constants. You define variables with such statements as these:

```
int     i, j;
int     m = 9;
float   x;
char    ara[ ] = "Tulsa";
```

These statements tell the program that these variables are needed, and you want them reserved. A function is defined when the C++ compiler reads its first statement that describes the name, and any variables that might have been passed to it. Never follow a function definition with a semicolon. Instead, always follow the statement that calls a function with a semicolon.

> **Note:** To some C++ purists, a variable is declared only when you write int i;, and it is truly defined only when you assign it a value, such as i = 7;. The variable is both declared and defined when you declare it and assign it a value at the same time, such as int i = 7;.

The following program contains two function definitions, main() and pr_it().

*The start of the main() function.*
   *Initialize the integer variable i to 5.*
   *Call the pr_it function, passing the i variable with*
      *the value of 5.*
   *Jump down to the function pr_it.*
      *Print the value of i to the screen, and return to*
      *the next line.*
      *Return to the main() function.*
   *Return to DOS.*

```
main()                  // The main() function definition
   {
   int  i = 5;          // Define an integer variable

   pr_it(i);            // Call the pr_it() function and
                        // pass it i
   return 0;            // Return to DOS
   }

void pr_it(int i)       // The pr_it() function definition
   {
   cout << i << "\n";   // Call the cout function
   return;              // Return to main()
   }
```

A passed parameter is treated as a local variable in the receiving function; therefore, the cout in pr_it() prints a 5, even though main() was the function that initialized this variable.

When you pass arguments to a function, the receiving function has no idea of the data types of the incoming variables. Therefore, in front of the name of the parameter, you must include its data type. In the preceding example, the definition of pr_it() (the first line of the function) contains the type, int, of the incoming variable i. Notice that the main() calling function does not need to indicate the variable type. In this example, main() already knows what type of variable i is (an integer); only pr_it() needs to know that i is an integer.

**Tip:** C++ requires that you declare the type of the parameters in the receiving function. Precede each parameter in the function's parentheses with its data type followed by a space.

## Examples

**1.** The following includes a `main()` function that contains three local variables. `main()` passes one of the variables to the first function, and two of them to the second function.

```
// Filename: C19LOC1.CPP
// Passes three local variables to functions

#include <iostream.h>
#include <iomanip.h>

void pr_init(char initial)      // NEVER put a semicolon after
                                // a function definition
    {
    cout << "Your initial is really " << initial << "? \n";
    return;                      // Return to main()
    }

void pr_other(int age, float salary)     // MUST type BOTH
                                         // parameters
    {
    cout << "You look young for " << age << "\n";
    cout << "And $"
      << setiosflags(ios::fixed) << setprecision(2) << salary
        << " is a LOT of money!";
    return;                      // Return to main()
    }

main()
    {
    char      initial;      // Three variables local to main()
    int       age;
    float     salary;

    // Fill these variables in main()
    cout << "What is your initial? ";
    cin >> initial;
    cout << "What is your age? ";
    cin >> age;
    cout << "What is your salary? ";
    cin >> salary;
    pr_init(initial);          // Call pr_init() and pass it the
                               // initial
    pr_other(age, salary);     // Call pr_other() and pass
                               // it the other two arguements
    return 0;
    }
```

**2.** A receiving function can contain its own local variables. As long as the names are not the same, these local variables do not conflict with the passed ones. In the following program, the second function receives a passed variable from `main()`, and also defines its own local variable named `price_per`.

```
// Filename: C19LOC4.CPP
// Second function has its own local variable

#include <iostream.h>
#include <iomanip.h>

void compute_sale(int gallons)
    {
    float     price_per = 12.45;  // Local to
                                  // compute_sale()

    cout << "The total is: $"
         << setiosflags(ios::fixed)  << setprecision(2)
         << (price_per * (float)gallons) << "\n";
    // Had to type cast gallons since it was integer
    return;                         // Return to main()
    }

main()
    {
    int  gallons;

    cout << "Richard's Paint Service\n";
    cout << "How many gallons of paint did you buy?";
    cin >> gallons;             // Get gallons in main()
    compute_sale(gallons);    // Compute total in function
    return 0;
    }
```

**3.** The following sample lines test your skill at recognizing calling and receiving functions. Being able to recognize the difference is half the battle in understanding them.

```
do_it()
```

The preceding code must be the first line of a new function. The reason is that no semicolon appears at the end of the line.

```
do_it2(sales);
```

The preceding code calls a function named `do_it2()`. The calling function passes the variable called `sales` to `do_it2()`.

```
pr_it(float total)
```

The preceding is the first line of a function that receives a floating-point variable from the calling function. All receiving functions must specify the type of each variable that is passed.

```
pr_them(float total, int number)
```

The preceding is the first line of a function that receives two variables; one is a floating-point variable, and the other is an integer. This line cannot be calling the function pr_them. The reason is that no semicolon appears at the end of the line.

# Automatic and Static Variables

The terms *automatic* and *static* describe what happens to local variables when a function returns to the calling procedure. By default, all local variables are automatic. This means that local variables are erased completely when their function ends. To declare a variable automatic, prefix its definition with the word auto. Because all local variables are automatic by default, the auto is optional. Study the two statements after main()'s opening brace:

```
main()
    {
    int          i;
    auto float   x;
    // Rest of main() goes here
```

Both statements declare automatic local variables. Because auto is the default, x does not really need it. C++ programmers rarely use the auto keyword, as all local variables are automatic by default.

Automatic variables are local, and disappear when their function ends. The opposite of an automatic variable is a static variable. All global variables are static. Local static variables are not erased when their functions end; they retain their value in case the function is ever called a second time. When defining a variable, place the keyword static in front of it when you want to declare it as static. The following section of code defines three variables: i, j, and k. The variable i is automatic. However, j and k are static.

```
my_fun()              // Start of new function definition
    {
    int          i;
    static int   j = 25;   // Both j and k are static
                           // variables
    static int   k = 30;
```

Always assign an initial value to a static variable when you declare it, as in the last two lines of the preceding code. That initial value will be placed there only the first time `my_fun()` executes. If you do not assign a static variable an initial value, C++ initializes the static variable to zero the first time it is executed.

> **Tip:** Static variables are good to use when you write functions that keep track of a count, or add to a total when called. If the variables that are used for either of these two purposes were local and automatic, their values would disappear when the function ended, destroying the totals.

# Rules for Automatic and Static Variables

A local automatic variable disappears when its block ends. All local variables are automatic by default. You can either prefix a variable (at its definition time) with the `auto` keyword, or leave it off; the variable will still be automatic, and its value will be destroyed when the block in which the variable is local ends.

A local static variable does not lose its value when its function ends. The static variable remains local to that function. If the function is called again, the static variable's value would still remain in place.

## Examples

**1.** Consider the following program:

```
// Filename: C19STA1.CPP
// Attempts to use a static variable without a static
// declaration
#include <iostream.h>

void triple_it(int ctr)
    {
    int  total, ans;    // Local automatic variables

    // Triple whatever value is passed to it and add up
    // the total

    total = 0;      // Will hold total of all numbers
                    // tripled

    ans = ctr * 3; // Triple number passed
    total += ans;  // Add up triple numbers while this is
                   // called

    cout << "The number " << ctr
         << ", multiplied by 3 is: " << ans << "\n";

    if (total > 300)
        {
        cout << "The total of the triple numbers ";
        cout << "is over 300\n";
        }
```

```
      return;
      }
  main()
      {
      int  ctr;        // Used by the for loop to call
                       // a function 25 times

      for (ctr = 1; ctr <= 25; ctr++)
          {
          triple_it(ctr);     // Pass the ctr to function called
                              // triple_it()
          }
      return 0;
      }
```

This program does not do much. However, if you study it, you might sense that something is wrong. The program passes numbers from 1 to 25 to the function called `triple_it`. The function triples the number, then prints it.

The variable named `total` is initially set to 0. The idea is to add up the triple numbers and print a message when the total of the triples goes over 300. However, that `cout` will never execute. Each of the twenty-five times this subroutine is called, `total` gets set back to 0 again. It is an automatic variable whose value is erased and initialized each time its procedure is called. The next example fixes this problem.

**2.** If you want `total` to retain its value, even after the procedure ends, you have to make it static. A local variable is automatic by default. Therefore, the `static` keyword overrides the default and makes the variable static. The variable's value is then retained each time the subroutine is called.

The following program corrects the intent of the preceding program:

```
// Filename: C19STA2.CPP
// Uses a static variable with the static declaration

#include <iostream.h>

void triple_it(int ctr)
    {
    static int    total = 0;    // Local and static
    int           ans;          // Local and automatic

    // Triple whatever value is passed to it, then add up
    // the total

    // total will be set to 0 only the FIRST time this
    // function is called

    ans = ctr * 3; // Triple number passed
    total += ans;  // Total triple numbers
```

```
    cout << "The number " << ctr
        << ", multiplied by 3 is: " << ans << "\n";

    if (total > 300)
        {
        cout << "The total of the triple numbers ";
        cout << "is over 300\n";
        }
    return;
    }

main()
    {
    int  ctr;        // Used by the for loop to call
                     // a function 25 times

    for (ctr = 1; ctr <= 25; ctr++)
        {
        triple_it(ctr);     // Pass the ctr to the function called
                            // triple_it()
        }
    return 0;
    }
```

Figure 19.3 shows this program's output. Notice that the function's cout is triggered, even though total is a local variable. It is static; therefore, its value is not erased when the function finishes. When the function is called a second time by main(), total's previous value (when you left the routine) is still there.

This does not mean that local static variables become global. The main program cannot refer to, use, print, or change total. The reason is that it is local to the second function. *Static* simply means that the local variable's value will still be there if the program calls that function again.

**Figure 19.3.**

The value of a
static variable is
not erased when
the function
finishes.

## Summary

The concept of parameter passing is important to know because local variables are better than global ones; local variables are protected in their own functions, but are shared among other functions. If the local data is to remain in those variables, in case the function is called again in the same program, the variables should be made static; if they are automatic, their values would disappear.

Most of the information in this chapter will become clearer as you use functions in your own programs. To understand functions, you need to learn three additional concepts:

- ♦ Passing arguments (variables) by value (or "by copy")
- ♦ Passing arguments (variables) by address (or "by reference")
- ♦ Returning values from functions

The first two items deal with the way local variables are passed and received. The third item describes the way that receiving functions send values back to the calling functions. The next chapter focuses on these methods of passing parameters and returning values.

## Review Questions

The answers to Review Questions are in Appendix B.

1. True or false: A function should always include a `return` statement as its last command.

2. How do you refer to a local variable that is passed—an argument or a parameter?

3. True or false: A function that is passed variables from another function cannot have its own local variables, as well.

4. What must appear inside the receiving function's parentheses, besides the variables passed to it?

5. Should the variable in the following situation be automatic or static: the variable is in a function that keeps track of a total or count every time it is called?

6. When would you pass a global variable to a function?

# Review Exercises

**1.** Write a program that asks for the following in `main()`:

```
The age of the user's dog
```

Write a second function, named `people()`, that computes the dog's age in "people" years (multiplying the dog's age by 7 to get the equivalent people years).

**2.** Write a function that counts the number of times the function is called. Name the function `count_it()`. Do not pass it anything. Print the following message in the body of `count_it()`:

```
The number of times this function has been called is: ##
## is the actual number.
```

> **Tip:** The variable must be local; therefore, make it static, and initialize it to zero when you first define it.

**3.** The following program contains several problems, some of which produce errors. One problem (for a hint, find all global variables) is not an error, but is a bad location of a variable declaration. See if you can spot some of the problems in the program, and rewrite it so that it works better.

```cpp
// Filename: C19BAD.CPP
// Program with bad uses of variable declarations

#include <iostream.h>

#define NUM 10

char city[ ] = "Miami";
int  count;

main()
    {
    int  abc;

    count = NUM;
    abc = 5;
    do_var_fun();

    cout << abc << " " << count << " " << pgm_var << " "
        << xyz;
    return 0;
    }

int  pgm_var = 7;
```

```
void do_var_fun(void)
    {
    char xyz = 'A';

    xyz = 'b';
    cout << xyz << " " << pgm_var << " " << abc << " "
        << city;
    return;
    }
```

# CHAPTER 20

# Passing Values

C++ provides two methods for passing variables between functions. This chapter explores both methods. The one you use depends on how you want the passed variables changed.

The concepts discussed here are not new to the C++ language. Other programming languages—such as Pascal, FORTRAN, and QBasic—pass parameters with similar techniques. A truly structured computer language has the capability to pass information between functions.

This chapter introduces the following topics:

♦ Passing variables by value

♦ Passing arrays by address

♦ Passing nonarrays by address

Pay close attention to this chapter as it explains these special passing issues. Most of the programs in the rest of the book rely on the methods described here.

## Passing by Value (or by Copy)

The phrases "passing by value" and "passing by copy" mean the same thing in computer terms. Some textbooks and C++ programmers say that arguments are passed by value, and some say that they are passed by copy. Both describe one of the two methods by which arguments are passed to receiving functions. (The other method, described later in this chapter, is called "passing by address" or "passing by reference.")

> **Note:** When an argument (local variable) is passed *by value*, a copy of the variable's value is assigned to the receiving function's parameter. If more than one variable is passed by value, a copy of each variable's value is assigned to the receiving function's parameters.

When passing by value, a copy of the variable's value is passed to the receiving function.

Figure 20.1 shows the action of passing an argument by value. The actual variable i is not passed, but the *value* of i (which is 5) is passed to the receiving function. There is not just one variable called i, but actually two variables. The first is local to main(), and the second is local to pr_it(). Both variables have the same name, but because they are local to their respective functions, no conflict exists. The variable does not have to be called i in both functions; the value of i is sent to the receiving function, so it does not matter what the receiving function called the variable that receives the value.

**Figure 20.1.**

Passing the variable *i* by value.

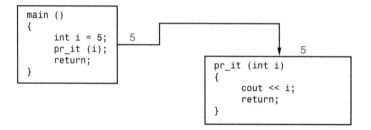

In this case, when passing and receiving variables among functions, you should retain the *same* names. Even though they are not the same variables, they hold the same value. In this example, the value of 5 is passed from main()'s i to pr_it()'s i.

Because a copy of i's value is passed to the receiving function (and *not* the actual variable), if pr_it() changed i, that function would be changing only its copy of i, not main()'s i. With this technique, you can pass a copy of a variable to a receiving function, but the receiving function cannot modify the calling function's variable. Thus, you have true separation of functions and variables.

All of the C++ nonarray variables that you have seen so far are passed by value. You do not have to do anything special to pass variables by value except to pass them in the calling function's argument list, and receive them in the receiving function's parameter list.

> **Note:** The default method for passing parameters is by value, as just described, unless you pass arrays. Arrays are always passed by address, the method described later in this chapter.

## Examples

1. The following program asks for the user's weight. The program then passes the weight to a function that calculates the equivalent weight on the moon. The second function uses the passed value and calculates with it. After the weight has been passed to the second function, that function can treat it as though it were a local variable.

*Comments to identify the program.*
*Include the header file iostream.h.*
*Start of the moon() function.*
    *Take the value of weight and divide it by 6.*
    *Print You weigh only X pounds on the moon! to the screen.*
    *Return out of the moon() function.*

*Start of the main() function.*
    *Declare the variable weight as an integer.*
    *Print How many pounds do you weigh? to the screen.*
    *Obtain an integer from the keyboard.*
    *Call the moon() function and pass it the variable weight.*
    *Return out of the main() function.*

```cpp
// Filename: C20PASS1.CPP
// Calculates the user's weight in a second function

#include <iostream.h>

void     moon(int weight)     // Declare the passed parameter
    {
    // Moon weights are 1/6th that of Earth weights
    weight /= 6;              // Divide the weight by 6

    cout << "You weigh only " << weight
         << " pounds on the moon!\n";
    return;                   // Return to main()
    }

main()
    {
    int     weight;   // main()'s local weight

    cout << "How many pounds do you weigh? ";
    cin >> weight;
    moon(weight);     // Call the moon() function and pass
                      // it the weight
    return 0;         // Return to DOS
    }
```

Here is the output of this program:

```
How many pounds do you weigh? 120
You weigh only 20 pounds on the moon!
```

**2.** You can rename a passed variable in the receiving function. That variable is distinct from the calling function's variable. The following program is the same program shown in example 1, except that the receiving function calls the passed variable earth_weight. A new variable, moon_weight, which is local to the receiving function, is used for the moon's equivalent weight.

```cpp
// Filename: C20PASS2.CPP
// Calculates the user's weight in a second function

#include <iostream.h>

void    moon(int earth_weight)         // Declare the passed
                                       // parameter
    {
    int    moon_weight;

    // Moon weights are 1/6th that of Earth weights
    moon_weight = earth_weight / 6;   // Divide the weight
                                      // by 6

    cout << "You weigh only " << moon_weight
         << " pounds on the moon!\n";
    return;                            // Return to main()
    }

main()
    {
    int     weight;    // main()'s local weight

    cout << "How many pounds do you weigh? ";
    cin >> weight;
    moon(weight);      // Call the moon() function and
                       // pass it the weight
    return 0;          // Return to DOS
    }
```

The resulting output is identical to that of the first program. Renaming the passed variable changes nothing.

**3.** The following program passes three variables, of three different types, to the receiving function. In the receiving function's parameter list, each of these variable types must be declared.

This program prompts the user for three values in the main() function. The main() function then passes those variables to the receiving function, which calculates and prints values related to those passed variables. When the

receiving function modifies a variable passed to it, it does *not* affect the
calling function's variable. When variables are passed by value, the *value*—
not the variable itself—is passed.

```cpp
// Filename: C20PASS3.CPP
// Gets grade information for a student

#include <iostream.h>

void     check_grade(char lgrade, float average, int tests)
     {
     switch (tests)
          {
          case    0:
               cout << "You will get your current grade of "
                    << lgrade << "\n";
               break;
          case 1:
               cout << "You still have time to ";
               cout << "bring your average ";
               cout << "of " << average <<
                    " up.  Study hard!\n";
               break;
          default:
               cout << "Relax -- You still have ";
               cout << "plenty of time.\n";
               break;
          }
     return;
     }

main()
     {
     char        lgrade;   // Letter grade
     int         tests;    // Number of tests yet taken
     float       average;  // Student's average based on
                           // 4.0 scale

     cout << "What letter grade do you want? ";
     cin >> lgrade;
     cout << "What is your current test average? ";
     cin >> average;
     cout << "How many tests do you have left? ";
     cin >> tests;

     check_grade(lgrade, average, tests);  // Call function
                              // and pass 3 variables by value

     return 0;
     }
```

# Passing by Address (or by Reference)

The phrases "passing by address" and "passing by reference" mean the *very same thing*. Some textbooks and C++ programmers say that arguments are passed by address, and some say that they are passed by reference. The first section of this chapter described the passing of arguments by value (or by copy). This section describes the passing of arguments by address (or by reference).

When you pass an argument (local variable) by address, the variable's address is assigned to the receiving function's parameter. (If you pass more than one variable by address, each of their addresses is assigned to the receiving function's parameters.)

All variables in memory (RAM) are stored at memory addresses. Figure 20.2 illustrates memory addresses. For more detail about your memory's internal representation, refer to Appendix A.

**Figure 20.2.**

Memory addresses.

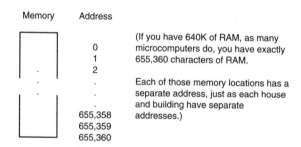

When you tell C++ to define a variable (such as int i;), you are requesting that C++ find a blank place in memory and assign that memory's address to i. When your program prints or uses the variable called i, C++ knows to go to i's address and print what is there.

Six variables are defined this way:

```
int        i;
float      x = 9.8;
char       ara[ 2 ] = {'A', 'B'};
int        j = 8;
int        k = 3;
```

C++ might arbitrarily place these variables in memory at the addresses shown in figure 20.3.

You don't know what is in the variable named i because you have not yet put anything in it. Before you use i, initialize it with a value. (All variables except character variables usually take more than one byte of memory.)

**Figure 20.3.**

After variables are
defined and placed
in memory.

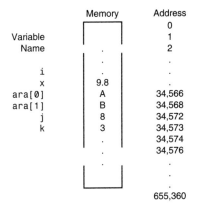

All C++ arrays are
passed by address.

The *address* of the variable—not its value—is copied to the receiving function
when you pass a variable by address. In C++, *all arrays are passed by address*.
(Actually, it's a copy of the array's address that gets passed, but you will understand
this better when you learn more about arrays and pointers in Part VI.) The following
important rule holds true for programs that pass by address:

**Note:** Every time you pass a variable by address, if the receiving function
changes the variable, it is also changed in the calling function.

If you pass an array to a function and that function changes the array, the change
will still be with the array when the function returns to the calling function. Unlike
passing by value, passing by address gives you the ability to change a variable in
the receiving function and keep the change in effect in the calling function as well.
The following sample program will help illustrate this concept.

```
// Filename: C20ADD1.CPP
// Program that passes by address

#include <iostream.h>
#include <string.h>

void     change_it(char c[ 4 ]) // You MUST tell the
                                // function that c is an array

    {
    cout << c << "\n";          // Print as it is passed
    strcpy(c, "USA");           // Change the array, both here
                                // AND in main()

    return;
    }

main()
    {
```

```
char      name[ 4 ] = "ABC";

change_it(name);       // Passed by address because it is
                       // an array
cout << name << "\n";  // Called function can change
                       // array
return 0;
}
Here is the output of this program:
ABC
USA
```

At this point, you should have no trouble understanding that the array is passed from main() to the function called change_it(). Even though change_it() calls the array c, that function refers to the same array passed to it, which was called name in the main() function.

Figure 20.4 shows how the array is passed. The value of the array is not passed from name to c, but both arrays are the same thing.

**Figure 20.4.**

Passing an array by address.

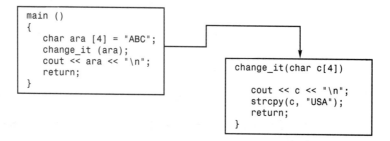

Because the actual address of name is passed to the function, even though the array is called c in the receiving function, c is still the same array as name. Figure 20.5 shows how C++ accomplishes this at the memory address level.

**Figure 20.5.**

The array being passed is the same as that of the receiving function, despite the different names.

```
                        Memory      Address
          Variable
          Name          .            .
                        .            .
                        .            .
name[0]--c[0]->         U          41,324      (Keep in mind that the
name[1]--c[1]->         S          41,325      actual address will depend
name[2]--c[2]->         A          41,326      on where your C++ compiler
                        .            .          puts the variables.)
                        .            .
                        .            .
```

The variable array is referred to as name in main(), but as c in change_it(). The address of name is copied to the receiving function, so the variable gets changed no matter what it is called in either function. Because change_it() changes the array, it is also changed in main().

## Examples

1. You can now use a function to fill an array with user input. The following program asks for the user's first name in the function called get_name(). As the user types the name in the array, the name is also being typed into main()'s array. main() then passes the array to pr_name(), where it is printed.

If arrays were passed by value, this program would not work; only the array value would be passed to the receiving functions.

```
// Filename: C20ADD2.CPP
// Gets a name in an array and then prints it,
// using separate functions

#include <iostream.h>

void    get_name(char name[ 25 ])    // Pass the array
                                     // by address
     {
     cout << "What is your first name? ";
     cin >> name;
     return;
     }

void    print_name(char name[ 25 ])
     {
     cout << "\n\n Here it is: " << name << "\n";
     return;
     }

main()
     {
     char    name[ 25 ];

     get_name(name);      // Get the user's name
     print_name(name);    // Print the user's name
     return 0;
     }
```

When you pass an array, be sure to specify the array's type in the receiving function's parameter list. If the preceding program declared the passed array with

```
get_name(char name)
```

the function get_name() would respond as if it were being passed a single character variable, *not* a character array.

You don't have to put the array size in the brackets. The following statement would work as the first line of get_name():

```
get_name(char name[ ])
```

2. Many programmers pass character arrays to functions in order to erase the arrays. The following function is called clear_it().

```
clear_it(char ara[ 10 ], int num_els)
    {
    int     ctr;

    for (ctr = 0; ctr <= num_els; ctr++)
        {
        ara[ ctr ] = '\0';
        }
    return;
    }
```

This function expects two parameters: a character array and the total number of elements declared for that array. The array is passed by address (as all arrays are), and the number of elements, num_els, is passed by value (as all nonarrays are). When the function finishes, the array will be cleared (all its elements will be set to null zero). Subsequent functions that use the array will then have a fresh array.

The ara brackets do not need to have a number. The 10 in this example simply serves as a placeholder for the brackets. Any value (or no value) that you want to substitute will work too.

## Passing Nonarrays by Address

You should now understand the difference between passing variables by value and by address. You can pass arrays by address and pass nonarrays by value. You can override the default passing by value for nonarrays if you want. This is not always the best choice because the called function can damage values in the calling function, but sometimes it is helpful.

You can pass nonarrays by address as well.

If you want a nonarray variable changed in a receiving function, and you want the change also kept in the calling function, you must override C++'s default (passing by value) and pass the variable by address. (You will understand this section better when you learn how arrays and pointers relate.) To pass a nonarray by address, you must do the following:

1. Precede the variable in the calling function with an ampersand (&) symbol.

2. Precede the variable in the receiving function with an asterisk (*) everywhere the variable appears.

This technique might sound strange, and it is at this point. Not many C++ programmers override the default passing by value. When you learn about pointers, you will have little need for this technique. Most C++ programmers do not like to clutter their code with those extra ampersands and asterisks, but they know they can use them if necessary.

## Examples

1. The following program passes a nonarray variable by address from `main()` to a function. The function changes the variable and returns to `main()`. Because the variable is passed by address, `main()` recognizes the new value.

```cpp
// Filename: C20ADD3.CPP
// Demonstrates passing nonarrays by address

#include <iostream.h>

void    do_fun(int *amt)      // Inform function of passing
                              // by address
    {
    *amt = 85;                // Assign new value to amt
    cout << "In do_fun(), amt is " << *amt << "\n";
    return;
    }


main()
    {
    int    amt;

    amt = 100;         // Assign a value in main()
    cout << "In main(), amt is " << amt << "\n";
    do_fun(&amt);      // The & means to pass it by address
    cout << "After return, amt is " << amt
         << " in main()\n";
    return 0;
    }
```

The output of this program is shown here:

```
In main(), amt is 100
In do_fun(), amt is 85
After return, amt is 85 in main()
```

Notice that `amt` changed in the receiving function. Because `amt` was passed by address, it gets changed also in the calling function.

2. You can use a function to get the user's keyboard values, and `main()` will recognize those values as long as you pass them by address.

The following program calculates the cubic feet in a swimming pool by requesting the length, width, and depth in one function; then calculates the cubic feet of water in another function; and then prints the answer in a third function. The purpose of `main()` is clearly to be a controlling function, passing variables between the functions by address.

```cpp
// Filename: C20POOL.CPP
// Calculates cubic feet in a swimming pool

#include <iostream.h>

void    get_values(int *length, int *width, int *depth)
    {
    cout << "What is the pool's length? ";
    cin >> *length;
    cout << "What is the pool's width? ";
    cin >> *width;
    cout << "What is the pool's average depth? ";
    cin >> *depth;
    return;
    }

void    calc_cubic(int *length, int *width,
                   int *depth, int *cubic)
    {
    // This may look confusing, but you MUST precede each
    // variable with an asterisk.
    *cubic = (*length) * (*width) * (*depth);
    return;
    }

void    print_cubic(int *cubic)
    {
    cout << "\nThe pool has " << *cubic << " cubic feet\n";
    return;
    }


main()
    {
    int     length, width, depth, cubic;

    get_values(&length, &width, &depth);
    calc_cubic(&length, &width, &depth, &cubic);
    print_cubic(&cubic);
    return 0;
    }
```

Here is the output of the program:

```
What is the pool's length? 16
What is the pool's width? 32
What is the pool's average depth? 6
The pool has 3072 cubic feet
```

# Summary

You now have a complete understanding of the ways you can pass data to functions in Borland C++. Because you will be using local variables as much as possible, you need to know how to pass them between functions so that they can share data, yet keep the data away from functions that don't need it.

There are two ways to pass data: by value and by address. When you pass data by value—the default method for nonarrays—only a copy of the variable's contents is passed. If the receiving function modifies its parameters, those variables are not modified in the calling function. When you pass data by address, as is done with arrays and nonarray variables preceded by an ampersand (&), the receiving function can change the data in both functions.

When passing values, you must ensure that they match in number and type. If they do not match, potential problems exist. For example, suppose that you pass an array and a floating-point variable, but in the receiving function, you receive a floating-point variable followed by an array. The data will not get to the receiving function properly because the parameter data types do not match the variables being passed. Chapter 21 shows you how to protect against such a disaster by prototyping all functions.

# Review Questions

Answers to Review Questions are in Appendix B.

1. What kind of variable is always passed by address?

2. What kind of variable is always passed by value?

3. True or false: If a variable is passed by value, it is also passed by copy.

4. If a variable is passed to a function by value and the function changes that variable, will it be changed in the calling function?

5. If a variable is passed to a function by address and the function changes that variable, will it be changed in the calling function?

6. What is wrong with the following function?

```
do_fun(x, y, z)
    {
    cout << "The variables are: " << x << ", " << y
        << ", and " << z;
    return;
    }
```

7. If you pass an array *and* a nonarray variable to a function at the same time, which of the following is correct?

    A. Both variables are passed by address.

    B. Both variables are passed by value.

    C. One variable is passed by address, and the other variable is passed by value.

## Review Exercises

1. Write a main() function and a second function that main() calls. Ask for the user's income in main(). Pass the income to the second function and print a congratulatory message if the user makes more than $50,000 or an encouragement message if the user makes less.

2. Write a three-function program, consisting of the following functions:

```
main()
fun1()
fun2()
```

Declare a 10-element character array in main(), fill it with the letters A through J in fun1(), and print that array backward in fun2().

3. Write a program whose main() function passes a number to a function called print_aster(). The print_aster() function prints that many asterisks on a line, across the screen. If print_aster() is passed a number greater than 80, display an error, because most screens will not be able to print more than that. When finished, return control to main() and then return to the operating system.

4. Write a function to which two integer values are passed by address. Make the function declare a third local variable. Use the third variable as an intermediate variable, and swap the values of both integers passed. In other words, if the calling function passes it old_pay and new_pay, as in

```
swap_it(old_pay, new_pay);
```

the function swap_it() should reverse the two values so that the old_pay and new_pay values are swapped when control is returned to the calling function.

# CHAPTER 21

# Function Return Values and Prototypes

So far, you have passed all variables to functions in one direction: from a calling function to a receiving function. You have yet to see how data is passed back *from* the receiving function to the calling function. When you pass variables by address, the data gets changed in both functions, but that is different from actually passing data back. This chapter shows you how to write function return values that improve your programming power.

Borland C++ requires that you prototype every function you write. Prototypes ensure data-type correctness of passed and returned values.

This chapter introduces the following topics:

♦ Returning values from functions

♦ Prototyping functions

♦ Understanding header files

After you complete your understanding of functions and how to use them, you will be writing better, more powerful, and more accurate programs.

# Function Return Values

Put the return value at the end of the return statement.

None of the functions described so far in this book returned values to the calling routine. Functions that return values offer a new opportunity. Instead being able to pass data in one direction—from calling function to receiving function—you can pass data back from a function to its calling function.

When you want to return a value from a function to its calling function, put the return value after the `return` statement. To make the return value clearer, many programmers put parentheses around the return value, like this:

```
return (return value);
```

> **Caution:** Do not return global variables. Not only will you confuse your compiler, but there is no need to do so because their values are already known throughout the code.

The calling function must have a use for the return value. Suppose, for example, that you wrote a function to calculate the average of three integer variables passed to it. If you return the average, the calling function will have to receive that return value. The following example helps illustrate this principle:

```cpp
// Filename: C21AVG.CPP
// Calculates the average of three input values

#include <iostream.h>

int    calc_av(int num1, int num2, int num3)
    {
    int    local_avg;   // Holds average for these numbers

    local_avg = (num1 + num2 + num3) / 3;
    return (local_avg);
    }


main()
    {
    int    num1, num2, num3;
    int    avg;     // Will hold the return value

    cout << "Please type three numbers ";
    cout << "(such as 23 54 85) ";
    cin >> num1 >> num2 >> num3;

    // Call the function, passing the numbers, and accept
    // return value
    avg = calc_av(num1, num2, num3);
    cout << "\n\nThe average is " << avg << "\n";
    return 0;
    }
```

Note this sample output from the program:

```
Please type three numbers (such as 23 54 85) 30 40 50
The average is 40
```

Study this program carefully. It is similar to many programs you have examined in this book, but a few additional points should be considered now that the function returns a value.

The early part of main() is similar to that of many programs in previous chapters. It declares its local variables—three for the user input and one for the calculated average. The cout and cin are familiar to you. The function call to calc_av() is familiar too; it passes three variables—num1, num2, and num3—to the calc_av() by value. (If the function passed them by address, an ampersand (&) would have to precede each argument, as discussed in the Chapter 20.)

**Put the function's return type before its name.**

The receiving function, calc_av(), looks like others you have seen, except that the first line, the function's definition line, has one addition: the int before its name. This is the type of the return value. Always precede a function name with its return data type. If you don't specify a type, C++ will assume that it is int, but the legibility of the program will suffer.

Because the variable local_avg, which is being returned from calc_av(), is an integer, the integer return type is placed before calc_av()'s name.

You also can see that the return statement of calc_av() includes the return value local_avg. This is the variable being sent back to the calling function main(). You can return only a single variable to a calling function.

> **Note:** Even though a function can receive more than one parameter, it can return only a single value to the calling function. If a receiving function is to modify more than one value from the calling function, you must pass the parameters by address; you cannot return multiple values by using a return statement.

After the receiving function calc_av() has returned the value, main() must do something with that returned value. So far, you have seen function calls on lines by themselves. Notice that in main() the function call appears on the right side of the following assignment statement:

```
avg = calc_av(num1, num2, num3);
```

When the calc_av() function returns its value (the average of the three numbers), that value *replaces* the function call. If the average computed in calc_av() is 40, the executing program "sees" the following statement in place of the function call:

```
avg = 40;
```

A function call had been indicated to the right of the equal sign, but the program replaces the function call with its return value when the return takes place. In other words, *a function that returns a value becomes that value.* You can only put such a function where you would put any variable or constant—usually to the right of an equal sign or in an expression or `cout`. The following line is an incorrect way to call `calc_av()`:

```
calc_av(num1, num2, num3);
```

If you used this line, C++ would have nothing to do with the return value.

> **Note:** Function calls that return values rarely appear on lines by themselves. Because the function call is replaced by the return value, you should do something with that return value—for example, assign it to a variable or use it in an expression. Return values can be ignored, but doing so usually defeats the purpose of using them.

## Examples

1. The following program passes a number to a function called `doub()`. The function doubles the number and returns the result.

```cpp
// Filename: C21DOUB.CPP
// Doubles the user's number

#include <iostream.h>

int     doub(int num)
    {
    int     d_num;

    d_num = num * 2;    // Double the number
    return (d_num);     // Return the result
    }


main()
    {
    int     number;     // Holds user's input
    int     d_number;   // Will hold double the user's input

    cout << "What number do you want doubled? ";
    cin >> number;
    d_number = doub(number);    // Assign return value
    cout << number << " doubled is " << d_number << "\n";
    return 0;
    }
```

The program produces output like this:

```
What number do you want doubled? 5
5 doubled is 10
```

**2.** Function return values can be used anywhere that constants, variables, and expressions are used. The following program is quite similar to the preceding one; the difference is in main(). The function call is performed, not on a line by itself, but from within a cout.

This call is a nested function call. You call the cout, using the return value from one of the program's functions, named doub(). Because the call to doub() is replaced by its return value, the cout has enough information to proceed as soon as doub() returns. This keeps main() a little cleaner from the extra variable called d_number.

```cpp
// Filename: C21DOUB2.CPP
// Doubles the user's number

#include <iostream.h>

int     doub(int num)
    {
    int     d_num;

    d_num = num * 2;     // Double the number
    return (d_num);      // Return the result
    }


main()
    {
    int     number;      // Holds user's input

    cout << "What number do you want doubled? ";
    cin >> number;
    // The 3rd cout parameter is replaced with
    // a return value
    cout << number << " doubled is " << doub(number)
        << "\n";

    return 0;
    }
```

You must use your own judgment about whether the program is easier to maintain. Sometimes it is wise to include function calls within other expressions. At other times, it may be clearer to call the function and assign its return value to a variable before using it.

**3.** The following program asks the user for a number. The number is then passed to a function called sum(), which adds together the numbers from 1 to that number. In other words, if the user types 6, the function returns the result of the following calculation:

```
1 + 2 + 3 + 4 + 5 + 6
```

This is known as the *sum-of-the-digits calculation*, and it is sometimes used for depreciation in accounting.

```cpp
// Filename: C21SUMD.CPP
// Computes the sum of the digits

#include <iostream.h>

int     sum(int num)
    {
    int     ctr;            // Local loop counter
    int     sumd = 0;       // Local to this function

    if (num <= 0) // Check to see if parameter is too small
        {
        sumd = num;         // Return parameter if too small
        }
    else
        {
        for (ctr = 1; ctr <= num; ctr++)
            {
            sumd += ctr;
            }
        }
    return (sumd);
    }


main()
    {
    int     num, sumd;

    cout << "Please type a number ";
    cin >> num;
    sumd = sum(num);
    cout << "The sum of the digits is " << sumd << "\n";
    return 0;
    }
```

Here is the output of this program:

```
Please type a number 6
The sum of the digits is 21
```

4. The following program contains two functions that return values. The first function, maximum(), returns the higher of two numbers entered by the user. The second function, minimum(), returns the lower number.

```cpp
// Filename: C21MINMX.CPP
// Finds minimum and maximum values in functions

#include <iostream.h>
```

```
int     maximum(int num1, int num2)
        {
        int     max;      // Local to this function only

        max = (num1 > num2) ? (num1) : (num2);
        return (max);
        }

int     minimum(int num1, int num2)
        {
        int     min;      // Local to this function only

        min = (num1 < num2) ? (num1) : (num2);
        return (min);
        }


main()
        {
        int     num1, num2;     // User's 2 numbers
        int     min, max;

        cout << "Please type two numbers (such as 46 75) ";
        cin >> num1 >> num2;
        max = maximum(num1, num2);  // Assign return value of
                                    // each function to variables
        min = minimum(num1, num2);
        cout << "The minimum number is " << min << "\n";
        cout << "The maximum number is " << max << "\n";
        return 0;
        }
```

Note the following output:

```
Please type two numbers (such as 46 75) 72 55
The minimum number is 55
The maximum number is 72
```

If the user types the same number twice, the minimum and maximum numbers will be the same.

These two functions can be passed any two integer values. In a simple example like this one, the user already knows which number is higher or lower. The purpose is to show how to code return values. You might want to use similar functions in a more useful application, such as finding the highest-paid employee from a payroll disk file.

# Function Prototypes

The word *prototype* is sometimes defined as "a model." In C++, a function prototype models the actual function. Before completing your study of functions, parameters, and return values, you must understand how to prototype each function in a program.

You must prototype all functions in your programs. By prototyping them, you inform C++ of the functions' parameter types and their return value, if any. Prototypes are mandatory.

A simple example will help clarify the need for prototyping. The following program asks the user for a temperature in Celsius and then converts that temperature to Fahrenheit. The parameter and the return type are both floating-point values. You know the return type is a floating-point value because of the word *float* before the function convert()'s definition. See if you can follow this program. Except for the Celsius calculation, the program is similar to those you have seen.

```
// Filename: C21TEMP.CPP
// Converts the user's Celsius to Fahrenheit

#include <iostream.h>
#include <iomanip.h>

main()
    {
    float     c_temp;    // Holds user's Celsius temperature
    float     f_temp;    // Holds converted temperature

    cout << "What is the Celsius temperature to convert? ";
    cin >> c_temp;

    f_temp = convert(c_temp);    // Convert the temperature

    cout << "The Fahrenheit equivalent is "
         << setprecision(1) << f_temp << "\n";
    return 0;
    }

float     convert(float c_temp)  // Return var and parameter
                                 // are both float
    {
    float     f_temp;            // Local variable

    f_temp = c_temp * (9.0 / 5.0) + 32.0;
    return (f_temp);
    }
```

*You must prototype all functions.*

If you run the preceding program, your C++ compiler will refuse to compile it. Yet this program seems like many others you have seen. The primary difference is the prototype.

To prototype a function, copy the function's definition line to the top of your program. (Immediately before or after the #include <iostream.h> line is fine.) Place a semicolon at the end of the copied line, and you have the prototype. Because the definition line (the function's first line) contains the return type, the function name, and the type of each argument, the function prototype serves (to the program) as a model of the function that is to follow.

If a function does not return a value, or if that function has no arguments passed to it, you must still prototype it. Use the keyword void in place of a return type or parameters. The following code shows the preceding program corrected with the prototype line.

```
// Filename: C21TEMP.CPP
// Converts the user's Celsius to Fahrenheit

#include <iostream.h>
#include <iomanip.h>

float    convert(float c_type);  int main(void);  // convert()'s
                                                  //  prototype

int    main()
    {
    float    c_temp;  // Holds user's Celsius temperature
    float    f_temp;  // Holds converted temperature

    cout << "What is the Celsius temperature to convert? ";
    cin >> c_temp;

    f_temp = convert(c_temp);    // Convert the temperature

    cout << "The Fahrenheit equivalent is "
         << setprecision(2) << f_temp << "\n";
    return 0;
    }

float    convert(float c_temp)  // Return var and parameter
                                //  are both float
    {
    float    f_temp;             // Local variable

    f_temp = c_temp * (9.0 / 5.0) + 32.0;
    return (f_temp);
    }
```

All functions must match their prototypes. You don't have to list individual parameter names in the function's prototype parentheses, only the data type of each parameter.

You can look at a prototype and tell whether it is a prototype or function definition (the function's first line) by the semicolon at the end.

## Improve Program Quality by Prototyping

Prototyping protects you from the possibility of your own programming mistakes. Suppose you write a function that expects two arguments: an integer followed by a floating-point value. Following is the definition line of such a function:

```
my_fun(int num, float amount)
```

What if you were to pass my_fun() incorrect data types? If you called this function by passing it two constants, a floating-point value followed by an integer, as in

*Prototyping protects your programs from function programming errors.*

```
my_fun(23.43, 5);   // Call the my_fun() function
```

the function would *not* receive correct parameters. The function is expecting an integer followed by a floating-point value, but you did the opposite.

Because of the power of your C++ compiler, you will get an error message if you do this. By prototyping such a function at the top of the program, as in

```
void    my_fun(int num, float amount);    // Prototype
```

you tell your compiler to check this function for accuracy. You inform the compiler to expect *nothing* after the return statement (because of the void keyword). You inform the compiler to expect an integer followed by a floating-point value in the parentheses. If you fail to follow the usage defined by the prototype, your compiler informs you of the problem, and you can correct it.

## Prototype All Functions

You must prototype every function in your program. The prototype defines for the program which functions follow, their return types, and their parameter types.

Think about how you would prototype cout. You don't always pass it the same types of parameters, because you print different data with each cout. Prototyping functions that you write is easy; the prototype is basically the first line in the function. Prototyping functions that you don't write may seem difficult. But it isn't—in fact, you have already done it in each program in this book!

The designers of C++ realized that all functions should be prototyped. They also realized that you cannot prototype library functions, so they did that for you by placing their prototypes in header files on your disk. You have been including the cout and cin prototype in each program with the following statement:

*Header files contain library function prototypes.*

```
#include <iostream.h>
```

Inside the file iostream.h is a prototype of many of C++'s input and output functions. By prototyping these functions, C++ ensures that you cannot pass bad values to such functions. If you do, the C++ compiler will catch the problem.

Prototyping is the primary reason you should always include the matching header file when using one of C++'s library functions. The strcpy() function you saw in earlier chapters requires the following line:

```
#include <string.h>
```

This is the header file for the `strcpy()` function. Without this file, you would have to enter all of the prototypes for the string library functions that you use. Otherwise, the compiler will give error messages.

### Examples

**1.** The following program asks the user for a number in `main()` and passes that number to `ascii()`. The `ascii()` function then returns the ASCII character of the user's number. This program illustrates a character return type. Functions can return any data type.

```
// Filename: C21ASC.CPP
// Prints the ASCII character of the user's number
// Prototypes follow

#include <iostream.h>

char    ascii(int num);

int     main()
     {
     int     num;
     char    asc_char;

     cout << "What is an ASCII number? ";
     cin >> num;

     asc_char = ascii(num);
     cout << "The ASCII character for " << num
          << " is " << asc_char << "\n";
     return 0;
     }

char    ascii(int num)
     {
     char    asc_char;

     asc_char = (char)num;
     return (asc_char);
     }
```

Here is the output of this program:

```
What is an ASCII number? 67
The ASCII character for 67 is C
```

**2.** Suppose you need to calculate net pay for a company. To compute this, you multiply the hours worked by the hourly pay and then deduct taxes. The following program includes a function that does these tasks. It requires three arguments: the hours worked, the hourly pay, and the tax rate (as a floating-point decimal, such as .30 for 30 percent). The function returns the net pay. The `main()` calling program tests this by sending three different payroll values to the function and then prints the three return values.

```cpp
// Filename: C21NPAY.CPP
// Defines a function that computes net pay

#include <iostream.h>
#include <iomanip.h>

float    netpayfun(float hours, float rate, float taxrate);

int    main()
    {
    float    net_pay;

    net_pay = netpayfun(40.0, 3.50, .20);
    cout << "The pay for 40 hours at $3.50/hr., ";
    cout << "and a 20% tax rate is: ";
    cout << setiosflags(ios::fixed) << setprecision(2) << net_pay
    ➥<< "\n";
    net_pay = netpayfun(50.0, 10.00, .30);
    cout << "The pay for 50 hours at $10.00/hr., ";
    cout << "and a 30% tax rate is: ";
    cout << setiosflags(ios::fixed) << setprecision(2) << net_pay
    ➥<< "\n";
    net_pay = netpayfun(10.0, 5.00, .10);
    cout << "The pay for 10 hours at $5.00/hr., ";
    cout << "and a 10% tax rate is: ";
    cout << setiosflags(ios::fixed) << setprecision(2) << net_pay
    ➥<< "\n";
    return 0;
    }

float    netpayfun(float hours, float rate, float taxrate)
    {
    float    gross_pay, taxes, net_pay;

    gross_pay = (hours * rate);
    taxes = (taxrate * gross_pay);
    net_pay = (gross_pay - taxes);
    return (net_pay);
    }
```

# Summary

You now have seen how to build your own collection of functions. When you write a function, you might want to use it in several programs; there is no need to reinvent the wheel. Many programmers write useful functions and use them in more than one program.

You now also understand prototyping functions. You must prototype all your own functions and include the appropriate header file when using one of the library functions.

The rest of this book uses the concepts presented in Parts I through IV to enable you to take advantage of separate functions and local data. You are ready to learn more about how C++ performs input and output. Chapter 22 shows you the theory behind C++'s I/O and introduces more library functions.

## Review Questions

Answers to Review Questions are in Appendix B.

1. How do you declare a function return type?

2. What is the maximum number of return values a function can return?

3. Name one reason for including header files.

4. What is the default function return type?

5. True or false: A function that returns a value can be passed only a single parameter.

6. How do prototypes protect the program from bugs?

7. Why do you not need to return global variables?

8. Consider the following function prototype:

```
float my_fun(char a, int b, float c);
```

What is the return type? How many parameters are being passed to `my_fun()`? What are their types?

## Review Exercises

1. Write a program that contains two functions. The first function returns the square of the integer passed to it, and the second function returns the cube. As with all programs from this point on, prototype all functions, including `main()`.

2. Write a function that returns the double-precision area of a circle, given the double-precision radius passed to it. The formula for calculating the area of a circle is this:

area = 3.14159 * radius * radius

**3.** Write a function that returns the value of a polynomial (the return value), given this formula:

$$9x^4 + 15x^2 + x1$$

Assume that x is passed from `main()` and was supplied by the user.

# Part V

*Input/Output*

# CHAPTER 22

# Device and Character I/O

Unlike many programming languages, C++ contains no input or output commands. C++ is an extremely *portable* language; this means that a C++ program that compiles and runs on one type of computer will be able to compile and run on another type of computer with minimal effort. Most incompatibilities between computers reside in their input/output devices. Each device requires a different method of performing input/output (I/O).

By putting all I/O capabilities in common functions supplied with each computer's compiler instead of in C++ statements, the designers of C++ ensured that programs were not tied to specific hardware for input and output. A compiler has to be modified for each target computer in order to work with all of its devices. The compiler designers write I/O functions for each machine, so when your C++ program writes a character to the screen, the program works whether you are on a DOS PC or a UNIX terminal.

This chapter shows you additional ways to perform input and output of data other than with the cin and cout operators you have seen so far. With its character-based I/O functions, C++ gives you the basic I/O functions needed for writing powerful data entry and printing routines.

This chapter introduces the following topics:

♦ Stream input and output

♦ Redirecting I/O

♦ Printing to the printer

♦ Character I/O functions

♦ Buffered and nonbuffered I/O

By the time you finish this chapter, you will understand the fundamental, built-in I/O functions available in C++. Performing "character input and output" (one character at a time) may sound like a slow I/O method, but you will soon see that character I/O actually gives you more power.

# Stream and Character I/O

*C++ views input and output from all devices as a stream of characters.*

C++ views all input and output as streams of characters. Whether your program gets input from the keyboard, a disk file, or a modem, C++ sees only a stream of characters. C++ does not know (or care) what type of device is supplying the input. C++ lets the operating system take care of the device specifics. The designers of C++ want your programs to operate on data without regard to the physical process that is taking place.

This stream I/O means that you can use the same functions to get input from the keyboard as you use to get input from the modem. You can use the same functions to write to a disk file, a printer, or the screen. Of course, you need some way of routing that stream input or output to the proper device, but each program's I/O functions work similarly. Figure 22.1 illustrates this concept.

**Figure 22.1.**

All I/O is viewed as character streams by C++.

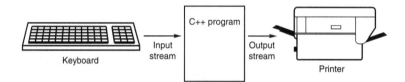

Keyboard — Input stream — C++ program — Output stream — Printer

---

**The Newline Special Character: \n**

Portability is the key to C++'s success. Few companies have the resources to rewrite every program they use when they change computer equipment. They need a programming language that works on many platforms (hardware combinations). C++ achieves portability better than other programming languages.

It is because of portability that C++ uses the generic newline character, \n, instead of the specific carriage return and linefeed sequences other languages use. This also is why C++ uses \t for tab, as well as all the other control characters used in I/O functions.

If C++ relied on specific ASCII code to represent these special characters, your programs would not be portable. You would be writing a C++ program on one type of computer, using a carriage return value such as 12. But 12 may not be the carriage return value on another type of computer.

> By using the newline character and the rest of the control characters available in C++, you ensure that your programs will work on any computer on which they are compiled. A specific compiler will substitute its computer's actual codes for the control codes in your programs.

## Standard Devices

Table 22.1 shows a listing of standard I/O devices. C++ always assumes that input will come from stdin, meaning the *standard input device*. It is usually the keyboard, although you can reroute this default. C++ assumes that all output will go to stdout, or the *standard output device*.

### Table 22.1. Standard devices in C++.

| Description | C++ Name |
| --- | --- |
| Screen | stdout |
| Keyboard | stdin |
| Printer | stdprn |
| Serial port | stdaux |
| Error messages | stderr |
| Disk files | None |

The reason that cout goes to the screen is simply that stdout is routed to the screen, by default, on most computers. The reason why cin gets input from the keyboard is that most computers consider the keyboard to be the standard input device, stdin. After compiling your program, C++ does *not* send data to the screen or get it from the keyboard. Instead, the program sends output to stdout and gets input from stdin. The operating system routes the data to the appropriate device.

## Printing Formatted Output to the Printer

ofstream lets your program write to the printer.

Sending program output to the printer is easy with ofstream objects and their member functions. The format of ofstream is

```
ofstream device(device_name);
```

> **Note:** ofstream uses the fstream.h header file.

The next example shows how you can combine cout and ofstream to write to both the screen and the printer.

## Example

> **Note:** The following example only works when compiled to a DOS target. (See Chapter 2, "The Borland C++ Environment.")

The following program asks for the user's first and last names. It then prints the full name, last name first, on the printer.

```
// Filename: C22FPR1.CPP
// Prints a name on the printer

#include <fstream.h>

main()
    {
    char    first[ 20 ];
    char    last[ 20 ];

    cout << "What is your first name? ";
    cin >> first;
    cout << "What is your last name? ";
    cin >> last;

    // Send names to the printer
    ofstream prn("PRN");
    prn << "In a phone book, your name looks like this: \n";
    prn << last << ", " << first << "\n";
    return 0;
    }
```

# Character I/O Functions

C++ provides many functions for performing character input and output. The cout and cin functions are called *formatted I/O operators*, which give you formatting control over your input and output. The cout and cin functions are not character I/O functions.

## The *get()* and *put()* Functions

get() inputs characters from any standard device; put() outputs characters to any standard device.

The most fundamental character I/O functions are get() and put(). The get() function inputs a single character from the standard input device (the keyboard, if you don't redirect it). The put() function outputs a single character to the standard output device (the screen, if you don't redirect it from the operating system).

The format of get() is

```
device.get(char_var);
```

The *device* can be any standard input device. If you were getting character input from the keyboard, you would use cin as the device. If you had initialized your modem and wanted to receive characters from it, you would use ifstream to open the modem device and read from it.

The format of put() is

```
device.put(char_val);
```

You output character data with put(). The *char_val* can be a character variable, expression, or constant. The *device* can be any standard output device. To write a character to your printer, you would open PRN with ofstream.

### Examples

1. The following program asks for the user's initials, one character at a time. Notice that the program uses both cout and put(). The cout is still very useful for formatted output, such as messages to the user. Writing individual characters is best achieved with put().

   The program has to call two get() functions for each character typed. When you answer a get() prompt, by typing a character and then pressing Enter, C++ sees that input as a stream of two characters. The get() first gets the letter you typed and then gets the \n (the newline character, supplied to C++ when you press Enter). Examples that follow fix this double get() problem.

   ```
   // Filename: C22CH1.CPP
   // Introduces get() and put()

   #include <fstream.h>

   main()
       {
       char    in_char;     // Holds incoming initial
       char    first, last; // Holds converted first and
                            // last initials

       cout << "What is your first name initial? ";
       cin.get(in_char);    // Wait for first initial
       first = in_char;
   ```

```
cin.get(in_char);       // Ignore newline
cout << "What is your last name initial? ";
cin.get(in_char);       // Wait for last initial
last = in_char;
cin.get(in_char);       // Ignore newline
cout << "\nHere they are: \n";
cout.put(first);
cout.put(last);
return 0;
}
```

Here is the output of this program:

```
What is your first name initial? G
What is your last name initial? P

Here they are:
GP
```

2. You can add carriage returns for better spacing of the output. To print the two initials on two separate lines, use put() to write a newline character to cout. The following program does this:

```
// Filename: C22CH2.CPP
// Introduces get() and put() and uses put() to output
// newline

#include <fstream.h>

main()
    {
    char    in_char;     // Holds incoming initial
    char    first, last; // Holds converted first and
                         // last initials

    cout << "What is your first name initial? ";
    cin.get(in_char);       // Wait for first initial
    first = in_char;
    cin.get(in_char);       // Ignore newline
    cout << "What is your last name initial? ";
    cin.get(in_char);       // Wait for last initial
    last = in_char;
    cin.get(in_char);       // Ignore newline
    cout << "\nHere they are: \n";
    cout.put(first);
    cout.put('\n');
    cout.put(last);
    return 0;
    }
```

**3.** It may be clearer to define the newline character as a constant. At the top of the preceding program, you could use this:

```
#define NEWLINE '\n'
```

The put() could then read

```
cout.put(NEWLINE);
```

Some programmers prefer to define their character-formatting constants and refer to them by name. It's up to you to decide whether this is clearer, or whether you want to continue using the '\n' character constant in put().

## Buffered and Unbuffered Character I/O

The get() function is a *buffered* input function; that is, as you type characters, the data does not immediately go into your program but instead goes into a buffer. The *buffer* is a section of memory managed by C++.

Figure 22.2 shows how a buffered input function works. When your program reaches a get() statement, the program temporarily waits as you type the input. The program doesn't see the characters at all, because they are going into the buffer of memory. When you press Enter, the computer releases the buffer to your program.

**Figure 22.2.**

get() input goes to a buffer, which is released when you press Enter.

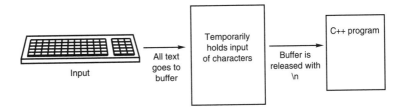

Most PCs allow either buffered or nonbuffered input. The getch() function, discussed later in this chapter, is nonbuffered. With get(), all input is buffered, which affects the timing of your program's input. The program receives no characters from get() until Enter is pressed. Therefore, if you ask a question, such as

```
Do you want to see the report again (Y/N)?
```

and use get() for input, the user can answer Y, but the program does not know it until the user presses Enter. The Y and the Enter keystroke are then sent, one character at a time, to the program, where the input is processed. If you want an immediate response to a user's typing, you will have to use getch().

> **Tip:** If you use buffered input, the user can, in response to a loop with `get()`, type a string of characters and correct the input with the Backspace key, if desired, before pressing Enter. If the input is nonbuffered, a Backspace keystroke is treated as just another character of data.

## Examples

**1.** C22CH2.CPP must discard the newline character. It did so by assigning the input character, from `get()`, to an extra variable. Obviously, the `get()` returns a value (the character typed). In this case, it's okay to ignore that return value by not using the character returned by `get()`. You know that the user will have to press Enter (to end the input), so discarding the character with an unused `get()` function call is acceptable.

**2.** `cin` is very limited when used for inputting strings, such as names and sentences. The `cin` operator allows only one word to be entered at a time. If you asked for a user's full name with the lines

```
cout << "What are your first and last names? ";
cin >> names;    // Get name into character array names
```

the array `names` would receive only the first name; `cin` ignores all data to the right of the first space.

**3.** Using `get()`, you can build your own input function that doesn't have a single-word limitation. When you want to get a string of characters from the user, such as first and last names, you can call the `get_in_str()` function, which is shown in the following program.

The `main()` function defines an array and prompts the user for a name. After the prompt, the program calls the `get_in_str()` function and builds the input array, one character at a time, using `get()`. The function keeps looping, using the `while` loop, until the user presses Enter (signaled by the newline character, `\n`) *or* until the maximum number of characters are typed.

You might want to use this function in your own programs. Be sure to pass it a character array and an integer that holds the maximum array size. (You don't want the input string to be longer than the character array that will hold it.) When control returns to `main()`, or to whatever function called `get_in_str()`, the array will have the user's full input, spaces and all.

```
// Filename: C22IN.CPP
// Program that builds an input string array, using get()

#include <fstream.h>

#define MAX 25      // Size of character array to be typed in

//*************************************************************
// The following function requires that a string and the
// maximum length of the string be passed to it. It accepts
// input from the keyboard and will send keyboard input into
// the string. On return, the calling routine has access to
// the string.
//*************************************************************

void     get_in_str(char str[ ], int len)
    {
    int      i = 0;          // Index
    char     input_char;     // Character typed

    cin.get(input_char);     // Get next character in string
    while (i < (len - 1) && (input_char != '\n'))
        {
        str[ i ] = input_char; // Build string a character
                               // at a time
        i++;
        cin.get(input_char);   // Get next character in
                               // string
        }
    str[ i ] = '\0';   // Make the char array into a string
    return;
    }


int     main(void)
    {
    char     input_str[ MAX ]; // Keyboard input will fill
                               // this
    cout << "What is your full name? ";
    get_in_str(input_str, MAX);     // String from keyboard
    cout << "After return, your name is " << input_str
        << "\n";
    return 0;
    }
```

**Note:** The loop checks for len - 1 to save room for the null terminating zero at the end of the input string.

# The *getch()* and *putch()* Functions

The functions `getch()` and `putch()` are slightly different than the preceding character I/O functions. Their formats are similar to those of `get()` and `put()`. `getch()` and `putch()` read from the keyboard and write to the screen, and they cannot be redirected, even from the operating system. Here are the formats for `getch()` and `putch()`:

```
int_var = getch();
putch(int_var);
```

`getch()` and `putch()` are not ANSI C standard functions but are nonbuffered functions. The `putch()` character-output function is a mirror image of the `getch()` character-input function. Because almost every output device made (except for the screen and modem) are inherently buffered, `putch()` effectively does the same thing as `put()`.

Another difference between `getch()` and the other character-input functions is that `getch()` does not echo the input characters on the screen as it receives them. When you type characters in response to `get()`, you see the characters as you type them (as they are sent to the buffer). If you want to see on the screen the characters received by `getch()`, you can follow a `getche()`. Echoing the characters on the screen enables the user to verify that what was entered was correct.

When you want your program to respond immediately to keyboard input, use `getch()`. Some programmers do not want to have the user press Enter after answering a prompt or selecting from a menu. Other programmers believe that buffered input gives users more time to decide whether they really want to input certain answers, since a user can press Backspace and correct the input before pressing Enter.

getch() and putch() offer nonbuffered input and output that grabs the user's characters immediately after the user types them.

**Note:** `getch()` and `putch()` use the `conio.h` header file.

Character input with getch() is not echoed to the screen as the user types the characters.

Other programmers like to grab the user's response to a single-character answer, such as a menu response, and act on it immediately. They think that pressing Enter is an added and unneeded burden for the user. The choice is yours. You should understand both buffered and nonbuffered input, however, so that you can use either when you need it.

**Tip:** You also can use `getche()`. It is a nonbuffered input identical to `getch()`, except that the input characters are echoed (displayed) to the screen as the user types them. Using `getche()` instead of `getch()` sometimes prevents you from having to call a `putch()` to echo the user's input to the screen.

### Example

The following program shows the getch() and putch() functions. The user is asked to enter five letters, which are added to the character array name letters, using a for loop. As you run this program, notice that the characters are *not* echoed to the screen as you type them. Because getch() is unbuffered, the program actually receives each character, adds it to the array, and loops again *as you type the characters*. (If this were buffered input, the program would not loop through the five iterations until you pressed Enter.)

> **Note:** The following example only works when compiled to a DOS target. (See Chapter 2, "The Borland C++ Environment.")

A second loop prints the five letters, using putch(). A third loop prints the five letters to the printer, using put().

```
// Filename: C22GCH1.CPP
// Uses getch() and putch() for input and output

#include <fstream.h>
#include <conio.h>

main()
    {
    int     ctr;         // for loop counter
    char    letters[ 5 ]; // Holds 5 input characters. No
                         // room is needed for the null
                         // zero since this array will
                         // never be treated as if it
                         // were a string.

    cout << "Please type five letters... \n";
    for (ctr = 0; ctr < 5; ctr++)
        {
        letters[ ctr ] = getche();  // Add input to array
        }
ofstream prn("PRN");
    for (ctr = 0; ctr < 5; ctr++)  // Print them to printer
        {
        prn.put(letters[ ctr ]);
        }
    return 0;
    }
```

When you run this program, do not press Enter after supplying the five letters. The getch() function does not use the Enter keystroke. The loop ends automatically after the fifth letter (because of the for loop). This is possible only because of the nonbuffered input allowed with getch().

## Summary

You should now understand the generic method that C++ programs use for input and output. By writing to standard I/O devices, you have portability with C++. If you write a program for one computer type, it will work on another. If C++ were to write directly to specific hardware, programs would not work on every computer.

If you still want to use the formatted I/O functions, such as cout, you can do so. The ofstream() function lets you write formatted output to any device, including the printer.

Although the methods of character I/O may seem primitive (and they are), they provide flexibility because you can build on them to create your own input functions. One of the C++ functions used most often, a string-building character I/O function, was demonstrated in the C22IN.CPP program in this chapter.

The next two chapters introduce many character and string functions, including string I/O functions. The string I/O functions build on the principles presented here. You will be surprised at the extensive character- and string-manipulation functions available in the language as well.

## Review Questions

Answers to Review Questions are in Appendix B.

1. Why are there no input or output commands in C++?

2. True or false: If you use the character I/O functions to send output to stdout, the output always goes to the screen.

3. What is the difference between getch() and get()?

4. What function sends formatted output to devices?

5. True or false: When using get(), the program receives your input as you type it.

6. Which keystroke releases the buffered input to the program?

## Review Exercises

1. Write a program that asks the user for five letters and prints them backwards, first to the screen and then to the printer.

2. Write a miniature typewriter program, using `get()` and `put()`. Loop while getting a line of input (until the user presses Enter without typing any text) and then write that line to the printer. Because `get()` is buffered, nothing goes to the printer until the user presses Enter at the end of each line of text. (Use the string-building input function shown in C22IN.CPP.)

3. Add a `putch()` inside the first loop of C22GCH1.CPP (this chapter's first `get()` program) so that the characters are echoed to the screen as the user types them.

4. A *palindrome* is a word or phrase that is spelled the same forward and backward. Two sample palindromes are

```
Madam, I'm Adam
Golf? No sir, prefer prison flog!
```

Write a C++ program that asks the user for a phrase. Build the input, one character at a time, using a character input function such as `get()`. Once you have the full string (store it in a character array), test the phrase to see whether it is a palindrome. You will have to filter out special (nonalphabetic) characters, storing only alphabetic characters to a second character array. You also must convert the characters, as you store them, to uppercase. The first palindrome becomes

```
MADAMIMADAM
```

Using one or more `for` or `while` loops, you now can test the phrase to see whether it is a palindrome. Print the result of the test on the printer. Sample output should look like this:

```
"Madam, I'm Adam" is a palindrome.
```

# CHAPTER 23

# Character, String, and Numeric Functions

C++ provides many built-in functions in addition to the strcpy() function. These library functions increase your productivity and save you programming time. You do not have to write as much code because they perform many useful tasks for you.

This chapter introduces the following topics:

- ♦ Character-testing functions
- ♦ Character-conversion functions
- ♦ String-testing functions
- ♦ String-manipulation functions
- ♦ Mathematical functions
- ♦ Trigonometric functions
- ♦ Logarithmic and exponential functions
- ♦ Random number processing

## Character Functions

This section explores many of the character functions available in the C++ language. Generally, you pass character arguments to the functions, and they return values you can store or print. By using these functions, you off-load a lot of work to C++, letting it do some of the tedious manipulation of your character and string data.

Several functions test for certain characteristics of your character data. With these functions, you can test whether your character data is alphabetic (uppercase or lowercase) or numeric, and much more. You must pass a character variable or constant argument to these functions (by placing the argument in the function parentheses) when calling them. All the functions return a True (nonzero) or False (0) result, so you can test their return values inside an `if` statement or a `while` loop.

The character functions return True (nonzero) or False (0) results, based on characters you pass to them.

> **Note:** All character functions discussed here are prototyped in the ctype.h header file. Be sure to include ctype.h at the top of any program that uses these functions.

## Alphabetic and Numeric Testing

The following functions test for alphabetic conditions:

◆ `isalpha(c)`. Returns True (nonzero) if *c* is an uppercase or a lowercase letter. A False (0) value is returned if anything other than a letter is passed to this function.

◆ `islower(c)`. Returns True (nonzero) if *c* is a lowercase letter. A False (0) value is returned if anything other than a lowercase letter is passed to this function.

◆ `isupper(c)`. Returns True (nonzero) if *c* is an uppercase letter. A False (0) value is returned if anything other than an uppercase letter is passed to this function.

In C++, any nonzero value is considered True and 0 is always False. If you use these functions' return values in a relational test, the True return value is not always 1 (it might be any nonzero value), but it will always be considered True for the test.

The following functions test for numeric characters:

◆ `isdigit(c)`. Returns True (nonzero) if *c* is a digit from 0 through 9. A False (0) value is returned if anything other than a digit is passed to this function.

> **Note:** Even though some of the character functions test for digits, the arguments are still considered character data and cannot be used in mathematical calculations, unless you want to calculate using ASCII values of characters.

♦ isxdigit(c). Returns True (nonzero) if *c* is any of the hexadecimal digits *0* through *9, A* through *F*, or *a* through *f*. A False (0) value is returned if anything other than a hexadecimal digit is passed to this function. (See Appendix A for more information about the hexadecimal numbering system.)

The following function tests for numeric or alphabetic arguments:

♦ isalnum(c). Returns True (nonzero) if *c* is a digit from 0 through 9 or an alphabetic character (either uppercase or lowercase). A False (0) value is returned if anything other than a digit or letter is passed to this function.

> **Caution:** You can pass only character values and integer values (holding ASCII values of characters) to these functions. You cannot pass an entire character array to a character function. If you want to test the elements of a character array, you must pass the array one element at a time.

## Example

The following program asks for the user's initials. If the user types anything other than alphabetic characters, the program displays an error and asks again.

*Comments to identify the program.*
*Include the header file iostream.h.*
*Include the header file ctype.h.*
*Start of the main() function.*
　*Declare the variable initial to a character.*
　*Print* What is your first initial? *to the screen.*
　*Obtain a character from the keyboard.*
　*While the character was not an alphabetic character, go through the loop.*
　　*Print* That was not a valid initial! *to the screen.*
　　*Print* What is your first initial? *to the screen.*
　　*Obtain another character from the keyboard.*
　*Print* Thanks! *to the screen.*
　*Return from the main() function.*

```
// Filename: C23INI.CPP
// Asks for initials and tests to ensure that they are
// correct

#include <iostream.h>
#include <ctype.h>
```

```
main()
    {
    char    initial;

    cout << "What is your first initial? ";
    cin >> initial;
    while (!isalpha(initial))
        {
        cout << "\nThat was not a valid initial!\n";
        cout << "\nWhat is your first initial? ";
        cin >> initial;
        }

    cout << "\nThanks!\n";
    return 0;
    }
```

This is one use of the ! (NOT) operator that is clear. The program continues to loop while the entered character is not alphabetic.

None of the character-testing functions change characters.

## Special Character-Testing Functions

Some character functions are useful if you need to read from a disk file, a modem, or another operating system device from which you route input. These functions are not used as much as the character functions you saw in the last section, but they may be useful for testing specific characters for readability.

Here are the rest of the character-testing functions:

◆ iscntrl(c). Returns True (nonzero) if c is a *control character* (any character numbered 0 through 31 from the ASCII table). A False (0) value is returned if anything other than a control character is passed to this function.

◆ isgraph(c). Returns True (nonzero) if c is a printable character (a non-control character), except a space. A False (0) value is returned if a space or anything other than a printable character is passed to this function.

◆ isprint(c). Returns True (nonzero) if c is a printable character (a non-control character) from ASCII 32 to ASCII 127, including a space. A False (0) value is returned if anything other than a printable character is passed to this function.

◆ ispunct(c). Returns True (nonzero) if c is any *punctuation character* (any printable character other than a space, letter, or digit). A False (0) value is returned if anything other than a punctuation character is passed to this function.

◆ isspace(c). Returns True (nonzero) if c is a space, newline (\n), carriage return (\r), tab (\t), or vertical tab (\v) character. A False (0) value is returned if anything other than a space character is passed to this function.

# Character-Conversion Functions

Two remaining character functions come in handy. Instead of testing characters, these functions can actually change characters to their lowercase or uppercase equivalents.

♦ `tolower(c)`. Converts *c* to lowercase. Nothing is changed if you pass `tolower()` a lowercase letter or a nonalphabetic character.

♦ `toupper(c)`. Converts *c* to uppercase. Nothing is changed if you pass `toupper()` an uppercase letter or a nonalphabetic character.

*tolower() and toupper() return lowercase arguments and uppercase arguments, respectively.*

These two functions return their changed character values. Typically, programmers change a character in the following ways:

```
c = tolower(c);
c = toupper(c);
```

In these two statements, the character variable *c* gets changed to its lowercase and uppercase equivalents.

These functions are quite useful for user input. Suppose that you ask the user a yes or no question, such as

```
Do you want to print the checks (Y/N)?
```

Without knowing `toupper()` and `tolower()`, you would have to check for both Y and y before printing the checks because the user may or may not type an uppercase letter for the answer. Instead of testing for both conditions, you can convert the character to uppercase and then test for Y.

## Example

Here is a program that prints an appropriate message for a user who is a girl or a user who is a boy. The program tests for G or B after converting the user's input to uppercase. No check for lowercase has to be done.

Comments to identify the program.
Include the header file iostream.h.
Include the header file ctype.h.
Start of the main() function.
> Declare the variable ans as a character.
> Print Are you a Girl or a Boy (G/B)? to the screen.
> Assign the variable ans to the value entered from the keyboard.
> Accept the Enter from the keyboard.
> Change the value of ans to uppercase.
> If ans is a G, print You look like a princess, today! to the screen and skip to the next line. Then break out of the switch.

*If* ans *is a B, print* You look handsome, today! *to the screen and skip to the next line. Then break out of the switch.*

*If a G or B is not entered, print* Your answer doesn't make sense! *to the screen and skip to the next line. Then break out of the switch.*

*Return from the main loop.*

```
// Filename: C23GB.CPP
// Tests if a G or a B is entered by user

#include <iostream.h>
#include <ctype.h>

main()
    {
    char     ans;       // Holds user's response
    char     c;         // To catch newline

    cout << "Are you a Girl or a Boy (G/B)? ";
    cin.get(ans);       // Get answer
    cin.get(c);         // Discard newline
    ans = toupper(ans);      // Convert answer to uppercase
    switch (ans)
        {
        case    'G':
            cout << "You look like a princess, today!\n";
            break;
        case    'B':
            cout << "You look handsome, today!\n";
            break;
        default:
            cout << "Your answer doesn't make sense!\n";
            break;
        }
    return 0;
    }
```

Here is the output from this program:

```
Are you a Girl or a Boy (G/B)? B
You look handsome, today!
```

# String Functions

Some of the most powerful built-in C++ functions are the string functions. They perform much of the tedious work you have been writing code for so far, such as inputting strings from the keyboard and comparing strings. You do not need to reinvent the wheel by writing code for tasks when built-in functions will do them for you. Use these functions as much as possible.

Now that you have a good grasp of the basics of C++, you can master the string functions. They let you concentrate on your program's primary purpose instead of spending time coding your own string functions.

## String Testing and Manipulation

A handful of string functions can be used for string testing and conversion. You have already seen one of the string functions, `strcpy()`, which copies a string of characters into a character array.

> **Note:** All string functions presented in this section are prototyped in the string.h header file. Be sure to include string.h at the top of any program that uses the string functions.

The string-manipulation functions work on character arrays that contain strings or on string constants.

Here are some string functions that test or manipulate strings:

♦ `strcat(s1, s2)`. Concatenates (merges) the string *s2* onto the end of the character array *s1*. The array *s1* must have enough reserved elements to hold both strings.

♦ `strcmp(s1, s2)`. Compares the string *s1* with *s2* on an alphabetic, element-by-element basis. If *s1* alphabetizes before *s2*, `strcmp()` returns a negative value. If *s1* and *s2* are exactly the same, `strcmp()` returns a 0. If *s1* alphabetizes after *s2*, `strcmp()` returns a positive value.

♦ `strlen(s1)`. Returns the length of *s1*. Remember that the length of a string is the number of characters up to but not including the null zero. The number of characters actually defined for the character array has nothing to do with the length of the string.

> **Tip:** Before using `strcat()` to concatenate (merge) strings, use `strlen()` to ensure that the target string (the string being concatentated to) is large enough to hold both strings.

## Conversion of Strings to Numbers

At times, you will need to convert numbers stored in character strings to a numeric data type. C++ provides the following functions:

♦ `atoi(s)`. Converts *s* to an integer. The name stands for *a*lphabetic *to i*nteger.

♦ `atol(s)`. Converts *s* to a long integer. The name stands for *a*lphabetic *to l*ong integer.

◆ `atof(s)`. Converts *s* to a floating-point number. The name stands for *a*lphabetic *to* *f*loating-point.

> **Note:** These three `ato()` functions are prototyped in the stdlib.h header file. Be sure to include stdlib.h at the top of any program that uses the `ato()` functions.

The string must contain a valid number. Here is a string that can be converted to an integer:

```
"1232"
```

The string must hold a string of digits short enough to fit in the target numeric data type. The following string cannot be converted to an integer with the `atoi()` function:

```
"-1232495.654"
```

This string can be converted to a floating-point number with the `atof()` function.

C++ cannot perform any mathematical calculations with such strings, even if they contain digits that represent numbers. Therefore, you must convert a string into its numeric equivalent before performing arithmetic with it.

> **Note:** If you pass a string to an `ato()` function and that string does not contain a valid representation of a number, the `ato()` function returns 0.

These functions will become more useful later, after you learn about disk files, pointers, and command-line arguments.

# Numeric Functions

In this section, you are introduced to some of the C++ numeric functions. Like string functions, these library functions save you time by converting and calculating numbers so that you don't have to write functions to do such tasks. Many of these functions are trigonometric and advanced math functions. You may use some of them rarely, but they are available if you need them.

## Mathematical Functions

Several built-in numeric functions return results based on numeric variables and constants passed to them. Even if you write very few science and engineering programs, some of these functions will be useful to you.

**Note:** All mathematical and trigonometric functions are prototyped in the math.h header file. Be sure to include math.h at the top of any program that uses these functions.

These numeric functions return double-precision values.

Here are the numeric functions:

♦ `ceil(x)`. Rounds up to the nearest integer. This function is sometimes called the *ceiling function*.

♦ `fabs(x)`. Returns the absolute value of $x$. The absolute value of a number is its positive equivalent.

> **Tip:** Absolute value is used for distances (which are always positive), accuracy measurements, age differences, and other calculations that require a positive result.

♦ `floor(x)`. Rounds down to the nearest integer.

♦ `fmod(x, y)`. Returns the floating-point remainder of (*x* divided by *y*), with the same sign as *x*. *y* cannot be zero. Because the modulus operator (%) works with integers only, this function was supplied to find the remainder of floating-point number divisions.

♦ `pow(x, y)`. Returns *x* raised to the *y* power, or *xy*. If *x* is less than or equal to zero, *y* must be an integer. If *x* equals zero, *y* cannot be negative.

♦ `sqrt(x)`. Returns the square root of *x*. *x* must be greater or equal to zero.

> **The *n*th Root**
>
> There are no functions that return the *n*th root of a number, only the square root. In other words, you cannot call a function that gives you the 4th root of 65,536. By the way, 16 is the 4th root of 65,536 because 16 times 16 times 16 times 16 equals 65,536.
>
> You can use a mathematical trick to simulate the *n*th root. C++ lets you raise a number to a fractional power, so with the `pow()` function, you can raise a number to the *n*th root by raising it to the (1/*n*) power. For example, to find the 4th root of 65,536, you type this:
>
> ```
> root = pow(65536.0, (1.0/4.0));
> ```

> **Caution:** The decimal points keep the numbers in floating-point format. If you left them as integers, as in
>
> ```
> root = pow(65536, (1/4));
> ```
>
> C++ would produce incorrect results. The `pow()` and most of the other mathematical functions require floating-point values as arguments.
>
> To store the 7th root of 78,125 in a variable called `root`, you type this:
>
> ```
> root = pow(78125.0, (1.0/7.0));
> ```
>
> This stores 5.0 in `root` because 5⁷ equals 78,125.
>
> Knowing how to compute the $n$th root comes in handy in scientific programs and financial applications, such as time value of money problems.

## Example

The following program uses the `fabs()` function to compute the difference between two ages.

```
// Filename: C23ABS.CPP
// Prints the difference between two ages

#include <iostream.h>
#include <math.h>

main()
    {
    float     age1, age2, diff;

    cout << "\nWhat is the first child's age? ";
    cin >> age1;
    cout << "What is the second child's age? ";
    cin >> age2;
    // Calculate the positive difference
    diff = fabs(age1 - age2);   // Determine the absolute
                                // value
    cout << "\nThey are " << diff << " years apart.\n";
    return 0;
    }
```

Here is this program's output:

```
What is the first child's age? 10
What is the second child's age? 12
They are 2 years apart.
```

Because of `fabs()`, the order of the ages does not matter. Without absolute value, this program would produce a negative age difference if the first age were less than the second age. Because the ages are relatively small, floating-point variables are used in this example. C++ automatically converts floating-point arguments to double when passing them to `fabs()`.

## Trigonometric Functions

The following functions are available for trigonometric applications:

♦ `cos(x)`. Returns the cosine of the angle *x*. *x* is expressed in radians.

♦ `sin(x)`. Returns the sine of the angle *x*. *x* is expressed in radians.

♦ `tan(x)`. Returns the tangent of the angle *x*. *x* is expressed in radians.

**Tip:** If you need to pass an angle, expressed in *degrees*, to these functions, convert the angle in radians to degrees by multiplying the radians by (pi / 180.0). Pi is approximately 3.14159.

## Logarithmic and Exponential Functions

Three highly mathematical functions are sometimes used in business and mathematics:

♦ `exp(x)`. Returns the base of the natural logarithm (e) raised to a power specified by *x* ($e^x$). e is approximately 2.718282.

♦ `log(x)`. Returns the natural logarithm of the argument *x*, mathematically written as `ln(x)`. *x* must be positive.

♦ `log10(x)`. Returns the base-10 logarithm of the argument *x*, mathematically written as `log10(x)`. *x* must be positive.

## Random Number Processing

*The* `rand()` *function produces random integer numbers.*

When simulating real events that contain a degree of randomness, we need to generate random numbers. In a factory simulation, we need to generate downtime in a random fashion to more closely resemble reality. Random events are especially important in games; part of the fun of games is the luck involved with the roll of the dice or the draw of a card, when combined with your playing skills.

The designers of C++ wrote a function, `rand()`, for generating random numbers. With it, you can get a random number to compute a dice roll or a card draw randomly.

To call the `rand()` function and assign the returned random number to test, you use the following line.

*Assign the variable test a random number returned from the rand() function.*

```
test = rand();
```

The `rand()` function returns an integer from 0 to 32767. Never use an argument in the `rand()` parentheses. If you do, the compiler will give you an error message. Each time you call `rand()` in the same program, you will get a random number.

If you run the *same* program that uses `rand()` over and over, `rand()` returns the same set of random numbers. If you want to get a different set of random numbers, you call the `srand()` function. Its format is

```
srand(seed);
```

where *seed* is an integer variable or constant. If you don't call `srand()`, C++ assumes a *seed* value of 1. The *seed* value reseeds (resets) the random number generator, so the *next* random number is based on the new *seed* value. If you run a program that uses `rand()` and you call `srand()` with a different *seed* value at the beginning of the program, `rand()` returns a different random number.

> **Note:** The `rand()` and `srand()` functions are prototyped in the stdlib.h header file. Be sure to include stdlib.h at the top of any program that uses `rand()` or `srand()`.

---

### Why Do They Make Us Do This?

There is much debate among C++ programmers about the random number generator. Many of them think that random numbers should be *truly* random and that programmers should not have to seed the generator themselves. Those programmers believe that C++ should do its own internal seeding when they ask for a random number, thereby taking the burden of *randomness* off the programmers' backs.

However, many applications would no longer work if the random number generator were seeded for you. Computer simulations are used all the time in business, engineering, and research to approximate the pattern of real-world events. Researchers need to be able to duplicate these simulations, over and over. Even though the events inside the simulations may be random to each other, the running of the simulations cannot be random if researchers are to study several different effects.

Mathematicians and statisticians also need to repeat random number patterns for their analyses, especially when working with risk, probability, and gaming theory.

Because so many computer users need to repeat their random number patterns, the designers of C++ have wisely chosen to give you, the programmer, the option of keeping the same random patterns or changing them. The advantages outweigh by far the burden of including an extra srand() function call!

If you want to produce a different set of random numbers every time your program runs, you can use randomize() to initialize the random number generator randomly. It is implemented as a macro that calls the time() function, so you should include time.h.

## Summary

By including the ctype.h header file, you can test and convert characters that the user types. There are many useful purposes for these character functions. Perhaps the most common use is to convert a user's responses to uppercase letters no matter how they are entered; that way, you can easily test the user's answers.

String functions give you ease of control over both string input and numeric input. You can get a string of digits from the keyboard and convert the digits to a number with the ato() functions. The string-comparison and concatenation functions let you test and change the contents of more than one string.

Functions save you programming time because they do some of the computing tasks for you, leaving you time to concentrate on your programs. This chapter has introduced you to numeric functions that round numbers, manipulate numbers, produce trigonometric and logarithm results, and produce random numbers.

## Review Questions

Answers to Review Questions are in Appendix B.

1. How do the character-testing functions differ from the character-conversion functions?

2. What is the difference between floor() and ceil()?

3. What will the following nested function return?

```
isalpha(islower('s'));
```

4. If the character array str1 contains the string Peter, and the character array str2 contains Parker, what does str2 contain after the following line of code?

```
strcat(s2, s1);
```

5. What is the output of the following cout?

```
cout << floor(8.5) << " " << ceil(8.5);
```

6. True or false: The isxdigit() and isgraph() functions could return the same value, depending on the character passed to them.

7. True or false: The following statements print the same results.

```
cout << pow(64.0, (1.0/2.0));
cout << sqrt(64.0);
```

# Review Exercises

1. Write a program that asks for the user's age. If the user types anything other than two digits, display an error message.

2. Write a program that stores a password in a character array called pass. Ask the user for the password. Use strcmp() to let the user know whether the proper password was typed.

3. Write a program that rounds the numbers –10.5, –5.75, and 2.75 in two different ways (up and down).

4. Write a program that asks for the user's name. Print the name in reverse case; in other words, print the first letter of each name in lowercase and print the rest of the name in uppercase.

5. Write a program that computes the square root, cube root, and fourth root of the numbers from 10 to 25.

6. Ask for the user's favorite song title. Discard all the special characters in the title. Print the words in the title, one word per line. If the title is *My True Love Is Mine, Oh, Mine!*, the output should look like this:

```
My
True
Love
Is
Mine
Oh
Mine
```

7. Ask the user for 10 first names of children divided into pairs. Using strcmp() on each pair of names, write a program to print the name (in each pair) that comes first in the alphabet.

# Part VI

*Arrays and Pointers*

# CHAPTER 24

# Arrays

This chapter discusses different types of arrays. You are already familiar with the character array, which is the only way to store a string of characters in C++. Character arrays are not the only kind of arrays you can use, however. There is an array for every data type in C++. Learning how to process these arrays will improve the efficiency and power of your programs.

This chapter introduces the following topics:

♦ Array basics: names, data types, and subscripts

♦ Initializing an array at declaration time

♦ Initializing an array during program execution

♦ Selecting elements from arrays

## Array Basics

*An array is a list of two or more variables with the same name and of the same data type.*

Although you have seen a special use of arrays as character strings, a little review is needed. An *array* is a list of two or more variables with the same name and of the same data type.

You might wonder how more than one variable can have the same name; that seems to violate the rules of variables. If two variables have the same name, how will C++ know which one you want when you use that name? Array variables are distinguished from each other by a *subscript*. A subscript is a number, within brackets, that differentiates one *element* of an array from another. Elements are the individual variables in an array.

Suppose you want to store a person's name in a character array called name. You can use either of the following definitions:

```
char name[ ] = "Ray Krebbs";
char name[ 11 ] = "Ray Krebbs";
```

Because C++ knows to reserve an extra element for the null zero at the end of every string, you don't have to specify the 11 as long as you initialize the array with a value. You know that the variable name is an array because brackets follow its name. The array has a single name called name, which contains 11 elements. The array is stored in memory (see figure 24.1). Each element is a character. You can manipulate individual elements in the array by using their subscripts.

**Figure 24.1.**

Storing a character array in memory.

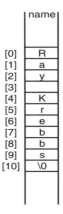

|       | name |
|-------|------|
| [0]   | R    |
| [1]   | a    |
| [2]   | y    |
| [3]   |      |
| [4]   | K    |
| [5]   | r    |
| [6]   | e    |
| [7]   | b    |
| [8]   | b    |
| [9]   | s    |
| [10]  | \0   |

**Note:** All array subscripts begin with 0.

For instance, the following cout function prints Ray's initials:

*Print the first and fifth elements of the array name.*

```
cout << name[ 0 ] << ". " << name[ 4 ];
```

You can define an array as any data type in C++. You can have integer arrays, long integer arrays, double floating-point arrays, short integer arrays, and so on. C++ knows that you are defining an array instead of a single nonarray variable when you put brackets after the array name. For example, the following line defines an array, called ages, of five integers:

```
int  ages[ 5 ];
```

The first element in the ages array is ages[ 0 ]. The second element is ages[ 1 ], and the last element is ages[ 4 ]. This declaration of ages does not assign values to the elements, so you do not know what is in ages, and your program cannot assume that it contains zeros or anything else.

Here are more array definitions:

```
int  weights[ 25 ], sizes[ 100 ]; // Declare 2 integer arrays

float     salaries[ 8 ];   // Declare 1 floating-point array

double    temps[ 50 ];     // Declare 1 double floating-point
                           // array

char letters[ 15 ];        // Declare a character array
```

When you declare an array, you instruct C++ to reserve a specific number of memory locations for that array. C++ will reserve those elements. In the preceding four lines of code, if you assign a value to letters[ 2 ], you will not overwrite any data in weights, sizes, salaries, or temps. If you assign a value to sizes[ 94 ], you will not overwrite data stored in weights, salaries, temps, or letters.

Each element in an array occupies the same amount of storage as a nonarray variable of the same data type. In other words, each element in a character array occupies 1 byte of memory. Each element in an integer array occupies 2 bytes of memory. The same is true for every other data type.

In your programs, you can reference elements by using formulas for subscripts. As long as the subscript can evaluate to an integer, you can use a constant, a variable, or an expression for the subscript. All of the following reference individual elements of arrays:

```
ara[ 4 ]
sales[ ctr + 1 ]
bonus[ month ]
salary[ month[ i ] * 2 ]
```

Array elements follow each other in memory, with nothing between them.

All array elements are stored in a contiguous, back-to-back fashion. This is important to remember, especially as you write more advanced programs. You can *always* count on an array's first element preceding the second, the second element placed immediately before the third, and so on. There is no "padding" of memory; that is, C++ ensures (and guarantees) that there is no extra space between array elements. This holds true for character arrays, integer arrays, floating-point arrays, and every other array data type. If a floating-point value on your computer occupies 4 bytes of memory, the *next* element in a floating-point array *always* begins 4 bytes after the preceding element.

---

**The Size of Arrays**

The `sizeof()` function returns the number of bytes needed to hold the functions argument. If you use `sizeof()` to request the size of an array name, `sizeof()` returns the number of bytes *reserved* for the entire array.

For instance, suppose you declared an integer array of 100 elements called `scores`. If you were to produce the size of the array, as in

```
n = sizeof(scores);
```

n would hold 200. `sizeof()` always returns the reserved amount of storage, no matter what data is in the array. Therefore, a character array's contents, even if the array holds a very short string, do not affect the size of the array that was originally reserved in memory.

If, however, you request the size of an individual array element, such as

```
n = sizeof(scores[ 6 ]);
```

n would hold 2.

---

You must never go out of bounds of an array. Suppose, for example, that you want to keep track of five employees' exemptions and their five salary codes. You can reserve two arrays to hold these data:

```
int  exemptions[ 5 ];    // Holds up to 5 employee exemptions
char sal_codes[ 5 ];     // Holds up to 5 employee codes
```

C++ reserves only as many array elements as you specify.

Figure 24.2 shows how C++ reserves memory for these arrays. Notice that C++ knows to reserve five elements for `exemptions` from the array declaration. C++ starts reserving memory for `sal_codes` after it reserves all five elements for the `exemptions`. If you were to declare several more variables, either locally or globally, after these two lines, C++ would always reserve the five elements for `exemptions` and `sal_codes`.

**Figure 24.2.**

Memory locations of two arrays.

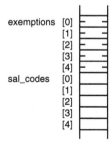

If you reserve five elements for `exemptions`, you have five integer array elements referred to as `exemptions[ 0 ]`, `exemptions[ 1 ]`, `exemptions[ 2 ]`, `exemptions[ 3 ]`, and exemptions[ 4 ]. *C++ will not reserve more than five elements for* exemptions*!* If you were to put a value into an exemptions element that you did not reserve, such as

```
exemptions[ 6 ] = 4;    // Assign a value to an out-of-range
                        // element
```

C++ lets you do so, but the results are damaging! C++ overwrites other data—in this case, sal_codes[ 2 ] and sal_codes[ 3 ], because they were reserved where the sixth element of the integer array exemptions would be placed. Figure 24.3 shows the damaging results of assigning a value to an out-of-range element.

**Figure 24.3.**

Memory storage after overwriting part of sal_codes.

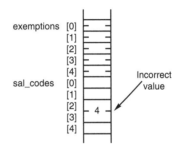

Although you can define an array of any data type, you cannot declare an array of strings. A string is not a C++ variable data type. You will learn how to hold multiple strings in an arraylike structure in Chapter 28, "Pointers and Arrays."

> **Caution:** Unlike some programming languages, C++ lets you assign values to out-of-range (nonreserved) subscripts. You must be careful not to do this, because you will overwrite other data or code.

## Initializing Arrays

You must assign values to array elements before using them. Here are the two ways to initialize elements in an array:

♦ Initialize the elements at declaration time.

♦ Initialize the elements in the program.

> **Note:** C++ automatically initializes global arrays to null zeros. All global character array elements are therefore null, and all numeric array elements contain zeros.

## Initializing Elements at Declaration Time

You already know how to initialize character arrays that hold strings when you define the arrays. You simply assign the array a string. For example, the following declaration reserves six elements in a character array called `city`:

```
char city[ 6 ];     // Reserve space for city
```

If you also want to initialize `city` with a value, you can use the following code:

```
char city[ 6 ] = "Tulsa"; // Reserve space and initialize city
```

The `6` is optional because C++ counts the elements needed to hold `Tulsa`, plus an extra element for the null zero at the end of the quoted string.

You can reserve a character array and initialize it, a single character at a time, by using braces around the character data. The following line of code declares an array called `initials` and initializes it with eight characters:

```
char initials[ 8 ] =
     { 'Q', 'K', 'P', 'G', 'V', 'M', 'U', 'S' };
```

The array `initials` is *not a string!* Its data does not end in a null zero. There is nothing wrong with defining an array of characters like this one, but you must remember that you cannot treat the array as if it were a string. Do not use string functions with it or attempt to print the array as a string.

Using the braces, you can initialize any type of array. For example, if you want to initialize an integer array that holds five children's ages, you can use the following declaration:

```
int  child_ages[ 5 ] =    { 2, 5, 6, 8, 12 }; // Declare and initialize
array
```

If you want to keep track of the last three years' total sales, you can declare an array and initialize it at the same time with this declaration:

```
double   sales[ ] =
     { 454323.43, 122355.32, 343324.96 };
```

As with character arrays, you do not have to state explicitly the array size when declaring and initializing an array of any type. C++ knows, in this case, to reserve three double floating-point array elements for `sales`. Figure 24.4 shows the memory representation of `child_ages` and `sales`.

> **Note:** You cannot initialize an array, using the assignment and braces, *after* you declare it. You can initialize arrays in this manner only when you declare them. If you want to fill an array with data after you declare the array, you must do so element by element, or by using functions as described later in this chapter.

**Figure 24.4.**

Memory
representation
of two arrays.

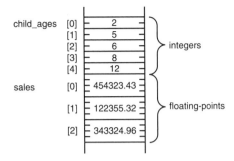

Although C++ does not automatically set array elements to zero (or initialize them to *any* value), if you initialize some but not all the elements when you declare the array, C++ will finish the job for you by assigning zero to the rest of the elements.

For instance, suppose you need to reserve array storage for profit figures from the three preceding months as well as for the next three months. You need to reserve six elements of storage, but you know values for only the first three elements. You can initialize the array in this way:

```
double    profit[ 6 ] =
     { 67654.43, 46472.34, 63451.93 };
```

Because you explicitly initialized the first three elements, C++ initializes the rest of them to zero. If you were to print the entire array, one element per line, with an appropriate cout, you would get the following:

```
67654.43
46472.34
63451.93
00000.00
00000.00
00000.00
```

**Tip:** To initialize all elements of a large array to zero at the same time, declare the entire array and initialize its first value to zero. C++ finishes assigning zeros to the rest of the array.

**Caution:** Always declare an array with the maximum number of subscripts, unless you initialize the array at the same time. The following array declaration is illegal:

```
int  count[ ];   // BAD array declaration!
```

*continues*

*continued*

C++ will not know how many elements to reserve for `count`, so it reserves *none*. If you then assign values to `count`'s nonreserved elements, you may (and probably will) inadvertently overwrite other data.

You can leave the brackets empty only when you assign values to the array, such as

```
int  count[ ] =
     { 15, 9, 22, -8, 12 };   // Good definition
```

C++ can tell, from the list of values, how many elements to reserve. In this case, C++ reserves five elements for `count`.

## Examples

1. Suppose you want to keep track of the stock-market averages for the preceding 90 days. Instead of storing the averages in 90 different variables, you can easily store them in an array:

```
float    stock[ 90 ];
```

The rest of the program can assign values to the averages.

2. You just finished taking classes at a local university and want to average your six class scores. The following program initializes an array for the school name and for the six classes. The body of the program averages the six scores.

```
// Filename: C24ARA1.CPP
// Averages six test scores

#include <iostream.h>

main()
    {
    char        s_name[ ] = "Tri Star University";
    float    scores[ 6 ] =
         { 88.7, 90.4, 76.0, 97.0, 100.0, 86.7 };
    float    average = 0.0;
    int          ctr;

    // Compute total of scores
    for (ctr = 0; ctr < 6; ctr++)
        {
        average += scores[ ctr ];
        }
```

```
// Compute the average
average /= (float)6;
cout << "At " << s_name << ", your class average is "
     << average << ".\n";
return 0;
}
```

Here is this program's output:

```
At Tri Star University, your class average is 89.8.
```

Notice that the use of arrays makes processing lists of information much easier. Instead of averaging six differently named variables, you can use a for loop to step through the array elements. The advantage of arrays is that you can average as many as 1,000 numbers with a simple for loop. If the 1,000 variables were not array elements but were individually named, you would have to write a lot of code just to add them together.

**3.** The following program is an expanded version of the one shown in Example 2. This program prints the six scores before computing the average. Notice that you have to print array elements individually; there is no way to print an entire array in a single cout. (Of course, you can print an entire character array, but only if it holds a null-terminated string of characters.)

```
// Filename: C24ARA2.CPP
// Prints and averages six test scores

#include <iostream.h>

void    pr_scores(float scores[ 6 ])
    {
    // Print the six scores
    int     ctr;

    cout << "Here are your scores:\n";       // Title
    for (ctr = 0; ctr < 6; ctr++)
        cout << scores[ ctr ] << "\n";
    return;
    }


int     main(void)
    {
    char        s_name[ ] = "Tri Star University";
    float    scores[ 6 ] =
        { 88.7, 90.4, 76.0, 97.0, 100.0, 86.7 };
    float    average = 0.0;
    int         ctr;

    // Call function to print scores
```

```
      pr_scores(scores);
      // Compute total of scores
      for (ctr = 0; ctr < 6; ctr++)
         {
         average += scores[ ctr ];
         }
      // Compute the average
      average /= (float)6;
      cout << "At " << s_name << ", your class average is "
           << average << ".\n";
      return 0;
      }
```

To pass any array to a function, you just specify the array's name. In the receiving function's parameter list, you must state the array type and provide brackets that tell the function that it is an array.

4. To improve the maintainability of your programs, define all array sizes with the #define preprocessor directive. What if you plan to take only four classes next semester but you want to use the same program you used when you took six classes? You could modify it by changing all the 6's to 4's. But if you have defined the array size with a defined constant, you will need to alter only one line to change the program's subscript limits. Notice how the following program uses a defined constant for the number of classes throughout the program:

```
// Filename: C24ARA3.CPP
// Prints and averages six test scores

#include <iostream.h>

#define     CLASS_NUM      (6)

void     pr_scores(float scores[ CLASS_NUM ])
     {
     int     ctr;

     cout << "Here are your scores:\n";      // Title
     for (ctr = 0; ctr < CLASS_NUM; ctr++)
          cout << scores[ ctr ] << "\n";
     return;
     }


int     main(void)
     {
     char          s_name[ ] = "Tri Star University";
```

```
float       scores[ CLASS_NUM ] =
    { 88.7, 90.4, 76.0, 97.0, 100.0, 86.7 };
float       average = 0.0;
int         ctr;

// Call function to print scores
pr_scores(scores);
// Compute total of scores
for (ctr = 0; ctr < CLASS_NUM; ctr++)
    {
    average += scores[ ctr ];
    }
// Compute the average
average /= (float)CLASS_NUM;
cout << "At " << s_name << ", your class average is "
     << average << ".\n";
return 0;
}
```

For a simple example such as this, using a defined constant for the maximum subscript may not seem like a big advantage. However, if you were writing a larger program that processed several arrays, changing the defined constant at the top of the program is much easier than searching the program for each occurrence of that array reference.

Using defined constants for array sizes has the added advantage of protecting you from going out of the subscript bounds. You don't have to remember the subscript when looping through arrays; you can use the defined constant instead.

## Initializing an Array in the Program

Rarely will you know the contents of arrays when you declare them. Usually, you fill an array with user input or from a disk file's data. The for loop is a perfect tool for looping through arrays once you fill them with values.

> **Caution:** An array name cannot appear on the left side of an assignment statement.

You cannot assign one array to another. Suppose that you want to copy an array called total_sales to a second array called saved_sales. You *cannot* do this with the following assignment statement:

```
saved_sales = total_sales;      // INVALID!
```

Instead, you have to copy the arrays one element at a time, using a loop, as in the section of code that follows:

*Initialize the variable* ctr *to 0 and increment it by 1 while the variable* ctr *is less than* ARRAY_SIZE.
*Write the* ctr'th *element of the* total_sales *array to the* ctr'th *element of the* saved_sales *array.*

```
for (ctr = 0; ctr < ARRAY_SIZE; ctr++)
    {

    saved_sales[ ctr ] = total_sales[ ctr ];

    }
```

The following examples illustrate methods for initializing arrays within the program. After learning about disk processing later in the book, you will learn to read array values from a disk file.

## Examples

**1.** The following program uses the assignment operator to assign 10 temperatures to an array:

```
// Filename: C24ARA4.CPP
// Fills an array with 10 temperature values

#include <iostream.h>

#define NUM_TEMPS 10

main()
    {
    float       temps[ NUM_TEMPS ];
    int         ctr;

    temps[ 0 ] = 78.6;      // Subscripts ALWAYS begin at 0
    temps[ 1 ] = 82.1;
    temps[ 2 ] = 79.5;
    temps[ 3 ] = 75.0;
    temps[ 4 ] = 75.4;
    temps[ 5 ] = 71.8;
    temps[ 6 ] = 73.3;
    temps[ 7 ] = 69.5;
    temps[ 8 ] = 74.1;
    temps[ 9 ] = 75.7;
    // Print the temps
    cout << "Daily temperatures for the last "
         << NUM_TEMPS << " days:\n";
    for (ctr = 0; ctr < NUM_TEMPS; ctr++)
        {
        cout << temps[ ctr ] << "\n";
        }
    return 0;
    }
```

**2.** The following program uses a `for` loop to assign eight integers from the user's input, using `cin`. The program then prints the total sum of the numbers.

```
// Filename: C24TOT.CPP
// Totals 8 input values from the user

#include <iostream.h>

#define NUM 8

main()
    {
    int     nums[ NUM ];
    int     ctr;
    int     total = 0;    // Holds total of user's 8 numbers

    for (ctr = 0; ctr < NUM; ctr++)
        {
        cout << "Please enter the next number...";
        cin >> nums[ ctr ];
        total += nums[ ctr ];
        }
    cout << "The total of the numbers is " << total << "\n";
    return 0;
    }
```

**3.** You don't have to access the elements of an array in the same order in which you initialized the array. Chapter 25, "Array Processing," shows you how to change the order of an array. You can use the subscript to "pick out" items from a list (array) of values.

The following program requests sales data for the last 12 months. The program then waits until the user types in a month number. Only that month's sales are then printed, without the values for the surrounding months getting in the way. This is how you would begin to build a search program to find requested data: store the data in an array (or in a disk file that can be read into an array, as you will learn in Chapters 31 and 32) and then wait for a request from the user to see only specific pieces of that data.

```
// Filename: C24SAL.CPP
// Stores 12 months of sales and prints selected ones

#include <iostream.h>
#include <ctype.h>
#include <conio.h>
#include <iomanip.h>
#define NUM 12

main()
    {
```

```
float    sales[ NUM ];
int      ctr, ans;
int      req_month;      // Holds user's request

cout.setf(ios::fixed);
cout.setf(ios::showpoint);
// Fill the array
cout << "Please enter the twelve monthly "
     << "sales values\n";
for (ctr = 0; ctr < NUM; ctr++)
    {
    cout << "What are sales for month number "
         << (ctr + 1) << "\n";
    cin >> sales[ ctr ];
    }
// Wait for a requested month
for (ctr = 0; ctr < 25; ctr++)
    cout << "\n";  // Clear the screen
cout << "*** Sales Printing Program ***\n";
cout << "Prints any sales from the last " << NUM
     << " months\n\n";
do
    {
    cout << "\nWhat month (1-" << NUM
         << ") do you want to see a sales value for?";
    cin >> req_month;
    // Adjust for zero-based subscript
    cout << "Month " << req_month << "'s sales are "
         << setprecision(2) << sales[ req_month - 1 ]
         << "\n";
    cout << "\nDo you want to see another (Y/N)? ";
    ans = getch();
    ans = toupper(ans);
    }
while (ans == 'Y');
return 0;
}
```

Figure 24.5 shows the second screen from this program. Once the 12 sales values are entered into the array, any or all of them can be requested, one at a time, simply by supplying the month number (the number of the subscript).

Notice the helpful screen-clearing routine that prints 25 newline characters. This routine scrolls the screen until it is blank.

**Figure 24.5.**

Printing sales
values entered
into the array.

```
*** Sales Printing Program ***
Prints any sales from the last 12 months


What month (1-12) do you want to see a sales value for?1
Month 1's sales are 3233.45

Do you want to see another (Y/N)?
What month (1-12) do you want to see a sales value for?5
Month 5's sales are 6535.64

Do you want to see another (Y/N)?
What month (1-12) do you want to see a sales value for?2
Month 2's sales are 6434.67

Do you want to see another (Y/N)?
What month (1-12) do you want to see a sales value for?8
Month 8's sales are 4598.79

Do you want to see another (Y/N)?
```

## Summary

You now know how to declare and initialize arrays of various data types. You can initialize an array when you declare it or in the body of your program. Array elements are much easier to process than many variables with different names.

Useful sorting and searching techniques are available to make your programs extremely powerful. The next chapter describes these techniques and shows you other ways to access array elements.

## Review Questions

Answers to Review Questions are in Appendix B.

1. True or false: A single array can hold several values of different data types.

2. How do C++ programs tell one array element from another if the elements have identical names?

3. Why must you initialize an array before using it?

4. Look at the following definition of an array called `weights`:

```
int    weights[ 10 ] = { 5, 2, 4 };
```

What is the value of weights[ 5 ]?

5. Recall how character arrays are passed to functions. If you change a passed integer array in a function, does the array also change in the calling function?

6. How does C++ initialize global array elements?

# Review Exercises

**1**

**1.** Write a program to store six of your friends' ages in a single array. Store each of the six ages by using the assignment operator. Print the ages on the screen.

**2.** Modify the program you created in Exercise 1 to print the ages backward.

**1  2**

**3.** Write a simple data program to track a radio station's ratings (1, 2, 3, 4, or 5) for the last 18 months. Use cin to initialize the array with the ratings. Print the ratings on the screen with an appropriate title.

**4.** Write a program to store the numbers from 1 to 100 in an array of 100 integer elements. Remember that the subscripts begin at 0 and end at 99.

**3**
**1  2**

**5.** Write a program that a small-business owner can use to track customers. Assign each customer a number (starting at 0). When a customer makes a purchase, store that customer's sales in an element that matches a number for that customer (the next, unused array element). When the store owner signals the end of the day, print a report with each customer number and matching sales, total sales at the bottom, and the average sales per customer.

# CHAPTER 25

# Array Processing

C++ provides many ways to access arrays. If you have programmed with other computer languages, some of C++'s array-indexing techniques may be unfamiliar to you. You learn how to search an array for one or more values, find the highest and lowest values in an array, and sort an array into numeric or alphabetic order.

This chapter introduces the following topics:

♦ Searching arrays

♦ Finding the highest and lowest values in arrays

♦ Sorting arrays

♦ Using advanced subscripting with arrays

## Searching Arrays

Many types of programs lend themselves to processing lists (arrays) of data, such as an employee payroll program, scientific research of several chemicals, or customer account processing. Upcoming chapters describe disk file processing. You should know how to manipulate arrays so that you see the data exactly the way you want to see it.

*Array elements do not always appear in the most appropriate order.*

In the preceding chapter, you learned how to print the elements of arrays in the same order in which you entered the data. This is sometimes done, but it is not always the best method for looking at data.

Suppose, for instance, that a high school uses C++ programs for its grade reports, and the principal wants to see the top 10 grade-point averages. You cannot print the first 10 grade-point averages in the list of student averages because the top 10 grade points may not (and probably do not) appear as the first 10 array elements. Because the grade points are not in any sequence, the program would have to sort the array elements into numeric order (from high to low grade points), or search the array for the 10 highest grade points.

You need a method for putting arrays in a specific order. This is called *sorting* an array. When you sort an array, you put that array's elements in a specific order, such as alphabetic order or numeric order. A dictionary is in alphabetic order, and so is a phone book.

You also can reverse the order of a sort, called a *descending sort*. For instance, if you wanted to look at a list of all employees in descending salary order, the names of the highest-paid employees would be printed first.

Figure 25.1 shows a list of eight numbers in an array called unsorted. The middle list of numbers is an ascending sorted version of unsorted. The third list of numbers is a descending sorted version of unsorted.

**Figure 25.1.**

A list of unsorted numbers sorted in both ascending and descending order.

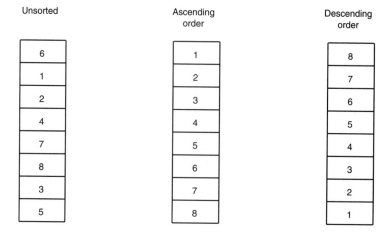

Before learning to sort, you need to know a preliminary step—how to search an array for a value. What if one of those students receives a grade change? The computer has to be able to access that student's grade in order to change it (without affecting the others). As the next section shows, programs can search for specific array elements.

# Searching for Values

You do not need to know any new commands to search an array for a value. Basically, the if and for loop statements are all you need. To search an array for a specific value, look at each element in the array, using the if statement to compare the elements to see whether they match. If they do not, keep searching down the array. If you run out of array elements before finding the value, it is not in the array.

You do not have to sort an array to find its extreme values.

You can perform several different kinds of searches. For example, you might need to find the highest or lowest value in a list of numbers. This is helpful when you have lots of data and you want to know the extremes of the data (such as the highest and lowest sales region in your division). In addition, you can search an array to see whether it contains a matching value. For instance, you can determine whether an item is already in an inventory by searching a part number array for a match.

The following example programs illustrate some of these array-searching techniques.

## Examples

1. To find the highest number in an array, compare each element with the first. If you find a higher value, it becomes the basis for the rest of the array. If you continue until you reach the end of the array, you get the highest value, as the following program shows:

```cpp
// Filename: C25HIGH.CPP
// Finds the highest value in the array

#include <iostream.h>

#define SIZE 15

main()
    {
    // Put a bunch of numbers in the array
    int     ara[ SIZE ] =
          { 5, 2, 7, 8, 36,
            4, 2, 86, 11, 43,
            22, 12, 45, 6, 85 };
    int     high_val, ctr;

    high_val = ara[ 0 ];      // Initialize with first array
                              // element
    for (ctr = 1; ctr < SIZE; ctr++)
         {      // Store current value if it is higher than
                // highest so far
         if (ara[ ctr ] > high_val)
             {
             high_val = ara[ ctr ];
             }
```

Here is this program's output:

```
The highest number in the list is 86.
```

You save the element only if it is higher than the one to which you are comparing the element. Finding the smallest number in an array is just as easy, except that you compare the elements to see whether each succeeding array value is less than the lowest value found so far.

**2.** The following program finds the highest and lowest values. It stores the first array element in *both* the highest and lowest variable to begin the search. This ensures that each element after that one is tested to see whether it is higher or lower than the first.

This example also uses the rand() function, discussed in Chapter 23, to fill the array with random values from 0 to 99. The modulus operator (%) and 100 are applied to whatever value rand() produces. The program prints the entire array before starting the search for the highest and lowest values.

```cpp
// Filename: C25HILO.CPP
// Finds the highest and lowest values in the array

#include <time.h>
#include <iostream.h>
#include <stdlib.h>

#define SIZE 15

main()
    {
    int     ara[ SIZE ];
    int     high_val, low_val, ctr;

    // Fill array with random numbers from 0 to 99
    randomize();
    for (ctr = 0; ctr < SIZE; ctr++)
        {
        ara[ ctr ] = rand() % 100;
        }
    // Print the array to the screen
    cout << "Here are the " << SIZE
         << " random numbers:\n";       // Title
    for (ctr = 0; ctr < SIZE; ctr++)
        {
        cout << ara[ ctr ] << "\n";
        }
    cout << "\n\n";               // Print a blank line
    high_val = ara[ 0 ];         // Initialize both high_val
                                 // and low_val to first element
    low_val  = ara[ 0 ];
    for (ctr = 1; ctr < SIZE; ctr++)
        {    // Store current value if it is higher than
             // the highest so far
        if (ara[ ctr ] > high_val)
            high_val = ara[ ctr ];
        if (ara[ ctr ] < low_val)
            low_val = ara[ ctr ];
        }
    cout << "The highest number in the list is "
         << high_val << ".\n";
    cout << "The lowest number in the list is "
```

```
        << low_val << ".\n";
    return 0;
    }
```

Figure 25.2 shows the output of this program.

**Figure 25.2.**

Printing the
highest and lowest
values in a list of
random numbers.

```
Here are the 15 random numbers:
    46
    38
    82
    90
    56
    17
    95
    15
    48
    26
     4
    58
    71
    79
    92

The highest number in the list is 95.
The lowest number in the list is 4.
```

**3.** The following program fills an array with part numbers from an inventory.
Use your imagination; the inventory array would normally fill more of the
array, be initialized from a disk file, and be part of a larger set of arrays
holding descriptions, quantities, costs, selling prices, and so on. For this
example, assignment statements initialize the array. The important idea to
learn from this program is not the array initialization, but the method for
searching the array.

> **Note:** If the newly entered part number is already on file, the program tells
> the user. Otherwise, the part number is added to the end of the array.

```cpp
// Filename: C25SERCH.CPP
// Searches a part number array for the input value. If
// the entered part number is not in the array, it is added.
// If the part number is in the array, a message is printed.

#include <iostream.h>

#define MAX 100

void    fill_parts(long int parts[ MAX ])
    {
    // Assign five part numbers to array for testing
    parts[ 0 ] = 12345;
    parts[ 1 ] = 24724;
```

```
        parts[ 2 ] = 54154;
        parts[ 3 ] = 73496;
        parts[ 4 ] = 83925;
        return;
        }


int     main(void)
    {
    long int     search_part;    // Holds user request
    long int     parts[ MAX ];
    int          ctr;
    int          num_parts = 5; // Beginning inventory count

    fill_parts(parts);        // Fill the first five elements



    do
        {
        cout << "\n\nPlease type a part number ";
        cout << "...(-9999 ends program) ";
        cin >> search_part;
        if (search_part == -9999)
            break;       // Exit loop if user wants
        // Scan array to see if part is in inventory
        for (ctr = 0; ctr < num_parts; ctr++)
            // Check each item
            {
            if (search_part == parts[ctr])
                // If in inventory...
                {
                cout << "\nPart " << search_part
                    << " is already in inventory";
                break;
                }
            else
                {
                if (ctr == (num_parts - 1))
                    // If not there, add it
                    {
                    parts[ num_parts ] = search_part;
                    // Add to end of array
                    num_parts++;
                    cout << "\n" << search_part
                        << " was added to inventory\n";
                    break;
                    }
                }
            }
        }
```

```
        while (search_part != -9999); // Loop until user
                                      // signals end

        return 0;
        }
```

Figure 25.3 shows the output of this program.

**Figure 25.3.**

Searching a table
of part numbers.

```
Please type a part number...(-9999 ends program) 25432

25432 was added to inventory

Please type a part number...(-9999 ends program) 12345

Part 12345 is already in inventory

Please type a part number...(-9999 ends program) 65468

65468 was added to inventory

Please type a part number...(-9999 ends program) 25432

Part 25432 is already in inventory

Please type a part number...(-9999 ends program) 43234
```

# Sorting Arrays

At times, you may need to sort one or more arrays. Suppose that you took a list of numbers, wrote each number on a separate piece of paper, and threw all the pieces into the air. The steps you would follow in trying to put the numbers in order, shuffling and changing the order of the pieces, are similar to what your computer goes through to sort numbers or character data.

Because sorting arrays requires exchanging values of elements, you should first learn the technique for swapping variables. Suppose that you have two variables named score1 and score2. What if you wanted to reverse their values (putting score2 into the score1 variable, and score1 into the score2 variable)? You could *not* use the following method:

```
score1 = score2;      // Does NOT swap the two values
score2 = score1;
```

Why doesn't this work? In the first line, the value of score1 is replaced with score2's value; when the first line finishes, both score1 and score2 contain the same value. Therefore, the second line cannot work.

To swap two variables, you need to use a third variable to hold one value temporarily. (That's the only purpose of the third variable.) For instance, to swap score1 and score2, use a third variable, called hold_score, as in the following code:

```
hold_score = score1;      // These 3 lines properly swap
score1 = score2;          // score1 and score2
score2 = hold_score;
This code exchanges the two values in the two variables.
```

There are several different ways to sort arrays. Some of the methods are the *bubble sort*, the *quick sort*, and the *shell sort*. The basic goal of each method is to compare each array element to another array element and then swap them if the higher one is less than the other one.

The theory behind these sorts is beyond the scope of this book; however, the bubble sort is one of the easiest methods to follow. Values in the array are compared to each other, a pair at a time, and swapped if they are not in back-to-back order. The lowest value eventually "floats" to the top of the array, like a bubble in a glass of soda.

*The lowest value in a list "floats" to the top with the bubble sort algorithm.*

Figure 25.4 shows a list of numbers before, during, and after a bubble sort. The bubble sort steps through the array, comparing pairs of numbers to see whether they need to be swapped. Several passes may have to be made through the array before it is finally sorted (that is, no more passes are needed). Other types of sorts improve on the bubble sort; its procedure is easy to program but slower than many of the other methods.

The example programs that follow show the bubble sort in action.

## Examples

1. This program assigns 10 random numbers, between 0 and 99, to an array and then sorts it.

A nested `for` loop, as shown in the `sort_array()` function, is perfect for sorting numbers in the array. Nested `for` loops provide a nice mechanism for working on pairs of values, swapping them if needed. As the outside loop counts down the list, referencing each element, the inside loop compares each of the remaining values with those array elements.

```
// Filename: C25SORT1.CPP
// Sorts and prints a list of numbers

#define MAX 10

#include <time.h>
#include <iostream.h>
#include <stdlib.h>


void     fill_array(int ara[ MAX ])
     {
     // Put random numbers in the array
     int     ctr;

     randomize();
     for (ctr = 0; ctr < MAX; ctr++)
          ara[ ctr ] = (rand() % 100);   // Force # to
                                         // 0-99 range
     return;
```

**Figure 25.4.**

Sorting a list of
numbers with the
bubble sort.

| First Pass | | | |
|---|---|---|---|
| 3 | 2 | 2 | 2 |
| 2 | 3 | 3 | 3 |
| 5 | 5 | 1 | 1 |
| 1 | 1 | 5 | 4 |
| 4 | 4 | 4 | 5 |

| Second Pass | |
|---|---|
| 2 | 2 |
| 3 | 1 |
| 1 | 3 |
| 4 | 4 |
| 5 | 5 |

| Third Pass | |
|---|---|
| 2 | 1 |
| 1 | 2 |
| 3 | 3 |
| 4 | 4 |
| 5 | 5 |

| Fourth Pass |
|---|
| 1 |
| 2 |
| 3 |
| 4 |
| 5 |

```
    }

void    print_array(int ara[ MAX ])
    {
    // Print the array
    int     ctr;
    for (ctr = 0; ctr < MAX; ctr++)
        cout << ara[ ctr ] << "\n";
    return;
    }

void    sort_array(int ara[ MAX ])
    {
    // Sort the array
    int     temp;        // Temporary variable to swap with
    int     ctr1, ctr2;  // Need 2 loop counters to swap
                         // pairs of numbers

    for (ctr1 = 0; ctr1 < (MAX - 1); ctr1++)
        {
        for (ctr2 = (ctr1 + 1); ctr2 < MAX; ctr2++)
            // Test pairs
            {
            if (ara[ ctr1 ] > ara[ ctr2 ])
                // Swap if this pair
                {
                temp = ara[ ctr1 ]; // is not in order
                ara[ ctr1 ] = ara[ ctr2 ];
                ara[ ctr2 ] = temp; // "float" the
                                    // lowest to highest
                }
            }
        }
    return;
    }


int     main(void)
    {
    int     ara[ MAX ];

    fill_array(ara);     // Put random numbers in the array
    cout << "Here are the unsorted numbers:\n";
    print_array(ara);    // Print the unsorted array
    sort_array(ara);     // Sort the array
    cout << "\n\nHere are the sorted numbers:\n";
    print_array(ara);    // Print the newly sorted array
    return 0;
    }
```

Figure 25.5 shows the output of this program. If any two randomly generated numbers are the same, the bubble sort works properly, placing them next to each other in the list.

**Figure 25.5.**

Printing a sorted
list of numbers.

```
Here are the unsorted numbers:
46
30
82
90
56
17
95
15
48
26

Here are the sorted numbers:
15
17
26
30
46
48
56
82
90
95
```

2. The following program is just like the preceding one, except that this program prints the list of numbers in descending order.

To produce a descending sort, use the < (less than) logical operator when swapping array elements.

A descending sort is as easy to write as an ascending sort. With the ascending sort (from low to high values), you compare pairs of values, testing to see whether the first value is greater than the second. With a descending sort, you test to see whether the first value is less than the second.

```cpp
// Filename: C25SORT2.CPP
// Sorts and prints a list of numbers in descending order

#define MAX 10

#include <time.h>
#include <iostream.h>
#include <stdlib.h>


void    fill_array(int ara[ MAX ])
    {
    // Put random numbers in the array
    int    ctr;

    randomize();
    for (ctr = 0; ctr < MAX; ctr++)
        ara[ ctr ] = (rand() % 100);      // Force # to
                                          // 0-99 range

    return;
    }

void    print_array(int ara[ MAX ])
    {
    // Print the array
    int    ctr;
```

```
        for (ctr = 0; ctr < MAX; ctr++)
            cout << ara[ ctr ] << "\n";
        return;
        }

void    sort_array(int ara[ MAX ])
    {
    // Sort the array
    int     temp;           // Temporary variable to swap with
    int     ctr1, ctr2;     // Need 2 loop counters to swap
                            // pairs of numbers

    for (ctr1 = 0; ctr1 < (MAX - 1); ctr1++)
        {
        for (ctr2 = (ctr1 + 1); ctr2 < MAX; ctr2++)
            // Test pairs
            // Notice the difference in descending (here)
            // and ascending
            {
            if (ara[ ctr1 ] < ara[ ctr2 ])
                // Swap if this pair
                {
                temp = ara[ ctr1 ]; // is not in order
                ara[ ctr1 ] = ara[ ctr2 ];
                ara[ ctr2 ] = temp; // "float" the
                                    // highest to lowest
                }
            }
        }
    return;
    }

int     main(void)
    {
    int     ara[ MAX ];

    fill_array(ara);        // Put random numbers in the array
    cout << "Here are the unsorted numbers:\n";
    print_array(ara);       // Print the unsorted array
    sort_array(ara);        // Sort the array
    cout << "\n\nHere are the sorted numbers:\n";
    print_array(ara);       // Print the newly sorted array
    return 0;
    }
```

> **Tip:** You can save the preceding programs' sort functions in two files named `sort_ascend` and `sort_descend`. When you need to sort two different arrays, `#include` these files in your own programs. Even better, compile each of these routines separately and link the one you need to your program.

You can sort character arrays as easily as you sort numeric arrays. C++ uses the ASCII table for its sorting comparisons. Look at the ASCII table in Appendix C, and you will see that numbers sort before letters and that uppercase letters sort before lowercase letters.

## Advanced Referencing of Arrays

*An array name is the address of the starting element of the array.*

The array notation you have seen so far is common in computer programming languages. Most languages use subscripts inside brackets (or parentheses) to refer to individual array elements. For instance, you know that the following array references describe the first and fifth elements of the array called sales (remember that the starting subscript is always 0):

```
sales[ 0 ]
sales[ 4 ]
```

C++ provides another approach to referencing arrays. In C++, an array's name is not just a label for you to use in programs. To C++, the array name is the actual address where the first element begins in memory. Suppose that you define an array called amounts with the following statement:

```
int     amounts[ 6 ] =
    { 4, 1, 3, 7, 9, 2 };
```

Figure 25.6 shows how this array is stored in memory. The figure shows the array beginning at address 405,332. (The actual addresses of variables are determined by the computer when you load and run your compiled program.) Notice that the name of the array, amounts, is located somewhere in memory and contains the address of amounts[ 0 ], or 405,332.

You can refer to an array by using its regular subscript notation or by modifying the address of the array. Both of the following items refer to the third element of amounts:

```
amounts[ 3 ]
(amounts + 3)[ 0 ]
```

**Figure 25.6.**

The array name
amounts holds
the address of
amounts[ 0 ].

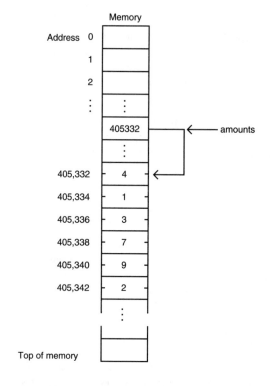

Because C++ considers the array name to be an address in memory that contains the location of the first array element, nothing keeps you from using a different address as the starting address and referencing from there. Taking this one step further, each of the following *also* refers to the third element of amounts:

```
(amounts + 0)[ 3 ]
(amounts + 2)[ 1 ]
(amounts - 2)[ 5 ]
(1 + amounts)[ 2 ]
(3 + amounts)[ 0 ]
(amounts + 1)[ 2 ]
```

You can print any of these array elements with a cout function.

> **Caution:** The hierarchy table in Appendix D shows that array subscripts have precedence over addition and subtraction. Therefore, you must enclose an array name in parentheses if you want to modify the name. The following examples are not equivalent:
>
> ```
> (2 + amounts)[ 1 ]
>
>  2 + amounts[ 1 ]
> ```
>
> The second example takes the value of `amounts[ 1 ]` (which is 1 in this sample array) and adds 2 to it (resulting in a value of 3).

This second method of array referencing might seem like more trouble than it is worth, but learning to reference arrays in this way will make your transition to pointers much easier. An array name is actually a pointer itself because the array contains the address of the first array element (it "points" to the start of the array).

When printing strings inside character arrays, referencing the arrays by their modified addresses is more useful than referencing the arrays with integers. Suppose that you stored three strings in a single character array. You could initialize the array with the following statement:

```
char names[ ] =
     { 'T', 'e', 'd', '\0',
       'E', 'v', 'a', '\0',
       'S', 'a', 'm', '\0' };
```

Figure 25.7 shows how this array might look in memory. The array name, `names`, contains the address of the first element, `names[ 0 ]` (the letter *T*).

**Figure 25.7.**

Storing more than one string in a single character array.

| names | [0] | T |
|-------|-----|---|
| | [1] | e |
| | [2] | d |
| | [3] | \0 |
| | [4] | E |
| | [5] | v |
| | [6] | a |
| | [7] | \0 |
| | [8] | S |
| | [9] | a |
| | [10] | m |
| | [11] | \0 |

You have yet to see a character array that holds more than one string, but C++ allows such an array. The problem is how you reference (especially how you print) the second and third strings. If you were to print this array (as you have been doing) with the following code fragment

```
cout << names;
```

C++ would print

```
Ted.
```

cout prints characters starting at the array's address until the null zero is reached.

As mentioned in Chapter 8, "Simple Input and Output," cout prints the string starting at the address of the specified array. Without a different way to reference the array, you would have no method of printing the three strings inside the single array (without resorting to printing them one element at a time).

Because cout requires a starting address, you can print the three strings with the following cout function calls:

```
cout << names;        // Print Ted
cout << names + 4;    // Print Eva
cout << names + 8;    // Print Sam
```

To test your understanding, what will the following cout function calls print?

```
cout << names + 1;
cout << names + 6;
```

The first cout prints ed, the string starting at the address specified (names + 1), and stops printing when it gets to the null zero. The second cout prints a. Adding 6 to the address at names produces the address where the a is located. The "string" is only one character long because the null zero appears in the array immediately after the a.

In summary of character arrays, the following refer to individual array elements (single characters):

```
names[ 2 ]
(names + 1)[ 1 ]
```

You can print both of these elements as characters but *not* as strings.

The following refer only to addresses:

```
names
(names + 4)
```

You can print both of these elements as strings but *not* as characters.

The next sample program is a little different from most of those you have seen. This example does not perform real-world work, but helps you become familiar with this new method of array referencing. The next few chapters expand on this method.

## Example

The following program stores the numbers from 100 to 600 (in increments of 100) in an array and then prints elements with the new method of array subscripting:

```
// Filename: C25REF1.CPP
// Prints elements of an integer array in different ways

#include <iostream.h>

main()
    {
    int    num[ 6 ] =
        { 100, 200, 300, 400, 500, 600 };

    cout << "num[0] is \t" << num[ 0 ] << "\n";
    cout << "(num + 0)[ 0 ] is \t" << (num + 0)[ 0 ]
        << "\n";
    cout << "(num - 2)[ 2 ] is \t" << (num - 2)[ 2 ]
        << "\n\n";
    cout << "num[ 1 ] is \t" << num[ 1 ] << "\n";
    cout << "(num + 1)[ 0 ] is \t" << (num + 1)[ 0 ]
        << "\n";
    cout << "(num - 3)[ 4 ] is \t" << (num - 3)[ 4 ]
        << "\n\n";
    cout << "num[ 5 ] is \t" << num[ 5 ] << "\n";
    cout << "(num + 5)[ 0 ] is \t" << (num + 5)[ 0 ]
        << "\n";
    cout << "(num + 2)[ 3 ] is \t" << (num + 2)[ 3 ]
        << "\n\n";
    cout << "(3 + num)[ 1 ] is \t" << (3 + num)[ 1 ]
        << "\n";
    cout << "3 + num[ 1 ] is \t" << 3 + num[ 1 ] << "\n";
    return 0;
    }
```

Figure 25.8 shows this program's output.

**Figure 25.8.**

The output of
various array
references.

```
num[0] is        100
(num+0)[0] is    100
(num-2)[2] is    100

num[1] is        200
(num+1)[0] is    200
(num-5)[4] is    200

num[5] is        600
(num+5)[0] is    600
(num+2)[3] is    600

(3+num)[1] is    500
3+num[1] is      203
```

## Summary

Arrays enable you to search and sort lists of values. Sorting and searching are what computers do best; they can quickly scan hundreds and even thousands of values, looking for a match. Scanning files of paper by hand to look for just the right number takes much more time. By stepping through arrays, your programs can quickly scan, sort, calculate, or print a list of values. You now have the tools to sort lists of numbers as well as to search for values in a list.

Chapter 26, "Multidimensional Arrays," shows you how to keep track of arrays in a different format, called a *matrix*. Not all lists of data lend themselves to matrices, but you should be prepared to use them when appropriate.

## Review Questions

Answers to Review Questions are in Appendix B.

1. True or false: You must access an array in the same order in which you initialized it.

2. Where did the bubble sort get its name?

3. Are the following values sorted in ascending or descending order?

```
33  55  78  78  90  102  435  859  976  4092
```

4. How does C++ use the name of an array?

5. Look at this array definition:

```
char teams[ ] =
    { 'E', 'a', 'g', 'l', 'e', 's', '\0',
      'R', 'a', 'm', 's', '\0' };
```

What is printed with each of the following statements?

```
A. cout << teams;
B. cout << teams + 7;
C. cout << (teams + 3);
D. cout << teams[ 0 ];
E. cout << (teams + 0)[ 0 ];
F. cout << (teams + 5);
G. cout << (teams - 200)[ 202 ]);
```

# Review Exercises

1. Write a program to store six of your friends' ages in a single array. Assign the ages in random order. Print the ages, from lowest to highest, on the screen.

2. Modify the preceding program to print the ages in descending order.

3. Using the new method of subscripting arrays, rewrite the programs in exercises 1 and 2. Always put a 0 in the subscript brackets, modifying the address instead. Use (ages + 3)[ 0 ] instead of ages[ 3 ].

4. Sometimes *parallel arrays* are used in programs that must track more than one list of values that are related. Suppose that you have to maintain an inventory, tracking the integer part numbers, prices, and quantities of each item. This task requires three arrays: an integer part-number array, a floating-point price array, and an integer quantity array. Each array has the same number of elements (the total number of parts in the inventory).

   Write a program to maintain such an inventory. Reserve enough elements for 100 parts in the inventory. Present the user with an input screen. When the user enters a part number, search the part number array. Once you locate the position of the part, print the corresponding price and quantity. If the part does not exist, let the user add it to the inventory, along with the matching price and quantity.

# Multidimensional Arrays

Some data fits into lists, as shown in the preceding chapters; other data is better suited for tables of information. The preceding chapters focused on single-dimensional arrays—that is, an array that represents a list of values but has only one subscript. This chapter takes arrays one step further by covering *multidimensional arrays*. These arrays, sometimes called *tables* or *matrices*, have at least two dimensions: rows and columns. Sometimes multidimensional arrays have even more dimensions.

This chapter covers the following topics:

♦ Declaring multidimensional arrays

♦ Reserving storage for multidimensional arrays

♦ Putting data into multidimensional arrays

♦ Using nested for loops to process multidimensional arrays

## Declaring Multidimensional Arrays

A multidimensional array has more than one subscript.

A *multidimensional array* is an array with more than one subscript. A single-dimensional array is a list of values, but a multidimensional array simulates a table of values, or even multiple tables of values. The most commonly used table is a two-dimensional table (an array with two subscripts).

Suppose that a softball team wants to keep track of its players' hits. The team played 10 games, and 15 players are on the team. Table 26.1 shows the team's record of hits.

### Table 26.1. A softball team's record of hits.

| Player Name | 1 | 2 | 3 | 4 | 5 | 6 | 7 | 8 | 9 | 10 |
|---|---|---|---|---|---|---|---|---|---|---|
| Adams | 2 | 1 | 0 | 0 | 2 | 3 | 3 | 1 | 1 | 2 |
| Berryhill | 1 | 0 | 3 | 2 | 5 | 1 | 2 | 2 | 1 | 0 |
| Downing | 1 | 0 | 2 | 1 | 0 | 0 | 0 | 0 | 2 | 0 |
| Edwards | 0 | 3 | 6 | 4 | 6 | 4 | 5 | 3 | 6 | 3 |
| Franks | 2 | 2 | 3 | 2 | 1 | 0 | 2 | 3 | 1 | 0 |
| Grady | 1 | 3 | 2 | 0 | 1 | 5 | 2 | 1 | 2 | 1 |
| Howard | 3 | 1 | 1 | 1 | 2 | 0 | 1 | 0 | 4 | 3 |
| Jones | 2 | 2 | 1 | 2 | 4 | 1 | 0 | 7 | 1 | 0 |
| Martin | 5 | 4 | 5 | 1 | 1 | 0 | 2 | 4 | 1 | 5 |
| Powers | 2 | 2 | 3 | 1 | 0 | 2 | 1 | 3 | 1 | 2 |
| Smith | 1 | 1 | 2 | 1 | 3 | 4 | 1 | 0 | 3 | 2 |
| Smithtown | 1 | 0 | 1 | 2 | 1 | 0 | 3 | 4 | 1 | 2 |
| Townsend | 0 | 0 | 0 | 0 | 0 | 0 | 1 | 0 | 0 | 0 |
| Ulmer | 2 | 2 | 2 | 2 | 2 | 1 | 1 | 3 | 1 | 3 |
| Williams | 2 | 3 | 1 | 0 | 1 | 2 | 1 | 2 | 0 | 3 |

Do you see that the softball table is a two-dimensional table? It has rows (the first dimension) and columns (the second dimension). Therefore, you would call this a two-dimensional table with 15 rows and 10 columns. (Generally, the number of rows is specified first.)

Each row has a player's name, and each column has a game number associated with it, but these are not part of the data. The data consists only of 150 values (15 rows times 10 columns equals 150 data values). The data in a two-dimensional table, just as with arrays, is always the same type of data; in this case, every value is an integer. If it were a table of salaries, every element would be a floating-point value.

A three-dimensional table has three dimensions: depth, rows, and columns.

The number of dimensions—in this case, two of them—corresponds to the dimensions in the physical world. The single-dimensional array is a line, or list of values. Two dimensions represent length and width. You write on a piece of paper in two dimensions; two dimensions represent a flat surface. Three dimensions represent length, width, and depth. You might have seen a 3-D movie. Not only do the images have length (height) and width, but they also (appear to) have depth. Figure 26.1 shows what a three-dimensional array looks like if it has a depth of four, six rows, and three columns. Notice that a three-dimensional table resembles a cube of blocks.

**Figure 26.1.**

A representation of a three-dimensional table (a cube).

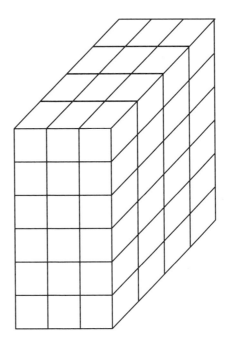

Visualizing more than three dimensions is difficult. You can think of each dimension after three, however, as another occurrence. In other words, you could store in a single-dimensional array a list of one player's season hit record. The team's hit record (as shown earlier) is two-dimensional. The league, made of up several teams' hit records, would represent a three-dimensional table. Each team (the depth of the table) would have rows and columns of hit data. If two leagues are involved, the second league could be considered another dimension (another set of data).

C++ gives you the capability to store several dimensions, although real-world data rarely requires more than two or three dimensions.

# Reserving Space for Multidimensional Arrays

When you reserve a multidimensional array, you must let C++ know that the array has more than one dimension. Put more than one subscript in brackets after the array name. You must put a different number, in brackets, for each dimension in the table. To reserve the team data from Table 26.1, for example, you use the following multidimensional array declaration:

*Declare the integer array teams with 15 rows and 10 columns.*

```
int  teams[ 15 ][ 10 ];      // Reserve a two-dimensional table
```

> **Caution:** Unlike other programming languages, C++ requires that you enclose *each* dimension in brackets. Do not reserve multidimensional array storage like this:
>
> ```
> int  teams[ 15, 10 ];    // INVALID table declaration
> ```

Properly reserving the teams table produces a table with 150 elements. The elements' subscripts look like those in figure 26.2.

If you needed to keep track of three teams, and each team had 15 players and played 10 games, you could dimension an array as

The far-right dimension always represents columns, the next dimension represents rows, and so on.

```
int  teams[ 3 ][ 15 ][ 10 ];  // Reserve a 3-dimensional
                              // table
```

This dimensions three occurrences of the teams table shown in figure 26.2.

When dimensioning a two-dimensional table, always put the maximum number of rows first, and the maximum number of columns second. C++ always uses 0 as the starting subscript of each dimension. The last element, the lower-right element of the teams table, would be teams[ 2 ][ 14 ][ 9 ].

## Examples

1. Suppose that you want to keep track of utility bills for the year. You can store 12 months of four utilities in a two-dimensional table of floating-point amounts, as shown in the following array declaration:

```
float    utilities[ 12 ][ 4 ];    // Reserve 48 elements
```

You can compute the total number of elements in a multidimensional array by multiplying the subscripts. Because 12 times 4 is 48, 48 elements are in this array (12 rows, 4 columns). Each of these elements is a floating-point data type.

**Figure 26.2.**

Subscripts for the softball team table.

| | | | | | | | | | |
|---|---|---|---|---|---|---|---|---|---|
| [0] [0] | [0] [1] | [0] [2] | [0] [3] | [0] [4] | [0] [5] | [0] [6] | [0] [7] | [0] [8] | [0] [9] |
| [1] [0] | [1] [1] | [1] [2] | [1] [3] | [1] [4] | [1] [5] | [1] [6] | [1] [7] | [1] [8] | [1] [9] |
| [2] [0] | [2] [1] | [2] [2] | [2] [3] | [2] [4] | [2] [5] | [2] [6] | [2] [7] | [2] [8] | [2] [9] |
| [3] [0] | [3] [1] | [3] [2] | [3] [3] | [3] [4] | [3] [5] | [3] [6] | [3] [7] | [3] [8] | [3] [9] |
| [4] [0] | [4] [1] | [4] [2] | [4] [3] | [4] [4] | [4] [5] | [4] [6] | [4] [7] | [4] [8] | [4] [9] |
| [5] [0] | [5] [1] | [5] [2] | [5] [3] | [5] [4] | [5] [5] | [5] [6] | [5] [7] | [5] [8] | [5] [9] |
| [6] [0] | [6] [1] | [6] [2] | [6] [3] | [6] [4] | [6] [5] | [6] [6] | [6] [7] | [6] [8] | [6] [9] |
| [7] [0] | [7] [1] | [7] [2] | [7] [3] | [7] [4] | [7] [5] | [7] [6] | [7] [7] | [7] [8] | [7] [9] |
| [8] [0] | [8] [1] | [8] [2] | [8] [3] | [8] [4] | [8] [5] | [8] [6] | [8] [7] | [8] [8] | [8] [9] |
| [9] [0] | [9] [1] | [9] [2] | [9] [3] | [9] [4] | [9] [5] | [9] [6] | [9] [7] | [9] [8] | [9] [9] |
| [10] [0] | [10] [1] | [10] [2] | [10] [3] | [10] [4] | [10] [5] | [10] [6] | [10] [7] | [10] [8] | [10] [9] |
| [11] [0] | [11] [1] | [11] [2] | [11] [3] | [11] [4] | [11] [5] | [11] [6] | [11] [7] | [11] [8] | [11] [9] |
| [12] [0] | [12] [1] | [12] [2] | [12] [3] | [12] [4] | [12] [5] | [12] [6] | [12] [7] | [12] [8] | [12] [9] |
| [13] [0] | [13] [1] | [13] [2] | [13] [3] | [13] [4] | [13] [5] | [13] [6] | [13] [7] | [13] [8] | [13] [9] |
| [14] [0] | [14] [1] | [14] [2] | [14] [3] | [14] [4] | [14] [5] | [14] [6] | [14] [7] | [14] [8] | [14] [9] |

2. If you were keeping track of five years' worth of utilities, you would have to add an extra dimension. The first dimension is the years, the second dimension is the months, and the last dimension is the individual utilities. You would reserve storage this way:

```
float      utilities[ 5 ][ 12 ][ 4 ]; // Reserve 240 elements
```

## Mapping Arrays to Memory

C++ approaches multidimensional arrays a little differently from most programming languages. A two-dimensional array is actually an *array of arrays*. You program multidimensional arrays as though they were tables with rows and columns. A two-dimensional array is really a single-dimensional array, and *each* of its elements is not an integer, floating-point, or character value, but is another array.

Knowing that a multidimensional array is an array of other arrays is critical when you're passing and receiving such arrays. C++ passes all arrays, including multidimensional arrays, by address. Suppose that you are using an integer array called scores, reserved as a five-by-six table. You can pass scores to a function called print_it():

```
print_it(scores);   // Pass table to a function
```

The function print_it() has to know the type of parameter being passed to it. print_it() also must know that the parameter is an array. If the table is one-dimensional, you can receive it as

```
print_it(int scores[ ])        // Works only if scores
                               // is 1-dimensional
```

or

```
print_it(int scores[ 10 ])     // Assuming scores has 10
                               // elements
```

If scores is a multidimensional table, you *must* designate each pair of brackets and put the maximum number of subscripts in the brackets, as in

```
print_it(int scores[ 5 ][ 6 ])  // Let print_it() know
                                // about dimensions
```

or

```
print_it(int scores[ ][ 6 ])    // Let print_it() know
                                // about dimensions
```

Notice that you do *not* have to explicitly state the number of elements in the first dimension when passing multidimensional arrays, but you must explicitly state the number of elements in the other dimensions. If scores were a three-dimensional table dimensioned as 10 by 5 by 6, for example, you would pass it to print_it() as

```
print_it(int scores[ 10 ][ 5 ][ 6 ])  // Let print_it() know
                                      // about dimensions
```

or

```
print_it(int scores[ ][ 5 ][ 6 ])     // Only first dimension
                                      // is optional
```

Generally, you do not need to worry much about the way tables are physically stored. Even though a two-dimensional table is an array of arrays (and each of *those* arrays would contain another array if the table were three-dimensional), you can program multidimensional arrays as if they were stored in row-and-column order by using subscripts.

C++ stores multidimensional arrays in row order.

Multidimensional arrays are stored in *row order*. Suppose that you want to keep track of a three-by-four table. Figure 26.3 shows how you can visualize that table (and its subscripts). Despite the tablelike feel of such a two-dimensional table, your memory is still sequential storage. C++ has to map multidimensional arrays to single-dimensional memory, and it does so in row order.

**Figure 26.3.**

Mapping a two-dimensional table to memory.

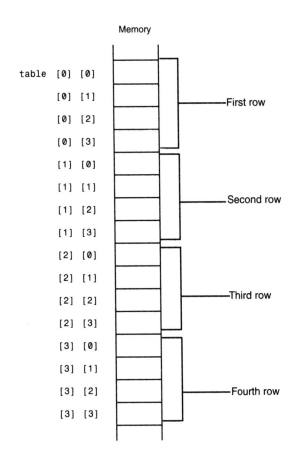

Memory

```
table  [0]  [0]
       [0]  [1]          ──First row
       [0]  [2]
       [0]  [3]
       [1]  [0]
       [1]  [1]          ──Second row
       [1]  [2]
       [1]  [3]
       [2]  [0]
       [2]  [1]
       [2]  [2]          ──Third row
       [2]  [3]
       [3]  [0]
       [3]  [1]
       [3]  [2]          ──Fourth row
       [3]  [3]
```

Each row fills memory before the next row is stored. The bottom of figure 26.3 shows how a three-by-four table is mapped to memory. The entire first row, `table[ 0 ][ 0 ]` through `table[ 0 ][ 3 ]`, is stored first in memory before any of the second row is stored. Because a table is an array of arrays, and, as you learned earlier, array elements are always stored sequentially in memory, the first row (array) completely fills memory before the second row is stored. Study figure 26.3 to learn how two-dimensional arrays map to memory.

## Defining Multidimensional Arrays

C++ is not picky about the way you define a multidimensional array when you initialize it at declaration time. As with single-dimensional arrays, you initialize multidimensional arrays with braces that designate dimensions. Because a multidimensional array is an array of arrays, you can nest braces when initializing them.

The following three array definitions fill the arrays ara1, ara2, and ara3, as shown in figure 26.4:

```
int   ara1[ 5 ] =
      { 8, 5, 3, 25, 41 };      // 1-dimensional array
int   ara2[ 2 ][ 4 ] =
      {
            { 4, 3, 2, 1 },
            { 1, 2, 3, 4 }
      };
int   ara3[ 3 ][ 4 ] =


      {

            { 1, 2, 3, 4 },

            { 5, 6, 7, 8 },

            {9, 10, 11, 12 }

      };
```

Notice that the multidimensional arrays are stored in row order. In ara3, the first row gets the first four elements of the definition (1, 2, 3, and 4).

**Tip:** To make a multidimensional array initialization match the array's subscripts, some programmers like to visualize how arrays are filled. Because C programs are free form, you can initialize ara2 and ara3 as

```
int ara2[2][4]={{4, 3, 2, 1},       // Does exactly the
                {1, 2, 3, 4}};      // same thing as
                                    // before
int ara3[4][4]={{1, 2, 3, 4},
                {5, 6, 7, 8},
                {9, 10, 11, 12},
                {13, 14, 15, 16}};  // Visually more
                                    // obvious
```

C++ does not mind if you initialize a multidimensional array as if it were a single-dimensional array. But you have to make sure that you keep track of the row order if you initialize this way. For instance, the following two definitions reserve storage and initialize ara2 and ara3:

```
int     ara2[ 2 ][ 4 ] =
      { 4, 3, 2, 1, 1, 2, 3, 4 };
int     ara3[ 4 ][ 4 ] =
      { 1, 2, 3, 4, 5, 6, 7, 8, 9, 10, 11, 12, 13, 14,
        15, 16 };
```

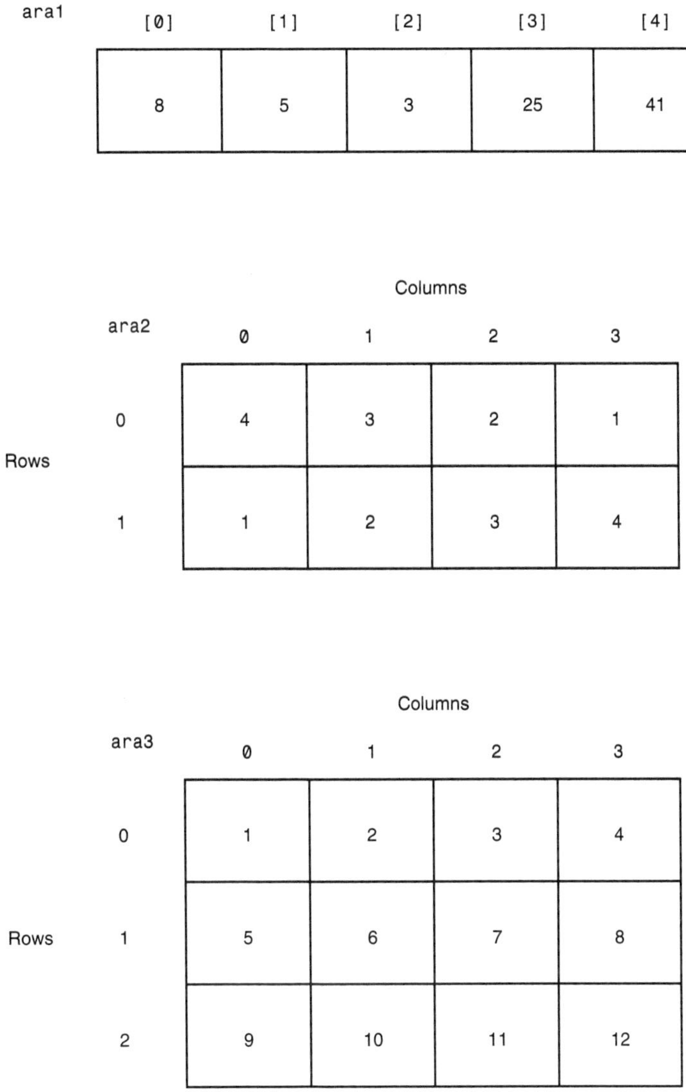

**Figure 26.4.**

Table contents
after initialization.

ara1

|  | [0] | [1] | [2] | [3] | [4] |
|---|---|---|---|---|---|
|  | 8 | 5 | 3 | 25 | 41 |

Columns

ara2

| Rows | | 0 | 1 | 2 | 3 |
|---|---|---|---|---|---|
|  | 0 | 4 | 3 | 2 | 1 |
|  | 1 | 1 | 2 | 3 | 4 |

Columns

ara3

| Rows | | 0 | 1 | 2 | 3 |
|---|---|---|---|---|---|
|  | 0 | 1 | 2 | 3 | 4 |
|  | 1 | 5 | 6 | 7 | 8 |
|  | 2 | 9 | 10 | 11 | 12 |

Initializing ara2 and ara3 with or without the nested braces is no different. The nested braces seem to show the dimensions and how C++ fills them a little better, but the choice of using nested braces is yours.

> **Tip:** Multidimensional arrays (unless they are global) are *not* initialized to specific values unless you assign them values at declaration time or in the program. As with single-dimensional arrays, if you initialize one or more of the elements but not all of them, C++ fills the rest with zeros. If you want to zero out an entire multidimensional array, you can use
>
> ```
> float     sales[ 3 ][ 4 ][ 7 ][ 2 ] =
>       { 0.0 };     // Fill all of sales with zeros
> ```

One last point to consider is how multidimensional arrays are viewed by your compiler. Many people program in C++ for years but never understand how tables are stored internally. As long as you use subscripts, a table's internal representation should not matter. After you learn about pointer variables, however, you might need to know how C++ stores your tables in case you want to reference them with pointers (as shown in the next few chapters).

Figure 26.5 shows the way C++ stores a three-by-four table in memory. Unlike the elements of a single-dimensional array, each element is stored contiguously, but look at how C++ views the data. Because a table is an array of arrays, the array name contains the address of the start of the primary array. Each of those elements points to the array it contains (the data in each row).

This coverage of table storage is for your information only. As you become more proficient in C++ and write more powerful programs that manipulate internal memory, you might want to review this method, used by C++ for table storage.

## Using Tables and *for* Loops

Nested `for` loops are good candidates for looping through every element of a multidimensional table. For instance, the code

```
for (row = 0; row < 2; row++)
    {
    for (col = 0; col < 3; col++)
        cout << row << "   " << col << "\n";
    }
```

produces the following output:

```
0     0
0     1
0     2
1     0
1     1
1     2
```

**Figure 26.5.**

Internal representation of a two-dimensional table.

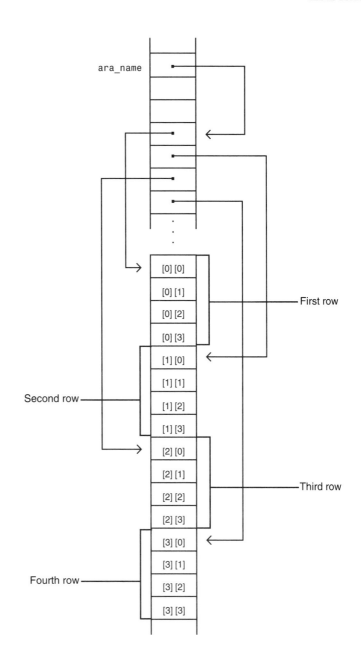

These numbers are exactly the subscripts, in row order, for a two-row by three-column table that is dimensioned with

```
int     table[ 2 ][ 3 ];
```

*Nested loops work well with multidimensional arrays.*

Notice that there are as many `for` loops as there are subscripts in the array (two). The outside loop represents the first subscript (the rows), and the inside loop represents the second subscript (the columns). The nested `for` loop steps through each element of the table.

You can use `cin()` to fill a table, or you can assign values to the elements when declaring the table. Usually, the data comes from data files on disk.

Regardless of what method stores values in multidimensional arrays, nested `for` loops are excellent control statements for stepping through the subscripts. The next examples illustrate how nested `for` loops work with multidimensional arrays.

## Examples

1. The following statement reserves enough memory elements for a television station's ratings (A through D) for one week:

```
char    ratings[ 7 ][ 48 ];
```

This statement reserves enough elements to hold 7 days (the rows) of ratings for each 30-minute time slot (48 of them in a day).

Remember that every element in a table is always the same type. In this case, each element is a character variable. You can initialize some of them with the following assignment statements:

```
shows[ 3 ][ 12 ] = 'B';    // Store B in 4th row, 13th column
shows[ 1 ][ 5 ] = 'A';     // Store A in 2nd row, 6th column
cin.get(shows[ 6 ][ 20 ]);
```

2. A computer company sells two sizes of diskettes: 3 1/2-inch and 5 1/4-inch. Each diskette comes in one of four capacities: single-sided, double-density; double-sided, double-density; single-sided, high-density; or double-sided, high-density.

The diskette inventory is well suited for a two-dimensional table. The company determined that the diskettes have the following retail prices:

|  | Single-Sided, Double-Density | Double-Sided, Double-Density | Single-Sided, High-Density | Double-Sided, High-Density |
|---|---|---|---|---|
| **3 1/2"** | 2.30 | 2.75 | 3.20 | 3.50 |
| **5 1/4"** | 1.75 | 2.10 | 2.60 | 2.95 |

The company wants to store the prices of the diskettes in a table for easy access. The following program does that with assignment statements:

```cpp
// Filename: C26DISK1.CPP
// Assigns diskette prices to a table

#include <iostream.h>
#include <iomanip.h>

main()
    {
    float         disks[ 2 ][ 4 ];  // Table of disk prices
    int           row, col;

    disks[ 0 ][ 0 ] = 2.30;    // Row 1, Column 1
    disks[ 0 ][ 1 ] = 2.75;    // Row 1, Column 2
    disks[ 0 ][ 2 ] = 3.20;    // Row 1, Column 3
    disks[ 0 ][ 3 ] = 3.50;    // Row 1, Column 4
    disks[ 1 ][ 0 ] = 1.75;    // Row 2, Column 1
    disks[ 1 ][ 1 ] = 2.10;    // Row 2, Column 2
    disks[ 1 ][ 2 ] = 2.60;    // Row 2, Column 3
    disks[ 1 ][ 3 ] = 2.95;    // Row 2, Column 4
           // Print the prices
                 cout.setf(ios::fixed);
                 cout.setf(ios::showpoint);

    for (row = 0; row < 2; row++)
        {
                 for (col = 0; col < 4; col++)
                     {
                         cout << setprecision(2);
                         cout << "$" << disks[ row ][ col ]
                         ➡<< "\n";
                     }
        }
    return 0;
    }
```

This program displays the following prices:

```
$2.30
$2.75
$3.20
$3.50
$1.75
$2.10
$2.60
$2.95
```

The program prints the prices one line at a time and without any descriptive titles. Although this output is not labeled, the program illustrates how you can use assignment statements to initialize a table and how nested for loops can print the elements.

**3.** You could display the preceding floppy disk inventory better if the output had descriptive titles. Before you add titles, you should know how to print a table in its native row-and-column format.

Typically, you use a nested `for` loop, like the one in the preceding example, to print rows and columns. You should not, however, output a newline character with every `cout`. If you do, you see one value per line, as in the preceding output, which is not the row-and-column format of the table.

You do not want to see every diskette price on one line, but you want each row of the table printed on a separate line. You must insert a `cout << "\n";` to send the cursor to the next line each time the row number changes. Printing newlines after each row prints the table in its row-and-column format, as the following program shows:

```
// Filename: C26DISK2.CPP
// Assigns diskette prices to a table and prints them in a
// table format

#include <iostream.h>
#include <iomanip.h>

main()
    {
    float       disks[ 2 ][ 4 ];  // Table of disk prices
    int         row, col;

    disks[ 0 ][ 0 ] = 2.30;       // Row 1, Column 1
    disks[ 0 ][ 1 ] = 2.75;       // Row 1, Column 2
    disks[ 0 ][ 2 ] = 3.20;       // Row 1, Column 3
    disks[ 0 ][ 3 ] = 3.50;       // Row 1, Column 4
    disks[ 1 ][ 0 ] = 1.75;       // Row 2, Column 1
    disks[ 1 ][ 1 ] = 2.10;       // Row 2, Column 2
    disks[ 1 ][ 2 ] = 2.60;       // Row 2, Column 3
    disks[ 1 ][ 3 ] = 2.95;       // Row 2, Column 4
    // Print the prices
        cout.setf(ios::fixed);
        cout.setf(ios::showpoint);
for (row = 0; row < 2; row++)
        {
        cout << setprecision(2);
        for (col = 0; col < 4; col++)
            cout << "$" << disks[row][col] << "\t";
        cout << "\n";       // Print a new line each row
        }
    return 0;
    }
```

The following shows the output of the disk prices in their native table order:

```
$2.30     $2.75     $3.20     $3.50
$1.75     $2.10     $2.60     $2.95
```

4. To add descriptive titles, simply print a row of titles before the first row of values and then print a new column title before each column, as shown in this program:

```cpp
// Filename: C26DISK3.CPP
// Assigns diskette prices to a table
// and prints them in a table format with titles

#include <iostream.h>
#include <iomanip.h>

main()
    {
    float    disks[ 2 ][ 4 ];    // Table of disk prices
    int      row, col;

    disks[ 0 ][ 0 ] = 2.30;  // Row 1, Column 1
    disks[ 0 ][ 1 ] = 2.75;  // Row 1, Column 2
    disks[ 0 ][ 2 ] = 3.20;  // Row 1, Column 3
    disks[ 0 ][ 3 ] = 3.50;  // Row 1, Column 4
    disks[ 1 ][ 0 ] = 1.75;  // Row 2, Column 1
    disks[ 1 ][ 1 ] = 2.10;  // Row 2, Column 2
    disks[ 1 ][ 2 ] = 2.60;  // Row 2, Column 3
    disks[ 1 ][ 3 ] = 2.95;  // Row 2, Column 4
    cout.setf(ios::fixed);
    cout.setf(ios::showpoint);

    // Print the top titles
    cout << "\tSingle-sided,\tDouble-sided,"
        << "\tSingle-sided,\tDouble-sided,\n";
    cout << "\tDouble-density\tDouble-density"
        << "\tHigh-density\tHigh-density\n";
    // Print the prices
    for (row = 0; row < 2; row++)
        {
        if (row == 0)
            cout << "3 1/2\"\t";
        else
            cout << "5 1/4\"\t";
        for (col = 0; col < 4; col++)
            cout << "$" << setprecision(2)
                << disks[row][col] << "\t\t";
        cout << "\n"; // Print a new line each row
        }
    return 0;
    }
```

The output from this program in shown in figure 26.6.

425

**Figure 26.6.**

The table of disk
prices with titles.

| | Single-sided, Double-density | Double-sided, Double-density | Single-sided, High-density | Double-sided, High-density |
|---|---|---|---|---|
| 3 1/2" | $2.30 | $2.75 | $3.20 | $3.50 |
| 5 1/4" | $1.75 | $2.10 | $2.60 | $2.95 |

## Summary

You now know how to create, initialize, and process multidimensional arrays. Although not all data fits into the compact format of tables, some data does. Using nested for loops makes stepping through a multidimensional array straightforward.

One of the limitations of a multidimensional array is that each element must be the same data type. This restriction keeps you from being able to store several kinds of data in tables. Upcoming chapters show you how to store data in different ways to overcome this limitation.

## Review Questions

Answers to Review Questions are in Appendix B.

**1.** What statement reserves a two-dimensional table of integers, called scores, with five rows and six columns?

**2.** What statement reserves a 3-dimensional array of 4 tables of character variables, called initials, with 10 rows and 20 columns?

**3.** Consider the following statement:

```
int    weights[ 5 ][ 10 ];
```

Which subscript (first or second) represents rows, and which represents columns?

**4.** How many elements are reserved with the following statement?

```
int    ara[ 5 ][ 6 ];
```

**5.** Examine the following table of integers in a table called ara:

| 4 | 1 | 3 | 5 | 9 |
|---|---|---|---|---|
| 10 | 2 | 12 | 1 | 6 |
| 25 | 42 | 2 | 91 | 8 |

What values do the following elements contain?

A. ara[ 2 ][ 2 ]

B. ara[ 0 ][ 1 ]

C. ara[ 2 ][ 3 ]

D. ara[ 2 ][ 4 ]

**6.** Consider this section of a program:

```
int     grades[ 3 ][ 5 ] = {80, 90, 96, 73, 65,
                             67, 90, 68, 92, 84,
                             70, 55, 95, 78, 100 };
```

What are the values of the following?

A. grades[ 2 ][ 3 ]

B. grades[ 2 ][ 4 ]

C. grades[ 0 ][ 1 ]

# Review Exercises

**1.** Write a program that stores and prints the numbers from 1 to 21 in a three-by-seven table. (*Hint:* Remember that C++ begins subscripts at 0.)

**2.** Write a program that reserves storage for three years' worth of sales data for five salespeople. Use assignment statements to fill the table with data and print it out, one value per line.

**3.** Instead of using assignment statements, use the cin function to fill the salespeople's data in the preceding exercise.

**4.** Write a program that tracks the grades for 5 classes, each having 10 students. Input the data, using the cin function. Print the table in its native row-and-column format.

# CHAPTER 27

# Pointers

C++ reveals its true power through pointer variables. *Pointer variables* (or *pointers*, as they are generally called) are variables that contain the addresses of values in memory. All variables that you have seen so far have held data values. You understand that variables hold values of various data types: character, integer, floating-point, and so on. A pointer variable contains the location of the value. In effect, a pointer variable *points* to the value because the variable holds the address of the value.

When first learning C++, students of the language tend to shy away from pointers, thinking that they are difficult. But pointers don't have to be difficult. In fact, after you work with them for a while, you might think that pointers are easier to use than arrays (and much more flexible).

This chapter introduces the following topics:

♦ What pointers are

♦ Pointers of different data types

♦ The "address of" (&) operator

♦ The dereferencing (*) operator

♦ Arrays of pointers

Pointers offer a highly efficient means of accessing and changing data. Because a pointer contains the address of data, your computer has less work to do when finding that value in memory. Pointers do not have to link data to specific variable names. A pointer can point to an unnamed data value. With pointers, you gain a "different view" of your data.

# Understanding Pointer Variables

Pointer variables do not contain the actual value; instead they contain the *address* of the value.

Pointers are variables and thus follow all the usual naming rules of regular, nonpointer variables. As with regular variables, you must declare pointer variables before you use them. A type of pointer exists for every data type in C++; you can use integer pointers, character pointers, floating-point pointers, and so on. You can declare global pointers (although global pointers, as with regular variables, are not usually recommended) or local pointers, depending on where you declare them.

The only difference between pointer variables and regular variables is what they hold. Pointers do not contain values per se, but the *address* of a value. If you need a quick review of addresses and memory, see Appendix A.

```
C++ has two pointer operators:

&     The "address of" operator

*     The dereferencing operator
```

Don't let these operators confuse you. You have seen them before! The & is the bitwise AND operator (see Chapter 13, "Bitwise Operators"), and the * means, of course, multiplication. C++ determines that the * and & operators are associated with pointers when they are used as unary operators—that is, when they precede a variable or expression, as in &(num) or *(p_age+3).

Whenever you see & used with pointers, think of the phrase "address of." The & operator provides the memory address of whatever variable it precedes. The * operator, when used with pointers, dereferences the pointer's value. When you see the * operator used, think of the phrase "value pointed to." The * operator retrieves the value that is "pointed to" by the variable it precedes.

# Declaring Pointers

If you need to declare a variable to hold your age, you might use the following variable declaration:

```
int     age = 30;     // Declare a variable to hold my age
```

Declaring age this way does several things. Because C++ knows that you need a variable called age, C++ reserves storage for that variable. C++ knows also that you will store only integers in age, not floating-point or double floating-point data. You also have requested that C++ store the value of 30 in age after reserving storage for that variable.

Where did C++ store age in memory? You, as programmer, do not really care where C++ decided to store age. You do not need to know the variable's address because you never need to refer to age by its address. If you want to calculate or print with age, you call it by its name, age.

Suppose that you want to declare a pointer variable, not to hold your age but to *point* to age, the variable that holds your age. (Why you would want to use such a pointer variable is made clear in this chapter and the next few chapters.) p_age might be a good name for this pointer variable. Figure 27.1 shows an illustration of what you want to do. This example assumes that C++ stored age at address 350,606, although your C++ compiler arbitrarily determines the address of age, and it could be anything.

**Figure 27.1.**

p_age contains the address of age; p_age points to the age variable.

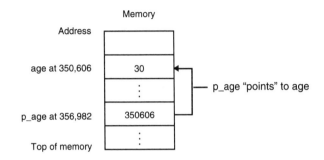

**Tip:** Give your pointer variables meaningful names.

The name p_age by itself has nothing to do with pointers except that it is the name selected for the pointer to age. p_age could just as easily be named house, x43344, space_trek, or whatever else you wanted to call it. You can name variables anything, as long as you follow the naming rules for variables. This naming flexibility reinforces the idea that a pointer is just a variable that you must reserve in your program. Make up meaningful variable names, even for pointer variables. p_age is a good name for a variable that points to age. The names ptr_age and ptr_to_age are good, too.

To declare the p_age pointer variable, you should do the following:

```
int     *p_age;      // Declare an integer pointer
```

As with the declaration for age, this line reserves a variable called p_age. It is not a normal integer variable, however. Because of the *, C++ knows that this variable is to be a pointer variable.

Remember that the * is *not* part of the variable name. When you later use p_age, you prefix the name with the * only when you are dereferencing (as later examples show).

**Tip:** Whenever an * appears in a variable definition, the variable being declared is *always* a pointer variable.

Consider the declaration for p_age if the asterisk were not there; C++ would think that you were declaring a regular integer variable. The * is important because it tells C++ to interpret p_age as a pointer variable rather than a normal, data variable.

# Assigning Values to Pointers

A pointer points to a value that is of the same type as was declared for the pointer.

p_age is an integer pointer. This is very important. p_age can point only to integer values, never to floating-point values, double values, or even characters. If you need to point to a floating-point variable, you might declare the pointer as

```
float      *point;      // Declare a floating-point pointer
```

As with any automatic variables, C++ does not initialize pointers when you declare them. If you declare p_age as previously described, and you want p_age to point to age, you have to assign p_age to the address of age explicitly:

```
p_age = &age;           // Assign the address of age to p_age
```

What value is now in p_age? You do not know exactly, but you do know that it is the address of age, wherever that is.

Instead of assigning the address of age to p_age with an assignment operator, you can declare and initialize pointers at the same time. The next two lines declare and initialize both age and p_age:

```
int     age = 30;       // Declare a regular integer
                        // variable, putting 30 in it
int     *p_age = &age;  // Declare an integer pointer,
                        // initializing it with the
                        // address of age
```

These two lines produce the variables described in figure 27.1.
If you want to print the value of age, you can use the following:

```
cout << age;            // Print the value of age
```

Or you can print the value of age like this:

```
cout << *p_age;         // Dereference p_age
```

The dereferencing operator gives you the value *to which the pointer points.* Without the *, the second cout would print an address (the address of age). The * means to retrieve the value at that address.

You can assign age a different value with the following statement:

```
age = 41;          // Assign age a new value
```

Or you can assign age a value in this way:

```
*p_age = 41;
```

This line says, "Take the memory location being pointed to by p_age, and assign it 41."

> **Tip:** The * appears before a pointer variable in only two places: when you declare a pointer variable and when you dereference a pointer variable (to find the data to which it points).

## Understanding Pointers and Parameters

You might recall from Chapter 20, "Passing Values," that you can override C++'s normal default of passing by copy (also known as passing by value) by passing a variable preceded by an &, and putting an asterisk before the parameter everywhere it appears in the receiving function. The following function call passes `tries` by address to the receiving function called `pr_it()`:

```
pr_it(&tries);    // Pass integer tries to pr_it() by address
                  // (tries would normally pass by copy)
The function pr_it() receives the address of tries, in effect, receiving
tries by address:
void    pr_it(int *tries)  // Receive tries by address
                           // (dereference its value)

    {
    *tries++;    // Change tries in calling AND
                 // receiving functions.

    return;
    }
```

Now that you understand the & and * operators, you can understand the passing of parameters to functions by address.

### Examples

**1.** The following section of a program declares three regular variables of three different data types, as well as pointers:

```
char        initial= 'Q';  // Declare three regular
int         num = 40;      // variables of three
                           // different types
float      sales = 2321.59;

char        *p_initial = &initial;  // Declare three
int         *ptr_num = &num;        // pointers
float       *sales_add = &sales;
```

**2.** As with regular variables, you can initialize pointers with assignment statements. You do not have to initialize pointers when you declare them. The next few lines of code are equivalent to the code in the preceding example:

```
char        initial;    // Declare three regular variables
int         num;        // of three different types
float       sales;

char        *p_initial; // Declare three pointers but
int         *ptr_num;   // do not initialize them yet
float       *sales_add;

initial = 'Q';          // Initialize the regular
num = 40;               // variables with values
sales = 2321.59;

p_initial = &initial;   // Initialize the pointers with
ptr_num = &num;         // the addresses of their
sales_add = &sales;     // corresponding variables
```

Notice that you do not put the * operator before the pointer variable names when assigning them values. You prefix a pointer variable with * only if you are dereferencing it.

> **Note:** In this example, the pointer variables could have been assigned the addresses of the regular variables before they were assigned values. The operation would not be any different. The pointers are assigned the addresses of the regular variables no matter what data is in the regular variables.

Keep the data type of each pointer consistent. Do *not* assign a floating-point variable to an integer's address. You cannot make the following assignment statement, for instance, because p_initial can point only to character data, not to floating-point data:

```
p_initial = &sales;     // INVALID pointer assignment
```

3. Examine the following program closely. It shows more about pointers and the pointer operators, & and *, than several pages of text could explain:

```cpp
// Filename: C27POINT.CPP
// Demonstrates the use of pointer declarations and
// operators

#include <iostream.h>

main()
    {
    int     num = 123;      // A regular integer variable
    int     *p_num;         // Declare an integer pointer

    cout << "num is " << num << "\n";  // Print value of num
    cout << "The address of num is "
         << (unsigned long)&num << "\n";
```

```
    p_num = &num;      // Put address of num in p_num,
                       // in effect, making p_num point
                       // to num (no * in front of p_num)
    cout << "*p_num is " << *p_num << "\n"; // Print value
                                            // of num
    cout << "p_num is " << (unsigned long)p_num << "\n";
                       // Print location of num
    return 0;
    }
```

The output of this program is the following:

```
num is 123
The address of num is 65522
*p_num is 123
p_num is 65522
```

If you run this program, you probably get different results for the value of p_num, because your compiler places num at a different location, depending on your memory setup. The actual address is moot, though. Because the pointer p_num always contains the address of num, and because you can dereference p_num to get num's value, the address is not critical.

4. The following program includes a function that swaps the values of any two integers passed to it. You might recall that a function can return only a single value. Therefore, you could not write, before now, a function that changed two different values and returned both values to the calling function.

To swap two variables (reversing their values for sorting as you saw in Chapter 25, "Array Processing"), you need the ability to pass both variables by address. Then, when the function reverses the variables, the calling function's variables also are swapped.

Notice the function's use of dereferencing operators before each occurrence of num1 and num2. You don't care which addresses num1 and num2 are stored at, but you have to make sure that you dereference whatever addresses were passed to the function.

Be sure to pass arguments with the prefix & to functions that receive by address, as shown here in main():

```
// Filename: C27SWAP.CPP
// Program that includes a function which swaps any two
// integers passed to it

#include <iostream.h>

void    swap_them(int *num1, int *num2)
    {
    int     temp;      // Variable that holds in-between
                       // swapped value
```

```
        temp = *num1;      // The asterisks ensure that the
                           // calling function's variables are
                           // ones worked on in this function
                           // and not copies of them.
        *num1 = *num2;
        *num2 = temp;
        return;
        }


int     main(void)
        {
        int i = 10, j = 20;

        cout << "\n\nBefore swap, i is " << i
             << " and j is " << j << "\n\n";
        swap_them(&i, &j);
        cout << "\n\nAfter swap, i is " << i
             << " and j is " << j << "\n\n";
        return 0;
        }
```

# Declaring Arrays of Pointers

If you need to reserve many pointers for many different values, you might want to declare an *array of pointers*. You know that you can reserve an array of characters, integers, long integers, and floating-point values, as well as an array of every other data type available. You also can reserve an array of pointers, with each pointer being a pointer to a specific data type.

The following line reserves an array of 10 integer pointer variables:

```
int     *iptr[ 10 ];   // Reserve an array of 10 integer
                       // pointers
```

Figure 27.2 shows how C++ views this array. Each element holds an address (after being assigned values) that *points* to other values in memory. Each value pointed to must be an integer. You can assign an element from iptr an address, just as you would for nonarray pointer variables. You can make iptr[ 4 ] point to the address of an integer variable named age by assigning it, as shown here:

```
iptr[ 4 ] = &age;  // Make iptr[ 4 ] point to address of age
```

The following line reserves an array of 20 character pointer variables:

```
char    *cpoint[ 20 ];    // Array of 20 character pointers
```

Again, the asterisk is not part of the array name. The asterisk serves to let C++ know that this array is an array of integer pointers and not just an array of integers.

**Figure 27.2.**

An array of 10
integer pointers.

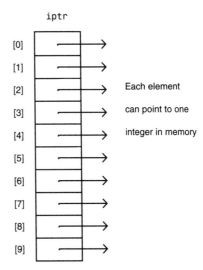

Some beginning C++ students start getting confused when they see such a declaration. Pointers are one thing, but reserving storage for arrays of pointers tends to bog down students. The concept, however, is easy to understand. Take away the asterisk from the last declaration, as in

```
char    cpoint[ 20 ];
```

Now what do you have? You have just reserved a simple array of 20 characters. Adding the asterisk informs C++ to go one step further: instead of wanting an array of character variables, you want an array of character-pointing variables. Instead of each element being a character variable, each element holds an address that points to characters.

Reserving arrays of pointers will be much more meaningful when you learn about structures in the next few chapters. As with regular, nonpointer variables, an array makes processing several variables much easier. You can use a subscript to reference each variable (element) without having to use a different variable name for each value.

## Summary

Declaring and using pointers might seem like a lot of trouble at this point. Why assign *p_num a value when assigning a value directly to num is easier (and clearer)? If you are asking yourself (and this book!) that question, you probably understand everything you should from this chapter, and you are ready to begin seeing the true power of pointers: combining array processing and pointers.

## Review Questions

Answers to Review Questions are in Appendix B.

1. What kind of variable is reserved in each of the following?

    A. `int *a;`

    B. `char *cp;`

    C. `float *dp;`

2. What words should spring to mind when you see the `&` operator?

3. What is the dereferencing operator?

4. How would you assign the address of the floating-point variable `salary` to a pointer called `pt_sal`?

5. True or false: You must define a pointer with an initial value when declaring it.

6. Examine the following two sections of code:

    ```
    int     i;
    int     *pti;
    i = 56;
    pti = &i;

    int     i;
    int     *pti;
    pti = &i;      // These two lines are reversed from the
    i = 56;        // preceding example.
    ```

    Is the value of `pti` the same after the fourth line of each section?

7. Now look at this section of code:

    ```
    float     pay;
    float     *ptr_pay;
    pay = 2313.54;
    ptr_pay = &pay;
    ```

    What is the value of each of the following (answer "Invalid" if it cannot be determined)?

    A. `pay`

    B. `*ptr_pay`

    C. `*pay`

    D. `&pay`

**8.** What does the following declare?

```
double     *ara[ 4 ][ 6 ];
```

A. An array of double floating-point values

B. An array of double floating-point pointer variables

C. An invalid declaration statement

> **Note:** Because this chapter is theory oriented, exercises are saved until you master the next chapter, "Pointers and Arrays."

# CHAPTER 28

# Pointers and Arrays

Arrays and pointers are closely related in the C++ programming language. You can address arrays as if they were pointers, and pointers as if they were arrays. Being able to store and access pointers and arrays means that you can store strings of data in array elements. Without pointers, you could not handle this task because no fundamental string data type exists in C++; you have no string variables, only string constants.

This chapter introduces the following topics:

♦ Arrays and pointers

♦ Character pointers

♦ Pointer arithmetic

♦ Ragged-edge arrays of string data

You will use the concepts presented here for much of your future programming in C++. Pointer manipulation is very important to the C++ programming language.

## Arrays as Pointers

An array is a pointer.

An array is just a pointer, nothing more. Suppose that you have the following array declaration:

```
int    ara[ 5 ] =
    { 10, 20, 30, 40, 50 };
```

If you printed ara[ 0 ], you would see 10. By now, you fully understand and expect this value to appear.

But what if you were to print *ara? Would that print anything? If so, what? If you thought that an error would print because ara is not a pointer but an array, you would be wrong. An array is a pointer. If you print *ara, you would also see 10.

Recall how arrays are stored in memory. Figure 28.1 reviews how ara is mapped in memory. The array, ara, is nothing more than a pointer that points to the first element of the array. If you dereference that pointer, you dereference the value stored at the first element of the array, which is 10. Dereferencing ara is exactly the same thing as referring to ara[ 0 ] because both produce the same value.

**Figure 28.1.**

Storing the array ara in memory.

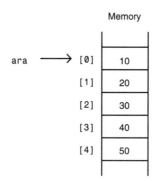

You now see that you can reference an array with subscripts or with pointer dereferencing. Can you use pointer notation to print the third element of ara? Yes, and you already have the tools to do so. The following cout prints ara[ 2 ] (the third element of ara) without using a subscript:

```
cout << *(ara + 2);     // Print ara[ 2 ]
```

The expression *(ara + 2) is not vague at all, as long as you remember that an array is just a pointer that always points to the array's first element. *(ara + 2) takes the address stored in ara, adds 2 to the address, and dereferences *that* location. All the following hold true:

```
ara + 0 points to ara[ 0 ]

ara + 1 points to ara[ 1 ]

ara + 2 points to ara[ 2 ]

ara + 3 points to ara[ 3 ]

ara + 4 points to ara[ 4 ]
```

Therefore, to print, store, or calculate with an array element, you can use either subscript notation or pointer notation. Because an array contains the address of the array's first element, you must dereference the pointer to get the element's value.

> **Internal Locations**
>
> C++ knows the internal data-size requirements of characters, integers, floating points, and the other data types on your computer. Therefore, because ara is an integer array and each element in an integer array consumes two bytes of storage, C++ adds 2 or 4 to the address if you reference arrays as just shown.
>
> Even though you might write *(ara + 3) to refer to ara[ 3 ], C++ really adds 6 to the address of ara to get the third element. C++ does not add an actual 3. You don't have to worry about this addition because C++ handles these internals. When you write *(ara + 3), you are requesting that C++ add 3 integer addresses to the address of ara. If ara were a floating-point array, C++ would add 3 floating-point addresses to ara.

# Examining Pointer Advantages

*An array is a pointer constant.*

Although arrays are really pointers in disguise, they are special types of pointers. An array is a *pointer constant*, not a pointer variable. You cannot change the value of an array pointer because you cannot change constants. This definition explains why you cannot assign new values to an array name during a program's execution. For instance, even if cname is a character array, the following is not valid in C++:

```
cname = "Christine Chambers";     // INVALID array assignment
```

You cannot change the array name, cname, because it is a constant. You would not attempt

```
5 = 4 + 8 * 2;                    // INVALID assignment
```

because you cannot change the constant 5 to any other value. C++ knows that you cannot assign anything to 5 and gives you an error if you attempt to change 5. C++ also knows that an array is a constant and that you cannot change an array to another value. You can assign values to an array at declaration time, one element at a time during execution, or by using functions such as strcpy().

The most important reason to learn pointers is this: pointers (except arrays referenced as pointers) are variables. You *can* store a new pointer value in a pointer variable, which means that you can process any data type more powerfully and efficiently than you can with arrays.

## Examples

1. By changing pointers, you make them point to different values in memory. The following program shows how to change pointers. The program first defines two floating-point variables. A floating-point pointer points to the first variable, v1, and is used in the cout. The pointer is then changed so that it points to the second floating-point variable, v2.

```
// C28PTRCH.CPP
// Changes the value of a pointer variable

#include <iostream.h>
main()
    {
    float    v1 = 676.54;       // Define 2 floating-point
                                // variables
    float    v2 = 900.18;
    float    *p_v;      // Define a floating-point pointer

    p_v = &v1;                   // Make pointer point to v1
    cout << "The first value is " << *p_v << "\n";   // Print 676.54
    p_v = &v2;      // Change the pointer so that it points to v2
    cout << "The second value is " << *p_v << "\n";   // Print 900.18
    return 0;
    }
```

Because they are able to change pointers, most C++ programmers use pointers rather than arrays. Sometimes, because arrays are easy to declare, programmers declare arrays and then use pointers to reference those arrays.

**2.** You can reference arrays with pointer notation, and you can reference pointers with array notation. The following program declares an integer array and an integer pointer that points to the start of the array. The array and pointer values are printed with subscript notation. Afterward, the program uses array notation to print the array and pointer values.

Study this program carefully. You can see the inner workings of arrays and pointer notation.

```
// Filename: C28ARPTR.CPP
// References arrays like pointers and references pointers
// like arrays

#include <iostream.h>

main()
    {
    int    ctr;
    int    iara[ 5 ] =
        { 10, 20, 30, 40, 50 };
    int    *iptr;

    iptr = iara; // Make iptr point to array's first element
    // This would also work: iptr = &iara[ 0 ];
    cout << "Using array subscripts:\n";
    cout << "iara\tiptr\n";
    for (ctr = 0; ctr < 5; ctr++)
```

```
          cout << iara[ ctr ] << "\t" << iptr[ ctr ] << "\n";
     cout << "\nUsing pointer notation:\n";
     cout << "iara\tiptr\n";
     for (ctr = 0; ctr < 5; ctr++)
          cout << *(iara + ctr) << "\t"
               << *(iptr + ctr) << "\n";
     return 0;
     }
```

This program's output is shown here:

```
Using array subscripts:
iara    iptr
10      10
20      20
30      30
40      40
50      50

Using pointer notation:
iara    iptr
10      10
20      20
30      30
40      40
50      50
```

# Using Character Pointers

The ability to change pointers is especially useful when you are working with character strings in memory. You have the ability to store strings in character arrays or to point to strings with character pointers. Consider the following two string definitions:

```
char    cara[ ] = "C++ is fun";    // An array holding
                                   // a string
char    *cptr = "C++ By Example"; // A pointer to
                                  // the string
```

**Note:** When first initialized, a character pointer points to the first character of a string.

Figure 28.2 shows how C++ stores these two strings in memory. C++ stores them basically the same way. You are familiar with the array definition. When assigning a string to a character pointer, C++ grabs enough free memory to hold the string and assigns the address of the first character to the pointer. Apart from the changeability of the two pointers (the array and the character pointers), the preceding two string definition statements do exactly the same thing.

**Figure 28.2.**

Storing two strings as arrays.

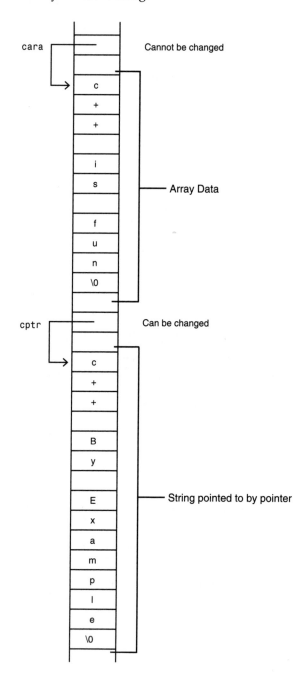

Because cout prints strings by starting at the array or pointer name until the null zero is reached, you can print each of these strings with the following cout statements:

```
cout << "String 1: " << cara << "\n";
cout << "String 2: " << cptr << "\n";
```

Notice that you print strings in arrays and strings pointed to in the same way. Up to this point, you might have wondered what advantage one method of storing strings has over the other. The seemingly minor difference between these stored strings makes a big difference when you change them.

Suppose that you want to store the string Hello in the two strings. You *cannot* assign the string to the array in this way:

```
cara = "Hello";     // INVALID
```

Because you cannot change the array, you cannot assign it a new value. The only way to change the contents of the array is to assign characters from the string to the array, one element at a time, or to use a built-in function such as strcpy(). You can, however, make the character pointer point to the new string, as in

```
cptr = "Hello";          // Change the pointer so that it points
                         // to the new string
```

> **Tip:** If you want to store user input in a string pointed to by a pointer, you first must reserve enough storage for that input string. An easy way to reserve the space is to reserve a character array and then assign a character pointer to the beginning element of that array, like this:
>
> ```
> char      input[ 81 ];   // Holds a string as long as
>                          // 80 characters
> char *iptr = input;      // Could also have done this:
>                          // char *iptr = &input[ 0 ];
> ```
>
> Now you can input a string by using the pointer, as in
>
> ```
> cin >> iptr;             // Make sure that iptr points
>                          // to the string typed by user
> ```
>
> You can use pointer manipulation, arithmetic, and modification on the input string.

## Examples

1. Suppose that you want to store your sister's full name and then print it. Instead of using arrays, you can use a character pointer. The following program does just that:

```
// Filename: C28CP1.CPP
// Stores a name in a character pointer
```

```
#include <iostream.h>

main()
    {
    char    *c = "Bettye Lou Horn";

    cout << "My sister's name is " << c << "\n";
    return 0;
    }
```

This program prints the following:

```
My sister's name is Bettye Lou Horn
```

**2.** Now suppose that you need to change a string pointed to by a character pointer. If your sister married, changing her last name to Henderson, your program can show both strings:

```
// Filename: C28CP2.CPP
// Illustrates changing a character string

#include <iostream.h>

main()
    {
    char    *c = "Bettye Lou Horn";

    cout << "My sister's maiden name was " << c << "\n";
    c = "Bettye Lou Henderson";   // Assign new string to c
    cout << "My sister's married name is " << c << "\n";
    return 0;
    }
```

Here is the output:

```
My sister's maiden name was Bettye Lou Horn
My sister's married name is Bettye Lou Henderson
```

**3.** Another way to accomplish the same task is to copy characters into the character string. For this task, declare an array large enough to hold any new characters, and then assign the string to it. Next, assign the address of the first character in the array to the pointer. Finally, use strcpy() to copy the updated last name into the position specified: c+10.

```
// Filename: C28CP3.CPP
// Illustrates modifying characters in a string

#include <iostream.h>
#include <string.h>

main()
    {
```

```
char       name[25]=     "Bettye Lou Horn";
char       *c=           name;

cout << "My sister's maiden name was " << c << "\n";

strcpy( c+10, "Henderson" );      // Copy in the new name

cout << "My sister's married name is " << c << "\n";

return 0;
}
```

The program changes the last name from Horn to Henderson. Here is the
output of this program:

```
My sister's maiden name was Bettye Lou Horn
My sister's married name is Bettye Lou Henderson
```

Figure 28.3 shows the memory layout from these string manipulations.

## Using Pointer Arithmetic

You saw an example of pointer arithmetic when you accessed array elements with
pointer notation. By now, you should be comfortable with the fact that both of these
array/pointer references are identical:

```
ara[ sub ]
*(ara + sub)
```

You can increment or decrement a pointer. If you increment a pointer, the
address inside the pointer variable increments. The pointer does not always
increment by 1, however.

Suppose that f_ptr is a floating-point pointer that points to the first element of
an array of floating-point numbers. f_ptr might be initialized like this:

```
float     fara[ ] =
    { 100.5, 201.45, 321.54, 389.76, 691.34 };
f_ptr = fara;
```

Figure 28.4 shows what these variables look like in memory. Each floating-point
value in this example takes four bytes of memory.

Incrementing a
pointer by 1 might
add more than
one byte to the
address contained
in the pointer.

If you print the value of *f_ptr, you see 100.5. Suppose that you incremented
f_ptr by 1 with the following statement:

```
f_ptr++;
```

**Figure 28.3.**

Two string constants appear in memory because two string constants are used in the program.

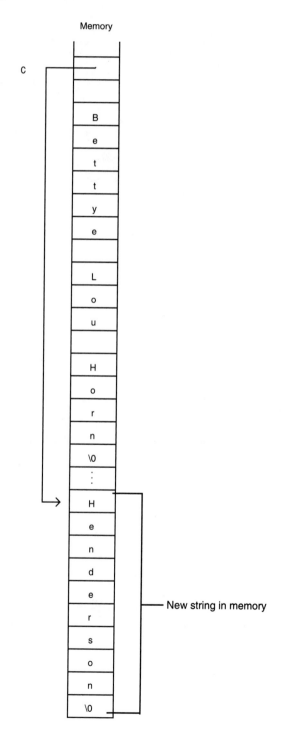

**Figure 28.4.**

A floating-point array and a pointer.

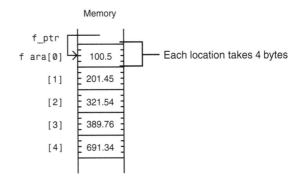

Memory

f_ptr

f ara[0]  100.5 — Each location takes 4 bytes

[1]  201.45

[2]  321.54

[3]  389.76

[4]  691.34

C++ does *not* add 1 to the address in f_ptr even though it seems as though 1 should be added. In this case, because floating-point values take four bytes each on this machine, C++ adds 4 to f_ptr. How does C++ know how many bytes to add to f_ptr? C++ knows from the pointer's type declaration how many bytes to increment.

If you were to print *f_ptr after you incremented it, you would see 201.45, which is the second element in the array. If C++ added only 1 to the address in f_ptr, f_ptr would point only to the second byte of 100.5, and you would see only garbage on-screen.

**Note:** When you increment a pointer, C++ adds one data type size (in bytes) to the pointer, not 1. When you decrement a pointer, C++ subtracts one data type size (in bytes) from the pointer.

## Examples

**1.** The following program defines an array with five values. An integer pointer is then initialized to point to the first element in the array. The rest of the program prints the dereferenced value of the pointer and then increments the pointer so that it points to the next integer in the array.

So that you can see what is going on, the size of integer values is printed at the bottom of the program. Because integers take two bytes, C++ increments the pointer by 2 in order to point to the next integer. (The integers are two bytes apart from each other.)

```
// Filename: C28PTI.CPP
// Increments a pointer through an integer array

#include <iostream.h>
```

```
main()
    {
    int    iara[ ] =
          { 10, 20, 30, 40, 50 };
    int    *ip = iara;      // The pointer points to
                            // the start of the array

    cout << *ip << "\n";
    ip++;      // 2 is actually added
    cout << *ip << "\n";
    ip++;      // 2 is actually added
    cout << *ip << "\n";
    ip++;      // 2 is actually added
    cout << *ip << "\n";
    ip++;      // 2 is actually added
    cout << *ip << "\n\n";
    cout << "The integer size is " << sizeof(int)
         << " bytes on this machine";
    return 0;
    }
```

The output of this program is

```
10
20
30
40
50
The integer size is 2 bytes on this machine
```

2. Here is the same program, but using a character array and a character pointer. Because a character takes only one byte of storage, incrementing a character pointer adds just 1 to the pointer; only 1 is needed because the characters are just one byte apart from each other.

```
// Filename: C28PTC.CPP
// Increments a pointer through a character array

#include <iostream.h>

main()
    {
    char    cara[ ] =
          { 'a', 'b', 'c', 'd', 'e' };
    char *cp = cara;        // The pointer points to
                            // the start of the array

    cout << *cp << "\n";
    cp++;      // 1 is actually added
    cout << *cp << "\n";
    cp++;      // 1 is actually added
    cout << *cp << "\n";
```

```
cp++;      // 1 is actually added
cout << *cp << "\n";
cp++;      // 1 is actually added
cout << *cp << "\n\n";
cout << "The character size is " << sizeof(char)
     << " byte on this machine";
return 0;
}
```

**3.** The following program shows the many ways you can add to, subtract from, and reference arrays and pointers. The program defines a floating-point array and a floating-point pointer. The body of the program prints the values from the array, using array and pointer notation.

```
// Filename: C28ARPT2.CPP
// Comprehensive reference of arrays and pointers

#include <iostream.h>
#include <iomanip.h>
main()
    {
    float    ara[ ] =
        { 100.0, 200.0, 300.0, 400.0, 500.0 };
    float    *fptr;      // Floating-point pointer

    // Make pointer point to array's first value
    fptr = &ara[ 0 ];      // Could also have been this:
                           // fptr = ara;
    cout <<setiosflags(ios::fixed)<<setprecision(1);
    cout << *fptr << "\n";         // Print 100.0
    fptr++;      // Point to NEXT  floating-point value
    cout << *fptr << "\n";         // Print 200.0
    fptr++;      // Point to NEXT  floating-point value
    cout << *fptr << "\n";         // Print 300.0
    fptr++;      // Point to NEXT  floating-point value
    cout << *fptr << "\n";         // Print 400.0
    fptr++;      // Point to NEXT  floating-point value
    cout << *fptr << "\n";         // Print 500.0
    fptr = ara;      // Point back to first element again
    cout << *(fptr + 2) << "\n";   // Print 300.00 but do
                                   // NOT change fptr
    // Reference both array and pointer, using subscripts
    cout << (fptr + 0)[ 0 ] << "  " << (ara + 0)[ 0 ]
         << "\n"; // 100.0  100.0
    cout << (fptr + 1)[ 0 ] << "  " << (ara + 1)[ 0 ]
         << "\n"; // 200.0  200.0
    cout << (fptr + 4)[ 0 ] << "  " << (ara + 4)[ 0 ]
         << "\n"; // 500.0  500.0
    // Reference both array and pointer, using subscripts
    // Notice that subscripts are based from addresses that
    // begin before the data in the array and pointer.
    cout << (fptr - 1)[ 2 ] << "  " << (ara - 1)[ 2 ]
```

```
              << "\n"; // 200.0  200.0
     cout << (fptr - 20)[ 23 ] << "   " << (ara - 20)[ 23 ]
              << "\n"; // 400.0  400.0
     return 0;
     }
                     This program's output is
100.0
200.0
300.0
400.0
500.0
300.0
100.0   100.0
200.0   200.0
500.0   500.0
200.0   200.0
400.0   400.0
```

## Storing Arrays of Strings

*An array of character pointers defines a ragged-edge array.*

You are now ready for one of the most useful applications of character pointers: storing arrays of strings. Actually, you cannot store an array of strings, but you can store an array of character pointers, and each character pointer can point to a string in memory.

By defining an array of character pointers, you define a *ragged-edge array*. This array is similar to a two-dimensional table, with one exception: instead of each row being the same length (the same number of elements), each row contains a different number of characters.

The term *ragged-edge* is derived from word processing. A word processor can typically print text fully justified or with a ragged-right margin. The columns in a newspaper are fully justified because both the left and the right columns align evenly. Letters you write by hand or type on typewriters (remember what a typewriter is?) generally have ragged-right margins.

All two-dimensional tables you have seen so far have been fully justified. If you declare a character table with 5 rows and 20 columns, for example, each row contains the same number of characters. You could define the table with the following statement:

```
char    names[ 5 ][ 20 ] =
   {
        { "George" },
        { "Michelle" },
        { "Joe" },
        { "Marcus" },
        { "Stephanie" }

   };
```

This table is shown in figure 28.5. Notice that much of the table is wasted space. Each row takes 20 characters, even though the data in each row has far fewer characters. The unfilled elements contain null zeros because C++ zeros out all elements that you do not initialize in arrays. This type of table uses too much memory.

**Figure 28.5.**

A fully justified table.

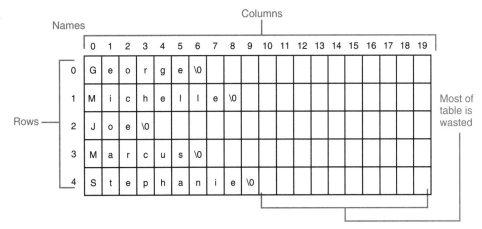

To fix the memory-wasting problem of fully justified tables, you should declare a single-dimensional array of character pointers. Each pointer points to a string in memory, and the strings do *not* have to be the same length.

The definition for such an array is

```
char *names[ 5 ] =
    {
        { "George" },
        { "Michelle" },
        { "Joe" },
        { "Marcus" },
        { "Stephanie" }

    };
or simply
char *names[] =
    {
        "George",
        "Michelle",
        "Joe",
        "Marcus",
        "Stephanie"
    };
```

These arrays are single-dimensional. The definition should not confuse you, although it is something you have not seen. The asterisk before names makes this array an array of pointers. The type of pointers is character. The strings are *not* being assigned to the array elements, but they are being *pointed to* by the array elements.

Figure 28.6 shows this array of pointers. The strings are stored elsewhere in memory. Their actual locations are not critical because each pointer points to the starting character. The strings waste no data; each string takes only as much memory as needed by the string and its terminating zero. This structure gives the data its ragged-right appearance.

**Figure 28.6.**

The array that points to each of the five strings.

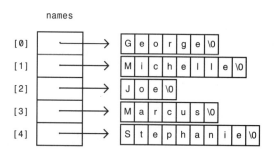

To print the first string, you can use the following cout:

```
cout << *names;        // Print George
```

To print the second string, you can use this cout:

```
cout *(names + 1);     // Print Michelle
```

Whenever you dereference any pointer element using the * dereferencing operator, you access one of the strings in the array. You can use a dereferenced element anywhere you use a string constant or character array (with strcpy(), strcmp(), and so on).

**Tip:** Working with pointers to strings is *much* more efficient than working with the strings. For instance, sorting a list of strings takes a lot of time if they are stored as a fully justified table. Sorting strings pointed to by a pointer array is much faster. During the sort, you just swap pointers, not entire strings.

## Examples

1. The following full program uses the pointer array with five names. The for loop controls the cout function, printing each name in the string data. You now can see why learning about pointer notation for arrays pays off!

```
// Filename: C28PTST1.CPP
// Prints strings pointed to by an array

#include <iostream.h>
```

```
main()
    {
    char *names[] =
            {
            "George",           // Define a ragged-edge array
            "Michelle",         // of pointers to strings
                "Joe",
            "Marcus",
            "Stephanie"
            };
    int     ctr;

    for (ctr = 0; ctr < 5; ctr++)
        cout << "String #" << (ctr + 1) << " is "
        << *(names + ctr) << "\n";

    return 0;
    }
*
String #1 is George
String #2 is Michelle
String #3 is Joe
String #4 is Marcus
String #5 is Stephanie
```

**2.** The following program stores the days of the week in an array. When the user types a number from 1 to 7, the day of the week that matches that number (with Sunday being 1) is displayed. The program dereferences the pointer that points to that string.

```
// Filename: C28PTST2.CPP
// Prints the day of the week based on an input value

#include <iostream.h>

main()
    {
    char    *days[ ] =
            {
            "Sunday",       // The seven separate sets
            "Monday",       // of braces are optional.
            "Tuesday",
            "Wednesday",
            "Thursday",
            "Friday",
            "Saturday"
            };
    int     day_num;

    do
        {
```

```
            cout << "What is a day number (from 1 to 7)? ";
            cin >> day_num;
            }
    while ((day_num < 1) || (day_num > 7));
            // Ensure accurate number
    day_num--;      // Adjust for subscript
    cout << "The day is " << *(days + day_num) << "\n";
    return 0;
    }
```

## Summary

You deserve a break! You now understand the foundation of C++'s pointer and array notation. After you master this material, you are on your way to thinking in C++ as you design your programs. C++ programmers know that C++'s arrays are pointers in disguise, and program them accordingly.

Using ragged-edge arrays offers two advantages. You can hold arrays of string data without wasting extra space, and you can quickly change the pointers without having to move the string data around in memory.

As you progress into advanced C++ concepts, you will appreciate the time you spent on pointer notation. The next chapter introduces a new topic, *structures*. Structures enable you to store data in a more unified way than simple variables allow.

## Review Questions

Answers to Review Questions are in Appendix B.

**1.** What is the difference between an array and a pointer?

**2.** Assume that ipointer points to integers that take two bytes of memory. If you performed the statement

```
ipointer += 2;
```

how many bytes are added to ipointer?

**3.** Which of the following items are equivalent, assuming that iary is an integer array and that iptr is an integer pointer that points to the start of the array?

A. iary and iptr

B. iary[ 1 ] and iptr + 1

C. iary[ 3 ] and *(iptr + 3)

D. (iary - 4)[ 9 ] and iary[ 5 ]

E. `*iary` and `iary[ 0 ]`

F. `iary[ 4 ]` and `*iptr + 4`

4. Why is it more efficient to sort a ragged-edge character array than a fully justified string array?

5. Look at the following array and pointer definition:

```
int     ara[ ] =
        { 1, 2, 3, 4, 5, 6, 7, 8, 9, 10 };
int     *ip1, *ip2;
```

Which of the following are allowed?

A. `ip1 = ara;`

B. `ip2 = ip1 = &ara[ 3 ];`

C. `ara = 15;`

D. `*(ip2 + 2) = 15;   // Assuming ip2 and ara are equal`

# Review Exercises

1. Write a program to store the names of your family members in a character array of pointers. Print the names.

2. Write a program that asks the user for 15 daily stock market averages and stores those averages in a floating-point array. Using only pointer notation, print the array forward and backward. Using only pointer notation, print the highest and lowest stock market quotes in the list.

3. Modify the bubble sort shown in Chapter 25, "Array Processing," so that it sorts with pointer notation. Add this bubble sort to the program in Exercise 2, printing the stock market averages in ascending order.

4. Write a program that requests 10 song titles from the user. Store the titles in an array of character pointers (a ragged-edge array). Print the original titles, print the alphabetized titles, and print the titles in reverse alphabetical order (from Z to A).

# Part VII

*Data Structures*

# CHAPTER 29

# Structures

Structures give you the ability to group data together and work with that data as a whole. Being able to manipulate several values of different data types in a single variable makes programs easier to write and maintain. In the past, business data processing used structures in almost every program. Recently, classes rather than structures have been used in most object-oriented programs, but a lot of code makes heavy use of structures that must be maintained and enhanced. For this reason, understanding structures well is important.

This chapter introduces the following topics:

♦ Structure definitions

♦ Structure initialization

♦ The dot operator (.)

♦ Structure assignment

♦ Nested structures

## Understanding Structure Variables

*Structures can have members of different data types.*

A *structure* is a collection of one or more values, each potentially of a different data type. As you know, the elements in an array must be the same data type, and you must refer to the entire array by its name. Each element (called a *member*) in a structure can be a different data type.

Suppose that you want to use a structure to keep track of your CD music collection. You might want to track the following pieces of information about each CD:

> Title
> Artist
> Number of songs
> Cost
> Date bought

This CD structure would have five members.

> **Tip:** If you have programmed in other computer languages or used a database program, keep in mind that C++ structures are analogous to file records, and members are analogous to fields in those records.

After deciding on the members, you must decide what data types to use for the members. Both the title and the artist can be character arrays, the number of songs can be an integer, the cost can be a floating-point value, and the date can be another character array. This information is represented here:

| Member Name | Data Type |
| --- | --- |
| Title | Character array of 25 characters |
| Artist | Character array of 20 characters |
| Number of songs | Integer |
| Cost | Floating-point |
| Date bought | Character array of 8 characters |

A structure tag is a label for the structure's format.

Each structure you define can have an associated structure name, called a *structure tag*. Structure tags are not required in most cases, but defining one for each structure in your program is generally a good idea. The structure tag is *not* a variable name. Unlike array names that reference arrays as variables, a structure tag is just a label for the structure's format.

You name structure tags yourself, using the naming rules of variables. If you give the CD structure a structure tag named cd_info, you are telling C++ that the tag called cd_info contains two character arrays, followed by an integer, a floating-point value, and a final character array.

A structure tag is actually a new data type that you, the programmer, define. When you want to store an integer, you do not have to define to C++ what an integer is. C++ already knows. When you want to store a CD collection's data, however, C++ does not know what format your CD collection will take. You have to tell C++ (using the example described here) that you need a new data type. That data type is your structure tag called cd_info, and it looks like the structure just described (two character arrays, an integer, a floating-point value, and another character array).

> **Note:** No memory is reserved for structure tags. A structure tag is your own data type. C++ does not reserve memory for the integer data type until you declare an integer variable. C++ does not reserve memory for a structure until you declare a structure variable.

Figure 29.1 contains the CD structure, graphically showing the data types within the structure. Notice that the structure includes five members, and each member is a different data type. The entire structure type is called cd_info, which is the structure tag.

**Figure 29.1.**

The format of the cd_info structure.

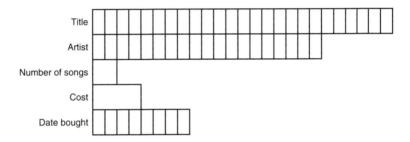

## Examples

**1.** Suppose that you are asked to write a program for a company's inventory system. The company had been using a card-file inventory system that tracks the following items:

> Item name
> Quantity in stock
> Quantity on order
> Retail price
> Wholesale price

This system is a perfect use for a structure containing five members. Before defining the structure, you need to determine the data type of each member by asking questions about the range of data. For example, you must know the largest item name and the most quantity that will ever be on order to ensure that your data types can hold the data. You then decide to use the following structure tag and data types:

**Structure tag: inventory**

| Member | Data Type |
| --- | --- |
| Item name | Character array of 20 characters |
| Quantity in stock | long int |
| Quantity on order | long int |
| Retail price | double |
| Wholesale price | double |

**2.** Suppose that the same company wants you to write a program to keep track of its monthly and annual salaries, printing a report at the end of the year that shows each month's individual salaries and the annual salaries at the end of the year.

What would the structure look like? Be careful! This type of data probably does not need a structure. Because all the monthly salaries are the same data type, a floating-point or double floating-point array holds the monthly salaries nicely without the complexity of a structure.

Structures are useful for keeping track of data of varying types that should be grouped together, such as inventory data, a customer's name and address data, or an employee data file.

# Defining Structures

To define a structure, you use the `struct` statement. `struct` defines a new data type for your program. The format of the `struct` statement is

```
struct [structure tag]
    {
    member definition;
    member definition;
       :
    member definition;
    } [one or more structure variables];
```

As mentioned earlier, the structure tag is optional (hence, the brackets in the format). Each member definition is a normal variable definition, such as `int i;` or `float sales[ 20 ];` or any other valid variable definition, including variable pointers if the structure requires a pointer as a member. At the end of the structure's definition and before the final semicolon, you can specify one or more structure variables.

If you specify a structure variable, C++ reserves space for that variable. C++ knows that the variable is not an integer, a character, or any other internal data type; C++ knows that the variable will be a type that looks like the structure. If you don't specify any structure variables, C++ does not reserve space for any instances of the structure.

You declare the CD structure this way:

```
struct cd_info
    {
    char        title[ 25 ];
    char        artist[ 20 ];
    int         num_songs;
    float       price;
    char        date_bought[ 8 ];
    } cd1, cd2, cd3;
```

Before going any further, you should be able to answer the following questions about this structure:

**1.** What is the structure tag?

**2.** How many members are there?

**3.** What are the member data types?

**4.** What are the member names?

**5.** How many structure variables are there?

**6.** What are their names?

The structure tag is called `cd_info`. Five members are included: two character arrays, an integer, a floating-point value, and a character array. The member names are `title`, `artist`, `num_songs`, `price`, and `date_bought`. The three structure variables are `cd1`, `cd2`, and `cd3`.

**Tip:** Often you can visualize structure variables as looking like a card-file inventory system. Figure 29.2 shows how you might keep your CD collection in a 3-by-5 card file, with each CD taking one card (representing each structure variable). The information about the CD (the structure members) is on each card.

If you had 1,000 CDs, you would have to declare 1,000 structure variables. Obviously, you would not want to list that many structure variables at the end of a structure definition. To help define structures for a large number of occurrences, you must define an *array of structures*. The next chapter, "Arrays of Structures," shows you how to do that. For now, just familiarize yourself with structure definitions.

**Figure 29.2.**

Using a card-file
CD inventory
system.

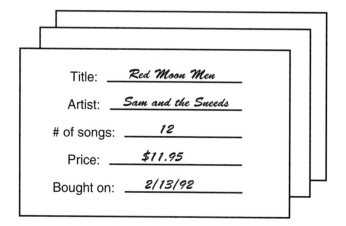

| | |
|---|---|
| Title: | *Red Moon Men* |
| Artist: | *Sam and the Sneeds* |
| # of songs: | *12* |
| Price: | *$11.95* |
| Bought on: | *2/13/92* |

## Examples

**1.** Here is a structure definition of the inventory application described earlier in this chapter:

```
struct inventory
     {
     char        item_name[ 20 ];
     long int    in_stock;
     long int    order_qty;
     float       retail;
     float       wholesale;
     } item1, item2, item3, item4;
```

Four inventory structure variables are defined. Each structure variable— item1, item2, item3, and item4—looks like the structure.

**2.** Suppose that a company wants to track its customer and personnel. The following two structure definitions create five structure variables for each structure. This example (with five employees and five customers) is limited but serves to show how you can define structures.

```
struct employee
     {
     char        emp_name[ 25 ];   // Employee full name
     char        address[ 30 ];    // Employee address
     char        city[ 10 ];
     char        state[ 2 ];
     long int    zip;
     double      salary;           // Annual salary
     } emp1, emp2, emp3, emp4, emp5;

struct customer
     {
     char        cust_name[ 25 ];  // Customer full name
     char        address[ 30 ];    // Customer address
```

```
char            city[ 10 ];
    char            state[ 2 ];
    long int        zip;
    double          balance;         // Balance owed to company
    } cust1, cust2, cust3, cust4, cust5;
```

Similar data is in each structure. A little later in this chapter, you learn how to consolidate similar member definitions by creating nested structures.

> **Tip:** Put comments to the right of members to document the purpose of the members.

## Initializing Structure Data

You can initialize a structure variable when you declare it.

You can initialize members of a structure in two ways. You can initialize members when you declare a structure, or you can initialize a structure within the body of the program. Most programs lend themselves to the second method because you do not always know structure data when you write your program.

The following example shows a structure declared and initialized at the same time:

```
struct cd_info
    {
    char            title[ 25 ];
    char            artist[ 20 ];
    int             num_songs;
    float           price;
    char            date_bought[ 8 ];
    } cd1 =
        {
        "Red Moon Men",
        "Sam and the Sneeds",
        12,
        11.95,
        "02/13/92"
        };
```

When you first learn about structures, you might be tempted to initialize members individually inside the structure, as in

```
char    artist[ 20 ] = "Sam and the Sneeds";      // INVALID
```

But you cannot initialize individual members because they are *not* variables. You can assign values to variables only. The only structure variable in the preceding structure is cd1.

Note that the braces must enclose the data when you initialize the structure variables, just as the braces enclose data when you initialize arrays.

This method of initializing structure variables gets tedious when several structure variables are involved (as is usually the case). Putting the data into several variables, with each set of data enclosed in braces, gets messy and takes too much space in your code.

More important, you usually do not know the contents of the structure variables. Generally, the user enters the data to be stored in structures, or you read the data from a disk file.

**Use the dot operator (.) to initialize members of structures.**

A better approach to initializing structures is to use the *dot operator* (.). With it, you can initialize individual members of a structure variable within the body of your program. You can treat each structure member almost as if it were a regular, nonstructure variable.

The format of the dot operator is

```
structure_variable_name.member_name
```

A structure variable name must always precede the dot operator, and a member name must always appear after the dot operator. Using the dot operator is quite easy, as the following examples show.

## Examples

1. The following simple program uses the CD collection structure and the dot operator to initialize the structure. Notice that the program treats members as if they were regular variables when combined with the dot operator.

```cpp
// Filename: C29ST1.CPP
// Structure initialization with the CD collection

#include <iostream.h>
#include <string.h>

main()
    {
    struct     cd_info
        {
        char        title[ 25 ];
        char        artist[ 20 ];
        int         num_songs;
        float       price;
        char        date_bought[ 8 ];
        } cd1;

    // Initialize members here
    strcpy(cd1.title, "Red Moon Men");
    strcpy(cd1.artist, "Sam and the Sneeds");
    cd1.num_songs = 12;
    cd1.price = 11.95;
    strcpy(cd1.date_bought, "02/13/92");
    // Print the data to the screen
```

```
cout << "Here is the CD information:\n\n";
    cout << "Title: " << cd1.title << "\n";
    cout << "Artist: " << cd1.artist << "\n";
    cout << "Songs: " << cd1.num_songs << "\n";
    cout << "Price: " << cd1.price << "\n";
    cout << "Date bought: " << cd1.date_bought << "\n";
    return 0;
    }
```

Note the output of this program:

Here is the CD information:

```
Title: Red Moon Men
Artist: Sam and the Sneeds
Songs: 12
Price: 11.95
Date bought: 02/13/92
```

2. By using the dot operator, you can get structure data from the keyboard with any of the data input functions you know, such as cin, get(), and getch().

The following program asks the user for student information. To keep the example reasonably short, only two students are defined in the program.

```cpp
// Filename: C29ST2.CPP
// Structure input with student data

#include <iostream.h>
#include <stdio.h>
#include <string.h>

main()
    {
    struct      students
        {
        char        name[ 25 ];
        int         age;
        float       average;
        } student1, student2;

    // Get two students' data
    cout << "What is first student's name? ";
    gets(student1.name);
    cout << "What is the first student's age? ";
    cin >> student1.age;
    cout << "What is the first student's average? ";
    cin >> student1.average;
    fflush(stdin);      // Clear input buffer for next input
    cout << "What is second student's name? ";
    gets(student2.name);
    cout << "What is the second student's age? ";
    cin >> student2.age;
    cout << "What is the second student's average? ";
```

```
cin >> student2.average;
// Print the data
cout << "\n\nHere is the student ";
cout << "information you entered:\n\n";
cout << "Student #1:\n";
cout << "Name:     " << student1.name << "\n";
cout << "Age:      " << student1.age << "\n";
cout << "Average: " << student1.average << "\n";
cout << "Student #2:\n";
cout << "Name:     " << student2.name << "\n";
cout << "Age:      " << student2.age << "\n";
cout << "Average: " << student2.average << "\n";
return 0;
}
```

Figure 29.3 shows the output of this program.

**Figure 29.3.**

For this program, the user has filled structure variables with values.

```
What is first student's name? Joe Sanders
What is the first student's age? 13
What is the first student's average? 78.4

What is second student's name? Mary Reynolds
What is the second student's age? 12
What is the second student's average? 98.9


Here is the student information you entered:

Student #1:
Name:    Joe Sanders
Age:     13
Average: 78.4

Student #2:
Name:    Mary Reynolds
Age:     12
Average: 98.9
```

3. When passed to functions, structure variables are passed by copy as are all other variables in C++. Therefore, if you pass a structure variable to a function that modifies one or more members of the structure, the calling function's structure variable is not automatically updated. This aspect distinguishes structures from arrays, in that a structure contains a composite of several values, like an array, yet structure members cannot be modified by a called function, and array elements can.

If you need to modify the members of a structure in a function, you can pass a pointer to the structure, you can have the function return the structure value, or you can simply update a global structure variable.

Define structures
globally; define
structure variables
locally.

If you choose to use either of the first two methods, you need to define
your structure globally and then define structure variables locally in each
function that needs them. Here is where the structure tag plays an important role. You should use the structure tag preceded by the word struct to
define local structure variables. All upcoming examples in this book use
this method.

The following program is similar to the preceding one. Notice that the
students structure is defined globally with *no structure variables*. In each
function, local structure variables are declared through references to the
structure tag. The structure tag keeps you from having to redefine the
structure members every time you define a new structure variable.

```cpp
// Filename: C29ST3.CPP
// Structure input with student data passed to functions

#include <iostream.h>
#include <stdio.h>
#include <string.h>

struct      students     // A global structure
    {
    char        name[ 25 ];
    int         age;
    float       average;
    };                    // No memory reserved yet

struct students     fill_structs(students student_var)
    {
    // Get students' data
    fflush(stdin);      // Clear input buffer for next input
    cout << "What is student's name? ";
    gets(student_var.name);
    cout << "What is the student's age? ";
    cin >> student_var.age;
    cout << "What is the student's average? ";
    cin >> student_var.average;
    return (student_var);
    }

void    pr_students(students student_var)
    {
    cout << "Name:    " << student_var.name << "\n";
    cout << "Age:     " << student_var.age << "\n";
    cout << "Average: " << student_var.average << "\n";
    return;
    }

int     main(void)
    {
    students       student1, student2;    // Define 2
                                          // local variables
```

```
                    // Call function to fill structure variables
                    student1 = fill_structs(student1);   // student1 is
                                                         // passed by copy, so it
                                                         // must be returned for
                                                         // main() to recognize it.
                    student2 = fill_structs(student2);
                    // Print the data
                    cout << "\n\nHere is the student ";
                    cout << "information you entered:\n\n";
                    pr_students(student1);    // Print first student's data
                    pr_students(student2);    // Print second student's data
                    return 0;
                    }
```

The definition of the fill_structs() function might seem complicated, but
they follow the same pattern you have seen throughout this book. Before
a function name, you must declare void or put the return data type if the
function returns a value. fill_structs() does return a value, and the type
of value it returns is struct students.

**4.** Because structure data is nothing more than regular variables grouped
together, feel free to calculate with structure members. As long as you use
the dot operator, you can treat structure members like other variables.

The following example asks for a customer's balance and uses a discount
rate (included in the customer's structure) to calculate a new balance. To
keep the example short, the structure's data is initialized at variable
declaration time.

This program does not actually require structures because only one
customer is used. You could use individual variables, but they do not
illustrate calculating with structures.

```
// Filename: C29CUST.CPP
// Updates a customer balance in a structure

#include <iostream.h>

struct      customer_rec
    {
    char        cust_name[ 25 ];
    double      balance;
    float       dis_rate;
    };

main()
    {
    customer_rec      customer =
        { "Steve Thompson", 2431.23, .25 };
```

```
cout << "Before the update, " << customer.cust_name;
cout << " has a balance of " << customer.balanc << "\n";
// Update the balance
customer.balance *= (1.0 - customer.dis_rate);
cout << "After the update, " << customer.cust_name;
cout << " has a balance of " << customer.balanc << "\n";
return 0;
}
```

**5.** You can copy the members of one structure variable to those of another structure variable as long as both structures have the same format. Some older versions of C required that you copy each member individually when you wanted to copy one structure variable to another, but ANSI C makes duplicating structure variables easy.

Being able to copy one structure variable to another will be more meaningful in the next chapter, "Arrays of Structures," but the concept is easy to apply.

The following program declares three structure variables but initializes only the first one with data. The other two structure variables are then initialized when the first structure variable is assigned to them.

```
// Filename: C29STCPY.CPP
// Demonstrates assigning one structure to another

#include <iostream.h>

struct      student
    {
    char        st_name[ 25 ];
    char        grade;
    int         age;
    float       average;
    };

main()
    {
    student     std1 =
        { "Joe Brown", 'A', 13, 91.4 };
    student     std2, std3;     // Not initialized

    std2 = std1;    // Copy each member of std1 to std2
    std3 = std1;    // and std3
    cout << "The contents of std2:\n";
    cout << std2.st_name << ", " << std2.grade << ", ";
    cout << std2.age << ", " << std2.average << "\n\n";
    cout << "The contents of std3:\n";
```

```
cout << std3.st_name << ", " << std3.grade << ", ";
    cout << std3.age << ", " << std3.average << "\n\n";
    return 0;
    }
```

This program's output is

```
The contents of std2
Joe brown, A, 13, 91.4

The contents of std3
Joe brown, A, 13, 91.4
```

Notice that each member of std1 is assigned to std2 and std3 with two single assignments.

# Nesting Structures

C++ enables you to nest one structure definition within another. This technique saves time when you are writing programs that use similar structures. You have to define the common members only once in their own structure and then use that structure as a member in another structure.

Consider the following two structure definitions:

```
struct     employee
    {
    char        emp_name[ 25 ];    // Employee full name
    char        address[ 30 ];     // Employee address
    char        city[ 10 ];
    char        state[ 2 ];
    long int    zip;
    double      salary;            // Annual salary
    };

struct     customer
    {
    char        cust_name[ 25 ];   // Customer full name
    char        address[ 30 ];     // Customer address
    char        city[ 10 ];
    char        state[ 2 ];
    long int    zip;
    double      balance;           // Balance owed to company
    };
```

These structures hold different data. One structure is for employee data, and the other structure is for customer data. Even though you should keep the data separate (you don't want to send a customer a paycheck!), the structure definitions have a lot of overlap and can be consolidated if you create a third structure:

```
struct      address_info
    {
    char           address[ 30 ];   // Common address
                                     // information
    char           city[ 10 ];
    char           state[ 2 ];
    long int       zip;
    };
```

You then can use this structure as a member in the other structures in this way:

```
struct      employee
    {
    char                    emp_name[ 25 ];   // Employee
                                              // full name
    address_info address;       // Employee address
    double          salary;        // Annual salary
    };

struct      customer
    {
    char                    cust_name[ 25 ];  // Customer
                                              // full name
    address_info address;       // Customer address
    double          balance;       // Balance owed
                                   // to company

    };
```

You must realize that a total of three structures exist, with the tags `address_info`, `employee`, and `customer`. How many members does the `employee` structure have? If you answered three, you are correct. `employee` and `customer` each have three members. `employee` has the structure of a character array, followed first by the `address_info` structure and then by the double floating-point member `salary`.

Figure 29.4 shows how these structures look graphically.

After you define a structure, it is then a new data type in the program, and you can use the structure anywhere that a data type (such as `int`, `float`, and so on) can appear.

You can assign values to members by using the dot operator. A structure variable named `cus` declared of type `customer` would refer to a member by the following notation.

```
us.balance = 5643.24;
```

Alternatively, you could use the pointer notation to achieve the same result. The following assignment statement is exactly equivalent to the preceeding one. If you declare a pointer in the following manner:

```
struct customer *cus_ptr;
Then the syntax of the assignment will be:
cus_ptr->balance = 5643.24;
```

**Figure 29.4.**

Defining a nested
structure.

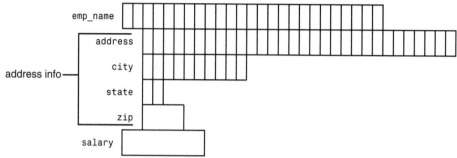

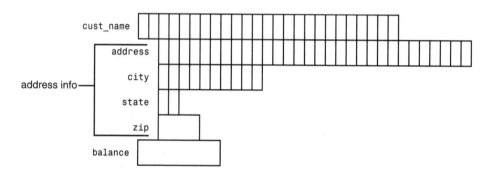

The nested structure might appear to pose a problem. How can you assign a value to one of the nested members? When you use the dot operator, you must nest it just as you nest the structure definitions. To assign a value to the customer's ZIP code, you use the following:

```
cus.address.zip = 34312;
```

Assuming a variable emp declared of type employee, you assign to the member that holds the ZIP code like this:

```
emp.address.zip = 59823;
```

## Summary

Structures enable you to group data in more flexible ways than arrays allow. The structures can contain members of different data types. You can initialize the structures either at declaration time or during the program with the dot operator (.).

Structures become even more powerful when you declare arrays of structures. The next chapter shows you how to declare arrays of structures so that you do not have to declare a new structure variable every time you need to store new information in a structure. You also can step through structures more quickly with loop constructs.

## Review Questions

Answers to Review Questions are in Appendix B.

1. What is the difference between structures and arrays?

2. What are the individual elements of a structure called?

3. What are the two ways to initialize members of a structure?

4. Do you pass structures by copy or by address?

5. True or false: The following structure definition reserves storage in memory:

```
struct      crec
    {
    char          name[ 25 ];
    int           age;
    float     sales[ 5 ];
    long          int num;
    }
```

6. Should you declare a structure globally or locally?

7. Should you declare a structure variable globally or locally?

8. How many members does the following structure declaration contain?

```
struct      item
    {
    int               quantity;
    struct part_rec   item_desc;
    float             price;
    char              date_bought[8];
    };
```

## Review Exercises

1. Write a structure that a video store can use in a program to track the video tape inventory. Make sure that the structure includes the tape's title, the length of the tape (in minutes), the cost of the tape, the rental price of the tape, and the date of the movie's release.

**2.** Write a program that uses the structure declared in the preceding exercise. Define three structure variables and initialize them *when you declare the variables* with data. Print the data to the screen.

**3.** Write a teacher's program that keeps track of 10 student names, ages, letter grades, and IQs. Use 10 different structure variable names and get the data for the students in a `for` loop from the keyboard. Print the data on the printer when the teacher finishes entering the information for all the students.

# CHAPTER 30

# Arrays of Structures

This chapter builds on the preceding one by showing you how you can create many structures for your data. After creating an array of structures, you can store multiple occurrences of your data values.

Arrays of structures are good for storing a collection of employees, information about several inventory items, or any other set of data that fits within the structure format. Whereas arrays provide a handy way to store several values of the same type, arrays of structures enable you to store together several values of different types, grouped as structures.

This chapter introduces the following topics:

♦ Creating arrays of structures

♦ Initializing arrays of structures

♦ Referencing elements from a structure array

♦ Using arrays as members

Many C++ programmers use arrays of structures as a prelude to storing data in a disk file. You can input and calculate your disk data in arrays of structures and then store those structures in memory. Arrays of structures also provide a means of holding data you read from the disk.

## Declaring Arrays of Structures

Declaring an array of structures is easy. You specify the number of reserved structures inside array brackets when you declare the structure variable. Consider the following structure definition:

```
struct    store
    {
    int           employees;
    int           registers;
    double        sales;
    } store1, store2, store3, store4, store5;
```

This structure is easy to understand because no new commands are used in the structure declaration, which creates five structure variables. Figure 30.1 shows how C++ stores these five structures in memory. Each of the structure variables has three members—two integers followed by a double floating-point value.

**Figure 30.1.**

The structure of store1, store2, store3, store4, and store5.

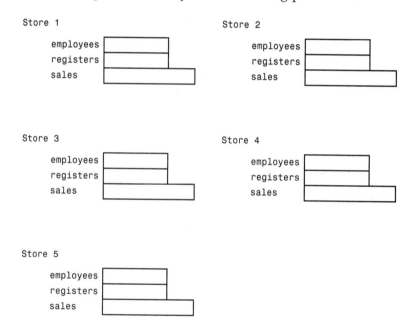

If the fourth store increases its employees by three, you can update the store's employee count with the following assignment statement:

```
store4.employees += 3;      // Add 3 to this store's
                            // employee count
```

Suppose that the fifth store just opened, and you want to initialize its members with data. If the stores are part of a chain, and the new store is similar to one of the others, you might begin initializing the store's data by assigning each of its members the same data as that of another store:

```
store5 = store2;            // Define initial values for the
                            // store5 members
```

Arrays of structures make working with large numbers of structure variables manageable.

Such structure declarations are fine for a small number of structures, but if the stores are part of a national chain, five structure variables are not enough. What if 1,000 stores are involved? You would not want to create 1,000 different store variables and work with each one individually. Creating an array of store structures would be much easier.

Consider the following structure declaration:

```
struct     store
    {
    int         employees;
    int         registers;
    double      sales;
    } stores[ 1000 ];
```

In one quick declaration, this code creates 1,000 store structures, each containing three members. Figure 30.2 shows how these structure variables appear in memory. Notice the name of each individual structure variable: stores[ 0 ], stores[ 1 ], stores [ 2 ], and so on.

**Caution:** Be careful that you do not run out of memory when creating a large number of structures. Arrays of structures quickly consume valuable memory. You might have to create fewer structures, storing more data in disk files and less data in memory.

**Figure 30.2.**

An array of the store structures.

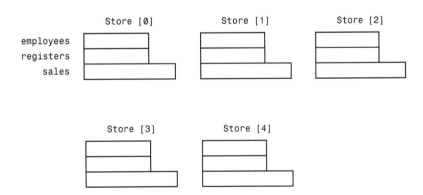

The value contained in the second element of stores (stores[ 1 ]) is unlike the others you have seen; it is a structure. It contains three members, each of which you can reference with the dot operator (.).

The dot operator works the same way for structure array elements as for regular structure variables. If the number of employees for the fifth store (stores[ 4 ]) increases by three, you can update the structure variable like this:

```
stores[ 4 ].employees += 3;      // Add 3 to this store's
                                 // employee count
```

You also can assign complete structures to one another by using array notation. To assign all the members of the 20th store to the 45th store, you can do this:

```
stores[ 44 ] = stores[ 19 ];     // Copy all members from the
                                 // 20th store to the 45th
```

The rules of arrays are still in force here. Each element of the array stores contains a value of the same data type, a value of type struct store. The data type for stores [ 316 ] is exactly the same as for stores[ 981 ] and stores[ 74 ].

The name of the array, stores, is a pointer constant to the starting element of the array, stores[ 0 ]. Therefore, you can use pointer notation to reference the stores. To assign stores[ 60 ] the same value as stores[ 23 ], you can reference the two elements like this:

```
*(stores + 60) = *(stores + 23);
```

You also can mix array and pointer notation, as in the following line, and get the same results:

```
stores[ 60 ] = *(stores + 23);
```

You can increase the sales of stores[ 8 ] by 40 percent with pointer or subscript notation as well:

```
stores[ 8 ].sales = (*(stores + 8)).sales * 1.40;
```

The extra pair of parentheses is required because the dot operator has precedence over the dereferencing symbol in C++'s hierarchy of operators (see Appendix D). Of course, in this case, the code is not helped by the pointer notation, and the following is a much clearer way to increase the sales by 40 percent:

```
stores[ 8 ].sales *= 1.40;
```

---

### Keep Your Array Notation Straight

You could never access the ninth store's **sales** member like this:

```
stores.sales[ 8 ] = 3234.54;     // INVALID
```

Array subscripts follow array elements only. **sales** is not an array; it was declared as being a double floating-point number. **stores** can never be used *without* a subscript (unless you are using pointer notation).

The corrected version of the preceding assignment statement is

```
stores[ 8 ].sales = 3234.54;     // Correctly assigns
                                 // the value
```

---

The following examples build an inventory data-entry system for a mail-order firm, using an array of structures. You don't have to learn much more than you already know to work with arrays of structures. Concentrate on the notation for accessing arrays of structures and their members so that you can get comfortable with this notation.

## Examples

1. Suppose that you work for a mail-order company that sells disk drives. You are given the task of writing a tracking program for the 25 different drives you sell. You must keep track of the following information:

   Storage capacity in megabytes

   Access time in milliseconds

   Vendor code (A, B, C, or D)

   Cost

   Price

   Because 25 different disk drives are in the inventory, the data fits nicely into an array of structures. Each array element is a structure containing the five members described in this list.

   The following structure definition defines the inventory:

   ```
   struct      inventory
       {
       long int    storage;
       int         access_time;
       char        vendor_code;
       double      code;
       double      price;
       } drive[ 25 ];      // Define 25 occurrences
                           // of the structure
   ```

2. When working with a large array of structures, your first concern should be how the data will be input into the array elements. The application determines the best method of data entry.

   If you are converting from an older computerized inventory system, for instance, you have to write a conversion program that reads the inventory file in its native format and saves it to a new file in the format needed by your C++ programs. This task is no easy one, requiring that you have extensive knowledge of the system from which you are converting.

   If you are writing a computerized inventory system for the first time, your job is a little easier because you do not need to worry about converting the old files. But you still must realize that someone has to type the data into the computer. You have to write a data-entry program that receives each inventory item from the keyboard and saves the item to a disk file. You should give the user a chance to edit inventory data to correct any data that might have been typed incorrectly.

One of the reasons that this book does not introduce disk files until the last chapters is that disk file formats and structures share a common bond. After you store data in a structure, or more often in an array of structures, you can easily write that data to a disk file with straightforward disk I/O commands.

The following program takes the array of disk drive structures shown in the preceding example and adds a data-entry function so that the user can enter data into the array of structures. The program is menu driven. The user has a choice, when starting the program, to add data, print data to the screen, or exit the program. Because you have yet to see disk I/O commands, the data in the array of structures goes away when the program ends. As noted, saving those structures to disk is easy after you learn C++'s disk I/O commands. For now, concentrate on the manipulation of the structures.

This program is longer than many you have seen in this book, but if you have followed the discussion of structures and the dot operator, you should have little trouble following the code.

```cpp
// Filename: C30DSINV.CPP
// Data-entry program for a disk drive company

#include <iostream.h>
#include <stdio.h>
#include <stdlib.h>
#include <conio.h>

struct      inventory      // Global structure definition
    {
    long int  storage;
    int       access_time;
    char      vendor_code;
    float     cost;
    float     price;
    };      // No structure variables defined globally

void      disp_menu(void)
    {
    cout << "\n\n*** Disk Drive Inventory System ***\n\n";
    cout << "Do you want to:\n\n";
    cout << "\t1. Enter new item in inventory\n\n";
    cout << "\t2. See inventory data\n\n";
    cout << "\t3. Exit the program\n\n";
    cout << "What is your choice? ";
    return;
    }
```

```
struct inventory        enter_data(void)
    {
    struct inventory      disk_item; // Local variable to
                                     // fill with input

    cout << "\n\nWhat is the next drive's ";
    cout << "storage in bytes? ";
    cin >> disk_item.storage;
    cout << "What is the drive's access time in ms? ";
    cin >> disk_item.access_time;
    cout << "What is the drive's vendor code ";
    cout << "(A, B, C, or D)? ";
    cin >> disk_item.vendor_code;
    cout << "What is the drive's cost? ";
    cin >> disk_item.cost;
    cout << "What is the drive's price? ";
    cin >> disk_item.price;
    return (disk_item);
    }

void     see_data(inventory disk[ 25 ],
                  int num_items)
    {
    int     ctr;

    cout << "\n\nHere is the inventory listing:\n\n";
    for (ctr = 0; ctr < num_items; ctr++)
        {
        cout << "Storage: " << disk[ ctr ].storage
             << "\t";
        cout << "Access time: " << disk[ ctr ].access_time
             << "\n";
        cout << "Vendor code: " << disk[ ctr ].vendor_code
             << "\t";
        cout << "Cost: $" << disk[ ctr ].cost << "\t";
        cout << "Price: $" << disk[ ctr ].price << "\n";
        }
    return;
    }

int     main(void)
    {
    inventory       disk[ 25 ];   // Local array
                                  // of structures
    int                     ans;
    int                     num_items = 0;       // Number of
                            // total items in the inventory

    do
        {
        do
            {
            disp_menu(); // Display menu of user choices
            cin >> ans;  // Get user's request
            }
```

```
            while ((ans < 1) || (ans > 3));
            switch (ans)
                {
                case 1:
                    // Enter disk data
                    disk[ num_items ] = enter_data();
                    num_items++; // Increment number of items
                    break;
                case 2:
                    // Display disk data
                    see_data(disk, num_items);
                    break;
                default:
                    break;
                }
            }
        while (ans != 3);  // Quit program when user is through
        return 0;
        }
```

Figure 30.3 shows an item being entered into the inventory file. Figure 30.4 shows the inventory listing being displayed on-screen. You can add many features and error-checking functions, but this program is the building block to a more comprehensive inventory system. You can easily adapt the program to a different type of inventory—such as a videotape collection, a coin collection, or any other tracking system—just by changing the structure definition and the member names throughout the program.

**Figure 30.3.**

Entering inventory information.

```
*** Disk Drive Inventory System ***

Do you want to:

        1. Enter new item in inventory

        2. See inventory data

        3. Exit the program

What is your choice? 1


What is the next drive's storage in bytes? 120000
What is the drive's access time in ms? 17
What is the drive's vendor code (A, B, C, or D)? A
What is the drive's cost? 121.56
What is the drive's price? 240.00
```

```
What is your choice? 2


Here is the inventory listing:

Storage: 120000 Access time: 17
Vendor code: A  Cost: $121.56   Price: $240.00
Storage: 320000 Access time: 21
Vendor code: D  Cost: $230.85   Price: $409.57
Storage: 280000 Access time: 19
Vendor code: C  Cost: $210.84   Price: $398.67


*** Disk Drive Inventory System ***

Do you want to:

        1. Enter new item in inventory

        2. See inventory data

        3. Exit the program

What is your choice? 3
```

# Using Arrays as Members

Members of structures can themselves be arrays. Array members pose no new problem, but you have to be careful when you access individual array elements. Keeping track of arrays of structures that contain array members might seem like a lot of work on your part, but there is really nothing to it.

Consider the following structure definition. This statement declares an array of 100 structures, with each structure holding payroll information for a company. Two of the members, name and department, are arrays.

```
struct     payroll
    {
    char        name[ 25 ];      // Employee name array
    int         dependents;
    char        department[ 10 ]; // Department name array
    float       salary;
    } employee[ 100 ];       // An array of 100 employees
```

Figure 30.5 shows what these structures look like. The first and third members are arrays. name is an array of 25 characters, and department is an array of 10 characters.

**Figure 30.5.**
The payroll data.

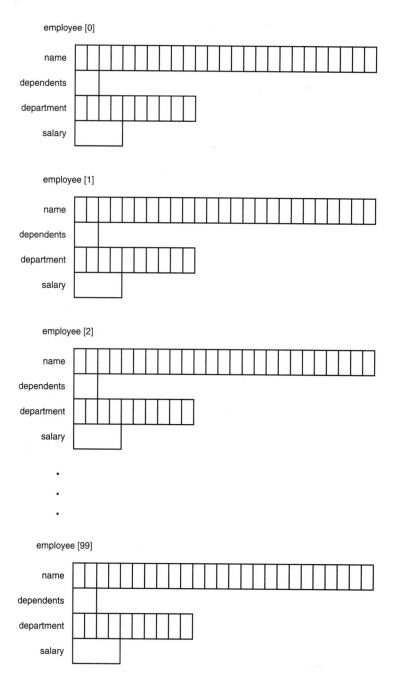

Suppose that you need to store the 25th employee's first initial to a character variable. Assuming that `f_initial` is already declared as a character variable, the following statement assigns the employee's first initial to `f_initial`:

```
f_initial = employee[ 24 ].name[ 0 ];
```

The double subscripts might look confusing, but the dot operator requires a structure variable on its left (employee[ 24 ]) and a member on its right (name's first array element). Being able to refer to member arrays makes the processing of character data in structures simple.

### Examples

1. Suppose that an employee gets married and wants her name changed in the payroll file. (She happens to be the 45th employee in the array of structures.) Given the payroll structure just described, the following line assigns a new name to her structure:

```
// Assign a new name
strcpy(employee[ 44 ].name, "Mary Larson");
```

When you refer to a structure variable with the dot operator, you can use regular commands and functions to process the data in the structures.

2. A bookstore wants to catalog its inventory of books. The following program creates an array of 100 structures. Each structure contains several types of variables, including arrays. This program is the data-entry portion of a larger inventory system. Study the references to the members to see how member arrays are used.

```
// Filename: C30BOOK.CPP
// Bookstore data-entry program

#include <iostream.h>
#include <stdio.h>
#include <ctype.h>

struct     inventory
    {
    char        title[ 25 ];        // Book's title
    char        pub_date[ 19 ];     // Publication date
    char        Steve[ 20 ];        // Author's name
    int         num;                // Number in stock
    int         on_order;           // Number on order
    float       retail;             // Retail price
    };

main()
    {
```

```
struct inventory    book[ 100 ];
int                 total = 0;  // Total books

                                // in inventory
char                ans;

do    // Program enters data into the structures
      {
      cout << "Book #" << (total + 1) << ":\n";
      cout << "What is the title? ";
      gets(book[ total ].title);
      cout << "What is the publication date? ";
      gets(book[ total ].pub_date);
      cout << "Who is the Author? ";
      gets(book[ total ].Author);
      cout << "How many books of this title are there? ";
      cin >> book[ total ].num;
      cout << "How many are on order? ";
      cin >> book[ total ].on_order;
      cout << "What is the retail price? ";
      cin >> book[ total ].retail;
      fflush(stdin);
      cout << "\nAre there more books? (Y/N) ";
      cin >> ans;
      fflush(stdin);            // Discard carriage return
      ans = toupper(ans);       // Convert to uppercase
      if (ans == 'Y')
         {
         total++;
         continue;
         }
      }
while (ans == 'Y');
return 0;
}
```

Much more is needed to make this program a usable inventory program.
An exercise at the end of this chapter recommends ways you can improve
this program (adding a printing routine and a title search). One of the first
things you should do is put the data-entry routine in a separate function to
make the code more modular.

3. This comprehensive example gives the steps you might go through to
   write a C++ program. You are getting to the point where you understand
   enough of the C++ language to start writing some advanced programs.

Assume that you are hired by a local bookstore to write a magazine
inventory system. You need to track the following:

Magazine title (maximum of 25 characters)

Publisher (maximum of 20 characters)

Month (1, 2, 3, ..., 12)

Publication year

Number of copies in stock

Number of copies on order

Price of magazine (dollars and cents)

Suppose that the store plans to carry a projected maximum of 1,000 magazine titles. Therefore, you need 1,000 occurrences of the structure, not a total of 1,000 magazines. The following example is a good structure definition for such an inventory:

```
struct       mag_info
{
char         title[ 25 ];
char         pub[ 25 ];
int          month;
int          year;
int          stock_copies;
int          order_copies;
float        price;
} mags[ 1000 ];     // Define 1,000 occurrences
```

Because this program consists of more than one function, the best approach is to declare the structure globally and the structure variables locally within the functions that need them.

The program needs three basic functions: a `main()` controlling function, a data-entry function, and a data-printing function. You can add a lot more, but these functions provide a good start for an inventory system. To keep the length of this example reasonable, assume that the user wants to enter several magazines and then print them out. (To make the program more usable, you would want to add a menu so that the user can control when to add and print the information, as well as add more error-checking and editing capabilities.)

The following code is an example of the complete data-entry and printing program. The arrays of structures are passed between the functions from `main()`.

```
// C30MAG.CPP
// Magazine inventory program for adding and displaying
// a bookstore's magazines

#include <iostream.h>
#include <stdio.h>
#include <ctype.h>
```

```
struct      mag_info
    {

    char        title[ 25 ];
    char        pub[ 25 ];
    int         month;
    int         year;
    int         stock_copies;
    int         order_copies;
    float       price;
    };


struct mag_info     fill_mags(struct mag_info mag)
    {
    cout << "\n\nWhat is the title? ";
    gets(mag.title);
    cout << "Who is the publisher? ";
    gets(mag.pub);
    cout << "What is the month (1, 2, ..., 12)? ";
    cin >> mag.month;
    cout << "What is the year? ";
    cin >> mag.year;
    cout << "How many copies in stock? ";
    cin >> mag.stock_copies;
    cout << "How many copies on order? ";
    cin >> mag.order_copies;
    cout << "How much is the magazine? ";
    cin >> mag.price;
    return (mag);
    }


void    print_mags(struct mag_info mags[], int mag_ctr)
    {
    int     i;

    for (i = 0; i <= mag_ctr; i++)
        {
        cout << "\n\nMagazine " << (i + 1) << "\n";
        cout << "\nTitle: " << mags[ i ].title << "\n";
        cout << "\tPublisher: " << mags[ i ].pub << "\n";
        cout << "\tPub. Month: "
            << mags[ i ].month << "\n";
        cout << "\tPub. Year: "
            << mags[ i ].year << "\n";
        cout << "\tIn-stock: "
            << mags[ i ].stock_copies << "\n";
        cout << "\tOn order: "
            << mags[ i ].order_copies << "\n";
        cout << "\tPrice: " << mags[ i ].price << "\n";
        }
    return;
    }
```

```
int     main(void)

{
    struct mag_info     mags[ 1000 ];
    int                 mag_ctr = 0; // Number of
                                     // magazine titles
    char                ans;

    do
        {       // Assume that at least
                // one magazine will be filled
        mags[ mag_ctr ] = fill_mags(mags[ mag_ctr ]);
        cout << "Do you want to enter another magazine? ";
        fflush(stdin);
        cin.get(ans);
        fflush(stdin);      // Discard carriage return
        if (toupper(ans) == 'Y')
            mag_ctr++;
        }
    while (toupper(ans) == 'Y');
    print_mags(mags, mag_ctr);
    return 0;       // Return to operating system
    }
```

## Summary

You have now mastered structures and arrays of structures. Many useful programs are ready to be written by you, using structures. Now that you can create arrays of structures, you can store and manipulate multiple occurrences of data.

The next step in the process of learning C++ is to master sequential files. This is the subject of the next chapter.

## Review Questions

Answers to Review Questions are in Appendix B.

1. True or false: All elements in an array of structures must be the same type.

2. What is the advantage of creating an array of structures instead of using individual variable names for each structure variable?

3. Consider the following structure declaration:

```
struct      item
    {
    char        part_no[ 8 ];
    char        descr[ 20 ];
    float       price;
    int         in_stock;
    } inventory[ 100 ];
```

A. How would you assign a price of 12.33 to the 33rd item's in-stock quantity?

B. How would you assign the first character of the 12th item's part number the value of 'x'?

C. How would you assign the 97th inventory item the same value as the 63rd?

4. Now look at this structure declaration:

```
struct     item
    {
    char        desc[ 20 ];
    int         num;
    float       cost;
    } inventory[ 25 ];
```

What is wrong with each of the following statements?

A. `item[ 1 ].cost = 92.32;`

B. `strcpy(inventory.desc, "Widgets");`

C. `inventory.cost[ 10 ] = 32.12;`

# Review Exercises

1. Write a program that stores an array of friends' names, phone numbers, and addresses and then prints them two ways: the full name and address, and just the name and phone number for a phone listing.

2. Add a sort function to the preceding program so that you can print your friends' names in alphabetic order. (*Hint:* You have to make the member holding the names a character pointer.)

3. Expand on the data-entry program (C30BOOK.CPP) by adding features to make it more usable, such as searching books by Steve and title, and printing an inventory of books on order.

# CHAPTER 31

# Sequential Files

So far, every example in this book has processed data that resided inside the program listing or that came from the keyboard. You assigned constants and variables to other variables and created new data values from expressions. The programs also received input with cin, gets(), and the character input functions.

The data that is created by the user and assigned to variables with assignment statements is sufficient for some applications. With the large volumes of data that most real-world applications need to process, however, you need a better way of storing that data. For all but the smallest computer programs, disk files offer the solution.

This chapter focuses on disk file processing concepts and shows you the first of two methods of disk access: *sequential file access.*

This chapter introduces the following topics:

♦ An overview of disk files

♦ The types of files

♦ Processing data on the disk

♦ Sequential file access

♦ File I/O functions

After reading this chapter, you will be ready to tackle the more advanced methods of accessing random files, covered in the next chapter. If you have programmed computerized data files with another programming language, you might be surprised at how C++ borrows from other programming languages, especially BASIC, when working with disk files. If you are new to disk file processing, you will find that disk files are simple to create and read.

## Why Use a Disk?

Disks hold more data than can fit in computer memory.

The typical computer system has much less internal memory (RAM) than hard disk storage space. Your hard disk drive certainly holds more data than can fit in your computer's RAM. In addition, the contents of your computer's RAM are cleared every time you turn your computer off, whereas your hard disk retains the data you store to it even when your computer is turned off.

For these two reasons, most programs store data to the hard disk or floppy diskette instead of maintaining it continually in memory.

By storing data on either type of disk, you assure that the amount of data you store and maintain is not limited by your computer's RAM. Your computer's hard disk can typically store several hundred times the amount of information that your computer can maintain at any one time in RAM. In addition, you can increase a computer's hard disk space much more easily than you can a computer's usable RAM.

## Examining Types of Disk File Access

Your programs can access files in two ways: through sequential access and through random access. The needs of your application determine the method you should choose. The access mode of a file determines how you read, write, change, and delete data from the file. Some of your files can be accessed in both ways, sequentially and randomly, as long as your programs are written properly and the data lends itself to both types of file access.

A sequential file has to be accessed in the same order in which the file was written. Thus a sequential file is analogous to a cassette tape: you play music in the same order it was recorded. (You can quickly fast-forward through or rewind songs that you do not want to listen to, but the order of the songs dictates what you do to play the song you want.)

Inserting data in the middle of a sequential file is difficult and sometimes impossible. How easy is it to insert a new song in the middle of two other songs on a tape? The only way to add or delete records from the middle of a sequential file is to create a completely new file that combines both old and new songs. You might be thinking that sequential files are limiting, but it turns out that many applications lend themselves to sequential file processing. Word processor files are sequential files.

Unlike sequential files, random-access files can be accessed in any order you want. Think of data in a random-access file as you would songs on a compact disc or record; you can go directly to any song you want without having to play or fast-forward through the other songs. If you want to play the first song, the sixth song, and then the fourth song, you can do so. The order of play has nothing to do with the order in which the songs were originally recorded. Random file access sometimes takes more programming but rewards that effort with a more flexible file access method. Chapter 32, "Random-Access Files," discusses how to program for random-access files.

## Understanding Sequential File Concepts

You can perform the following operations on sequential disk files:

♦ Create disk files

♦ Add to disk files

♦ Read from disk files

Again, the needs of your application determine what you should do. If you are storing information to a particular disk file for the first time, you must specifically create the file. Suppose that you want to start a customer data file. You need to create the new file and begin writing customer data to that file. The customer data is likely to be typed in by the user or imported from some other file.

As your customer base grows, you can add new customers to the file. When you add to the end of a file, you *append* to that file. As customers return to your store, you can retrieve their information from the customer data file.

This thought brings up one disadvantage of sequential files. Suppose that a customer moves and wants you to change his or her address in your files. Changing the information that is stored in a sequential access file is difficult. Removing information from sequential files is also difficult. Random files, described in the next chapter, provide a much easier approach to changing and removing data.

The primary approach to changing or removing data from a sequential access file is to create a new one based on the old one with the appropriate changes incorporated in the new file. You use this method when you modify and then save your AUTOEXEC.BAT file by using DOS Edit.

Because the existing data in sequential files is not easily updated, this chapter concentrates on creating, reading, and adding to sequential files. The next chapter covers the updating of files under the topic of random-access files.

## Opening and Closing Files

Before you can create, write to, or read from a disk file, you must open the file. Opening a file is analogous to opening a file cabinet before working with a file stored in the cabinet. After you are done with a cabinet's file, you close the file door. You must also close a disk file when you finish with it.

When you open a disk file, you inform C++ of the file name and what you want to do with it (write to, add to, or read from). C++ and the operating system work together to make sure that the disk is ready and to create an entry in your file directory (if you are creating a file) for the file name. When you close a file, C++ writes any remaining data to the file, releases the file from the program, and updates the file directory to reflect the file's new size.

To open a file, call the open() member function with one of the file stream objects. To close a file, call the close() member function. The formats of these two member function calls look like this:

```
fs_obj.open(file_name, access);
fs_obj.close();
```

The fs_obj is an object that represents a file. Your operating system handles the exact location of your data in the disk file. You don't want to worry about the exact track and sector number of your data on the disk. You need only the fs_obj, and then you can let C++ take care of locating the physical data for you.

The file_name is a string (or a character pointer that points to a string) containing a valid file name for your computer. The file_name can contain a complete disk and directory path name. You can specify the file name in uppercase or lowercase letters.

The access can be any value from table 31.1 or a combination of values, using the bitwise OR (¦) operator.

## Table 31.1. Possible access modes.

| Mode | Description |
| --- | --- |
| ios::app | Open the file for appending (adding to it) |
| ios::ate | Seek to end of file on opening it |
| ios::in | Open file for reading |
| ios::out | Open file for writing |
| ios::binary | Open file in binary mode |
| ios::trunc | Discard contents if file exists |
| ios::nocreate | If file doesn't exist, open fails |
| ios::noreplace | If file exists, open fails unless appending or seeking to end of file on opening |

Assuming a file stream object `cus_fs`, you can open the file called TRANSACT.LOG for appending with this line:

```
cus_fs.open( "TRANSACT.LOG", ios::app );
```

If, for instance, you want the `open()` to fail if the TRANSACT.LOG file does not exist, use `ios::noreplace` combined with `ios:app`, as in

```
cus_fs.open( "TRANSACT.LOG", ios::app | ios::noreplace );
```

**Caution:** If you open a file for writing by using `ios::out`, C++ simply creates the file. If a file by that name already exists, C++ overwrites the old file with no warning. You must be careful when opening files so that you do not overwrite existing data you want to save.

The default mode for file access is ASCII text. An ASCII text file is compatible with most programming languages and applications. Programs that can read ASCII files can read ASCII text files that you create using C++. One such program that reads and writes ASCII text files is DOS Edit. In addition, you can display the contents of an ASCII text file by using the DOS TYPE command at the DOS prompt:

```
C:\> TYPE TRANSACT.LOG
```

### Binary Modes

If you specify binary access, C++ creates or reads the file in a binary format. Binary data files differ from text data files in that they can contain the '\0' character. Other than including the access mode in the **open()** function, you use no additional commands to access binary files with your C++ programs.

Binary data files are smaller; they take less space than text files. Thus the advantage of binary files is that you save disk space because your data files are more compact. The disadvantage of using binary files is that other programs cannot always read the data files. Only C++ programs that are written to access binary files can read and write to them.

The binary format is a system-specific file format. Generally, other types of computers cannot read a binary file created on another computer.

If an error occurs when you attempt to open a file, the file stream object will be equal to zero. If you open a file for `ios::nocreate`, for example, but the file does not exist, C++ does not open the file. You can test for an error of this type in the following manner:

```
if ( !cus_fs ) cerr << "File TRANSACT.LOG does not exist."
```

Always check the file stream object when writing disk file programs to ensure that the file opened properly.

> **Tip:** Beginning programmers like to open all files at the beginning of their programs and close them at the end. But this approach is not always best. You should consider opening files immediately before you access them and closing them as soon as you are done with them. This way, you provide more protection for your files in the unlikely (but possible) event of a power failure or computer breakdown.

The following examples help illustrate these concepts.

## Examples

1. Suppose that you want to create a file for storing your house payment records for the last year. The following lines are the first few lines in the program, which would create a file called HOUSE.DAT on your disk:

```
#include <fstream.h>
main()
    {
    ofstream      fs_obj;               // Declare a file stream
                                        object
                                     // for writing
    fs_obj.open("house.dat", ios::out); // Create the file
```

The rest of the program writes data to the file. The program never has to refer to the file name again but uses the fs_obj variable to refer to the file. Examples in the next few sections illustrate how this referral is done. The name fs_obj is nothing special. You can name file stream object variables XYZ or a908973 if you like, but providing meaningful names for your variables is a better idea.

You must include the fstream.h header file because it contains the definition for the ofstream and ifstream declarations. You don't have to worry about the physical specifics. The fs_obj manages the data in the file for you as you write it. Put the declarations in your programs where you declare other variables and arrays.

Before finishing with the program, you should close the file. The following close() function closes the house file:

```
    fs_obj.close();      // Close the house payment file
```

**2.** If you like, you can put the complete path name in the file's name. The following line opens the household payment file in a subdirectory on the d: disk drive:

```
fs_obj.open("d:\mydata\house.dat", ios::out);
```

**3.** You can store a file name in a character array or point to it with a character pointer. Each of the following sections of code are equivalent:

```
char    fn[ ] = "house.dat"; // File name in character array
fs_obj.open(fn, ios::out);        // Create the file

char    *myfile = "house.dat";     // File name pointed to
fs_obj.open(myfile, ios::out);   // Create the file

// Let the user enter the file name
cout << "What is the name of the household file? ";
gets(filename);      // File name must be an array
                     // or character pointer
fs_obj.open(filename, ios::out);  // Create the file
```

No matter how you specify the file name when opening the file, close the file with the file stream object. The following close() function closes the open file, regardless of which method you used to open the file:

```
fs_obj.close();       // Close the house payment file
```

**4.** You should check the return value from open() to ensure that the file opened properly. This code after open() checks for an error:

```
#include <fstream.h>

main()
    {
    ofstream    fs_obj;         // Declare a file stream object

    fs_obj.open("house.dat", ios::out); // Create the file
    if (!fs_obj)
        cerr << "Error opening file.\n";
    else
        {

        // Rest of output commands go here

        }
```

**5.** You can open and write to several files in the same program. Suppose that you want to read data from a payroll file and create a backup payroll data file. You would have to open the current payroll file by using the in reading mode, and the backup file in the out output mode.

For each open file in your program, you must declare a different file stream object. The file stream objects that your input and output statements use determine on which file they operate. If you need to open several files, you also can declare an array of file stream objects.

You can open the two payroll files this way:

```
#include <fstream.h>

ifstream       file_in;      // Input file
ofstream       file_out;     // Output file

main()
    {
    file_in.open("payroll.dat", ios::in);      // Existing file
    file_out.open("payroll.BAK", ios::out);    // New file
```

When you finish with these files, be sure to close them with the following two `close()` function calls:

```
file_in.close();
file_out.close();
```

# Writing to a File

Any of the I/O functions that reference a device can perform input and output with files. You have seen most of these functions already. The most common file I/O functions are

```
get()
put()
gets()
puts()
```

You also can use file stream objects like you have used `cin` and `cout`. The following function call reads three integers from a file pointed to by `fs_obj`:

```
fs_obj >> num1 >> num2 >> num3;    // Read three variables
```

You always have more than one way to write data to a disk file. For instance, you can use `put()`, `puts()`, or `fs_obj <<` to write to a file. You should use whichever method that you feel is most appropriate for the data being written. If you need a newline character (`\n`) at the end of each line in your file, `fs_obj <<` and `puts()` are probably easier to use than `put()`, but any of the three can do the job.

> **Tip:** Each line in a file is called a *record*. By writing a newline character at the end of each record, you create a sequential file that is easier to read back into your program at a later time. This type of file is an ASCII text file.

## Examples

1. The following program creates a file called NAMES.DAT. The program writes five names to a disk file, using `fp <<`.

```
// Filename: C32WR1.CPP
// Writes five names to a disk file
#include <fstream.h>
ofstream      fp;
main()
    {
    fp.open("NAMES.DAT", ios::out);   // Create a new file
    fp << "Michael Langston\n";
    fp << "Sally Redding\n";
    fp << "Jane Kirk\n";
    fp << "Stacy Grady\n";
    fp << "Paula Hiquet\n";
    fp.close();                       // Release the file
    return 0;
    }
```

For simplicity, no error checking was done on the `open()`. The next few examples check for the error.

NAMES.TXT is a text data file. If you like, you can read this file into your word processor (use the word processor's command for reading ASCII files), or you can use the MS-DOS TYPE command to display the file on-screen. If you display NAMES.TXT, you see the following:

```
Michael Langston
Sally Redding
Jane Kirk
Stacy Grady
Paula Hiquet
```

2. The following file writes the numbers from 1 to 100 to a file called NUMS.1:

```
// Filename: C32WR2.CPP
// Writes 1 to 100 to a disk file

#include <fstream.h>

ofstream      fp;

main()
    {
    int    ctr;

    fp.open("NUMS.1", ios::out);      // Create a new file
    if (!fp)
        cerr << "Error opening file.\n";
```

```
        else
            {
            for (ctr = 1; ctr < 101; ctr++)
                fp << ctr << " ";
            }
        fp.close();
        return 0;
        }
```

The numbers are not written one per line, but with a space between them. The way that you invoke the fp << determines the format of the output data. When writing data to disk files, keep in mind that you have to read the data later. You will likely need to write functions that can read the files that your output functions created.

# Writing to a Printer

The open() function and other output functions were not designed just to write to files. They were designed to write to any device, including files, the screen, and the printer. If you need to write data to a printer, you can treat it as if it were a file. The following program opens a file stream object, using the MS-DOS name for a printer located at LPT1 (the first parallel printer port):

```
// Filename: C32PRNT.CPP
// Prints to the printer device
#include <fstream.h>
ofstream    prnt;     // Will point to the printer
main()
    {
    prnt.open("LPT1", ios::out);
    prnt << "Printer line 1\n";     // 1st line printed
    prnt << "Printer line 2\n";     // 2nd line printed
    prnt << "Printer line 3\n";     // 3rd line printed
    prnt.close();
    return 0;
    }
```

Make sure that your printer is turned on and has paper before you run this program. When you run it, the following lines are printed on the printer:

```
Printer line 1
Printer line 2
Printer line 3
```

# Adding to a File

You can easily add data to an existing file or create new files by opening the file in append access mode. Data files on the disk are rarely static; they grow almost daily as business increases. Being able to add to data already on the disk is very useful indeed.

When you open a file for append access (using `ios::app`), the file does not have to exist already. If the file does exist, C++ opens the file such that any data written appends to the end of the file. If the file does not exist, C++ simply creates the file (just as when you open a file for write access).

### Example

The following program adds three more names to the NAMES.DAT file created earlier:

```
// Filename: C32AP1.CPP
// Adds three names to a disk file

#include <fstream.h>
ofstream     fp;
main()
    {
    fp.open("NAMES.DAT", ios::app);     // Add to file
    fp << "Johnny Smith\n";
    fp << "Laura Hull\n";
    fp << "Mark Brown\n";
    fp.close();     // Release the file
    return 0;
    }
```

The file now looks like this:

```
Michael Langston
Sally Redding
Jane Kirk
Stacy Grady
Paula Hiquet
Johnny Smith
Laura Hull
Mark Brown
```

**Note:** If the file did not exist, C++ would create it and store the three names in the file.

Basically, you have to change only the `open()` function's access mode to turn a file-creation program into a program that appends to a file.

# Reading from a File

After the data is in a file, you probably need to read that data at some point. To do so, you must open the file in a read access mode. You have several ways to read data. You can read character data a character at a time or a string at a time. The choice depends on the format of the data.

Files you open for read access (using `ios::in`) must exist already; C++ does not create the file for you. Obviously, you cannot read a file that does not exist. `open()` returns zero if the file does not exist when you open it for read access.

If you read a file sequentially, you eventually read *all* the data in the file. If you attempt to read data after you have reached the end-of-file, C++ returns the value of zero. To find the end-of-file condition, be sure to check for zero when performing input from files.

## Examples

1. The following program asks the user for a file name and prints the contents of the file to the screen. If the file does not exist, the program displays an error message.

```
// Filename: C32RE1.CPP
// Reads and displays a file

#include <fstream.h>
#include <stdlib.h>
ifstream     fp;
main()
    {
    char     filename[ 12 ];   // Will hold user's file name
    char     in_char;          // Input character
    cout << "What is the name of the file ";
    cout << "you want to see? ";
    cin >> filename;
    fp.open(filename, ios::in);
    if (!fp)
        {
        cerr << "\n\n*** That file does not exist ***\n";
        exit(0);    // Exit program
        }
    while (fp.get(in_char))
        cout << in_char;
    fp.close();
    return 0;
    }
```

Figure 31.1 shows what happens when the NAMES.DAT file is requested. Because newline characters are in the file at the end of each name, the names appear on-screen, one name per line.

**Figure 31.1.**

Reading and
displaying a
disk file.

```
What is the name of the file you want to see? names.dat
Michael Langston
Sally Redding
Jane Kirk
Stacy Grady
Paula Hiquet
Johnny Smith
Laura Hull
Mark Brown
```

If the user attempts to read a file that does not exist, the program displays
the following message:

```
*** That file does not exist ***
```

2. The following program reads one file and copies it to another file. You
might want to use such a program to back up important data in case the
original file gets damaged.

This program must open two files, the first for reading and the second for
writing. The file stream object determines which of the two files is being
accessed.

```cpp
// Filename: C32RE2.CPP
// Makes a copy of a file

#include <fstream.h>
#include <stdlib.h>

ifstream    in_fp;
ofstream    out_fp;

main()
    {
    char    in_filename[ 12 ];  // Will hold original
                                // file name
    char    out_filename[ 12 ]; // Will hold backup
                                // file name
    char    in_char;            // Input character

    cout << "What is the name of the file ";
    cout << "you want to back up? ";
    cin >> in_filename;
    cout << "What is the name of the file ";
    cout << "you want to copy " << in_filename
        << " to? ";
    cin >> out_filename;
    in_fp.open(in_filename, ios::in);
    if (!in_fp)
        {
```

```
            cerr << "\n\n*** %s does not exist ***\n";
            exit(0);      // Exit program
            }
     out_fp.open(out_filename, ios::out);
     if (!out_fp)
         {
         cerr << "\n\n*** Error opening %s ***\n";
         exit(0);      // Exit program
         }
     cout << "\nCopying...\n";      // Waiting message
     while (in_fp.get(in_char))
         out_fp.put(in_char);
     cout << "\nThe file is copied.\n";
     in_fp.close();
     out_fp.close();
     return 0;
     }
```

# Summary

This chapter showed you how to perform two of the most important requirements of data processing: writing to and reading from disk files. Before now, you could store data only in variables. The short life of variables (they last only as long as your program is running) made long-term storage of data impossible. Now you can save large amounts of data in disk files for later processing.

Reading and writing sequential files involve learning more concepts than actual commands or functions. The `open()` and `close()` functions are the most important ones discussed in this chapter. You were already familiar with most of the I/O functions needed to get data to and from disk files.

The next chapter, which concludes this book's discussion of disk files, shows you how to create and use random-access files. By programming with such files, you are able to read selected data from a file, as well as change data without having to rewrite the entire file.

# Review Questions

Answers to Review Questions are in Appendix B.

1. What are the three ways to access sequential files?

2. What advantages do disk files have over holding data in memory?

3. How do sequential files differ from random-access files?

4. What happens if you open a file for read access and the file does not exist?

5. What happens if you open a file for write access and the file already exists?

6. What happens if you open a file for append access and the file does not exist?

7. How does C++ inform you that you have reached the end-of-file condition?

# Review Exercises

1. Write a program that creates a file containing the following data:

    Your name

    Your address

    Your phone number

    Your age

2. Write a second program that reads and prints the data file created in the preceding exercise.

3. Write a program that takes that same data and writes it to the screen, one word per line.

4. Write a program for PCs that backs up two important files: AUTOEXEC.BAT and CONFIG.SYS. Call the backup files AUTOEXEC.SAV and CONFIG.SAV.

5. Write a program that reads a file and creates a new file with the same data, with one exception: reverse the case on the second file. Everywhere uppercase letters appear in the first file, write lowercase letters to the new file. Everywhere lowercase letters appear in the first file, write uppercase letters to the new file.

# CHAPTER 32

# Random-Access Files

Random file access enables you to read or write data in a disk file without having to read or write every piece of data that comes before the data you want. You can quickly add, retrieve, change, and delete information in a random-access file. Although you need to learn a few new functions to access files randomly, you will find that the extra effort pays off in flexibility, power, and speed of disk access.

In this chapter, you learn about the following topics:

♦ Random-access files

♦ File records

♦ The seekg() function

♦ Special-purpose file I/O functions

## Understanding Random File Records

Random files exemplify the power of data processing with C++. Sequential file processing is inconvenient unless you read the entire file into arrays and process them in memory. As explained in the preceding chapter, however, you have much more disk space than RAM, and most disk files do not even fit in your RAM at one time. Therefore, you need a way to read individual pieces of data from a file quickly in any order needed and to process them one at a time.

A record to a file is like an element to an array of structures.

Generally, you read and write file records. A record to a file is analogous to a C++ structure. A *record* is a collection of one or more data values (called *fields*) that you read and write to disk. A *structure* is a collection of one or more data values (also called *fields*) that you store in random access memory and process with executable code and write to disk. Generally, you store data in structures and write the structures to disk, where they are called records. When you read a record from disk, you generally read that record into a structure variable and process it with your program.

Unlike most programming languages, C++ does not require that all disk data be stored in record format. Typically, you write a stream of characters to a disk file and access that data either sequentially or randomly by reading it into variables and structures.

The process of randomly accessing data in a file is simple. Think about the data files of a large credit card organization, for example. When you make a purchase, the store calls the credit card company to get an authorization. The records of millions of people are contained in the credit card company's files. The credit card company could not possibly read every record from the disk that comes before yours (sequentially) in a timely manner. Sequential files do not lend themselves to quick access. In many instances, looking up individual records in a data file with sequential access is not feasible.

The credit card company must use a random file access so that its computers can go directly to your record, just as you go directly to a song on a compact disk or record album. The functions you use are different from the sequential functions, but the power that results from learning the added functions is worth the effort.

**You do not have to rewrite the entire file to change random-access file data.**

Reading and writing files randomly are similar to thinking of the file as a big array. With arrays, you know that you can add, print, or remove values in any order. You do not have to start at the first array element, sequentially looking at the next one, until you get the element you need. You can view your random-access file in the same way, accessing the data in any order.

Most random file records are fixed-length records. That is, each record (usually a row in the file) takes the same amount of disk space. Most of the sequential files you read and wrote in the preceding chapter were variable-length records (except for the examples that wrote structures to the disks). When you are reading or writing sequentially, you have no need for fixed-length records because you input each value one character, word, string, or number at a time, looking for the data you want. With fixed-length records, your computer can better calculate exactly where the search record is located on the disk.

Although you waste some disk space with fixed-length records (because of the spaces that pad some of the fields), the advantages of random file access sometimes make up for the "wasted" disk space.

> **Tip:** With random-access files, you can read or write records in any order. Therefore, even if you want to perform sequential reading or writing of the file, you can use random-access processing and "randomly" read or write the file in sequential record number order.

# Opening Random-Access Files

Just as with sequential files, you must open random-access files before reading or writing to them. You can use any of the read access modes mentioned in the preceding chapter (such as `ios::in`) if you plan *only* to read a file randomly. To modify data in a file, however, you must open the file in one of the update modes listed in the last chapter and repeated in table 32.1.

**Table 32.1. Random-access update modes.**

| Mode | Description |
|------|-------------|
| app | Open the file for appending (adding to it) |
| ate | Seek to end of file on opening it |
| in | Open file for reading |
| out | Open file for writing |
| binary | Open file in binary mode |
| trunc | Discard contents if file exists |
| nocreate | If file doesn't exist, open fails |
| noreplace | If file exists, open fails unless appending or seeking to end of file on opening |

Sequential files and random files in C++ are really no different. The difference between the files is not physical but lies in the method you use to access and update them.

## Examples

1. Suppose that you want to write a program to create a file of friends' names. The following `open()` function call does the job, assuming that `fp` is declared as a file pointer:

```
fp.open("NAMES.DAT", ios::out);
if (!fp)
    cerr << "\n*** Cannot open file ***\n");
```

If you are simply creating a file and not reading data from it, you need only specify `ios::out` as an `open()` access mode. But what if you want to create a file, write data to it, and give the user a chance to change any of the data before closing the file? You would then have to open the file like this:

```
fp.open("NAMES.DAT", ios::in | ios::out);
if (!fp)
cerr << "\n*** Cannot open file ***\n");
```

This version enables you to create the file and then change the data you wrote to the file.

2. As with sequential files, with random files the only difference in using a binary open() access mode is that the file you create is more compact and saves disk space. You cannot, however, read that file from other programs as an ASCII text file. You can rewrite the preceding open() function to create and allow updating of a binary file. All other file-related commands and functions work for binary files just as they do for text files. The modified code is

```
fp.open("NAMES.DAT", ios::in | ios::out | ios::binary);
if (!fp)
cerr << "\n*** Cannot open file ***\n");
```

# Using the *seekg()* Function

C++ provides a function that enables you to read to a specific point in a random-access data file. This function is seekg(). The format of seekg() is

```
fs_obj.seekg(long_num, origin);
```

The *fs_obj* is the file stream object for the file you want to access, initialized with an open() statement.

The long_num is the number of bytes in the file you want to skip. C++ then does not read this many bytes but literally skips the data by the number of bytes specified in long_num. Skipping the bytes on the disk is much faster than reading them. If long_num is negative, C++ skips backward in the file (enabling you to reread data several times). Because data files can be large, you must declare long_num as a long integer to hold a large amount of bytes.

The origin is a value that tells C++ where to begin the skipping of bytes specified by long_num. The origin can be xany of the three values shown in table 32.2.

You can use seekg() to read forward or backward from any point in a file.

**Table 32.2. Possible origin values.**

| Mode | Description |
|------|-------------|
| `ios::beg` | Beginning of file |
| `ios::cur` | Current file position |
| `ios::end` | End of file |

The mode identifiers `ios::beg`, `ios::cur`, and `ios::end` are defined in `iostream.h`.

**Note:** The file stream object plays an important role in processing the file. In conjunction with the operating system, the file stream object keeps track of the next byte to read or write. In other words, as you read data, from either a sequential file or a random-access file, the file pointer increments with each byte read. By using `seekg()`, you can move the file pointer forward or backward in the file.

## Examples

**1.** No matter how far into a file you have read, the following `seekg()` function positions the file pointer back to the beginning of a file:

```
fp.seekg(0L, ios::beg);  // Position the file pointer
                         // at the beginning
```

The constant `0L` passes a long integer `0` to the `seekg()` function. Without the `L`, C++ would pass a regular integer, which would not match the prototype for `seek()` that is located in `fstream.h`. (Chapter 5, "Variables and Constants," explains the use of data type suffixes on numeric constants, but the suffixes have not been used again until now.)

This `seekg()` function literally reads "move the file pointer 0 bytes from the beginning of the file."

**2.** The following example reads a file named MYFILE.TXT twice, once to send the file to the screen and once to send the file to the printer. Three file pointers are used, one for each device (the file, the screen, and the printer).

```
// Filename: C33TWIC.CPP
// Writes a file to the screen, rereads it, and sends it
// to the printer
```

```
#include <fstream.h>
#include <stdlib.h>
#include <stdio.h>

ifstream    in_file;   // Input file pointer
ofstream    scrn;      // Screen pointer
ofstream    prnt;      // Printer pointer

main()
    {
    char     in_char;

    in_file.open("NAMES.DAT", ios::in);
    if (!in_file)
        {
        cerr << "\n*** Error opening MYFILE.TXT ***\n";
        exit(0);
        }
    scrn.open("CON", ios::out);     // Open screen device
    while (in_file.get(in_char))
        scrn << in_char;            // Output characters
                                    // to the screen
    scrn.close();                   // Close screen since
                                    // it is no longer needed
    in_file.seekg(0L, ios::beg);    // Reposition file pointer
    prnt.open("LPT1", ios::out);    // Open printer device
    while (in_file.get(in_char))
        prnt << in_char;            // Output characters
                                    // to the printer

        prnt.close();               // Always close all
                                    // open files

    in_file.close();
    return 0;
    }
```

You also can close and then reopen a file to position the file pointer back at the beginning, but using seekg() is a more efficient method.

Of course, you could use regular I/O functions to write to the screen instead of opening the screen as a separate device.

3. The following seekg() function positions the file pointer at the 30th byte in the file. (The next byte read will be the 31st byte.)

```
fs_obj.seekg(30L, ios::beg);     // Position file pointer
                                 // at the 30th byte
```

This seekg() function literally reads "move the file pointer 30 bytes from the beginning of the file."

If you write structures to a file, you can quickly seek any structure in the file by using the `sizeof()` function. Suppose that you want the 123rd occurrence of the structure tagged with `inventory`. You would search with this `seekg()` function:

```
fs_obj.seekg((123L * sizeof(struct inventory)), ios::beg);
```

4. The following program writes the letters of the alphabet to a file called ALPH.TXT. The `seekg()` function is then used to read and display the 9th and 17th letters (I and Q).

```cpp
// Filename: C33ALPH.CPP
// Stores the alphabet in a file and then reads two letters
// from it

#include <fstream.h>
#include <stdlib.h>
#include <stdio.h>

fstream     fp;

main()
    {
    char      ch;       // Will hold A through Z

    // Open in update mode so that you can read
    // file after writing to it
    fp.open("alph.txt", ios::in | ios::out);
    if (!fp)
        {
        cerr << "\n*** Error opening file ***\n";
        exit(0);
        }
    for (ch = 'A'; ch <= 'Z'; ch++)
        fp << ch;       // Write letters
    fp.seekg(8L, ios::beg);    // Skip 8 letters, point to I
    fp >> ch;
    cout << "The first character is " << ch << "\n";
    fp.seekg(16L, ios::beg);  // Skip 16 letters, point to Q
    fp >> ch;
    cout << "The second character is " << ch << "\n";
    fp.close();
    return 0;
    }
```

5. To point to the end of a data file, you can use the `seekg()` function to position the file pointer at the last byte. Subsequent `seekg()` functions should then use a negative `long_num` value to skip backward in the file.

The following `seekg()` function makes the file pointer point to the end of the file:

```
fs_obj.seekg(-1L, ios::end);     // Position file pointer
                                 // at the end
```

This `seekg()` function literally reads "move the file pointer 0 bytes from the end of the file." The file pointer now points to the end-of-file marker, but you can then `seekg()` backward to get to other data in the file.

6. The following program reads the ALPH.TXT file (created in example 4) backward, printing each character as it skips back in the file:

```
// Filename: C33BACK.CPP
// Reads and prints a file backward

#include <fstream.h>
#include <stdlib.h>
#include <stdio.h>

ifstream    fp;

main()
    {
    int      ctr;     // Step through the 26 letters
                      // in the file
    char     in_char;

    fp.open("ALPH.TXT", ios::in);
    if (!fp)
        {
        cout << "\n*** Error opening file ***\n";
        exit(0);
        }
    fp.seekg(-1L, ios::end);    // Point to last byte
                                // in the file
    for (ctr = 0; ctr <= 25; ctr++)
        {
        fp >> in_char;
        fp.seekg(-2L, ios::cur);
        cout << in_char;
        }
    fp.close();
    return 0;
    }
```

This program also uses `ios::cur` for the origin. The last `seekg()` in the program seeks two bytes backward from the *current* position—not the beginning or end, as in the previous examples. The `for` loop toward the end of the program performs a "skip two bytes back, read one byte forward" method to skip backward through the file.

7. The following program performs the same actions as example 4 (C33ALPH.CPP), but with one addition. When the letters I and Q are found, the letter *x* is written over the I and Q. The seekg() must be used to back up one byte in the file to overwrite the letter just read.

```cpp
// Filename: C33CHANG.CPP
// Stores the alphabet in a file, reads two letters from it,
// and changes each of them to x

#include <fstream.h>
#include <stdlib.h>
#include <stdio.h>

fstream     fp;

main()
    {
    char    ch;      // Will hold A through Z

    // Open in update mode so that you can read file
    // after writing to it
    fp.open("alph.txt", ios::in | ios::out);
    if (!fp)
        {
        cout << "\n*** Error opening file ***\n";
        exit(0);
        }
    for (ch = 'A'; ch <= 'Z'; ch++)
        fp << ch;        // Write letters
    fp.seekg(8L, ios::beg);   // Skip 8 letters, point to I
    fp >> ch;
    // Change the I to an x
    fp.seekg(-1L, ios::cur);
    fp << 'x';
    cout << "The first character is " << ch << "\n";
    fp.seekg(16L, ios::beg);   // Skip 16 letters, point to Q
    fp >> ch;
    cout << "The second character is " << ch << "\n";
    // Change the Q to an x
    fp.seekg(-1L, ios::cur);
    fp << 'x';
    fp.close();
    return 0;
    }
```

The file named ALPH.TXT now looks like this:

ABCDEFGHxJKLMNOPxRSTUVWXYZ

This program forms the basis of a more complete data file management program. After you master the seekg() function and become more familiar with disk data files, you can begin to write programs that store more advanced data structures and access them.

The mailing list application in Appendix F is a good example of what you can do with random file access. The user is given a chance to change name and address information for people already in the file. The program uses random-access seeks and writes to change selected data without having to rewrite the entire disk file.

# Using Other Helpful I/O Functions

Several more disk I/O functions are available that you might find useful. They are mentioned here for completeness. As you write more powerful programs in C++, you will find uses for many of these functions when performing disk I/O. Each of the following functions is prototyped in the `fstream.h` header file:

- ◆ `read(array, count)`. Reads the amount of data specified by the integer `count` into the array or pointer specified by `array`. `read()` is called a *buffered I/O* function. `read()` enables you to read a lot of data with a single function call.

- ◆ `write(array, count)`. Writes `count` array bytes to the file specified. `write()` is also a buffered I/O function. `write()` enables you to write a lot of data in a single function call.

- ◆ `remove(filename)`. Erases the file named by `filename`. It returns a 0 if the file was successfully erased or –1 if an error occurred.

Many of these functions, as well as other built-in I/O functions you will learn in your C++ programming career, are helpful functions that you can duplicate by using what you already know.

The buffered I/O file functions enable you to read and write entire arrays (including arrays of structures) to the disk in a single function call.

## Examples

1. The following program requests a file name from the user and erases the file from the disk, using the `remove()` function.

```
// Filename: C33ERAS.CPP
// Erases the file specified by the user

#include <stdio.h>
#include <iostream.h>

main()
    {
    char    filename[ 12 ];

    cout << "What is the filename you want me to erase? ";
    cin >> filename;
    if (remove(filename) == -1)
```

```
        cout << "\n*** I could not remove the file ***\n";
     else
        cout << "\nThe file " << filename <<
             " is now removed\n";
     return 0;
     }
```

**2.** The following function could be part of a larger program that gets inventory data, in an array of structures, from the user. This function is passed the array name and the number of elements (structure variables) in the array. The `write()` function then writes the complete array of structures to the disk file pointed to by `fp`. `fp` is declared globally in this case.

```
void write_str(struct inventory items[ ], int inv_cnt)
    {
    fp.write(items, inv_cnt * sizeof(struct inventory);
    return;
    }
```

If the inventory array had 1,000 elements, this one-line function would still write the entire array to the disk file. You can use the `read()` function to read the entire array of structures from the disk in a single function call.

## Summary

C++ supports random-access files with several functions. These include error checking, file pointer positioning, opening of files, and closing of files. You now have the tools you need to save your C++ program data to the disk for storage and retrieval.

The mailing list application in Appendix F offers a complete example of random-access file manipulation. The program enables the user to enter names and addresses, store them to disk, edit them, change them, and print them from the disk file. The mailing list program combines almost every topic from this book into a complete application that "puts it all together."

## Review Questions

Answers to Review Questions are in Appendix B.

**1.** What is the difference between records and structures?

**2.** True or false: You have to create a random-access file before reading from it randomly.

**3.** What happens to the file pointer as you read from a file?

**4.** What are the two buffered file I/O functions?

**5.** What are two methods for positioning the file pointer at the beginning of a file?

**6.** What are the three starting positions (the origins) in the seekg() function?

**7.** What is wrong with the following program?

```
#include <fstream.h>

ifstream    fp;

main()
    {
    char    in_char;

    fp.open(ios::in | ios::binary);
    if fp.get(in_char))
        cout << in_char;      // Write to the screen
    fp.close();
    return 0;
    }
```

# Review Exercises

**1.** Write a program that asks the user for a list of five names and writes the names to a file. Rewind the file and display its contents on-screen, using the seekg() and get() functions.

**2.** Rewrite the preceding program so that it displays every other character in the file of names.

**3.** Write a program that reads characters from a file. If the input character is a lowercase letter, change it to uppercase. If the input character is uppercase, change it to lowercase. Do not change other characters in the file.

**4.** Write a program that displays the number of nonalphabetic characters in a file.

**5.** Write a grade-keeping program for a teacher. Let the teacher enter up to 10 students' grades. Each student has 3 grades for the semester. Store the student names and their 3 grades in an array of structures and store the data on the disk. Make the program menu-driven. Let the teacher have the options of adding more students, looking at the file's data, or printing the grades to the printer with a calculated class average.

# Part VIII

*Object-Oriented Programming*

# CHAPTER 33

# Objects and Classes

Borland C++ gives you the capability to do object-oriented programming. *Object-oriented programming* enables the programmer to group together data and the code that uses data into discrete units. Objects in C++ are defined using C++ classes. Classes, which allow the programmer to define new data types, are a powerful part of Borland C++. Classes distinguish C++ from C. In fact, before the name C++ was coined, it was called "C with classes."

This chapter covers the following topics:

♦ The nature of object-oriented programming

♦ What an object is

♦ What a class is

♦ Data members and member functions

## What Is Object-Oriented Programming?

Object-oriented programming (OOP) is a different way of thinking about programming. In procedural programming, you think about functions and the execution flow through these functions. You think separately about data and how the functions interact with data. Object-oriented programming, however, forces you to think in terms of objects and the interaction between objects. An *object* is a self-contained entity that describes not only certain data but the procedures to manipulate the data.

Why use object-oriented programming? The answer to this question isn't simple. OOP enables you to model more closely whatever real-world problem the program is being written to solve. In addition, because objects are discrete entities, you can debug, modify, and maintain them more easily. Finally, if your objects are thought-fully designed, you can reuse much more of your code than with procedural programming.

Objects are the means that you use to implement object-oriented programming and to obtain the resulting benefits.

## Objects

An *object* is a self-contained abstraction of an item. The item could be a student record or a screen window. An object includes all the data necessary to represent the item and the functions, or methods, that manipulate this data. The perfect object knows everything about itself, including how to input, output, and manipulate its data.

In Borland C++, objects are implemented using classes.

## Classes

A *class* is a user-defined data type used to implement an abstract object, giving you the capability to use object-oriented programming with Borland C++. A class includes members. A *member* can be either data, known as a *data member*, or a function, known as a *member function*.

Data members can be of any type, including C++ defined types such as int and double or user-defined types, including other classes. Member functions manipulate the data members, create and destroy class variables, and even redefine C++ operators to act on the class objects.

## Members

Like a structure, a class has one or more variable types, called *members*. The two kinds of members are data members and member functions. Members have a new attribute: visibility. Just as global variables are visible to all functions and local variables are not, individual members of a class can be made visible everywhere or not. A member's visibility is determined by the visibility label, which will be discussed fully in Chapter 34.

> **Note:** If this sounds like something discussed earlier, it should. A class of nothing but data members, all of which are visible outside the class, has another name: a *structure*.

## Data Members

*Data members* of a class are exactly like the variables in a structure. To describe a sphere, for example, you need to know the sphere's radius and the coordinates describing its center. A sphere class would look like the following:

```
// A data only sphere class
class Sphere
 {
    public:
        float      r;         // Radius of sphere
        float      x, y, z;   // Coordinates of sphere
 };
```

The Sphere class has four data members: r, x, y, and z. So far, not much distinguishes the sphere class from a struct. Notice, however, that the class has a label—the word public:. This label is explained later in the chapter.

## Member Functions

*Member functions* are functions defined within a class that act on the data members in the class. The use of member functions distinguishes a class from a struct. The following is the updated Sphere class, which includes some member functions:

```
// A sphere class
class Sphere
{
    public:
        float      r;         // Radius of sphere
        float      x, y, z;   // Coordinates of sphere
        Sphere(float xcoord, float ycoord,
               float zcoord, float radius)
        { x = xcoord; y = ycoord; z = zcoord; r = radius; }
        ~Sphere() { }
        float volume()
        {
            return (r * r * r * 4 * M_PI / 3);
        }
        float surface_area()
        {
            return (r * r * 4 * M_PI);
        }
 };
```

The member functions added to the Sphere class are Sphere, ~Sphere, volume, and surface_area. The class is definitely not a struct anymore.

After you define your class, you can create variables of the class type. You can create class variables anywhere you can create a variable of a built-in type. The following code shows how to declare a Sphere class variable:

```
Sphere      sphereVariable;
```

## Constructors and Destructors

The Sphere function is unique. Sphere is a constructor function used primarily in declaring a new instance of the class. A *constructor function*, which always has the same name as the class, is used to create and initialize a class variable all at once. Class variables can be relatively complex to create and initialize. Class constructors automate the procedure of creating and initializing class variables, eliminating the likelihood of missing a step or performing a step incorrectly.

Constructors are used to initialize the data members of the class. If you have data members that must be initialized, you must have a constructor. In your constructor, you should not do something that can fail because the constructor doesn't return a value. If you do something that fails, such as a memory allocation, you have no way to indicate that to the function creating the class.

The other special function is ~Sphere—the destructor function. The destructor also has the same name as the class, but includes a tilde (~) as a prefix.

Whereas the constructor function allocates memory to create a class variable, the *destructor function* gives back the memory, effectively destroying the class variable. The destructor can perform other activities, such as printing out final values of the class data members. (These are useful for debugging.)

The destructor function takes no arguments and returns no value. Notice also that ~Sphere does nothing, which is true of most destructors. A destructor's main processing job is to free any memory that the class allocates for itself.

> **Note:** If your destructor function does nothing, you don't need to create it. As soon as the class variable no longer exists, the memory allocated for the object is returned to the system. Similarly, if you don't need to do anything specific for a constructor, you don't need to include a constructor; Borland C++ allocates memory for a class variable when you create the variable.

### Examples

1. The program in listing 33.1 shows a complete program that uses the Sphere class. It shows that the constructor creates and initializes a Sphere class variable s.

**Listing 33.1. A Program Demonstrating the Use of a Constructor**

```
// Filename: C33CON.CPP
// Demonstrates use of a class constructor function

#include  <iostream.h>
#include  <math.h>
// M_PI (value of pi) is defined in MATH.H

// A sphere class
class Sphere
```

```
      {
public:
     float      r;          // Radius of sphere
     float      x, y, z;    // Coordinates of sphere
     Sphere(float xcoord, float ycoord,
            float zcoord, float radius)
       { x = xcoord; y = ycoord; z = zcoord; r = radius; }
     ~Sphere() { }
     float volume()
       {
       return (r * r * r * 4 * M_PI / 3);
       }
     float surface_area()
       {
       return (r * r * 4 * M_PI);
       }
     };

void  main(void)
     {
     Sphere     s(1.0, 2.0, 3.0, 4.0);

     cout << "X = " << s.x
          << " Y = " << s.y
          << " Z = " << s.z
          << " R = " << s.r
          << "\n";
     }
```

Figure 33.1 shows the output of this program.

**Figure 33.1.**

A class construc-
tor in use.

```
d:\bcppbe\chap33>c33con
X = 1 Y = 2 Z = 3 R = 4

d:\bcppbe\chap33>
```

**2.** This example demonstrates that a destructor is called and can do something. Listing 33.2 shows the modified Sphere program. This new program
announces that the destructor has been called.

**Listing 33.2. A Program Demonstrating the Use of a Destructor**

```
// Filename: C33DES.CPP
// Demonstrates use of a class destructor function

#include  <iostream.h>
#include  <math.h>
// M_PI (value of pi) is defined in MATH.H
```

*continues*

**Listing 33.2. Continued**

```cpp
// A sphere class
class Sphere
    {
public:
    float     r;          // Radius of sphere
    float     x, y, z;   // Coordinates of sphere
    Sphere(float xcoord, float ycoord,
          float zcoord, float radius)
      { x = xcoord; y = ycoord; z = zcoord; r = radius; }
    ~Sphere()
        {
        cout << "Sphere (" << x << ", " << y << ", "
             << z << ", " << r << ") destroyed\n";
        }
    float volume()
      {
      return (r * r * r * 4 * M_PI / 3);
      }
    float surface_area()
      {
      return (r * r * 4 * M_PI);
      }
    };

void  main(void)
    {
    Sphere    s(1.0, 2.0, 3.0, 4.0);

    cout << "X = " << s.x
         << " Y = " << s.y
         << " Z = " << s.z
         << " R = " << s.r << "\n";
    }
```

Figure 33.2 shows the output of this program.

**Figure 33.2.**

A class destructor
in use.

```
d:\bcppbe\chap33>c33des
X = 1 Y = 2 Z = 3 R = 4
Sphere (1, 2, 3, 4) destroyed

d:\bcppbe\chap33>
```

## Using Member Functions

After you create a class variable, you can access the data members and member functions of that class. Because the data members and member functions are part of the class, you must access them through the variable you created.

```
// create a Sphere variable
Sphere      s;

// access the data members and member functions
float       LocalX;
float       Volume;
LocalX = s.x;             // access a data member
Volume = s.volume();      // access a member function
```

The class members are accessed using the dot (.) operator. This operator tells C++ to access a member of the class of which the variable is an instance. Each instance of a class has its own set of data, and the member functions operate on the variable's specific set of data.

## Example

This version of the Sphere program demonstrates using the member functions volume and surface_area. It calls both functions to display the volume and surface area of the sphere defined. This program is given in listing 33.3.

**Listing 33.3. A Program Demonstrating Member Function Usage**

```
// Filename: C33MEM.CPP
// Demonstrates use of class member functions

#include  <iostream.h>
#include  <math.h>
// M_PI (value of pi) is defined in MATH.H

// A sphere class
class Sphere
    {
public:
    float     r;        // Radius of sphere
    float     x, y, z;  // Coordinates of sphere
    Sphere(float xcoord, float ycoord, float zcoord,
           float radius)
      { x = xcoord; y = ycoord; z = zcoord; r = radius; }
    ~Sphere()
        {
        cout << "Sphere (" << x << ", " << y << ", "
             << z << ", " << r << ") destroyed\n";
        }
    float volume()
      {
```

*continues*

**Listing 33.3. Continued**

```
        return (r * r * r * 4 * M_PI / 3);
        }
        float surface_area()
        {
        return (r * r * 4 * M_PI);
        }
    };

void  main(void)
    {
    Sphere    s(1.0, 2.0, 3.0, 4.0);

    cout << "X = " << s.x
         << " Y = " << s.y
         << " Z = " << s.z
         << " R = " << s.r << "\n";
    cout << "The volume is " << s.volume() << "\n";
    cout << "The surface area is "
         << s.surface_area() << "\n";
    }
```

The output of this program is shown in figure 33.3.

**Figure 33.3.**

Class member
functions in use.

```
d:\bcppbe\chap33>c33mem
X = 1 Y = 2 Z = 3 R = 4
The volume is 268.083
The surface area is 201.062
Sphere (1, 2, 3, 4) destroyed

d:\bcppbe\chap33>
```

## In-Line Member Functions

Most member functions can be made to be *in-line*. A function is defined as being in-line; its implementation is substituted into the code where the function call was made. In the Sphere class, the volume and surface_area functions could be made in-line, as shown in the following:

```
// A sphere class with in-line member functions
class Sphere
{
    public:
        float        r;          // Radius of sphere
        float        x, y, z;  // Coordinates of sphere
        Sphere(float xcoord, float ycoord,
               float zcoord, float radius)
        { x = xcoord; y = ycoord; z = zcoord; r = radius; }
        ~Sphere() { }
        inline float volume()
        {
            return (r * r * r * 4 * M_PI / 3);
        }
        inline float surface_area()
```

```
        {
            return (r * r * 4 * M_PI);
        }
};
```

Using this class definition, the line of code

```
cout << "The volume is " << s.volume() << "\n";
```

is expanded into

```
cout << "The volume is " << (s.r * s.r * s.r * 4 * M_PI / 3 ) << "\n";
```

This expansion is done automatically by Borland C++ when your code is compiled.

In-line functions can speed up a program significantly, but if not used wisely can cause the size of the program to become huge. You must consider the speed-versus-size tradeoff when deciding whether a function should be in-line.

## Example

The program in listing 33.4 shows the use of in-line functions. The volume member function is declared in-line. Notice that the use of the function in the main program does not change.

**Listing 33.4. A Program Demonstrating In-Line Member Functions**

```
// Filename: C33MEM1.CPP
// Demonstrates use of in-line class member functions

#include  <iostream.h>
#include  <math.h>
// M_PI (value of pi) is defined in MATH.H

// A sphere class
class Sphere
    {
public:
    float     r;        // Radius of sphere
    float     x, y, z;  // Coordinates of sphere
    Sphere(float xcoord, float ycoord, float zcoord,
           float radius)
      { x = xcoord; y = ycoord; z = zcoord; r = radius; }
    ~Sphere()
        {
        cout << "Sphere (" << x << ", " << y << ", "
             << z << ", " << r << ") destroyed\n";
        }
    inline float volume()
        {
        return (r * r * r * 4 * M_PI / 3);
        }
```

*continues*

**Listing 33.4. Continued**

```
    float surface_area()
      {
      return (r * r * 4 * M_PI);
      }
    };

void  main(void)
    {
    Sphere    s(1.0, 2.0, 3.0, 4.0);

    cout << "X = " << s.x
         << " Y = " << s.y
         << " Z = " << s.z
         << " R = " << s.r << "\n";
    cout << "The volume is " << s.volume() << "\n";
    cout << "The surface area is " << s.surface_area()
         << "\n";
    }
```

Figure 33.4 shows the output of this program.

**Figure 33.4.**

In-line class
member in use.

```
d:\bcppbe\chap33>c33mem1
X = 1 Y = 2 Z = 3 R = 4
The volume is 268.083
The surface area is 201.062
Sphere (1, 2, 3, 4) destroyed

d:\bcppbe\chap33>
```

## Default Member Function Arguments

Member functions also can take default arguments. In the Sphere class, assume that, by default, the y coordinate of a sphere is 2.0, the z coordinate is 2.5, and the radius is 1.0. The rewritten constructor function now looks like the following:

```
Sphere( float xcoord, float ycoord = 2.0,
      float zcoord = 2.5, float radius = 1.0)
{
    x = xcoord; y = ycoord; z = zcoord; r = radius;
}
```

You can create a sphere with any of the following instructions:

```
Sphere     s(1.0);                    // Use all defaults
Sphere     t(1.0, 1.1);               // Override y coord
Sphere     u(1.0, 1.1, 1.2);          // Override y and z
Sphere     v(1.0, 1.1, 1.2, 1.3);     // Override all defaults
```

Notice that when you use a default value, you must use all the other default values to the right. Similarly, after you define a function's parameter as having a default value, every parameter to the right must have a default value as well.

## Example

This example shows the use of default member function arguments. The constructor of Sphere has default argument values assigned for ycoord, zcoord, and radius. listing 33.5 shows this program.

**Listing 33.5. This Program Demonstrates Member Function Default Arguments**

```
// Filename: C33DEF.CPP
// A program that demonstrates use of default arguments in
// class member functions

#include  <iostream.h>
#include  <math.h>
// M_PI (value of pi) is defined in MATH.H

// A sphere class
class Sphere
    {
public:
    float     r;        // Radius of sphere
    float     x, y, z;  // Coordinates of sphere
    Sphere(float xcoord,
           float ycoord = 2.0,
           float zcoord = 2.5,
           float radius = 1.0)
      { x = xcoord; y = ycoord; z = zcoord; r = radius; }
    ~Sphere()
        {
        cout << "Sphere (" << x << ", " << y << ", "
             << z << ", " << r << ") destroyed\n";
        }
    inline float volume()
      {
      return (r * r * r * 4 * M_PI / 3);
      }
    float surface_area()
      {
      return (r * r * 4 * M_PI);
      }
    };

void  main(void)
    {
    Sphere    s(1.0);              // Use all defaults
    Sphere    t(1.0, 1.1);         // Override y coord
    Sphere    u(1.0, 1.1, 1.2);    // Override y and z
    Sphere    v(1.0, 1.1, 1.2, 1.3); // Override all
                                   // defaults
```

*continues*

**Listing 33.5. Continued**

```
      cout << "s: X = " << s.x
           << " Y = " << s.y
           << " Z = " << s.z
           << " R = " << s.r << "\n";
      cout << "The volume of s is " << s.volume() << "\n";
      cout << "The surface area of s is "
           << s.surface_area() << "\n";
      cout << "t: X = " << t.x
           << " Y = " << t.y
           << " Z = " << t.z
           << " R = " << t.r << "\n";
      cout << "The volume of t is " << t.volume() << "\n";
      cout << "The surface area of t is " <<
              t.surface_area() << "\n";
      cout << "u: X = " << u.x
           << " Y = " << u.y
           << " Z = " << u.z
           << " R = " << u.r << "\n";
      cout << "The volume of u is " << u.volume() << "\n";
      cout << "The surface area of u is "
           << u.surface_area() << "\n";
      cout << "v: X = " << v.x
           << " Y = " << v.y
           << " Z = " << v.z
           << " R = " << v.r << "\n";
      cout << "The volume of v is " << v.volume() << "\n";
      cout << "The surface area of v is " <<
              v.surface_area() << "\n";
}
```

Figure 33.5 shows the output of this program.

**Figure 33.5.**

Various defaults
in use; all four
spheres are
destroyed.

```
d:\bcppbe\chap33>c33def
s: X = 1 Y = 2 Z = 2.5 R = 1
The volume of s is 4.18879
The surface area of s is 12.5664
t: X = 1 Y = 1.1 Z = 2.5 R = 1
The volume of t is 4.18879
The surface area of t is 12.5664
u: X = 1 Y = 1.1 Z = 1.2 R = 1
The volume of u is 4.18879
The surface area of u is 12.5664
v: X = 1 Y = 1.1 Z = 1.2 R = 1.3
The volume of v is 9.20277
The surface area of v is 21.2372
Sphere (1, 1.1, 1.2, 1.3) destroyed
Sphere (1, 1.1, 1.2, 1) destroyed
Sphere (1, 1.1, 2.5, 1) destroyed
Sphere (1, 2, 2.5, 1) destroyed

d:\bcppbe\chap33>
```

## Overloading Constructor Functions

You also can have more than one constructor; this is called *overloading the constructor*. Overloading gives a function more than one thing to do while using the same function name for each of the different things it does. How do you (and the Borland C++ compiler) know which version of the overloaded function to use? You create a different *context* for each of the different purposes.

With more than one constructor, each having the name of the class, you must give the constructors different parameter lists so that the compiler can determine which constructor you intend to use. This supplies the context to the compiler and informs the compiler which constructor you intend to use.

## Example

This example demonstrates a common usage of overload constructors. Here one constructor initializes all the data members; the other constructor leaves all the data members uninitialized. Listing 33.6 shows this program.

**Listing 33.6. This Program Demonstrates Overloaded Constructors**

```
// Filename: C33OVCON.CPP
// Demonstrates use of overloaded constructors

#include  <iostream.h>
#include  <math.h>
// M_PI (value of pi) is defined in MATH.H

// A sphere class
class Sphere
    {
public:
    float     r;          // Radius of sphere
    float     x, y, z;   // Coordinates of sphere
    Sphere() {  } // doesn't do anything...
    Sphere(float xcoord, float ycoord,
           float zcoord, float radius)
      { x = xcoord; y = ycoord; z = zcoord; r = radius; }
    ~Sphere()
        {
        cout << "Sphere (" << x << ", " << y << ", "
             << z << ", " << r << ") destroyed\n";
        }
    inline float volume()
      {
      return (r * r * r * 4 * M_PI / 3);
      }
    float surface_area()
      {
      return (r * r * 4 * M_PI);
```

*continues*

**Listing 33.6. Continued**

```
        }
    };

void  main(void)
    {
    Sphere    s(1.0, 2.0, 3.0, 4.0);
    Sphere    t;   // No parameters - an uninitialized
                   // sphere

    cout << "X = " << s.x
         << " Y = " << s.y
         << " Z = " << s.z
         << " R = " << s.r << "\n";
    t = s;
    cout << "The volume of t is " << t.volume() << "\n";
    cout << "The surface area of t is "
         << t.surface_area() << "\n";
    }
```

Figure 33.6 shows the output of this program.

**Figure 33.6.**

Overloaded constructors in use.

```
d:\bcppbe\chap33>c33ovcon
X = 1 Y = 2 Z = 3 R = 4
The volume of t is 268.083
The surface area of t is 201.062
Sphere (1, 2, 3, 4) destroyed
Sphere (1, 2, 3, 4) destroyed

d:\bcppbe\chap33>
```

# Summary

This chapter introduced you to object-oriented programming. You learned how to define and use classes, data members, and member functions. You now have the foundation needed to move on to more advanced object-oriented programming concepts.

The next three chapters discuss additional aspects of object-oriented programming: data hiding, inheritance, and polymorphism.

# Review Questions

Answers to Review Questions are in Appendix B.

1. Why is it advantageous to use object-oriented programming?

2. What enables you to implement objects in C++?

3. What are the two types of class members?

4. Is a constructor always necessary?

5. Can you have multiple constructors?

6. Is a destructor always necessary?

7. How do you define default argument values?

# Review Exercises

1. Construct a class for handling a CD collection database. Use the following data members:

```
char     cd_title[40];
char     group[40];
int      number_of_tracks;
int      total_time;
```

Define two constructors: one that initializes the data members and another that creates an uninitialized class.

2. Construct a class for handling personnel records. Use the following data members:

```
char     name[ 25 ];
float    salary;
char     date_of_birth[ 9 ];
```

In addition to the constructor, create member functions to alter the individual's name, salary, and date of birth.

3. Construct a class that handles your to-do list. Use the following data members:

```
char     todo_description[60];
char     date_due[9];
int      priority;
```

Define multiple constructors and a full set of member functions to manipulate the data members. Assign default values to each member function argument.

# CHAPTER 34

# Data Hiding and the Public Interface

Object-oriented programming requires you to consider several specific paradigms. Objects are implemented as classes in C++. Within each class, these new paradigms make it easier to derive the specific benefits of object-oriented programming. The concepts of data hiding and an object's public interface comprise the first paradigm to be covered.

This chapter covers the following topics:

♦ What data hiding is

♦ How class member visibility works

♦ What a class's public interface is

## What Is Data Hiding?

A goal of object-oriented programming is to separate the use of an object from the implementation of that object. One way to accomplish this is through the use of data hiding. *Data hiding* enables you to completely encapsulate an object's data members. Data hiding prevents an object's users from directly accessing the data members of the class. Use of data hiding provides the following benefits:

♦ Users of the class are insulated from the actual representation of the data.

♦ Class programmers can change how data is represented or even where data comes from without affecting applications that use the class.

These benefits are derived by using C++ class member visibility. *Visibility* enables you to specify which class members—either data or functions—can be accessed by users of the class. If all data members of a class are hidden, as is convention, you must define a set of member functions used to access, modify, and process the data members. These accessible member functions are known as the class's *public interface*.

To create a class using data hiding, you must first understand how to make class members either hidden or visible outside the class.

## Class Member Visibility

As mentioned in Chapter 33, "Objects and Classes," each member function and data member of a class has an attribute known as its visibility. A class member's visibility determines who can use that member. C++ has three levels of visibility: public, private, and protected. Public and private visibility are discussed in this section, but protected visibility is beyond the scope of this book.

Recall the Sphere class from the last chapter.

```
class Sphere
{
    public:
                float     r;        // Radius of sphere
                float     x, y, z;  // Coordinates of sphere
                Sphere(    float xcoord, float ycoord,
                      float zcoord, float radius );
            ~Sphere();
            inline float volume();
            float surface_area();
};
```

This class contains the class visibility label public:. By declaring a class member *public*, you make that member accessible to both member and non-member functions. The data hiding paradigm does not allow non-member functions to access data members. Consider this new declaration of Sphere:

```
class Sphere
{
    public:
                Sphere(    float xcoord, float ycoord,
                      float zcoord, float radius );
            ~Sphere();
            inline float volume();
            float surface_area();
    private:
                float     r;        // Radius of sphere
                float     x, y, z;  // Coordinates of sphere
            float cube();
            float square();
};
```

Here the data members of Sphere are declared as *private*. Private members can be accessed only by a member function of that class. They cannot be accessed by any non-member functions; the data is hidden from the outside world. Two private member functions also are declared. Because they are private, neither cube nor square can be called outside the Sphere class.

Implementation of the data hiding paradigm uses class member visibility to prevent non-member functions from directly accessing the class data. It is good object-oriented programming practice to make all your data members private, while defining a good public interface for the object.

## Example

This example demonstrates the use of public and private members. The program shown in listing 34.1 makes the Sphere data private and implements two private member functions, cube and square.

Notice that the line that displayed the class's data members was removed from main(). The data members now are private and no longer directly accessible except by a member function of class Sphere.

**Listing 34.1. This Program Demonstrates Class Visibility**

```
// Filename: C34VISIB.CPP
// Demonstrates use of class visibility labels

#include   <iostream.h>
#include   <math.h>
// M_PI (value of pi) is defined in MATH.H

// A sphere class
class Sphere
    {
private:
    float     r;        // Radius of sphere
    float     x, y, z;  // Coordinates of sphere
    float cube() { return (r * r * r); }
    float square() { return (r * r); }
public:
    Sphere(float xcoord, float ycoord,
           float zcoord, float radius)
      { x = xcoord; y = ycoord; z = zcoord; r = radius; }
    ~Sphere()
        {
        cout << "Sphere (" << x << ", " << y << ", "
             << z << ", " << r << ") destroyed\n";
        }
    float volume()
      {
      return (cube() * 4 * M_PI / 3);
      }
```

*continues*

**Listing 34.1. Continued**

```
    float surface_area()
      {
      return (square() * 4 * M_PI);
      }
    };

void  main(void)
    {
    Sphere    s(1.0, 2.0, 3.0, 4.0);

    cout << "The volume is " << s.volume() << "\n";
    cout << "The surface area is "
        << s.surface_area() << "\n";
    }
```

Figure 34.1 shows the output of this program.

**Figure 34.1.**

Class visibility
labels in use.

```
d:\bcppbe\chap34>c34visib
The volume is 268.083
The surface area is 201.062
Sphere (1, 2, 3, 4) destroyed

d:\bcppbe\chap34>
```

# What Is a Public Interface?

The use of class member public and private visibility enables you to hide class members from non-member functions. A class can have both public and private members. The public members define how a non-member function can use the class. These public class members are known as the class's public interface.

The well-designed public interface usually includes member functions that do the following:

♦ Initialize a variable of the class type. Constructors are always `public:`.

♦ Free the memory used by a class variable. Destructors are always `public:`.

♦ Set the value of a class's private data members.

♦ Get the value of a class's private data members.

♦ Perform the real work of the object.

Here is an updated `Sphere` declaration that includes a complete public interface:

```
class Sphere
{
    public:
        Sphere(float xcoord, float ycoord,  float zcoord, float radius);
        ~Sphere();
        float volume();
        float surface_area();
        void    SetX( float newX );
        void    SetY( float newY );
        void    SetZ( float newZ );
        void    SetRadius( float newRadius );
        float    GetX();
        float    GetY();
        float    GetZ();
        float    GetRadius();
    private:
        float    r;         // Radius of sphere
        float    x, y, z;   // Coordinates of sphere
        float cube() ;
        float square();
};
```

In this class, a total of twelve functions make up the public interface. The functions `Sphere` and `~Sphere` are the class's constructor and destructor. Next, `volume` and `surface_area` do the actual work for which the class was designed. Finally, the eight `Get...` and `Set...` functions allow non-member functions to retrieve and modify the values of the private data members.

By defining these data access functions in the public interface instead of allowing direct access to the data members, the class program can change how the data members are stored without affecting programs that use the class. This is the main goal of data hiding and proper definition of a class public interface.

### Example

This example shows a version of the Sphere program with an expanded public interface. Listing 34.2 shows the program. It implements a full set of public member functions that give main() access to the private data members.

**Listing 34.2. This Program Implements a Full Public Interface**

// Filename: C34PUBIF.CPP
// Demonstrates use of class public interface

```
#include  <iostream.h>
#include  <math.h>
// M_PI (value of pi) is defined in MATH.H

// A sphere class
class Sphere
{
    private:
        float      r;        // Radius of sphere
        float      x, y, z;  // Coordinates of sphere
        float cube() { return (r * r * r); }
        float square() { return (r * r); }
    public:
        Sphere(float xcoord, float ycoord,
                   float zcoord, float radius)
            { x = xcoord; y = ycoord; z = zcoord; r = radius; }
        ~Sphere()
        {
            cout << "Sphere (" << x << ", " << y << ", "
                 << z << ", " << r << ") destroyed\n";
        }
        float volume()
        {
            return (cube() * 4 * M_PI / 3);
        }
        float surface_area()
        {
            return (square() * 4 * M_PI);
        }
        void    SetX( float newX )
        {
            x = newX;
        }
        void    SetY( float newY )
        {
            y = newY;
        }
        void    SetZ( float newZ )
        {
            z = newZ;
        }
```

```
        void      SetRadius( float newRadius )
        {
            r = newRadius;
        }
        float     GetX()
        {
            return( x );
        }
        float     GetY()
        {
            return( y );
        }
        float     GetZ()
        {
            return( z );
        }
        float     GetRadius()
        {
            return( r );
        }
};

void  main(void)
{
    Sphere    s(1.0, 2.0, 3.0, 4.0);

    cout << "X = " << s.GetX()
         << " Y = " << s.GetY()
         << " Z = " << s.GetZ()
         << " R = " << s.GetRadius() << "\n";

    cout << "The volume is " << s.volume() << "\n";
    cout << "The surface area is "
         << s.surface_area() << "\n";

    s.SetX( 5.0 );
    s.SetY( 6.0 );
    s.SetZ( 7.0 );
    s.SetRadius( 8.0 );

    cout << "X = " << s.GetX()
         << " Y = " << s.GetY()
         << " Z = " << s.GetZ()
         << " R = " << s.GetRadius() << "\n";

    cout << "The volume is " << s.volume() << "\n";
    cout << "The surface area is "
         << s.surface_area() << "\n";
}
```

Figure 34.2 shows the output of this program.

**Figure 34.2.**

Demonstration of
a public interface.

```
d:\bcppbe\chap34>c34pubif
X = 1 Y = 2 Z = 3 R = 4
The volume is 268.083
The surface area is 201.062
X = 5 Y = 6 Z = 7 R = 8
The volume is 2144.66
The surface area is 804.248
Sphere (5, 6, 7, 8) destroyed

d:\bcppbe\chap34>
```

## Summary

This chapter introduced the data hiding paradigm. You learned how class member visibility is used to implement data hiding. The chapter discussed a class's public interface, and you learned how to use the public interface along with class member visibility to insulate class data members from the applications that use them.

## Review Questions

Answers to Review Questions are in Appendix B.

1. What is the default visibility of a class member?

2. How do you make a class member visible outside its class?

3. What is an object's public interface?

4. Why is a public interface used?

# Review Exercises

1. Construct a class to represent a window on a computer screen. Use the following data members:

```
int     left_side;
int     top_side;
int     right_side;
int     bottom_side;
```

Create a constructor to initialize the window structure with the necessary values. Create member functions to return the height and width of the window. The data members should not be accessible outside the class.

2. Construct a class for handling accounts receivable records. Use the following data members:

```
char    name[ 25 ];
char    date_of_sale[8];
float   amount_due;
```

Create a constructor to initialize the record with its necessary values and a constructor that simply creates an uninitialized record. Create member functions to modify and retrieve the individual's name, salary, and date of birth. Use data hiding to insulate the data members from an application that uses the class.

# CHAPTER 35

# Class Inheritance

One advantage of object-oriented programming is code reuse. The capability to define custom data types using classes enables you to reuse the code you develop. This works well if you always need exactly the same object. In the real world, however, you may need an object that is almost the same as an already developed object—but not quite. *Inheritance* enables you to more readily reuse an object, making slight adjustments where necessary.

This chapter discusses the following topics:

♦ What inheritance is

♦ How inheritance is implemented in Borland C++

♦ How derived classes can override base class members

## What Is Inheritance?

People usually think of inheritance as a child receiving certain traits from his/her parents. This is true whether you are talking about people or about C++ class objects. C++ enables you to define parent, or *base*, classes and child, or *derived*, classes. The derived class inherits all the public data members and public member functions from the base class. This, in effect, makes them part of the derived class's public interface.

How C++ uses inheritance is discussed in the following section.

## Implementing Inheritance

Consider the class Shape. It defines an object that has x, y, and z coordinates. Its public interface enables you to create a shape, setting the coordinates of the shape. It also enables you to Set and Get each coordinate separately.

```
class Shape
{
    protected:
        float      x, y, z;                    // coordinates of the shape
    public:
        Shape( float xcoord, float ycoord, float zcoord  )
        ~Shape();
        void     SetX( float newX );
        void     SetY( float newY );
        void     SetZ( float newZ );
        float    GetX();
        float    GetY();
        float    GetZ();
};
```

The most important point to notice about the Shape class is the new visibility label *protected*. A protected class member is accessible to a derived class as if it were a public member. However, the protected class member is not accessible to non-class members as if it were a private member.

Now look at a new Sphere class. This time the Sphere class is derived from the Shape class.

```
class Sphere : public Shape
{
    private:
        float      r;        // Radius of sphere
        float      cube();
        float      square();
    public:
        Sphere(float xcoord, float ycoord,  float zcoord, float radius);
        ~Sphere();
        float      volume();
        float      surface_area();
        void     SetRadius( float newRadius );
        float      GetRadius();
};
```

Notice several important things about the new Sphere class. First, the class name is followed by a colon and then the name of the base class. This is how you can inherit from a base class in C++. Second, Sphere no longer defines the x, y, and z coordinates. It inherits them from Shape and can use them just like it defined them itself.

When you create a Sphere class variable, its constructor is called to initialize itself. Because the Sphere object is derived from the Shape object, the Shape constructor also needs to be called. This is done in one of the two following ways:

♦ You can specify the parameters to use in calling the base class constructor.

♦ Borland C++ automatically calls a base class's constructor that takes no arguments.

The first option is better because it gives you both control of the base class's creation and explicit documentation of the base class's construction. The constructor for the Sphere class looks like this:

```
Sphere(float xcoord, float ycoord, float zcoord, float radius)
    : Shape( xcoord, ycoord, zcoord )
{
    x = xcoord; y = ycoord; z = zcoord; r = radius;
}
```

Notice that it now includes a call to the constructor of Shape, its base class. This call to Shape's constructor is listed after the declaration of Sphere's constructor but before its opening brace. A base class's constructor is always executed before its derived class's constructor. However, for destructors, the derived class's destructor is executed before the base class's.

This constructor also shows that you can use the data members and member functions of Shape as if they were defined directly in the Sphere class.

## Example

This example demonstrates the use of class inheritance. In the constructor and destructor for both Sphere and Shape, a message displays showing the order of object construction and destruction. The program is given in listing 35.1.

### Listing 35.1. This Program Implements Class Inheritance

```
// Filename: C35INHRT.CPP
// Demonstrates use of class inheritance
```

```
#include  <iostream.h>
#include  <math.h>
// M_PI (value of pi) is defined in MATH.H

// A shape base class
class Shape
{
    protected:
        float     x, y, z;                    // coordinates of the shape
    public:
        Shape(float xcoord, float ycoord, float zcoord )
        {
            x = xcoord; y = ycoord; z = zcoord;
            cout << "Shape (" << x << ", " << y << ", "
                 << z << ") created\n";
        }
        ~Shape()
        {
            cout << "Shape (" << x << ", " << y << ", "
                 << z << ") destroyed\n";
```

*continues*

**Listing 35.1. Continued**

```
        }
        void    SetX( float newX )
        {
            x = newX;
        }
        void    SetY( float newY )
        {
            y = newY;
        }
        void    SetZ( float newZ )
        {
            z = newZ;
        }
        float   GetX()
        {
            return( x );
        }
        float   GetY()
        {
            return( y );
        }
        float   GetZ()
        {
            return( z );
        }
};

// A sphere class
class Sphere : public Shape
{
    private:
        float   r;          // Radius of sphere
        float cube() { return (r * r * r); }
        float square() { return (r * r); }
    public:
        Sphere(float xcoord, float ycoord,
                float zcoord, float radius)
            : Shape( xcoord, ycoord, zcoord )
        {
            x = xcoord; y = ycoord; z = zcoord; r = radius;
            cout << "Sphere (" << x << ", " << y << ", "
                << z << ", " << r << ") created\n";
        }
        ~Sphere()
        {
            cout << "Sphere (" << x << ", " << y << ", "
                << z << ", " << r << ") destroyed\n";
        }
        float volume()
        {
            return (cube() * 4 * M_PI / 3);
```

```
            }
            float surface_area()
            {
                return (square() * 4 * M_PI);
            }
            void    SetRadius( float newRadius )
            {
                r = newRadius;
            }
            float    GetRadius()
            {
                return( r );
            }
};

void  main(void)
    Sphere    s(1.0, 2.0, 3.0, 4.0);

    cout << "X = " << s.Shape::GetX()
        << " Y = " << s.GetY()
        << " Z = " << s.GetZ()
        << " R = " << s.GetRadius() << "\n";

    cout << "The volume is " << s.volume() << "\n";
    cout << "The surface area is "
        << s.surface_area() << "\n";

    s.SetX( 5.0 );
    s.SetY( 6.0 );
    s.SetZ( 7.0 );
    s.SetRadius( 8.0 );

    cout << "X = " << s.GetX()
        << " Y = " << s.GetY()
        << " Z = " << s.GetZ()
        << " R = " << s.GetRadius() << "\n";

    cout << "The volume is " << s.volume() << "\n";
    cout << "The surface area is "
        << s.surface_area() << "\n";
}
```

Figure 35.1 shows the output of this program.

**Figure 35.1.**

Output showing
class inheritance.

```
d:\bcppbe\chap35>c35inhrt
Shape (1, 2, 3) created
Sphere (1, 2, 3, 4) created
X = 1 Y = 2 Z = 3 R = 4
The volume is 268.083
The surface area is 201.062
X = 5 Y = 6 Z = 7 R = 8
The volume is 2144.66
The surface area is 804.248
Sphere (5, 6, 7, 8) destroyed
Shape (5, 6, 7) destroyed

d:\bcppbe\chap35>
```

# Overriding Base Class Member Functions

A main reason for using inheritance is to change an object that is almost what you need into an object that is exactly what you need. To do this, you must *override* some of the base class functions. This gives you the capability to either completely replace a base class member or to use the base class member function and add functionality with your new member function. In Borland C++, you can override base member functions by defining new member functions in the derived class. The new member functions have the same name, argument list, and return type as the base class functions they are overriding.

The Shape class defined below includes a new function named IsA(). This function returns a pointer to a char array that contains the name of the class. This type of function can be useful at run-time to determine the type of object you are working with.

```
class Shape
{
    protected:
        float    x, y, z;                    // coordinates of the shape
    public:
        Shape(float xcoord, float ycoord, float zcoord );
        ~Shape();
        char * IsA();
        void    SetX( float newX );
        void    SetY( float newY );
        void    SetZ( float newZ );
        float   GetX();
        float   GetY();
        float   GetZ();
};
```

When using the Shape class as a base for Sphere, you want your new class to return that it is a Sphere, not a Shape. You can accomplish this by adding the member function IsA() to the Sphere class also, as shown in the following code. Now when a Sphere object is created, it returns a pointer to the string "Sphere".

```
class Sphere : public Shape
{
    private:
        float     r;          // Radius of sphere
        float cube();
        float square();
    public:
        Sphere(float xcoord, float ycoord, float zcoord, float radius);
        ~Sphere();
        char * IsA();
        float volume();
        float surface_area();
        void     SetRadius( float newRadius );
        float     GetRadius();
};
```

If you create a variable s, which is a Sphere object, you can code a line like the following:

```
cout << "Object s is a " << s.IsA() << " derived from a " <<
s.Shape::IsA() << "\n";
```

This line displays the message

```
Object s is a Sphere derived from a Shape
```

This code shows that when you call s.IsA(), the string "Shape" is returned. However, by using *scope resolution*—that is, s.Shape::IsA()—you can still access the base member functions overridden in the derived class. This is useful for calling the base class member when it does most of what you want done, but you still need to do some processing in the derived class before or after the base class processing.

## Example

This example demonstrates how to override base member functions. It adds the function IsA to both the Shape and Sphere classes. It then uses these new functions to display a line about the class of the variable created in main().

**Listing 35.2. This Program Demonstrates Derived Class Member Function Overriding**

```
// Filename: C35OVRRD.CPP
// Demonstrates use of derived class overrides


#include   <iostream.h>
#include   <math.h>
```

*continues*

**Listing 35.2. Continued**

```cpp
// M_PI (value of pi) is defined in MATH.H

// A shape base class
class Shape
{
    protected:
        float      x, y, z;                  // coordinates of the shape
    public:
        Shape(float xcoord, float ycoord, float zcoord )
        {
            x = xcoord; y = ycoord; z = zcoord;
            cout << "Shape (" << x << ", " << y << ", "
                << z << ") created\n";
        }
        ~Shape()
        {
            cout << "Shape (" << x << ", " << y << ", "
                << z << ") destroyed\n";
        }
        char * IsA()
        {
            return( "Shape" );
        }
        void    SetX( float newX )
        {
            x = newX;
        }
        void    SetY( float newY )
        {
            y = newY;
        }
        void    SetZ( float newZ )
        {
            z = newZ;
        }
        float   GetX()
        {
            return( x );
        }
        float   GetY()
        {
            return( y );
        }
        float   GetZ()
        {
            return( z );
        }
};

// A sphere class
```

```
class Sphere : public Shape
{
    private:
        float    r;            // Radius of sphere
        float cube() { return (r * r * r); }
        float square() { return (r * r); }
    public:
        Sphere(float xcoord, float ycoord,
                  float zcoord, float radius)
            : Shape( xcoord, ycoord, zcoord )
        {
            x = xcoord; y = ycoord; z = zcoord; r = radius;
            cout << "Sphere (" << x << ", " << y << ", "
                 << z << ", " << r << ") created\n";
        }
        ~Sphere()
        {
            cout << "Sphere (" << x << ", " << y << ", "
                 << z << ", " << r << ") destroyed\n";
        }
        char * IsA()
        {
            return( "Sphere" );
        }
        float volume()
        {
            return (cube() * 4 * M_PI / 3);
        }
        float surface_area()
        {
            return (square() * 4 * M_PI);
        }
        void    SetRadius( float newRadius )
        {
            r = newRadius;
        }
        float    GetRadius()
        {
            return( r );
        }
};

void  main(void)
{
    Sphere    s(1.0, 2.0, 3.0, 4.0);

    cout << "Object s is a " << s.IsA() <<
            " derived from a " << s.Shape::IsA() << "\n";

    cout << "X = " << s.Shape::GetX()
         << " Y = " << s.GetY()
         << " Z = " << s.GetZ()
         << " R = " << s.GetRadius() << "\n";
```

*continues*

**Listing 35.2. Continued**

```
        cout << "The volume is " << s.volume() << "\n";
        cout << "The surface area is "
             << s.surface_area() << "\n";

        s.SetX( 5.0 );
        s.SetY( 6.0 );
        s.SetZ( 7.0 );
        s.SetRadius( 8.0 );

        cout << "X = " << s.GetX()
             << " Y = " << s.GetY()
             << " Z = " << s.GetZ()
             << " R = " << s.GetRadius() << "\n";

        cout << "The volume is " << s.volume() << "\n";
        cout << "The surface area is "
             << s.surface_area() << "\n";
}
```

Figure 35.2 shows the output of this program.

**Figure 35.2.**

Output showing
overriding of a
member function.

```
d:\bcppbe\chap35>c35ovrrd
Shape (1, 2, 3) created
Sphere (1, 2, 3, 4) created
Object s is a Sphere derived from a Shape
X = 1 Y = 2 Z = 3 R = 4
The volume is 268.083
The surface area is 201.062
X = 5 Y = 6 Z = 7 R = 8
The volume is 2144.66
The surface area is 804.248
Sphere (5, 6, 7, 8) destroyed
Shape (5, 6, 7) destroyed

d:\bcppbe\chap35>
```

# Summary

This chapter discussed the concept of inheritance. You saw how to inherit base classes in Borland C++. Class member overrides also were demonstrated.

In the next chapter, polymorphism—one of the most important topics in object-oriented programming—is discussed.

# Review Questions

Answers to Review Questions are in Appendix B.

1. What is inheritance?

2. How is inheritance implemented in C++?

3. In what order are the base and derived class constructors executed?

4. How do you override a base class member function?

5. Why is it important to be able to access overridden base class member functions?

# Review Exercises

1. Define a base class that can be used to track general information about the books in your library. Use the following fields:

```
char     title[ 64 ];
char     Tim[ 64 ];
int      year_of_copyright;
int      number_of_pages;
```

Make the data members accessible to any classes derived from your class. Define two constructors: one that initializes the data members, and one that leaves them uninitialized. Create member functions that can set and get the values of the data members.

2. Using the base class defined in Exercise 1, define a derived class that tracks technical books. Use the additional fields:

```
char     technical_level;
char     disk_included;
char     tutorial;
```

Define a single constructor that takes all the arguments necessary to initialize the derived class. Create member functions to set and get all of each book's information.

3. Using the classes defined in exercises 1 and 2, add a new member function to the derived class that overrides the function defined in the base class to get the book name. The new function should call the base class's function, add the string " - Technical" to the end of the title, and return the new string.

# CHAPTER 36

# Polymorphism

At this point, you can implement the basic principles of object-oriented programming, including C++ classes, class visibility, and inheritance. The last paradigm of object-oriented programming is polymorphism. Polymorphism enables you to deal with different types of objects as if they were all the same type.

This chapter discusses the following topics:

♦ What polymorphism is

♦ Why to use polymorphism

♦ How to implement polymorphism

## What Is Polymorphism?

*Poly* means many or multiple; *morph* means to change from one thing to another; and *ism* means the process of something. The word *polymorphism*, derived from these three definitions, describes C++'s capability to deal with multiple derived classes as if they were all the same class.

Polymorphism uses the base class as the common type to manipulate multiple derived types. To understand polymorphism, you must remember one important fact: A pointer to a derived class is a pointer to the base class. Using the Shape and Sphere classes used in the preceding chapter, you can define some variables like this:

```
Sphere      sphere1( 1, 2, 3, 4 );
Sphere      *sphere_ptr;
Shape       *shape_ptr;
```

These variables can then be used like this:

```
sphere_ptr = &sphere;
shape_ptr = sphere_ptr;
```

Notice that you can assign the pointer to a Sphere object to the pointer to a Shape object without using casting. You can do this because any pointer to a Sphere object is a pointer to a Shape object.

You can derive several excellent benefits from using polymorphism, including the following:

◆ Simpler code that does not have to check for the type of object you are working with

◆ Easier addition of new types of objects to the program

◆ Easier debugging because the code implementing a specific type of object is localized to that object's methods

# Implementing Polymorphism

Borland C++ includes everything you need to develop programs that use polymorphism. You already learned about classes and inheritance; polymorphism is just an extension of these concepts. In C++, polymorphism is implemented using *virtual member functions*.

## What Is a Virtual Function?

A virtual member function is a member function defined in the base class as being *virtual*. This virtual member function is then overridden in each derived class. This is different from the normal overriding of functions shown in Chapter 35 because when you refer to a derived object as a pointer to the base class, calling a virtual function causes the derived class's member function to be executed rather than the base class's.

A virtual function is declared in the class definition as shown in this new Shape class.

```
class Shape
{
    protected:
        float      x, y, z;                 // coordinates of the shape
    public:
        Shape(float xcoord, float ycoord, float zcoord );
        virtual ~Shape();
        virtual char * IsA();
        void      SetX( float newX );
        void      SetY( float newY );
        void      SetZ( float newZ );
```

```
        float    GetX();
        float     GetY();
        float     GetZ();
        virtual float volume();
        virtual float surface_area();
};
```

Notice that the functions ~Shape, IsA, volume, and surface_area are declared virtual. These functions will exhibit polymorphic behavior when they are called through a pointer to a Shape object.

## Using Virtual Functions

To use the virtual functions defined in Shape, you must derive multiple classes from the base class. Following are definitions for two derived classes. The first is Sphere:

```
class Sphere : public Shape
{
    private:
        float    r;         // Radius of sphere
        float cube();
        float square();
    public:
        Sphere(float xcoord, float ycoord, float zcoord, float radius);
        virtual ~Sphere();
        virtual char * IsA();
        virtual float volume();
        virtual float surface_area();
        void    SetRadius( float newRadius );
        float     GetRadius();
};
```

The next is Cube:

```
class Cube : public Shape
{
    public:
        Cube(float xcoord, float ycoord, float zcoord );
        virtual ~Cube();
        virtual char * IsA();
        virtual float volume();
        virtual float surface_area();
};
```

Notice that both derived classes override all four virtual functions. This allows them to exhibit polymorphic behavior. Assume that you created the following variables:

```
Sphere    sphereVar( 1.0, 2.0, 3.0 4.0 );
Shape     *shapePtr;
```

You can then write the following code:

```
shapePtr = &sphereVar;
cout << "Object shapePtr is a " << shapePtr->IsA() << " derived from a "
        << shapePtr->Shape::IsA() << "\n";
```

These lines of code demonstrate the polymorphic behavior for which you are looking. When you call the IsA function through the base class pointer, the IsA function of the derived class is executed. This enables you to write code independent of the object on which it is working. The output of the preceding line of code is:

```
Object shapePtr is a Sphere derived from a Shape
```

## Example

This program demonstrates the use of polymorphism and virtual functions. Several member functions of the Shape object are declared virtual. The program defines two derived classes, Sphere and Cube. Each of these classes declares the same member functions virtual.

The program also demonstrates defining member functions outside the class definition. Finally, the main program creates a Sphere and a Cube and stores pointers to them in an array of Shape pointers. The IsA, volume, and surface_area functions are called to illustrate polymorphism.

```
// Filename: C36POLYM.CPP
// Demonstrates use of polymorphism

#include   <iostream.h>
#include   <math.h>
// M_PI (value of pi) is defined in MATH.H

// A shape base class
class Shape
{
    protected:
        float      x, y, z;                  // coordinates of the shape
    public:
        Shape(float xcoord, float ycoord, float zcoord )
        {
            x = xcoord; y = ycoord; z = zcoord;
            cout << "Shape (" << x << ", " << y << ", "
                << z << ") created\n";
        }
        virtual ~Shape()
        {
            cout << "Shape (" << x << ", " << y << ", "
                << z << ") destroyed\n";
        }
        virtual char * IsA()
        {
```

```
            return( "Shape" );
        }
        void     SetX( float newX )
        {
            x = newX;
        }
        void     SetY( float newY )
        {
            y = newY;
        }
        void     SetZ( float newZ )
        {
            z = newZ;
        }
        float    GetX()
        {
            return( x );
        }
        float    GetY()
        {
            return( y );
        }
        float    GetZ()
        {
            return( z );
        }
        virtual float volume()
        {
            return( 0.0 );
        }
        virtual float surface_area()
        {
            return( 0.0 );
        }
};

// A sphere class
class Sphere : public Shape
{
    private:
        float    r;           // Radius of sphere
        float cube() { return (r * r * r); }
        float square() { return (r * r); }
    public:
        Sphere(float xcoord, float ycoord,
                float zcoord, float radius)
            : Shape( xcoord, ycoord, zcoord )
        {
            x = xcoord; y = ycoord; z = zcoord; r = radius;
            cout << "Sphere (" << x << ", " << y << ", "
                << z << ", " << r << ") created\n";
        }
        virtual ~Sphere()
```

```
        {
            cout << "Sphere (" << x << ", " << y << ", "
                 << z << ", " << r << ") destroyed\n";
        }
        virtual char * IsA()
        {
            return( "Sphere" );
        }
        virtual float volume()
        {
            return (cube() * 4 * M_PI / 3);
        }
        virtual float surface_area()
        {
            return (square() * 4 * M_PI);
        }
        void    SetRadius( float newRadius )
        {
            r = newRadius;
        }
        float    GetRadius()
        {
            return( r );
        }
};

// A cube class
class Cube : public Shape
{
    public:
        Cube(float xcoord, float ycoord, float zcoord );
        virtual ~Cube();
        virtual char * IsA();
        virtual float volume();
        virtual float surface_area();
};

Cube::Cube(float xcoord, float ycoord, float zcoord )
    : Shape( xcoord, ycoord, zcoord )
{
    x = xcoord; y = ycoord; z = zcoord;
    cout << "Cube (" << x << ", " << y << ", " << z << ") created\n";
}
Cube::~Cube()
{
    cout << "Cube (" << x << ", " << y << ", " << z << ") destroyed\n";
}
char * Cube::IsA()
{
    return( "Cube" );
}
float Cube::volume()
{
```

```
        return ( x * y * z );
}
float Cube::surface_area()
{
    return ( (2 * (x * y)) + (2 * (x * z)) + (2 * (y * z)) );
}

void  main(void)
{
    Sphere      *SpherePtr;
    Cube       *CubePtr;
    Shape       *ShapePtr[ 2 ];

    SpherePtr = new Sphere( 1.0, 2.0, 3.0, 4.0 );
    CubePtr = new Cube( 5.0, 6.0, 7.0 );

    ShapePtr[0] = SpherePtr;
    ShapePtr[1] = CubePtr;

    for ( int i = 0; i < 2; i++ )
        cout << "Object ShapePtr[ " << i << " ] is a "
                << ShapePtr[i]->IsA() << " derived from a "
                << ShapePtr[i]->Shape::IsA() << "\n";

    for ( i = 0; i < 2; i++ )
    {
        cout << "The volume of the " << ShapePtr[i]->IsA()
                << " is " << ShapePtr[i]->volume() << "\n";
        cout << "The surface area of the " << ShapePtr[i]->IsA()
                << " is " << ShapePtr[i]->surface_area() << "\n";
    }

    delete ShapePtr[1];
    delete ShapePtr[0];
}
```

The output from this program is shown in figure 36.1.

## Summary

This chapter discussed the reasoning behind polymorphism. You saw how to use Borland C++'s virtual functions to implement polymorphism and learned how to write code specific to a particular type of object.

**Figure 36.1.**

Demonstrates C++
polymorphism.

```
d:\bcppbe\chap36>c36polym
Shape (1, 2, 3) created
Sphere (1, 2, 3, 4) created
Shape (5, 6, 7) created
Cube (5, 6, 7) created
Object ShapePtr[ 0 ] is a Sphere derived from a Shape
Object ShapePtr[ 1 ] is a Cube derived from a Shape
The volume of the Sphere is 268.083
The surface area of the Sphere is 201.062
The volume of the Cube is 210
The surface area of the Cube is 214
Cube (5, 6, 7) destroyed
Shape (5, 6, 7) destroyed
Sphere (1, 2, 3, 4) destroyed
Shape (1, 2, 3) destroyed

d:\bcppbe\chap36>
```

# Review Questions

Answers to Review Questions are in Appendix B.

**1.** What is polymorphism?

**2.** What mechanism does C++ give you to implement polymorphism?

**3.** What happens when you call a virtual function through a base class pointer?

**4.** Why would you use polymorphism in your applications?

# Review Exercises

**1.** Write a base class to represent the common characteristics of the four card suits. Use the following field:

```
int     card_value;     // 2 - 10, 11 - 14 for Jack, Queen, King,
and Ace
```

Define a constructor to initialize the value of a card. Member functions should include a function to return the suit of the card and the value of the card. Both these member functions should exhibit polymorphic properties. Make sure that the destructor also is virtual.

**2.** Write four classes derived from the class in Exercise 1. These classes should override the member functions defined for polymorphism to exhibit the proper behavior for each derived class.

**3.** Write an application that defines a full deck of cards, sorts the cards, and displays the sorted deck.

# Part IX

*Borland's ObjectWindow's Library*

# CHAPTER 37

# Introduction to ObjectWindows Library 2.0

One of the hottest computer environments in use today is Microsoft Windows. Until recently, programmers developing software for Windows had to learn the Microsoft Windows Software Development Kit and hundreds of Windows functions and messages. Now Borland makes software development for Windows easier with the *ObjectWindows Library (OWL)* included with Borland C++.

This chapter introduces the following topics:

♦ What the ObjectWindows Library is

♦ How to use the Borland IDE to develop OWL programs

♦ How To Code a simple OWL program

## What Is ObjectWindows Library 2.0?

ObjectWindows Library is a set of classes that contain the *Microsoft Windows Software Development Kit (SDK)* functions and messages. The OWL classes also extend the functionality of the basic Windows SDK. OWL offers many benefits to those doing Windows application development, including the following:

- Simpler application development
- An easier learning curve
- More built-in functionality
- Improved code reusability

ObjectWindows Library classes make it easier for you to use standard Windows application items, including:

- Windows
- Button bars
- Status lines
- Dialog boxes
- Child windows and controls

Now, you can plunge right into developing an OWL program.

# A Simple OWL Program

To start learning about the structure of OWL applications, you will develop one of the simplest applications possible. This application creates an application object, creates a main window, and displays a "Hello World!" message in the center of the main window. To make the development of this application as simple as possible, use the *Borland C++ 4.0 Integrated Development Environment (IDE)*.

## Using the Borland IDE

The Borland IDE is a Windows-based development environment that includes the following elements:

- A *project manager* that helps you to keep track of all the pieces of an application.
- A *code editor* that enables you to enter your source code.
- A *make utility* that enables you to compile only the pieces of your application that have been modified.
- A *debugger* that enables you to trace through your application and to locate bugs.

To develop an OWL application under the IDE, you must first define a project. The project manager is used to track all the component pieces of your application, including source code files and resource and module definition files. To start a new project, first start the Borland IDE by clicking the IDE's icon in the Program Manager (see fig. 37.1). The main IDE window appears.

**Figure 37.1.**

The Borland C++ Integrated Development Environment Icon.

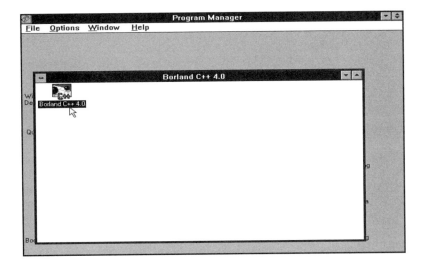

Click the new project icon on the IDE toolbar (see fig. 37.2) to open the New Project dialog box (see fig. 37.3). This dialog box enables you to define your project. For an OWL application, you need to enter a **P**roject Path and Name, select a Target **T**ype and a **P**latform, and select Standard Libraries to include. Figure 37.3 shows the proper settings for most OWL applications.

**Figure 37.2.**

Clicking the New Project button on the IDE toolbar.

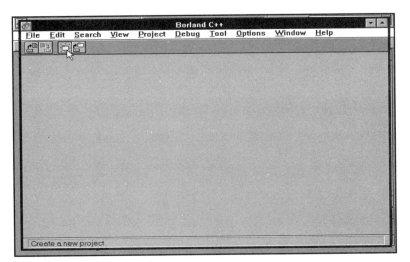

**Figure 37.3.**

The New Project
dialog box.

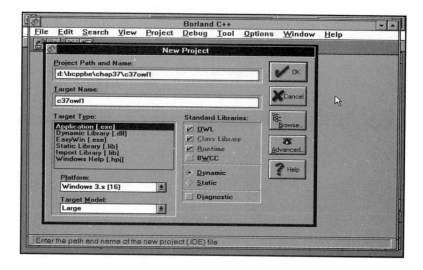

For this particular application, you need to set some of the advanced settings.
Choose the **Advanced** button to open the Advanced Options dialog box (see fig.
37.4). This dialog box enables you to specify the default files that will be included
in the project being created. This application does not use *.rc* (resource) or *.def*
(module definition) files, so click each of these check boxes to clear them (so Borland
C++ doesn't add the files to the project). After making this change, click OK in both
the Advanced Options dialog box and the New Project dialog box.

**Figure 37.4.**

The New Project
Advanced Options
dialog box.

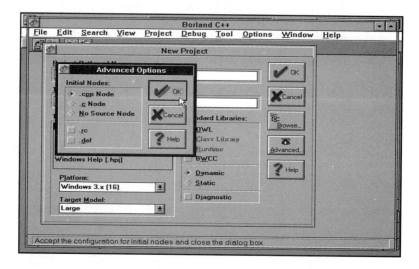

After you click OK in the New Project dialog box, the project window (see fig. 37.5) is created within the IDE. This window provides you with an easy way to access and organize the files that are included in your project. It groups together all the files used to create each particular executable or library. Double-clicking a source file name brings up the selected file in an edit window. If you double-click the file c37owl1 [.cpp], for example, an edit window like the one shown in figure 37.6 appears. You use this window to enter the code for your application.

**Figure 37.5.**

The Borland IDE project window.

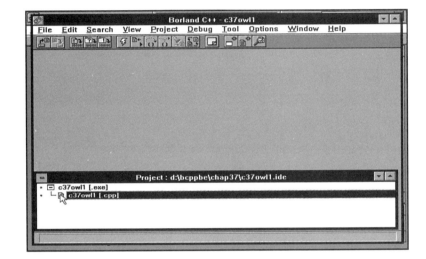

**Figure 37.6.**

The c37owl1.CPP edit window.

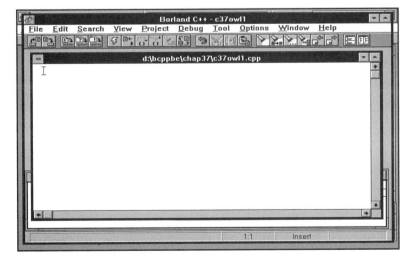

## Coding a Simple OWL Program

A simple OWL program contains three parts: the *application class*, the *main window class*, and the *OwlMain function*. You define the two classes, both of which are derived from the standard OWL classes, *TApplication* and *TFrameWindow*. The OwlMain function is a replacement for the DOS `main()` function and the normal Windows WinMain function.

The first part that you must create is the application class. Your application class is derived from OWL's TApplication class, which contains the functionality needed by every application (such as initializing an application, creating a main window, and performing the main application message loop). For your first OWL application, use the following application class definition:

```
class     HelloApplication : public TApplication
{
    public:
        HelloApplication() : TApplication()
        {
        }
        virtual void InitMainWindow( void );
};
```

Notice that in the HelloApplication class, the constructor simply calls the TApplication constructor rather than doing any processing itself. This technique can't be used in all applications, but in a simple application there is nothing for the derived application constructor to do. Also notice that you have overridden the InitMainWindow function. It is used to create the main window class and to save a pointer to it in an application class data member.

The implementation of InitMainWindow follows:

```
void HelloApplication::InitMainWindow( void )
{
    SetMainWindow( new HelloWindow( 0, "Borland C++ By Example" ) );
}
```

In this routine, you call SetMainWindow to save the pointer to the main window of your application. The main window of this application is being instantiated directly within the call to SetMainWindow. HelloWindow, your main window class, is derived from the OWL class TFrameWindow, as seen below:

```
class     HelloWindow : public TFrameWindow
{
    public:
        HelloWindow( TWindow *parent, const char far *title ) :
            TFrameWindow( parent, title )
        {
        };
        void Paint( TDC &tDC, BOOL bErase, TRect &invalidRect );
};
```

Your `HelloWindow` class defines a constructor and overrides the `Paint` function. The constructor takes two arguments, a pointer to the window's parent window and a pointer to the title to be used for the class. Like the previous constructor, this constructor simply calls the constructor of its base class. The parent window pointer and the title pointer are passed on to the `TFrameWindow` constructor.

The `Paint` function has also been overridden. This function is called whenever Windows needs to redisplay the information appearing in an application window. Every Windows application must be capable of redisplaying the information appearing in its windows at any time. Windows does not take any responsibility for saving a window's display when that window is either minimized or covered with another window. The `Paint` function is called whenever Windows determines that your window needs to be redrawn. The `Paint` function for `HelloWindow` follows:

```
#pragma argsused
void HelloWindow::Paint( TDC &tDC, BOOL bErase, TRect &invalidRect )
{
    TRect     clientArea;

    GetClientRect( clientArea );

    tDC.SetTextAlign( TA_CENTER );
    tDC.TextOut( clientArea.Width() / 2, clientArea.Height() / 2,
    [ic:ccc] "Hello World!" );
}
```

The first line of this code segment is a directive informing the Borland C++ compiler that it should consider all arguments in the next defined function as being used. This code ensures that the compiler does not issue a warning to the effect that you haven't used an argument to a function. Paint accepts the following three arguments:

- **tDC**, a device context used to draw items on the screen

- **bErase**, a Boolean which indicates if the screen should be erased before it is redrawn

- **invalidRect**, a rectangle which defines the part of the window which needs to be redrawn

These three arguments completely define a redraw operation. For the purposes of this program, you can ignore the `bErase` and `invalidRect` parameters.

Most Windows programs draw only to the area defined by `invalidRect`; this routine does not. It begins by asking Windows for the client area of the window. The *client area* of a window is the area within that window's borders and under its menu—the area which is used by the application to actually display its information. This area is the only area for which a Windows application is responsible. This routine uses the full client area to draw on.

Next, the routine uses the tDC argument to display information in the client area. A TDC object is an OWL wrapper around a Windows device context. A *device context* defines a program's display area on-screen and tracks information about how to draw text, lines, and other graphic elements. Using a TDC object simplifies the process of displaying information on-screen.

This program calls the tDC member function SetTextAlign to inform Windows that you want to display information centered on the pixel given in the TextOut call. The TextOut member function is used to display a string on the device context. It accepts the x and y coordinates where the string should be displayed and the string itself. In this program, the location is the center of the client area and the string is "Hello World!".

The final portion of this simple OWL program is the OwlMain function, which replaces the main function of a normal C++ program and the WinMain function of a normal Windows program. The OwlMain function, as shown below, instantiates the HelloApplication class. It then calls the Run member function of the HelloApplication class, which in turn calls all the initialization routines, including InitMainWindow. The OwlMain function then enters the application's message-processing loop. Under Windows, every application contains a loop that receives messages from Windows and dispatches those messages to the application's windows.

```
#pragma argsused
int OwlMain( int argc, char *argv[] )
{
    HelloApplication      *theApp;

    theApp = new HelloApplication();

    return theApp->Run();
}
```

## Compiling and Running an OWL Program

After you enter a program into the IDE's source code editor, you can compile it from within the IDE. Figure 37.7 shows the Make button being pressed. This button causes any source code listed in the project to be compiled if it has changed since the last compile. After you press it, the IDE displays the Compile Status window, which shows you what is happening during the compile process. After compilation is complete, the Compile Status window displays a final status of Success (see fig. 37.8) if all went well, or There are errors if the source code contains syntax errors.

**Figure 37.7.**

Compiling from within the Borland IDE.

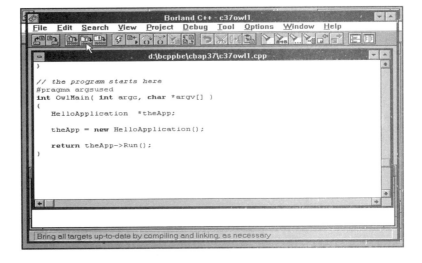

**Figure 37.8.**

Successful compilation in Borland C++.

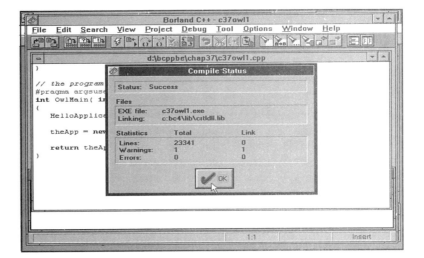

After you click OK to close the Compile Status window, the Message window appears. If you had compile errors, the error messages are displayed here. You can double-click an error message to examine the source code that contains the error. With this program, only one warning has been issued (see fig. 37.9); no errors have been issued.

**Figure 37.9.**
One compiler
warning is issued,
but no compiler
errors.

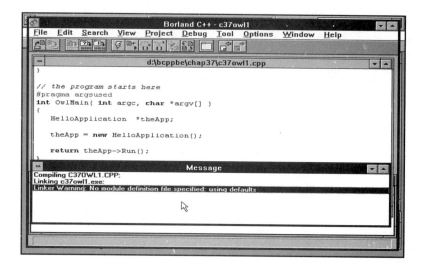

After your program has compiled without errors, you can run it without having to leave the IDE. Figure 37.10 in the following Example section shows the Run button on the toolbar being pressed. This button makes the project, if the source code has been modified, and then runs the application. Figure 37.11 in the following Example section shows the window created by this program. This window is a complete window that can be resized, moved, minimized, and maximized. The client area is properly repainted whenever necessary.

## Example

This example is the basic "Hello World!" program that every new programmer starts with. This OWL version demonstrates how to derive an application class from TApplication and a main window class from TFrameWindow. It also shows the basic implementation of the OwlMain function. The program is shown in listing 37.1.

**Listing 37.1. The OWL Hello World Program**

```
//
//      C37OWL1.CPP
//          program to demonstrate the basics of OWL 2.0
//

// OWL include files
#include     <owl\applicat.h>
#include <owl\framewin.h>
#include <owl\dc.h>

// define the main window class
class     HelloWindow : public TFrameWindow
{
```

```
    public:
        HelloWindow( TWindow *parent, const char far *title ) :
            TFrameWindow( parent, title )
        {
        };
        void Paint( TDC &tDC, BOOL bErase, TRect &invalidRect );
};

#pragma argsused
void HelloWindow::Paint( TDC &tDC, BOOL bErase, TRect &invalidRect )
{
    TRect       clientArea;

    GetClientRect( clientArea );

    tDC.SetTextAlign( TA_CENTER );
    tDC.TextOut( clientArea.Width() / 2, clientArea.Height() / 2,
    [ic:ccc] "Hello World!" );
}

// define the application class
class       HelloApplication : public TApplication
{
    public:
        HelloApplication() : TApplication()
        {
        }
        virtual void InitMainWindow( void );
};

void HelloApplication::InitMainWindow( void )
{
    SetMainWindow( new HelloWindow( 0, "Borland C++ By Example" ) );
}

// the program starts here
#pragma argsused
int OwlMain( int argc, char *argv[] )
{
    HelloApplication       *theApp;

    theApp = new HelloApplication();

    return theApp->Run();
}
```

**Figure 37.10.**

The Run
button depicts
a lightning bolt.

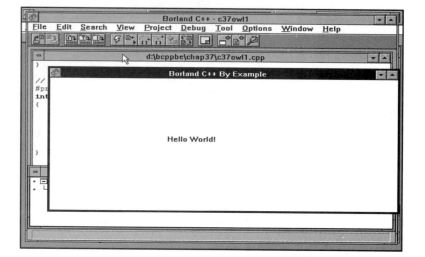

**Figure 37.11.**

The results of
executing a simple
OWL program.

## Summary

In this chapter, you were introduced to Borland's ObjectWindows Library. The reasons for using OWL were discussed, and you learned which classes are necessary for producing an OWL application. You also learned how to use Borland's IDE to develop an OWL application. Finally, you examined a complete, simple OWL application.

# Review Questions

**1.** What is the Borland ObjectWindows Library?

**2.** What OWL class is an application class derived from?

**3.** What OWL class can a main window class be derived from?

**4.** What is the purpose of the Paint function?

# Review Exercises

**1.** Define a window class to be used as an OWL's program main window. This class should override the Paint member function.

**2.** Define an application class for an OWL application. This application should override the function which creates the main window. The implementation of that member function should create a window of the class defined in Exercise 1.

**3.** Create a complete application using the window class defined in Exercise 1 and the application class defined in Exercise 2. The window class should display the string "Borland C++ ObjectWindows Library" in the upper-left corner of the screen and your name in the center of the screen.

# CHAPTER 38

# Handling Applications, Windows, and Events

Windows applications must be written in a way that enables them to respond to Windows events. OWL handles such *event-driven programming* extremely well. The OWL layered approach to application development—applications, windows, and controls—enables you to handle different Windows events at the appropriate level.

This chapter introduces the following topics:

- The TApplication class

- How to create different types of windows

- Events and event processing

## The TApplication Class

Every Windows application must handle a number of basic tasks in one way or another. These tasks include things like:

- Application initialization

- Instance initialization

- Main window creation

- Windows message loop processing

Borland has incorporated the functionality required to handle these basic tasks in the OWL TApplication class. The basic functionality provided by OWL is sometimes sufficient, but in many cases you must add your own functionality to OWL's.

## Instantiating an Application

You need to derive a new application class from TApplication for almost every Windows application that you write using OWL. This step enables you to enhance OWL's general functionality or to replace it entirely. The function that you are most likely to override is main window creation. The following code shows a new application class:

```
class NewApplication : public TApplication
{
    NewApplication( const char far *AppName = NULL );
    ~NewApplication();
    virtual void InitApplication();
    virtual void InitInstance();
    virtual void InitMainWindow();
}
```

The NewApplication class has defined both a constructor and a destructor, as well as three virtual member functions. These member functions, InitApplication, InitInstance, and InitMainWindow, enable you to override the common functionality built into the TApplication class.

The constructor for NewApplication takes a single argument consisting of a far pointer to a string representing the application's name. The constructor also defines a default value of NULL for the application's name. If the pointer is NULL, then the application does not have a name. OWL uses this name as the caption for the main window (if you do not override InitMainWindow) and as an application label in error messages. As shown in the code below, the implementation of the NewApplication constructor calls the constructor for TApplication.

```
NewApplication::NewApplication( const char far *AppName )
    : TApplication( AppName )
{
}
```

Every time you derive an application class from TApplication, you must call the TApplication constructor also. After you have derived a new application object, you will instantiate it within the OwlMain function. As described in Chapter 37, OwlMain replaces main from a C++ program and WinMain from a Windows program. As seen below, in OwlMain you instantiate the application object and then call the Run member function to cause the application to execute.

```
int OwlMain( int argc, char *argv[] )
{
    NewApplication      *theApp =
    ➡new NewApplication( "New Application Name " );

    return theApp.Run();
}
```

The Run member function returns a value, which in this case is also the value returned from OwlMain. Run initially calls the InitApplication and InitInstance member functions. Then it enters into OWL's common message loop. This message loop is adequate for most Windows applications; extending it is beyond the scope of this book.

## Application Initialization

Because Windows is a multitasking system, it enables you to run more than one copy of an application at the same time. Under Windows, each running copy of an application is known as an *instance*. When you start an OWL application one of two functions is called, depending upon which instance of the program is being initialized.

### Initializing the First Instance

The Run member function initially checks to see if this is the first instance of the program. If it is, the member function InitApplication is called. You need to override InitApplication if you have special processing to do the first time an application is called. The following is a simple override of InitApplication:

```
void NewApplication::InitApplication()
{
    firstInstance = TRUE;
}
```

The preceding code sets a data member called firstInstance to TRUE if this is indeed the first instance of this program. In the constructor of NewApplication, firstInstance would be set to FALSE. This method ensures that firstInstance remains FALSE if this is a subsequent instance of the program.

### Initializing All Instances

OWL enables you to do some initialization every time an application starts. The InitInstance member function is called either immediately (for instances other than the first instance) or after the InitApplication member returns (for the first instance). InitInstance is a very important member function. The following code shows the InitInstance implementation for your NewApplication class:

```
void NewApplication::InitInstance()
{
    strcpy( WindowTitle, "Main Window Title" );
    TApplication:InitInstance();
}
```

This implementation first copies a string into a data member which is used to hold the main window's title, then calls TApplication's InitInstance. Every time you override the InitInstance member function, you must call TApplication's InitInstance. The standard functionality provided by TApplication::InitInstance calls InitMainWindow to create the application's main window.

## Creating a Main Window

After TApplication's InitInstance is called, it in turn calls InitMainWindow. Almost every OWL application you write overrides this member function to enable you to create a more appropriate main window.

```
void NewApplication::InitMainWindow()
{
    SetMainWindow( new TFrameWindow( 0, "Window Title" );
}
```

The NewApplication::InitMainWindow shown above uses the TApplication member function SetMainWindow to save a pointer to the window being created. Here, you are creating a TFrameWindow to use as the main window. Your applications should instantiate a main window class derived from TFrameWindow or one of the other OWL window classes that can be used as main windows.

### Example

This example shows an application that displays the message First Instance for the first instance of the program. If you run a second instance of the program while the first is still running, the message displayed is 2nd or later instance.

The AppExerApplication class is derived from TApplication and shows how to override both InitApplication and InitMainWindow. The class also adds two member functions for setting and getting a pointer to the message to be displayed.

The AppExerWindow class has only one important feature. It calls the TWindow member function GetApplication. GetApplication returns a pointer to the current application object. You can then use the returned pointer to access application class data members and member functions.

```
//
//      C38APP.CPP
//          program to demonstrate the TApplication class
```

```
//

// OWL include files
#include     <owl\applicat.h>
#include <owl\framewin.h>
#include <owl\dc.h>

// define the application class
class    AppExerApplication : public TApplication
{
    public:
        AppExerApplication();
        virtual void InitMainWindow( void );
        virtual void InitApplication( void );
        virtual void SetDisplayMsg( char * );
        virtual char *GetDisplayMsg( void );

    private:
        char    *DisplayMsg;
};

// define the main window class
class    AppExerWindow : public TFrameWindow
{
    public:
        AppExerWindow( TWindow *parent, const char far *title ) :
            TFrameWindow( parent, title )
            {
            };
        void Paint( TDC &tDC, BOOL bErase, TRect &invalidRect );
};

// implement the application class
AppExerApplication::AppExerApplication()
    : TApplication()
{
    SetDisplayMsg( "2nd or later Instance" );
}
void AppExerApplication::InitApplication( void )
{
    SetDisplayMsg( "First Instance" );
}

void AppExerApplication::InitMainWindow( void )
{
    SetMainWindow( new AppExerWindow( 0, "Application Class Example" ) );
}

void AppExerApplication::SetDisplayMsg( char *NewMsg )
{
    DisplayMsg = NewMsg;
}
```

```
char * AppExerApplication::GetDisplayMsg( void )
{
    return( DisplayMsg );
}


// implement the main window class
#pragma argsused
void AppExerWindow::Paint( TDC &tDC, BOOL bErase, TRect &invalidRect )
{
    TRect      clientArea;
    char       *displayMsg = ((AppExerApplication*)GetApplication())->
    ➡GetDisplayMsg();

    GetClientRect( clientArea );

    tDC.SetTextAlign( TA_CENTER );
    tDC.TextOut( clientArea.Width() / 2, clientArea.Height() / 2,
    ➡ displayMsg );
}


// the program starts here
#pragma argsused
int OwlMain( int argc, char *argv[] )
{
    AppExerApplication      *theApp;

    theApp = new AppExerApplication();

    return theApp->Run();
}
```

The window created by the first instance of this program is shown in figure 38.1.

**Figure 38.1.**

First Instance of
the Application
Example Program.

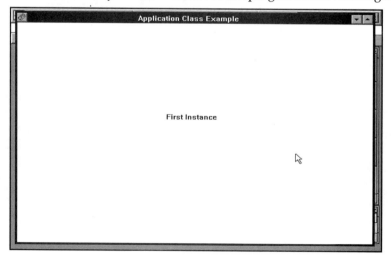

The window created by all subsequent instances of the example program is shown in figure 38.2.

**Figure 38.2.**

Subsequent
Instances of the
Application
Example Program.

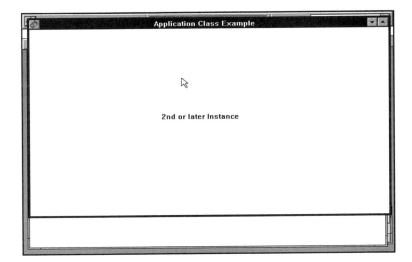

## Windows under OWL

Applications that run under Windows use rectangular areas of the screen, called windows, to communicate with the user. The real job of a Windows application, then, is to manage its windows to help the user perform whatever job the program is designed to do. OWL helps you to create, display, paint, destroy, and otherwise manage an application's windows. You already saw how the TApplication class gives you the opportunity to create an application's main window.

### Interface Objects and Interface Elements

When you created a TFrameWindow object, a window magically appeared on-screen. It seems reasonable to ask at this time how the creation of a C++ object caused a window to be displayed. The real answer is that it didn't. The relationship between a C++ object you instantiate and a window that is created on-screen is defined by the concepts of interface objects and interface elements.

An *interface object* is a C++ object that we can instantiate and thereafter use its member functions and data members just like any other instantiated object. An interface object encapsulates an interface element. An *interface element* is a window, control, or dialog box that you can see on-screen. Interface elements are defined and created by Windows under the control of your application.

You control an interface element using the data members and member functions of an interface object you have instantiated. So what really happened when you instantiated the main window interface object during the InitMainWindow call? The member function SetMainWindow saved the pointer to the interface object you instantiated. Then InitInstance, which called InitMainWindow, called two TFrameWindow member functions, Create and Show. The Create member function created the actual interface element—the window—and Show displayed that window on-screen. Every time you instantiate an interface object, Create and Show have to be called to actually see the interface element on-screen.

## Main Window Objects

Every OWL application has to have a main window. Windows under OWL are all derived from TWindow. Several types of window objects derived from TWindow can be used as your main window. The TFrameWindow object is discussed in this chapter. You will derive a class for your main window from TFrameWindow, as seen in the following section of code:

```
class MainWindow : public TFrameWindow
{
    public:
        MainWindow( char far *WindowTitle );
        ~MainWindow();
};
```

When you instantiate this class, you create an interface object. If you do the instantiation from within the TApplication SetMainWindow call, the interface element corresponding to this object is automatically created (as described above). This method is demonstrated in the code below:

```
void MyApplication::InitMainWindow()
{
    SetMainWindow( new MainWindow( "Window Title" ) );
}
```

Many member functions are available from TFrameWindow. Table 38.1 lists and describes some of the more important functions.

### Table 38.1. TFrameWindow member functions.

| Function Name | Function Description |
| --- | --- |
| CanClose | Enables you to determine if it is OK to close a window before you actually close it. |
| Create | Creates the interface element associated with this interface object. |
| GetClientRect | Gets the size of the window's client area. |

| Function Name | Function Description |
|---|---|
| GetParent | Gets a pointer to the parent interface object. |
| Invalidate | Makes the whole client area invalid so it will be repainted. |
| InvalidateRect | Makes part of the client area invalid so only that area will be repainted. |
| Paint | Overriding this function enables you to display your information on-screen. |
| SetCaption | Changes the window's title. |
| SetCursor | Changes the cursor that is being displayed. |
| Show | Displays or hides a window on-screen. |
| UpdateWindow | Forces the client area of the window to be repainted immediately. |

The main window of an application does not have a parent window. It can, of course, have child windows.

## Child Window Objects

A *child window* belongs to its parent. It can be created immediately upon creation of the parent window, or it can be created later. A child window is destroyed automatically whenever the parent window is destroyed. The parent-child relationship is set in the construction of the child window. The constructor of the TFrameWindow class takes a pointer to the parent window's interface object. The child uses this pointer to add itself to the parent's list of children. This list enables you to search for a particular child window, to send a message to all child windows, and to destroy the child windows when the parent is destroyed.

Almost any type of OWL window can be a child window. OWL offers a nice mechanism for automatic creation of child windows. Consider the parent window constructor shown here:

```
ParentWindow::ParentWindow( TWindow *parent, char far *WindowName )
    : TFrameWindow( parent, WindowName )
{
    ChildWindowPtr = new ChildWindow( this, "Child Window Name" );
}
```

This constructor instantiates a new ChildWindow interface object and saves a pointer to it. Notice that the parent window pointer passed to ChildWindow is this. The instance of ParentWindow being created is now the parent of the new ChildWindow.

ChildWindow automatically adds itself to ParentWindow's child list. Because ChildWindow has been added to the child list before the ParentWindow interface element has been created, the ChildWindow interface element is created when ParentWindow's interface element is created.

You can disable this automatic creation by calling the member function DisableAutoCreate. You can turn automatic creation on, which is the default for all windows except dialog boxes, by calling the member function EnableAutoCreate.

## Example

This example program demonstrates the automatic creation and destruction of a child window. The child window's interface object, a TEdit object, is created in the constructor for the main window. The interface elements for both the main window and the TEdit window are created automatically.

```
//
//      C38WNDW.CPP
//            program to demonstrate OWL windows
//

// OWL include files
#include     <owl\applicat.h>
#include <owl\framewin.h>
#include <owl\dc.h>
#include <owl\edit.h>

// define the application class
class     WindowExerApplication : public TApplication
{
     public:
          WindowExerApplication( char far *name = 0 )
               : TApplication( name )
               {
               };
          virtual void InitMainWindow( void );
};

// define the main window class
class     WindowExerMainWindow : public TFrameWindow
{
     public:
          WindowExerMainWindow( TWindow *parent, char far *WindowName );
          void Paint( TDC &tDC, BOOL bErase, TRect &invalidRect );
     private:
          TEdit     *Child1;
};

// implement the application class
void WindowExerApplication::InitMainWindow( void )
{
```

```
      SetMainWindow( new WindowExerMainWindow( 0,
      ➡ "Window Example - Parent Window" ) );
}

// implement the main window class
WindowExerMainWindow::WindowExerMainWindow( TWindow *parent,
➡ char far *WindowName )
      : TFrameWindow( parent, WindowName )
{
      Child1 = new TEdit( this, 101, "A Sample Child Window", 10,
      ➡ 10, 200, 30, 0, FALSE );
};

#pragma argsused
void WindowExerMainWindow::Paint( TDC &tDC, BOOL bErase, TRect &invalidRect
)
{
      TRect     clientArea;

      GetClientRect( clientArea );

      tDC.SetTextAlign( TA_CENTER );
      tDC.TextOut( clientArea.Width() / 2, clientArea.Height() / 2,
      ➡ "Window Exercise Parent Window" );
}

// the program starts here
#pragma argsused
int OwlMain( int argc, char *argv[] )
{
      WindowExerApplication     *theApp;

      theApp = new WindowExerApplication();

      return theApp->Run();
}
```

The window created by this program is shown in figure 38.3.

# Event Processing

As mentioned earlier, all Windows applications are event-driven. An event is a message that Windows sends to your application to tell it that something of importance has occurred. The message might indicate that the user has selected an item from a menu, that an edit control has changed, or that the window has been resized or activated. Windows can generate hundreds of different events.

OWL provides a standard method for defining which events you are interested in processing. This processing is done using an event method which you define in your class.

**Figure 38.3.**

The child window creation example.

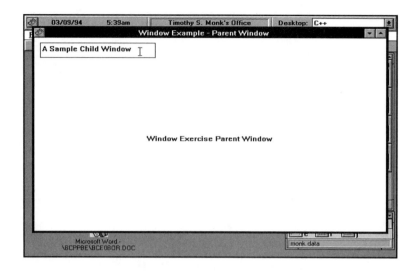

## Defining an Event Response Table

The response table is a member of the window class that is going to use the table. As such, the response table must be declared within the class:

```
class EventWindow : public TFrameWindow
{
    .
    .
    .
    DECLARE_RESPONSE_TABLE( EventWindow );
};
```

OWL provides a series of macros that help you to declare and define a response table. As seen in the preceding code, you declare the response table within the class definition using the DECLARE_RESPONSE_TABLE macro. This macro takes a single argument which consists of the name of the class in which it is being used.

After you declare the response table, it must also be defined. The response table is defined outside the class. OWL again provides you with a series of macros which can be used to define the response table. The following code shows a response table definition:

```
DEFINE_RESPONSE_TABLE1( EventWindow, TFrameWindow )
    EV_WM_LBUTTONDOWN,
    EV_WM_SIZE,
    EV_COMMAND( CM_MENUOPT, ProcessMenuOpt ),
END_RESPONSE_TABLE;
```

A response table definition starts with a DEFINE_RESPONSE_TABLEx macro. The x is the number of classes that the class defining the response table is immediately derived from. This macro requires x + 1 arguments; the first argument is the name of the class defining the response table and the rest are the names of the direct base classes. In the example above, EventWindow defines the response table and TFrameWindow is the only direct base class of EventWindow.

Each event you want to handle has to be defined in the response table. Depending on the type of event you are handling, you can use several different methods to define a response table entry. Window message handling is discussed in this chapter. Command and notification messages are discussed in Chapter 39, "Controls, Gadgets, and Dialog Boxes."

OWL defines a macro for every Windows message. Simply add the appropriate macro to the response table if you want to respond to a particular message. The macro name for a Windows message always begins with EV_ and concludes with the full Windows message. In the response table above, EV_WM_LBUTTONDOWN indicates that you want to process the Windows message WM_LBUTTONDOWN.

After defining the response table, you have to implement an event response member function for each event you intend to process.

## Implementing Event Response Member Functions

Each event that you listed in the response table has to have an event response member function defined in the class. For the EventWindow class and its response table defined above, you need to define an event response member function such as the following:

```
class EventWindow : public TFrameWindow
{
    void EvLButtonDown( UINT modkeys, TPoint &point );
    void EvSize( UINT SizeType, TSize &size );
    void ProcessMenuItem();

    DECLARE_RESPONSE_TABLE( EventWindow );
};
```

For Windows message response functions, the name of the event response function is created by beginning with the characters Ev and adding the Windows message *except* for the initial WM_. The remainder of the Windows message begins with a capital letter; each full word should also begin with a capital letter. The event response function for the Windows message WM_LBUTTONDOWN, for example, is EvLButtonDown.

The return value and arguments for the event response functions are defined by OWL. These function signatures are listed in the OWL Reference Guide, which is included in the Borland C++ package.

## Example

This example demonstrates OWL event processing. The main window class defines two event processing routines. These routines, EvTimer and EvSize, process the WM_TIMER and WM_SIZE messages, respectively.

This example also shows the use of the SetupWindow function to perform window initialization that requires a legal window handle.

```cpp
//
//      C38EVENT.CPP
//          program to demonstrate OWL event processing
//

// OWL include files
#include     <owl\applicat.h>
#include <owl\framewin.h>
#include <owl\dc.h>

// Borland C++ include files
#include     <time.h>

// define the application class
class     EventExerApplication : public TApplication
{
    public:
        EventExerApplication( char far *name = 0 )
            : TApplication( name )
        {
        };
        ~EventExerApplication()
        {
        };
        virtual void InitMainWindow( void );
};

// define the main window class
class     EventExerWindow : public TFrameWindow
{
    public:
        EventExerWindow( TWindow *parent, char far *WindowName )
            : TFrameWindow( parent, WindowName )
        {
        };
        ~EventExerWindow();
        void Paint( TDC &tDC, BOOL bErase, TRect &invalidRect );
        void EvTimer( UINT TimerID );
        void EvSize( UINT sizeType, TSize &size );

        DECLARE_RESPONSE_TABLE( EventExerWindow );
    protected:
        virtual void SetupWindow();
};
```

```
DEFINE_RESPONSE_TABLE1( EventExerWindow, TFrameWindow )
    EV_WM_TIMER,
    EV_WM_SIZE,
END_RESPONSE_TABLE;


// implement the application class
void EventExerApplication::InitMainWindow( void )
{
    SetMainWindow( new EventExerWindow( 0, "Event Demonstration" ) );
}

// implement the main window class
EventExerWindow::~EventExerWindow()
{
    KillTimer( 1 );
};

void EventExerWindow::SetupWindow()
{
    UINT TimerId = SetTimer( 1, 1000 );
    if ( TimerId != 1 )
        MessageBox( "Error Creating Timer", "C38EVENT" );
}

#pragma argsused
void EventExerWindow::Paint( TDC &tDC, BOOL bErase, TRect &invalidRect )
{
    TRect         ClientArea;
    time_t     CurrentTime;
    char          *TimeString;

    time( &CurrentTime );
    TimeString = ctime( &CurrentTime );
    TimeString[ 24 ] = '\0';

    GetClientRect( ClientArea );

    tDC.SetTextAlign( TA_CENTER );
    tDC.TextOut( ClientArea.Width() / 2, ClientArea.Height() / 2,
    ➥ TimeString  );
}

#pragma argsused
void EventExerWindow::EvTimer( UINT TimerID )
{
    Invalidate( FALSE );
    UpdateWindow();
}

#pragma argsused
void EventExerWindow::EvSize( UINT sizeType, TSize &size )
{
```

```
        Invalidate();
        UpdateWindow();
}


// the program starts here
#pragma argsused
int OwlMain( int argc, char *argv[] )
{
    EventExerApplication      *theApp;

    theApp = new EventExerApplication();

    return theApp->Run();
}
```

The window created by this example is shown in figure 38.4.

**Figure 38.4.**

The event
processing
example window.

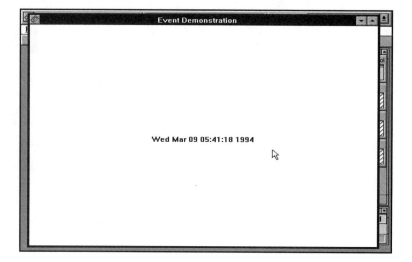

## Summary

This chapter took a close look at the TApplication class and the initializations it performs. You learned how to define a main window class, deriving it from TFrameWindow. You also explored the parent-child window relationship. Finally, this chapter discussed setting up event response tables and writing event response member functions.

# Review Questions

1. From which class do you derive an application class?

2. What member function is used to create an application's main window?

3. Why do you use the Create member function?

4. What do you use to tell OWL that you want to process Windows messages?

5. How can child windows be created automatically?

# Review Exercises

1. Define a new application class that sets a flag which is True if it is the first instance and False otherwise. A member function should be provided to return this flag. The application class should also be able to instantiate a main window.

2. Define a main window class which displays a message in its window. The original message should indicate whether or not this is the first instance of the window.

   The class should also respond to the Windows messages WM_LBUTTONDOWN and WM_RBUTTONDOWN. When one of these buttons is pressed, the message in the window should change to indicate which button was pressed.

3. Write a full application that uses the classes defined in exercises 1 and 2.

# CHAPTER 39

# Controls, Gadgets, and Dialog Boxes

In looking at OWL so far, you have learned how to specify an application and a main window. You have also learned how to do some event processing. But OWL also gives you the ability to make use of additional visual items that are either connected to, or a child of, the windows you have already seen.

This chapter introduces the following topics:

- ♦ Adding menus to a window
- ♦ Using controls within a window
- ♦ Adding a toolbar and status bar to a window
- ♦ Incorporating dialog boxes to simplify using controls

## Menus

Almost every Windows application has a menu bar from which you can choose commands to be executed. OWL provides you with an easy way to add a menu to an OWL window—the TMenu class. This class also offers a set of member functions that you can use to manipulate menus.

## Adding a Menu to a Window

You must take the following steps before you can add a menu to a window:

◆ Define values to use for the menu items.

◆ Define a menu resource.

◆ Attach the menu resource to your window.

Each menu item must be assigned a unique identification value. These values are usually defined in a header file. Header files, usually having a .h extension, are included in both the resource definition file and your source code file. This practice ensures that the ID values used by your code and the resource file are consistent.

Your menu resource is defined in a file called a *resource definition file*. These files usually have an .rc extension. You can create this resource definition file in two different ways. The first option is to enter the menu resource code manually. The better option is to use Borland's *Resource Workshop*, which is included with Borland C++. Figure 39.1 shows the menu resource creation screen from Resource Workshop. Full coverage of the uses of Resource Workshop is beyond the scope of this book.

**Figure 39.1.**
Borland's
Resource
Workshop.

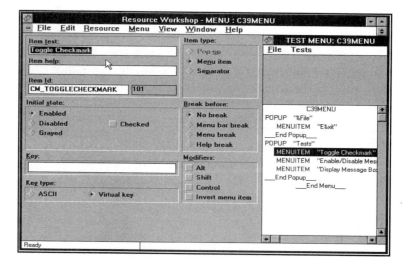

The resource definition file that you create has to be included in your Borland C++ project so that it is compiled and added to the executable file. The easiest way to accomplish this task is to add the resource definition file when you create your project. Click the Advanced button in the New Project dialog box to display the Advanced Options dialog box (see fig. 39.2). Then check the .rc check box to add a resource definition node to the project. Double-clicking that node automatically starts Resource Workshop.

**Figure 39.2.**

The Advanced
Options dialog box
for a new project.

After defining a menu resource, you have to attach it to your OWL window. Recall from Chapter 38, "Handling Applications, Windows, and Events," that you instantiate your main window interface object in the `InitMainWindow` member function. The `TFrameWindow` class includes the member function `AssignMenu`. This member function takes the name of a menu resource, loads the menu, and attaches it to the instance of the window class. The code below shows a sample `InitMainWindow` implementation:

```
void SampleApplication::InitMainWindow( void )
{
    SetMainWindow( new MainWindow( 0, "Main Window Title" ) );
    GetMainWindow()->AssignMenu( "MENUNAME" );
}
```

After you have assigned a menu to the window, you will receive `WM_COMMAND` events every time the user selects a menu item.

## Processing Menu Commands

When a user chooses one of the menu items from the menu you have added to a window, Windows generates `WM_COMMAND` messages. You might assume that you must add an `EV_WM_COMMAND` macro to the response table to be able to process these messages (as you would for other messages). OWL, however, makes it easier for you to process individual menu items. The following line can be used as a model for response table entries:

```
EV_COMMAND( CM_FILEEXIT, CmExit );
```

This line causes the member function `CmExit` to be called every time the user chooses the menu item that corresponds to `CM_FILEEXIT`. In this example, `CM_FILEEXIT` is one of the unique menu IDs assigned to each menu item in the resource definition file. By enabling you to add each menu item response function directly to the response table, OWL makes it unnecessary for you to process the `WM_COMMAND` directly.

The member function that is listed in the `EV_COMMAND` macro must have the following signature:

```
void CmExit();
```

This signature is adequate for most WM_COMMAND messages you will want to process. OWL also provides you with an EV_COMMAND_AND_ID macro (see example below) which takes a response function with a single argument. This macro gives you the option of receiving the WM_COMMAND message's WPARAM for additional processing. Windows uses WPARAM to pass additional information about a command to the program processing the command.

```
EV_COMMAND_AND_ID( CM_FILEEXIT, CmExit );

void CmExit( WPARAM wParam );
```

Now that you can process a menu item after a user chooses it, you might find it useful to manipulate the menu in various ways (depending on your application).

## Manipulating Menu Items

OWL has encapsulated the ability to manipulate menus into the TMenu class. The menu manipulations that you can perform using TMenu include the following actions:

♦ Adding menu items

♦ Removing menu items

♦ Enabling, disabling, and graying menu items

♦ Adding/removing check marks next to menu items

To use TMenu, you must first create a TMenu variable. TMenu has a constructor, as shown here, that enables you to create the interface object for an interface element that already exists. This constructor, called from within a member function in a window class, gets a menu handle using the GetMenu member function:

```
TMenu menuVar( GetMenu() );
```

After you have instantiated the TMenu class, you can use that variable to manipulate the menu. Windows enables you to display a check mark to the left of any menu item. You can use this check mark to show the user that an option is active. Using the CheckMenuItem member function, you can easily add or remove this check mark:

```
menuVar.CheckMenuItem( CM_MENUCOMMAND, MF_CHECKED );
```

This member function takes two arguments—the ID of the menu item that you want to manipulate and either MF_CHECKED or MF_UNCHECKED to set the new state of that menu item. The other manipulations available through TMenu are just as simple to implement. The ultimate manipulation of a menu item, of course, is to disable it completely.

# Enabling and Disabling Menu Items

OWL provides you with a built-in method for enabling and disabling menu items. This mechanism, known as a *command enabler event*, is handled automatically for most menu items. If an EV_COMMAND or EV_COMMAND_AND_ID entry appears in the response table for a menu item, that menu item is automatically enabled.

If you want to be able to disable and enable a menu item that has a response table entry, you need to add yet another event to the response table, as shown here:

```
EV_COMMAND_ENABLE( CmExit, CmExitEnable );
```

The member function that corresponds to this response table entry has the following signature:

```
void CmExitEnable( TCommandEnabler &commandEnabler );
```

The most important TCommandEnabler class member function is Enable. Enable takes a single Boolean argument—either TRUE to enable the menu item or FALSE to disable it. This mechanism enables you to determine when a menu object is enabled or disabled.

## Example

This example program demonstrates OWL menu processing. The program adds a simple menu to the application. The menu contains four menu items to be processed. The first, CM_FILEEXIT, causes the program to exit. The next, CM_TOGGLECHECKMARK, demonstrates how to display a check mark next to a menu item.

The final two menu items, CM_ENABLEDISABLEMSG and CM_DISPLAYMBOX, work together. Choosing the CM_ENABLEDISABLEMSG menu item sets a data member flag that determines whether CM_DISPLAYMBOX is enabled. Using the command enabler mechanism, the CM_DISPLAYMBOX menu item is enabled/disabled based on this Boolean flag. If CM_DISPLAYMBOX is enabled, choosing it causes a simple message box to be displayed.

The C++ code for this program is given in listing 39.1. Listing 39.2 shows the header file for this program, and listing 39.3 shows the resource definition file.

**Listing 39.1. Menu Processing Example Program Source File**

```
//
// C39MENU.CPP
//          demonstration of OWL menu processing
//

// OWL include files
#include <owl\applicat.h>
#include <owl\framewin.h>
#include <owl\dc.h>
```

*continues*

**Listing 39.1. Continued**

```
#include <owl\menu.h>

// Borland C++ include files
#include    <time.h>

// Local include files
#include "c39menu.h"

// define the application class
class    MenuExerApplication : public TApplication
{
    public:
        MenuExerApplication( char far *name = 0 )
            : TApplication( name )
        {
        };
        ~MenuExerApplication()
        {
        };
        virtual void InitMainWindow( void );
};

// define the main window class
class    MenuExerWindow : public TFrameWindow
{
    public:
        MenuExerWindow( TWindow *parent, char far *WindowName )
            : TFrameWindow( parent, WindowName )
        {
            MBoxEnabled = TRUE;
        };
        ~MenuExerWindow();
        void Paint( TDC &tDC, BOOL bErase, TRect &invalidRect );
        void EvTimer( UINT TimerID );
        void EvSize( UINT sizeType, TSize &size );
        void CmToggleCheckmark();
        void CmEnableDisableMsg();
        void CmDisplayMBox();
        void CmDisplayMBoxEnable( TCommandEnabler &tce );

        DECLARE_RESPONSE_TABLE( MenuExerWindow );
    protected:
        virtual void SetupWindow();
    private:
        BOOL    MBoxEnabled;
};

DEFINE_RESPONSE_TABLE1( MenuExerWindow, TFrameWindow )
    EV_WM_TIMER,
    EV_WM_SIZE,
    EV_COMMAND( CM_FILEEXIT, CmExit ),
    EV_COMMAND( CM_TOGGLECHECKMARK, CmToggleCheckmark ),
    EV_COMMAND( CM_ENABLEDISABLEMSG, CmEnableDisableMsg ),
    FV_COMMAND( CM_DISPLAYMBOX, CmDisplayMBox ),
```

```
    EV_COMMAND_ENABLE( CM_DISPLAYMBOX, CmDisplayMBoxEnable ),
END_RESPONSE_TABLE;

// implement the application class
void MenuExerApplication::InitMainWindow( void )
{
    SetMainWindow( new MenuExerWindow( 0, "Menu Demonstration" ) );
    GetMainWindow()->AssignMenu( "C39MENU" );
}

// implement the main window class
MenuExerWindow::~MenuExerWindow()
{
    KillTimer( 1 );
};

void MenuExerWindow::SetupWindow()
{
    UINT TimerId = SetTimer( 1, 1000 );
    if ( TimerId != 1 )
        MessageBox( "Error Creating Timer", "C38EVENT" );
}

#pragma argsused
void MenuExerWindow::Paint( TDC &tDC, BOOL bErase, TRect &invalidRect )
{
    TRect         ClientArea;
    time_t      CurrentTime;
    char          *TimeString;

    time( &CurrentTime );
    TimeString = ctime( &CurrentTime );
    TimeString[ 24 ] = '\0';

    GetClientRect( ClientArea );

    tDC.SetTextAlign( TA_CENTER );
    tDC.TextOut( ClientArea.Width() / 2, ClientArea.Height() / 2,
    ➡ TimeString   );
}

#pragma argsused
void MenuExerWindow::EvTimer( UINT TimerID )
{
    Invalidate( FALSE );
    UpdateWindow();
}

#pragma argsused
void MenuExerWindow::EvSize( UINT sizeType, TSize &size )
{
    Invalidate();
```

*continues*

**Listing 39.1. Continued**

```
    UpdateWindow();
}

void MenuExerWindow::CmToggleCheckmark()
{
    TMenu     MenuObj( GetMenu() );

    UINT    CurrentMenuState = MenuObj.GetMenuState(CM_TOGGLECHECKMARK,
    ➥ MF_CHECKED );

    MenuObj.CheckMenuItem(      CM_TOGGLECHECKMARK,
                CurrentMenuState ? MF_UNCHECKED : MF_CHECKED );

    DrawMenuBar();
}

void MenuExerWindow::CmEnableDisableMsg()
{
    MBoxEnabled = !MBoxEnabled;
}

void MenuExerWindow::CmDisplayMBox()
{
    MessageBox( "You selected the Display MessageBox menu item",
    ➥ "C39MENU" );
}

void MenuExerWindow::CmDisplayMBoxEnable( TCommandEnabler &tce )
{
    tce.Enable( MBoxEnabled );
}

// the program starts here
#pragma argsused
int OwlMain( int argc, char *argv[] )
{
    MenuExerApplication      *theApp;

    theApp = new MenuExerApplication();

    return theApp->Run();
}
```

**Listing 39.2. Menu Processing Example Program Header File**

```
//
//    C39MENU.H
//

#ifndef    _C39MENU_H
#define    _C39MENU_H
```

```
// define constants for the menu
#define     CM_FILEEXIT               24338
#define     CM_TOGGLECHECKMARK          101
#define     CM_ENABLEDISABLEMSG         102
#define     CM_DISPLAYMBOX              103


#endif
```

## Listing 39.3. Menu Processing Example Program Resource Definition File

```
/*
    C39MENU.RC
        resource file for menu demonstration
*/

#include "c39menu.h"

C39MENU MENU
{
    POPUP "&File"
    {
        MENUITEM "E&xit", CM_FILEEXIT
    }

    POPUP "Tests"
    {
        MENUITEM "Toggle Checkmark", CM_TOGGLECHECKMARK
        MENUITEM "Enable/Disable Message", CM_ENABLEDISABLEMSG
        MENUITEM "Display Message Box", CM_DISPLAYMBOX, GRAYED
    }
}
```

Figure 39.3 shows the window created by this program.

**Figure 39.3.**

The window created by the menu processing example.

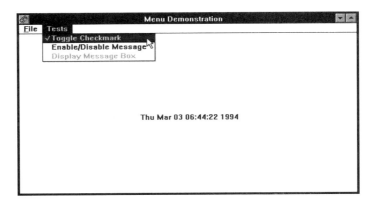

# Controls

Controls are specialized windows that perform a single particular function. These windows define the functionality for a set of standard controls. OWL has encapsulated these controls in a series of classes, all of which are derived from the TControl class. The standard controls provided are:

- Static text
- Edit controls
- Buttons
- Check boxes
- Radio buttons
- List boxes
- Combo boxes

OWL's classes give you the ability to create, manipulate, and destroy controls. They also enable you to make processing decisions based on the events a control generates.

## Creating Controls

The creation of controls is a two-step process (as with other OWL windows). You first instantiate the interface object and then create the interface element. OWL controls are always instantiated as child windows of another window. This instantiation of the control interface object is done in the constructor of the parent window, as seen below:

```
ParentWindow::ParentWindow( TWindow *parent, char far *WindowName )
    : TFrameWindow( parent, WindowName )
{
    // create the control interface objects
    // the interface elements will be autocreated
    editControl = new TEdit( this, IDC_EDIT_CONTROL, "Default Text",
    ➥ 10, 10, 100, 25, 0 );
    buttonControl = new TButton( this, IDC_BUTTON, "OK", 20, 45, 80,
    ➥ 30, TRUE );
};
```

As you create these two control interface objects, you specify the this pointer as the parent window. The controls automatically add themselves to ParentWindow's child window list. The other important argument of the control constructor is the control ID. Each control created in a parent window must have a unique ID. These IDs are used to manipulate the control and to identify the control's notifications to the parent window.

One of the nicest features of OWL is the automatic creation of child windows. If you instantiate the control interface objects in the parent window's constructor, the interface elements for the controls are automatically created when the parent window's interface element is created. Conversely, the control interface elements are automatically destroyed when the parent's interface element is destroyed.

You can override the default behavior and turn off autocreation of controls by calling the `DisableAutoCreate` member function individually for each control. Autocreation can then be turned back on using `EnableAutoCreate`.

Controls generate events to which the parent window must be able to respond. These events, known as control notifications, are handled within the response table structure.

## Control Notification Processing

Controls generate *notifications* that are sent to their parent window. These notifications inform the parent window that something of importance has happened to the control. Common notifications include the following:

- ♦ `BN_CLICKED`, which indicates that a button control was clicked.

- ♦ `EN_CHANGE`, which indicates that an edit control's text has changed.

- ♦ `LBN_DBLCLK`, which indicates that an item in a list box has been double-clicked.

In an OWL program, these notifications are handled as part of a Windows response table. A macro that corresponds to each notification is used in the response table definition, as seen below. The arguments for each macro are the control ID, as given in the control's constructor, and the name of the member function that will handle the event.

```
DEFINE_RESPONSE_TABLE1( ParentWindow, TFrameWindow )
    EV_BN_CLICKED( IDC_BUTTON, EvButtonClicked ),
    EV_EN_CHANGE( IDC_EDIT_CONTROL, EvEditControlChange ),
END_RESPONSE_TABLE;
```

The signature of the response member functions is the same for all these events. For example:

```
void EvButtonClicked();
```

The processing that occurs in these response functions can vary widely. Control manipulations are often handled in response functions.

## Control Manipulation

By encapsulating control interface elements in interface objects, OWL enables you to manipulate controls without dealing directly with the Windows API. The available manipulations include reading text from edit controls, putting text into edit controls, initializing list boxes, getting the current selection from a list box, and changing the text displayed on a button. The code below shows how you can read the text from an edit control:

```
editControl->GetText( buffer, buffer_size );
```

All the OWL control classes have member functions available for the types of manipulations listed above, as well as a host of others.

## Example

This program demonstrates the use of OWL's controls. The main window of this program instantiates three controls: two edit boxes and a button. When the button is clicked, the text in the top edit box control is copied into the bottom edit box control. An edit box control enables the user to type text in it.

This example demonstrates the processing of button notification codes. It also demonstrates control manipulation using the control member functions in the process of copying the edit control text.

The source code for this example is given in listing 39.4; the header file is shown in listing 39.5.

**Listing 39.4. Control Example Source Code**

```
//
// C39CNTRL.CPP
//              demonstration of OWL control processing
//

// OWL include files
#include <owl\applicat.h>
#include <owl\framewin.h>
#include <owl\dc.h>
#include <owl\edit.h>
#include <owl\button.h>

// Local include files
#include "c39cntrl.h"

// define the application class
class    ControlExerApplication : public TApplication
{
    public:
        ControlExerApplication( char far *name = 0 )
            : TApplication( name )
        {
        };
        ~ControlExerApplication()
        {
        };
```

```
                 virtual void InitMainWindow( void );
};

// define the main window class
class     ControlExerWindow : public TFrameWindow
{
    public:
        ControlExerWindow( TWindow *parent, char far *WindowName );
        ~ControlExerWindow();
        void EvButtonClicked();

        DECLARE_RESPONSE_TABLE( ControlExerWindow );
    private:
        TEdit              *editControl1;
        TEdit              *editControl2;
        TButton          *buttonControl;
};

DEFINE_RESPONSE_TABLE1( ControlExerWindow, TFrameWindow )
    EV_BN_CLICKED( IDC_BUTTON, EvButtonClicked ),
END_RESPONSE_TABLE;

// implement the application class
void ControlExerApplication::InitMainWindow( void )
{
    SetMainWindow( new ControlExerWindow( 0,
    ➡ "Control Demonstration" ) );
}

// implement the main window class
ControlExerWindow::ControlExerWindow( TWindow *parent,
➡ char far *WindowName )
    : TFrameWindow( parent, WindowName )
{
    // create the control interface objects
    // the interface elements will be autocreated
    editControl1 = new TEdit( this, IDC_EDIT1, "Copy From", 10, 10,
    ➡ 100, 25, 0 );
    editControl2 = new TEdit( this, IDC_EDIT2, "Copy To", 10, 85,
    ➡ 100, 25, 0 );
    buttonControl = new TButton( this, IDC_BUTTON, "Copy", 20, 45,
    ➡ 80, 30, TRUE );
};

ControlExerWindow::~ControlExerWindow()
{
};

void ControlExerWindow::EvButtonClicked()
{
    char     TempBuffer[256];
```

*continues*

**Listing 39.4. Continued**

```
        if ( editControl1->GetText( TempBuffer, sizeof( TempBuffer ) ) )
            editControl2->SetText( TempBuffer );
}

// the program starts here
#pragma argsused
int OwlMain( int argc, char *argv[] )
{
    ControlExerApplication     *theApp;

    theApp = new ControlExerApplication();

    return theApp->Run();
}
```

**Listing 39.5. Control Example Header File**

```
//
//      C39CNTRL.H
//

#ifndef      _C39CNTRL_H
#define      _C39CNTRL_H

// define constants for the menu
#define      IDC_EDIT1      101
#define      IDC_EDIT2      102
#define      IDC_BUTTON     103

#endif
```

The window created by this program is shown in figure 39.4.

**Figure 39.4.**

Control example program.

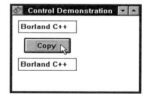

## Gadgets

OWL provides you with a simple way to add advanced user interface features to your applications. These advanced features, including control (or tool) bars, status bars, and toolbox windows, are used in better Windows applications.

Under OWL, these special features are referred to as *gadget windows*; the controls contained in them are called *gadgets*. If you plan to use gadgets, the first change needed is a modification of your main window.

## Creating Windows To Use Gadgets

In all of the examples up to this point, you have used a main window which is derived from TFrameWindow. To be able to use a gadget window, you must change the way you create your window. The first modification, as shown below, is to change the base class of your derived window to TWindow.

```
class     ExampleWindow : public TWindow
{
    public:
        ExampleWindow( TWindow *parent, char far *WindowName );
        ~ExampleWindow();
        void EvExitGadget();

        DECLARE_RESPONSE_TABLE( ExampleWindow );
};
```

This change enables you to use the created window as a client window. A client window is a specialized child window, which when used with a main window derived from TFrameWindow allows usage of gadgets with the main window.

To use a gadget window with your window, the window you create must be a TDecoratedFrame or one derived from it. The InitMainWindow that appears below shows how to create a main window in which gadget windows can be used.

```
void YourApplication::InitMainWindow( void )
{
    TDecoratedFrame *mainWindow = new TDecoratedFrame( 0, "Gadget
Example", new ExampleWindow( 0, NULL ), TRUE );

    // Construct any gadgets
    // Insert gadgets into the frame window

    // Set the main window and its menu
    SetMainWindow( mainWindow );
}
```

The first thing to notice is that the main window is now an instantiation of TDecoratedFrame. This is the first time that you have instantiated the main window outside the actual call to SetMainWindow. Next, the arguments to TDecoratedFrame are different from the ones you have seen before. They are as follows:

♦ A pointer to the parent window

♦ A pointer to the window title

♦ A pointer to the client window

♦ A Boolean telling if automatic status bar tracking should take place

The client window being instantiated here gives the program its actual functionality. By putting the functionality into a client window, you can easily add gadget windows to the main window, giving you simple access to these advanced application features.

# Control Bars

A control bar, also known as a toolbar, enables you to give users easier access to commands than they get when using the menu. A control bar can contain a variety of controls, including buttons, bitmaps, and text controls.

## Creating a Control Bar

A control bar for use in the main window is created in the InitMainWindow member function, as seen below. The first step is to instantiate a TControlBar, giving the TDecoratedFrame as the parent window. This TControlBar is your gadget window, which is inserted into your frame window.

```
void YourApplication::InitMainWindow( void )
{
    TDecoratedFrame *mainWindow = new TDecoratedFrame( 0,
    ➥"Gadget Example", new ExampleWindow( 0, NULL ), TRUE );

    // Construct a control bar
    TControlBar *controlBar = new TControlBar( mainWindow );
    controlBar->Insert( *new TButtonGadget(IDC_BUTTON, IDC_BUTTON ) );
    controlBar->Insert( *new TSeparatorGadget() );
    controlBar->Insert( *new TButtonGadget(IDC_EXIT, IDC_EXIT ) );

    // Insert the control bar into the frame window
    mainWindow->Insert(*controlBar, TDecoratedFrame::Top);

    // Set the main window and its menu
    SetMainWindow( mainWindow );
}
```

After creating the control bar object, you insert gadgets into the gadget window. The preceding sample code inserts three gadgets—two button gadgets and a separator gadget. Each button gadget is constructed with two arguments. The first is the resource ID of the bitmap to be displayed in the gadget button. The second is the control ID that will be used to access this button and to identify its notifications. The resource ID and the control ID don't have to be the same value. Making them the same is useful during debugging.

The bitmaps used for a TButtonGadget are defined in the resource definition file. This file can be created by hand or with Borland's Resource Workshop (a much better option).

The TSeparatorGadget is used to put space between gadgets. The argument indicates the number of pixels to put between the gadgets. Gadgets produce notifications similar to controls.

After you have inserted all the gadgets into the gadget window, you must insert the control bar into the frame window. This step is accomplished using the `TDecoratedFrame::Insert` member function. This function accepts a pointer to the control bar and a location indicator. You can place the control bar at the top or bottom of the window or at its left or right side.

### Control Bar Event Processing

When you press a button gadget, a notification is generated and sent to the frame's client window. The notifications generated by gadgets are the same as the notifications generated by controls; they are handled in exactly the same way (using the response table).

## Status Bars

A status bar is a specialized control bar that primarily uses text gadgets. Status bars are used to display messages to the user, often including automated help for menu and gadget items.

### Creating a Status Bar

You create a status bar for the main window in the `InitMainWindow` member function, as seen below:

```
void YourApplication::InitMainWindow( void )
{
    TDecoratedFrame *mainWindow = new TDecoratedFrame( 0,
    ➥"Gadget Example", new ExampleWindow( 0, NULL ), TRUE );

    // Construct a status bar
    TStatusBar* statusBar = new TStatusBar( mainWindow,
    ➥ TGadget::Recessed, TStatusBar::CapsLock ¦
    ➥ TStatusBar::NumLock ¦ TStatusBar::Overtype );

    // Insert the status bar into the frame window
    mainWindow->Insert(*statusBar, TDecoratedFrame::Bottom);

    // Set the main window and its menu
    SetMainWindow( mainWindow );
}
```

You begin by instantiating a `TStatusBar`. The first argument accepted in this case is the parent window. The next argument indicates whether the text fields should be recessed into or raised above the status bar. The last argument is a list of indicators that you want to add to the status bar. The indicators entered above enable you to track the status of the Num Lock key, the Caps Lock key, and the Overtype/Insert key. The status bar changes these indicators automatically whenever the appropriate keys are pressed.

After creating the status bar, you need to insert it into the frame window. This task is accomplished using the TDecoratedFrame::Insert member function. This function accepts a pointer to the status bar and a location indicator. The status bar can be placed either at the top or bottom of the window.

## Automatic Menu and Gadget Tracking

If you created the TDecoratedWindow with automatic tracking turned on, OWL uses the status bar to display help information about the menu item or gadget that has been selected. This automatic tracking uses the application's string table resource.

A string table is defined in the resource definition file. You can use Resource Workshop to easily create a string table, as seen in figure 39.5. If OWL finds a string in the string table that has an ID which matches the ID of a selected menu item or a gadget, it displays that string on the status bar.

**Figure 39.5.**

Resource Workshop's String Table Editor.

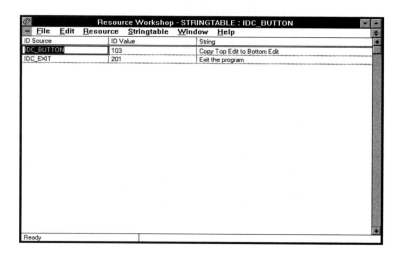

## Example

This example program adds a control bar and status bar to the control example program. It creates and adds a control bar and status bar in the InitMainWindow function.

It also demonstrates how to process the events generated by the gadget buttons. Listings 39.6, 39.7, and 39.8 show the source code, header file, and resource definition file, respectively.

**Listing 39.6. Gadget Example Program**

```
//
// C39GADGT.CPP
//          demonstration of OWL gadget control processing
//

// OWL include files
#include    <owl\applicat.h>
#include <owl\decframe.h>
#include <owl\edit.h>
#include <owl\button.h>
#include <owl\controlb.h>
#include <owl\buttonga.h>
#include <owl\statusba.h>


// Local include files
#include "c39gadgt.h"

// define the application class
class    GadgetExerApplication : public TApplication
{
    public:
        GadgetExerApplication( char far *name = 0 )
                : TApplication( name )
            {
            };
            ~GadgetExerApplication()
            {
            };
            virtual void InitMainWindow( void );
};

// define the main window class
class    GadgetExerWindow : public TWindow
{
    public:
        GadgetExerWindow( TWindow *parent, char far *WindowName );
        ~GadgetExerWindow();
        void EvButtonClicked();
        void EvExitGadget();

        DECLARE_RESPONSE_TABLE( GadgetExerWindow );
    private:
        TEdit            *editControl1;
        TEdit            *editControl2;
        TButton          *buttonControl;
};

DEFINE_RESPONSE_TABLE1( GadgetExerWindow, TWindow )
```

*continues*

**Listing 39.6. Continued**

```
        EV_BN_CLICKED( IDC_BUTTON, EvButtonClicked ),
        EV_BN_CLICKED( IDC_EXIT, EvExitGadget ),
END_RESPONSE_TABLE;

// implement the application class
void GadgetExerApplication::InitMainWindow( void )
{
    TDecoratedFrame *mainWindow = new TDecoratedFrame( 0,"Gadget Example",
    new GadgetExerWindow( 0, NULL ), TRUE );

    // Construct a control bar
    TControlBar *controlBar = new TControlBar( mainWindow );
    controlBar->Insert( *new TButtonGadget(IDC_BUTTON, IDC_BUTTON ) );
    controlBar->Insert( *new TSeparatorGadget() );
    controlBar->Insert( *new TButtonGadget(IDC_EXIT, IDC_EXIT ) );

    // Construct a status bar
    TStatusBar* statusBar = new TStatusBar( mainWindow,
 ➥TGadget::Recessed,TStatusBar::CapsLock ¦
 ➥TStatusBar::NumLock ¦ TStatusBar::Overtype );

    // Insert the status bar and control bar into the frame
    mainWindow->Insert(*statusBar, TDecoratedFrame::Bottom);
    mainWindow->Insert(*controlBar, TDecoratedFrame::Top);

    // Set the main window and its menu
    SetMainWindow( mainWindow );
}

// implement the main window class
GadgetExerWindow::GadgetExerWindow( TWindow *parent, char far *WindowName )
    : TWindow( parent, WindowName )
{
    // create the control interface objects
    // the interface elements will be autocreated
    editControl1 = new TEdit( this, IDC_EDIT1, "Copy From", 10, 10,
    ➥ 100, 25, 0 );
    editControl2 = new TEdit( this, IDC_EDIT2, "Copy To", 10, 85,
    ➥ 100, 25, 0 );
    buttonControl = new TButton( this, IDC_BUTTON, "Copy", 20, 45,
    ➥ 80, 30, TRUE );
};

GadgetExerWindow::~GadgetExerWindow()
{
};

void GadgetExerWindow::EvButtonClicked()
```

```
{
    char    TempBuffer[256];

    if ( editControl1->GetText( TempBuffer, sizeof( TempBuffer ) ) )
        editControl2->SetText( TempBuffer );
}

void GadgetExerWindow::EvExitGadget()
{
    CloseWindow();
}

// the program starts here
#pragma argsused
int OwlMain( int argc, char *argv[] )
{
    GadgetExerApplication    *theApp;

    theApp = new GadgetExerApplication();

    return theApp->Run();
}
```

**Listing 39.7. Gadget Example Header File**

```
//
//      C39GADGT.H
//

#ifndef      _C39GADGT_H
#define BITMAP_1      1
#define      _C39GADGT_H

// define constants for the menu
#define    IDC_EDIT1      101
#define    IDC_EDIT2      102
#define    IDC_BUTTON      103

#define    IDC_EXIT         201

#endif
```

**Listing 39.8. Gadget Example Resource Definition File**

```
/*
    C39GADGT.RC
        resource definition for gadget example
*/

#include "c39gadgt.h"

IDC_BUTTON BITMAP
{
'42 4D F6 00 00 00 00 00 00 00 76 00 00 00 28 00'
'00 00 10 00 00 00 10 00 00 00 01 00 04 00 00 00'
'00 00 80 00 00 00 00 00 00 00 00 00 00 00 00 00'
'00 00 10 00 00 00 00 00 00 00 00 00 00 80 00 00 80'
'00 00 00 80 80 00 80 00 00 00 80 00 80 00 80 80'
'00 00 C0 C0 C0 00 80 80 80 00 00 00 FF 00 00 FF'
'00 00 00 FF FF 00 FF 00 00 00 FF 00 FF 00 FF FF'
'00 00 FF FF FF 00 CC CC CC CC CC CC CC CC CC CC'
'CC CC CC CC CC CC CC CC CC CC CC CC CC CC CC CC'
'CC CC CC CC CC CC CC CC CB BB BC CC CC CC CC CC'
'BC CC CB CC CC CC CC CC BC CC CC CC CC CC CC CC'
'BC CC CC CC CC CC CC CC BC CC CC CC CC CC CC CC'
'BC CC CC CC CC CC CC CC BC CC CC CC CC CC CC CC'
'BC CC CB CC CC CC CC CC CB BB BC CC CC CC CC CC'
'CC CC CC CC CC CC CC CC CC CC CC CC CC CC CC CC'
'CC CC CC CC CC CC'

}

IDC_EXIT BITMAP
{
'42 4D F6 00 00 00 00 00 00 00 76 00 00 00 28 00'
'00 00 10 00 00 00 10 00 00 00 01 00 04 00 00 00'
'00 00 80 00 00 00 00 00 00 00 00 00 00 00 00 00'
'00 00 10 00 00 00 00 00 00 00 00 00 00 80 00 00 80'
'00 00 00 80 80 00 80 00 00 00 80 00 80 00 80 80'
'00 00 C0 C0 C0 00 80 80 80 00 00 00 FF 00 00 FF'
'00 00 00 FF FF 00 FF 00 00 00 FF 00 FF 00 FF FF'
'00 00 FF FF FF 00 CC CC CC CC CC CC CC CC CC CC'
'CC CC CC CC CC CC CC CC CC CC CC CC CC CC CC CC'
'CC CC CC CC CC CC CC CC CC BB BB BC CC CC CC CC'
'CC BC CC CC CC CC CC CC CC BC CC CC CC CC CC CC'
'CC BC CC CC CC CC CC CC CC BB BB CC CC CC CC CC'
'CC BC CC CC CC CC CC CC CC BC CC CC CC CC CC CC'
'CC BC CC CC CC CC CC CC CC BB BB BC CC CC CC CC'
'CC CC CC CC CC CC CC CC CC CC CC CC CC CC CC CC'
'CC CC CC CC CC CC'

}


STRINGTABLE
{
 IDC_BUTTON, "Copy Top Edit to Bottom Edit"
 IDC_EXIT, "Exit the program"
}
```

The window created by this program is shown in figure 39.6.

**Figure 39.6.**

The window created by the example gadget program.

# Dialog Boxes

Earlier in this chapter, you learned how to add controls to OWL windows. Even with OWL's autocreation feature, adding controls this way can be tedious because you have to manually place each control in the window. Windows and OWL provide you with an easier way to create windows that include controls. These special windows, known as dialog boxes, are used to provide the user with information or to get information from the user.

## Defining a Dialog Box

Dialog boxes are created using a template that is stored in your resource definition file. The easiest way to create a dialog box template is to use a dialog editor such as the one provided by Resource Workshop (see fig. 39.7). You can also enter a dialog box template manually into your resource definition file.

**Figure 39.7.**

Resource Workshop's Dialog Editor.

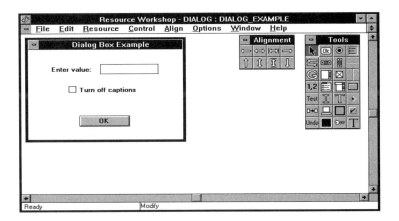

Your dialog box template defines the size of the dialog box, the title of the dialog box, and the controls to be created in the dialog box. Each control has a unique ID that enables you to manipulate that control and to receive its notifications. After you have defined a dialog box template, you can use it to create a dialog box in your application.

## Executing a Dialog Box

A dialog box can be either modal or modeless. A *modal* dialog box stops the rest of the application until it is closed. A *modeless* dialog box executes independently of the rest of the application. This chapter examines only modal dialog boxes.

OWL provides the TDialog class, which encapsulates the concept of a dialog box. You will derive a new class from the class TDialog to encapsulate your dialog box, as seen here:

```
class ExampleDialog : public TDialog
{
    public:
            ExampleDialog( TWindow *parent, TResId resId );
            ~ExampleDialog();
};
```

In this derived class, you handle any events related to the dialog box controls and window. The derived class is also used to set up automatic data transfer, which is discussed in the next section.

After you have defined this new class, instantiate it using the resource ID of the dialog box template. You then use the class variable to actually execute the dialog box. Program execution continues with the statement after the Execute statement. Execute returns a value from the dialog box which indicates how the dialog box was closed.

```
ExampleDialog     exampleDialog( this, "DIALOG_EXAMPLE" );
return_value = exampleDialog.Execute();
```

This dialog class is minimal because it uses OWL's automatic data transfer.

## Automatic Dialog Box Data Transfer

OWL gives you a simple way to automatically transfer data to and from the controls in a dialog box. This data transfer is very simple to set up. The first step in the process is to define a structure that includes a field for each control in the dialog box. The structure shown here defines fields for two controls—an edit control and a check box.

```
struct DataTransferStruct
{
    char      editControl[1024];
    WORD      checkBox;
} DialogTransferBuffer;
```

The field for the edit control is a character buffer used to hold the text of the edit control. The field for the check box is a WORD which contains either MF_CHECKED or

MF_UNCHECKED. This buffer variable must be accessible by both the dialog box and the function executing the dialog box.

After you have a buffer variable, you define the data transfer within the dialog box class constructor, as seen below. You must create an interface object for each control involved in the data transfer. You do not need to save the pointers to these classes, unless you are going to manipulate the controls directly.

```
ExampleDialog::ExampleDialog( TWindow *parent, TResId resId )
    : TDialog( parent, resId )
{
    new TEdit( this, IDD_EDITBOX, 1024 );
    new TCheckBox( this, IDD_CAPTION );

    DialogTransferBuffer.editControl[0] = '\0';
    DialogTransferBuffer.checkBox = BF_UNCHECKED;

    SetTransferBuffer( &DialogTransferBuffer );
}
```

You can either initialize the data transfer structure in the constructor or before you get to the constructor. The member function SetTransferBuffer accepts a pointer to the transfer structure and turns the automatic data transfer on. When the interface element is constructed, the data in the transfer structure will be used to initialize the control elements. When the dialog box is destroyed, the data in the control elements will be saved in the transfer structure.

## Example

This example program has a menu item which executes a dialog box. It uses automatic data transfer to initialize the dialog box controls, and to return the values from them.

If you press the OK button to exit the dialog box, the final values of the dialog box controls are displayed in a series of message boxes. The source code is given in listing 39.9. The header file is shown in listing 39.10 and the resource definition file in listing 39.11.

### Listing 39.9. Dialog Box Example Code

```
//
// C39DIALG.CPP
//          demonstration of OWL dialog box processing
//

// OWL include files
#include    <owl\applicat.h>
#include <owl\framewin.h>
#include <owl\dc.h>
#include <owl\menu.h>
```

*continues*

**Listing 39.9. Continued**

```
#include <owl\dialog.h>
#include <owl\edit.h>
#include <owl\checkbox.h>

// Borland C++ include files
#include     <time.h>

// Local include files
#include "c39dialg.h"

// define the dialog data transfer structure
struct DataTransferStruct
{
    char      editControl[1024];
    WORD      checkBox;
} DialogTransferBuffer;

// define the application class
class     DialogExerApplication : public TApplication
{
    public:
        DialogExerApplication( char far *name = 0 )
            : TApplication( name )
        {
        };
        ~DialogExerApplication()
        {
        };
        virtual void InitMainWindow( void );
};

// define the main window class
class     DialogExerWindow : public TFrameWindow
{
    public:
        DialogExerWindow( TWindow *parent, char far *WindowName )
            : TFrameWindow( parent, WindowName )
        {
        };
        ~DialogExerWindow();
        void Paint( TDC &tDC, BOOL bErase, TRect &invalidRect );
        void EvTimer( UINT TimerID );
        void EvSize( UINT sizeType, TSize &size );
        void EvDialogOpen();

        DECLARE_RESPONSE_TABLE( DialogExerWindow );
    protected:
        virtual void SetupWindow();
};
```

```
DEFINE_RESPONSE_TABLE1( DialogExerWindow, TFrameWindow )
    EV_WM_TIMER,
    EV_WM_SIZE,
    EV_COMMAND( CM_FILEEXIT, CmExit ),
    EV_COMMAND( CM_OPENDIALOG, EvDialogOpen ),
END_RESPONSE_TABLE;

// define the dialog box class
class DialogExerDialog : public TDialog
{
    public:
        DialogExerDialog( TWindow *parent, TResId resId );
        ~DialogExerDialog()
        {
        };
};

// implement the application class
void DialogExerApplication::InitMainWindow( void )
{
    SetMainWindow( new DialogExerWindow( 0, "Dialog Box Example" ) );
    GetMainWindow()->AssignMenu( "DIALOG_MENU" );
}

// implement the main window class
DialogExerWindow::~DialogExerWindow()
{
    KillTimer( 1 );
};

void DialogExerWindow::SetupWindow()
{
    UINT TimerId = SetTimer( 1, 1000 );
    if ( TimerId != 1 )
        MessageBox( "Error Creating Timer", "C38EVENT" );
}

#pragma argsused
void DialogExerWindow::Paint( TDC &tDC, BOOL bErase, TRect &invalidRect )
{
    TRect        ClientArea;
    time_t    CurrentTime;
    char        *TimeString;

    time( &CurrentTime );
    TimeString = ctime( &CurrentTime );
    TimeString[ 24 ] = '\0';

    GetClientRect( ClientArea );

    tDC.SetTextAlign( TA_CENTER );
```

*continues*

**Listing 39.9. Continued**

```
        tDC.TextOut( ClientArea.Width() / 2, ClientArea.Height() / 2,
        ➥ TimeString  );
    }

    #pragma argsused
    void DialogExerWindow::EvTimer( UINT TimerID )
    {
        Invalidate( FALSE );
        UpdateWindow();
    }

    #pragma argsused
    void DialogExerWindow::EvSize( UINT sizeType, TSize &size )
    {
        Invalidate();
        UpdateWindow();
    }

    void DialogExerWindow::EvDialogOpen()
    {
        DialogExerDialog     exmpleDialog( this, "DIALOG_EXAMPLE" );
        if ( exmpleDialog.Execute() == IDOK )
        {
            MessageBox( DialogTransferBuffer.editControl, "Dialog Results" );
            if ( DialogTransferBuffer.checkBox == BF_CHECKED )
                MessageBox( "Caption CheckBox was checked", "Dialog Results" );
            else
                MessageBox( "Caption CheckBox was not checked",
                ➥"Dialog Results" );
        }
    }

    // implement the dialog class
    DialogExerDialog::DialogExerDialog( TWindow *parent, TResId resId )
        : TDialog( parent, resId )
    {
        new TEdit( this, IDD_EDITBOX, 1024 );
        new TCheckBox( this, IDD_CAPTION );

        DialogTransferBuffer.editControl[0] = '\0';
        DialogTransferBuffer.checkBox = BF_UNCHECKED;

        SetTransferBuffer( &DialogTransferBuffer );
    }

    // the program starts here
    #pragma argsused
```

```
int OwlMain( int argc, char *argv[] )
{
    DialogExerApplication     *theApp;

    theApp = new DialogExerApplication();

    return theApp->Run();
}
```

## Listing 39.10. Dialog Box Example Header File

```
//
//      C39DIALG.H
//

#ifndef     _C39DIALG_H
#define     _C39DIALG_H

// define constants for the menu
#define     CM_FILEEXIT          24338
#define     CM_OPENDIALOG     101

// define constants for the dialog box
#define IDD_EDITBOX     101
#define IDD_CAPTION     102

#endif
```

## Listing 39.11. Dialog Box Example Resource Definition

```
/*
    C39DIALG.RC
        resource definition for dialog example
*/

#include "c39dialg.h"

DIALOG_MENU MENU
{
 POPUP "&File"
 {
  MENUITEM "E&xit", CM_FILEEXIT
 }

 POPUP "&Dialog Test"
 {
  MENUITEM "&Open Dialog Box", CM_OPENDIALOG
 }

}
```

*continues*

**Listing 39.11. Continued**

```
DIALOG_EXAMPLE DIALOG 7, 19, 152, 111
STYLE DS_MODALFRAME | WS_POPUP | WS_VISIBLE | WS_CAPTION | WS_SYSMENU
CAPTION "Dialog Box Example"
FONT 8, "MS Sans Serif"
{
 LTEXT "Enter value:", -1, 23, 20, 42, 8
 EDITTEXT IDD_EDITBOX, 71, 18, 57, 12
 CHECKBOX "Turn off captions", IDD_CAPTION, 40, 43, 71, 12,
 ➥BS_AUTOCHECKBOX | WS_TABSTOP
 PUSHBUTTON "OK", IDOK, 50, 81, 50, 14
}
```

The main window created by this application is shown in figure 39.8. The dialog box is shown in figure 39.9.

**Figure 39.8.**

The main window created by the dialog box example program.

**Figure 39.9.**

The dialog box created by this example program.

## Summary

This chapter covered many of OWL's features. You learned how to add menus, controls, control bars, and status bars to your OWL windows. Finally, you learned how to add dialog boxes to your applications.

This section just touched the surface of the numerous features that Borland's ObjectWindows Library gives you. With this background, you should be able to continue developing better Windows applications faster using OWL!

# Review Questions

**1.** What are the IDs of menu items, controls, and gadgets used for?

**2.** When should you add a menu to a main window?

**3.** What are dialog boxes used for?

**4.** What type of window can a gadget window be inserted into?

**5.** When do you instantiate control interface objects to allow for automatic creation of the interface elements?

**6.** How do you run a modal dialog box?

**7.** When do you need to save a pointer to a dialog box control's interface object?

**8.** What is automatic data transfer used for?

# Review Exercises

**1.** Define a dialog box class and dialog template that will allow the user to enter the following data:

```
char    name[40];
char    address[40];
char    city[20];
char    state[3];
char    zip[6];
```

The dialog box should allow for automatic data transfer.

**2.** Define a main window class and a client window class with the following features:

♦ A menu bar that enables you to exit the program and open a dialog box.

♦ A control bar that includes buttons for each menu command.

♦ A status bar that tracks the menu item and gadget selections.

**3.** Write a complete OWL application that uses the classes defined in exercises 1 and 2. This application should allow the user to enter names and addresses, and should then save these fields in a text file.

# Part X

*Appendixes*

# Memory Addressing, Binary, and Hexadecimal Review

You do not have to understand the concepts in this appendix to become well versed in C++. The only way you can master C++, however, is to spend some time learning about the "behind the scenes" roles played by binary numbers. The material presented here is not difficult, but many programmers do not take the time to study it. Hence, only a handful of C++ masters learn this material and understand how C++ works "under the hood," and others will never be as expert in the language as they could be.

Take the time to learn about addressing, binary numbers, and hexadecimal numbers. These fundamental principles are presented here for your benefit. Although a working knowledge of C++ is possible without understanding them, this information will greatly enhance your C++ skills (and your skills in every other programming language).

After reading this appendix, you will better understand why different C++ data types hold different ranges of numbers. You also will see the importance of being able to represent hexadecimal numbers in C++, and you will better understand C++ array and pointer addressing.

## Computer Memory

Each memory location inside your computer holds a single character called a *byte*. A byte is any character, whether it is a letter of the alphabet, a digit, or a special character such as a period, question mark, or even a space (a blank character). If your computer contains 640K of memory, it can hold a total of approximately 640,000 bytes of memory. This means that when you fill your computer's memory with 640K, you have no room for an additional character unless you overwrite something else.

Before describing the physical layout of your computer's memory, it may be best to take a detour and explain what 640K means.

## Memory and Disk Measurements

K means approximately 1,000 and exactly 1,024.

By appending the *K* (from the metric word *kilo*) to memory measurements, the manufacturers of computers do not have to attach as many zeros to the end of numbers for disk and memory storage. The K stands for approximately 1,000 bytes. As you are about to see, almost everything inside your computer is based on a power of 2. Therefore, the K of computer memory measurements actually equals the power of 2 closest to 1,000, which is two to the tenth power, or 1,024. Because 1,024 is very close to 1,000, computerists often think of K as meaning 1,000, even though they know it equals *approximately* 1,000.

Think for a moment what 640K exactly equals. Practically speaking, 640K is about 640,000 bytes. To be exact, however, 640K equals 640 times 1,024, or 655,360. This explains why the PC DOS command CHKDSK returns 655,360 as your total memory (assuming that you have 640K of RAM) rather than 640,000.

Because extended memory and many disk drives can hold such a large amount of data (typically several million characters), an additional memory measurement shortcut is used, called *M*, which stands for *meg*, or *megabytes*. The M is a shortcut for approximately one million bytes. Therefore, 20M is approximately 20,000,000 characters, or bytes, of storage. As with K, the M literally stands for 1,048,576 because that is the closest power of 2 (2 to the 20th power) to one million.

How many bytes of storage is 60 megabytes? It is approximately 60 million characters, or 62,914,560 characters, to be exact.

## Memory Addresses

Like each house in your town, each memory location in your computer has a unique *address*. A memory address is simply a sequential number, starting at zero, that labels each memory location. Figure A.1 shows a diagram of how your computer's memory addresses are numbered if you have 640K of RAM.

**Figure A.1.**

Memory addresses for a 640K computer.

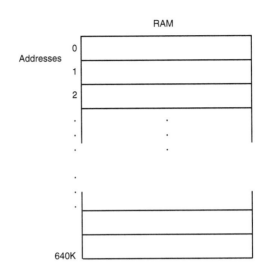

By using unique addresses, your computer keeps track of memory. When the computer stores a result of a calculation in memory, it finds an empty address, or one matching the data area where the result is to go, and stores the result at that address.

Your C++ programs and data share computer memory with DOS. DOS must always reside in memory while you operate your computer; otherwise, your programs would have no way to access disks, printers, the screen, or the keyboard. Figure A.2 shows computer memory being shared by DOS and a C++ program. The exact amount of memory taken by DOS and a C++ program is determined by the version of DOS you use, how many DOS extras (such as device drivers and buffers) your computer uses, and the size and needs of your C++ program and data.

**Figure A.2.**

DOS, your C++ program, and your program's data share the same memory.

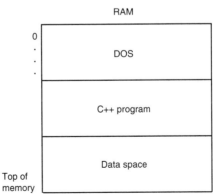

# Bits and Bytes

You now know that a single address of memory might contain any character, called a byte. You know that your computer holds many bytes of information, but it does not store those characters in the same way that humans think of characters. For example, if you press the letter W on your keyboard while working in your C++ editor, you see the W on the screen, and you also know that the W is stored in a memory location at some unique address. Actually, your computer does not store the letter W; it stores electrical impulses that stand for the letter W.

Electricity, which is what runs through the components of your computer to make it understand and execute your programs, can exist in only two states: on and off. As with a light bulb, electricity is either flowing (it is on) or not flowing (it is off). Even though you can dim some lights, the electricity is still either on or off.

Today's modern digital computers use this on/off concept. Your computer is nothing more than millions of on and off switches. You may have heard about integrated circuits, transistors, and even vacuum tubes that computers over the years have contained. These electrical components are nothing more than switches that rapidly turn electrical impulses on and off.

This two-state (on and off) mode of electricity is called a *binary* state of electricity. Computer people use a 1 to represent an on state (a switch in the computer that is on) and a 0 to represent an off state (a switch that is off). These numbers, 1 and 0, are called binary digits. The term *binary digits* is usually shortened to *bits*. A bit is either a 1 or a 0, representing an on or off state of electricity. Different combinations of bits represent different characters.

The binary digits 1 and 0 (called bits) represent on and off states of electricity.

Several years ago, someone listed every single character that might be represented on a computer, including all uppercase letters, all lowercase letters, the digits 0 through 9, the many other characters (such as %, *, {, and +), and some special control characters. When you add up the total number of characters that a PC can represent, you get 256. These are listed in Appendix C's ASCII (pronounced "ask-ee") table.

The order of the ASCII table's 256 characters is basically arbitrary, just as radio's Morse code table is arbitrary. With Morse code, different sets of long and short beeps represent different letters of the alphabet. In the ASCII table, a different combination of bits (1s and 0s strung together) represents each of the 256 ASCII characters. The ASCII table is a standard table used by almost every PC in the world. Its letters form the acronym for *American Standard Code for Information Interchange*. (Some minicomputers and mainframes use a similar table, called the EBCDIC table.)

If you take every different combination of eight 0s strung together all the way to eight 1s strung together (that is, from 00000000, 00000001, 00000010, and so on, until you get to 11111110, and last, 11111111), you will have a total of 256 of them! (256 is 2 to the 8th power.) Each memory location in your computer holds eight bits each.

These bits can be any combination of eight 1s and 0s. This brings you to the following fundamental rule of computers:

Because it takes a combination of eight 1s and 0s to represent a character, and because each byte of computer memory can hold exactly one character, it holds true that eight bits equal one byte.

For a better perspective on this, consider that the bit pattern needed for the uppercase letter A is 01000001. No other character in the ASCII table "looks" like this to the computer because each of the 256 characters is assigned a unique bit pattern.

Suppose that you press the A key on your keyboard. Your keyboard does *not* send a letter A to the computer; instead, it looks in its ASCII table for the on and off states of electricity that represent the letter A. As Figure A.3 shows, when you press the A key, the keyboard actually sends 01000001 (as on and off impulses) to the computer. Your computer simply stores this bit pattern for A in a memory location. Even though you can think of the memory location as holding an A, it really holds the byte 01000001.

**Figure A.3.**

Your computer keeps track of characters by their bit patterns.

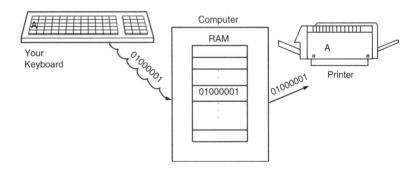

If you were to print that A, your computer does not send an A to the printer but sends the 01000001 bit pattern for an A. The printer receives that bit pattern, looks up the correct letter in the ASCII table, and prints an A.

From the time you press the A until the time you see it on the printer, it is *not* the letter A! It is the ASCII pattern of bits the computer uses to represent an A. Because a computer is electrical and electricity is easily turned on and off, this is a very nice way for the computer to manipulate and move characters, and it can do so very quickly. Actually, if it were up to the computer, you would enter everything by its bit pattern and look at all the results in their bit patterns! This would not be good, so devices such as the keyboard, screen, and printer work part of the time with letters as we know them. That is why the ASCII table is such an integral part of a computer.

At times, your computer treats two bytes as a single value. Even though memory locations are typically eight bits wide, many CPUs access memory two bytes at a time. In that case, the two bytes are called a *word* of memory. On other computers (commonly mainframes), the word size may be four bytes (32 bits) or even eight bytes (64 bits).

---

**A Summary of Bits and Bytes**

A bit is either a 1 or a 0 that represents an on or off state of electricity.

Eight bits represent a byte.

A byte, or eight bits, represents one character.

Each memory location of your computer is eight bits (a single byte) wide. Therefore, each memory location can hold one character of data. A list of all possible characters can be found in the ASCII table in Appendix C.

If the CPU accesses memory two bytes at a time, those two bytes are called a word of memory.

---

# The Order of Bits

To further understand memory, you should know how programmers refer to individual bits. Figure A.4 shows a byte and a two-byte word. Notice that the far right bit is called bit 0. From bit 0, keep counting by 1s as you move left. For a byte, the bits are numbered 0 to 7, from right to left. For a double byte (a 16-bit word), the bits are numbered from 0 to 15, from right to left.

Bit 0 is called the *least-significant bit*, or sometimes the *low-order bit*. Bit 7 (or bit 15 for a 2-byte word) is called the *most-significant bit*, or sometimes the *high-order bit*.

**Figure A.4.**

The order of bits in a byte and a two-byte word.

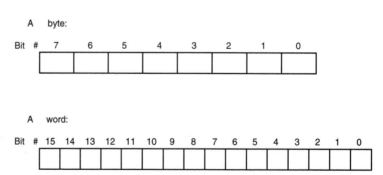

# Binary Numbers

Because a computer works best with 1s and 0s, its internal numbering method is limited to a *base-2* (binary) numbering system. People work in a *base-10* numbering system in the real world. The base-10 numbering system is sometimes called the decimal numbering system. There are always as many different digits as the base in a numbering system. For example, the base-10 system has ten digits, 0 through 9. As soon as you count to 9 and run out of digits, you have to combine some that you already used. The number 10 is a representation of 10 values, but combines the digits 1 and 0.

The same is true of base-2. Base-2 has only two digits, 0 and 1. As soon as you run out of digits, after the second one, you have to reuse digits. The first seven binary numbers are

0       1     10     11     100     101     110

If you do not understand how these numbers were derived, that is OK; you will see in a moment. For the time being, realize that no more than two digits, 0 and 1, can be used to represent any base-2 number, just as no more than 10 digits, 0 through 9, can be used to represent any base-10 number in the regular "real world" numbering system.

You should know that a base-10 number, such as 2,981, does not really mean anything by itself. You must assume what base it is. You get very used to working with base-10 numbers because that is what the world uses. However, the number 2,981 actually represents a quantity based on powers of 10. For example, figure A.5 shows what the number 2,981 represents. Notice that each digit in the number stands for a certain number of a power of 10.

**Figure A.5.**

The base-10 breakdown of the number 2,981.

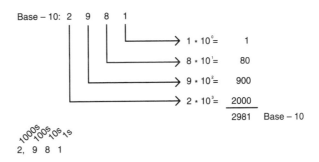

This same concept applies when you work in a base-2 numbering system. Your computer uses this numbering system, so the power of 2 is just as common to your computer as the power of 10 is to you. The only difference is that the digits in a base-2 number represent powers of 2 and not powers of 10. Figure A.6 shows what the binary numbers 10101 and 10011110 are in base-10. This is how you convert any binary number to its base-10 equivalent.

## Figure A.6.

The base-2 breakdown of the numbers 10101 and 10011110.

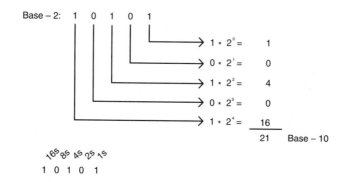

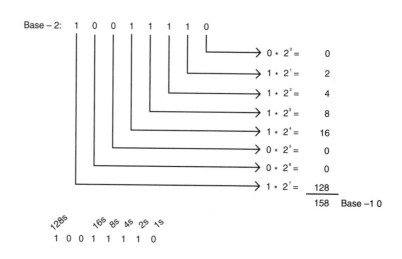

A binary number can contain only the digits 1 and 0.

A base-2 number contains only 1s and 0s. To convert any base-2 number to base-10, add each power of 2 everywhere a 1 appears in the number. The base-2 number 101 represents the base-10 number 5; there are two 1s in the number—one in the 2 to the 0th power (which equals 1), and one in the 2 to the 2nd power (which equals 4). Table A.1 shows the first 17 base-10 numbers and their matching base-2 numbers.

### Table A.1. The first 17 base-10 (decimal) and base-2 (binary) numbers.

| Base-10 | Base-2 | Base-10 | Base-2 |
|---------|--------|---------|--------|
| 0 | 0 | 9 | 1001 |
| 1 | 1 | 10 | 1010 |

| Base-10 | Base-2 | Base-10 | Base-2 |
|---------|--------|---------|--------|
| 2 | 10 | 11 | 1011 |
| 3 | 11 | 12 | 1100 |
| 4 | 100 | 13 | 1101 |
| 5 | 101 | 14 | 1110 |
| 6 | 110 | 15 | 1111 |
| 7 | 111 | 16 | 10000 |
| 8 | 1000 | 17 | 10001 |

You do not have to memorize this table; you should be able to figure the base-10 numbers from their matching binary numbers by adding the powers of 2 over each 1 (on bit). Many programmers do memorize the first several binary numbers, however, which comes in handy in advanced programming techniques.

What is the largest binary number a byte can hold? The answer is all 1s, or 11111111. If you add the first eight powers of 2, you get 255.

A byte holds either a number or an ASCII character, depending on how it is accessed. For example, if you were to convert the base-2 number 01000001 to a base-10 number, you would get 65. However, this also happens to be the ASCII bit pattern for an uppercase letter A. Check out the ASCII table, and you see that the A is ASCII code 65. Because the ASCII table is so closely linked with the bit patterns, the computer knows (by the context of how they are used) to work with a number 65 or a letter A.

Unlike an ASCII character, a binary number is not limited to a byte. Sixteen or 32 bits at a time can represent a binary number (and usually do). There are more powers of 2 to add when converting that number to a base-10 number, but the process is the same. By now, you can figure out (although it may take a little time to calculate) that 1010101010101010 is 43,690 in the base-10 decimal numbering system.

To convert from decimal to binary takes a little more effort. Luckily, you rarely need to convert in that direction. Converting from base-2 to base-10 is not covered here.

## Binary Arithmetic

At their lowest level, computers can only add and convert binary numbers to their negative equivalents. Computers are not truly able to subtract, multiply, and divide, although they simulate these operations through judicious use of the addition and negative-conversion techniques.

If a computer were to add the numbers 7 and 6 (it can do so at the binary level), the result is 13. If the computer is instructed to subtract 7 from 13, it cannot do so. However, it can take the negative value of 7 and add that to 13. Because –7 plus 13 equals 6, the result is a simulated subtraction.

To multiply, computers perform repeated addition. To multiply 6 by 7, the computer adds seven 6s together and gets 42 as the answer. To divide 42 by 7, a computer keeps subtracting 7 from 42 repeatedly until it gets to a 0 answer (or less than 0 if there is a remainder), and then counts the number of times it took to reach 0.

All math is done at the binary level, so the following additions are possible in binary arithmetic:

```
0 + 0 = 0
0 + 1 = 1
1 + 0 = 1
1 + 1 = 10
```

Because these are binary numbers, the last result is not the number 10, but the binary number 2. (Just as the binary 10 means "no ones, and carry an additional power of two," the decimal number 10 means "no ones, carry a power of ten.") There is no binary digit to represent a 2, so you have to combine the 1 and the 0 to form the new number.

Because binary addition is the foundation of all other math, you should learn how to add binary numbers. You will then understand how computers do the rest of their arithmetic.

Using the binary addition rules previously shown, consider the following binary calculation:

```
  01000001    (65 decimal)
 +00101100    (44 decimal)
  01101101    (109 decimal)
```

The first number, 01000001, is 65 decimal. This also happens to be the bit pattern for the ASCII A, but if you add with it, the computer knows to interpret it as the number 65 rather than the character A.

The following binary addition requires a carry into bit 4 and bit 6:

```
  00101011    (43 decimal)
 +00100111    (39 decimal)
  01010010    (82 decimal)
```

Typically, you have to ignore bits that carry past bit 7, or bit 15 for double-byte arithmetic. For example, both of the following binary additions produce incorrect positive results:

| | | | |
|---|---|---|---|
| 10000000 | (128 decimal) | 1000000000000000 | (65536 decimal) |
| +10000000 | (128 decimal) | +1000000000000000 | (65536 decimal) |
| 00000000 | (0 decimal) | 0000000000000000 | (0 decimal!) |

There is no 9th or 17th bit for the carry, so both these additions produce incorrect results. Because the byte and 16-bit word cannot hold the answers, the magnitude of both these additions is not possible. The computer must be programmed at the bit level to perform *multiword arithmetic*, which is beyond the scope of this book.

## Binary Negative Numbers

Because subtracting requires understanding binary negative numbers, you need to learn how computers represent them. The computer uses 2's *complement* to represent negative numbers in binary form. To convert a binary number to its 2's complement (to its negative), you must do the following:

**1.** Reverse the bits (the 1s to 0s, and the 0s to 1s).

**2.** Add 1.

Negative binary numbers are stored in their 2's complement format.

This may seem a little strange at first, but it works very well for binary numbers. To represent a binary −65, you need to take the binary 65 and convert it to its 2's complement, such as

| | |
|---|---|
| 01000001 | (65 decimal) |
| 10111110 | (Reverse the bits) |
| +1 | (Add 1) |
| 10111111 | (−65 binary) |

By converting the 65 to its 2's complement, you produce −65 in binary. You might wonder what makes 10111111 mean the negative 65, but by the 2's complement definition, it means −65.

If you were told that 10111111 is a negative number, how would you know which binary number it is? You perform the 2's complement on it. Whatever number you produce is the positive of that negative number. Note the following example:

| | |
|---|---|
| 10111111 | (−65 decimal) |
| 01000000 | (Reverse the bits) |
| +1 | (Add 1) |
| 01000001 | (65 decimal) |

Something might seem wrong at this point. You just saw that 10111111 is the binary −65, but isn't 10111111 *also* 191 decimal (adding the powers of 2 marked by the 1s in the number, as explained in a previous section)? It depends on whether the number is *signed* or *unsigned*. If a number is signed, the computer looks at the most-significant bit (the leftmost bit), called the *sign bit*. If the most-significant bit is a 1, the number is negative. If it is 0, the number is positive.

Most numbers are 16 bits in length. That is, two-byte words are used to store most integers. This is not always the case for all computers, but it is true for most PCs.

In the C++ programming language, you can designate numbers as either signed integers or unsigned integers (they are signed by default if you do not specify otherwise). If you designate a variable as a signed integer, the computer interprets the high-order bit as a sign bit. If the high-order bit is on (1), the number is negative. If the high-order bit is off (0), the number is positive. If, however, you designate a variable as an unsigned integer, the computer uses the high-order bit as just another power of 2. That is why the range of unsigned integer variables goes higher (generally from 0 to 65536, but it depends on the computer) than for signed integer variables (generally from −32768 to +32767).

After so much description, a little review is in order. Assume that the following 16-bit binary numbers are unsigned:

```
0011010110100101    1001100110101010    1000000000000000
```

These numbers are unsigned, so bit 15 is not the sign bit, but just another power of 2. You should practice converting these large 16-bit numbers to decimal. The decimal equivalents are

```
13733      39338      32768
```

If, however, these numbers are signed numbers, the high-order bit (bit 15) indicates the sign. If the sign bit is 0, the number is positive, and you convert the numbers to decimal in the usual manner. If the sign bit is 1, you must convert the numbers to their 2's complement to find what they equal. Their decimal equivalents are

```
+13733      −26197      −32768
```

To compute the last two binary numbers to their decimal equivalents, take their 2's complement and convert it to decimal. Put a minus sign in front of the result, and you find what the original number represents.

**Tip:** To make sure that you convert a number to its 2's complement correctly, you can add the 2's complement to its original positive value. If the answer is 0 (ignoring the extra carry to the left), you know that the 2's complement number is correct. This is just like saying that decimal opposites, such as −72 + 72, add up to zero.

# Hexadecimal Numbers

All those 1s and 0s are confusing to people. If it were up to your computer, you would enter *everything* as 1s and 0s! This is unacceptable because people don't like to keep track of all those 1s and 0s. Therefore, a *hexadecimal* numbering system (sometimes called *hex*) was devised. The hexadecimal numbering system is based on base-16 numbers. As with other bases, 16 unique digits are in the base-16 numbering system. Here are the first 19 hexadecimal numbers:

| 0 | 1 | 2 | 3 | 4 | 5 | 6 | 7 | 8 | 9 | A | B | C | D | E | F | 10 | 11 | 12 |

Hexadecimal numbers use 16 unique digits, 0 through F.

Because there are only 10 unique digits as we know them (0 through 9), we must use the letters A through F to represent the remaining six digits. (Anything could have been used, but the designers of the hexadecimal numbering system decided to use the first six letters of the alphabet.)

To understand base-16 numbers, you should know how to convert them to base-10, so that they represent numbers people are familiar with. You perform the conversion to base-10 from base-16 in the same way that you did with base-2, but instead of representing powers of 2, each hexadecimal digit represents powers of 16. Figure A.7 shows how to convert the number 3C5 to decimal.

**Figure A.7.**

Converting hexadecimal 3C5 to its decimal equivalent.

Base –16:   3   C   5

$$5 * 16^0 = 5 * 1 = 5$$
$$C * 16^1 = 12 * 16 = 192$$
$$3 * 16^2 = 3 * 256 = 768$$
$$965 \quad \text{Base –10}$$

256s  16s  1s
3  C  5

**Tip:** Calculators are available for programmers to do conversions between numbers in base-16, base-10, and base-2, as well as perform 2's complement arithmetic.

You ought to be able to convert 2B to its decimal 43 equivalent and convert E1 to decimal 225 in the same manner. Table A.2 shows the first 20 decimal, binary, and hexadecimal numbers.

**Table A.2. The first 20 base-10 (decimal), base-2 (binary), and base-16 (hexadecimal) numbers.**

| Base-10 | Base-2 | Base-16 | Base-10 | Base-2 | Base-16 |
|---------|--------|---------|---------|--------|---------|
| 1 | 1 | 1 | 11 | 1011 | B |
| 2 | 10 | 2 | 12 | 1100 | C |

*continues*

**Table A.2. Continued**

| Base-10 | Base-2 | Base-16 | Base-10 | Base-2 | Base-16 |
| --- | --- | --- | --- | --- | --- |
| 3 | 11 | 3 | 13 | 1101 | D |
| 4 | 100 | 4 | 14 | 1110 | E |
| 5 | 101 | 5 | 15 | 1111 | F |
| 6 | 110 | 6 | 16 | 10000 | 10 |
| 7 | 111 | 7 | 17 | 10001 | 12 |
| 8 | 1000 | 8 | 18 | 10010 | 13 |
| 9 | 1001 | 9 | 19 | 10011 | 14 |
| 10 | 1010 | A | 20 | 10100 | 15 |

# Why Learn Hexadecimal?

Hexadecimal notation is extremely efficient for describing memory locations and values because of its close association to the actual binary numbers your computer uses. It is much easier for you (and more important, at this level, for your *computer*) to convert from base-16 to base-2 than from base-10 to base-2. Therefore, you sometimes want to represent data at the bit level, but using hexadecimal notation is easier (and requires less typing) than using binary numbers.

To convert from hexadecimal to binary, convert each hex digit to its 4-bit binary number. You can use Table A.2 as a guide for this. For example, the hexadecimal number

```
5B75
```

can be converted to binary by taking each digit and converting it to four binary numbers. If you need leading zeros to "pad" the four digits, use them. The number becomes

```
0101 1011 0111 0101
```

It turns out that the binary number 0101101101110101 is equal to the hexadecimal number 5B75. This was much easier than converting them both to decimal first.

To convert from binary to hexadecimal, reverse this process. If you are given the binary number

```
1101000011110111111010
```

you can convert it to hexadecimal by grouping the bits into groups of four, starting with the right bit. Because there is not an even number of groups of four, pad the leftmost one with 0s. You then have the following:

```
0011 0100 0011 1101 1111 1010
```

Now you just have to convert each group of four binary digits into their hexadecimal number equivalents. You can refer to Table A.2 for help. You then get the following base-16 number:

```
343DFA
```

The C++ programming language also supports the base-8 *octal* representation of numbers. Because octal numbers are rarely used in today's computers, they are not covered here.

# How This Relates to C++

The material presented here may seem foreign to many programmers. The binary and 2's complement arithmetic reside deep in your computer and are shielded from most programmers (except assembly language programmers). Understanding this level of your computer, however, explains everything else you learn.

Many C++ programmers learn C++ before delving into binary and hexadecimal representation. For them, much about the C++ language seems strange, but could be explained very easily if they understood these basic concepts.

For example, a signed integer holds a different range of numbers from that of an unsigned integer. You now know the reason for this: the sign bit is used in two different ways, depending on whether the number is designated as signed or unsigned.

The ASCII table should make more sense to you after this discussion as well. The ASCII table is an integral part of your computer. Characters are not actually stored in memory and variables; instead, their ASCII bit patterns are. That is why C++ can move between characters and integers with ease. The following two C++ statements are allowed, although they probably would not be in another programming language:

```
char c = 65;    // Put the ASCII letter A in c
int ci = 'A';   // Put the number 65 in ci
```

The hexadecimal notation taught to many C++ programmers also makes more sense when they truly understand base-16 numbers. For example, if you saw the line

```
char a = '\x041';
```

you could convert the hex 41 to decimal (65 decimal) if you wanted to know what was really being assigned. In addition, C++ system programmers find that they can better interface with assembly language programs if they understand the concepts presented here.

If you gain even a cursory knowledge of this material at this point, you will be very much ahead of the game when you program in C++.

# Answers to Review Questions

## Chapter 1 Answers

1. Low-level languages express a problem and its solution in a language that is very close to the computer's native machine language. High-level languages allow you to express a problem and its solution in a language you can understand.

2. It has aspects of both.

3. C++ embodies some of the object-oriented model and allows the user to define data types not possible under C.

4. It offered an integrated programming environment, providing both the compiler and the source code editor in one program.

5. DOS and Windows, and Windows NT.

## Chapter 2 Answers

1. It is the set of all files and settings necessary to build executables on all of the projects that target operating systems.

2. The operating system that will run the finished program.

3. Click **Help** and then **Contents**. Or press Alt+F+C.

**4.** It means that the help screen you bring up is a response to whatever the cursor is on.

**5.** You use the shortcut keys as an alternative to having to go through the levels of menus.

**6.** It is a set of programming support tools (i.e. the editor, debugger, compiler, linker, browsers) that facilitate the development of software. They work together to speed coding and debugging.

**7.** An EasyWin target is a text application running in a window under Microsoft Windows. A DOS application runs without Microsoft windows loaded.

**8.** In the IDE, you select Project | New project. When the New Project dialog box appears, click on the Advanced button. Using the Initial Node radio buttons, select either .c or .cpp to indicate a C or C++ program, respectively.

# Chapter 3 Answers

**1.** A set of detailed instructions that tells the computer what to do.

**2.** A program editor.

**3.** .CPP

**4.** To get the errors out of your program.

**5.** False. You must compile a program before linking it. Most compilers link the program automatically.

# Chapter 4 Answers

**1.** /* before and */ after.

**2.** A holding place for data that can be changed.

**3.** A value that cannot be changed.

**4.** False

**5.** +, -, *, and /.

**6.** = (the assignment operator).

7. False. There can be floating-point and many more variable data types.

8. A variable name. By convention, constant names are entirely in uppercase.

9. All C++ reserved words must be in lowercase.

# Chapter 5 Answers

1. `my_name` and `sales_89`.

2. Characters: `'X'` and `'0'`.

   Strings: `"2.0"` and `"X"`.

   Integer: `0` and `-708`.

   Floating-point constants: -12.0 and 65.4.

3. Seven variables are declared—3 integers, 3 characters, and 1 floating-point variable.

4. A null zero, also called a binary zero.

5. True

6. 1

7. As a series of ASCII values, representing the characters and blanks in the string, ending in a binary 0.

8. As a single binary 0.

# Chapter 6 Answers

1. `char my_name[ ] = "This is C++";`

2. 11

3. 12

4. Binary zero.

5. Two character arrays are declared, each with 25 elements.

6. False. The keyword `char` must precede the variable name.

7. True. The binary zero terminates the string.

8. False. The characters do not represent a string because there is no terminating zero.

# Chapter 7 Answers

1. False. You can define constants only with the `#define` preprocessor directive.

2. `#include`

3. `#define`

4. True

5. The preprocessor changes your source code before the compiler sees the source code.

6. Use angle brackets when the include files reside in the compiler's include subdirectory. Use quotation marks when the include file resides in the same subdirectory as the source program.

7. Defined constants are easier to change because you just have to change the line with `#define`, not several other lines in the program.

8. `iostream.h`

9. False. You cannot define constants enclosed in quotation marks (as `"MESSAGE"` is in the `cout` operator).

10. Amount is 4.

# Chapter 8 Answers

1. `cout` sends output to the screen, and `cin` gets input from the keyboard.

2. The prompt informs the user of what is expected.

3. Four values will be entered.

4. The `cin` function gets its value(s) from the keyboard, and the assignment statement gets its value from data in the program.

5. The backslash, `"\"` character is special

6. The following value prints (with one leading space): 123.456.

# Chapter 9 Answers

1. **A.** 5

   **B.** 6

   **C.** 5

2. **A.** 2

   **B.** 7

3. **A.** a = (3 + 3) / (4 + 4);

   **B.** x = (a - b) * ((a - c) * (a - c));

   **C.** f = (a1 / 2) / (b1 / 3);

   **D.** d = ((8 - x * x) / (x - 9)) - ((4 * 2 - 1)
      / (x * x * x));

4. ```
   #include <iostream.h>
   #define PI 3.14159
   int  main(void)
       {
       cout << (PI * (4 * 4));
       return 0;
       }
           5.
   r = 100 % 4;
   cout << r;
   ```

# Chapter 10 Answers

1. ==

2. **A.** False

   **B.** True

   **C.** True

   **D.** True

3. True

4. The if statement determines what code executes if the relational test is true. The if-else statement determines what happens for both the true and the false relational tests.

5. No
   ```

6. **A.** True

   **B.** False

   **C.** True

# Chapter 11 Answers

1. `&&`, `¦¦`, and `!`

2. **A.** False

   **B.** False

   **C.** True

   **D.** True

3. **A.** True

   **B.** True

   **C.** True

4. g is 25 and f got changed to 35.

# Chapter 12 Answers

1. The `if-else` statement.

2. The conditional operator is the only C++ operator with three arguments.

3. ```
   if (a == b)
       ans = c + 2;
   else
       ans = c + 3;
   ```

4. True

5. The increment and decrement operators compile into single assembly instructions.

6. A comma (,) operator that forces a left-to-right execution of the statements on either side.

7. The output cannot reliably be determined. Do not pass an increment operator as an argument.

8. The size of name is 20.
   ```

# Chapter 13 Answers

1. ~, &, ^, |, &=, ^=, |=, <<, and >>

2. **A.** 1

   **B.** 1

   **C.** 0

   **D.** 0

3. True

4. The 2's complement converts a number to its negative; the 1's complement simply reverses the bit pattern.

# Chapter 14 Answers

1. The `while` loop tests for a true condition at the top of the loop, and the `do-while` loop tests at the bottom.

2. A counter variable increments by one, and a total variable increments by the addition to the total you are performing.

3. `++`

4. True. The braces are not required if the body of the loop is a single statement, but the braces are always recommended.

5. There are no braces. The second `cout` will always execute no matter what the `while` loop's relational test results in.

6. `stdlib.h`

7. One time.

8. By returning a value inside the `exit()` function's parentheses.

9. `This is the outer loop`

   `This is the outer loop`

   `This is the outer loop`

   `This is the outer loop`

10. The program could have executed a divide by zero.

# Chapter 15 Answers

1. A sequence of one or more instructions executed repeatedly.

2. False

3. A loop within a loop.

4. The expressions may be initialized elsewhere, such as before the loop or in the body of the loop.

5. The inside loop.

6.

```
10
7
4
1
```

7. True

8. The body of the `for` loop stops repeating.

9. False, because of the semicolon after the first `for` loop.

10. There is no output. The value of `start` is already less than `end` when the loop begins; therefore, the `for` loop's test is immediately false.

# Chapter 16 Answers

1. To force a program to pause.

2. Some computers are faster than others.

3. If the `continue` and `break` statements are unconditional, there would be little use for them.

4. There is no output because of the unconditional `continue` statement.

5. *****

6. A single variable rarely can hold a large enough value for the timer's count.

# Chapter 17 Answers

1. The program does not execute sequentially, as it would without `goto`.

2. The `switch` statement.

**3.** The break statement.

**4.** False

**5.**
```
switch (num)
      {
      case 1:
            cout << "Alpha";
            break;
      case 2:
            cout << "Beta";
            break;
      case 3:
            cout << "Gamma";
            break;
      default:
            cout << "Other";
   break;
    }
```

**6.**
```
do
      {
      cout << "What is your first name? ";
      cin >> name;
      }
   while ((name[ 0 ] < 'A') ¦¦ (name[ 0 ] > 'Z'));
```

# Chapter 18 Answers

**1.** True

**2.** main()

**3.** Several smaller functions, so that each function performs a single task.

**4.** Function names always end with a set of parentheses.

**5.** By putting separating comments between functions.

**6.** The function sq_25() cannot be nested within calc_it().

**7.** A function call.

## Chapter 19 Answers

1. True

2. A local variable is passed as an argument.

3. False

4. The variable data types.

5. Static

6. You should never pass global variables; they do not need to be passed.

## Chapter 20 Answers

1. Arrays are always passed by address.

2. Nonarray variables are always passed by value (unless you override the default with & before each variable name).

3. True

4. No

5. Yes

6. The data types of variables x, y, and z are not declared in the receiving parameter list.

7. C

## Chapter 21 Answers

1. By putting the return type to the left of the function name.

2. One

3. To prototype library functions.

4. `int`

5. False

6. Prototypes ensure that the correct number and type of parameters are being passed.

7. Global variables are known across functions already.

8. The return type is float. Three parameters are being passed—a character, an integer, and a floating-point variable.

# Chapter 22 Answers

1. To achieve portability between different computers.

2. False. The standard output can be redirected to any device through the operating system.

3. `get()` assumes `stdin` for the input device.

4. `cout`

5. False. The input from `get()` goes to a buffer as you type it.

6. <Enter>

# Chapter 23 Answers

1. The character-testing functions do not change the characters passed to them.

2. `floor()` rounds down, and `ceil()` rounds up.

3. False (the inner function returns 1).

4. `ParkerPeter`

5. `8 9`

6. True

7. True

# Chapter 24 Answers

1. False

2. The array subscripts differentiate array elements from one another.

3. C++ does not initialize or zero-out arrays for you automatically.

4. `0`

5. Yes. All arrays are passed by address because an array name is nothing more than an address to that array.

6. C++ initializes all global variables (and every other static variable in your program) to zero or null zero.

## Chapter 25 Answers

1. False

2. From the low numbers "floating" to the top of the array like bubbles.

3. Ascending order.

4. The name of an array is an address to the starting element of that array.

5. **A.** Eagles

   **B.** Rams

   **C.** les

   **D.** E

   **E.** E

   **F.** s

   **G.** g

## Chapter 26 Answers

1. `int scores[ 5 ][ 6 ];`

2. `char initials[ 4 ][ 10 ][ 20 ]`

3. The first subscript represents rows, and the last subscript represents columns.

4. 30

5. **A.** 2

   **B.** 1

   **C.** 91

   **D.** 8

6. **A.** 78

   **B.** 100

   **C.** 90

# Chapter 27 Answers

1. **A.** Integer pointer.

   **B.** Character pointer.

   **C.** Floating-point pointer.

2. Address of.

3. *

4. `pt_sal = &salary;`

5. False

6. Yes

7. **A.** 2313.54

   **B.** 2313.54

   **C.** Invalid

   **D.** Invalid

8. B

# Chapter 28 Answers

1. Array names are pointer constants, not pointer variables.

2. Four

3. A, B, C, D, and E. (Parentheses are needed around `iptr + 4` to make F valid.)

4. You just have to move pointers, not entire strings.

5. A, B, and D.

# Chapter 29 Answers

1. Structures hold groups of more than one value, each of which can be a different data type.

2. Members

3. At declaration time and at runtime.

4. Structures are passed by copy.

5. False. Memory is reserved only when structure variables are declared.

6. Globally

7. Locally, in most cases.

8. Four

# Chapter 30 Answers

1. True

2. Arrays are easier to manage.

3. **A.** `inventory[32].price = 12.33;`

   **B.** `inventory[11].part_no[0] = 'X';`

   **C.** `inventory[96] = inventory[62];`

4. **A.** `item` is not a structure variable.

   **B.** `inventory` is an array and must have a subscript.

   **C.** the subscript must precede the `(.)`.

# Chapter 31 Answers

1. Write, append, and read.

2. Disks hold more data than can fit in memory.

3. You can access sequential files only in the order in which they were originally written.

4. An error condition occurs.

5. The old file is overwritten.

6. The file is created.

7. The `eof()` function returns true when an end-of-file condition is met.

# Chapter 32 Answers

1. Records are stored in files, and structures are stored in memory.

2. False

3. The file pointer continually updates to point to the next byte to read.

4. `write()` and `read()`

5. `rewind()` and `seekg(0, beg);`

6. `beg` (or 0), `cur` (or 1), and `end` (or 2).

7. No file name is specified.

# Chapter 33 Answers

1. More realistic designs, better code encapsulation for easier debugging, more code reuse capabilities.

2. Classes

3. data members and member functions.

4. No, the compiler will create a default constructor.

5. Yes, by changing the argument signatures.

6. No, you only need to define a destructor if it has specific things to do. The compiler will create a default destructor.

7. You add the default value to the member function declaration. For example, `void MFunc( int arg1 = 5 );`.

# Chapter 34 Answers

1. Private

2. By adding the Public: label to the class definition before the member function.

3. The public member functions that are available to users of the object.

4. To enforce data hiding and encapsulation.

# Chapter 35 Answers

1. Inheritance is the ability to derive a class from a base class and use the base class's data members and member functions as if they were defined in the derived class.

2. Inheritance is implemented in the class definition statement. For example, `class Dclass : public Bclass.`

3. Base class constructors are executed first and then the derived class's constructor.

4. By defining a member function in the derived class with the same return type and argument list signature.

5. To be able to use the functionality already built into the base class. This allows better code reuse.

# Chapter 36 Answers

1. Polymorphism allows you to deal with an object as a pointer to its base class.

2. Virtual functions.

3. The proper derived class's member function is executed.

4. To be able to write code that does not depend of the type of object being manipulated.

# Chapter 37 Answers

1. A set of classes that makes it easier to develop applications for Microsoft Windows.

2. TApplication

3. TFrameWindow

4. To give the application a single place to be able to update its screen.

# Chapter 38 Answers

1. TApplication

2. InitMainWindow()

3. To create an interface object's interface elements.

4. The event response table.

5. By creating their interface objects in the parent class's constructor.

# Chapter 39 Answers

1. To uniquely define the control that is creating the event.

2. In `InitMainWindow()`

3. To allow the user to enter data

4. `TDecoratedFrame`

5. In the constructor of the parent window.

6. With its `Execute()` member function.

7. If you want to be able to access the dialog box's controls.

8. To allow the controls of a dialog to be automatically initialized and automatically return the final values of the controls.

# ASCII Table

(Including IBM Extended Character Codes)

| Dec $X_{10}$ | Hex $X_{16}$ | Binary $X_2$ | ASCII Character | Ctrl | Key |
|---|---|---|---|---|---|
| 000 | 00 | 0000 0000 | null | NUL | ^@ |
| 001 | 01 | 0000 0001 | ☺ | SOH | ^A |
| 002 | 02 | 0000 0010 | ● | STX | ^B |
| 003 | 03 | 0000 0011 | ♥ | ETX | ^C |
| 004 | 04 | 0000 0100 | ◆ | EOT | ^D |
| 005 | 05 | 0000 0101 | ♣ | ENQ | ^E |
| 006 | 06 | 0000 0110 | ♠ | ACK | ^F |
| 007 | 07 | 0000 0111 | ● | BEL | ^G |
| 008 | 08 | 0000 1000 | ■ | BS | ^H |
| 009 | 09 | 0000 1001 | ○ | HT | ^I |

| Dec $X_{10}$ | Hex $X_{16}$ | Binary $X_2$ | ASCII Character | Ctrl | Key |
|---|---|---|---|---|---|
| 010 | 0A | 0000 1010 | ■ | LF | ^J |
| 011 | 0B | 0000 1011 | ♂ | VT | ^K |
| 012 | 0C | 0000 1100 | ♀ | FF | ^L |
| 013 | 0D | 0000 1101 | ♪ | CR | ^M |
| 014 | 0E | 0000 1110 | ♪♪ | SO | ^N |
| 015 | 0F | 0000 1111 | ☼ | SI | ^O |
| 016 | 10 | 0001 0000 | ► | DLE | ^P |
| 017 | 11 | 0001 0001 | ◄ | DC1 | ^Q |
| 018 | 12 | 0001 0010 | ↕ | DC2 | ^R |
| 019 | 13 | 0001 0011 | ‼ | DC3 | ^S |
| 020 | 14 | 0001 0100 | ¶ | DC4 | ^T |
| 021 | 15 | 0001 0101 | § | NAK | ^U |
| 022 | 16 | 0001 0110 | – | SYN | ^V |
| 023 | 17 | 0001 0111 | ↨ | ETB | ^W |
| 024 | 18 | 0001 1000 | ↑ | CAN | ^X |
| 025 | 19 | 0001 1001 | ↓ | EM | ^Y |
| 026 | 1A | 0001 1010 | → | SUB | ^Z |
| 027 | 1B | 0001 1011 | ← | ESC | ^[ |
| 028 | 1C | 0001 1100 | ∟ | FS | ^\ |
| 029 | 1D | 0001 1101 | ↔ | GS | ^] |
| 030 | 1E | 0001 1110 | ▲ | RS | ^^ |
| 031 | 1F | 0001 1111 | ▼ | US | ^_ |
| 032 | 20 | 0010 0000 | Space | | |
| 033 | 21 | 0010 0001 | ! | | |
| 034 | 22 | 0010 0010 | " | | |
| 035 | 23 | 0010 0011 | # | | |
| 036 | 24 | 0010 0100 | $ | | |
| 037 | 25 | 0010 0101 | % | | |
| 038 | 26 | 0010 0110 | & | | |
| 039 | 27 | 0010 0111 | ' | | |
| 040 | 28 | 0010 1000 | ( | | |

| Dec $X_{10}$ | Hex $X_{16}$ | Binary $X_2$ | ASCII Character |
|---|---|---|---|
| 041 | 29 | 0010 1001 | ) |
| 042 | 2A | 0010 1010 | * |
| 043 | 2B | 0010 1011 | + |
| 044 | 2C | 0010 1100 | , |
| 045 | 2D | 0010 1101 | - |
| 046 | 2E | 0010 1110 | . |
| 047 | 2F | 0010 1111 | / |
| 048 | 30 | 0011 0000 | 0 |
| 049 | 31 | 0011 0001 | 1 |
| 050 | 32 | 0011 0010 | 2 |
| 051 | 33 | 0011 0011 | 3 |
| 052 | 34 | 0011 0100 | 4 |
| 053 | 35 | 0011 0101 | 5 |
| 054 | 36 | 0011 0110 | 6 |
| 055 | 37 | 0011 0111 | 7 |
| 056 | 38 | 0011 1000 | 8 |
| 057 | 39 | 0011 1001 | 9 |
| 058 | 3A | 0011 1010 | : |
| 059 | 3B | 0011 1011 | ; |
| 060 | 3C | 0011 1100 | < |
| 061 | 3D | 0011 1101 | = |
| 062 | 3E | 0011 1110 | > |
| 063 | 3F | 0011 1111 | ? |
| 064 | 40 | 0100 0000 | @ |
| 065 | 41 | 0100 0001 | A |
| 066 | 42 | 0100 0010 | B |
| 067 | 43 | 0100 0011 | C |
| 068 | 44 | 0100 0100 | D |
| 069 | 45 | 0100 0101 | E |
| 070 | 46 | 0100 0110 | F |
| 071 | 47 | 0100 0111 | G |
| 072 | 48 | 0100 1000 | H |
| 073 | 49 | 0100 1001 | I |

| Dec $X_{10}$ | Hex $X_{16}$ | Binary $X_2$ | ASCII Character |
|------|------|-----------|-----------|
| 074 | 4A | 0100 1010 | J |
| 075 | 4B | 0100 1011 | K |
| 076 | 4C | 0100 1100 | L |
| 077 | 4D | 0100 1101 | M |
| 078 | 4E | 0100 1110 | N |
| 079 | 4F | 0100 1111 | O |
| 080 | 50 | 0101 0000 | P |
| 081 | 51 | 0101 0001 | Q |
| 082 | 52 | 0101 0010 | R |
| 083 | 53 | 0101 0011 | S |
| 084 | 54 | 0101 0100 | T |
| 085 | 55 | 0101 0101 | U |
| 086 | 56 | 0101 0110 | V |
| 087 | 57 | 0101 0111 | W |
| 088 | 58 | 0101 1000 | X |
| 089 | 59 | 0101 1001 | Y |
| 090 | 5A | 0101 1010 | Z |
| 091 | 5B | 0101 1011 | [ |
| 092 | 5C | 0101 1100 | \ |
| 093 | 5D | 0101 1101 | ] |
| 094 | 5E | 0101 1110 | ^ |
| 095 | 5F | 0101 1111 | – |
| 096 | 60 | 0110 0000 | ` |
| 097 | 61 | 0110 0001 | a |
| 098 | 62 | 0110 0010 | b |
| 099 | 63 | 0110 0011 | c |
| 100 | 64 | 0110 0100 | d |
| 101 | 65 | 0110 0101 | e |
| 102 | 66 | 0110 0110 | f |
| 103 | 67 | 0110 0111 | g |
| 104 | 68 | 0110 1000 | h |
| 105 | 69 | 0110 1001 | i |

| Dec $X_{10}$ | Hex $X_{16}$ | Binary $X_2$ | ASCII Character |
|---|---|---|---|
| 106 | 6A | 0110 1010 | j |
| 107 | 6B | 0110 1011 | k |
| 108 | 6C | 0110 1100 | l |
| 109 | 6D | 0110 1101 | m |
| 110 | 6E | 0110 1110 | n |
| 111 | 6F | 0110 1111 | o |
| 112 | 70 | 0111 0000 | p |
| 113 | 71 | 0111 0001 | q |
| 114 | 72 | 0111 0010 | r |
| 115 | 73 | 0111 0011 | s |
| 116 | 74 | 0111 0100 | t |
| 117 | 75 | 0111 0101 | u |
| 118 | 76 | 0111 0110 | v |
| 119 | 77 | 0111 0111 | w |
| 120 | 78 | 0111 1000 | x |
| 121 | 79 | 0111 1001 | y |
| 122 | 7A | 0111 1010 | z |
| 123 | 7B | 0111 1011 | { |
| 124 | 7C | 0111 1100 | ¦ |
| 125 | 7D | 0111 1101 | } |
| 126 | 7E | 0111 1110 | ~ |
| 127 | 7F | 0111 1111 | Delete |
| 128 | 80 | 1000 0000 | Ç |
| 129 | 81 | 1000 0001 | ü |
| 130 | 82 | 1000 0010 | é |
| 131 | 83 | 1000 0011 | â |
| 132 | 84 | 1000 0100 | ä |
| 133 | 85 | 1000 0101 | à |
| 134 | 86 | 1000 0110 | å |
| 135 | 87 | 1000 0111 | ç |
| 136 | 88 | 1000 1000 | ê |
| 137 | 89 | 1000 1001 | ë |

| Dec $X_{10}$ | Hex $X_{16}$ | Binary $X_2$ | ASCII Character |
|---|---|---|---|
| 138 | 8A | 1000 1010 | è |
| 139 | 8B | 1000 1011 | ï |
| 140 | 8C | 1000 1100 | î |
| 141 | 8D | 1000 1101 | ì |
| 142 | 8E | 1000 1110 | Ä |
| 143 | 8F | 1000 1111 | Å |
| 144 | 90 | 1001 0000 | É |
| 145 | 91 | 1001 0001 | æ |
| 146 | 92 | 1001 0010 | Æ |
| 147 | 93 | 1001 0011 | ô |
| 148 | 94 | 1001 0100 | ö |
| 149 | 95 | 1001 0101 | ò |
| 150 | 96 | 1001 0110 | û |
| 151 | 97 | 1001 0111 | ù |
| 152 | 98 | 1001 1000 | ÿ |
| 153 | 99 | 1001 1001 | Ö |
| 154 | 9A | 1001 1010 | Ü |
| 155 | 9B | 1001 1011 | ¢ |
| 156 | 9C | 1001 1100 | £ |
| 157 | 9D | 1001 1101 | ¥ |
| 158 | 9E | 1001 1110 | Pt |
| 159 | 9F | 1001 1111 | *f* |
| 160 | A0 | 1010 0000 | á |
| 161 | A1 | 1010 0001 | í |
| 162 | A2 | 1010 0010 | ó |
| 163 | A3 | 1010 0011 | ú |
| 164 | A4 | 1010 0100 | ñ |
| 165 | A5 | 1010 0101 | Ñ |
| 166 | A6 | 1010 0110 | a̲ |
| 167 | A7 | 1010 0111 | o̲ |
| 168 | A8 | 1010 1000 | ¿ |
| 169 | A9 | 1010 1001 | ⌐ |

| Dec $X_{10}$ | Hex $X_{16}$ | Binary $X_2$ | ASCII Character |
|---|---|---|---|
| 170 | AA | 1010 1010 | ⌐ |
| 171 | AB | 1010 1011 | ½ |
| 172 | AC | 1010 1100 | ¼ |
| 173 | AD | 1010 1101 | ¡ |
| 174 | AE | 1010 1110 | « |
| 175 | AF | 1010 1111 | » |
| 176 | B0 | 1011 0000 | ░ |
| 177 | B1 | 1011 0001 | ▒ |
| 178 | B2 | 1011 0010 | ▓ |
| 179 | B3 | 1011 0011 | │ |
| 180 | B4 | 1011 0100 | ┤ |
| 181 | B5 | 1011 0101 | ╡ |
| 182 | B6 | 1011 0110 | ╢ |
| 183 | B7 | 1011 0111 | ╖ |
| 184 | B8 | 1011 1000 | ╕ |
| 185 | B9 | 1011 1001 | ╣ |
| 186 | BA | 1011 1010 | ║ |
| 187 | BB | 1011 1011 | ╗ |
| 188 | BC | 1011 1100 | ╝ |
| 189 | BD | 1011 1101 | ╜ |
| 190 | BE | 1011 1110 | ╛ |
| 191 | BF | 1011 1111 | ┐ |
| 192 | C0 | 1100 0000 | └ |
| 193 | C1 | 1100 0001 | ┴ |
| 194 | C2 | 1100 0010 | ┬ |
| 195 | C3 | 1100 0011 | ├ |
| 196 | C4 | 1100 0100 | ─ |
| 197 | C5 | 1100 0101 | ┼ |
| 198 | C6 | 1100 0110 | ╞ |
| 199 | C7 | 1100 0111 | ╟ |
| 200 | C8 | 1100 1000 | ╚ |
| 201 | C9 | 1100 1001 | ╔ |

| Dec $X_{10}$ | Hex $X_{16}$ | Binary $X_2$ | ASCII Character |
|---|---|---|---|
| 202 | CA | 1100 1010 | ╩ |
| 203 | CB | 1100 1011 | ╦ |
| 204 | CC | 1100 1100 | ╠ |
| 205 | CD | 1100 1101 | ═ |
| 206 | CE | 1100 1110 | ╬ |
| 207 | CF | 1100 1111 | ╧ |
| 208 | D0 | 1101 0000 | ╨ |
| 209 | D1 | 1101 0001 | ╤ |
| 210 | D2 | 1101 0010 | ╥ |
| 211 | D3 | 1101 0011 | ╙ |
| 212 | D4 | 1101 0100 | ╘ |
| 213 | D5 | 1101 0101 | ╒ |
| 214 | D6 | 1101 0110 | ╓ |
| 215 | D7 | 1101 0111 | ╫ |
| 216 | D8 | 1101 1000 | ╪ |
| 217 | D9 | 1101 1001 | ┘ |
| 218 | DA | 1101 1010 | ┌ |
| 219 | DB | 1101 1011 | █ |
| 220 | DC | 1101 1100 | ▄ |
| 221 | DD | 1101 1101 | ▌ |
| 222 | DE | 1101 1110 | ▐ |
| 223 | DF | 1101 1111 | ▀ |
| 224 | E0 | 1110 0000 | α |
| 225 | E1 | 1110 0001 | β |
| 226 | E2 | 1110 0010 | Γ |
| 227 | E3 | 1110 0011 | π |
| 228 | E4 | 1110 0100 | Σ |
| 229 | E5 | 1110 0101 | σ |
| 230 | E6 | 1110 0110 | μ |

| Dec $X_{10}$ | Hex $X_{16}$ | Binary $X_2$ | ASCII Character |
|---|---|---|---|
| 231 | E7 | 1110 0111 | τ |
| 232 | E8 | 1110 1000 | Φ |
| 233 | E9 | 1110 1001 | θ |
| 234 | EA | 1110 1010 | Ω |
| 235 | EB | 1110 1011 | δ |
| 236 | EC | 1110 1100 | ∞ |
| 237 | ED | 1110 1101 | ø |
| 238 | EE | 1110 1110 | ∈ |
| 239 | EF | 1110 1111 | ∩ |
| 240 | F0 | 1111 0000 | ≡ |
| 241 | F1 | 1111 0001 | ± |
| 242 | F2 | 1111 0010 | ≥ |
| 243 | F3 | 1111 0011 | ≤ |
| 244 | F4 | 1111 0100 | ⌠ |
| 245 | F5 | 1111 0101 | ⌡ |
| 246 | F6 | 1111 0110 | ÷ |
| 247 | F7 | 1111 0111 | ≈ |
| 248 | F8 | 1111 1000 | ° |
| 249 | F9 | 1111 1001 | • |
| 250 | FA | 1111 1010 | · |
| 251 | FB | 1111 1011 | √ |
| 252 | FC | 1111 1100 | η |
| 253 | FD | 1111 1101 | 2 |
| 254 | FE | 1111 1110 | ■ |
| 255 | FF | 1111 1111 | |

# C++ Precedence Table

| Precedence Level | Symbol | Description | Associativity |
|---|---|---|---|
| 1 | ++ | Prefix increment | Left to right |
| | — | Prefix decrement | |
| | ( ) | Function call and subexpression | |
| | [ ] | Array subscript | |
| | -> | Structure pointer | |
| | . | Structure member | |
| 2 | ! | Logical negation | Right to left |
| | ~ | 1's complement | |
| | - | Unary negation | |
| | + | Unary plus | |
| | (type) | Type cast | |
| | * | Pointer dereference | |
| | & | Address of | |
| | sizeof | Size of | |
| 3 | * | Multiplication | Left to right |
| | / | Division | |
| | % | Modulus (int remainder) | |
| 4 | + | Addition | Left to right |
| | - | Subtraction | |

| Precedence Level | Symbol | Description | Associativity |
|---|---|---|---|
| 5 | << | Bitwise left shift | Left to right |
|  | >> | Bitwise right shift |  |
| 6 | < | Less than | Left to right |
|  | <= | Less than or equal to |  |
|  | > | Greater than |  |
|  | >= | Greater than or equal to |  |
| 7 | == | Equal test | Left to right |
|  | != | Not equal test |  |
| 8 | & | Bitwise AND | Left to right |
| 9 | ^ | Bitwise exclusive OR | Left to right |
| 10 | ¦ | Bitwise inclusive OR | Left to right |
| 11 | && | Logical AND | Left to right |
| 12 | ¦¦ | Logical inclusive OR | Left to right |
| 13 | ?: | Conditional test | Right to left |
| 14 | = | Assignment | Right to left |
|  | += | Compound add |  |
|  | -+ | Compound subtract |  |
|  | *= | Compound multiply |  |
|  | /= | Compound divide |  |
|  | %= | Compound modulus |  |
|  | <<= | Compound bitwise left shift |  |
|  | >>= | Compound bitwise right shift |  |
|  | &= | Compound bitwise AND |  |
|  | ^= | Compound bitwise exclusive OR |  |
|  | ¦= | Compound bitwise inclusive OR |  |
| 15 | , | Sequence point | Left to right |
|  | ++ | Postfix increment |  |
|  | — | Postfix decrement |  |

# Keyword and Function Reference

Here are the 64 Borland C++ keywords:

| | | | |
|---|---|---|---|
| asm | _ds | interrupt | short |
| auto | else | _loadds | signed |
| break | enum | long | sizeof |
| case | _es | _near | _ss |
| catch | _export | near | static |
| _cdecl | extern | new | struct |
| cdecl | _far | operator | switch |
| char | far | _pascal | template |
| class | float | pascal | this |
| const | for | private | typedef |
| continue | friend | protected | union |
| _cs | goto | public | unsigned |
| default | huge | register | virtual |
| delete | if | return | void |
| do | inline | _saveregs | volatile |
| double | int | _seg | while |

The following are the library function prototypes, listed by their header files. The prototypes describe how you use them in your programs.

```
<alloc.h>
int brk (void *);
void *calloc (size_t, size_t);
unsigned coreleft (void);
unsigned long coreleft (void);
void far *farcalloc (unsigned long, unsigned long);
unsigned long farcoreleft (void);
void farfree (void far *);
int farheapcheck (void);
int farheapcheckfree (unsigned int);
int farheapchecknode (void far *);
int farheapfillfree (unsigned int);
int farheapwalk (struct farheapinfo *);
void far *farmalloc (unsigned long);
void far *farrealloc (void far *, unsigned long);
void free (void *);
int heapcheck (void);
int heapcheckfree (unsigned int);
int heapchecknode (void *);
int heapchecknode (void far *);
int heapfillfree (unsigned int);
int heapwalk (struct heapinfo *);
int heapwalk (struct farheapinfo far *);
void *malloc (size_t);
void *realloc (void *, size_t);
void *sbrk (int);
<assert.h>
void assert(int p);
void __assertfail(char *, char *, char *, int);
<bcd.h>
bcd abs (bcd&);
bcd acos (bcd&);
bcd asin (bcd&);
bcd atan (bcd&);
bcd cos (bcd&);
bcd cosh (bcd&);
bcd exp (bcd&);
bcd log (bcd&);
bcd log10 (bcd&);
bcd pow (bcd&, bcd&);
long double real (bcd&);
bcd sin (bcd&);
bcd sinh (bcd&);
bcd sqrt (bcd&);
bcd tan (bcd&);
bcd tanh (bcd&);
long double pascal __bcd_log10(bcd far *);
void pascal __bcd_pow10(int n, bcd far *);
long double pascal __bcd_tobinary(const bcd far *);
void pascal __bcd_todecimal(long double, int, bcd far *);
<bios.h>
int bioscom(int, char, int);
```

```
int biosdisk(int, int, int, int, int, int, void *);
int biosequip(void);
int bioskey(int);
int biosmemory(void);
int biosprint(int, int, int);
long biostime(int, long);
```

**<complex.h>**
```
double abs(complex&);
complex acos(complex&);
double arg(complex&);
complex asin(complex&);
complex atan(complex&);
complex conj(complex&);
complex cos(complex&);
complex cosh(complex&);
complex exp(complex&);
double imag(complex&);
complex log(complex&);
complex log10(complex&);
double norm(complex&);
complex polar(double, double);
complex pow(complex&, double);
complex pow(double, complex&);
complex pow(complex&, complex&);
double real(complex&);
complex sin(complex&);
complex sinh(complex&);
complex sqrt(complex&);
complex tan(complex&);
complex tanh(complex&);
```

**<conio.h>**
```
char cgets (char *;
void clreol (void);
void clrscr (void);
int cprintf (const char *, ...);
int cputs (const char *);
int cscanf (const char *, ...);
void delline (void);
int getch (void);
int getche (void);
char getpass (const char *);
int gettext (int, int, int, int, void *);
void gettextinfo (struct text_info *);
void gotoxy (int, int);
void highvideo (void);
void insline (void);
int kbhit (void);
void lowvideo (void);
int movetext (int, int, int, int, int, int);
void normvideo (void);
int putch (int);
int puttext (int, int, int, int, void *);
void textattr (int);
void textbackground (int);
```

```
void textcolor (int);
void textmode (int);
int ungetch (int);
int wherex (void);
int wherey (void);
void window (int, int, int, int);
void _setcursortype (int);
```
**<ctype.h>**
```
int isalnum (int);
int isalpha (int);
int isascii (int);
int iscntrl (int);
int isdigit (int);
int isgraph (int);
int islower (int);
int isprint (int);
int ispunct (int);
int isspace (int);
int isupper (int);
int isxdigit (int);
int toascii (int);
int tolower (int);
int toupper (int);
```
**<dir.h>**
```
int chdir (const char *);
int findfirst (const char *, struct ffblk *, int);
int findnext (struct ffblk *);
void fnmerge (char *, const char *, const char *, const char *,
              const char *);
int fnsplit (const char *, char *, char *, char *, char *);
int getcurdir (int, char *);
char getcwd (char *, int);
int getdisk (void);
int mkdir (const char *);
char mktemp (char *);
int rmdir (const char *);
char searchpath (const char *);
int setdisk (int);
```
**<dos.h>**
```
int absread (int, int, long, void *);
int abswrite (int, int, long, void *);
int allocmem (unsigned, unsigned *);
int bdos (int, unsigned, unsigned);
int bdosptr (int, void *, unsigned);
struct COUNTRY *country (int, struct COUNTRY *);
void ctrlbrk (int (*)(void));
void delay (unsigned);
void disable (void);
int dosexterr (struct DOSERROR *);
long dostounix (struct date *, struct time *);
void enable (void);
unsigned FP_OFF (void far *)
unsigned FP_SEG (void far *)
int freemem (unsigned);
void geninterrupt (int);
```

```
int getcbrk (void);
void getdate (struct date *);
void getdfree (unsigned char, struct dfree *);
char far *getdta (void);
void getfat (unsigned char, struct fatinfo *);
void getfatd (struct fatinfo *);
unsigned getpsp (void);
int getswitchar (void);
void gettime (struct time *);
void interrupt (far *getvect(int))(void);
int getverify (void);
void harderr (int(*)());
void hardresume (int);
void hardretn (int);
unsigned char inp (int);
int inport (int);
unsigned char inportb (int);
int int86 (int, union REGS *, union REGS *);
int int86x (int, union REGS *, union REGS *, struct SREGS *);
int intdos (union REGS *, union REGS *);
int intdosx (union REGS *, union REGS *, struct SREGS *);
void intr (int, struct REGPACK *);
void keep (unsigned char, unsigned);
void far *MK_FP (void _seg *, void near *)
void nosound (void);
void outp (int, unsigned char);
void outport (int, int);
void outportb (int, unsigned char);
char *parsfnm (const char *, struct fcb *, int);
int peek (unsigned, unsigned);
char peekb (unsigned, unsigned);
void poke (unsigned, unsigned, int);
void pokeb (unsigned, unsigned, char);
int randbrd (struct fcb *, int);
int randbwr (struct fcb *, int);
void segread (struct SREGS *);
int setblock (unsigned, unsigned);
int setcbrk (int);
void setdate (struct date *);
void setdta (char far *);
void setswitchar (char);
void settime (struct time *);
void setvect (int, void interrupt (far *)());
void setverify (int);
void sleep (unsigned);
void sound (unsigned);
void unixtodos (long, struct date *, struct time *);
int unlink (const char *);
int far _OvrInitEms (unsigned, unsigned, unsigned);
int far _OvrInitExt (unsigned long, unsigned long);
void __cli__ (void);
void __emit__ (int);
unsigned char __inportb__ (int);
void __int__ (int);
```

```
void __outportb__ (int, unsigned char);
void __sti__ (void);
```
**<float.h>**
```
unsigned int _clear87 (void);
unsigned int _control87 (unsigned int, unsigned int);
void _fpreset( void);
unsigned int _status87 (void);
```
**<fstream.h>**
```
filebuf* attach (int);
void attach (int);
filebuf* close ();
void close ();
int fd ();
int is_open ();
filebuf* open (const char*, int, int);
void open (const char*, int, int);
virtual int overflow (int);
filebuf* rdbuf ();
virtual streampos seekoff (streamoff, seek_dir, int);
virtual streambuf* setbuf (char*, int);
void setbuf (char*, int);
virtual int sync ();
virtual int underflow ();
```
**<graphics.h>**
```
void far arc (int, int, int, int, int);
void ATT_driver (void);
void far bar (int, int, int, int);
void far bar3d (int, int, int, int, int, int);
void CGA_driver (void);
void far circle (int, int, int);
void far cleardevice (void);
void far clearviewport (void);
void far closegraph (void);
void far detectgraph (int far *, int far *);
void far drawpoly (int, int far *);
void EGAVGA_driver (void);
void far ellipse (int, int, int, int, int, int);
void far fillellipse (int, int, int, int);
void far fillpoly (int, int far *);
void far floodfill (int, int, int);
void far getarccoords (struct arccoordstype far *);
void far getaspectratio (int far *, int far *);
int far getbkcolor (void);
int far getcolor (void);
struct palettetype far *far getdefaultpalette (void);
char *far getdrivername (void);
void far getfillpattern (char far *);
void far getfillsettings (struct fillsettingstype far *);
int far getgraphmode (void);
void far getimage (int, int, int, int, void far *);
void far getlinesettings (struct linesettingstype far *);
int far getmaxcolor (void);
int far getmaxmode (void);
int far getmaxx (void);
```

```
int far getmaxy (void);
char *far getmodename (int);
void far getmoderange (int, int far *, int far *);
void far getpalette (struct palettetype far *);
int far getpalettesize (void);
unsigned far getpixel (int, int);
void far gettextsettings (struct textsettingstype far *);
void far getviewsettings (struct viewporttype far *);
int far getx (void);
int far gety (void);
void gothic_font (void);
void far graphdefaults (void);
char *far grapherrormsg (int);
int far graphresult (void);
void Herc_driver (void);
void IBM8514_driver (void);
unsigned far imagesize (int, int, int, int);
void far initgraph (int far *, int far *, char far *);
int far installuserdriver (char far *, int huge (*)(void));
int far installuserfont (char far *);
void far line (int, int, int, int);
void far linerel (int, int);
void far lineto (int, int);
void far moverel (int, int);
void far moveto (int, int);
void far outtext(char far *);
void far outtextxy (int, int, char far *);
void PC3270_driver (void);
void far pieslice (int, int, int, int, int);
void far putimage (int, int, void far *, int);
void far putpixel (int, int, int);
void far rectangle (int, int, int, int);
int registerbgidriver (void (*)(void));
int registerbgifont (void (*)(void));
int far registerfarbgidriver (void far *);
int far registerfarbgifont (void far *);
void far restorecrtmode (void);
void sansserif_font (void);
void far sector (int, int, int, int, int, int);
void far setactivepage (int);
void far setallpalette (struct palettetype far *);
void far setaspectratio (int, int);
void far setbkcolor (int);
void far setcolor (int);
void far setfillpattern (char far *, int);
void far setfillstyle (int, int);
unsigned far setgraphbufsize (unsigned);
void far setgraphmode (int);
void far setlinestyle (int, unsigned, int);
void far setpalette (int, int);
void far setrgbpalette (int, int, int, int);
void far settextjustify (int, int);
void far settextstyle (int, int, int);
void far setusercharsize (int, int, int, int);
```

```
void far setviewport (int, int, int, int, int);
void far setvisualpage (int);
void far setwritemode (int);
void small_font (void);
int far textheight (char far *);
int far textwidth (char far *);
void triplex_font (void);
void far _graphfreemem (void far *, unsigned);
void far *far _graphgetmem (unsigned);
```

**<io.h>**

```
int access (const char *, int);
int chmod (const char *, int);
int chsize (int, long);
int close (int);
int creat (const char *, int);
int creatnew (const char *, int);
int creattemp (char *, int);
int dup (int);
int dup2 (int, int);
int eof (int);
long filelength (int);
int getftime (int, struct ftime *);
int ioctl (int, int, ...);
int isatty (int);
int lock (int, long, long);
long lseek (int, long, int);
int open (const char *, int, ...);
int read (int, void *, unsigned);
int setftime (int, struct ftime *);
int setmode (int, int);
int sopen (const char *, int, int, unsigned);
long tell (int);
unsigned umask (unsigned);
int unlink (const char *);
int unlock (int, long, long);
int write (int, void *, unsigned);
int _chmod (const char *, int, ...);
int _close (int);
int _creat (const char *, int);
int _open (const char *, int);
int _read (int, void *, unsigned);
int _write (int, void *, unsigned);
```

**<iostream.h>**

```
int allocate ();
int bad ();
char* base ();
int blen ();
void clear (int);
void dbp ();
ios& dec (ios&);
virtual int doallocate ();
signed char do_get ();
int do_ipfx (int);
int do_opfx ();
```

```
void do_osfx ();
virtual int do_sgetn (char*, int);
int do_snextc ();
virtual int do_sputn (const char*, int);
void eatwhite ();
char* eback ();
char* ebuf ();
char* egptr ();
ostream& endl (ostream&);
ostream& ends (ostream&);
int eof ();
char* epptr ();
int fail ();
char fill (char);
long flags (long);
ostream& flush ();
ostream& flush (ostream&);
void gbump (int);
int gcount ();
int get ();
istream& get (signed char&);
istream& get (signed char*, int, char);
istream& get (streambuf&, char);
istream& get (unsigned char&);
istream& get (unsigned char*, int, char);
istream& getline (signed char*, int, char);
istream& getline (unsigned char*, int, char);
int good ();
char* gptr ();
ios& hex (ios&);
istream& ignore (int, int);
void init (streambuf*);
int in_avail ();
int ipfx (int);
int ipfx0 ();
int ipfx1 ();
long & iword (int);
ios& oct (ios&);
int opfx ();
void osfx ();
void outstr (const signed char*, const signed char*);
int out_waiting ();
virtual int overflow (int);
virtual int pbackfail (int);
char* pbase ();
void pbump (int);
int peek ();
char* pptr ();
int precision (int);
ostream& put (char);
istream& putback (char);
void* & pword (int);
streambuf* rdbuf ();
int rdstate ();
```

```
istream& read (signed char*, int);
istream& read (unsigned char*, int);
int sbumpc ();
istream& seekg (streampos);
istream& seekg (streamoff, seek_dir);
virtual streampos seekoff (streamoff, seek_dir, int);
ostream& seekp (streamoff, seek_dir);
ostream& seekp (streampos);
virtual streampos seekpos (streampos, int);
void setb (char*, char*, int);
streambuf* setbuf (unsigned char*, int);
long setf (long, long);
void setg (char*, char*, char*);
void setp (char*, char*);
void setstate (int);
int sgetc ();
int sgetn (char*, int);
int skip (int);
int snextc ();
int sputbackc (char);
int sputc (int);
int sputn (const char*, int);
void stossc ();
virtual int sync ();
int sync ();
streampos tellg ();
streampos tellp ();
ostream* tie (ostream*);
int unbuffered ();
void unbuffered (int);
virtual int underflow ();
long unsetf (long);
void usersize (int);
int width (int);
ostream& write (const signed char*, int);
ostream& write (const unsigned char*, int);
istream& ws (istream&);
```

**<locale.h>**

```
struct lconv *localeconv (void);
char *setlocale (int, const char *);
```

**<math.h>**

```
int abs (int);
double acos (double);
double asin (double);
double atan (double);
double atan2 (double, double);
double atof (const char *);
double cabs (struct complex);
double ceil (double);
double cos (double);
double cosh (double);
double exp (double);
double fabs (double);
double floor (double);
```

```
double fmod (double, double);
double frexp (double, int *);
double hypot (double, double);
long labs (long);
double ldexp (double, int);
double log (double);
double log10 (double);
int matherr (struct exception *);
double modf (double, double *);
double poly (double, int, double[]);
double pow (double, double);
double pow10 (int);
double sin (double);
double sinh (double);
double sqrt (double);
double tan (double);
double tanh (double);
double _matherr (_mexcep, char *, double *, double *, double);
```
**<mem.h>**
```
void *memccpy (void *, const void *, int, size_t);
void *memchr (const void *, int, size_t);
int memcmp (const void *, const void *, size_t);
void *memcpy (void *, const void *, size_t);
int memicmp (const void *, const void *, size_t);
void *memmove (void *, const void *, size_t);
void *memset (void *__s, int __c, size_t __n);
void movedata (unsigned, unsigned, unsigned, unsigned, size_t);
void movmem (void *, void *, unsigned);
void setmem (void *, unsigned, char);
```
**<process.h>**
```
void abort (void);
int execl (char *, char *, ...);
int execle (char *, char *, ...);
int execlp (char *, char *, ...);
int execlpe (char *, char *__, ...);
int execv (char *, char *[]);
int execve (char *, char *[], char **);
int execvp (char *, char *[]);
int execvpe (char *, char *[], char **);
void exit (int);
int spawnl (int, char *, char *, ...);
int spawnle (int, char *, char *, ...);
int spawnlp (int, char *, char *, ...);
int spawnlpe (int, char *, char *, ...);
int spawnv (int, char *, char *[]);
int spawnve (int, char *, char *[], char **);
int spawnvp (int, char *, char *[]);
int spawnvpe (int, char *, char *[], char **);
int system (const char *);
void _exit (int);
```
**<setjmp.h>**
```
void longjmp (jmp_buf, int);
int setjmp (jmp_buf);
```
**<signal.h>**

```
int raise(int);
void (*signal(int, void (*)(int)))(int);
<stdio.h>
void clearerr (FILE *);
int fclose (FILE *);
int fcloseall(void);
FILE *fdopen (int, char *);
int feof (FILE *);
int ferror (FILE *);
int fflush (FILE *);
int fgetc (FILE *);
int fgetchar (void);
int fgetpos (FILE *, fpos_t *);
char *fgets (char *, int, FILE *);
int fileno (FILE *);
int flushall (void);
FILE *fopen (const char *, const char *);
int fprintf (FILE *, const char *, ...);
int fputc (int, FILE *);
int fputchar (int);
int fputs (const char *, FILE *);
size_t fread (void *, size_t, size_t, FILE *);
FILE *freopen (const char *, const char *, FILE *);
int fscanf (FILE *, const char *, ...);
int fseek (FILE *, long, int);
int fsetpos (FILE *, const fpos_t *);
long ftell (FILE *);
size_t fwrite (const void *, size_t, size_t, FILE *);
int getc (FILE *);
int getchar (void);
char *gets (char *);
int getw (FILE *);
void perror (const char *);
int printf (const char *, ...);
int putc (const int, FILE *);
int putchar (const int);
int puts (const char *);
int putw (int, FILE *);
int remove (const char *);
int rename (const char *, const char *);
void rewind (FILE *);
int scanf (const char *__format, ...);
void setbuf (FILE *, char *);
int setvbuf (FILE *, char *, int, size_t);
int sprintf (char *, const char *, ...);
int sscanf (const char *, const char *, ...);
char *strerror (int);
FILE *tmpfile (void);
char *tmpnam (char *);
int ungetc (int, FILE *);
int unlink (const char *);
int vfprintf (FILE *, const char *, void *);
int vfscanf (FILE *, const char *, void *);
int vprintf (const char *, void *);
```

```
int vscanf (const char *, void *);
int vsprintf (char *, const char *, void *);
int vsscanf (const char *, const char *, void *);
int _fgetc (FILE *);
int _fputc (char, FILE *);
char *_strerror (const char *);
```

**<stdiostr.h>**

```
virtual int overflow (int);
virtual int pbackfail (int);
stdiobuf *rdbuf ();
virtual streampos seekoff (streamoff, seek_dir, int);
FILE *stdiofile ();
virtual int sync ();
virtual int underflow ();
```

**<stdlib.h>**

```
void abort (void);
int abs (int);
int atexit (atexit_t);
double atof (const char *);
int atoi (const char *);
long atol (const char *);
void *bsearch (const void *, const void *, size_t, size_t, int
               (*)(const void *, const void *));
void *calloc (size_t, size_t);
div_t div (int, int);
char ecvt (double, int, int *, int *);
void exit (int);
char *fcvt (double, int, int *, int *);
void free (void *);
char *gcvt (double, int, char *);
char getenv (const char *);
char itoa (int, char *, int);
long labs (long);
ldiv_t ldiv (long, long);
void *lfind (const void *, const void *, size_t *, size_t, int
             (*)(const void *, const void *));
void *lsearch (const void *, void *, size_t *, size_t, int
               (*)(const void *, const void *));
char *ltoa (long, char *, int);
void *malloc (size_t);
int max (int, int);
int mblen (const char *, size_t);
size_t mbstowcs (wchar_t *, const char *, size_t);
int mbtowc (wchar_t *, const char *, size_t);
int min (int, int);
int putenv (const char *);
void qsort (void *, size_t, size_t, int (*)(const void *,
            const void *));
int rand (void);
int random(int);
void randomize(void);
void *realloc (void *, size_t);
void srand (unsigned);
double strtod (const char *, char **);
```

```
long strtol (const char *, char **, int);
unsigned long strtoul (const char *, char **, int);
void swab (char *, char *, int);
int system (const char *);
char *ultoa (unsigned long, char *, int);
size_t wcstombs (char *, const wchar_t *, size_t);
int wctomb (char *, wchar_t);
void _exit (int);
unsigned long _lrotl (unsigned long, int);
unsigned long _lrotr (unsigned long, int);
unsigned _rotl (unsigned, int);
unsigned _rotr (unsigned, int);
int __abs__ (int);
```
**<stream.h>**
```
int allocate ();
int bad ();
void checkskip (int&, int&);
char *chr (int, int);
void clear (int);
int close ();
char *dec (long, int);
void eatwhite (istream&);
int eof ();
int fail ();
ostream& flush ();
char *form (char * ...);
istream& get (char&);
istream& get (char *, int, int);
long get_long (int);
int good ();
char *hex (long, int);
char *oct (long, int);
filebuf *open ( char *, int );
virtual int overflow ();
ostream& put (char);
void putback (char);
int rdstate ();
streambuf *setbuf ( char *, int, unsigned);
int skip (int);
int snextc ();
virtual int snextc ();
virtual void sputbackc (char);
void sputbackc (char);
int sputc (int);
virtual int sputc (int);
char *str (const char *, int);
virtual void terminate ();
void terminate ();
ostream *tie (ostream *)
virtual int underflow ();
```
**<string.h>**
```
void *memccpy (void *, const void *, int, size_t);
void *memchr (const void *, int, size_t);
int memcmp (const void *, const void *, size_t);
```

```
void *memcpy (void *, const void *, size_t);
int memicmp (const void *, const void *, size_t);
void *memmove (void *, const void *, size_t);
void *memset (void *, int, size_t);
void movedata (unsigned, unsigned, unsigned, unsigned, size_t);
char *stpcpy (char *, const char *);
char *strcat (char *, const char *);
char *strchr (const char *, int);
int strcmp (const char *, const char *);
int strcmpi (const char *, const char *);
int strcoll (const char *, const char *);
char *strcpy (char *, const char *);
size_t strcspn (const char *, const char *);
char *strdup (const char *);
char *strerror (int);
int stricmp (const char *, const char *);
size_t strlen (const char *);
char *strlwr (char *);
char *strncat (char *, const char *, size_t);
int strncmp (const char *, const char *, size_t);
int strncmpi (const char *, const char *, size_t);
char *strncpy (char *, const char *, size_t);
int strnicmp (const char *, const char *, size_t);
char *strnset (char *, int, size_t);
char *strpbrk (const char *, const char *);
char *strrchr (const char *, int);
char *strrev (char *);
char *strset (char *, int);
size_t strspn (const char *, const char *);
char *strstr (const char *, const char *);
char *strtok (char *, const char *);
char *strupr (char *);
size_t strxfrm (char *, const char *, size_t);
char *_strerror (const char *);
```
**<strstrea.h>**
```
void *(*allocf) (long);
virtual int doallocate ();
void (*freef) (void *);
void freeze (int);
void init (signed char *, int, signed char *);
virtual int overflow (int);
int pcount ();
strstreambuf *rdbuf ();
virtual streampos seekoff (streamoff, seek_dir, int);
virtual streambuf *setbuf (char*, int);
char *str ();
virtual int underflow ();
```
**<sys\stat.h>**
```
int fstat (int, struct stat *);
int stat (char *, struct stat *);
```
**<sys\timeb.h>**
```
void ftime (struct timeb *);
```

```
<time.h>
char *asctime (const struct tm *);
char *ctime (const time_t *);
clock_t clock (void);
double difftime (time_t, time_t);
struct tm *gmtime (const time_t *);
struct tm *localtime (const time_t *);
time_t mktime (struct tm *);
int stime (time_t *);
size_t strftime (char *, size_t, const char *,
                 const struct tm *);
time_t time (time_t *);
void tzset (void);
```

# The Mailing List Application

This appendix collects *in one complete program* most of the commands and functions you learned throughout the book. This program manages a mailing list for your personal or business needs.

When you run the program, you are presented with a menu of choices that guides you through the program's operation. Comments throughout the program offer suggested improvements you might want to make. As your knowledge and practice of Borland C++ improve, you might want to expand this mailing list application into an entire database of your contacts. You should build this to a DOS target and run it from a command line, not from the Debug menu in the IDE.

Note that a code continuation character (➥) appears on a few of the code lines in this program. This character indicates a continuing line of code that should *not* be broken when you type the program. These lines have been broken here because of the book's margin restrictions. When you encounter this character in your typing, simply leave one space and continue typing the second line.

Here is the listing of the complete program:

```
// Filename: MAILING.CPP
// Mailing list application
// ----------------------

// This program lets the user enter, edit, maintain, and print a
// mailing list of names and addresses.

// All commands and concepts included in this program are
// explained throughout the text of Borland C++ 4 By Example.
```

```
// These are items you might want to add or change:
// 1. Find your compiler's clear-screen function to
//    improve on the screen-clearing function.
// 2. Add an entry for the 'code' member to track different types
//    of names and addresses (such as business codes, personal
//    codes, and so on).
// 3. Search for a partial name (for example, typing "Sm" finds
//    "Smith" and "Smitty" and "Smythe" in the file).
// 4. When searching for name matches, ignore case (for example,
//    typing "smith" finds "Smith" in the file).
// 5. Print mailing labels on your printer.
// 6. Allow for sorting a listing of names and addresses by name
//    or ZIP code.
// 7. Separate the names into first, middle, and last.

// Header files used by the program

#include <conio.h>
#include <ctype.h>
#include <fstream.h>
#include <iostream.h>
#include <string.h>

#define    FILENAME   "ADDRESS.DAT"

// Prototype all of this program's functions

char get_answer(void);
void disp_menu (void);
void clear_sc (void);
void change_na (void);
void print_na (void);
void err_msg (char err_msg[ ]);
void pause_sc (void);

#define    NAME_SIZE (25)
#define    ADDRESS_SIZE (25)
#define    CITY_SIZE (12)
#define    STATE_SIZE (3)
#define    ZIPCODE_SIZE (6)
#define    CODE_SIZE (7)

// Class of a name and address
class      Mail
       {
private:
     char name[ NAME_SIZE ];   // Name stored here, should be
                               // last, first order
     char address[ ADDRESS_SIZE ];
     char city[ CITY_SIZE ];
     char state[ STATE_SIZE ];      // Save room for null zero
     char zipcode[ ZIPCODE_SIZE ];
```

```
        char code[ CODE_SIZE ];  // For additional expansion. You
                                 // might want to use this member
                                 // for customer codes, vendor
                                 // codes, or holiday card codes
public:

void pr_data(Mail *item)
     {
     // Print the name and address sent to it
     cout << "\nName    : " << (*item).name << "\n";
     cout << "Address: " << (*item).address << "\n";
     cout << "City    : " << (*item).city << "\tState: "
          << (*item).state << "   ZIP code: " << (*item).zipcode
          << "\n";
     }

void get_new_item(Mail *item)
     {
     Mail temp_item;      // Holds temporary changed input

     cout << "\nEnter new name and address information below\n"
          << "(Press the Enter key without typing data to "
          << "retain old information)\n\n";
     cout << "What is the new name? ";
     cin.getline(temp_item.name, NAME_SIZE);
     if (strlen(temp_item.name))   // Save new data only if user
                                   // types something
          strcpy((*item).name, temp_item.name);
     cout << "What is the address? ";
     cin.getline(temp_item.address, ADDRESS_SIZE);
     if (strlen(temp_item.address))
          strcpy((*item).address, temp_item.address);
     cout << "What is the city? ";
     cin.getline(temp_item.city, CITY_SIZE);
     if (strlen(temp_item.city))
          strcpy((*item).city, temp_item.city);
     cout << "What is the state? (2 letter abbreviation only) ";
     cin.getline(temp_item.state, STATE_SIZE);
     if (strlen(temp_item.state))
          strcpy((*item).state, temp_item.state);
     cout << "What is the ZIP code? ";
     cin.getline(temp_item.zipcode, ZIPCODE_SIZE);
     if (strlen(temp_item.zipcode))
          strcpy((*item).zipcode, temp_item.zipcode);
     (*item).code[ 0 ] = 0;   // Null out the code member
                              // (unused here)

     }

void add_to_file(Mail *item);
void change_na(void);
void enter_na(Mail *item);
void getzip(Mail *item);
     };

void Mail::change_na(void)
     {
```

```
// This search function can be improved by using the code
// member to assign a unique code to each person in the
// list. Names are difficult to search for because there
// are so many variations (such as Mc and Mac and St. and
// Saint).

Mail item;
fstream    file;
int  ans;
int  s;                    // Holds size of structure
int  change_yes = 0;       // Will be TRUE if user finds a
                           // name to change
char test_name[ 25 ];

cout << "\nWhat is the name of the person you want to "
     << "change? ";
cin.getline(test_name, NAME_SIZE);
s = sizeof(Mail);   // To ensure that fread() reads properly
file.open(FILENAME, ios::in | ios::out);
if (!file)
     {
     err_msg("*** Read error - Ensure file exists before
     ➥reading it ***");
     return;
     }
do
     {
     file.read((unsigned char *)&item, sizeof(Mail));
     if (file.gcount() != s)
          {
          if (file.eof())
               break;
          }
     if (strcmp(item.name, test_name) == 0)
          {
          item.pr_data(&item);      // Print name and address
          cout << "\nIs this the name and address to "
               << "change? (Y/N) ";
          ans = get_answer();
          if (toupper(ans) == 'N')
               break;               // Get another name
          get_new_item(&item);      // Let user type new
                                    // information
          file.seekg((long)·s, ios::cur);   // Back up one
                                             // structure
          file.write((const unsigned char *)(&item),
               sizeof(Mail));   // Rewrite information
          change_yes = 1;          // Changed flag
          break;    // Finished
          }
     }
while (!file.eof());
if (!change_yes)
```

```
            err_msg("*** End of file encountered before finding
           ➥the name ***");
      }

void Mail::getzip(Mail *item) // Ensure that ZIP code is all
                              // digits
   {
   int  ctr;
   int  bad_zip;

   do
         {
         bad_zip = 0;
         cout << "What is the ZIP code? ";
         cin.getline((*item).zipcode, ZIPCODE_SIZE);
         for (ctr = 0; ctr < 5; ctr++)
               {
               if (isdigit((*item).zipcode[ ctr ]))
                     continue;
               else
                     {
                     err_msg("*** The ZIP code must consist
                    ➥of digits only ***");
                     bad_zip = 1;
                     break;
                     }
               }
         }
   while (bad_zip);
   }

void Mail::add_to_file(Mail *item)
   {
   ofstream  file;

   file.open(FILENAME, ios::app);      // Open file in append
                                       // mode
   if (!file)
         {
         err_msg("*** Disk error - please check
        ➥disk drive ***");
         return;
         }
   // Add structure to file
   file.write((const unsigned char *)(item), sizeof(Mail));
   }

void Mail::enter_na(Mail *item)
   {
   char ans;

   do
         {
         cout << "\n\n\n\n\nWhat is the name? ";
```

```
             cin.getline((*item).name, NAME_SIZE);
             cout << "What is the address? ";
             cin.getline((*item).address, ADDRESS_SIZE);
             cout << "What is the city? ";
             cin.getline((*item).city, CITY_SIZE);
             cout << "What is the state? (2 letter abbreviation "
                  << "only)";
             cin.getline((*item).state, STATE_SIZE);
             getzip(item);  // Ensure that ZIP code is all digits
             strcpy((*item).code, " ");    // Null out the code
                                           // member
             add_to_file(item);  // Write new information to disk
                                 // file
             cout << "\n\nDo you want to enter another name and "
                  << "address? (Y/N)";
             ans = get_answer();
             }
         while (toupper(ans) == 'Y');
         }


//******************************************************************

// Defined constants
// MAX is total number of names allowed in memory for reading
// mailing list

#define    MAX   250
#define    BELL  '\x07'

//******************************************************************

int  main(void)
     {
     char ans;
     Mail item;

     do
         {
         disp_menu();    // Display the menu for the user
         ans = get_answer();
         switch (ans)
             {
             case '1':
                 item.enter_na(&item);
                 break;
             case '2':
                 item.change_na();
                 break;
             case '3':
                 print_na();
                 break;
             case '4':
                 break;
             default:
```

```
                      err_msg("*** You need to enter
                      ➥1 through 4 ***");
                      break;
                  }
           }
      while (ans != '4');
      return 0;
      }

//****************************************************************

void disp_menu(void)      // Display the main menu of program
      {
      clear_sc();     // Clear the screen
      cout << "\t\t*** Mailing List Manager ***\n";
      cout << "\t\t   ------------------\n\n\n\n";
      cout << "Do you want to:\n\n\n";
      cout << "\t1. Add names and addresses to the list\n\n\n";
      cout << "\t2. Change names and addresses in the list\n\n\n";
      cout << "\t3. Print names and addresses in the list\n\n\n";
      cout << "\t4. Exit this program\n\n\n";
      cout << "What is your choice? ";
      }

//****************************************************************

void clear_sc()      // Clear the screen by sending 25 blank lines
                     // to it
      {
      int  ctr; // Counter for the 25 blank lines

      for (ctr = 0; ctr < 25; ctr++)
           cout << "\n";
      }

//****************************************************************

void print_na(void)
      {
      Mail       item;
      ifstream   file;
      int        s;
      int        linectr = 0;

      s = sizeof(Mail);   // To ensure that fread() reads properly
      file.open(FILENAME);
      if (!file)
          {
          err_msg("*** Read error - Ensure file exists
          ➥before reading it ***");
          return;
          }
      do
          {
```

```
            file.read((signed char *)&item, s);
            if (file.gcount() != s)
                {
                if (file.eof())       // If EOF, quit reading
                    break;
                }
            if (linectr > 20)    // Screen is full
                {
                pause_sc();
                linectr = 0;
                }
            item.pr_data(&item);      // Print the name and address
            linectr += 4;
            }
        while (!file.eof());
        cout << "\n- End of list -";
        pause_sc();    // Give user a chance to see names remaining
// on screen
        }

//***************************************************************

void err_msg(char err_msg[ ])
        {
        cerr << "\n\n" << err_msg << BELL << "\n";
        pause_sc();    // Give user a chance to see names remaining

        }

//***************************************************************

void pause_sc()
        {
        cout << "\nPress the Enter key to continue...";
        while (getch() != '\r')
            ;
        }

//***************************************************************

char get_answer(void)
        {
        char ans;

        ans = getch();
        while (kbhit())
            getch();
        putch(ans);
        return ans;
        }
```

# Glossary

**address**  Each memory (RAM) location (each byte) has a unique address. The first address in memory is 0, the second address is 1, and so on, until the last address (which comes thousands of bytes later).

**argument**  The value sent *to* a function or procedure. This can be either a constant or a variable and is enclosed in parentheses.

**array**  A list of variables, sometimes called a table of variables.

**ASCII**  Acronym for *American Standard Code for Information Interchange*.

**ASCII file**  A file containing characters that can be used by any program on most computers. Sometimes the file is called a text file or an ASCII text file.

**AUTOEXEC.BAT**  A batch file in PCs that executes a series of commands whenever you start or reset the computer.

**backup file**  A duplicate copy of a file that preserves your work in case you damage the original file. Files on a hard disk are commonly backed up onto floppy disks or tapes.

**binary**  A numbering system based on only two digits. The only valid digits in a binary system are 0 and 1. See also *bit*.

**binary zero**  Another name for null zero.

**bit**  Binary digit, the smallest unit of storage on a computer. Each bit can have a value of 0 or 1, indicating the absence or presence of an electrical signal. See also *binary*.

**bitwise operators**  C++ operators that manipulate the binary representation of values.

**block**  Two or more statements treated as though they are a single statement. A block is always enclosed in braces ({ }).

**boot**  To start a computer with the operating system software in place. You must boot your computer before using it.

**bubble sort**  A type of sorting routine.

**bug**  An error in a program that prevents it from running correctly. Originated when a moth short-circuited a connection in one of the first computers, preventing the computer from working!

**byte**  A basic unit of data storage and manipulation. A byte is equivalent to 8 bits and can contain a value ranging from 0 through 255.

**cathode ray tube (CRT)**  The televisionlike screen, also called the *monitor*. One place to which the output of the computer can be sent.

**central processing unit (CPU)**  The controlling circuit responsible for operations within the computer. These operations generally include system timing, logical processing, and logical operations. The central processing unit controls every operation of the computer system. On PCs, the central processing unit is called a microprocessor and is stored on a single integrated circuit chip.

**class**  A C++ user-defined data type that can consist of data members and member functions.

**code**  A set of instructions written in a programming language. See *source code*.

**compile**  Process of translating a program written in a programming language such as C++ into machine code that your computer understands.

**concatenation**  The process of attaching one string to the end of another or combining two or more strings into a longer string.

**conditional loop**  A series of C++ instructions that occurs a fixed number of times.

**constant**  Data that remains the same during a program run. It cannot be modified by either the program or the user.

**constructor**  The function executed when the program declares an instance of a class.

**CPU**  See *central processing unit*.

**CRT**  See *cathode ray tube*.

**data**  Information stored in the computer as numbers, letters, and special symbols such as punctuation marks. Data also refers to the characters you input into your program so that it can produce meaningful information.

**data member**   A data component of a class or structure.

**data processing**   What computers really do. They take data and manipulate it into meaningful output, called *information*.

**data validation**   The process of testing the values input into a program—for example, testing for a negative number when you know the input cannot be negative, or ensuring that a number is within a certain range.

**debug**   Process of locating an error (bug) in a program and removing it.

**declaration**   A statement that declares the existence of a data object or function. A declaration reserves memory.

**default**   A predefined action or command that the computer chooses unless you specify otherwise.

**definition**   A statement that defines the format of a data object or function. A definition reserves no memory.

**demodulate**   To convert an analog signal into a digital signal for use by a computer. See also *modulate*.

**dereference**   The process of finding a value pointed to by a pointer variable.

**destructor**   The function called when a class instance goes out of scope.

**digital computer**   A computer that operates on binary (on and off) digital impulses of electricity.

**directory**   A list of files stored on a disk. Directories within existing directories are called subdirectories.

**disk**   A round, flat magnetic storage medium. Floppy disks are made of flexible material enclosed in 5 1/4-inch or 3 1/2-inch protective cases. Hard disks consist of a stack of rigid disks housed in a single unit. A disk is sometimes called *external memory*. Disk storage is nonvolatile. When you turn off your computer, the disk's contents do not go away.

**disk drive**   Device that reads and writes data to a floppy or hard disk.

**diskette**   Another name for a removable floppy disk.

**display**   A screen or monitor.

**display adapter**   Located in the system unit, the display adapter determines the amount of *resolution* and the possible number of colors on the screen.

**DOS**   Acronym for *Disk Operating System*.

**dot-matrix printer**   One of the two most common PC printers. (The *laser* printer is the other.) A dot-matrix printer is inexpensive and fast; it uses a series of small dots to represent printed text and graphics.

**element**   An individual variable in an array.

**execute**   To run a program.

**expanded memory**   RAM above and beyond the standard 640K. It is accessed with special software and can be copied in and out of memory below 1M. Expanded memory can be obtained through special hardware or through emulation by extended memory drives.

**extended memory**   RAM above and beyond the standard 640K. It is accessed with special software and is found only on PCs with 80286, 80386, and 80486 microprocessors.

**external modem**   A modem that sits in a box outside your computer. See also *internal modem*.

**file**   A collection of data stored as a single unit on a floppy or hard disk. A file always has a file name that identifies it.

**file extension**   Used by PCs and consists of a period followed by one to three characters. The file extension follows the file name.

**filename**   A unique name that identifies a file. File names can contain up to eight characters and may have a period followed by an extension (usually three characters long).

**fixed disk**   See *hard disk*.

**fixed-length record**   Each of this record's fields takes the same amount of disk space, even if that field's data value does not fill the field.

**floppy disk**   See *disk*.

**format**   Process of creating on the disk a "map" that tells the operating system how the disk is structured. This is how the operating system keeps track of where files are stored.

**function**   A self-contained coding segment designed to do a specific task. All C++ programs must have at least one function called main(). Some functions are library routines that manipulate numbers, strings, and output.

**function keys**   The keys labeled F1 through F12 (some keyboards go only to F10 ).

**global variable**   A variable that can be seen from (and used by) every statement in the program.

**hard copy**  The printout of a program (or its output); also a safe backup copy for a program in case the disk is erased.

**hard disk**  Sometimes called *fixed disks*, they hold much more data and are many times faster than floppy disks. See also *disk*.

**hardware**  The physical parts of the machine. Hardware has been defined as "anything you can kick" and consists of the things you can see.

**header files**  A file created with the intent of using a #include to place it in a C++ program. Declarations of variables, typedefs, prototypes, and classes are the most common residents. This is done to hide some detail from the program and also to guarantee that the same declaration is used in all files in the product or system.

**hexadecimal**  A numbering system based on 16 elements. Digits are numbered 0 through F (0, 1, 2, 3, 4, 5, 6, 7, 8, 9, A, B, C, D, E, and F).

**hierarchy of operators**  See *order of operators*.

**indeterminate loop**  Unlike the for loop, a loop whose number of cycles is not known in advance.

**infinite loop**  The never-ending repetition of a block of C++ statements.

**information**  The meaningful product from a program. Data goes *into* a program to produce meaningful output (information).

**inline function**  A function that compiles as inline code each time the function is called.

**input**  The entry of data into a computer through a device such as the keyboard.

**input-process-output**  The foundation of everything that happens in your computer. Data is input; it is then processed by your program in the computer; and finally information is output.

**I/O**  Acronym for *Input/Output*.

**integer variable**  A variable that can hold an integer.

**internal modem**  A modem that resides inside the system unit. See also *external modem*.

**kilobyte (K)**  A unit of measurement that is 1,024 bytes.

**laser printer**  A type of printer that is generally faster than a dot-matrix printer. Laser printer output is much sharper than that of a dot-matrix printer because a laser beam actually burns toner ink into the paper. Laser printers are more expensive than dot-matrix printers.

**least significant bit**   The rightmost bit of a byte. For example, a binary 00000111 has a 1 as the least significant bit.

**line printer**   Another name for your printer.

**local variable**   A variable that can be seen from (and used by) only the block in which it is defined.

**loop**   The repeated execution of one or more statements.

**machine language**   The series of binary digits that a microprocessor executes to perform individual tasks. People seldom, if ever, program in machine language. Instead, they program in assembly language, and an assembler translates their instructions into machine language.

**main module**   The first function of a modular program, called `main()`, which controls the execution of the other functions.

**maintainability**   The computer industry's word for the capability to change and update programs written in a simple style.

**manipulator**   A value used by a program to tell the stream to modify one of its modes.

**math operator**   A symbol used for addition, subtraction, multiplication, division, or other calculations.

**megabyte (M)**   A unit of measurement that is approximately a million bytes (1,048,576 bytes).

**member**   A piece of a structure variable that holds a specific type of data, a piece of a class variable that holds a specific type of data, or a class variable function acting on class data.

**member function**   A function of a class.

**memory**   Storage area inside the computer; used to store data temporarily. The computer's memory is erased when the power is turned off.

**menu**   A list of commands or instructions displayed on the screen. A menu organizes commands and makes a program easier to use.

**menu-driven**   Describes a program that provides menus for choosing commands.

**microchip**   A small wafer of silicon that holds computer components and occupies less space than a postage stamp.

**microcomputer**   A small computer, such as a PC, that can fit on a desktop. The microchip is the heart of the microcomputer. Microcomputers are much less expensive than their larger counterparts.

**microprocessor**   The chip that does the calculations for PCs. Sometimes this chip is called the central processing unit (CPU).

**modem**   A piece of hardware that modulates and demodulates signals so that your computer can communicate with other computers over telephone lines. See also *external modem* and *internal modem*.

**modular programming**   The process of writing your programs in several modules rather than as one long program. By breaking a program into several smaller programlike routines, you can isolate problems better, write correct programs faster, and produce easy-to-maintain programs.

**modulate**   Before your computer can transmit data over a telephone line, the information to be sent must be converted (modulated) into analog signals. See also *demodulate*.

**modulus**   The integer remainder of division.

**monitor**   A televisionlike screen that lets the computer display information. The monitor is an output device.

**mouse**   A hand-held device that you move across the desktop to move a corresponding indicator, called a mouse pointer, across the screen. Used instead of the keyboard to select and move items (such as text or graphics), execute commands, and perform other tasks.

**MS-DOS**   An operating system for IBM and compatible PCs.

**multidimensional array**   An array with more than one dimension. Two-dimensional arrays are sometimes called tables or matrices, which have rows and columns.

**nested loop**   A loop within a loop.

**null string**   An empty string whose first character is the null zero and whose length is zero.

**null zero**   The string-terminating character. All C++ string constants and strings stored in character arrays end in null zero. The ASCII value for the null zero is 0.

**numeric functions**   Library routines that work with numbers.

**object code**   A "halfway step" between source code and executable machine language. Object code consists mostly of machine language, but is not directly executable by the computer. Such code must first be linked to resolve external references and address references.

**operator**   An operator works on data and might perform math calculations or change data to other data types. Examples include `+`, `-`, and `sizeof()`.

**order of operators** Sometimes called the *hierarchy of operators* or the *precedence of operators*, this order determines exactly how C++ computes formulas.

**output device** The device where the results of a program are output, such as the screen, the printer, or a disk file.

**parallel arrays** Two arrays working side by side. Each element in each array corresponds to an element in the other array.

**parallel port** A connector used to plug a device, such as a printer, into the computer. Transferring data through a parallel port is much faster than through a serial port.

**parameter** A list of variables enclosed in parentheses that follow the name of a function or procedure. Parameters indicate the number and type of arguments to be sent to the function or procedure.

**passing by address** Also called *passing by reference*. When an argument (a local variable) is passed by address, the variable's address in memory is sent to and assigned to the receiving function's parameter list. (If more than one variable is passed by address, each variable's address is sent to and assigned to the receiving function's parameters.) A change made to the parameter within the function also changes the value of the argument variable.

**passing by copy** Another name for *passing by value*.

**passing by reference** Another name for *passing by address*.

**passing by value** By default, all C++ variable arguments are passed *by address*. When the value contained in a variable is passed to the parameter list of a receiving function, changes made to the parameter within the routine do *not* change the value of the argument variable. Also called *passing by copy*.

**path** The route that the computer "travels" from the root directory to any subdirectories when locating a file. The path refers also to the subdirectories that MS-DOS examines when you type a command requiring the operating system to find and access a file.

**peripheral** A device attached to the computer, such as a modem, disk drive, mouse, or printer.

**personal computer** A microcomputer; sometimes called a PC, which stands for *pe*rsonal *c*omputer.

**pointer** A variable that holds the address of another variable.

**precedence of operators** See *order of operators*.

**preprocessor directive**   A command, preceded by a #, that you place in your source code to direct the compiler to modify the source code in some way. The two most common preprocessor directives are #define and #include.

**printer**   A device that prints data from the computer to paper.

**private class member**   A class member inaccessible except to the class's member functions.

**program**   A group of instructions that tells the computer what to do.

**programming language**   A set of rules for writing instructions for the computer. Popular programming languages include BASIC, C, Visual Basic, C++, and Pascal.

**prototype**   The definition of a function. The prototype includes the function's name, return type, and parameter list.

**public class member**   A class member accessible to any functions.

**RAM**   Acronym for *random-access memory*.

**random-access file**   A file in which records can be accessed in any order.

**random-access memory (RAM)**   What your computer uses to store data and programs temporarily. RAM is measured in kilobytes and megabytes. Generally, the more RAM a computer has, the more powerful the programs it can run.

**read-only memory (ROM)**   A permanent type of computer memory. It contains the BIOS (*Basic Input/Output System*), a special chip used to provide instructions to the computer when you turn it on.

**real numbers**   Numbers that have decimal points and a fractional part to the right of the decimal.

**record**   An individual row in a file.

**relational operators**   Operators that compare data, telling how two variables or constants relate to each other. Relational operators can tell whether two variables are equal, or which variable is less than or more than the other.

**ROM**   Acronym for *read-only memory*.

**scientific notation**   A shortcut method of representing numbers of extreme values.

**sectors**   A pattern of pie-shaped wedges on a disk. Formatting creates a pattern of tracks and sectors where your data and programs are stored.

**sequential file**   A file that must be accessed one record at a time, beginning with the first record.

**serial port**   A connector used to plug in a serial device, such as a modem or mouse.

**single-dimensional array**   An array that has only one subscript. A single-dimensional array represents a list of values.

**software**   The data and programs that interact with your hardware. The C++ language is an example of software.

**sorting**   A method of putting data in a specific order (such as alphabetical or numerical order), even if that order is not the same order in which the elements were entered.

**source code**   The C++ language instructions, written by humans, that the C++ compiler translates into object code.

**spaghetti code**   Term used when too many gotos are in a program. If a program branches all over the place, it is difficult to follow, and the logic resembles a bowl of spaghetti.

**stream**   A stream of characters, one following another, flowing between devices in the computer.

**string constant**   One or more groups of characters that end in a null zero.

**string literal**   Another name for a *string constant*.

**structure**   A unit of related information containing one or more members, such as an employee number, employee name, employee address, employee pay rate, and so on. See also *class*.

**subscript**   A number inside brackets that differentiates one element of an array from another element.

**syntax error**   An error that is the result of an incorrect statement in the code.

**system unit**   The large box component of the computer. The system unit houses the PC's microchip, (the CPU).

**tracks**   A pattern of paths on a disk. Formatting creates a pattern of tracks and sectors where your data and programs are stored.

**truncation**   The fractional part of a number (the part of the number to the right of the decimal point) is taken off the number. No rounding is done.

**two's complement**   A method your computer uses to take the negative of a number. This method, when used with addition, allows the computer to simulate subtraction.

**unary operator**   The addition or subtraction operator used before a single variable or constant.

**user-friendly**   Describes programs that make the user comfortable and simulate what the user is already familiar with.

**variable**   Data that can change as the program runs.

**variable-length records**   This record's fields waste no space on the disk. As soon as a field's data value is saved to the file, the next field's data value is stored immediately after it. Usually, a special separating character appears between the fields so that your program knows where the fields begin and end.

**variable scope**   Sometimes called the *visibility of variables*, this describes how variables are "seen" by your program. See also *global variable* and *local variable*.

**volatile**   Temporary. For example, when you turn the computer off, all the RAM is erased.

**word**   In PC usage, two consecutive bytes (16 bits) of data.

# Index

Index

## K

## L

# Index